For Colin

For 1970

Quelle Année !

Ginger Evans

The Reverend GR Gleig MA, Chaplain-General and first Inspector-General of Army Schools

Mars and Minerva

A History of Army Education

Leslie Wayper

The Royal Army Educational Corps Association

First published in 2004 by
The Royal Army Educational Corps Association
Worthy Down, Winchester
Hampshire SO21 2RG

ISBN 0-9540898-0-4

Printed by
Antony Rowe Limited

CONTENTS

ACKNOWLEDGEMENTS

I have been fortunate enough to know many RAEC officers, not a few of whom were my pupils in the courses run at Fitzwilliam College in the 1960s for the officers who were to teach International Relations. I hope they will think as kindly of me as I do of them and will forgive me for not thanking them by name for all I learned from them. Some I cannot forebear naming. There is Roy Fairclough whose friendship I have treasured for years and whose ability to remove log-jams forwarded the production of this book. There is Peter Reese, a greatly valued friend since we were officer tutors together in Hong Kong, Singapore, Malaya and Cyprus, and with whom I drank happily and at ease while incognito with EOKA B terrorists in the fastnesses of the Trudos Hills. There is Stanley Mullin under whom I served and whose drive and fertility of mind were so impressive, Elaine Smith whose unrivalled knowledge of the Corps' archives she so kindly put at my disposal and whose writings on the early days of Army Education have been so valuable, Brigadier Allan Thompson and his successor as head of the Educational and Training Services Branch of the Adjutant-General's Corps, Brigadier Chris Horsfall whose views on present developments and those of his colleagues at Worthy Down I have been privileged to share, Lieutenant-Colonel Keith Bryan, Regimental Secretary of the RAEC Association, for kindness far beyond the call of duty. Finally it is my great pleasure and privilege to acknowledge my debt to, and to record my grateful thanks for the help received from, the Directors of Army Education who fought so hard and so well for the Corps in recent times. General Foxton is no longer with us; he was an old friend who kindly put himself at my disposal. I was royally entertained by Generals Cliff Kinvig, Stuart Lee, Denis Ryan and Tony Trythall in the In and Out Club whose precincts I had not entered since I was drinking there in uniform during a doodle-bug visitation. General Lloyd Howell was unable to be with us, being off colour; he was kind enough, as were his colleagues, to send me his written reflections. General Kinvig, the last Director of the RAEC and the first Head of the Education and Training Services Branch, collated this material to which he added his thoughts on his own more recent experience. I had not been unaware of the limitations of documentary evidence but this was forcibly brought home to me by the wide-ranging and uninhibited discussions, to which we all understood Chatham House rules would apply, in which, over an excellent lunch table, we then engaged. Those not bearing the heat and burden of the day cannot know the pressures on those who do and I am well aware how privileged I have been to share their reflections. The errors, heresies and enormities remain my own. They would have been greater but for them. To them all and to the great unmentioned my most grateful thanks.

To Margaret

FOREWORD

Education is perhaps not the first activity with which armies are associated in the mind of the general public. However, it is one of considerable importance for their efficient operation. This is a consequence of the singular position which armies occupy in society and the central purposes they exist to serve. These features are exemplified most obviously by their wearing of distinctive uniform and occupying separate barrack accommodation, but they stem in essence from their members' acceptance of a unique contract of unlimited liability in the service of the state. It is not surprising that theirs is a role which, except in times of dire national emergency, only a minority of citizens are prepared to take up: that of acting under orders in situations which the Army itself hopes will never occur, but for which it must continuously train – the risking of its members' lives in war. This also makes the military profession largely the province of the young and physically fit. The singularity of armies as social institutions is underscored by the all-important if sometimes uncomfortable fact that they are generally the sole repository of significant force within the state and in some cases the best organised institution within it. History, and sadly the contemporary world as well, is replete with examples of armies using their monopoly of force not to support the interests of the state but to supplant its legitimate government. The realisation of this truth is never entirely absent from the consciousness of statesmen, even those of some relatively advanced European states, and provides a historical perspective if nothing more cautionary than the fact that the 'bayonet count' in the British Army is still subject to annual approval by Parliament.

It is the features of this uniqueness in society of the British Army which account for the significant place which education occupies within it. The Army cannot 'head-hunt' appropriately trained talent for its ranks in the way civilian organisations do; it is of necessity a 'through structure' which must educate and train for its highest appointments those who enter at its lowest levels. Furthermore, it must often take special measures, and providing particular educational facilities is generally one of them, to attract sufficient entrants to fill its ranks and enough high calibre people to rise ultimately to the top of them.

Since a military career is relatively short and many of the skills it imparts are distinctive, not to say esoteric, special educational provision has to be made for the resettlement of the ex-soldier into a civilian working life at the end of his military service. Nor is this mere altruism on the part of the Army's high command: such measures not only serve the national interest in making the best use of available manpower, but have particular implications for Army recruiting as well, for the successfully resettled ex-regular soldier is likely to prove the best recruiting sergeant. In some armies, generally those of nations where the society at large and its young people in particular are noted for their anti-military sentiments, the needs of recruiting and resettlement tend to play a powerful role in determining the professional military curriculum. The principal rationale of the in-service graduate training programme of the Bundeswehr and at least part of that of the Japanese Self-Defence Force is determined by these recruiting and resettlement imperatives.

A similar rationale explains the prevalence of the policy of recruiting school-leavers under the usual military age into Britain's 'Junior Army'. Despite the high cost of the education and training provided in junior units, since the Second World War the Army has seldom been able to meet its manpower targets without recourse to the recruitment of those making their first career choice as they left school. This was as true in the days of conscription for a 'Cold War' army with residual colonial commitments as it is today for the much smaller force needed after the end of empire and the collapse of the USSR. The realisation that the moment when schoolboys are making their first decision about a future occupation, is for many the sole occasion when they will even consider a career in the Army, has come late to the authorities, who tried to dispense with the Junior Army altogether. This avenue has traditionally proved a source of long-service NCOs and officers, and, with its strong educational component, an invaluable route to advancement and personal development for many whose school careers have been undistinguished and in some cases intermittent.

The Junior Army shares much of the distinctive character of its adult equivalent and both find a particular need to spend considerable time on that aspect of education and training best, if least elegantly, described as 'professional socialisation'. This is a process concerned with the inculcation of the professional values and behaviour which are (sadly, in the view of some commentators) not shared by the larger society from which both are drawn – the spirit of service, the primacy of the community interest, a high degree of discipline and self-control and the creation of that particular kind of group homogeneity generally known as *esprit de corps*.

War may be the least likely, certainly the least to be welcomed, of international eventualities for the British state. It is nevertheless one for which its Army must routinely prepare. All armies spend the bulk of their time in such preparation. With the growing technical complexity of modern warfare it is only to be expected that such emphasis on training should require a significant educational underpinning. Given the substantial investment in training and education which the British Army makes, it is perhaps a natural consequence that it should have acquired an enviable reputation for the systematic approach it has developed to the design and management of its training and for the quality and originality of some of its educational activities, ranging from basic literacy schemes through personal development programmes for NCOs, to intensive foreign language training and the well-respected syndicate system at its Staff College. It is similarly unsurprising that over the years the Army should have developed an educational service of uniformed staff, sharing the ethos and professional mores of the Army at large, to provide and manage a range of its educational activities. The British Army, in common with those of major Commonwealth countries, formed a specialist Corps to carry out this work.

When the idea of commissioning a new history of education in the British Army was first conceived, those concerned with the decision had two main purposes in mind. It was their hope that a fresh history might enlarge upon the pioneering and well-regarded account, *The Story of Army Education*, by Colonel ACT White VC (1963), to which several other hands had contributed. However, the principal end in view was not simply a more detailed description of the activities which Colonel White's book records, but to have his history, which concluded in the early 1960s and for some educational functions rather earlier still, brought closer to modern times. What the Trustees of the RAEC Museum could not possibly have appreciated was how soon after commissioning the work the Cold War would end, transforming the military environment within which Army Education operated and radically restructuring the organisations through which it was to be delivered. Although the author of the history was already engaged upon his task, there seemed no sensible alternative for him but to extend the period covered by his work so that it comprehended the revolutionary changes which took place in the early 1990s following the reforms which the Government's 'Options for Change' programme introduced. But the Trustees were under no illusions about the problems this would present for the author.

In asking Dr Leslie Wayper to undertake the task of writing the new history, the Trustees were engaging the services of an academic with extensive experience of adult education in the civilian environment. Sometime President and now Life Fellow of Fitzwilliam College and for many years Director of Extramural Studies at Cambridge, Dr Wayper was not only a distinguished academic who bestrode the worlds of undergraduate teaching at Fitzwilliam and extramural work beyond it, but one who shared in the policy-making for local authority provision as well. His links with the Army are also of long standing. He served in the AEC during the Second War and was later closely associated with the development of several Services' programmes of officers' education, particularly the Defence and Service Fellowship Schemes and especially the very successful and popular Master of Philosophy programme in International Relations at Cambridge of which he was a principal academic architect. Many of the Army's senior officers, serving and retired, have benefited from these educational initiatives and in some cases from his tutorial counsel as well. Not a few RAEC officers have profited from the post-graduate courses which Dr Wayper ran as part of their training as officers' education tutors and as many have enjoyed his company and friendship thereafter. It would be no exaggeration to say that officers' education in the Army has been a passionate interest of his for many years and an enthusiasm which he had retained in his retirement from active teaching. The pernickety who may search for omissions from Dr Wayper's history will discover only one significant lacuna: this is the contribution, in advising, assisting, teaching and examining, which the good doctor himself has made to the development of its officers' education programmes, whose retrenchment he, like many other erstwhile practitioners in the field, so earnestly regrets.

In so far as Dr Wayper's book can be considered a regimental history of the Royal Army Educational Corps (RAEC) and its antecedents (and it is clearly a much broader study than this), it was never intended that it should conform to the traditional mould. Regimental histories are written as much to sustain the morale and *esprit de corps* of the cap-badged members concerned, as to present a faithful, warts-and-all record of the actions of their forebears. The Museum Trustees were looking rather for an independent examination and evaluation of the activities with which the Corps and its predecessors had been associated. This Dr Wayper has given us, and in the context of the wider educational, social and political currents which he, as historian as well as teacher, is well able to provide. This is a personal view of the development and achievements of Army Education and I commend it to all past members of the RAEC and their successors in the AG Corps as well as to the public at large.

5 January 2004   Major General CA Kinvig
                                              Chairman RAEC Museum Trustees

CHAPTER 1

THE ORIGINS OF ARMY EDUCATION

The English and Their Army

When the Army Educational Corps became the Royal Army Educational Corps (RAEC) a fitting tribute was paid to its important role in the Second World War and in the years thereafter. It had helped, in its Army Bureau of Current Affairs discussions, to maintain the morale of a vastly expanded army during the long months of training and waiting before many of its soldiers could be in action. It had been confronted with a problem of illiteracy, the major size of which had shocked and surprised it, and its handling of that problem was one of its outstanding achievements. During the post-war conscript years its continuing contribution to the maintenance of morale was of a high order. Its studies of ways of instruction improved weapon-training. It established a relationship with the universities the like of which had never been seen before. In its schemes of officer education it made a major contribution to adult education. It fashioned a highly successful resettlement service for officers and men leaving the Army. It arranged courses for the training of foreign troops on British military equipment sold abroad – an important component of successful arms sales. In an army more professional than it had ever hitherto been it was, by any standard, a major part that the RAEC now played.

The British love old things. The greatest honour they could pay to one of their courts was to say of it '*si dignitatem spectemus est honoratissima, si vetustatem antiquissima*', 'if we consider its dignity it is one of the most honourable, if we look at its age it is one of the most ancient in the land'.[1] They could say this of neither their Army nor of the RAEC, its present significant role being a very recent development in an army itself the youngest of the great European armies.

There was a military revolution in the century 1560–1660, during which period we see the modern army, together with the modern system of diplomacy and indeed the modern state itself, of which these are its two essential arms, struggling to emerge. Armies greatly increased in size in these years. Philip II dominated Europe with an army which did not exceed 40,000 men; Louis XIV needed 400,000. By 1660 there were mass armies, strict discipline, the conjoint ascendancy in military matters of financial power and applied science, the use of propaganda for military purposes and psychological warfare. In the 18th Century we have the development of modern standing armies and in the 19th Century the evolution within them of a professional officer corps. But these are things not to be seen in Britain. The history of the British Army is the history of an institution which the British have done their best to persuade themselves they did not need. It is not the story of a continuous development of a national army such as we can see on the continent. It is the history of recurrent need dispelling the anti-military illusions of the nation. It is a history of sudden expansion to meet particular emergencies followed by relapse into peacetime stagnation and national neglect.

For as long as possible England would have no army. It looked to the Navy as its first line of defence and for its second it turned to the fyrd or general muster of the people, the so-called Trained or Train Bands – the nomenclature suggesting an expertise which nothing else about them would. Obvious though it ought to have been, what would have happened, had Alva's Spanish veterans met them in 1588, that grand old Elizabethan soldier, Sir John Norris, declared that he could see no man in the kingdom afeared but himself at the prospect.[2] Even in this matter of the Train Bands the English expressed their disapproval of too great military effort. In the year of the Armada Queen Elizabeth was 'not a little amazed' that not all counties had produced their due quota of armed men,[3] while in the late 17th Century bodies of men made a living by tramping the country to let themselves out as dummy soldiers for muster parades.[4] At the time of the French Revolution the English were still putting their trust in these Train Bands, which were now called the Militia. Even in the 19th Century it was maintained that if there was an invasion 'The Colliers of Northumberland could be whirled from the north to the south by the fuel their sturdy hands have brought to the surface and they alone would be a host to sweep the aggressor from our earth.'[5] The English saw no need for military reform or even for military preparation. They put their trust in their Navy and in their own pre-eminent valour, in their abiding conviction that, as Shakespeare expressed it, 'Upon one pair of English legs did march three Frenchmen.' For them the army was only a third line of defence and one to which they need pay little attention. Indeed not all looked upon it even as that. Many MPs were sure that we needed no army in peacetime. After the Restoration of 1660 Parliament demanded the total disbandment of the Army, which was saved only by the disturbances occasioned by the 5th Monarchy men. Perhaps the Army was unnecessary even in wartime, Swift suggested. For after all, no-one likes foreigners and, as there were many different kinds of them, it followed that they would dislike each other. So if one set of foreigners attacked England another could always be hired to attack them.

When England produced its first fully organised force which constituted an army, Cromwell's New Model of 1645, England became a great military power and Englishmen aware of a great problem. For highly as their Army was respected abroad it was even more greatly feared and disliked at home. They were already saying of soldiers in the reign of Queen Elizabeth:

> We care not for your soldier men
> Who do the State disdain
> But we care for your sailor boys
> Who do the State maintain

They were to say that with greater fervour and conviction thereafter. For the New Model Army not only dispensed with King Charles's head, a dispensation which offended them, it also deprived them of Parliament and of the rule of law, a deprivation which offended them still more. They found themselves under the rule of Cromwell's Major-Generals, who ruled them very well, better undoubtedly than they were to be ruled for many years thereafter. It would have been better had these been typical soldiers. But they were not. If they were not soldierly saints they were at least saintly soldiers. It is highly likely that Englishmen would have rejected the rule of soldiers even if they had not been saints. It is even more likely that they would have resented the rule of saints even if they had not been soldiers. But the combination was more than English flesh and blood could bear. Old Adam, who would put up with a little rough and ready smartening up, was not prepared to be made too good, and those whose task it was to keep him in order knew this, being well-aware both of his limitations and of their own. They were the English squirearchy and they were well versed not only in the chasing of the fox but of Old Adam too. As Justices of the Peace they had chased him off every ale-bench in the kingdom and in a world in which ale-benches continued to be they were unconvinced of his perfectibility. They put up with him and he put up with them. But to use the sword to make him saintly, that was overdoing it, and his howls of wrath have gone ringing down the centuries to the discomfort not of all military men but at least of all military Englishmen. That such recollection of sworded saints should carry with it lasting dislike of other sworded gentlemen whose claim to sainthood is not immediately apparent may seem surprising. But it ought not to be forgotten that while Englishmen have often been accused of paying excessive attention to their past, it has never been said of them that they have an excessive regard for logic.

Thus from the first modern army the English inherited a problem which was to plague them and their army throughout the years. That was the problem now usually referred to as that of civil-military relations. Soldiers, as Plato pointed out, must by the very nature of their calling lead a life somewhat apart from that of their fellow citizens. Not only their function, but their preparation to discharge it, their discipline, their ranks, their uniforms and rituals, their barrack and mess life, sets them more than any other profession apart from the community. Yet the power in their hands, armed power, is the most highly developed and most immediately obtainable power to be found within the state. For as a 17th Century pamphlet put it 'He that is armed is always master of him that is unarmed.'[6] Hamilton, one of the greatest of the American Founding Fathers, maintained that the perennial problem of politics is how to give the government sufficient power to govern without at the same time giving it also the power to deprive the governed of their liberties.[7] A greater problem would appear to be how to prevent armed power taking over the state. For that power cannot be dispensed with, for not all interests are easily reconcilable, not all men are good and it is always as well to keep an eye on Old Adam. States have always needed the soldier for the securing and forwarding of their interests, for the retention of their independence, for the maintenance of peace, for the maintenance of internal order. Those states which sought too long to dispense with his services or which neglected to give him the arms which would give him a reasonable chance of successfully resisting his enemies, did not profit thereby – Athens going down before Philip of Macedon, Poland being wiped from the map of 18th Century Europe, and 19th Century China forced to put up with the unpleasing presence and bitterly resented attentions of the West. It was the very nature of things that made this so, for the international world was made up of sovereign states which had conflicting interests. These could not be sorted out by due process of law for sovereign states could not enjoy the privilege of living under the rule of law. Nor could what men called morality or fair play smooth away conflicting interests. Not only did states disagree as to what action was moral and fair, but in the international world dire necessity laid even upon good people, if they took upon themselves the leadership of their countries, the obligation from time to time of doing bad things, as for instance sinking the ships of a defeated ally at Oran and Dakar lest they fall into the hands of a dangerously powerful enemy. This being a world in which power was always present, the soldier was as indispensable as the statesman. He was a necessary and powerful servant but he might believe himself to be more powerful than his master, as he might indeed be, and if that were so, how long would he remain the servant?

Here was the problem which is summed up in the old Latin tag which even the most resistant of schoolboys learned, *quis custodiet ipsos custodes* – 'who will guard against the guards themselves?' Perhaps the more appropriate English rendering would be 'How can we keep those confounded soldiers whom we will need from time to time to keep our enemies from our throats, always at our feet?' This was the problem that we inherited from the days of the Commonwealth in the 17th Century and which has loomed so large thereafter in the relationship between the British Army and British society. No people has ever been so concerned with this problem as the British. For a people proud of its determination never, never, never to be slaves, the British have been extraordinarily afraid that it is their Army's purpose ever, ever, ever to make them so.

Thus they honoured Sir William Blackstone when in his commentaries on the Laws of England he taught them that the condition of the Army was akin to servitude and that free nations should not allow the establishment of slavery in their midst. Their statutes forbade the raising or keeping of a standing army in time of peace unless it be with the assent of Parliament and they adopted the practice of legalising the Army for only one year at a time, the idea being that if the soldiers did not behave, Parliament would disband them. They allowed their pride in the great victories of their best loved soldier, Corporal John, John Churchill, Duke of Marlborough, to evaporate even before the ending of his astonishing military career. They would not allow soldiers in towns where assizes were held lest even-handed justice be displaced by the sword. They confined troops to barracks on election days, and where there were no barracks, as too often there were not, required them to get out of town. It is difficult to think of a corrupt practice from which they themselves would shrink on these great occasions. But the corrupting presence of soldiers was something they were not prepared to risk. They would not build more barracks as the Younger Pitt wanted them to do. For as Pulteney said 'if the soldiers were all kept in barracks the people would be insensible of their numbers', whereas if they were billeted out in the countryside, people would be 'sensible of the fetters which are preparing for them and put an end to too numerous an army before it be too late'.[8] And so it went on. When two Whig peers were halted in the Mall by a sentry, they raised a debate in the Lords declaring that the constitution was in danger. MPs feared a military coup after

Waterloo. One of them uncovered evidence of officers caballing together against civilians and no doubt to blow up Parliament, their greater familiarity with gunpowder enabling them to attend to this business more effectively than did Guy Fawkes. They were, he said, meeting together 'in an institution of which I cannot speak with too much reprobation, where military men are alone admitted and where the general topic of conversation must be of a military nature', this revolutionary institution being the newly-founded United Services Club in the Mall. Half-pay officers in the London Clubs who, it was said, wanted both full employment for themselves and to take over the affairs of the state, were blamed in retrospect for the war scarc of 1847 when it was feared that the French were about to land on British shores. When Wellington said of his Peninsula soldiers that he did not know if they scared the enemy but they certainly scared him, he was speaking with the authentic voice of English society, forever ready to be more scared of its own Army than of its external foes.[9]

Such was the regard of the British for their Army that even after Waterloo soldiers were excluded from the public parks and gardens in London under a regulation dating from the days of Charles II, and in the 1870s Randolph Churchill expressed concern lest garrisoning a regiment in Oxford would, by the 'mingling of learned professors and thoughtful students with roystering soldiers and licentious camp followers', destroy that ancient university.[10] When it could no longer be pretended that an Army was unnecessary it was certain that as the British people feared it so much they would insist on having the smallest of armies. The British Army had to conform to this requirement. When grave international emergencies arose the size of the Army had to be increased, and this was done by means so weird and wonderful as to cast doubt on the proposition that the British are a practical people who value common sense whatever they may think of abstract and high-faluting reasoning. But as soon as the emergency passed the Army was hastily cut down to size again. That is why, heraldically speaking, the device that should be emblazoned on the standard of every regiment is the concertina, for it is only that which contracts and expands as quickly as the British Army. This is also why, since it is not possible for armies to achieve their maximum efficiency overnight, the British Army has displayed a preference for winning its last battles rather than its first. It is, however, an ill wind that blows nobody any good. The vicissitudes which the Army met in its earlier campaigns have enabled the politicians who occasioned them to convince themselves of their wisdom in not giving more to those who so ill-used what they had got. Such indeed was the determination of the British people to keep their Army small that it is difficult to resist the conclusion that they love to get into holes in order to display their great virtuosity in getting out of them.

Given this fear it was also certain that the British would not tolerate a professional army with its own standards which rigidly separated it from the rest of the nation. To this requirement the British Army also had to conform. The slow development of professionalism in it was one of its outstanding characteristics in the 19th Century. There were examinations for officers in the Prussian Army seeking promotion in the early 19th Century. In 1810 the Kriegsakademie was established in Berlin, its effect being apparent in the middle years of the century when it was estimated that 50% of the military literature was produced in Germany, 25% in France and only 1% in Britain. A Royal Military College was set up in Sandhurst in 1802 and a Staff College at Camberley in 1857, but neither of these establishments enjoyed the reputation of the Berlin academy, or indeed anything like it. And as late as 1890, General Wolseley could still say that the Army was divided between those who clung to the Wellington tradition and those who wished to make it a profession.

What kept the British Army amateur, not professional, was the practice of buying and selling commissions which persisted in Britain long after it had been dropped elsewhere. Of course not all commissions were bought and sold. Promotion above the rank of Lieutenant-Colonel and appointment to the Staff was by selection. The Gunners and the Engineers belonged to non-purchase regiments; chances were not to be taken here on inadequate expertise. Some, but far fewer than in European armies, were commissioned from the ranks, and after 1842 cadets from Sandhurst could become officers without purchasing their commissions. Yet as late as 1871, when purchase was ended, three out of every four officers had bought their commissions.

The drawbacks of this practice were obvious. Not all officers who bought commissions would soldier seriously. Many joined for the social round and said 'The Army is all right so long as it is limited to the mess and the band but the troops are a damned nuisance.' Some knew little about their regiments; as witness the officer who, on being asked what was his regiment, answered 'Upon my soul, I don't know; but they wear green facings and you get to 'em from Waterloo Station.' Many knew little about duty. Wellington said that only when he went on active service in India did he learn what not to do, and he added 'Nobody in the British Army ever reads a regulation or an order as if it were to be a guide for his conduct, or in any other manner than as an amusing novel.'[11]

With this a not uncommon practice it is easy to believe Lord Chesterfield when he said in 1746 that the British Army was the worst officered in all Europe. Campaigns were wrecked by incompetent generals who, having bought their way as high as they could in the Army, then owed their command to influence. Lord Sackville, court-martialled for his performance at Minden, was judged unfit to serve His Majesty in any capacity thereafter, something which did not prevent his later appointment as Secretary of State for War. When Minorca was besieged in 1756 no fewer than thirty-five officers, including the Colonels of the four regiments stationed there, were absent from their posts. Britain declared war on France in 1793 and Sir Ralph Abercombie took a British force to Flanders, two regiments of which had to be left behind as being unfit to appear in the presence of the enemy. There was only one battalion that he dare risk in the line. General Craig wrote of his army on active service in Holland in 1794:

> That we are the most undisciplined, the most ignorant, the worst-provided army that
> ever took the field is certain; but we are not to blame for it. There is not a young man
> in the Army that cares one farthing whether his Commanding Officer, his brigadier
> or his Commander-in-Chief himself approves of his conduct or not. His promotion
> depends not on their smiles or frowns. His friends can give him a thousand pounds

and in a fortnight he becomes a Captain. Out of the fifteen regiments of cavalry and twenty-six of infantry which we have here, twenty-one are literally commanded by boys or idiots.

Not surprisingly the campaign of 1794 was a conspicuous failure, eight more years being required before a strong British Army could be created.[12]

Purchase, nevertheless, had its ardent advocates. It was pointed out that it helped the promising to get ahead; Wellington got his start in this way. And its most seamy side was frowned on. Eyebrows were raised when the Duke of York's mistress sold commissions at cut prices. Many oddities were then considered to be 'the thing', but this was not among them.[13] Above all it was emphasised that commissions were expensive and the practice of purchase thus established a property qualification for military rank which was consciously designed to ensure an identity of interest between army and society, and thus to make a second military dictatorship impossible. Palmerston thought it desirable to connect the higher classes of society with the Army, and he did not know any more effective way of doing this than by allowing members of high families to get on with greater rapidity than they would by mere seniority. If the connection between the Army and the upper class of society was dissolved, the Army would assume a very dangerous and unconstitutional appearance. It was only when the Army was unconnected with those whose property gave them an interest in the welfare of the country, and was commanded by unprincipled military adventurers, that it could ever become formidable to the liberties of the nation.[14] Purchase would ensure acceptable behaviour on the part of the officer who was practically bound over in the price of his commission, which he forfeited if cashiered. It was this, Wellington said, 'which exempts the British Army from the character of being a mercenary army, it has rendered its employment for nearly a century and a half not only consistent with the constitutional privileges of the country but safe and beneficial'.[15] There were safeguards and these were thought to be adequate. A serving officer could only purchase a higher rank if no objection was lodged by his Commanding Officer or by the Commander-in-Chief. It is obvious, however, that the meshes of this particular safety net were very wide. Purchase, too, was beloved of the Treasury. It was economical as the officer's pay little exceeded the interest on the money paid for his commission. The Treasury, moreover, did not have to find money for officers' pensions as the officer sold his commission on retirement. The officer's pay and the man's pay being very low, military budgets were also low. Here we have the obvious reason why conditions in the Army remained unchanged for so long. Change was bound to cost more and therefore was bound to be resisted by Government and Parliament. There may not have been much sense but there was at least some consistency in the philosophy of mid-Victorian governments. Believing as they did that the Army should never interfere in politics, they also believed that the politicians should never interfere with the Army. 'Leave the old army alone and don't make war' was their slogan. Only when they began to doubt if they could continue to refuse to make war did they also begin to doubt the wisdom of leaving the Army alone.

Purchase ensured that in an aristocratic society the British Army should be officered, in Wellington's words, by 'the gentlemen of England'. 'The way of thinking of a gentleman' was Sir John Moore's requirement for a commission. 'The British officer should be a gentleman first and an officer second,' the Duke of Cambridge held. The officer was ill-paid, getting half a day's pay for half a day's work. He was not well trained and was expected to be neither industrious nor particularly intelligent. But he was expected to have the values of the country gentleman – courage, toughness, a sensitive sense of honour – and as long as he had these values it was held that he had enough. The thought that he might be the better for having professional, technical qualities might be entertained by the artilleryman and the engineers, it being somewhat doubtful if gentlemen would turn their hands to such black arts. There were times when the Army did not sufficiently value brains. But it never undervalued birth and breeding and Wavell quoted as the best confidential report he had seen the comment by one Horse Guards officer on another 'Personally I would not breed from this officer', a confidential report possibly not made known to the officer in question.[16]

In yet another way this Army insured against the danger of becoming professional. Its administration could be relied on to prevent that. It has been described as being in a state of 'exquisite confusion'. Military affairs were the concern of fifteen distinct and jealous offices, each conducting its relations with the others through the most formal and leisurely correspondence. In 1782 the Secretary at War was appointed, his title being appropriate as he was at war with many people much of the time. He was responsible to Parliament for Army finances. He was responsible for drawing up plans of campaign and for moving troops. He selected billeting areas, issued commissions and, at one time, even granted leave to officers without reference to their Commanding Officers, another practice which could hardly be said to promote military efficiency. The Board of Ordnance was responsible for military stores and for the engineer and artillery branches of the Army. The Paymaster issued pay, was responsible for Chelsea Hospital and Army pensions and for the payment to foreign rulers of subsidies for the hire of their troops. In case the Secretary at War ran out of people to fight, there was created in 1794 a Secretary of State for War. Fortunately in 1801 this Secretary became Secretary of State not only for War but also for the Colonies. Since his time became fully occupied with colonial matters, he lacked the time that otherwise he would no doubt have had to put much heart into fighting the Secretary at War. Even so it gradually became clear that if the purpose was not primarily to comfort the enemy, there had better be only one Secretary of State for War who would have sole responsibility for the Army and for nothing but the Army. Otherwise letters would remain unanswered, guns inadequate, palisades better fitted for hen-coops than for fortification and huts burned for fuel, as the Governor of Gibraltar complained.[17]

Before unified control could be established, however, yet another difficulty, which the year 1798 had produced, would have to be overcome. Since Monk's death in 1670 no Commander-in-Chief of the British Army had been appointed in peacetime. But in 1798 the Horse Guards had been created by the Crown and the office of Commander-in-Chief again appeared. So that Parliament through the Secretaries of

State for War and at War now controlled the finances and the discipline of the Army while the Crown was in charge of its command and organisation. Thus two authorities shared its higher direction. The relationship between them lacked clear definition, although it was understood that the one, representing the government of the day, should make policy while the other, representing the royal prerogative, should issue orders. It was a case of two authorities being up, neither supreme, and, as Coriolanus emphasised, in such a situation confusion was always likely to enter twixt the gap of both and take the one by the other. In the early 19th Century the Commander-in-Chief tried to insist that the Secretary at War must be subordinate to the Commander-in-Chief. The Secretary at War was Lord Palmerston and the Commander-in-Chief would have been better advised to have picked someone else to have a tussle with. Palmerston pointed out that the Secretary, too, was responsible to the Crown and could not be so if he was not a free agent; he could not be that if he was subordinate to the Commander-in-Chief. However, the failure of the Commander-in-Chief to assert his authority over the Secretary of State was followed years later by the failure of the Secretary of State to reduce the Commander-in-Chief to subordination. This time the Commander-in-Chief was a cousin of Queen Victoria and this time the Prime Minister was again Palmerston, with whom she had already crossed swords in the matter of her prerogative and against whom she could be relied on to tolerate no further diminution of her prerogative powers. Thus when the Secretary of State wished to appoint a brilliant young artillery officer, Lieutenant-Colonel Lefroy, Inspector-General of Military Education and to bring under his direction all education in the Army, the Commander-in-Chief, the Duke of Cambridge, objected. If education was brought under the Secretary of State it would be taken away from the Commander-in-Chief. He therefore drew up his own scheme for a new Department of Education in the Army which would be responsible to him and not to Lord Panmure, the Secretary of State. Palmerston was popularly known as Lord Pumice Stone for his ability to rough up foreigners, something which did not diminish his popularity in the country. He could not, however, rough up the Queen nor effectively answer her contention that 'If for his military proficiency and moral discipline the officer is to be responsible to his military chiefs, and for his mental requirements to a civil department, the unity of the system will be broken and the army ruined.' Duality thus continued and although it could hardly be said to have ruined the Army its contribution to the unity of the system was unimpressive.[18]

All of this might have appeared to be a carefully thought-out system of 'divide and rule' on the part of a people ever more afraid of its own Army than of the enemy, determined to keep the Army divided in order not to be ruled by it. It would seem, however, that it is Topsy, who just growed, and not Machiavelli, who is the patron saint of this development, and that what we have here is the typical English capacity to live with congenial chaos, not the untypical taking of timely thought to minimise and control an untimely problem. As a way of minimising professionalism and maximising amateurism in the Army there was, however, much to be said for it.

One further thing must be said about this peculiar, if not eccentric, Army: it did its job. For all its faults it produced great leaders and developed adequate military capacity. Had it not done so, Britain would never have attained its greatness. Had it not done so, Britain might not have survived. And having successfully defeated the French and chased the cannibals, having shown its mettle as well as demonstrated its faults to the Russians, it proved itself able to adapt to meet a far more formidable foe in the Germans.

It served society, too, as well at home as abroad. In the absence of an organised police force it suppressed smuggling, enforced the law, and dealt with riot. Indeed, however little Government and society might think they needed the Army to cope with the foreigner, they thought it as well to have sufficient armed power to put down civil disturbance. Perhaps the Army would have had to wait still longer for its barracks had it not had to deal with the Luddites. For if dispersed in pubs the troops would not be as easy to assemble as they would be if concentrated in barracks. Nor could it be felt that they would be as politically reliable.[19] And, be it noted, the aid the Army gave to the civil power enhanced the rule of law, not only in suppressing the lawless but also in keeping that suppression always within the law. For the soldier had no special privileges in enforcing the law. He remained under it in doing so. He could be court-martialled and shot if he refused to use the force he was ordered to and hanged by the civil power if in so doing he committed murder. It was undoubtedly tough on the soldier but the thought must occur to us how indebted we are to him for bearing that load as we still greatly value the fact that the policeman, who has taken over from the soldier the task of upholding the law, continues to be bound by it.

The Pressures Making For and Against Army Education

This was the Army that throughout the 19th Century was engaged in a two-fold struggle. There was the struggle between the Army and society, the struggle in which it had always been engaged, the struggle to find an acceptable place in society and to discharge an important role in the state. There was also the struggle within the Army between those who understood the increasingly imperative need to educate it to meet the ever more formidable challenges of an ever more dangerous world and those who saw little need of change because, being blind to the new challenges, they were content with things as they were. It is to that second struggle that we must now turn. Throughout the century we see power greater than man had ever known being put into his hands by the scientific, the industrial and the technological revolutions that were transforming the world. We see that these things were producing throughout Europe and indeed throughout the world uneven concentrations of that power and that this inevitably destroyed old balances and created new patterns of power. We see having a similar effect the spread of the nationalism which insisted that the greatest political allegiance be given to the nation which must now be organised as a state, if necessary at the expense of existing states. The impact on all men's thinking and on the conduct of states of these developments was bound eventually to be very great. But new realities do not always produce immediate changes in old appearance, entrenched positions are rarely quickly evacuated and the alternative to action, namely inaction, has for many a strong appeal. It is not therefore surprising that it took many years for these changes to have their cumulative effect. So we see both of the struggles in which the Army was engaged, the struggle of education to find an acceptable position and discharge an important role in it and the struggle of the Army to find an acceptable position and discharge an important role in society and the state, lasting through the century, each affecting the other. It could not in the long run be doubted what the outcome would be, for the world was undeniably becoming more dangerous for Britain and a better Army in consequence was necessary for it too. The Army would win its place in the affections of the British people and education its place in the Army. But this was to be achieved not without heat and toil.

It is in the early stages of the struggle to win for education an important place in the Army that we find the ancestry of the RAEC. We must, then, consider it, for if we see things in their first beginnings we learn a lot about their nature, as Aristotle taught us, and if we look at their development we see their strengths and weaknesses, the pressures to which they have to adjust and the adjustment they have made necessary in these pressures. And we will remind ourselves that, highly important as the RAEC's contribution to the modern Army has been, that of its predecessors to the well-being of their Army was never negligible.

The pressures making for Army Education soon showed themselves. Some might continue to believe with Frederick the Great that the essence of military education consisted in making the soldiers fear the Corporal's rod more than the enemy's bullet.[20] One suspects that Wellington might have thought so too and be grateful, bearing in mind his contempt for his men, that it was not in the first flush of their revolutionary ardour that he had to deal with the soldiers of France. Cromwell knew better. The best had to be got out of men and this was not the way to get it. 'The mind is the man,' he said and he warned John Hampden that he would be defeated unless he could get men of spirit into the Parliamentary forces. How, he wondered, could 'old decayed servicemen and tapsters and such kind of fellows' be expected to encounter 'gentlemen that have honour and courage and resolution'?[21] The soldier must know what he was fighting for and love what he knew. So he established the practice of holding 'Councils of War' to explain to the soldiers what was happening and why, and thus in 1643 the *Soldier's Pocket Bible* was issued and in the following year the *Soldier's Catechism*. There were to be regular discussions based on these books, for good morale was essential and this was the way in which education could contribute to it. Moreover, following the texts to which their attention would so frequently be drawn must have helped men to read. Proselytism is not education, but many roads lead to Rome, little though Cromwell would have welcomed that. Cromwell's Army was not typically English and, though the call for those who know what they were fighting for and who loved what they knew was to be revived in the 20th Century British Army, the early 19th Century recruiting Sergeant who tells us that he never recruited anyone who wasn't drunk didn't expect it to be heard by those he brought to the Colours.[22] Yet, though what Cromwell wanted was more akin to proselytism than to education, it led to education of a somewhat restricted kind and of a nature of which he would have disapproved. As discussion leaders know too well, groups do not always keep to the subjects under discussion. Those attended by the New Model soldiers did not. The appearance, to the dismay of their officers, of the 'agitators', the selected representatives of the Horse and the Foot who, as Fairfax tells us, almost took over the Army and who were very familiar with the ideas of Lilbourne and the Levellers show they learned more than bible stories could have taught them.[23]

There were, it soon became apparent, stronger reasons than Cromwell's desire to improve morale, for the furthering of Army Education. The problems raised by the need to administer and train larger bodies of men left no doubt about that. It was important for NCOs at least to be able to read, write and add up. In the 18th Century Army the administration of the units was becoming increasingly complex. There were reports, rosters, returns and accounts to be attended to. Thus NCOs in the Queen's Royal Regiment were required to have certain educational qualifications. It was said that the Sergeant-Major 'should be a man of real merit, a complete Sergeant and a good scholar ... and must be ready at his pen and expert at making out details and rosters'. It was expected that the Corporal 'should have a quickness of comprehension and a knowledge of reading, writing, and accounts'.[24] There were few barracks at this time and men were billeted in local inns and taverns under a Sergeant or Corporal. Innkeepers had to provide straw for beds, candles, food and drink in return for stoppages from the soldier's pay. In such matters the soldier was frequently cheated and he needed somebody literate who would understand, as the Soldier in Sheridan's play *St Patrick's Day* says 'Our figures and such like auxiliaries in scoring.'[25] This system of scattered billets often meant that one unit would be stationed in as many as six villages, which not only made training and the maintenance of discipline difficult, but also meant that orders had to be read by NCOs and copied by them to be read later to their men.

Slowly but surely the advance of weapons technology was beginning to have its effect and the demand for more skilful, more intelligent and better educated men was being raised. As fire-power became more effective troops had to be dispersed and this demanded more initiative and self-reliance in the men, and particularly in the NCOs. Such initiative had been discouraged in Braddock's army when officers forced their men who were firing from behind trees, as the French *coureurs de bois* and their Huron allies were doing, back into line to be the more effectively mown down by that deadly accurate fire. Braddock's defeat had a salutary effect and when, largely in consequence, Sir John Moore trained the Light Division he stressed the role of education in developing the initiative that could not now be dispensed with. The Standing Orders of the Rifle Brigade 1801 decreed that a school be set up 'for the instruction of those who wished to become non-commissioned officers and to ensure that every Sergeant would be literate and also numerate'. Soldiers were so instructed as to be 'capable of doing their duty efficiently because they knew what they were doing'. It was more important, he insisted, to promote the good in the soldier, than to punish the bad in him. The emotion felt at Corunna is easily understood.[26]

A difficulty developed in finding enough instructors to train men in the use of the musket. This was ascribed to the widespread 'deficiency in reading and writing' in the Army.[27] Moreover, the technology that was affecting the development of weapons inevitably also affected accepted tactical ideas. With the coming into use of the rifle the traditional infantry square become more deadly to its occupants than to their enemies, dispersing the men into open formations became essential, problems of command and control became greater, and the demands on the soldier and on the NCO more onerous. This the Army acknowledged, the Royal Commission of 1870 emphasising that as there must now be greater demands on 'the intelligence and self-reliance' of the soldier he must have 'at least a rudimentary education'.[28] Indeed, frequent as were advances in weapons technology, they were not more frequent than the assertions of the leaders of the Army that to cope with them the soldier must have the sharpened mind that education would give him. Persistent and sustained attention to providing the sharpened mind that education would produce was not, however, forthcoming. The Army may have had the possibly not misplaced conviction that drawing attention to a problem repeatedly, and in the event it turned out to be for more than a century and a half, would eventually facilitate its solution.

There were in the early 19th Century educational stirrings in the civilian world of which the Army could not but be conscious. It is estimated that only about one in thirty children received any organised education at that time. Education was never, however, synonymous with schooling: there were undoubtedly those whose education was sound but not of a scholastic kind. There were many who believed that nothing should be altered. In the debate on the Parochial Schools Bill in 1807 one MP declared 'Giving education to the labouring classes would be prejudicial to their happiness', as 'it would lead them to despise their lot in life.' It would also, it seems, be prejudicial to the happiness of their betters as it would render the lower classes 'insolent to their superiors'.[29] Nevertheless, as Brougham told the House of Commons, 'The anxiety of the poor for education daily increases.'[30] Sunday Schools were spreading apace and the Mechanics Institute Movement was begun in 1800. It was not as yet thought that education should be a state responsibility. Adam Smith typifies the thinking of the time. State endowments, he thought, made for inefficiency and the public contribution to education should be limited to making good any deficiency left by other sources – as was done in 1833 when for the first time a grant of public money was made to add to the sum raised by private subscriptions. Unimpressive as for some years these educational rumblings in the civilian world were, they continued. Dr Bell, during his chaplaincy in Madras, had been superintendent of an orphanage and he made use of the older children there to teach the younger. That practice was perhaps no worse, and conceivably was better, than the instruction at many of the small private schools. It involved much repetition but it was at least the recognition that ignorance ought not to be allowed to remain unspotted, the acknowledgement that it is better that some things should be learned by rote than not to be learned at all. Yet much knowledge cannot be imparted by those whose stock of it is small and it was more likely to inhibit than to promote thought. What was taught was of the simplest as it had to be, given the nature of the teachers and of the taught. Dr Bell's was a secular education but one in which religious training bulked large. Morality, religion, reading, writing and simple arithmetic were the whole of the curriculum. It must be remembered that few, apart from a handful of radicals, believed at this time that there could be a clear distinction between the secular and the religious in matters educational.

No doubt strengthened by the bitter battle between church and chapel which filled these years, interest in education grew and prompted the thinking of more original minds than that of Dr Bell. David Stow was pondering on ways in which to improve the standard of teaching. He was campaigning against the monitorial system, declaring that monitors cannot train minds although they might teach facts and that apprenticeship was as necessary for the profession of teachers as it was for that of any other. Teacher-training was indeed attracting attention at this time. In 1839 there was only a handful of training colleges in England. These included that of Borough Road established by the British and Foreign Schools Society. The following year Kay-Shuttleworth founded his college at Battersea; in 1841 the National Society opened with Non-Conformity pressing hard on the heels of the Church. An Army that had the children of its soldiers as well as its young soldiers to care for and that was acutely aware that many of its mature soldiers were illiterate could not afford to be indifferent to these developments in civilian education.

There was a further pressure strongly pushing for education in the Army. This was the great force of evangelical humanitarianism so impressive in and so characteristic of early 19th Century Britain. Ending the slave trade, emancipating slaves, greatly strengthening missionary societies, it turned its attention to the poor and distressed at home, to alleviating the sufferings occasioned by the spawning of the dark satanic mills as in the great novels of Dickens. Evangelical humanitarianism affected the Army in two ways. It also felt the urge to pay increasing attention to its men. One beneficial result of the purchase of commissions was that officers had a pecuniary interest in the welfare of their men. Every soldier lost through sickness, death or desertion had to be replaced and recruits cost money. But of course officers had much more than a pecuniary interest in the welfare of their men. It was a general and a very real interest that they took in it. Officers looked after their men, as they have always had to do, and more particularly when there was no one else to do so. That feeling of care became a sacred duty. And it is worth remembering that in the whole range of literature the most beautiful, touching and humorous picture of friendship and trust between master and man is that given us by a child of the barrack-yard, Sterne, in his immortal picture of a Captain, Uncle Toby, and a Corporal, Corporal Trim, both crippled by wounds received in action. Always in looking after their men it was the officers who led the way and the state which limped sulkily behind. They taught classes at times and coached promising soldiers. They promoted temperance societies and introduced savings banks into the regiments. They started unit hospitals. They inaugurated the first married quarters by raising funds to buy property. However thick their heads, there was never much wrong with their hearts. Whatever the oddities of the British Army, there was never any doubt how well served it was by the spirit, the pride and the self-respect of its regiments.

Their zeal and their liberality, as Palmerston acknowledged, paid for these things. Nor were they lacking in the necessary ingenuity in providing for all the unconsidered trifles essential to the functioning of an Army and for which the state would not pay, as it ought to have done. The Army has never been entirely unpractised in ways at which the meticulously righteous might conceivably look askance. For if help is indeed essential and is not forthcoming from those who might reasonably be expected to give it, ingenuity in its provision on the part of those who cannot do without it is not to be unexpected. So the regiments developed the system of 'contingent men', fictitious privates borne on the roll whose pay went to the upkeep of Chelsea Hospital, to the provision of pensions for war widows and even to the remounting of the cavalry. These contingent men, or 'false musters', lasted into the 19th Century. Twice yearly every regiment marched in single file before an aged official known as the 'Muster Master', whose function it was to see that things were not overdone. And if his eyesight was not expected to be overly sharp, who could forget that the nation heartily approved of the inability of its best-loved sea-son to see Admiral Hyde Parker's signal of recall at Copenhagen? Moreover, in an age which was becoming less brutal and less indifferent to suffering the pitiable condition of the families of soldiers was coming to be seen as an intolerable evil. There was, moreover, in the Army a new Department of Army Chaplains. This was Wellington's answer to the spreading of Methodism in the Army of the Peninsula. He took unkindly to officers being asked to confess their sins. The new Army Chaplains brought to the fore the social problems to which the Army had hitherto turned a blind eye.[31]

Evangelical humanitarianism now prompted officers to find new ways of helping their men, ways genuinely sought for the good they would do but also wanted for the contribution they would make to improving the Army's image in the public eye, the strengthening of the desire to do so being the second of the ways in which evangelical humanitarianism affected the Army.

The cat was frequently used in civilian gaols and it was generally believed that conditions in them should act as a deterrent to the criminally inclined. Even so, society was looking askance at the brutal punishments inflicted on the soldiery, and as no-one believed that punishment earned should be dispensed with, thoughts turned to ways of ensuring that it would not be so frequently earned. The sea-shanty reminds us that the sailor likes his bottle-o. So does the soldier. Such was his liking for it that in 1876 it was for drunkenness that 28% of defaulters were punished. It must not be forgotten that sobriety was not a characteristic of civilian society at this time. No doubt the 18th Century appeal to the sybaritic drunk, 'drunk for a penny, dead drunk with straw for twopence' was no longer in such evidence. Alcohol, however, was as much in demand. It may therefore be thought that soldiers were not more often drunken than civilians but were more punished for not being less or at least for not occasioning less trouble in public to the discredit of the Colours.[32] If soldiers could be induced to curtail their natural desire to get away from the Sergeant-Major and to resist a little more frequently the attractions of the town, where they often occasioned as much trouble as universities did when they were established and indeed for long thereafter, this would also reduce the necessity for punishing them. So libraries were opened in units, as later games were arranged in the hope of keeping the soldiers in barracks and out of trouble.[33] This spreading of libraries owed more to the concern of senior officers for the welfare and the reputation of their troops than for their education. Libraries nevertheless gave a fillip to Army Education as we shall see. Not all that was read would be educative. How many of us use libraries exclusively to further our education? But the pleasures of reading are not only to be found in works of fiction; browsing among books is itself an education and may, though we had not intended it to, lead us to a fuller education.

These pressures on the Army making for the further development of education in it were continuous and strong. Sooner or later they would prevail. But there were other pressures on the Army making against Army Education and they also were continuous and strong. They were determined to make the successful impact of the former pressures occur later rather than sooner, much later than sooner, as late indeed as they could contrive. What these pressures were we must now see.

They all sprang from the same source, the hostile attitude to Army Education of many influential officers. Generally speaking there were four categories of such officers. There were the root-and-branchers whose whole-hearted opposition could always be relied on. They never doubted the undesirability of Army Education. Captain Plume, who said 'a fellow that can write can draw petitions' and who feared that the consequences of their concomitant contumacy would be the promotion of the Jacobinism and of its later embodiments Chartism and Radicalism, fear of which was widespread in society, spoke for many officers more influential than he was.[34] They were also afraid that the more educated a soldier became the more difficult he might be to control. It was a commonplace to say, as Colonel Eltrington did, that 'the art of governing people in the ranks is not to be learnt at school' and that 'if men were taught too much their heads only become addled'.[35] They could point the moral and adorn the tale. Two Grenadiers engaged in 'a discussion regarding forms of government' were so uplifted by it as to act in a way that led them to be charged with mutiny and to be committed to the Tower.[36] Such root-and-branch opponents of Army Education saw in it another difficulty too, although they were well aware of the advantages of not making it widely known. Le Marchant's scheme for Other-Rank Education had been rejected among other grounds because it was 'inconsistent with the habits of the country to raise private soldiers to so close an equality with their officers'.[37] Aware of the educational achievements of the officer and unwilling to face the formidable task of making them more impressive, they could not but be conscious of the strength of this argument against educating the other ranks. It was essentially the same argument, in another context, which led to the changing of the Army Schoolmaster's original uniform; its power had not diminished over the years.

In the second category of the opponents of Army Education were those who opposed it in private but who on occasion were prepared to give it their reluctant support. Prominent among them was the Duke of Wellington. His ideal officers were 'gentlemen fitted for command by their breeding and education ... willing to serve the Crown for honour and not material gain'. As long as the officer had 'the education given to English gentlemen', that would suffice. Deprived of it, European Armies had to depend on their military academies which produced 'pedants and coxcombs'. Such academies and Staff Colleges, if introduced in Britain, would lower the tone of the Army and impair the cohesion of the Officer Corps. It was said that Wellington treated the Army Schools 'to the last as mischievous innovations, and the not improbable *foci* of mutiny'. Gleig assures us that his old friend Sir George Brown could be relied on in saying that he heard Wellington exploding 'If there is ever a mutiny in the Army – and in all probability we shall have one – you'll see that these new-fangled schoolmasters will be at the bottom of it.' However, if we rely on Gleig's authority or believe with Colonel White that this is merely 'part of the enormous Wellington apocrypha', we cannot take this as his considered view of the Schoolmasters or of Army Education. As the years went by he saw the necessity of moving with the times. We cannot forget his most important support of Gleig and his support of the proposal to 'raise the position of the Schoolmaster'. His statement that 'time alone would tell if the setting up of schools was justified' best sums up his position.[38] Army Education would have developed much more slowly than it did had Wellington, and the many who thought as he did, been its only supporters.

Then there were the many who believed Army Education to be unnecessary. Typical of them was the Commander-in-Chief, the Duke of Cambridge, who told a parliamentary committee that the examinations for the Certificates of Education which aspiring NCOs had to pass were too difficult and that only elementary reading and writing should be required of the NCO.[39] Their readiness to think Army Education unnecessary was strengthened by their awareness of the difficulty of providing it, Lord William Paulet when Adjutant-General thinking this insuperable.[40] This conviction that the soldier did not need education was further strengthened by the belief widespread after Forster's Education Act of 1870 that what he needed he would in any case get elsewhere. When, with the abandoning in 1888 of the 4th Class Army Certificate, compulsory attendance at school for recruits was ended on the grounds that in the few weeks devoted to recruit training he could not be expected to reach the standard required for the 3rd Class Certificate, it was concluded that the soldier need reach no educational standard at all. He could be accepted as a soldier and left in his unlettered state. His military training could proceed and, although General Orders continued to stress that it was as important that he should be able to read and write as to do his drill, as long as he could do that his inability to read and write could be overlooked. No doubt the Army hoped it could train him into adequacy and that somehow, somewhere along the line, he would, as it were, pick up from the ambient air the minimum of education needed to consolidate that achievement. Misplaced or justified as that hope might be, it at least left no doubt of the widespread conviction in the Army that Army Education was unnecessary.

There were others in the Army who, while believing Army Education to be necessary, thought it could not have priority and who hoped and believed that the years and the changes they would bring would eventually remove the need for it. Lord Wolseley, a distinguished supporter of Army Education, spoke for them. He called attention to Colonel Gleig's view that the 4th Class Army Certificate was worthless and stressed the priority training must have, now that Cardwell's reforms had brought in the short-service man who, when he returned to civilian life, would continue to provide a reserve for the Army and whose training must have priority if the Army was to get from him any worthwhile service at all. Army Education must await its turn if Forster's Education Act did not remove the necessity for it.[41]

The Professor of Military Science at the Royal Military College said in June 1855 'Military education is but little valued by the greater part of the high military authorities.'[42] Twenty years later it was still the same. The findings of an 1887 Parliamentary Committee showed with what little esteem education was still generally regarded by the Army leaders. Those who, in Wolseley's words, saw the Army as a tradition and not as a profession were strong. They wanted no changes. They had been appalled when in the early 19th Century the Duke of York introduced the confidential report. They said this was 'wicked' and 'degrading', 'dark' and 'foul'. It turned the Army 'whose constitution is based on the most scrupulous adherence to the highest and nicest principles of honour into a graduated corps of spies from the ensign up to the general'. They opposed the Cardwell reforms. The traditionalists were strongly supported for it could be maintained, as Kipling did, that attempts to reform the Army adversely affected its capacity to discharge its function overseas. He believed that Cardwell's short-service enlistment lowered the morale of the soldiers of the Raj. In the *Drums of the Fore and Aft* he tells of a regiment which broke and fled in the face of the enemy because its short-service men lacked the toughness and endurance which had been instilled by longer service into their predecessors.[43]

Unfortunately, outstanding Minister of War as he was, Cardwell was of those who work against rather than with the grain of things. Wolseley said of him 'There was nothing in common between him and the fighting British soldiers. The ambitions, the prospects, the feelings and prejudices of our officers were not known to him.'[44] Lord Haldane, a later and greater Minister of War, won over the High Command as Cardwell never did. Had Haldane not done so he could never have fashioned in so short a time the magnificent Expeditionary Force which went to France in 1914. Cardwell did not carry the Army enthusiastically with him, with the result that for the next quarter of a century Army reform stagnated. Those who, like Wolseley, wanted it were a small and isolated group. The great majority of officers remained opposed to reform. Moreover, the view was by no means confined to the Army that it was in lands sunnier than Europe that its worth had to be demonstrated and that if the Navy did its job, as who could doubt that it would, the Army would do adequately what it was called upon to do, as the suppression of the Indian Mutiny had shown. 'We could not dispense with command of the sea but having that why should we bother about command of the land?' Winston Churchill asked. 'If we had command of the sea', he added, 'we required fewer soldiers; if we had it not we want more ships.'[45] That was the attitude that made it so difficult to keep up the pressure for Army reform and that even strengthened those who opposed it. Given this unresolved conflict in the Army and this persistent struggle between the forces working for and against Army Education, we can easily understand its chequered course in the 19th Century Army. Circumstances favoured now the one and now the other side in the fight and it is to these we must look for understanding of the changes and chances of Army Education in it.

The Protracted Struggle for Army Education in the 19th Century

In the first part of the 19th Century the pressures working for Army Education were much stronger than those opposing it and therefore it showed slow but steady and cumulatively impressive progress. This we can see in the setting up of regimental schools. In 1662 the East India Company seems to have led the way by requesting a schoolmaster for Madras when the officers of Fort St George asked it to provide a school. However, the first record of such a school is the garrison school in Tangier founded in 1675. It would be wrong, however, to think that Kirke's Lambs stationed there acquired a scholarly reputation. The first regimental school in England was that of the Grenadier Guards, established in 1762 in the Tower. The Royal Hibernian School in Dublin was set up in 1789 as a result of a public petition got up by those who were appalled by the poverty of the families of soldiers quartered in Ireland and at that of the families left behind by Irish Regiments serving overseas. The Royal Military Asylum at Chelsea was founded in 1801 by Frederick, Duke of York. This was 'for the management and education of a certain number of orphans and other children of NCOs and soldiers of our army'. There was also in later years schooling for a number of children in institutions maintained by the Royal Victoria Patriotic Fund, a charity founded after the Crimean War for the families of servicemen.

The Dublin and Chelsea schools were maintained from the public purse but in the closing years of the 18th Century the practice was widespread of regiments establishing their own schools. Thus, besides the Grenadiers, the Royal Artillery opened its regimental schools in Woolwich in 1797, the Coldstream Guards theirs in St George's Barracks, Charing Cross, in 1784. So well thought of was the school of the Royal Scots that the Stirling magistrates asked that local children might join it.[46] Regimental schools were set up abroad, too. The 52nd Foot opened one in Sicily in 1807 – with remarkably beneficial results, it seems, since it was said that 'there was not a soldier of the 52nd guilty of any of those atrocious crimes which were then so frequent in the army'.

In 1811 the Duke of York asked Palmerston, then Secretary at War, to establish regimental schools throughout the Army 'for the education of young soldiers and the soldiers' children', and it was recommended that schools should now be set up in every battalion or corps. They were to be taught by schoolmaster Sergeants and each regiment was required to nominate a 'suitably qualified' NCO to be trained as such at Chelsea.[47] This was followed by a letter from the Adjutant-General to Commanding Officers of Regulars and of the Militia saying that the Government contemplated providing cash for establishing regimental schools and informing them that they would be pleased to look out for someone to take charge of them. The responses of the regiments varied considerably. Some were pleased to report that this had already been done, the North Yorkshire Militia proudly announcing that 'one William Hutchinson had for several years acted as Schoolmaster to the Regiment and given the greatest satisfaction in that capacity'. Others declined to be pleased to look. They may, however, have been encouraged to do so by the announcement of 1 January 1812 that Generals and Commanding Officers would take the schools under their special protection. Regimental chaplains were to keep an eye on them too, and to ensure that girls also should be taught 'whenever the circumstances would so permit'.

By 1821 the post of Schoolmaster Sergeant was a recognised appointment on the strength of every regiment. His rate of pay was that of a Staff-Sergeant. A second general order of July 1812 required a room to be set aside in each barracks for a school and authorised an allowance of coal for heating it. The Schoolmaster Sergeant was to teach the children and the young soldiers. Enlisted boys could be seen in Marlborough's army as trumpeters, drummers and buglers, but it was only in the Revolutionary and Napoleonic Wars that they became numerous. Faced with a shortage of recruits, the Army raised four line regiments of boys and in 1813 every line battalion was authorised to recruit up to fifty boys.[48] And, *mirabile dictu*, Palmerston in 1812 made available £20,000, a sum which he considered to be 'neither useless nor lavish', to run the schools.[49] This was twenty years before Parliament approved a grant to help set up civilian elementary schools. The Army schools were pioneering ventures and it was the Army that was giving the lead to civilian education.

The movement to a national system of compulsory education was very slow in 19th Century Britain, not being fully established until 1891. Long before then every Army child was receiving compulsory education. The Army conscience in this matter of education was sufficiently tender to prompt it to open a school, which they had to attend for eight hours a day, a very heavy load with which they would probably have wished to dispense, for the 1,300 boys who were employed making cartridges at the Royal Arsenal, a precedent at which mill and factory owners would have looked askance.[50] Fees had at first to be paid for attendance at school. Two pence a month was charged for one child, three half-pence for each child if three or four children from the same family came. Eight pence a month was paid by Sergeants attending school, six pence for Corporals and four pence for privates. These fees were abolished, as the Royal Commission recommended in 1871, in this provision of free education, too, the Army breaking the trail for civilians.

In 1850 two new types of Army school were opened. These were infant schools and so-called 'industrial schools'. Schoolmistresses looked after the infant schools; when Macaulay was Secretary at War he signed a Royal Warrant appointing a Schoolmistress to every regiment or regimental depot. It was to be upon their looks and character, not upon their scholastic achievements, that their suitability was to be judged. It would suffice for them to be 'a good plain woman, who might be the wife of a Sergeant'. Teaching experience was not thought a desirable extra. When, however, a professional Corps of Teachers was established and high standards demanded from its members, the Schoolmistresses whose teaching would be closely associated with them would have to be professionally trained, this also being insisted on in 1847.[51]

The naming of the industrial school was the most industrial thing about it; it could, however, have been important. In the afternoons the regimental Schoolmasters took the older boys, giving them what training they could provide in trades, while the Schoolmistresses taught the girls sewing. A great opportunity was missed here. Training in trades could have been developed and could have led to the breakthrough in technical and vocational education that would so much have benefitted the soldier, the Army and indeed the nation. Such a breakthrough would never result from reliance on what skilled teaching might be available. It needed skilled craftsmen; if the regiments thought of paying for them, they decided they could not be afforded. Without that support it was decline, not development, that faced the industrial schools, as was borne out by the Royal Commission's regret that there was virtually no technical training given to Army children.

The standard of those schools was varied. In some it was very good. In 1861 the Council of Military Education said that Army children were as well educated as children attending a national school. In the same year the Newcastle Commission reported favourably on Army Schools. The Reverend George Robert Gleig, one of the greatest supporters of Army Education, who was critical of some of the teaching he saw, nevertheless was convinced that 'The army schools are very superior to those in civil life.' 'The educational results of the schools', the Royal Commission of 1870 said, 'are decidedly successful, as compared with those of civil schools of a similar class.' And when Colonel Gleig, the nephew of the Reverend Gleig, retired in 1881 after many years' service as Inspector of Schools, they were said to be 'in a high state of efficiency'. Its schools served the Army well, as a significant proportion of recruits were Army children and they, unlike other recruits, could be relied on to be educated. Nor should we forget that the knowledge that his children would be educated would enhance the attraction of military life to the soldier.[52]

Efforts were made, not always successfully, to keep the schools under such supervision as to ensure they kept up to scratch.[53] Commanding Officers were reminded to keep a close eye on their schools and Chaplains were to visit them regularly. In 1846 the Chaplain-General to the Forces, the Reverend Gleig, assumed responsibility for the schools on becoming the first Inspector General of Army Schools. Lieutenant-Colonel Lefroy succeeded him as Inspector General for three years. The Council of Military Education, originally created to supervise Officer Education, assumed responsibility for Army Education in general, including the schools. And when in 1870 the post of Director-General of Military Education was created, schools came under his control until his post was abolished in 1898.

Standards in schools were not always as high. Perhaps abroad conditions were always likely to be more difficult. When compulsory education was accepted in Britain the comfort of children was rarely considered. Neither did it bulk large in the thinking of the providers of regimental schools. In 1896 the Director-General of Military Education reported that large numbers of younger children were risking deformity by sitting in chairs and using desks made for adults. The British do indeed, as Burke said, retain much of the old when they change. After the Second World War University Extra-Mural and WEA classes were sometimes held in schools and the adults attending them often had to sit in chairs and before desks made for children. More often than not in Army schools heating and lighting were inadequate in winter. The Treasury was obdurately unhelpful. As late as 1815 it maintained that 'the allowance of candles to regimental schools should in no case be granted' and when gas arrived it was only turned on half an hour after sunset. Abroad, the comfort of those attending school was often even less of a consideration. The School in Malta was 'dark, comfortless and uninviting' and in Hong Kong 300 men were crowded into a room designed for 50. When, as frequently occurred, arrangements for the supply of equipment broke down it almost seemed that greater effort went into emptying than filling schoolrooms.

At home, too, the teaching could be very bad. The Commander-in-Chief India was impressed by Dr Bell and his monitorial system. It became the standard practice there and in many of the larger schools in Britain. In those adopting this system there was a Schoolmaster Sergeant who would be helped by a boy Sergeant and perhaps by a boy Corporal too. In one visited by Gleig, dullness o'er all exerted her ancient right, no ray of light piercing the prevailing gloom. The teachers did not know what to teach or how to teach it. How could they, they plaintively asked, as no one had taught them. Elsewhere, too, it was obvious how limited was the success of birch and bawl.

Attendance was irregular. Boys were supposed to be compelled to attend; they often exercised their ingenuity in keeping out of the classroom. NCOs were expected to attend but their duties often took them elsewhere. Privates were encouraged to attend but a great majority felt themselves more encouraged to attend to other things. When there were other and more important tasks to be done, schools were not attended at all. In 1896 the Director General of Army Education criticised the lack of interest in the Schools shown by some Commanding Officers; those in the earlier part of the century who thought as they did were not a few.[54] The advocates of Army Education were discouraged by the judiciary, too. An attempt was made to make attendance of NCOs at regimental schools compulsory on a fee-paying basis. An NCO objected and was gaoled after court-martial for disobeying an order. A series of law-suits followed and in the course of an appeal the judge ruled 'It is no part of military duty to attend a school and to learn to read and write.' It was a little odd that a judge and not the Army should determine what constituted military duty; the judgement was later overturned.[55]

The schools certainly needed improving but they could not be improved if they had not been established. In the struggle between the forces pushing for and those holding back education in the Army the establishment of the schools registered the victory of the former, and it was a great victory. Nor was it the only victory for education at this time.

If men were to be encouraged to read, the view was bound to be expressed that they ought to have access to books. Thus libraries began to be thought of for regiments as well as schools. In 1793 a garrison library was opened in Gibraltar, in 1800 the Rifle Corps established its library, and in 1813 the Royal Engineers founded their library at Chatham. These were mainly for officers, but when the Coldstream Guards opened their school in 1804 a lending library supplied by the officers was attached to it for the use of the men. By 1816 the Royal Engineers had opened reading rooms for NCOs and they had got together small travelling libraries for their scattered detachments. A library was opened in Malta in 1825; four years earlier the East India Company had provided libraries for their European troops. Sir Charles Gordon of the Black Watch curtailed the hours of the 'wet' canteen and started a regimental library in 1830, his two-fold action marking, as it were, the opening round in the long-continuing battle between the bottle and the book. To seek to put men and women into rigidly exclusive categories is to ignore the richness of human nature; the drinking man may enjoy the library and the thinking man be at home in the 'wet' canteen. Sir Charles's hope was, nevertheless, a reasonable one that the hours spent in the one would reduce the time spent in the other. A dozen regiments had followed suit by 1830, in which year Lord Hill, the Commander-in-Chief, asked that a furnished reading room be established in every barracks and a library in every large barracks. By 1876 there were no fewer than 150 libraries for the troops at home and abroad.[56]

In 1840 the Army allotted £2,000 for the provision of thirty-one station libraries. All soldiers on payment of one penny per month could use them. By 1844 there were thirty-eight libraries at home and forty abroad, no foreign station being without one. In the Crimean War Florence Nightingale ensured that home-going ships carrying the sick and the wounded should take with them the books she would provide. Clearly, books were becoming part of Army life. A report of 1859 showed that an average of £1,744 was spent each year on them. In 1857 Prince Albert began the systematic purchase of books for the education of officers, this being the beginning of the Prince Consort's Library, for many years the jewel in the crown of the Army's library services. There was a constant increase too in the number of Army libraries. 'Over the dust and the glory of the day constantly brooded the shadow of the cat', Dickens writes of the soldiery. The part libraries played in lifting that shadow was no small one, and this at a time when there were virtually no public libraries. Even after the Public Libraries Act of 1850, not many were set up. The role of the libraries in the development of Army Education is not to be underestimated.

This spreading of libraries throughout the Army was not unopposed. Like the extension of education generally, it was slower than it might have been because of the widespread belief that it would disturb social stability. Lord Hill had his initial doubts before giving the opening of libraries his support. The Duke of York, a good friend of Army Education, thought that libraries were unnecessary and objectionable institutions. Perhaps he had a premonition of Andrew Carnegie gibbering away on future horizons, expressing the hope that the funding of the Carnegie Libraries would so deprive the British Army of recruits as to lead to its demise. In any case the Duke's fear was as silly as Carnegie's hope was stupid. There were indeed radical pamphlets about, exhorting soldiers to disobey their officers and desert, but whoever expected the shelves of regimental libraries to be sagging under their weight? Nor should it be forgotten that the outstanding characteristic of many of these pamphlets was a manifest daftness and that they, for the most part, had the great virtue of being unreadable. The Duke, however, was prepared to approve the issue of certain 'selected and safe' books such as *Kind Caution to Profane Swearers, Companion for the Aged, Disclosure on a Death-Bed Repentance*. Even those who doubted the desirability of exhorting the soldiery to live a more sober, righteous and godly life would have approved of those things which might have bred in them a greater immunity to the bottle. But if the Duke had read the books he recommended he might have had a greater understanding than seemed to be the case that such reading would in all likelihood add to the attractions both of illiteracy and of drink.[57]

There was to be another and still greater success for the forces pushing Army Education on. This was the appointment to significant office of perhaps the most outstanding man ever associated with education in the Army. This was the Rev George Robert Gleig who in 1846 was appointed Inspector-General of Army Schools, all of which were now under his authority.[58] He had been appointed Principal Chaplain in 1844. He became Chaplain-General as well as Inspector-General of Schools in 1846 and was to hold both offices until 1857 and the former until 1875. An Exhibitioner of Balliol College, Oxford at the age of fifteen, he left a year later to become an ensign in the Light Infantry. He was wounded both in the fighting in Spain against the French and in the fighting around New Orleans against the Americans.

He left the Army after Waterloo and was ordained in 1820 after completing his studies at Oxford. A man of immense energy, he turned to the pen to supplement his stipend. He wrote well and prolifically, and one of his books, *The Subaltern*, brought him to the attention of the Duke of Wellington, with whom he became friendly. This and his contributions to the important magazines of the day such as *Blackwoods*, *Fraser's Magazine* and *The Quarterly Review* brought him into sufficient notice for him to be appointed Chaplain of the Royal Hospital at Chelsea. Lord Russell told him later that the offer of the chaplaincy had been made to him 'not for your sake, but for the sake of the old pensioners, who I thought would like better a man who had seen battles, than a high and dry Churchman'.[59] Chelsea gave Gleig an important London pulpit and brought him into contact with influential people in education, in politics and in the Army – hence no doubt, his later appointments as Chaplain-General and Inspector-General of Schools.

He was not a man of original ideas. But he could appreciate the original thinking of others and see its relevance to what he wanted to do. What was original was his successful development within the Army of these original and indeed radical ideas. He had the great capacity for hard work, the outstanding determination and drive that enabled him to overcome the problems in the way of the application of these ideas to his own special circumstances. There is, however, a proverb 'God says take what you want from the world and pay for it.' Drive and energy have to be paid for and part of the price is often an impatient unwillingness to pay existing complexity the attention without which difficulties will undoubtedly multiply. Yet a circumspect compliance, indeed an unexpected flexibility, can sometimes be seen in him. He was for a moment willing to appease Lord Panmure by agreeing that the Secretary of State and not the Army should control Army Education – despite his earlier and his later opposition to this. This is not to say that there was anything of the time-server in him. There was not. He would have agreed whole-heartedly with Burke when Burke told his recalcitrant constituents that it would be absurd for him to renounce his objects in order to obtain his seat. Gleig valued his friendship with Wellington but went on pushing for what he wanted even though he knew that this would cost him that friendship. His fault was not in his occasional compliance but in his usual lack of it. A greater flexibility might have provided a greater impetus for his work and might have made it possible for it to continue longer. It was because he did so much for Army Education and had the capacity to do still more if he had been permitted to do so, that it is to be regretted there was an inherent arrogance in him, the absence of which might have profited Army Education.

The moment was ripe for the man. He had the luck which Napoleon said was essential for success in public life. Without Wellington he might never have arrived; without Sir Sidney Herbert he might never have achieved. As Secretary to the Admiralty, Sir Sidney had shown his interest in Service education by reorganising the Royal Naval School at Greenwich. As Secretary at War in 1845–46 he pushed through Gleig's greatest achievement, the founding in 1846 of the Corps of Army Schoolmasters, a new body, entry to which was only open initially to civilians. Gleig knew that he could not raise the standards in the Army schools unless he could have as his teachers there those who were carefully selected, trained and inspected. They were to be chosen after rigorous competitive examination and they were to attend a two-year course in which, as with the post-1945 BEd., there would be both academic study and teaching practice. They would, on enlistment, rank next to the Sergeant-Major. They were not to be subjected to corporal punishment 'in the very improbable case of gross misconduct'. They were to wear a distinctive uniform. This was to be a blue frock coat with gold shoulder knots, smart trousers and boots, a cap with a crown of gold thread on the front, a sash, sword-belt and sword. They were to receive 2s.6d. a day, with a further 6d. a day for efficiency and good conduct.[60]

Gleig's school, known as the Normal School, opened at the Royal Military Asylum, Chelsea, in 1847. It was the forerunner of the Army Schools of Education at Shorncliffe and at Belgaum in India. Gleig's would-be teachers were twenty-four in number. It was, however, soon agreed that NCOs could present themselves for examination and, if they successfully passed it, join the course. That the course was no sinecure is evident from the high drop-out rate, only thirteen of the initial intake completing their training and enlisting as Army Schoolmasters. They must have been a great improvement on the former Sergeant Schoolmasters. One Commanding Officer wrote that 'the new system of education was very popular'. His men were spending less time in the 'wet' canteen and this he attributed to the school.[61] It was a good beginning and it was well followed up. As the years went by it became evident that the schools fostered in the children who attended them a sense of belonging to the Army, which helped recruitment. The Schoolmasters' work with adults was impressive, too. As the Council of Military Education reported in 1870, they halved in a decade the startling rate of illiteracy in the Army, an undoubted achievement even if one is tempted to wonder how literate the standard of literacy was.[62]

Noteworthy as this was, it was, nevertheless, a chequered future which the Schoolmaster faced. It was still to be a very long haul indeed before education won an assured place in the Army. Events were to happen which would strengthen those who knew that the Army must be brought up-to-date to meet the challenges of a manifestly more dangerous world and who understood that education had its part to play in adding to the effectiveness of the Army. Unfortunately, other events were to strengthen those who were convinced that the Army could very well remain as it was. And so the long battle which was fought throughout the century between those who wanted reform in the Army and who wanted the pace of that reform to be quickened, and those who doubted its necessity and who thought, when it seemed to them it could not longer be avoided, that its implementation should be delayed as much as possible, took on a new urgency.

Ironically, too, the reforms which were adopted tended to frustrate the attempts which accompanied them to develop education. Above all, it gradually became evident that the circumstances which had given greater strength to the advocates than to the opponents of Army Education in the earlier part of the century had now so changed that the opponents of education in the Army had the upper hand in its later stages. Moreover, two events added great bitterness and ferocity to that struggle and boded ill for Army Education.

One was the Crimean War, which showed how needful it was to modernise the Army. The heroism and sufferings of its troops in the Crimea brought to the country's attention by an outstanding war correspondent, William Russell, and by the devoted work of a great lady who touched its heart-strings, Florence Nightingale, evoked bitter condemnation of those who had so ill-prepared for their needs and whose leadership was so appallingly deficient. Lions led by donkeys, fussy old women masquerading as generals, these were the headlines that leaped out of the pages of the press. This was an intolerable situation and the British people were no longer prepared to tolerate it. Hitherto determined to keep their army weak, they were at last anxious to make it strong. It was a startling innovation for the British to want a better army and this was bound to have its effects, even though they were unlikely to want it long. A much more lasting effect was the alienation of those who were described by the gentlemen of the press as the donkeys who led the lions in the Crimea. Officers who could never have been thus described would no doubt ensure that they never could be thereafter. But those who were rightly thus labelled would not think well of their tormentors. They would be greatly indignant and only too apt to see in the spread of education in their units the intrusion of the hated pen into the legitimately exclusive realm of the sword.

The other event which greatly embittered many officers was the abolition of the purchase of commissions, which was bitterly opposed. It is no accident that it followed the Reform Act of 1867 which far more than the Great Reform Act of 1832 marked the transition in Britain from aristocratic to middle-class rule. Abolition of purchase raised the issue on which the vast majority of senior ranks in the Army united with the landed gentry against the reformers. The resistance in Parliament was bitter in the extreme. The abuse of Parliamentary procedure which is associated with the behaviour of the Irish members in the 1880s now first appeared. The opposition in the Lords was even stronger than in the Commons. It was specifically declared that an inefficient Army was better than one which might pave the way to the setting up of an authoritarian state to which a non-purchase Army might lead. In the end Gladstone could only secure abolition of purchase by the use of the Royal Warrant.[63] That bitterness seems to have resulted in the determination to ensure that reforms should be as little effective as possible. How else can the acceptance of such a situation as that described by Lord Wolseley be explained? He said after his Egyptian campaigns of 1882–85 that 'Splendid battalions were kept in the rear while others of inferior quality were sent to the front because the General commanding did not dare to use against the enemy a Corps whose Commanding Officer was manifestly incompetent.'[64] Against that degree of entrenched bitterness it was hard for the reformers to make headway.

Nevertheless, it was not at once apparent that the educational tide was on the turn. The need for education was obvious. Lord Panmure at the War Office was impressed by the fact that continental armies attached more importance to scientific training than did the British Army, that in those armies schools were far more important, that they employed a much greater number of teachers, that they spent a great deal more money on military education.[65] Who could say we were justified on spending less when the educational standard of our recruits was so low? In 1871 the Fourth Class Army Certificate was introduced as something which all recruits must acquire. Its standard was described as being about equal to that reached by a child of eight. The unseemliness of comparing a soldier with a child of eight may have had something to do with its abolition in 1887 on the grounds that it was not worth having, as no doubt was the fact that in 1882 over 40% of recruits were unable to attain it. Ten years later the Director of Military Education reported that the educational standard of the recruit was 'at a low ebb' and that 'a number had probably had no schooling at all'.[66] Sir Richard Biddulph when Director-General ruefully admitted that 'the day when schools for adults can be dispensed with seems to be as far off as ever'. It was obvious to him that the level of education of the adult civilian was so low that recruits could not be expected to be adequately educated and that Army Education remained a vital necessity.[67]

Moreover, there were persistent attempts to make the most of education by strengthening the control over it. When Gleig retired in 1857 Lord Panmure had become dissatisfied with his work[68] and was glad to appoint as Inspector-General of Military Schools Lieutenant-Colonel John Lefroy. It was an inspired choice. He was a gunner who was known for his scientific studies. He was a man of great drive and energy and great imagination. He got on well with those with whom he had to work and he was soon the confidant of the Schoolmasters. He succeeded in getting the help of Her Majesty's Inspectors of Schools and he soon presented shattering evidence of the very low standard of soldiers' education and of the unhelpful attitude of many regiments to it. 'Men have been called out of school by the Regimental Sergeant-Major for the purpose of trying on clothing or on other trivial grounds for which no one would dream of interrupting a parade', he said. He classified schools in four grades. For the lowest to which Wellington's 1849 order compelled recruits to attend for two hours daily, he abolished fees and by 1870 all fees were got rid of. The hope that free attendance would encourage it was not borne out; every report on regimental schools by the Council of Military Education between 1862 and 1870 emphasised how poorly they were attended and called for compulsory teaching at least of recruits. Nevertheless, as we have seen his measures, which the Council of Military Education continued after his three years in office, halved the rate of illiteracy in the Army.[69]

His contribution to Army Education would have equalled Gleig's had he not fallen foul of the dualistic system of Army control, its sharing by the War Office and the Commander-in-Chief. To some extent this was Gleig's fault. He had persuaded

Lord Panmure to grade soldiers by making use of intelligence tests, the first time such tests were used in the Army. Gleig got two garrisons to try the tests and the results, he gleefully reported, 'struck consternation into the Horse Guards'.[70] His pleasure in so doing, was doubtless dimmed by it precipitating a great row between the War Office and the Commander-in-Chief. The Commander-in-Chief had not been told of the test; he believed his responsibility for reporting on the state of the Army was being ignored and thus undermined and he forbade garrisons to take further part in the tests. Lord Panmure had to climb down; hence his letter to the Queen expressing his dissatisfaction with Gleig. Matters did not, however, end here. Lord Panmure wanted Lefroy to draw up a plan which would unify education in the Army and bring it under the control of the Secretary of State. This, as we have seen, the Duke would not accept and with the support of the Queen he prevailed. Lefroy was not appointed Inspector-General of Military Education. He remained in post only until 1860 when he turned his attention to planning Britain's coastal defences and the Army, having been offered two different schemes to forward its education, found, no doubt not to its surprise, that both were soon forgotten. No one in matters educational in the Army in what remained of the century had Lefroy's promise, though only when the office of Director-General of Military Education was abolished was the effort to forward the cause of Army Education by keeping it under firm control given up. For nearly thirty years before then education was in the control of the Director-General, it was stable and it enjoyed the advantages stability brings.

When Lefroy ceased to be Inspector-General of Schools the control of Army Education passed into the hands of the Council of Military Education. With their usual determination to live with anomalies long after others have ended them, the British made this Council responsible to the Secretary of State and made its President the Commander-in-Chief. This was either to ensure that its responsibility would be discharged as contentiously as possible or that it would be careful always to avoid contentious issues. It is likely it was the latter that was intended as this was how the Council acted. In so doing the British were listening to the still, small voice which so often speaks to them in matters educational but to which they seem uncharacteristically deaf today and being convinced by it that, as Talleyrand said of diplomacy, too great zeal was to be deplored.

There was one civilian, a mathematician called Canon Moseley, on the Council and the few commissioned Supervisory Schoolmasters were also members. Its conduct of business was somewhat haphazard. It had no agenda, dealing with matters as they arose and acting only when all were agreed. It had few officials on whom it could rely to carry out whatever decisions it came to. At home three assistant inspectors were responsible to it; abroad a Staff Officer acted as its agent for the time being. It hardly needed its lack of financial power to demonstrate that it was not the strongest of bodies and that it was an inadequate replacement for the energetic, imaginative and well thought-of Lefroy. In fact it did surprisingly well. It made compellingly the utilitarian case for Army Education. It stressed how important it was for NCOs to be able to keep accounts and make returns. It insisted they must be better qualified educationally and, to ensure they would be, it introduced the Army Certificates of

Education, its most important achievement. Nor did it leave unmentioned the higher and broader grounds on which the case for education rested, namely the improved moral and intellectual standards which can in general be expected to result from it. It took its supervision of the schools seriously. It believed, as Colonel Wilson did in the Interim Scheme of Education after the Second World War, that the best way to achieve success in the Army for any special instruction was not to arrange regular classes during the normal working week, but to send men on courses during which they would be exempted from their normal duties. It seemed to be useless to arrange classes for large numbers of men most of whom, if they ever appeared, did so very irregularly. There would be only a few keen students who should attend classes for six or seven weeks and be free of all duties. Such special classes became a standard feature of military schools and undoubtedly the few benefitted from them. In 1858 Lefroy had arranged the first analysis of literacy in the Army. It showed that one-fifth of the troops could neither read nor write and that another fifth could read but not write; these he called uneducated. The Council's courses for the few would leave many soldiers in Lefroy's category 'uneducated'. However it was of the opinion that a full return for the money spent on education would never be obtained until compulsory education is the rule of the Service, a view which encouraged the advocates of Army Education.[71]

After ten not unprofitable years the Council was abolished, its supervision of all forms of military education now being undertaken by a Director-General of Military Education. The first holder of the officer was one of our most distinguished soldiers, Lord Napier, and his choice must greatly have raised the spirits of those who hoped for the further development of Army Education. How much it benefitted from a control that was centralised and continuous became obvious after 1898, in which year his office was abolished.

There were in these years developments in Army Education which further encouraged its supporters. There was the introduction by the Council of Military Education in 1860 of the Army Certificate of Education. Self-help always characterised the regiments and while officers would know who were potential NCOs, the advantage of some method of selection which could claim a degree of objectivity and which would eliminate the possibility of favouritism soon became apparent. Sometimes regiments set up a standing promotion board which the Schoolmasters sat on. Some regiments instituted their own tests, as the Green Howards did after the Crimean War.[72] The First Class Certificate, which the Army considered 'a superior education', was awarded as a result of periodic examinations. The Second and Third Class Certificates were presented on the recommendations of the Schoolmaster and later of the Commanding Officer. For the Second Class Certificate a soldier had 'to read a book of moderate difficulty and to write fairly a passage dictated from the same' and keep Mess Books, Ledger and Regimental Savings' Bank Books, and to cope with 'reasonably advanced' arithmetic. For the Third Class Certificate the soldier had to read an easy narrative and to do elementary arithmetic. More and more regiments turned to the Certificates since tests for prospective NCOs seemed a sensible way of assessing them. It was the obvious desirability of standardising them that led to the

Council of Military Education instituting the Army Certificates of Education. Not untypically, in introducing these Certificates the Council of Military Education had judged it best to leave Commanding Officers 'free to adopt them or not at their discretion'. In 1871 that discretion was removed and regimental certificates abolished.

There were further developments to encourage the supporters of Army Education. In 1881 promotion above the rank of Colour Sergeant was made dependant on the holding of a First Class Certificate. In the 1880s there was additional assistance given to potential NCOs. A booklet, *Second Class Certification of Education* was published and in 1886 *A Guide to Obtaining a First Class Certificate of Education* appeared. In 1889 there followed *The Third Class Army School Certificate Made Easy*.[73] This was little enough inducement to the soldier to take the certificates, but it was better than none. The standard to be reached to gain the certificates was not high. In particular the ability to read which had to be shown to achieve the Third Class was insufficient to give the soldier enjoyment in reading and learning. But the certificates called for effort and slog from those who sought them and we should not forget the reflection of one Army Schoolmaster: 'I used to wonder how many of the ordinary men in the street could pass such a test as the young NCO was asked to before his second stripe.' At worst the gaining of the certificates demanded effort and concentration from the soldier, at best it could have given a good teacher opportunity to open and strengthen minds. And much as the Army Schoolmasters disliked 'certificate grinding', the work for them kept them in the field and this gave them the opportunity to promote their extra-mural work, which the Army always appreciated and the contribution of which to their survival was significant. In this they could find the excitement and the culture denied to them in much of their teaching.[74]

There were indications, too, that the general education of the soldier was not being entirely neglected. In the late 1850s lectures were provided for the troops by officers, padres and Schoolmasters. They proved popular in Aldershot Camp and they soon spread, regiment vying with regiment in their provision. It was a good way of encouraging the others, perhaps more so than of encouraging the men, regimental rivalry being, as always, intense. But the men attended and interest was there. In 1866 more than 1,700 lectures were given to the troops at home and abroad. Aware that competition between the regiments in the number of lectures arranged could easily result – when the numbers game was being played – in the decline in their quality, and that if this happened lectures would be given to increasingly empty benches, the War Office in 1870 ceased to publish details of the lectures given. When the recommendation of the Royal Commission that the recruit should be compelled to attend school until he had reached a minimum educational standard was at once implemented, when in the new barracks being built there were classrooms provided, when it was arranged that HMIs should visit and report on Army schools, those pressing for Army Education could not believe their cause was lost.[75]

Important as these things were, however, still more important was the fact that became evident in the late 19th Century, that the tide in Army Education was now fully on the ebb. Centralised direction of Army Education would have needed a much greater faith in it and a much greater determination to forward it than there was on the part of the centralised authority to hold back this tide. What followed that centralised direction, when the office of Director-General of Military Education was abolished, was much more suited to the times and only in one matter was the set of the tide not apparent. Reform played its part in strengthening the tide making against Army Education. The Cardwell reforms did not weaken the arguments of the stalwarts fighting for it. They pointed out that as soldiers would now be returning more frequently to civilian life it would enhance the reputation of the Army and thus help recruiting if the education of discharged soldiers was such as to bring them acceptable civilian employment. Such arguments, sound as they are, have begun to appeal to the Army only now, after a century and a quarter. They failed at this time to impress those who insisted that to get the best from the short-service soldier he must be trained as quickly as possible, and in the new and pressing circumstances training must have priority. A similar situation developed with a similar effect on Army Education when the conscript had to be trained quickly on the outbreak of the Korean War. Another reform, that introduced by Forster's Education Act of 1870, had the same unfortunate effect on Army Education. It greatly strengthened those who said that whatever may have been the case in the past, in the future the Army would have no need to educate the troops as this Act would ensure they would be educated before joining the Colours. Lord Wolseley sincerely desired to see a more educated soldier but after the Forster's Education Act he, too, looked to the State to relieve the Army of the need to produce him. 'The time will come', he said in 1898 'when we shall be able to dispense with Army Schoolmasters.'[76] It was an understandable hope which could only be disproved by bitter experience, which strongly suggested that the recruit who could not find a way of slipping through the meshes of the civilian education net seemed to be among the perpetually unborn.

The assault on Army Education was strong, steady and persistent. In 1879 compulsory education was restricted to the first two years of a soldier's service, in 1882 it was deemed enough for the soldier to attend 220 hours of education, in 1885 it was only in his first six months he had to attend school. And this, as we have seen, ended when the Fourth Class Army Certificate of Education was abolished. The abolition of that disgracefully low standard certificate need not have ended the compulsory education of the recruit. For soldiers can legitimately be forced to attend school if that is necessary for them to acquire skills without which they will be inadequate soldiers and the Army had often declared that unless they reached a minimum educational standard they could not be so. It preferred to ignore what it had said and end its attack on the illiteracy of its soldiers. As the Newcastle Commission conceded, it had a case. For if the object of education was not just to enable soldiers to acquire the skills without which they would be useless, but to so develop their minds that they would become more alert and more intelligent and in this way better soldiers, and it could not be doubted that this was what the educators hoped for, this could not be achieved without their cooperation and consent. The mind which is not prepared to make the effort without which this objective cannot be achieved will never become alert, intelligent and disciplined. The Harris Committee reported in 1887 that it was not uncommon for men to prefer to sit six months in school, heedless of the Schoolmaster, than to try to get a certificate.[77] One must hope their slumbers were as disturbed as irate teachers could make them, yet wonder why those who ordered them there tolerated their continued attendance for six unprofitable months. But what of the view so often propounded that a minimum education was needed to produce the competent soldier? If there had ever been any truth in this, presumably there still was. And if the Army had a case for refusing to continue the effort to educate those who persistently refused to be educated, it had none for making no attempt to encourage soldiers to attend classes and in this way to secure the essential voluntary effort.

It is to be regretted when a desirable objective is not itself sufficient to induce the effort needed for its attainment. However, if it is not, the resources of civilisation can still be of assistance. Increased pay for soldiers improving their education might prompt at least some soldiers to make an effort initially seen as unjustified. Yet it was only in 1906 that this obvious truth was acted upon by giving proficiency pay to soldiers possessing a Third Class Certificate of Education. And such was the belief at that time that the vocational was not to be regarded as education that we cannot be surprised that a way of increasing the attraction of schools in the eyes of the soldiery that seems obvious to us today was not thought of then. The Royal Commission of 1870 was least interested in what would have interested the soldier most, its indifference to vocational matters typical of the priorities in the minds of those pushing at this time for the wider spreading of civilian education. In the Army in the 19th Century technical training was provided only for the small percentage of soldiers for whom this was necessary.[78] Such training would have cost money and the Army never had money to spare. As important as the lack of money was the failure to realise that vocational training had any importance for the Army. It got as far as appointing the Crawford Committee in 1862 to consider the instruction of soldiers and their children in trades.[79] The Committee favoured this but the opposition was too strong. It was said the soldiers lacked the time for additional instruction, that if employed as tradesmen they could not continue to be good soldiers and that civilian tradesmen would take unkindly to military competition. The Commander-in-Chief, the Duke of Cambridge, agreed and added his fear that if fully trained soldiers acquired trade qualifications they would want to leave the Army as soon as possible. After Parliamentary demands for a review of the situation, a further committee reported in 1871 that the number of craftsmen per battalion was most inadequate. The opposition to the employment of soldiers in any but military duties remained too strong. No further attempts to give the troops technical or vocational education were made until well into the 20th Century. As late as 1904, a War Office report on Army Schools rejected the idea that they should teach a trade. In this the Army was reflecting the society from which it sprang. Not until the 1880s was there the beginning of civilian interest in technical education and even then it was a mockery of what was being done by our increasingly formidable industrial rivals, the USA and Germany. Our educational ideal remained that of the cultured gentleman which we derived from the Greeks, and like them we looked down on the education needed by the craftsman, an unbelievable folly in a great industrial nation. Yet the Army was becoming aware of the need to prepare soldiers for resettlement and in 1906 technical classes were held in some garrisons. Had the schools addressed themselves to this, their decline might well have been arrested.[80]

It seemed in these years that the objective sought was to discourage attendance at school. School premises deteriorated. They fell below the standard laid down by the Education Department for State Schools and the Director-General of Military Education thought them far from satisfactory. The supervision of the schools became much less satisfactory. The Privy Council Order of 25 February 1856, which arranged for Her Majesty's Inspectors of Schools to visit Army Schools, was never implemented. Colonel A.G. Gleig, nephew of the former Inspector-General and Chaplain-General, had brought over twenty years' experience as Assistant Inspector and as Inspector of Army Schools to the job. Following his retirement in 1881 an Assistant Director of Military Education was appointed and under him schools were run by a quickly changing succession of staff officers. In 1887 the number of School Inspectors was reduced, a reduction not compensated for by the insistence of the Director-General that inspectors must make surprise visits to schools and by his exhortation to Commanding Officers to visit them too. There was some improvement in 1892 when a Director of Schools was appointed, but in 1903 his office disappeared together with the office of Director of Military Training and Education, which had been created in 1902 and to which the education both of officers and other ranks was entrusted. On the suppression of the latter post the schools became the responsibility of the Adjutant-General, his being a very loose rein as it was emphasised that General Officers Commanding would see to the schools and 'not, except in special circumstances, refer to the War Office any matter connected therewith'. Such continuous and erratic change is more suggestive of St Vitus's Dance than of coherent and rational thought, and it would be eccentric to see in it a strong and steady support of the schools. It is, however, an ill-wind that blows nobody any good. Those responsible for the schools were at least spared the embarrassment of reading reports which could not but have been scathing when adult attendance at them was so frequently derisory. Colonel Pocklington told the Royal Commission he could not even give a rough idea of the numbers attending school as many soldiers registered for it but never attended. In Gibraltar the average attendance was twice to three times a month, in Malta some regiments managed only half-an-hour per week.[81] The inadequacy of the supervision over them and the general losing of interest in them led the children's schools, too, to fall behind civilian schools. Since soldiers and their families were often on the move it was thought essential to have strict uniformity in the curriculum of all Army Schools and this compared unfavourably with the much more imaginative curriculum now adopted in State Schools. There were more facilities in State Schools than the Army had the money to provide. It seemed in keeping with the general decline in Army Schools that less concern was now shown to maintain high standards in the teaching of the infants. In 1887 acting Schoolmistresses were appointed to infant schools; they received a small salary, were given no allowances and earned no pension. Their appointment, as it could not be thought they were of the calibre of the trained Army Schoolmistresses they replaced, indicates how much the drive for education was slackening in the face of the strong desire to economise.

The one matter in which the set of the educational tide was not apparent was the matter of the Army Certificates of Education. Even these were thought undesirable by some. There were those who believed Commanding Officers would have too restricted a pool from which to draw if they could only choose from the educationally qualified. There were those who thought the time needed for the acquisition of the certificates could not be afforded. There were those who held the tests to be unnecessary as they could not reveal the qualities looked for in the good NCO and why should trouble be taken to reveal qualities they did not need?[82] Most, however, disagreed. They did not accept the view that the contemporary soldier was expected to be intelligent and self-reliant which he could not be if he had 'not mastered the rudiments of education and ... been subject to no mental training'. They nevertheless thought it essential to concentrate on the education of the NCO and particularly on that of senior NCOs who were potentially capable of handling more advanced weapons. In this the Army had an urgent need and also a reasonable hope that what it wanted could be achieved, for those seeking promotion would be as anxious to cooperate as those not wanting education never would be if it was thrust upon them. This, however, was the only educational need the greater part of the Army felt and it could not greatly qualify the anti-education set of the military mind in the later years of the 19th Century.

The Corps of Army Schoolmasters

It was this ebbing of the tide of Army Education in the second half of the 19th Century that made it impossible for Gleig's great achievement in establishing the Corps of Army Schoolmasters to have the effect that could be expected from it. The Corps was established by Royal Warrant of 2 July 1846. That same day Gleig was appointed Inspector General of Army Schools. A second Royal Warrant of November 1846 set up the Normal School in Chelsea to train Schoolmasters and a Model School there for regimental schools to copy. Army Schoolmasters had to be between twenty and twenty-five years old. They had to pass a stiff examination. If civilians, they had to hold a certificate of proficiency issued by the Committee of the Council of Education or to have been employed as an assistant teacher in an Army School.

If soldiers they were initially required to hold Sergeant's rank but by 1870 any soldier who had his Commanding Officer's support could apply. They had to pay what universities would later have called 'caution money', a £50 bond returned if they enlisted after training, similar to that demanded by the teacher training colleges. They enlisted in the first place for twelve years. Their first year of training was spent at the Normal School, their second year learning teaching at the Model School of the Asylum. Later, their initial training was reduced to eighteen months. Not surprisingly the requirement to undergo this training when they were already trained teachers occasioned much resentment in civilians seeking entry into the Corps. One Schoolmaster said that the Normal School taught him nothing about the running of Army Schools and nothing useful he did not already know. He failed to see why his civilian qualifications were not enough and believed that this requirement to repeat training was the main reason for civilian reluctance to join the Corps.[83] To begin with their pay was low. It was £54 a year on appointment and it rose biannually by sixpence a day. At this time the average civilian teacher's pay was £93 a year. However the Army Schoolmaster received food, clothing and keep. This low pay was a grievance but it was never the Schoolmaster's greatest grievance. It was substantially increased by the Royal Warrant of 1854. The Royal Commission of 1870 acknowledged that there was general dissatisfaction in the Corps. This it attributed to the decline in the Schoolmaster's status, to unsatisfactory conditions of service and to inadequate pay and pensions. It proposed to increase his pay to £73 a year and that he should retire on half-pay after serving twenty-one years. Leaver, who served as a Schoolmaster from 1898–1919 tells us that his stipend of £120 a year was very little less than that of his father who was Headmaster of a Church School. By Civil Service standards this was very good; it was better than London teachers received. Their salary was £90 a year and London paid more than elsewhere.[84]

The fact that out of the original twenty-four applicants only thirteen made the grade and enlisted shows how great were the demands on them. In view of the rapid increase in their numbers, and the fact that prior to the 1870 Royal Commission there were 250 Army Schoolmasters serving all over the world, it seems probable that the very high standards required from the first Schoolmasters were later considerably lowered.[85]

Those seeking to join were good candidates. Civilian education was developing, if slowly. As trained teachers those who became Army Schoolmasters would not have lacked civilian employment. While entering into an unfamiliar world, they were not ignorant of what would be expected of them. They knew the Army spent much of its time abroad and as fit young men they probably saw it as an advantage that they should see the world at Her Majesty's expense. They must have been keen to become Army Schoolmasters as the process of becoming one was not made easy for them. They had to pass a gruelling examination when the examinations they had to take to become qualified teachers were happily behind them. They faced further months of training which they could not have expected to be palatable as much of it would involve going over again what they had already done in the training colleges they had attended. Their lack of pay during this additional training would not add to their pleasure in contemplating it. They could not know the full extent of their commitments until they had experienced them, but they were well aware that they could not look forward to a life of leisure, nor be comforted by the thought that a princely pay awaited them. Once mustered in the Army they would have advantages denied to civilians. They would have bed and board, and a little later it was agreed they should have a reasonable pension. Those who found the pay a paltry pittance did not join the Corps; low pay became an Army Schoolmaster's grievance only when other and more significant discontents arose. Gleig tells us that most of them came from well-connected backgrounds, from clerical, Army Officer and medical backgrounds.[86]

Theirs was a heavy workload. They had to teach children during a full working day and then soldiers in the evening. They had to work on Saturday mornings and they had Sunday School responsibilities, if not teaching there, as often happened, then at least in accompanying the children to church and seeing they were well-behaved there. Living with regiments' extra-mural duties would come their way.

Cameron, an Army Schoolmaster between 1881 and 1920 tells us that as a pupil teacher he worked a thirteen-hour day and three hours on Saturday. He tells us that at times he was studying until the 'wee small hours'. It was the pattern of his life. 'Overworked and underpaid', he said, 'described his life.' 'But I enjoyed it all', he added, 'as did most of my colleagues.'[87] One can understand the relief of Ruthwen, who joined the Corps in 1890, on hearing he would no longer be required to teach on Saturdays.[88] The pressure from those who did not want to be taught on that day, even more than consideration for those who would as soon not teach on it, was no doubt the more important factor in bringing this about. To help the Schoolmaster he had the assistance of the Army Schoolmistresses. Since 1840 they had been appointed to every major unit. They were required to hold a proficiency certificate issued by the Council of Education, or to have taught as an assistant teacher in an Army School. However, they received no additional training at the Normal School.

Much thought had gone into the establishing of the Corps. Men's foresight, however, being limited, it is not surprising that such further adjustments had to be made to what had been agreed on in 1846 as experience dictated. There were unanticipated problems. Some were solved by common need and common sense, some by time and sympathetic understanding, some not at all. Three difficulties emerged.

The first was the easiest to deal with. The Army Schoolmaster was to have a full-time job. The Regimental Schoolmaster whom he replaced had had that too, yet had found time to do whatever private teaching came his way. Officers would often call on his help for their families and themselves. Such work was not and could not have been officially required of him for its amount and its remuneration would vary from individual to individual, from time to time and from place to place. It could not have been done by the Regimental Schoolmaster unpaid, for that would have established a relationship between the parties concerned which would have been improper. Yet such extra duty by the Schoolmaster was a present help to the regiment which showed and increased its appreciation of him and which must have helped him in his official work. Regimental Schoolmasters might become Army Schoolmasters who in any case must be expected in course of time to replace them. The services of Army Schoolmasters would similarly be sought by the regiment which would no more wish to be deprived of them than the Schoolmaster would be of the opportunity to provide them should he be asked and able to render them. In any case how could the Army insist that the Schoolmaster indulge in no paid activities beyond his official duties? He wrote books for which he was paid; they were of benefit to his colleagues, they increased his prestige in the regiment, they brought kudos to the Corps. Too much was at stake here for the heavy hand which would have ensured the greatest unhappiness for the greatest number. The Army had no desire to peer too closely into the private activities of the Schoolmasters. Not for the first time in their history the Armed Service found advantage in impaired vision. The Army benefitted greatly from the many unpaid activities of the Schoolmaster; it was happy that he should be remunerated for this particular extra-mural activity.

The second problem which presented itself was much more difficult to solve for it concerned not money but status and, much as money meant to the Victorians, place in society meant more; the Army Schoolmaster had status and it could be considerable. There were four classes of Schoolmasters. The First Class Schoolmaster was given Warrant Officer status, which was rare at the time. This placed him above the Sergeant-Major who held the rank of Staff Sergeant. At Regimental Balls it was the Schoolmaster's wife with whom the Commanding Officer first danced.[89] The Schoolmaster had better accommodation than that provided for the Sergeant-Major. He wore, as we have seen, a splendidly distinctive uniform, a frock coat embellished with three stars marked in gold thread on his collar and a waisted girdle. The remaining three classes of Schoolmasters were Staff Sergeants or Sergeants. The Second and Third Class Schoolmasters wore on their uniform two stars and a single gold star respectively and Assistant Schoolmasters shoulder knots and red sashes, and they had a gold thread crown on the front of their caps. All could hope for promotion to the First Class. To this extent it would seem they were what Gleig wanted them to be, neither commissioned officers nor non-commissioned officers. Yet despite their dignity, and they were to be addressed and referred to as 'Mr' by all ranks, and despite the fact that they must always in public wear white gloves and carry a swagger cane, they were more akin to non-commissioned officers and this was resented. Schoolmaster John Little did not speak for himself only in saying 'It appears unreasonable that well-educated men such as they are, and with responsibilities of a moral character resulting from the very nature of their duties, should not be rated higher than the grade of non-commissioned officers.'[90] This in all probability would not have constituted too serious a problem had not circumstances led to a lowering of their status.

They had a mixed reception when they joined the regiments. A year after doing so, as we have seen, a Parliamentary Committee was told that Commanding Officers believed the scheme had already justified itself. One Commanding Officer was quoted as saying 'Men have been able to fit themselves for promotion who were previously unable to do so. Others have learned to read and write and have found occupation for time that was formerly spent in public houses. It is very popular.' Crime, he said, had diminished and there were few defaulters, this he ascribed to the Schoolmaster's influence. Other regiments had other feelings. They did not appreciate the Schoolmaster. If he was less learned than his officers, it seems he was regarded by them as insufficient; if he was more learned he was thought insufferable. He was often looked on as American Presidents seem to view the State Department, as the representative, that is, of a hostile interest. It was said in 1862 'It is a notorious fact that Army Schoolmasters are the most unpopular body in the whole service. Two-thirds of them are regarded by their Commanding Officers as a nuisance, by the officers generally as upstarts who ape to be what they are not, by the non-commissioned officers as men who are too well-paid, have too many privileges, and consequently think too much of themselves.'[91] It was a catholic distaste thus shown for the

Schoolmaster and unfortunately he was not given time to live it down or to see if that could be done. It was the dissatisfaction he caused among the NCOs which seems to have convinced the Army that it had a serious problem to deal with and one in the tackling of which it could brook no delay.

When the Schoolmasters joined their units the NCOs must have been greatly taken aback. The Regimental Schoolmaster they knew and had no difficulty in getting on with. The Army Schoolmaster was another breed. He was obviously occupying an important position and those doing so in a hierarchical society are not to be taken lightly. The NCOs needed time to assess what they had in their midst. When they had time to weigh matters up they were far from satisfied. They had earned their rank in hard service, hard and bloody service in the case of those returning from the Alma, from Balaclava and Inkermann, and now they found young men, often considerably younger than themselves, men new to the Army and ignorant of its ways, posted over them and enjoying privileges to which they never could aspire. Sympathetic tolerance and understanding do not always characterise young men who wield an authority hitherto beyond their grasp and not all the newly-appointed Schoolmasters behaved with befitting decency and decorum. 'Often their conduct and manner', it was said 'give much occasion for the resentment their position created.' In 1862 Major-General Eyre said their 'extreme youth' told against them. He added 'Superior in dress and pay, and generally in acquirements, to the non-commissioned officers of the garrison, they are naturally looked upon by those with some feelings of enmity and dislike, and often their conduct and manner give much occasion for this prejudice.' Civilians, too, spoke of them as conceited and lacking in reverence.[92] Perhaps it was a mistake to give such status to young men. But if it was, it was a difficult mistake to rectify. For men always resent the loss of privileges once enjoyed. Yet when it was said that the Schoolmaster was the most unpopular man in the regiment and when he acknowledged his isolation, saying he was neither fish nor fowl nor good red herring,[93] something had to be done. Since there were more NCOs than Schoolmasters to be considered it was the latter who had to suffer. They lost their status and were deprived of their uniform.[94] All were offered higher pay and the prospect of a commission. There were to be two categories of Schoolmasters, ordinary Schoolmasters and Superintending Schoolmasters who would hold the commissioned rank of Ensign. Prospects of reaching the latter rank were poor as there were to be only eighteen of them. There was, however, no great haste in promoting them and a year after their introduction only seven had been appointed.[95] They were now to wear a blue frock coat which, it was said, would be 'more in accordance with the military rank of the Schoolmaster and which could not be mistaken, as the original Schoolmaster's uniform might be, for the undress uniform of a Commanding Officer which it too much resembled'. There might have been more difficulty in determining what was the appropriate dress had it been foreseen that in the Great War a properly attired Schoolmaster could be mistaken for Lord Kitchener and saluted accordingly by high-ranking allied officers. The Schoolmaster's demotion could not be concealed.[96] He had hoped for a higher status and had now to accept a lower one. The Royal Commission was right in saying how bitterly this was resented. The fact that in 1870 there were only sixteen student Schoolmasters and only three of these were civilians speaks for itself.[97]

The Schoolmasters had joined the Corps on the understanding that, though they would not be officers, theirs would be the highest non-commissioned rank. They would be or become Warrant Officers, of whom there were very few, an honourable status which underlined the important nature of their work. They had paid a high price for that status in meeting the conditions of their appointment. They had fulfilled their part of the contract and the Army, having difficulties which it had not foreseen when drawing up the contract, could not fulfil its. It believed the best way out of its difficulties would be to draw up a new contract and face the consequences of dishonouring the old one. Those consequences were the compulsion on it to honour the old contract in the case of those who would not accept the new one until such time as their engagement, which would not be renewed, ran out, and to live with the bitterness of those staying on but having to leave before they had been led to expect to, and of those others who, *faute de mieux*, agreed to stay. The Army could not have been unaware that taking this way out of its difficulties would have an adverse effect on the morale of the Schoolmasters and it must have been surprised that they stood up to it so well. It was the status of a gentleman which the Schoolmaster desired. This, which he felt had been in his grasp, was no longer so after the 1863 revision of his terms of service. It is not to be expected that he would not feel this deeply and resent it bitterly.

If the Army might have been wiser in dealing with the problem occasioned by the attitude of many officers and more NCOs to the newly-established Corps of Schoolmasters, it could not have been more unfortunate in its timing in so doing. For it did this when civilian teachers were demanding a truly professional status equal to that of the doctor, the clergyman, the lawyer. It was never likely that they would get it but their agitation attracted a great deal of attention.[98] And it was at its height when the status of Army Schoolmasters which, encouraged by their civilian colleagues, they hoped would be raised, was lowered. The Gods, it seems, were adding to the Army's troubles. The Army faced a real problem when it took what must have been the unpleasant and difficult decision to demote the Schoolmasters. A better way of dealing with it might have been found if the Army's interest in the education of its soldiers had been greater. Schoolmasters could not but be aware of the fact that the Army's way out of its difficulties was an indication of the value it attached to them. Half of the original Schoolmasters rejected the new offer, preferring, as they were contractually entitled to, to soldier on for the few years left before their contract expired.[99] This was a heavy blow to the morale of the Corps. This difficult and damaging question of status nevertheless eased with the passing years. A younger generation forgot the cares of an older and was grateful when in 1881 a common rank of Warrant Officer was introduced for the Sergeant-Major, the Bandmaster, and the Schoolmaster who had served for twelve years. Though this problem of status eased, it continued to trouble the Schoolmaster, who resented the fact that he was excluded from the Club in India to which officers had entry. There were times also when members of the AEC and the RAEC had occasion to realise that some officers and gentlemen regarded them as not quite the thing.

The third of the problems facing the Schoolmaster was the most important; it has never yet been solved. It was the problem of convincing an Army, which always had too much to do and never enough time to do it in or resources to do it with, that whatever it required from the education which was primarily instructional, it could not dispense with the education which was fructifying.

The Schoolmasters liked the teaching of the children. There was a rigidity about it which they would have been happier without, but they recognised the reason for it. Every child in every Army School had an arithmetic book and readers, literary, geographical and historical, appropriate to its standard chosen not by the Headmaster but by the War Office. This was to enable children to cope with the many family postings which occurred; in new schools they could take up where they had left in the old. It was not difficult for the Schoolmaster to cope with this. One, when asked if this did not mean being in a rut, replied 'Being in a rut you do know where you are going. It's better to be in a rut than drifting about on an uncharted ocean.'[100] Being generalists and not specialists they had plenty of opportunity for the change without which rigid syllabuses might easily have dulled teaching.

It was the teaching of the soldier that was the Schoolmaster's greatest trial for this did have the deadening effect he was able to avoid in the teaching of the child. This was not an unavoidable consequence of the fact that the low standard of the taught meant that the teaching must be at a very low level. Low-level teaching would be a challenge to the Schoolmaster who would have made every effort to interest his pupils and win their cooperation. He was denied the chance to do so for he soon ceased to be tasked with the soldier's general education. For when the Army gave up its attack on the illiteracy of the troops, at last convinced that it should no longer try to teach those who so persistently demonstrated their determination to remain unteachable, the only adult teaching left to the Schoolmaster was the certificate classes for would-be NCOs. That certificate education need not have become the deadly and deadening experience it often became. What was taught was of concern to the soldiers and good teaching, for which the Schoolmasters were noted, could have maintained a lively interest in teacher and taught. A good mixture of certificate teaching with the attempt to educate the soldier more generally would have given the Schoolmaster a good balanced diet. It would have kept him fresh and constantly aware that the purpose of education is to train the minds, not to fill the memory. Aware as he must always have been of the necessity of getting as many of his pupils as possible through their certificate examinations, he must always have been tempted to gear all his teaching to getting good examination results and to confine it to the question-spotting kind. This would not be true of his teaching for the First Class Certificate. 'The First Class Certificate', Schoolmaster Leaver tells us, 'was a great advance on the Second and Third Class which were in no way a preparation for it. It was a leap into other regions.'[101] Schoolmasters must have prayed that more would attempt that leap, but as more were content to make only Corporal or Sergeant many Schoolmasters would teach only Third and Second Class Certificate candidates and all would teach these for most of the time. What made things worse for the Schoolmasters was the extraordinary degree to which certificate syllabuses became narrow and rigid. At one time the exact number of words was prescribed for the essay for the Second Class Certificate, a regulation of unbelievable stupidity which made it evident how little education meant to those who introduced it. The effect of this was soon clear. As one Schoolmaster tells us 'there was much hostility to attendance at school'. He was undoubtedly right in adding 'generally examination cramming was unavoidable'. Leaver tells us there was an expression for it in the Corps – 'delivering the tale of the bricks'. This unfortunately was the way to promotion as Inspector of Army Schools and he says this was how some of his less cultured colleagues were promoted. Since cramming involves effort on the part of the crammed, that at least was a desirable effect on them of their certificate work. It had effects on the Army which were not so desirable. There was, a Schoolmaster tells us, 'a lack of anything humanising' in the process of gaining the Certificates that would lose nothing in the telling and if it was, as that Schoolmaster thought, 'no small contributory factor to the general hostility to education', then the price paid by the Army for this was perhaps not as negligible as, had it given any thought to it, it would undoubtedly have concluded.[102]

The effect of such teaching on the Schoolmasters can well be imagined. Leaver tells us 'It was a rigid system in which there was little room for individuality or initiative and little room for self-culture.' Good men, he says, were resigning from the Corps and he comments 'From 1898 to 1919 my mind was much at a standstill.'[103] Yet their achievements in class continued to win high praise. Her Majesty's Inspectors in the early 20th Century said that they were 'unequalled as teachers'.[104] Their extra-mural work, a reliable barometer of their morale, was as impressive as their teaching. Leaver tells us that when he served with the 12th Lancers he played the piano after dinner every Sunday and most of the Sergeants remained to listen. 'Nothing came amiss to them', he says, 'I frequently had requests which surprised me.' He adds that when he was in Dublin in 1912 'The Sergeants of the City of London Regiment would always ask for music if I called in after night school.'[105] He won their confidence and proved that even those whose opportunities to appreciate good music were limited could do so when they came their way. What he achieved outside the classroom was a most important educational complement to what he achieved in it. As the leisure that was not entirely unknown in the rest of the Army was rarely theirs it is a puzzle to know how the Schoolmasters found the time and the energy to be so distinguished in extra-mural activities. They organised, coached and played games, promoted plays and concerts and arranged expeditions. Schoolmaster James Wells founded the largest of the Army's voluntary societies, the Royal Temperance Association.

Leaver tells us they were once referred to by the press in his time as that 'pitiful outfit'.[106] No such absurd underestimation of them was made by the civilian educators who appointed retiring Schoolmasters to Headships or by those who like General Wilson, Director-General of Military Education, were in a position to know the quality of their work and who spoke in 1896 of their 'steady devotion to duty, their emulation and zeal ... and their highly satisfactory general conduct'.[107] Their memoirs leave us in no doubt they numbered in their ranks men of wide culture and impressive understanding. The first James Turner belonged to their Corps, but his *City of Dreadful*

Night is not dedicated to it. If there were times when they might have thought of themselves, in his words, as 'battling in black floods without an ark', they never looked on themselves as 'melancholy Brethren'. They did not lose heart and despite their many frustrations remained a determined and outstanding body of men. Wavell was right in saying they had much more to offer than they were allowed to give; it is to the discredit as well as to the disadvantage of the Army that it prevented them giving it. Nevertheless it was a strongly-burning torch that those who tended the flickering flame of Army Education in the early days handed on to their successors. And in that it could be as truthfully said of them, as of the Army as a whole, that they manifested the virtues of adversity encountered and adversity resisted, they were a faithful reflection of the Army they served – not unaware of the difficulty nor dismayed by the prospect.

The Education of the Officer: the Epitome of the Struggle for Army Education in the 19th Century

We have considered the forces making for and against Army Education in the 19th Century. We have seen the protracted struggle between them and its varying fortunes throughout that century. We have looked at the founding of the Corps of Schoolmasters, its effect on and how it was affected by that struggle. It remains to be seen what happened to Officer Education, the epitome of that struggle.

The Army is a reflection of society. When a country looks at its fighting forces it is looking in a mirror. Anomalies abound in British life. Without them the British would not feel at home. There is, therefore, no occasion for surprise at the anomalies to be found in the British Army. One such was, however, sufficiently striking to cause comment. Sir Lacy Evans drew attention to it when he said '£46,000 is spent on the education of other ranks and their children, £1,300 on education of officers.'[108] One way of ending the anomaly was to end the expenditure and many, in and out of uniform, would have been happy to do that. But that would have been to go against the grain of things. Irresistible forces were to insist that it be removed another way, uncongenial although that other way was to a majority of those whom it concerned. Education was one enemy the 19th Century British officer was unable to put to flight.

He put up a gallant fight against it. Some training of the officer was acknowledged to be essential, even though failure to undergo it was looked upon with an extraordinary tolerance. Wellington said that if you put 70,000 men into Hyde Park, possibly half-a-dozen officers might know how to get them out again. No one, he thought, should receive a commission unless proved on examination to have good average ability and to have received the education of a gentleman. He added that no ensign or cadet should be promoted to a lieutenancy, nor lieutenant to a captaincy, unless he has satisfied a competent tribunal of his fitness to hold these ranks. He nevertheless continued to look with kindly indulgence on the great majority of officers whom he judged unable to cope with Hyde Park. As for the education of the officer, that was something he was strongly against. He said that the military academies of France produced 'pedants and coxcombs' and thought that such academies and even Staff Colleges would lower the tone of the Army and impair the cohesion of the officer corps. 'The education usually given to English gentlemen was all the officer need possess.'

Not all were convinced that this should remain so. Gleig, that apostle of Army Education, was gravely dissatisfied. He thought poorly of the Woolwich education for the Artillery and the Engineers. He thought even more poorly of the officer selection at Sandhurst, saying of applicants there 'Their stupidity, be it ever so flagrant, is not regarded as a bar to their entrance into the service.'[109] In this he felt, Britain compared badly with Europe. The French École Polytechnique and the School of Application of the Corps d'Etat Major were very good. In Prussia courses of study were prescribed and examinations were essential for would-be officers. The Dutch insisted on a reasonable level of education for candidates for the Military Academy at Breda and on a regular course of study on entry. He therefore urged the setting up of a body of commissioners to examine candidates for commissions in the British Army. The Army 'officered by interest, by purchase or else by chance', was not good enough. Personal chivalry, 'on which we too much rely', was no substitute for professional ability. The Army could well do without those who did not 'consider themselves as undertaking an onerous obligation to the country'. 'The materials of which the British Army is composed are excellent', he wrote,

> ... and so are the precision and steadiness of regiments under arms; but was not this equally the case in 1793? And yet what followed? We are so dazzled by the successes of the last six years in the war of the French Revolution, that we entirely overlook the fifteen of disaster and disgrace which preceded them. We are old enough to recollect the time when British commanders, though nobody questioned their honour nor gallantry and heaven knows, the pluck of their soldiers could never be doubted, were considered the very worst in Europe and we cannot say that there is anything in the annals of the campaigns of '94, '95, '96 and '99 which goes far to cleanse them of that stain ... Is the country, which is taking so much pains to educate the private soldier and to raise him by this and other means in the scale of social life, prepared to act upon a similar principle in its dealings with his officer? ... Why should command in the Army be the only post of power to which young gentlemen may aspire, without the slightest inquiry being made in regard to their fitness for the exercise of power?

He said that if this was the case there was a problem. 'We shall soon require from the private soldier more than the subaltern was expected to know when the Duke began his career. Will it be safe either to leave the officer behind, or to trust to his voluntary exertions to prevent this misfortune?'[110] Such a situation demanded attention. The Junior Department of Sandhurst's Senior Department should be developed so that its contribution to the education of the officer could begin to compare to that available to the officers of European armies. Sandhurst at this time, it should be recalled, was in great need of attention. It languished under severe financial restrictions. It lost its Parliamentary grant altogether in 1832. It never enrolled its established quota of 400 cadets. It reached its maximum of 330 in 1818. By 1855 its numbers had fallen to fifteen and with few officers coming from Sandhurst its educational standards had declined.

The English, long inclined to believe with Burke that if it is not necessary to change, it is necessary not to change, have usually been slow to be convinced that change is necessary. It has sometimes been suggested that only when they are hit hard over the head do they think that it is timely to bestir themselves. But when things no longer seem satisfactory the thought occurs to them that perhaps they should no longer be left as they are. And as inadequate performance by his soldiery in the Azov campaign convinced Peter the Great of the desirability of reform, so the tribulations of their army in the Crimea suggested to the British that they must pay more attention to reforming it than they had hitherto thought necessary. The electric telegraph, the press, the modern postal service, showed the nation what kind of army it had. The press made much of 'the gross ignorance of the officer corps'. *The Times* said that French officers, unlike British officers, understood the science of their profession.[111] A Committee set up in 1856 on the training of officers for the Scientific Corps thought so too. The education of the officers of foreign armies was 'conducted on a more complete system'.[112] This, the Committee believed, should be copied and it proposed that all officers must pass a general examination and undertake professional studies. It was, indeed, returning to the ideas which Sir Sidney Herbert had advanced when he was Minister of War in 1854. He proposed then the setting up of a Board of Examiners to supervise examinations for commission and for promotion. He recommended that a military instructor be appointed in each Division to prepare officers for promotion and that a classroom and a library for this purpose should be provided at public expense. Those obtaining high passes in these examinations should be noted for appointment to the Staff. He had no intention, Sir Sidney had emphasised then, of converting the officers into pedants, still less of turning the hardy, active and daring officers into learned recluses and the like. He wanted the Senior Department at Sandhurst to be converted into a Staff College. These ideas were accepted by the Government but were suspended on the outbreak of the Crimean War. That war greatly strengthened such thinking. Lord Panmure, when he succeeded Sir Sidney at the War Office, was determined to promote education in the Army and at least in the matter of the Staff College royal pressure strengthened his resolve. The Prince Consort pressed the case for setting up a Staff College to train officers and the Duke of Cambridge, appointed Commander-in-Chief in 1856, wanted this too. The Committee of Military Education established in 1857 to report on the educational work of the Army had as its first task consideration of the proposed reorganisation of the Sandhurst Senior Department as a Staff College. In December 1857 it recommended that this be done and on 1 April 1858 the first Staff College course began.[113]

Only a minority of officers would go to the Staff College but all officers were affected by the cold winds now blowing. Hitherto the belief had been firmly held that education would corrupt the officers, replacing the power of leadership, that initiative, that moral and physical courage, that gentlemanly instinct which had enabled them to lead their men to victory on countless battlefields in countless wars.[114] General Sir

William Codrington warned of the danger of 'getting a man whose mind is a complex dictionary instead of a man whose mind is created for energy and action'. Earl Grey was sure that too much learning weakened the mind. Moreover he was able to point the moral and adorn the tale. 'Brain disease', he said, was 'decimating the military cadets of France.'[115] It was, however, one thing, and no doubt a correct thing, to say 'The art of governing people in the ranks is not to be learnt at school.' It was another thing, and a very stupid thing, to maintain that education was incompatible with the qualities necessary for leadership or that it would not raise them to higher order where they already existed. There were to be found in increasing numbers those who did not believe that the best of recipes for future military success was merely to watch the officers of potential enemies being destroyed by education while ensuring that the invincible ignorance of your own rendered them immune to its fatal attack. As early as 1848 the *Quarterly Review* had wondered how long the country could allow its armed forces to be officered by 5,000 honourable and gallant blockheads. Perhaps it was the pressure of those who thought in this way that induced the Duke of Wellington to lay it down in 1849, as we have seen, that no-one should be given or allowed to purchase a commission 'unless he could prove by examination to have good abilities and to have received the education of a gentleman'. Since seven years later Sir Sidney Herbert could say that 'ignorance of military matters has become a sort of badge of gentility'[116] among officers, a comment the truth of which Crimean experience seemed to confirm, more was needed, and it was forthcoming. Sandhurst, attended by those destined for the cavalry and the infantry, and Woolwich to which the artillery and engineer cadets went, were now to insist on better, more rigid, standards, although they did not, as did West Point and St Cyr, seek to give the equivalent of a university education. There were to be examinations to get out of them with a commission and there were soon to be examinations to get into them too. In 1885 entrance examinations were held at Woolwich and shortly thereafter at Sandhurst. By the end of the century examinations were to be taken for every promotion from Lieutenant up to the rank of Lieutenant-Colonel. The shadow of examinations had at last fallen upon the officer.

It can only be said that the inauguration of the Staff College and the introduction of examinations for officers proved most disappointing in their results. Despite the part played by the Duke of Cambridge in bringing the Staff College into being, the high military authorities still had little use for it or for officer education. They considered that as far as his education went 'It will not make the slightest difference in regard to his qualities as an officer.'[117] On leaving the Staff College, Smith-Dorrian, who became Military Secretary to the Commander-in-Chief, India, asked if he had done himself any good by going to Staff College. The reply was 'Well, I shouldn't say you have done yourself any harm, for if there were two candidates for an appointment, one with a p.s.c. and one without, and the Chief knew neither of them, it is possible, though I couldn't vouch for it, that he would select the p.s.c. man.'[118] That attitude was well known throughout the Army and it explains why the Staff College was vigorously kept away from for so long. An officer in the Royal Welsh Fusiliers said 'Training and keenness and Staff College were suspect in the Fusiliers.'

Prior to 1879, only one officer in the Coldstream Guards applied to go to Staff College.[119] By the end of the 19th Century things had improved in that all of the Foot Guards and all but six regiments of infantry had at least one officer with p.s.c. after his name, although none of the Household Cavalry and only seventeen out of the other twenty-eight cavalry regiments had been represented there.

Nor did exposure to examinations do much to prepare for the coming of the reading and of the thinking officer. Colonel John Bayne said that 'the officer had done his reading for life' when he joined his regiment and General Sir William Butler commented in 1911 on 'the entire absence of the thinking faculty in nine out of ten of the higher-grade officers with whom I was associated'.[120] The British officer was not what the French called *instruit*. To meet difficulties as they arose, instead of by foresight, to learn by hard experience rather than by reflection or premeditation, were national traits. As a soldier commented in the Boer War on Boer and British leaders 'They've got more brains nor we.' Generals, then, knew how to inspire their men in battle, and they seldom missed the opportunity to seize their swords and lead a charge, but in planning a battle, in the deployment of troops, in the coordination of the available arms and services and their best employment, in the use of the increasing technology which was now available to them – in all these matters, the knowledge and skill of most generals was deficient.[121] It cannot be denied that attempts to educate the British officer in the 19th Century were even less impressive than the efforts to educate the men.

The claims that nations have a monopoly, or even an excess, of original sin are always to be looked at askance. The oddities of the British Army that seem to bulk so large are seen in truer proportion when the practice of other armies is observed. Most of the faults that are so glaring in the British Army in the 18th and 19th Centuries were paralleled, or even exceeded, in European armies. Here is a description of the French Army in the Seven Years' War:

> There was no discipline, no subordination, no order on the march, in the camp or even on the battlefields. The very subalterns had their mistresses with them, and officers often left their men to accompany them on the march in their carriages. Everything that could contribute to the luxury of the officers was found in the French camps. At one time there were 12,000 waggons accompanying Soubise's army which belonged to sutlers and shopkeepers, though the army was not 50,000 strong. Balls were given in camp and officers left their posts to dance a minuet. They laughed at the orders of their leaders and only obeyed when it suited them.[122]

The British clung to their absurdities longer than did their neighbours not only because they are a more conservative people but also because it was safe, if costly, for them to do so. Nor can it be forgotten that the Army, like the law, is a reflection of the structure and the outlook of society. Through most of the 19th Century, British society remained aristocratic and through all of it the ideal of the amateur prevailed. Lord Salisbury once said that there were only two offices in the British Empire too difficult to be filled adequately by men of good average ability – the premiership and the foreign secretaryship. Service was expected and paid for, but not in cash. By the middle of the 19th Century, the pay of the British officer had not been increased since the reign of William III.[123] Similarly, the pay of the Foreign Office was outrageously little. In each case the quality of life was its own reward. And in each case those living that life were gentlemen by birth, habits and feeling. In each case a common background and education, similar habits of behaviour and thought, and a powerful *esprit de corps* combined to provide a congenial life-style. In each case it was a life-style not deprived of leisure. Bruce wrote of his life as diplomatist in pre-war Vienna 'We had an occasional busy day.'[124] For the rest there was hunting, as there was in the Army. As for the Army, birth and breeding were required for the Foreign Office. Brains were an optional extra in both.

To see how bad men can be in any profession is to learn little about it worth knowing. It is easy to become impatient at the slow pace of reform in the 19th Century British Army, and in particular to become indignant at the up-hill fight of the educators in it. But that may well have been the price to be paid for the avoidance of dangerous social strain. And what was finally secured was worth securing – an Army which was well on the way to overcoming the traditional antipathy to it of the society it served and an educational service which had survived the traditional antipathy to it of the soldiers themselves and which had convinced the best of them that its role must become still more important in the years ahead.

We have every reason to regret the low level of education of so many soldiers in the 19th Century and the slow development of Army Education then. Yet in this we must remember how faithfully the Army reflected society. By English standards the development of Army Education was not unduly long drawn-out. Whatever may be thought of the kind of education, the necessity of which was accepted, however much we may regret that only functional education interested the Army, that it turned its back resolutely on the education that would fructify, that it ignored the vocational education which soldiers would have welcomed, it acknowledged the indispensability of Army Education and of the uniformed instructors who could provide it. It did this over a span of years which bears comparison with the development of civilian education and with the working out in Britain of Parliamentary reform. Like them it is no mean achievement.

CHAPTER 2

THE FIRST WORLD WAR AND
EDUCATION AT HOME, 1920–1939

War is the rolling of the iron dice; its chances manifold, its consequences unknown. No one foresaw that the First World War would result in the collapse of the Russian, the Austro-Hungarian and the German Empires, on opposite sides of the fighting as they were. As unexpected was the great fillip war gave to education. We see this in the way it gave rise to the Pei Wei movement, the great challenge to the illiteracy of the common people of China. The traditional Chinese method of writing was long the exclusive preserve of the scholar. The Pei Wei movement was the attempt to simplify it so as to bring it within the comprehension of the common people. It began when one of the officers of the Chinese coolies brought to help with the digging on the Western Front scribbled simplified Chinese characters or idiograms on magic lantern slides and showed them to relieve the boredom of his men. The overwhelming response with which he met made him devote his life to the development of the new simplified Chinese script. The Chinese interest in education will surprise no one, for the scholar has long been esteemed in Chinese society. 'Tread not upon the shadow of your teacher' is a Chinese admonition, venerable with age, which members of the teaching profession elsewhere, particularly today, wish was more widely acted upon. That this interest should be shared by the soldiers of an army predominantly English is, however, occasion for surprise. English interest in, and concern for, education has been restrained, as witness the saying that the Scots will do anything to get education and the Welsh are keen on it too, while the English have nothing particular against it, a saying which does justice to the Scots and the Welsh but not to the English, who seem to have a great deal against it. The rise and development of the educational movement in the British armed forces towards the end of the war and in the months following it, indeed, in the words of the Adult Education Committee of the Ministry of Reconstruction in its 1919 report, 'stand out as one of the most striking and unpredictable' of the events of the war.[1]

The by no means impressive educational activity of the British Army came to a halt in 1914 for it soon became evident that the British war commitment was to be a predominantly continental one, although it had been hoped, as it was to be again twenty-five years later, that this would be avoided. It was soon obvious that it would be on a scale that baffled imagination and the High Command was acutely aware of the necessity of changing civilians into soldiers as quickly as possible. It is doubtful if the thought ever occurred to it that the stimulation of the minds in its care might help it to do so; if it did it was resolutely put aside. It was unimpressed by, and it brought to an end, the White City experiment, the attempt to provide evening educational facilities for the soldiers stationed there.[2] By 1917, however, a problem was developing which demanded its attention. That was the immaturity and very poor intelligence of many of the young men of eighteen who were joining up. As they would not be sent abroad until they were nineteen, it was decided that part of their training should be elementary education of the kind provided in the Army schools. A much more imaginative and ambitious version of this was begun in March 1917 in Brockton Camp, Cannock Chase. It attracted the enthusiastic attention of *The Times*, perhaps not surprisingly as A. L. Smith, Master of Balliol College, Oxford, was associated with it. It aimed to provide a liberal education to develop in the young soldiers intelligence, initiative, self-control and discipline. It sought to teach clear exposition and logical reasoning, to call forth the capacity to interpret ideas and situations aright. If these aims could be achieved, *The Times* was sure, the nation as a whole would benefit enormously thereby.[3] It would indeed. Some of the young soldiers no doubt did, but what the majority made of it is another matter. We can agree that a man's reach should exceed his grasp or what's a heaven for, and yet feel sympathy with those who believed that this was so much over the heads of the young men that vocational training should takes its place. Greatly to the regret of the Master of Balliol this was done.

Should we share his regret? We can notice that throughout the war and demobilisation years a constant tussle was taking place between those who believed that what the soldier both wanted and needed was greater vocational guidance to fit him for the civilian job to which he was looking at the end of hostilities, and those who were sure that his wants and his needs as a citizen of a great democracy must have precedence. It was a curious notion that these needs were mutually exclusive and an even greater oddity that so many should be convinced that they were. But just as the Army had so long insisted that an officer must be a gentleman first and an officer second, so English society had convinced itself that the liberal education which produced the qualities of the gentleman was the only sort worthy of the name. And just as the insistence that the gentleman must take precedence over the officer seemed for so long to have the absurd and illogical consequence that the professional qualities appropriate to the officer were felt by many officers to be hardly worth acquiring, so the deep-rooted belief that the best of all educations was of a liberal nature, that which produced the 'kalokagathos', or the ideal fully developed gentleman, seemed to have the equally absurd and illogical consequence that the qualities appropriate to the citizens of a great industrial nation, the technical qualities that would keep that nation in the forefront of the industrial world, were to be looked at askance. In the early 19th Century the Army had led the way in its provision for the education of its children. Perhaps in these war and post-war years it lost a great opportunity of teaching it the outstanding significance of technical and vocational education, a much needed lesson when the British economy was faltering and could be expected to falter still more when the cold winds of competition again began to blow with the inevitable re-emergence of the conquered.

The liberal education initially provided at Brockton Camp was seen again at Brentwood, when one of the Brockton officers was posted there.[4] One of its organisers was a former Professor of Education and another a former Workers' Educational Association tutor with experience of the tutorial classes, the best of the work done by that Association. Classes of a similar nature were begun in Colchester and in

Canterbury, attended by young soldiers for eight hours every fortnight. Schemes of this kind remained, however, the product of unit initiative. It was the unit and not the War Office which was responsible for them. They had the goodwill of the War Office but nothing more substantial; not until 21 August 1918 did they have its official support.

Self-help, practised on so wide a scale that it can almost be referred to as spontaneous combustion, was also a characteristic of the fighting armies at this time. On the Western Front the boredom of the trenches in the long periods of inaction had somehow to be borne, the monotony of protracted waiting elsewhere to be coped with. In France, newspapers, typical of which was the *Wypers Times* which began distribution in February 1916, helped.[5] To help, too, officers in the trenches arranged classes for their men, using duck-boards as blackboards and writing on them with the chalk they could find in trench walls. There were engineering classes behind the lines and Arabic classes in Haifa, while an artillery battery specialised in classes in music appreciation, these being the concern of Lieutenant Ralph Vaughan Williams.[6] The phrase *déjà vu* so often springs to mind when contemplating education in the Army. The work of Lieutenant Vaughan Williams recalls the excellent classes in music run during the Second World War by the amanuensis of Delius, Warrant Officer Eric Fenby; one wonders whether there was then a Sergeant-Major, as there was on that later occasion, who ushered in the pupils, bawling 'Hi there, you bloody Toscaninis. Get fell in for your music lesson.'

Impressed by these general stirrings, GHQ France appointed a staff officer, Captain Borden-Turner, to lecture to the fighting troops, supplying 'such information on the current topics of the time as could be accurately gathered and safely given'.[7] These lectures were so much in demand that he had to seek assistance. For this the YMCA, which had even before the war taken a keen interest in the welfare of the soldier and which as early as 1915 was organising education in whatever back areas were open to it, was turned to. It gave great help. In 1918 it set up the YMCA University Committee on which were represented all the British universities and many professional and educational bodies besides. At this call for help from the Army it sent to the various fronts many lecturers and it bore the whole cost of so doing, some £¼ million.[8] From time to time a perfunctory civilian interest had hitherto been expressed in education in the Army, usually to deplore its inadequacy at times of crisis occasioned not by the soldier but by the statesman, the adequacy of whose education none saw fit to question. There had, however, never been such sustained and high-level participation in Army Education as this. The highest educational interests in the land were now concerning themselves with it and this was bound to strengthen those who believed it to be important and to give pause to those whose inclination was to insist that it was not. It was a precedent which might become, as it did, of great significance in later years.

It is, nevertheless, worth pointing out that it was the Army, not as it is often said, the YMCA, which generated these war-time educational ventures. For at this time, in the phrase uttered by the Director of Education for the Canadian Expeditionary Force, education 'was in the air'.[9] It was plucked out of the ambient air rather more quickly by the Dominion than by the British forces. But even before the final German offensive, made possible and inevitable by the collapse of the Russian Front and the subsequent transfer of the German divisions there to the Western Front, the British High Command was attending to it. From the summer of 1917 the morale of the BEF was beginning to cause concern. It was noticed that war-weariness and the desire for peace were spreading.[10] Major-General Sir Charles Bonham-Carter believed it would help if lecturers visited units to explain why the war must be continued and to hold out to the men the benefits which would be theirs when it was won.[11] A panel of lecturers was accordingly drawn up. By the end of the year a still more comprehensive scheme to provide education and technical training for all in the BEF who wanted it was put forward. The calls on troops and on Staff Officers were, however, such that these schemes were put aside, but early in 1918 Haig, increasingly worried by reports of the lowering of Army morale, by unrest at the Étaples Base Camp in September 1917 and by a mutiny at a Calais training depot in which a Soldiers and Workers Council was set up in April 1918,[12] insisted that an educational scheme be at once set up to give the troops a clearer understanding of their responsibilities as citizens of a great empire and which should help them in their work after the war. The German offensive put all at risk but with its failure a wave of interest in education, gathering momentum as peace approached, swept over the troops. Suitably qualified officers were attached to formations for educational purposes. Soon there were classes in all sorts and conditions of subjects, even in Latin and Chinese. In the early days of peace a correspondent of *The Times* was to express his surprise at 'the weight of extensive and peculiar learning hidden in the ranks of our civilian Army'.[13] Officers, concerned as always with the well-being of their men, shared what knowledge they had with them and 'outline lectures', the precursors of the Army Bureau of Current Affairs in the Second World War, eked out the knowledge of the less well-informed. Consumer research has become something of a bogy but it would be interesting to know how the outline lecture on the Spirit of the Middle Ages was received. He seems not to have been an untypical Commanding Officer who wrote 'The education goes pretty well, I think, though text-books, maps and note-books are a bit of a difficulty. Subalterns have written home for old school-books. I've got classes going in English, History, Geography, Arithmetic, French, Shorthand, Physics, Electricity, Farming, Market-Gardening, Carpentry, Shoe-Making, Tailoring, Cookery and others.'[14] Variety ruled supreme, for as one officer indignantly wrote when it was thought that his unit might have copied what was happening in others 'we've done it all on our own'. As for vocational education, Lord Gorell tells us, 'There was hardly a trade or occupation in which we were not at one time or another asked to train men.'[15]

The scale of things becomes clear when we realise that 50,000 copies of any book were needed if it was to be in general use. A raised eyebrow is, nevertheless, not entirely out of place when the spreading zeal for education appears to be of too wholesale a nature, as it seems to have been when, the day after the Armistice, a Brigadier told a parade of his whole brigade that education was now the thing and when he ordered any who had no wish for it to fall out. It is comforting to think that the two who did so fell out not because they had developed a remarkable indifference to uncongenial fatigues but because they were, if not early advocates of human rights, at least incipient village Hampdens willing as true-born Englishmen to strike a blow for freedom. Like the sergeant who in the 19th Century gave rise to great legal battles because he refused to attend at his own expense the classes his Commanding Officer instructed him to, they restore one's faith in human nature. Besides, the Brigadier in question is very reminiscent of the Chinese Christian General who paraded his men, turned the hose-pipe on them and informed them that they were all now baptised Christians, the conversion of his men doubtless being as lasting as the educational interest of the Brigadier's troops. Nevertheless, when *Blackwood's Magazine* in July 1919 wrote of 'the Army's clamour for knowledge', we cannot say that it was being absurd, however aware we may be that this was a noise hitherto unobserved by military men. H.A.L. Fisher, President of the Board of Education, whose capacity for exaggeration was not minimal, cannot have been far from the truth when he said 'I do not think there has ever been in the whole history of education ... an educational experiment conducted on so large a scale.'[16]

One task was urgent in the early days of peace. That, in Lord Gorell's words, was 'the conversion of the local go-as-you-please, do-the-best-you-can, diversities of the past eighteen months into an educational system which should yet have in it sufficient elasticity to be adaptable to all the varied opportunities and circumstances of life on active service'. Ireland, Egypt and the Indian North-West Frontier still had to be pacified. It was, however, for the majority of the troops no longer on active service but impatiently awaiting demobilisation, for the troops in the Army of Occupation on the Rhine, for those still in hospital in Great Britain, that an educational scheme had primarily to be fashioned. Since there were nearly four million men to be discharged and since demobilisation would have to be tightly controlled and carefully supervised if appalling chaos were to be avoided (and in the event it was not until September 1920 that the last of the war-time soldiers could be returned to civilian life), the preparation of an appropriate education scheme was manifestly a task as gigantic as it was urgent. It was entrusted to Lord Gorell and it was his work which culminated in a world-wide scheme of education to which, as he believed, some three million men were exposed. A Staff Officer Grade II on the staff of General Bonham-Carter, who was in charge of training at GHQ France, Major Gorell, a former adjutant of a battalion in the trenches, was appointed to the War Office 'to take charge of the direction and coordination of the education scheme in the Army'.[17]

It was an inspired appointment. He had the initiative, the imagination, the drive and not least the contacts that enabled him to achieve outstanding success. In this he was helped by his title, of which he made excellent use. It was not only that the English then still loved a lord. He was personally acquainted with the great in the land. At a critical moment in his negotiations he could later record 'The next day Lord Milner [Secretary of State for War] happened to meet me in the House of Lords.' It does not do to underestimate the value of personal contacts of this kind, for Milner was of the greatest importance. It was Milner who secured the support of Bonar-Law, the Chancellor of the Exchequer, for the scheme.[18]

Indeed, without Milner's interest the scheme would never have begun; without his continued support it would never have survived. For in December 1918, by which time the education scheme was launched, a crisis occurred from which it might not have recovered. In that month the Government decided that students and teachers then in uniform could be demobilised immediately. These were now the teachers of the new scheme. Commanding Officers had been urged to look elsewhere than to the teachers when classes were begun, but perhaps inevitably full use continued to be made of them, since they were best able to promote the new scheme. How could it survive without them? Lord Gorell at once called on the Minister and it was his visit that saved the day. Army Order of 20 December 1918 was then published and this laid down that every Cavalry and Infantry Brigade was to have an Education Officer who would be responsible for organising education in it, that there should be four officers and twelve non-commissioned officer instructors to every thousand men, that there should be extra pay for these if their appointment was unaccompanied by promotion, that officers agreeing to remain for twelve months would retain their rank, pay and enrolments plus their extra duty pay at the time of general demobilisation and that NCOs similarly staying on would be given the rank of Warrant Officer Class 1. Lord Gorell writes of another crucial occasion 'I received a kind little note from Haldane ... telling me that he had happened to meet Mr Churchill [Milner's successor as Secretary of State for War] and had found him keen to go on with the education system in principle.' Whether or not Haldane or H.A.L. Fisher, with whom Gorell, was intimate, carried the weight in government to which they pretended, knowledge that Gorell had such contacts won for him a greater consideration than a lone and lowly attached officer at the War Office could expect to have.

He needed all the support he could get, for his was an uphill road. His very arrival at the War Office must have convinced him that that would be the case. Treasury opposition then compelled him to relinquish his rank as Staff Officer II, it being as infantry Captain not as staff Major that he assumed his task. Here we have once again the authentic harsh voice of the Treasury croaking over the years. In the early 19th Century it would not pay for candles in schools; a century later it was less interested in forwarding a highly important experiment in education than in saving the nation the difference between the pay of a Staff Officer Grade II and an infantry Captain. Such was its determination to spare the nation's pocket that it almost seemed to look upon the saving of a ha'porth of tar as the first step towards ending expenditure on the ship. And if Treasury opposition to a scheme which, whilst costly, seemed from its point of view to have the great advantage of being transitory, might be coped with, that opposition was bound to increase greatly when the outlines of a permanent scheme of education that would entail a continuing cost began to emerge. Thus there was vigorous Treasury opposition to the creation of a special education corps to forward the education of the Regular Army. Such a proposal it looked upon as 'a device for creating staff officers',[19] a strongly-to-be-resisted means of prising open Treasury coffers. From other quarters, too, the opposition that had seemed appropriate to a passing inconvenience would change its nature when a lasting incubus was in prospect. The Adjutant-General, Sir George Macdonagh, was as opposed to that proposal as was the Treasury. When overruled in his opposition, he was, we are told, 'so furious that he wouldn't speak to anyone'. It was said by those whose indignation blinded them to the undesirability of mixing metaphors that 'he continued to put spokes in the educational wheel' and that he 'fired shattering broadsides' against it. When the Selection Boards met to appoint the members of the Army Educational Corps (AEC) it appears that he instructed his representative to state his objections to this and then to walk out of the room. He was supported by Sir Travers Clarke, the Quartermaster-General. Well might Gorell say that he was engaged in 'one long fight' in the War Office.[20] Doubts about the desirability of having an AEC persisted. MPs were afraid that the teaching of citizenship might become party political propaganda and Churchill sought to reassure them by emphasising that 'the most work connected with citizenship would be purely factual in nature' and that AEC personnel would 'avoid the ordinary controversies of politics as far as possible'. In the debate it was said that many unit Commanding Officers opposed the founding of the Corps.

As had been evident in the case of the Army reforms of the late 19th Century there was unit as well as War Office opposition to be overcome. Not all Commanding Officers welcomed the importance now given to education in the Army. One Commanding Officer was appalled at the idea that NCOs who agreed to remain for a year teaching should be made up to Warrant Officer Class 1. He said 'The prospect of some of my present instructors as Warrant Officers is laughable – and you can't have a laughable Warrant Officer without diminishing the prestige of all Warrant Officers.'[21] Here, too, is an instance of that striking continuity which is to be seen in the story of education in the Army. History does not repeat itself as the incident, the hour and the individual are infinitely varied. But the history of Army Education is stamped with similarity. A Commanding Officer in Emergency Malaya was so convinced that an AEC sergeant was diminishing the prestige of all sergeants that he denied him admission to the Sergeants' Mess.[22] There were doubtless others like the Commanding Officer who feared the undermining of the authority of Sergeant-Majors and whose ingenuity would not have been greatly taxed in finding ways of effectively non-cooperating with the education scheme. Permanent officials in the War Office, too, were no friends of Gorell. One said that he had seen several earlier attempts at educating the soldier and where were the snows of yesteryear? He thought that it was only to the Army as it was immediately after the war, and not to the permanent Army, that education schemes applied and, as far as he and those who thought like him were concerned, it would have been, had they had their way.[23]

The developments which were so largely due to Gorell are indeed impressive. He had initially proposed to set up a separate education branch in the War Office, but he accepted the advice, as did Milner, of General Lyndon Bell, Director of Staff Duties in the War Office and a keen supporter of education, that since a small education branch would be 'frozen out' among the big and purely military directorates, and as education had come to be associated with the Directorate of Staff Duties, it would be better for it to remain there. There was a Treasury suggestion which Gorell tells us, 'for a few hundred pounds would have greatly weakened the whole organisation', but this was successfully resisted. The new branch, Staff Duties 8, soon showed its calibre. Gorell drafted and secured assent to the proposals which appeared in Army

Order 295 of 24 September 1918, the order which so greatly influenced subsequent education in the Army. It emphasised the importance of education in raising morale, in developing the intelligence of the soldier and in preparing him for resettlement after his service. It acknowledged a highly significant characteristic of the wartime Army, namely that 'The educational standards of many men now serving in the ranks are little, if at all, inferior to those of officers.'[24] The pace was kept up. Six days before the Armistice the number of Education Officers detailed to organise education was increased and authority obtained for the expenditure of considerable sums on books and equipment. Yet another Army Order of 9 December 1918 emphasised that educational training 'can no longer be regarded as a secondary consideration, and as much time as can be made available from the necessities of military service should be devoted to it'. It authorised the appointment of officers to supervise education and of instructors to carry it on. It provided for education in military hospitals at home. It authorised the issue of Active Service Certificates which recorded what courses had been attended and what examinations passed. It established at Corpus Christi College in Cambridge and at Trinity and Hertford in Oxford Schools of Education to train the officers and NCOs from the regiments, who were in their turn to teach their men. The former cadet schools at Newmarket and Shorncliffe were used for this purpose too. Schools of Instruction at Bedford and at Catterick had already been opened to give courses in professional and technical subjects to officers awaiting demobilisation. The universities, also, were persuaded to accept the Army's Special Certificate as exempting from matriculation or other entrance examinations.

Gorell's influence is clearly to be seen in Army Order 7 dated 13 May 1919 and in the pamphlet which accompanied it, *Educational Training – Armies of Occupation*. H.A.L. Fisher said of this that it was 'a very remarkable statement and it marks a great development in the history of the Army'.[25] It was a fine assertion of the great importance of education in any army worthy of the name and it is well worth quoting, lest we forget:

> Educational training is not to be regarded as a secondary consideration, nor for spare hours as a form of recreation; but as an essential element in the making of a soldier in an army. This principle is based upon three main considerations: the variety and the real difficulty of the battle training of the modern soldier render it necessary that he should be quick, intelligent and, as far as possible, of a ready understanding. It is a waste both of time and of energy to have to impart military and battle training to men whose minds, in the great majority of cases, have lain almost idle since the elementary school years. Educational training will produce a more or less cultivated soil in which the advanced stages of the military training will take root more quickly and more easily. Further, it is demanded nowadays that a man should understand what he is being taught, and the reasons for his instruction; he must not merely learn by rule of thumb. Unless his general intelligence is being developed, specialised instruction must remain largely a learning by rote and the mental self-confidence that any crisis may demand will never be created. Together with its bearing upon military efficiency the bearing of educational training upon morale had from the first

been kept in view. Diversion and occupation of the mind are to be found at their best in systematic classes, wherein men feel that they have, for their spare time, something well worth doing. Closely connected with the foregoing is the consideration that educational training provides a link with civil life, with the nation at large, which both from the point of view of the individual man and from that of the army generally, is of vital importance. In armies constituted as modern armies must be, it is inevitable that men should be concerned about their re-entry into civil life. It is of incalculable value that they should feel that their term of service has not handicapped them, but has given them opportunities of education which in the long hours of a factory or a shop they might never have found.

An equally fine peroration ended this convincing claim for the place of education in the Army:

The Scheme answers also to the national requirements of today. The Education Act of 1918 has established for the nation as a whole, the principle that training of the mind shall not cease as for the great majority it has ceased hitherto, in comparatively early boyhood, but shall be continued to an age at which everyone shall have had his chance to develop his abilities to their highest degree. With the Educational Training Scheme the Army takes its proper place alongside this movement. No man need in the Army fall behind his civilian fellows, or be debarred from his own advancement by lack of education.[26]

Nor did these seem to be empty words. When Churchill spoke to the Young Soldier Battalions about to embark for the Army of the Rhine he told them 'Your education will be continued',[27] and it was. In that Army the number of instructors allotted to each battalion had been increased to four officers and eight NCOs. General subjects formed part of training in every unit. And while the technical education necessary to meet the needs of young soldiers whose apprenticeship had been broken by the call-up could not be provided in the units, it was available in three GHQ colleges established to ensure that they would not be handicapped on their return to civilian life. A General and Commercial College was opened in Cologne in January 1919; a Science College in Bonn in March; and a Technical College in Seiburg in August. So that a soldier could continue the studies begun at these places on returning to his unit, a GHQ Correspondence School was also opened in June.

Gorell can claim credit for yet another development of the greatest importance. This was the assumption by his Department, Staff Duties 8, of responsibility for the Corps of Army Schoolmasters. When Gorell's department had been set up, this had remained the responsibility of A.G.4b, a small sub-section of one of the Departments of the Directorate of Personal Services, one of the Adjutant-General's Directorates. The Army Schoolmasters had played little part in the war and post-war Army Education scheme.[28] That scheme could call upon their services only 'wherever they can be made available', as officialdom decreed. Their availability was limited as they still had their schools to look after. Most of these at the outbreak of war, especially those at home, were ordered to continue their peace-time function; if they had been allowed to transfer to fighting units many of the garrison schools would have had to close. It was only by evasion and at risk of being court-martialled that a few found their way to the front. They must have felt frustrated, and when in the developing scheme of Army Education, in which they could play so restricted a part, they saw those who had taught in civilian elementary schools being commissioned, a bitter sense of grievance could not but have been added to their frustration. Little could be done for them as long as the future of the education scheme remained uncertain. While it did, they could not obtain regular commissions, for it was not known if there would be fully established Education Officers in the Regular Army. They might conceivably have been given temporary commissions. This could, however, have been to do them a great disservice for if the scheme was abandoned they would then have been demobilized. By accepting temporary commissions they would have forfeited their right to a Warrant Officer's pension and would have found themselves out of employment in possession only of a short-service gratuity. It was clearly not going to be easy to look after their interests, but there was no reason to think that they would be better safeguarded by the very small branch responsible for doing so than by the bigger and much more important department which Gorell was running. Moreover it could hardly be claimed that Army Schools were not part of Army Education and the case for having two separate departments concerned with it, however typical this was of the ways of the old Army and its administration, was unconvincing. Accordingly, in early 1919 the Corps of Army Schoolmasters came under Gorell's wing, thus strengthening him.

We are advised to drink deeply or taste not the Peirian spring and reminded that shallow draughts intoxicate the brain. It seems, however, that the intoxicating effect of what must frequently have been shallow draughts in many of the classes organised under the war-time and post-war education scheme is to be found in the eminent observers of the scheme rather than in its participants. Perhaps more simply we should think it a case of the unaccustomed spectacle of hundreds of thousands, possibly of millions, of Englishmen exposing themselves to education, affecting judgement and upsetting balance. But when we find one of the most experienced of workers in the field of adult education calling the Army Education scheme 'a movement which is destined to have a profound effect upon the life of the whole nation', when we find Albert Mansbridge, that grand educator, speaking of the Army Education Services as 'the greatest adult education institutions which have yet been created', when we find H.A.L. Fisher referring to that scheme as 'one of those great steps forward in the social progress of the world for which the war has been responsible', saying 'I do not think that in our time there has been any movement more promising than this', when we find General Sir William Robertson claiming that 'Education in the Army is a living and growing force, and its results should have a permanent effect on the life of the nation', we know that we are in the realm of hyperbole.[29] What happened was fascinating and perhaps even fantastic. But it was not what these eminent gentlemen claimed it to be, one of the great formative movements of history. It was the product of particular circumstances and when they were no longer there it would be absent too.

This is not to deny its importance, which was great and perhaps even crucial. We can easily convince ourselves of that by imagining what would have happened had British soldiers at this time felt not this interest in education, but the interests that gripped the soldiers of the Tsar in 1917 instead. There was fear that they might. After a great war men expect great rewards. The great effort required, the great suffering entailed, the great cost exacted, make their ultimate demands greatly exceed both those which first involved them in fighting and the existing capacity to satisfy them. The homes fit for heroes which it was thought desirable to promise them had to be paid for, as had the happenings that had called forth the heroes for whom the homes had to be fit. Reality has a habit of getting in the way of open-handedness, yet there is danger in greatly dissatisfying those who have become expert in the application of violence. Government was the more aware of the danger because of what had happened in Russia in 1917. Russian revolutionaries were determined to spread their revolution and the Government must have known of the efforts they were making to do so in Germany. There was sympathy for them, and interest in their doings, in the British Labour movement, and reluctance to admit the truth of the reports of their excesses which soon began to circulate. There was a mutiny of troops on draft for Archangel and while this was, and was thought to be, less motivated by the troops' love of the Bolshevik brother and desire to emulate him in ridding themselves of their government than by their dislike of the Sergeant-Major and their longing to rid themselves of him, it was not to be taken lightly.

The danger was felt to be the greater because of developments in the later 19th Century and the fears they occasioned. A great English historian, Froude, delivered a remarkable lecture in 1887 in which he said:

> In the condition at which we have arrived, as the wise man is, so the fool is; as the rich man is, so the poor man is. It is one man and one vote. And as the poor and ignorant are the majority, and the wise and the rich are the few, I think it perfectly certain – and it is only consistent with all one has ever read or heard of human nature – that those who have the power will use it to bring about a more equitable distribution of the good things of this world. I do not see how it can be otherwise.

Then, Froude said, come 'factions and quarrels, confiscations and civil disturbances and the convulsions of war'. At the end of that road, he warned us, was 'disunion, violence and finally an end to liberty'. It has, he said, always been so. The City States of Ancient Greece were free, cultivated, ingenious, prosperous and in every way remarkable. As they grew richer there came a division of classes into rich and poor, those who had and those who wanted to have. As democracy came it brought about a situation in which wealth came to be in some hands and power in others. And a struggle began between, on the one hand, those who had property, and on the other, those who had none and who wished to take it away from those who had it. 'So it always was and the end was always the same', Froude said. Human society, he added, cannot develop where industry, skill and the qualities which make men prosperous are not secure of their reward. And that, he said, is why that development of political liberty which takes the form of an attack upon property has never succeeded in destroying property, but has always contrived to destroy itself. 'In these Greek states property survived, but the free constitutions were eaten up by the Macedonians and the Romans.' The same occurred in Rome. 'The state again became more democratic and the eloquent orator came, and the rights of man, with revolutions and confiscations and bribery and faction and civil war.' And the end of it all? 'The Empire remained, but the liberty and the eloquent orators were gone for ever.' Froude is sure that society will always know how to save itself. 'Society and property always manage to save themselves in the end', he tells us, but constitutional liberty, unfortunately, lacks that survivability.[30]

Would we be immune to this process? Lord Acton, the learned Cambridge historian who disagreed with Froude in so many things, shared his fear that we would not be. With the coming of democracy, he pointed out, power passes to the masses who do not value liberty and have no good reason to:

> For the old notions of civil liberty and of social order did not benefit the mass of the people. Wealth increased without relieving their wants. The progress of knowledge left them in absolute ignorance. Religion flourished, but failed to reach them. Society, whose laws were made by the upper class alone, announced that the best thing for the poor is not to be born, and the next best, to die in childhood, and suffered them to live in misery and crime and pain. Liberty for the mass is not happiness; and institutions are not an end but a means. The thing they seek is a force sufficient to sweep away scruples, and the obstacle of rival interests, and in some degree, to better their condition.

They demand that power be concentrated to secure the good things of which they had hitherto been deprived. And wherever power is concentrated, whether it be exercised by the majority or by the delegate of the majority, the State is absolute and liberty destroyed.[31] The increasing violence that characterised Edwardian England seemed to confirm such fears and even a radical Prime Minister who had never shared them, who was strengthened by victory but not released thereby from dependence on those who were much more conservative than he would ever be, must have been aware of Jacobinical tendencies, however slight, in Britain and must have wondered whether they had been dangerously strengthened by the war. These fears were undoubtedly exaggerated for the British were victorious, their constitution seemed stable enough, and never since the 17th Century had they looked kindly on revolution. They had developed a way of life in which freedom was greatly valued and they would not lightly put it at risk. The price they had to pay for that way of life was a willingness not to push things to extremes, to be prepared to co-operate with time and to acknowledge that prudence was the god of this nether world, not to rush into change, however desirable, until opposition to it had grown less – but to be prepared, nevertheless, to accept the necessity of timely change. Resistance to irresistible pressure had destroyed others; to indulge in such resistance was not the British way. They knew the importance of safety valves; a conservative people, they have shown a remarkable capacity to judge soundly when adjustments had to be made to prevent the development of a dangerous situation or to defuse it if it seemed to be upon them. These were the qualities they demonstrated at the end of the war. The changes then introduced strengthened the popular attachment to the old established way of evolution and weakened what little appeal the way of revolution had. They turned to electoral reform and added eight million men and women to the electorate as a result of the Reform Act of 1918, which gave women over thirty and men over twenty-one years of age the vote. And as there was now a new need to educate our masters, they made better provision for the education of the masses in Fisher's Education Act of that same year, which raised the school leaving age, to 'diffuse' in Fisher's words, 'a steadier judgement and a better informed opinion throughout the community'.[32] They gave a wider representation to the interests of labour in a new and rapidly growing political party.

It is as one of these post-war adjustments to prevent difficulty arising or to smooth it away if it had arisen, that we should look upon the education scheme fashioned for the huge British Army awaiting demobilisation at the end of the war. It is no accident that the Army Order published in December 1918, which emphasised that education was no longer a secondary consideration, followed the disturbances that had broken out on several base camps when the Release Scheme, including what to many seemed unacceptable injustices, was made known. Nor is it an accident that it was with the politicians, not with the soldiers, that Gorell's influence was of the greatest importance; without the support of the politicians his scheme would have ended. Yet had the High Command determined to destroy it, it could not have continued. Despite his difficulties he managed to get on with it and he acknowledged that its support was 'as necessary as it was surprising'.[33] Bitterly opposed as it was, the AEC would never have come into being without its support. Matters, however, would not have got this far but for the support of the politicians. When the Treasury refused to sanction the education establishment without which education could not have been carried on in the Armies of Occupation (and if that had been the case it is highly improbable that there would ever have been an AEC), it was overridden by the Cabinet. Not surprisingly it was the politicians who were most acutely aware of what could have become the greatest of political problems and who were most anxious to avoid this happening.[34] Not that this in any way minimises the magnitude of Gorell's achievement. If he had not shaped and directed, sustained and fought for it as he did, the educational movement in the Army would not have appeared politically significant. Gorell's work was, then, of national importance, although not in the way that Fisher, Mansbridge and Robertson said that it was.

It was of the greatest importance on another and not so exalted level as well. For those who in the early post-war days were so sure that education had a great future in the Army were labouring under a great delusion, the delusion that the British people, after all the nonsensical years, would now be pleased to have a great Army. It was in an Army which would be a credit to the nation and of which the nation would be proud that they believed there would be an educational activity which would be a credit to the Army and of which it would be proud. It was, however, one thing to say that modern armies must make full provision for the education of the soldier when it was unwisely assumed that the British people would continue to have an Army of which they could be justly proud. It was another thing to see that there was such provision in the British Army when it became evident that old ways of thinking would prevail and that, far from having an Army of which they could be proud, the British people would do their best to have no Army at all. If little was to be spent on the Army, the competition between its various arms and branches would be of a cut-throat nature and education might well go to the wall. It soon became obvious how little money would come the Army's way. From the early 1920s disarmament and financial retrenchment was the order for all three Services. Of them all, the Army was the Cinderella service, the main victim of the financial stringency. In the decade 1923–1933 it spent some £2 million a year on weapons and stores – less, that is, than 9% of the very small sums then devoted to the Services. The Army became smaller than it was before 1914. In the mid-1930s the average age of its High Command was seven years older than in the pre-war years. It suffered from poor recruiting yet few inducements were offered either in pay or amenities to young men who might have thought of joining it. Home units were under strength and were disrupted every autumn to provide drafts for the foreign service battalions. In the mid-1920s the Government had signed the Locarno Treaties and thus assumed a Continental commitment which the Army told the Government it was unable to carry out; the Government retained both its equanimity and the commitments but hardly its honour. The British people did not seek an Army which would be fit to fight in Europe: the Army's primary purpose was Imperial policing. A great part of it was in India and there it was subject to the Government of India and was not directly responsible to the Home Government. India wanted an Army that would cope with frontier operations and maintain internal security in the cities. An Army strong in tanks, an Army training for a major war, had little appeal for it.

To the 'Blue Water' school of strategists, those convinced that British military power could be used with most decisive effect across seas broader than the English Channel, this was an acceptable Army; to the 'Continentalists' who argued that, when the chips were down and it was a question of national survival, the greatest British effort must be made in the quarter from which alone a mortal blow could come, the European land mass, it was not. The Ten Year Rule, according to which major war was not to be expected for at least ten years, renewed year after year until 1932 so that until then the Army seemed to be facing an indefinite future in which it was not exposed to the pressures of preparing for war, constituted no problem for the Blue Water school but it gravely weakened the Continentalists. This being so it is not surprising that the Army was not better prepared for what faced it in 1939 than it turned out to be. What is surprising is the high standard of its thinking, as becomes evident when the quality of many of the officers who taught at Staff College between the wars is considered – men like Alanbrooke, O'Connor, Slim, Auchinleck, Montgomery, Fuller, of whom any army would be justly proud. What is surprising is that so much was achieved; it is worth remembering that the British Army in 1939 was the only European army to go to war with completely mechanised transport. If in these years much of the spirit of the old Army survived, it must be admitted that a forgetful people gave it every opportunity to do so.

How much of that old spirit did survive, however, becomes clear when it is realised that as late as 1934 only some half-dozen regiments would accept young officers without private means, though off-setting this it must be remembered that from 1922 there was a great increase in the number of officers coming from the ranks, these by 1938 constituting 17% of the army's total officer strength. In the mid-1930s Frederick Morgan, not then the General he became, was responsible for the selection of officers for staff training, for the examination for entrance to the Staff Colleges, for the training there and for subsequent appointment to the Staff in all grades up to Brigadier. He tells us that there were a number of staff appointments that could be filled only by officers who could command considerable private fortunes, and he adds 'In the records of service of the officers with whom we dealt special prominence was always given to the names of those who had functioned as Masters or Whips to the Staff College Drag Hunt'. He reminds us that when the Commandant of the Staff College, Lord Gort, wanted to abolish the Drag and substitute for it a Flying Club, he was virtually accused of blasphemy.[35] It would be silly to make too much of these things and sillier to be sure that such survivals were totally insignificant anachronisms, never likely to bring with them old ways of thinking about the unimportance of education in the Army. They had their effect and it was the second of Gorell's outstanding achievements that it was so limited.

'By the middle of 1919', he said, 'military opinion had ripened sufficiently to make the inclusion of educational facilities in the Regular Army a practical possibility'.[36] There was, however, an immediate problem to be tackled. The Regular Army was still in process of being formed, its size was undetermined, the details of its life not yet settled. The particulars of the part must remain unknown until the particulars of the whole into which it must fit had become clearer. However, it was an unprecedented interest in education which made the inclusion of educational facilities in the Regular Army a practical possibility, and if that interest faded, so too would the prospects of education in the Regular Army. So that although optimism could believe that education in it was a practical possibility, caution must acknowledge that its exclusion was too. Did Army Order of 13 May 1919 which provided for Educational Training in the Armies of Occupation apply to the Regular Army? Were its battalions going overseas without instructors and without it being made clear to them that educational training was to be part of their life? No one knew. Field-Marshal Sir Henry Wilson could say in June 1919 that education in the Army 'must go on',[37] but so did the uncertainty as to whether it would or not. The Indian Army had expressed its interest in the war and post-war education scheme, but the classes that had sprung up in other armies had no place in it. Consequently, if regiments moving to India after the war were to continue their education they would have to be accompanied by those who would help them to do so. Yet almost until they were due to embark no provision had been made for this, something which at least demonstrates how easily education in the Army might have dropped out of the scheme of things almost by default. In July, Gorell feared that it would. 'Things can drift no longer and yet live' he said.[38] The distinguished educators who submitted their report on adult education in 1921 were right in saying that unless teachers accompanied moving regiments 'there is danger that the experience of the war may be to a large extent dissipated, whilst the present personnel upon whose knowledge and enthusiasm the success of the work so largely depends will be compelled by reason of uncertainty to return to civil life'. More needed to be done to ensure that the opportunity to give education an important role in the Regular Army would not pass away. Hopes that it would not rose when in December 1919 the Army Council determined that education 'should have precedence even if some other services more closely allied with the combatant side of the Army have to be sacrificed or curtailed'. Only a public commitment, however, would remove the doubt that what it had determined, it might undetermine on further reflection. This came when Churchill told the Commons 'It has been decided that education is henceforth to be regarded as an integral part of Army training.'[39] Gorell had won his point, even though the following months, which were devoted to working out the way in which this principle should be implemented by the establishment of the AEC, were not without anxiety. *The Times* thought it 'strange indeed, in view of the experiences of the War and the certainty that trained minds must supplement courage in all future military operations that there should have been any doubt or any delay in making this decision'.[40] Whether or not this ending of the temporary education scheme and its translation into an accepted part of training was 'the biggest step the Army has ever taken', or even 'a very vast step forward', as Sir Henry Wilson was kind enough to write to Gorell, there is no doubt how much was due, as Sir Henry added, to him. The Army's debt to him is as great as is the nation's.

On 15 June 1920 the Royal Warrant was published which authorised the establishment of the AEC and the disbanding of the Corps of Army Schoolmasters.[41] The new Corps, reflecting the increased importance now attached to education in the Army, was considerably larger than the old. Its total strength was 1,023 of whom twelve were Lieutenant-Colonels, thirty Majors, seventy-six Captains, 310 Lieutenants, 297 Warrant Officers and 298 Sergeants. Twenty-three inspectors of Army schools and seventy Army schoolmasters were commissioned in it. It is interesting that the Selection Boards had some 7,000 applicants for commissions from whom to choose.[42] It is always difficult for the disappointed to believe that justice has been done and it is understandable that among the former schoolmasters who were not promoted the view should be expressed that 'the old Corps should have been expanded to absorb the new blood and not vice versa', that it should even be said that 'the Warrant came at a time when Haig was agitating for the employment of ex-officers and there was a heaven-sent opportunity of disposing of some of the otherwise unemployable'.[43] But with so many to choose from the standard must have been high and care was taken to keep it so. In future, officers would be honours graduates or those who could demonstrate that they were peculiarly well-fitted for educational work, and Warrant Officers who passed a qualifying examination could be commissioned too. Soldiers who held the Special Army Certificate of Education and civilians its equivalent could join the Corps as NCOs.

If education were to become an integral part of Army training it followed that the AEC must be an integral part of the Army. Thus its members, unlike those of the old Corps, were 'not to be regarded in any other light than as a combatant corps of the Army'.[44] Every unit was to have one of its members on its strength. They were 'to assist by all means in their power in the maintenance of a high spirit of devotion and well-being within their units'. They were 'to accompany the unit to which they are attached, wherever and upon whatever duty it may be sent'. In wartime they had to carry out such duties as were allotted by their Commanding Officers. And to emphasise that they were indeed an integral part of the Army they were to wear the uniform of the Infantry and their Corps badge depicted an open book representing learning against the background of the rifles and lances of the Infantry. Their officers were to take the same examinations for promotion as those facing all officers. Like all line officers they were eligible to go to Staff College, the Chief of the Imperial General Staff indeed expressing his belief that 'it was highly desirable that officers with such high mental qualities as well as in many cases fine war records should attend the Staff College, as they were obviously likely to turn out valuable Staff Officers'.[45]

Whilst the majority of members of the Corps were attached to units, Corps personnel were also appointed to headquarters to supervise educational training there. They were posted to the garrison schools to teach the older children, and to military boarding schools, in this discharging the responsibility of the former Corps of Army Schoolmasters for the teaching of the Army's children as well as for that of the troops. They were attached to the training establishments for boy soldiers and to the Army Vocational Training Centres to prepare the soldier for resettlement, whilst a small number took up more specialist appointments at the Army School of Education at Shorncliffe and at the Royal Military College at Sandhurst; at the latter they taught general subjects to the cadets, by way of preparing the regimental officer to play the part envisaged for him in the programme of educational training. Finally, the more senior and experienced officers of the Corps were attached to the War Office as Inspectors of Educational Training. By 1923 members of the Corps were active in Great Britain, Northern Ireland, Aden, Bermuda, Ceylon, Egypt, Germany, Gibraltar, Hong Kong, India, Iraq, Jamaica, Malaya, Malta, Sierra Leone and Tientsin. Thus the Corps' function was a twofold one. It had an important teaching role and an even more important supervisory role, to organise, co-ordinate, direct and sustain a most ambitious educational scheme.

How ambitious that scheme was is spelled out in the *Manual, Educational Training, Part 1: General Principles*, which was published at the same time as the Royal Warrant which brought the Corps into being.[46] Educational training, it emphasised, was not new but it had gained, as a result of experience, a much greater importance relative to training as a whole. It insisted that every means must be taken to ensure that the same attention was paid to strengthening the mental capacity of a soldier as was devoted to ensuring that he was at all times physically capable of enduring the strain of active service. It declared its conviction that 'it is within the power of the Army to develop the mind of the recruit on such lines as to give him a wide outlook and power to improve'. It was sure that 'it is also possible to secure to a unique degree concentration of a highly efficient Army, composed of individuals who are both excellently trained soldiers and capable citizens'. Educational training would help to do this and would also ensure that the soldier at the end of his service would be fully qualified to find useful, profitable and congenial employment. It warned that 'modern educational opinion regards with disfavour the attachment of excessive importance to examinations and to their results as expressed by certificates', saying that their acquisition should be considered 'only as evidence of stages passed in an educational progress'. Above all it is stressed that educational training must develop 'the training faculties of officers and of NCOs'. For these were called upon more frequently to train than to lead, and experience of educational training would greatly improve their ability to carry out other forms of military training. The officer, it stated categorically, 'cannot excel unless he cultivates his power of instruction'.

It is a breath-takingly broad and liberal view of education that we find in *The Manual*, a view of the benefits it would bring that lacked nothing in optimism. It would improve the taught and make the soldier a better soldier and one more able to cope with the civilian life to which he would eventually return. It would improve the teacher, developing in him the gift of clear exposition. It would improve the Army by making its training easier and more effective. It would improve the nation both by its efforts and its example: by its efforts which would return to it good citizens; and by its example which would show to the nation what it itself could do if only it would embrace education with similar enthusiasm.

Perhaps all this was too great an underestimation of the British immunity to such contagion. It was at all events too great an overestimation of the Army's zeal for education. Unfortunately the birth of the AEC came at a time of economic crisis. With a slump in trade and rising unemployment, the Government appointed a special economic committee under the chairmanship of Sir Eric Geddes to review national expenditure. It recommended drastic cuts in public expenditure and the 'Geddes Axe', as it was nicknamed, dealt its severest blows on the Armed Forces. The AEC was cut more drastically than any other part of the Army, being reduced to less than half of its original complement of officers and losing many of its Warrant Officers and Sergeants.[47] Such a heavy loss was itself an acid commentary on the reality of the Army's interest in education. That disproportionate cut must have made the Corps aware that it had been misled into thinking that it had become a highly valued part of the Army. Further developments must have increased that awareness and added to its bitterness. One was the taking away of a privilege recently conferred and greatly appreciated: despite the view of one CIGS that members of the Corps would make 'valuable staff officers', his successor was unable to resist Treasury insistence that they be deprived of the opportunity to become such. This led to the anomaly that they took no formal part in preparing officers for the Staff College examinations, although the book *Imperial Military Geography* written by Captain D.H. Cole, one of their number, was essential reading for officers taking the promotion and Staff College examination. Another was the easing of pressure on the soldier to take his education beyond the level required for the Second Class Certificate. When it was Army policy that all soldiers should continue their education as far as their abilities allowed, there was at least a presumption that they would be encouraged to go beyond the Second Class Certificate. When, however, in 1924 it was decided that it would suffice if their abilities brought them the Second Class Certificate, the presumption would rather be that feet that went unwillingly to school would be left unencouraged to do so. It was, moreover, becoming increasingly difficult for the Corps to come by the tools of the trade. In 1924 unit libraries had been set up, one for each regiment of cavalry, brigade of artillery, brigade of infantry, tank battalion and infantry depot. There was a Command Education Library, too, and a Central Lending Library in the War Office, besides officers' mess libraries, libraries that were the private property of regiments, the old barrack libraries which the Victorian Army had begun and Command Libraries of a general nature, usually well-stocked with books on military history. There was, however, no central book supply or library service and the supply of books dwindled steadily until in 1931 the War Office Central Lending Library closed. Discouraged by all this, the AEC must have been discouraged too by what was happening in the field of vocational training.

The Manual of Educational Training, 1920, had outlined the system of vocational training that was to be introduced, with great emphasis being put on those in non-technical units who found most difficulty in obtaining employment on leaving the Colours. Members of such units were to develop their technical skills in three progressive stages: within the unit, within the garrison and at vocational training centres. Initial work would be done in units where there would be training in gardening, wood-work, sheet metal-work, elementary electrical work and so on, this being part of the soldier's general education. There would be similar but more intensive classes in garrisons, intended primarily for those nearing the end of their service. Finally there were full-time courses for those within six months of their discharge. The two Army Vocational Training Centres at Hounslow and Catterick, which had been established in 1919, were improved, the former specialising in engineering and the latter in agriculture. Both, like the Military Trade Centre at Aldershot, were staffed by members of the AEC. Many of the trainees secured immediate employment on discharge, thus justifying the scheme. However in the 1920s only some 5,000 men a year, that is about one-third of those leaving the Colours, applied for vocational courses, itself a disappointingly small proportion, and what was even more unfortunate, of those only about 2,000 were allotted places. What was done was well worth doing; nevertheless, the scheme fell far short of what had been intended. The AEC, which had initially been responsible for planning and setting up the vocational training centres, lost control of them by the early 1930s to the Ministry of Labour. There were regrettable consequences of this. Much of the impetus behind the scheme was lost and was not to be regained until after the Second World War. The Corps, too, witnessed a further diminution of its role and of its numbers. Before it lost its vocational work those of its members concerned with it and those attending to general education were pulling apart. The latter accused the former of being indifferent to the general education of their pupils. They said that 'a general education of a good standard is indispensable if the soldier is to reap the full benefit of the opportunities afforded by Vocational Training Centres, while any falling below the educational levels of those with whom he finds himself in competition when he obtains civil employment will prove a serious handicap to him.' Those engaged in vocational work did not take kindly to such criticism and the two groups were unable to bridge the gap between them. The suggestion that they should meet in annual conference and seek the intimacy of the dinner table thereafter was not taken up; the technically and vocationally inclined members of the Corps gladly joined the Ministry of Labour and with their departure the interest of the Corps in vocational education unfortunately but inevitably declined.[48] Yet another development, closely associated with this, also reduced the status of the Corps. The 1923 *Manual of Educational Training* had laid great stress on the importance of resettlement, which was to be the Corps' responsibility. It was this which had most endeared it to many Commanding Officers. The 1931 edition of the *Manual* made no further reference to resettlement. The Corps' loss of responsibility for this was not the least of the blows it suffered at this time.

A former CIGS had said of education in the Regular Army 'It is essential also that the close co-operation between the Army and the rest of the nation which has played so great a part in the victory of our arms during these years of war should be established on a permanent educational basis in peace.' The Corps, however, soon found that this insistence on the continuity of the intimate contact that had been established with civilian education was a thing of the past. Civilians were no longer interested in keeping it up. The Ministry of Reconstruction, set up in 1917 to help mould a 'better world', had shown a keen interest in Gorell's plans, but the educators within the Ministry soon became occupied exclusively with Fisher's Education Act, whilst the Ministry itself dwindled and vanished. Nor was the Army concerned to maintain this connection. In this it is difficult not to feel sympathy for it. For in 1921 an unfortunate report on adult education was published. It was drawn up by a committee of eminent civilian educators, chaired by the Master of Balliol. It concerned itself not only with civilian adult education but with military education, too, yet it was thought superfluous to include anyone in uniform among its members.

The Committee strongly urged that 'educational training should form an integral part of the daily life of members of the Forces'. It stressed the need for 'a more permanent organisation' in the Army which should attend to this. It suggested that the permanent organisation that was required 'should stand in the same relation to the Army as the Royal Army Medical Corps; that is to say it should be organised as an education corps for the performance of specific duties'. Such a Corps should be composed of 'specially equipped teachers with wide powers of initiative and the utmost freedom of action within the sphere of their duties'. It urged that 'in order that the teachers should retain their vigour, enthusiasm and intellectual interests, it is important that opportunities should be provided for teachers with the Forces to go into residence at a university for, say, a term every three years'. 'The value', it said, 'of a period of continuous study and of the opportunities for personal contact with students and scholars would be very considerable and would do much to safeguard the educational system of the Navy, the Army and the Air Force from becoming sterile, mechanical and stereotyped.' The education the committee thought desirable was education 'in the humane studies'. 'Certain forms of technical education', it somewhat grudgingly conceded, 'could be usefully carried on', but it was 'education on broad lines' that was of 'fundamental importance' and it was of the opinion that 'in future, non-technical studies should be given a prominent place in the curriculum'. 'Attendance at a minimum of classes would be obligatory', the committee insisted.

So far, despite the cavalier attitude to technical education, the Army would not have taken strong exception to the committee's views, although the Army authorities would doubtless have raised an eyebrow at the cost of all this and would certainly have wanted more information about 'the powers of initiative' and 'the utmost freedom of action' within the sphere of their duties which, it was thought, must be secured for the teachers. However, when the High Command read on, they must have been more taken aback at what followed:

> We would also venture to suggest that every effort should continue to be made to ensure that there is freedom of teaching and of discussion. There is a suspicion in the minds of many people that education in the Army is hampered by restraints upon free discussion. There is a danger that the educational opportunities which are provided may be used for ulterior purposes, such as the dissemination of 'sound' knowledge and the eradication of unpopular views. It would, in our opinion, be the gravest mistake if any action were taken which would lead to a suspicion that an education scheme for the Forces was being utilised to 'manufacture' public opinion. We believe that officers of all grades are becoming more and more convinced of the value of education, but it is desirable that arrangements should be made which will effectively prevent any injudicious action on the part of those in authority.[49]

This outburst was the more to be regretted as, even before the fighting was over, education in the British Army was never straightforward propaganda of the kind that passed for education in the German Army at this time. Unfit for further active service because of his wounds, Hitler became one of its educational agents and regard for impartiality is not to be suspected in him. The offensive and uncalled-for comments of the committee were a reflection of the old antagonism between the British people and their Army, an antagonism to which soldiers had contributed their share, too. It is always unwise to nourish a generic contempt, if only because it is so difficult to keep it concealed. When a Permanent Under-Secretary at the Foreign Office, Cadogan, confides to his diary that he hates all politicians, he must not be surprised if politicians sense that and fail to hold him in high esteem.[50] When a reforming soldier like Wolseley writes to his wife telling her that he yearns for the day when 'the license of democracy and socialism will be conquered by the sword and succeeded by cruel military despotism', adding 'then it will be that the man of talk will give way to the man of action, and the Gladstones, Harcourts, Morleys and all that most contemptible of God's creatures will black the boots of some successful cavalry colonel. A new Cromwell will clear the country of these frothing talkers, and the soldiers will rule. Would that my lot could have been cast in such an era', the silliness of soldiers must be seen to be as impressive as the stupidity of politicians and of civil servants.[51]

There was much soldierly silliness at this time. That the soldiers had a grievance cannot be denied. The nature of the war threatening in Europe in the early 20th Century had not been unperceived by them. As early as 1906 Haig had said it would be 'a great war requiring the whole resources of the nation to bring it to an end' and that it would be 'a war of several years'. Kitchener thought so too, thinking it would last three to four years and that it would only be won with the help of 'the last million men whom Great Britain could raise, train, equip and haul into the fight'. They had not been heeded and Kitchener's bitterness can be sensed in the question he asked in 1915 'Did they [the Government] remember when they went headlong into a war like this that they were without an Army and without any preparations to equip one?'[52] But what sense did it make when Sir Henry Wilson told Austin Chamberlain in 1921 'it was, to say the least, unwise for the frocks to try the Army too high, that we soldiers and sailors ... strongly objected to the relations with Krassin and Lenin, that we strongly objected to the Cabinet's Greek policy, to the Irish, Egyptian and Indian policy' and when in a blanket condemnation he accused the Cabinet of working with the King's enemies and took it upon himself to define who they were.[53]

For if soldiers but thinly veil their contempt for their political masters, they cannot wonder if their political masters feel impelled to say, as Bonar-Law did, that the military may be good servants but would be bad masters. Soldiers at the time of the Curragh troubles spoke of 'those swine of politicians' and toyed with the treasonable notion that their loyalty was to the Crown, not to its duly constituted ministers. Kitchener at the War Office, expressing his contempt for his Cabinet colleagues, said that they all told secrets to their wives. All except one, that is, and he told them to other people's wives. The High Command plunged with the onset of hostilities into that close relationship with the Monarch behind the back of the Prime Minister which was of more than dubious constitutional propriety. These things were bound to revive in some measure the old English suspicion of the soldier. It is not to be expected that a nation will be suspicious of itself and in the war and immediate post-war days the Army was the Nation-in-Arms. Those who sang, with gusto 'When this old war is over, O how happy I will be. When I get my civvy suit on, no more soldiering for me', those who conveyed in those immortal lines their special regard for the Sergeant-Major, were of the true blood and above suspicion. They who longed only to be more fully part of it would not challenge the supremacy of the civil power. But what of the bemedalled Commanders about whose behaviour in Flanders the poets had had a word or two to say? The extent of their challenge to the civil power was not fully known at the time. The nature of their regard for it was. Contempt and suspicion are highly contagious diseases and when the war was over it was soon apparent that the 'frocks' had no immunity to them, as the committee's report made plain.

The High Command could not be expected to welcome the suggestion that it was malevolently autocratic. If the dissemination of 'sound' knowledge and the eradication of 'unpopular' views were to be avoided, it would wonder if the dissemination of 'unsound' knowledge and the eradication of popular views were to be the objectives sought. What standards, it would want to know, were to be applied and who would apply them? What arrangements would effectively prevent injudicious behaviour on the part of those in authority, who would make them and who would determine the injudiciousness of the behaviour? Still worse was to come. 'The men should be allowed', the committee went on, 'to form their own reading circles and literary and similar societies'. 'Spontaneous organisation for an educational end', it said, 'is most desirable and would give a deeper meaning and value to the training courses provided by the authorities.' Spontaneous organisation was not to go without assistance. For the committee emphasised that education in the Army 'would benefit by co-operation with voluntary educational organisations'. This would 'encourage studies for which provision would not normally be made in the official scheme of education'. By this time authority could have been in no doubt whatever about that. There would indeed have been provision for such studies. It would have been supplied by the Workers' Educational Association. The committee did not advocate developing WEA classes by name in the Army. But that is what was meant. The WEA takes pride in the fact that it has no affiliation with any political party. But not all of its tutors have been as careful as they should have been that that pride would be apparent in their teaching. Nor is the impartiality of Professor Tawney, who was a member of the committee, as unquestioned today as many thought it was then. In any case the idea of WEA activities in the Army would inevitably raise hackles. Vision of the Soviets that had broken out in the famous regiments of the Tsar, and that had been fashioned in the once proud Imperial German Navy, appearing in the British Army could not but disturb the mind of the High Command.

Perhaps a still earlier happening remained in the collective memory of the British Army. Those calling themselves the Agitators, the representatives of the soldiers of the Puritan Army were at one time very close to seizing control of the whole Army. Fairfax, the General Officer Commanding, wrote in December 1647 'the power I once had was usurped by the Agitators' and in that same month Lilburne, the Leveller, wrote 'The whole Army by agreement and joint consent cashiered all officers at Newmarket Heath that would not associate with them and engage to stand for common right and freedom, though against the Parliament, and so they hooted diverse officers out of the field, unhorsed some and rent their clothes and beat them; and this in the face of the General, all of which acts were death by court martial.'[54]

The Adjutant-General had accused Gorell of bolshevising the Army.[55] Would not this accusation have been raised to high heaven if there had been WEA classes in the Forces at the time of the Invergordon Mutiny? On that occasion British Intelligence, wrongly as it now seems, blamed communists and their Soviet supporters. Would it not equally have blamed Service education and can we feel confident that education would have survived had it done so? Nevertheless if we can be glad that silly civilian suggestions were not taken up, we can greatly regret the lessening of contact between the worlds of civilian and of Army Education, for the interest of the civilians lay largely in liberal studies, the importance of which we must acknowledge, however much we may think that technical studies are important too. Without their support, interest in civic studies rapidly diminished in the Army and was not to be revived for another twenty years.

It was the proud hope of the *Manuals of Educational Training* published in the early 1920s that attention to their exhortations would produce the best of soldiers and the best of citizens. But have we not to say of these that what they gave us was an enchanting picture of an enchanted world? It was straight out of the pages of Hans Anderson. Armies at least should know that who wills the end must also will the means, something which was thought superfluous at this time. What we had here was an inversion of the old military rule, plan with the greatest of caution and execute with the greatest of resolution. Here caution can be seen only in the means of execution; the objective was as unlimited as the means to achieve it were restricted, apart, that is to say from the good fairy's wand without which what was sought could never be secured, given the less esoteric means that alone were contemplated. It was an essential part of the educational scheme then envisaged that it was on the shoulders of the regimental instructors, officer and NCO alike, that the burden of the teaching would fall. Any form of instruction, the 1923 *Manual* laid it down, that presented special difficulty would be left to the experts in the AEC The education in citizenship which was to make of the soldier the finest of citizens did not, it was assumed, present special difficulty, as this was the job of the unit instructors. To comfort them they were reminded that 'every form of proficiency is amenable to methodological instruction'[56] and no doubt it was envisaged that members of the AEC attached to units would be approached to divulge, as it were, a few tricks of the trade, although this was not thought sufficiently important to warrant attention being directed to it.

It was an excellent thing for the *Manual* to insist that 'every form of proficiency is amenable to methodological instruction'. In this, too, the Army was leading the way. What was being done, in particular, at the Army School of Education in Shorncliffe was of great importance. Regimental officers appointed to teach at Sandhurst, Woolwich and the Army Technical Schools went there for instruction in teaching method, such instruction also being made available to those who were training the various Arms and Corps. Here we have the building up of a great deal of knowledge about the teaching of adults. University Extra-mural Boards were beginning to concern themselves with this, not, however, with any pronounced sense of urgency. For the best of their work, the tutorial class, attended regularly by the same students for three years, the lecture, followed by question and answer and discussion, remained the accepted approach. Yet Shorncliffe, which could not aim at such a high standard, pioneered a more varied approach and was, in consequence, probably making at this time a more significant contribution to adult education than were the universities, at least in investigating ways of teaching appropriate to the unacademically inclined.

Nevertheless, in the educational scheme as outlined in the *Manuals*, too much was being made of technique. Technique can enable us to make the best use of knowledge but it can never replace it. Here was the conviction that it could. Training in the arts of instruction can greatly improve the instruction given by experts in musketry or equitation or in whatever else it was. But its help would be of little avail if the instructors were not already expert. The Army would not have entrusted its weapons training to those who were not proficient in arms nor the teaching at its Staff College to those unlettered in tactics and strategy. But it happily entrusted its education to those who had no such expertise in matters educational. In the limited time at his disposal the unfortunate unit officer was expected to achieve what no trained teacher would have believed to be possible. However much we may believe that civilian adult education could have profited from the insistence that 'every form of proficiency is amenable to methodological instruction', we have still to say that it was experienced teachers and those who were well abreast of their subjects who worked as adult teachers in the highways and byways of the country. And it was a more grievous mistake to think that those who do not know can be taught to teach effectively than it was to think that those who do know and who are professional teachers stand in no need of being made better teachers.

It was beyond doubt desirable that officers should learn to express themselves clearly, concisely and cogently. Borden-Turner, who had done much to promote education in France during the war, recalled his days at GHQ there, saying that few things had given greater delight than to listen to a brilliant exposition of a situation by a great commander and few things had been more depressing than to hear – from those of whose soldierly qualities there could be no question – halting, muddled statements of operations about to be carried out.[57] Clarity of exposition when added to the mastery of their craft would, as Borden-Turner emphasised, have been an asset to the commanders whom he found so disappointing; he would never have been silly enough to think that it could be a substitute for it. Yet he recalls these experiences in support of the view that the regimental officer must himself be ready to teach his men in matters in which it could not be assumed that he was knowledgeable. If a sufficient number of senior officers were so lacking in the capacity to give clear expositions of the matters with which they were dealing as to constitute a problem, that pointed to the desirability of having the AEC teaching at the Staff College to do a job which it could do well there; it did not point to having the regimental officer doing a job for which, for the most part, it would be found that he was ill-prepared and which he was unlikely to do well. No doubt Gorell was right in saying 'No proposals advocating an adequate number [of teachers] for the whole Army could conceivably have been entertained for a moment.' That did not, however, mean that the regimental officer could do the job thus assigned to him; it meant that the job, as the event was to prove, could not be adequately done. This is not to deny that there was the germ of fruitful development here. It is not fanciful to see here the outlines of a later and at least partially successful scheme, the ABCA scheme of the Second World War. But much greater thought, much greater effort and much greater expenditure went into that than into this scheme of the 1920s. Nor is this to say that nothing worthwhile was done by the regimental instructor at this time. It is, however, to say that the job that was enthusiastically addressed in the *Manuals*, the job that was said to be the object of the exercise, was not done and could not have been done in the way envisaged.

In this the Geddes Committee made things worse. The 'Geddes Axe' crippled the reforms introduced in the 1918 Fisher Education Act and not only did it make it impossible to rectify the inadequacies that characterised the educational scheme of the 1920s, it also removed, by removing the AEC members attached to units, whatever help might have been given to unit officers. It was the junior members of the Corps, those attached to the units, who became redundant; henceforth the regimental instructor could expect little aid in his fashioning of the citizens of the future. Here is an AEC

NCO's view of what all too easily the regimental officer might make of his class-room:

> I had to organise Second and Third Class instruction, each Battery running its own educational training under its own officers and NCOs, in accordance with the tenet that all officers and NCOs should share in all forms of training. I made out a weekly programme for each Battery. It was a failure. I well remember going over to a Battery class to give a 'demonstration lesson' in reading. The subaltern in charge, who should have listened awe-struck to my expert demonstration, immediately left me to take the lesson and, wishing me a courteous good-morning, took his leave. I couldn't blame him ... he had joined the Army to be a soldier not a teacher of semi-illiterates. No matters how I tried, as a missionary for the new scheme I made few converts.[58]

Who could be surprised? Not *The Times* which concluded that 'ordinary regimental officers and NCOs have been constrained to take a much larger share [of teaching] than could reasonably be expected of them' and which was sure that 'it was easier to obtain qualified graduates who could effectively combine educational and military activities than to make the regimental officer and NCO an adequate educationalist'. The Army, it had been said, might come to be regarded as 'the people's university course'. If ever that could be so, it would not be until another way of providing instruction had been found.[59]

The term 'educational training' had been coined in 1917.[60] It no doubt satisfied those who then held that there was no time for anything but training and those who believed that there must be education if the training was to be satisfactory. It was a term which became standard usage. It was a term, however, which could convey different meaning according to the placing of the stress. If the stress was placed on education, that suggested the calling forth and strengthening of the faculties of the individual. If the stress was placed on training, that suggested the adjustment of the individual to a required pattern, conformity with the response desired from a group. The phrase 'educational training' implied that education would not be sacrificed to training, nor training to education. They were, as the 1923 *Manual* said, 'indivisible parts of one process'. Military reality soon revealed that this unity was more apparent than real and that as there was a lesser and a greater here, the lesser, and there could be little doubt which that would be, would eventually be sacrificed to the greater.

It is no matter of surprise, then, that as it became apparent how little reality there was in the vision of an educational scheme that would produce the fully developed citizen as well as the efficient soldier, the emphasis in educational training should increasingly be on the making of the efficient soldier. When the Director of Military Training was given in 1928 responsibility for Army education on the grounds that 'he had only half the training of the Army under him, unless he had educational training as well', the element of training in educational training bulked still larger. The 1931 edition of the *Manual of Educational Training* underlined that fact. It declared the aims of educational training to be to develop the mental and moral qualities of the soldier and to make it easier to train him for specific duties, to heighten his loyalty and morale, to make him a more efficient leader and trainer, to return him to civil life a better citizen with improved prospects of earning a living. It was a more realistic, if also much less ambitious, document than the *Manuals* of the 1920s, and if it made mention of making the soldier a better citizen and improving his prospects of earning a living at the end of his service, there was no doubt that it was the making of a better soldier that was the target aimed at. The 1923 *Manual*, associating itself with what it referred to as 'modern educational opinion', had looked 'with disfavour' on the attachment of 'excessive importance to examinations and to their results as expressed by certificates'. Whether the importance now attached to certificates was excessive or not, it certainly seemed to be exclusive and preparing, and helping to prepare for them, became the main occupation of many members of the AEC. For the acquisition of Army Certificates of Education, based upon the aim of supporting military training and on syllabuses often, as for instance, in history, geography, map-reading, exclusively military in nature, now became, as before 1914, the crucial feature of the whole Army Educational scheme.

The art of analysis can be mastered by the study of any subject: critical and vigorous minds can be nurtured by thinking about military matters as well as by thinking about the classics. It is, moreover, an old and sound educational gambit to approach the unknown via the known and it made good sense for much of the work for the Army certificates to be of a military nature. One might, indeed, go further and suggest that concentration on geography, on history and on imperial strategy was an education more relevant to the world in which we were living than that which neglected these things, as in many public schools at this time they were neglected. Nevertheless, the broadening of interests is a way of broadening minds and it is difficult to resist the conclusion that much of the formal Army Education in the years between the wars, as distinct from the extra-mural activities of the AEC of which this could certainly not be said, was too narrow to give to the teachers the challenge they would have liked or to arouse in the taught the interest without which adult education can never thrive. If, however, the AEC could have done a better job had it been allowed to do so, it did what the Army required of it and it did it very well. An old need was in the between-war years pressing upon the Army with a new urgency. The use of the long-bow, the English secret weapon at Crécy, Poitiers, and Agincourt, had required sufficient intelligence in the archer to make due allowance for windage, and with every advance in weapons since then more intelligence had been demanded in the soldier. Now developing technology was advancing the level of intelligence and awareness which alone would allow the soldier to do his job properly. He had now to keep mechanised transport moving, to service new and intricate means of communication, to be familiar with and to rectify the faults which might occur in new weapons. If increasingly he had to think with his hands, it was highly desirable that he should be able to think with something else too.

Yet how could it be hoped that new methods of communication could be mastered when the old way, reading and writing, was beyond many of the Army's recruits? Of the 25,000 men enlisting in 1935, 2,300 were beyond question illiterate and another 6,000 next to it. In the years between 1926 and 1938 those who were unable to do more than read and write a few simple words and do a few simple sums, were never less than 25% of the whole intake and at the time of Munich they constituted no less than 34% of it.[61] If the Army could not get better recruits, it had to be able to effect an immediate transformation in those it was able to get. It was the great achievement of the AEC that it succeeded in doing this. In these years the number of soldiers unable to reach the level of the Third Class Certificate fell from 16% to 6% of the Army, those reaching the Second Class standard rose from 40% to 60%. Given the material on which it had to work, these figures represent a greater triumph for the AEC than does its success, in these same years, in increasing the percentage of those gaining First Class Certificates from 5% to 10%.[62] The circumstances in which teaching was done were often far from ideal. One AEC NCO described his education centre in Egypt thus: 'A hut with matted and wired walls; a floor of virgin desert; a wooden roof – and very old and decayed wood it is; an extra matting roof to hold back some of the continued never-to-be-escaped sun's heat; an indoor temperature of 100 degrees; a khamsin blowing, filling our eyes, ears, mouth, nose and covering our books, papers, everything with sand'. Another found conditions in Sierra Leone even worse. There, it seems, they suffered from 'Coast Memory'. When this attacked, the forgettery became so highly developed that what had just been said was immediately forgotten. In the rainy season the roar of the wind was such that only by shouting could one ensure that what would be immediately forgotten could at least be heard.[63]

Material conditions in the training depots were much better, and the strain perhaps worse. The instructor who said 'week by week and month by month we go over the same ground as squads come and go' would have greatly benefitted had it been possible to do as the Committee on Adult Education wanted in 1921 and have such teachers spend a term in a university every three years. However when we read that 'one who had fifteen years experience with Standard II and Third Class Certificate men was put into the padded ward' this seems to have been a unique occurrence.[64] Regrettable as the phrase 'educational training' may appear, there is little doubt that education greatly facilitated training in these difficult years. Just as there can be no doubt that, dull and repetitive as so much of it was, it was genuine education and it was a challenge to the nation. These below average recruits were a reflection of the nation; not all of their low standard joined the Army, and who was improving the minds of those who did not? Since examinations for officers seeking promotion were resumed in 1920 and for those wishing to go to Staff College, now a prestigious institution, in 1921, it might similarly be asked what comparable pressures were being brought on civilians in their late twenties and early thirties to turn to education and to bestir their minds? Perhaps after all it was a contribution to citizenship that Army Education was making.

In the apprentice tradesmen schools, the forerunners of the Army Apprentices Colleges, too, the AEC was ensuring that the soldier on turning to civil life would be a more valuable member of the community than he had been when he enlisted. The first of these was opened at Chepstow in 1924 and by 1939 the number had risen to four. As well as providing technical and military training these schools devoted much time to general education. At Chepstow the educational staff comprised one officer and nine Warrant Officers and Sergeants.

Teaching the soldier was not the sole concern of the AEC, which kept a fatherly eye on, and directly participated in, the teaching of his children as well. In 1920 it took over from the Corps of Army Schoolmasters responsibility for children's schools. There were 170 infant and older children's schools when the AEC assumed responsibility for them.[65] The majority were overseas, in India, the Middle and Far East as well as Europe. Only a third were in the United Kingdom and these were usually centred around large garrison towns. Most of the children came from the families of other ranks, for although the children of officers had never been barred from the Army's schools, officers preferred sending their children to civilian boarding schools.

Commanding Officers continued to be responsible for school administration and attendance, whilst Command Education Officers were to ensure that proper educational standards were maintained by frequent informal visits to the schools as well as through more formal inspections by AEC inspectors. Teaching was undertaken by members of the Corps in schools which were 'not staffed completely' by the Corps of Army Schoolmistresses. During these years Army children's schools increasingly forged closer links with the civilian school system, partly in the interests of economy, but also to ensure that they were able to provide as good an education as civilian schools, and from the outset they reflected the more modern approach to elementary education as laid down in the Board of Education's Code from 1904 to 1926 and reproduced in its 1927 *Handbook of Suggestions for Teachers*. The *Manual of Educational Training 1920*, for example, pointed out that the purpose of the infant school was 'not to give young children intellectual drill or any such ordered body of knowledge, capable of being tested, as may reasonably be expected of boys and girls in the higher classes' because the 'minds of little children are as delicate and unstable as their bodies'. Indeed, 'in no circumstances' were children in the infant school to be expected to reach a given standard in the three Rs, though 'very simple' lessons could be given in these subjects. Instead, there was to be emphasis given to the all-round development of the child through the provision of as much space as possible for play and the supply of materials for the 'spontaneous creative instincts of the child'. It is interesting that it was in the children's rather than the adult schools that progressive educational thought was put into practice. This has been attributed, no doubt correctly, to the quality and *esprit de corps* of the schoolmistresses themselves, but it was also perhaps because, unlike the adult soldier, Army children were increasingly attending civilian schools at home and thus the military authorities could hardly fail to keep abreast of civilian developments, at least at the elementary level. Even so by 1923 the idea of retaining an Army school everywhere was no longer official policy, for they were now to be maintained only where no civilian suitable school was accessible. A year later, the report of the Auditor-General endorsed this, when he drew attention to the fact that some Army schools were being maintained where there were adequate civilian facilities within reasonable distance and that this was contrary to the regulations.

The question of whether greater use should be made of civilian schools was not new but it was one that was becoming more pressing and complicated, there being sound arguments in favour of as well as against such a course. It was to address this problem that a committee was appointed in 1926 under the chairmanship of the Under Secretary of State for War, the Earl of Onslow,[66] and its report highlighted many of the issues surrounding the education of Army children during the inter-war years. On the one hand it recognised the disadvantages of sending children to local civilian schools: there was the danger of Army children mixing with children who might hold seditious views; they might catch infectious diseases which could rapidly spread within barracks; they might have to travel long distances; there were curricula differences between the two systems; and civilian school classes were usually larger. There was also, of course, the question of cost. If Army schools were abolished there would be an obvious saving for the Army, but not for the Treasury as the burden would simply be transferred to the Board of Education's Vote. At the same time, the Committee had to accept that civilian schools were better placed to provide more facilities, such as gardening, handicraft and cookery, which were beyond the means of Army schools, and also, especially, more comprehensive instruction at the top of the school. Perhaps, however, it was the need to maintain a rotation system for its schoolmasters and mistresses overseas that tipped the balance in favour of retaining the Army's own schools.

At the time, they served about one year at home for every year abroad. In December 1925 there were 137 schoolmistresses overseas and 202 at home. In 1938 there were 175 serving abroad and 160 at home. They were, incidentally, in 1927 given the designation of 'Queen's Army Schoolmistresses'. Since much of their service would be in isolated and perhaps insalubrious areas there had to be provision for home posting to keep their profession attractive. As there could be no question of abolishing schools overseas the authorities were in the curious position of having to maintain Army schools at home simply in order to maintain them overseas! Thus the Committee concluded that there should be no fundamental changes to the system, although it conceded that if the numbers of children were not large and there were convenient civilian schools, Army children should attend them rather than having special schools built for them.

In the longer term, however, there was one issue that could not simply be ignored and that was the provision of secondary education, which had been touched upon by the Onslow Committee, and which ultimately, in 1948, led to the closing of the Army's schools at home. The 1902 and 1918 Education Acts had paved the way for the local educational authorities to provide an education 'other than elementary' and this need was recognised by the military authorities, and only six years after the founding of the Corps, the problem of post-primary education came very much to the forefront with the publication of the Hadow Report.[67] Under the chairmanship of Sir Henry Hadow, the consultation committee of the Board of Education, which had been commissioned by the first Labour Government, was set up and as one writer put it was 'as variously eminent as any minister could desire'. As far as Army Education was concerned its composition was interesting for, in addition to its chairman, who had played such a prominent part in the wartime Army Education scheme, it included Lord Gorell himself. The Hadow Report on The Education of the Adolescent has been described as one of the milestones in the development of English education for it was the first endorsement of the principle of secondary education for all, with primary and secondary education being viewed as two consecutive stages following on from one another and not as parallel systems each for different social classes. In place of the existing system there would be a single and continuous process from five to fifteen, divided into primary and secondary stages with a break at eleven, the change in nomenclature from 'elementary' to 'primary' being deliberate in order to signify that the primary school was but the first stage in the education process.

The Army did its best to reorganise its schools along similar lines with the traditional infant and elder children's schools being replaced by infant, junior mixed and senior schools. Aldershot was one of the first to do this and in 1930 Catterick followed suit with a new secondary school being established within the garrison. But in most garrisons the secondary school population was too small to provide separate secondary schooling and so many children had to remain as 'tops' in the primary school. Alternatively, they could attend civilian schools, as happened at Chatham in 1935 when the garrison re-organised its schools. But a number of civilian schools were also facing the problem of inadequate numbers of pupils of secondary age, especially in rural areas and by 1939 only two-thirds of civilian children were in the reorganised secondary schools.

If these years were characterised by change in the Army's garrison schools, this was equally true of the military boarding schools which, after 1920, included members of the AEC amongst the staff. For those members of the Corps who taught at the Royal Hibernian School in Dublin, their stay was short-lived, for when in 1922 British troops withdrew from Ireland the school evacuated the ancient site in the Phoenix Park to find a temporary home in Somerset Barracks at Shorncliffe. No new boys were admitted and when in 1924 the remainder numbered just 200, they were transferred to better accommodation at its sister school, the Duke of York's School at Dover, thus bringing to a close the story of a great school, despite the terms of its Charter which in 1769 had established it 'in perpetuity'. Meanwhile, at the Duke of York's School further changes were taking place. Throughout its history the school had endeavoured to keep abreast of educational developments, not without success, and in 1923 an upper school was formed to replace the old students' training establishment which had been rendered redundant with the new entrance requirements of the AEC. With the introduction of secondary education and the creation of house and school prefects, the school felt justified in considering itself as a military public school, taking boys from the age of nine to eighteen and making available to its older students scholarships to the Royal Military College and the Royal Military Academy. The third of the military boarding schools, the Queen Victoria School, Dunblane, for the sons of Scottish Sailors and Soldiers, had been founded by Royal Charter in 1902 as a memorial to Queen Victoria and to those who fell during the South African War. Opened by the King in 1908, it, too, developed after the First World War into a secondary boarding school, by then open also to the sons of Scotsmen who had served or were serving in the Air Force.

It is a testimony to the standard reached in all the Army schools that from 1914 qualified teachers in them could count such service as meeting civilian teacher superannuation requirements. From 1921 qualified teachers in the AEC could similarly count teaching in an apprentice training centre or in the military schools at Dover or Dunblane, such service, too, counting for increments on the Burnham scale should they return to civilian teaching, while from 1927 all service in the AEC could similarly be reckoned on the production of a statement from the War Office that this was comparable with service under a Local Education Authority.[68] One anomaly remained however, and it constituted a serious problem. Ex-regimental instructors who transferred to the AEC – and they were numerous – were not similarly protected. This was a grievance with which they had to live until the ending of the Second World War. An even greater grievance, and one affecting the whole of the Corps, had to be lived with too. This was the problem of promotion, or rather lack of it. It was a problem which was far worse for the AEC than for any other part of the Army, in no part of which was it unknown. 99% of the officers appointed when the AEC was formed in 1920 already held commissions and all had participated in the war-time education scheme. Having all had war service they were of much the same age, being in the 30–39 age bracket. There would be no significant and regular retirement by age for years to come and therefore promotion prospects were bleak indeed. If the Geddes Axe had removed the older officers it would have been helpful; as it removed the younger officers instead it was not. There was some change in 1930, unhelpful in that by increasing the proportion of NCOs to officers it reduced the few opportunities to teach that officers had, helpful in that it created a new commissioned rank of quartermaster-type, the Education Officer, and in that promotion to Captain was made automatic after a certain length of service. Until this was done it seemed that there was a return almost to the days of Smollett who gives us a picture, in his novel, *Humphrey Clinker*, of an elderly officer who had purchased an ensigncy thirty years ago and only risen to be a Lieutenant, for there were Lieutenants with ten and even with sixteen years' service. But these changes only tinkered with the problem and in one way made it worse, as the retirement age was now raised to sixty and senior appointments were unlimited in duration. Some at the top blocked promotion for seventeen years. For thirteen years no new officer was appointed in the Corps. Even in 1939, by which time the Corps was expanding, there were only twenty officers who had not been in it since its beginning. By 1938 half of its majors had had no promotion since the founding of the Corps. Eighteen of its original captains were captains still and nearly all of them had twenty-three years' service. Among them were many with good degrees and decorations, such as the VC, DSO and MC. There was no provision in the Corps for anyone to reach the rank of Major-General. Barely 5% of its members could become Lieutenant-Colonels, as compared with 33% of the Chaplain's Department, nearly 20% of the Pay Corps, 11% of the Veterinary Corps and 8% of the Dental Corps. Whereas the Chief Chaplains and Paymasters in command were Colonels, none of the Command Education Officers were Colonels and only two were Lieutenant-Colonels.

Well might *The Times* say that the soldier's mind and its care were of considerably less importance to War Office than care of his pay, his teeth, his horses, his soul. *The Times* believed that eighteen years of almost stagnant promotion had had a deadening effect on the individuals concerned. Its effect on the Army, it also felt, was as unfortunate. It found that at a majority of large garrisons there was only one AEC officer. In one case he had to look after sixteen major units, auxiliary services and a children's school. *The Times* was sure that urgent action was necessary to 'restore the sense of just treatment and due recognition without which efficiency cannot be expected and present expenditure becomes uneconomic'. In conscript armies, it said, there would always be a representative contingent of citizens coming into the ranks which would raise the army's intellectual standard. But Regular Armies would not have that prospect and 'we cannot hope to recruit so high a mental average in peacetime'. 'For us', it concluded, 'the remedy is to raise the level of those enlisted by developing education in the Army.'[69]

The tribulations of the AEC before the Second World War reflect those of the Schoolmasters before the First. A greater lip-service to the importance of education in the Army was given before 1939 than before 1914, but if we agree with Burke that conduct is the only language that never lies we must conclude that the role of education in the Army was still insufficiently appreciated. Nevertheless we do well to bear in mind the admonition 'Say not the struggle naught availeth, the labour and the wounds are vain.' The AEC had succeeded in effecting a greater lodgement for education in the Army than had hitherto been achieved. That is to be seen in the fact that in 1931, by which time the Services were readying themselves to insist on the ending of the notorious Ten Year Rule, which they succeeded in doing in the following year, the AEC was given its war-time role. It was ordered then to take over from the Royal Corps of Signals responsibility for ciphers.[70] Moreover, that lodgement was not a shelf on which that which might occasionally be required could be stacked away without attracting undue attention. It was a spring-board which would make possible significant advance. It was thus of the greatest importance that by the time the lowering international storm clouds had suggested even to the British people the desirability of having a strong Army, there was a strong enough educational administration in it and a sufficiently vivid recollection of the education that would be required by and could be provided for a mass Army to ensure that education would have an important role to play in it, should such an Army again prove necessary as the predictable failure of the war to end all wars made certain that it would.

That in itself was an achievement. It would not be surprising if the somewhat ill-tempered 1924 *Torch* editorial already referred to was right in saying that the majority of the Corps had become apathetic, that it accepted all that was done for it with more or less appreciation but contributed nothing to the common pool. Events then and later would do nothing for its morale. But that editorial was certainly right in saying that there was a 'group in the Corps, perhaps, small in numbers, but active in furthering the Corps to the best of its powers and ability'. That group was strongly represented in the HQ Depot of the Corps and in the Army School of Education at Shorncliffe where it was located. Shorncliffe's morale was no doubt greatly strengthened by the handsome acknowledgement of it as what the *Morning Post* called 'the soldier's university'. The HQ Depot was responsible for the publication of the Corps' annual *Journal*, which played a major part in fostering its collective identity. Among its first intake the Corps numbered men of stature, determination and readiness to tackle any job that presented itself, as was the Captain in the recently created AEC who came to the help of some quarter of a million refugees from Eastern Thrace who arrived in Dedegetch in Greece in the winter of 1922. Nothing had been prepared for them and chaos and confusion reigned. With the help of two tough Tommies he sorted things out, got accommodation which, primitive as it was, saved lives, and arranged for rations sufficient to keep body and soul together.[71] There were in the Corps enough like him to hold it together through the dim and difficult days until once again it could in an even greater war preside over a yet more extraordinary flowering of education than that which had brought it into being.

CHAPTER 3

THE AEC OVERSEAS IN THE INTERWAR YEARS, 1920–1939

M ark Twain was fond of saying that the English were mentioned in The Bible in the phrase 'the meek shall inherit the earth'. They had inherited such a vast amount of it that they themselves came to believe that it was with a very fitting sense of shame that so much of the map had blushed red, to think that if the sun never set on the British Empire this was because God, seeing what the English were doing in the full light of day, could not afford to let them cloak their manifold activities in the shadow of night lest Heaven itself fall within the compass of their colonising zeal. When they lost their first Empire, they built up another in Canada, Australia, New Zealand and South Africa and they maintained a network of bases which, in the long years in which no formidable enemy threatened them, significantly added to their imperial power. They acquired a third Empire in what is normally referred to as Late Victorian Imperialism in the latter years of the 19th Century, some 1¾ million square miles of tropical territory with a population of about 51 million people. Those were the days in which we were at one with Rosebery when he declared:

> We have to look forward beyond the chatter of platforms and the passion of parties to the future of the race of which we are at present the trustees, and we should, in my opinion, grossly fail in the task that has been laid upon us did we shrink from responsibilities and decline to take our share in a partition of the world which we have not forced on, but which has been forced upon us.[1]

To those who could see only the inevitable part that pike and cannonade had played in the acquisition of empire, its extent did not seem to be proof that Britain was fulfilling its responsibilities but rather to be evidence that it was indulging its grosser appetites. However, whether the Empire was said to be a trust, or whether it was indignantly said of Britain that

> Her pirate flag it is flying where the East and the West are one
> And her drums when the day is dying salute the rising sun
> Her clothes are of purple and scarlet and kings have bent their knees
> To the gemmed and jewelled harlot that sitteth by many seas,

its impressive power seemed to be beyond dispute, its maintenance dear to the hearts of the British people, its security their abiding concern.

Hubris to the ancient Greeks was a deadly sin. The gods would not forgive, and would suitably deal with, those who pretended to too much power. And if with the arrival of the popular press, which led Lord Salisbury to say that Harmsworth had produced first a paper for those who could read but not think and secondly, with the coming of the illustrated press, one for those who could see but not read,[2] one of Harmsworth's closest collaborators had found that 'one of the greatest forces almost untapped at the disposal of the press was the depth and volume of public interest in Imperial questions',[3] nemesis was at hand. It was not with effortless ease that we had held our Empire. Isandhlwana will remind us of that and Kipling, lest we forget, had drawn attention to the fuzzy-wuzzies who broke a British square. We knew only too well the truth of the old frontier saying 'ten years of peace on the frontier and you have war' and we would have been surprised to find in Afghans and Pathans attachment to the ways of peace. But the call 'to have and to hold' sounded sweetest in our ears when we did not have to make a major effort to hold what we had, and that we had to do in the Boer War. That war was of the greatest importance to us for it made of us reluctant imperialists.

In the 17th Century the poet Andrew Marvell had reminded us, in the *Horatian Ode to Cromwell*, that 'the same arts that did gain a power must it maintain'. Power had acquired the Empire and power alone would maintain it. That we had thoroughly understood when in the Mutiny Indian sepoys had sought to deprive us of it. We did not then say 'You can do anything with bayonets except sit on them.' We said instead 'Government could not condescend to exist upon the moral sufferance of its subjects' and we acted accordingly. But thereafter the nakedness of power increasingly offended us. We became ever more reluctant to provide the power, the cost of which had always appalled us but the reality and the need of which we had not hitherto questioned. Indeed, the odd idea that the jungle, which everyone knew to be dangerous, would not exist if we convinced ourselves that there was no such place, began to make that siren appeal, response to which almost destroyed us in the halcyon days of the League of Nations. We liked to think that we had become so civilised that we could always count heads instead of breaking them. We genuinely did not want to break them as we thought that an uncivilised procedure. With the Boer War, however, we became aware of a dilemma. If we were going to rule those who had decided that they would rather break our heads than be ruled by us, then either we would have to overcome our reluctance to break heads, or forget about ruling those who were no longer prepared to put up with us.

There was, moreover, something else that demanded thought, something that suggested that we had not as completely lost touch with reality as their attitude to jungles showed that some of our people had done. If we were going to forget about being squeamish and get into the business of breaking heads again, had we in fact the power to do it? As the sun never set on the British Empire it never set on an impressive number of heads that might have to be broken. And if we had to spend all our time chasing the sun around in order to keep in the business of breaking heads, would not that present us with a major problem? Had we an Army strong enough to do it and if we had, could we get it to where it would have to deal with the waiting heads? To meet the menace of Germany's High Seas Fleet we had concentrated the Royal Navy in home or near-home waters. It seemed obvious, when German threats forced France to get rid of a Foreign Minister, Delcassé, whom Germany disliked, that Germany was seeking to establish that 'political dictatorship' in Europe to which Sir Eyre Crowe had said we must always be opposed.[4] It must in consequence have seemed to us that one of the reasons for the building of the German High Seas Fleet was to inhibit us from that intervention in the affairs of Europe which a serious threat to the balance of power there had always entailed. Since it was unlikely that we would allow our diplomacy to be as hamstrung as the Germans apparently hoped, there seemed little prospect of the Royal Navy significantly reducing its strength in home waters, as it would have to if required to transport troops from one troubled area to the next, and less that we would be able to divert from Europe formidable military might. The desire to avoid using force will always be strengthened by the doubt that the force which would be needed may not be available. Yet India, as well as South Africa, was making it apparent that we might have to use more force in the future than had been needed in the past.

At the very moment when we were becoming aware of the domestic troubles we might have to deal with in our overseas territories we were also becoming aware of the increasingly significant external threats to them, from Russia, France and Germany in the Far East and Africa. One of our greatest fears at the end of the 19th Century and the beginning of the 20th was that when the ever-more menacing European situation was compelling us to concentrate our forces at home we might be called upon to make a major effort in defence of our widely scattered imperial lands. We were fortunate then in finding a way of dealing with our mounting troubles. A deal with Japan ensured that we would not meet the hostility of that aggressively expanding power in the Pacific. A deal with France involving Morocco and Egypt led to the Anglo-French entente, and another with Russia over Persia in 1907 to our improving relations with that country. We succeeded, moreover, in easing our situation in South Africa and India, and although opposition continued to mount in India we managed to cope with it without too much difficulty, and years went by before we met serious trouble elsewhere. Nevertheless, our fears had been sufficiently acute to reduce our Imperial fervour, and that was something of great importance to the Army in the years after 1918.

A further characteristic of the British as imperialists was of significance to the Army too. They had allowed themselves to become improvident as well as reluctant imperialists. This had not always been the case. In the 18th Century the British Empire embodied a theory which made good sense at the time, and which gave strength and brought prosperity to it as a whole. This was the theory known as Mercantilism. According to it, foreigners were not allowed to trade in the colonies. Foreign goods could only be allowed in the colonies if they first came to England; certain colonial articles, known as enumerated articles, could only be exported to England, while others, non-enumerated articles such as agricultural provisions, fish, sugar and rum, could be sent only to countries in which there was no manufacturing industry and from which, therefore, there was no danger of manufactures which could compete with those of England being sent to the colonies in return payment. England was determined to have her colonies accept only her own manufactures and English ships to do the carrying. Mercantilism, too, provided for colonial goods coming into England

and paying less duty than foreign goods, which gave them practically a monopoly in the English market. It also prohibited the growth in England of things of which a sufficient supply could be got from the colonies. Thus, in 1690, 6,000 tobacco plantations in England were destroyed and not surprisingly troops had to be sent to destroy them. This was the mercantilist empire, a 'self-sufficing empire of customers' in which the colonies produced raw materials and England manufactured them, while in the process imperial power developed and protected the Empire. Within this framework of Empire Englishmen could feel 'citizens of no mean country'.

Thus there was nothing improvident about England's imperialism at that time and no-one doubted the wealth and the power that accrued from England's possessions overseas. Such wealth and such power, it was fully understood, were essential to the maintenance of the European balance of power. A pamphlet published in this country in 1727 said of England and of Holland 'whoever destroys their commerce, that is to say their wealth and their power, at the same time destroys the balance which can alone keep Europe in tolerable order', a view to which even other Europeans could subscribe. A Göttingen historian, for instance, put forward the idea that an England outside the balance system could draw from the areas outside Europe the strength to keep the pans in the scales properly balanced, emphasising that it was 'essential for the balance of power in Europe that England should retain its favourable position'. Those who, like the French, took strong exception to English power and who had it in mind to upset the balance of power in Europe to their own advantage, maintained indeed that mercantilism had so dangerously increased England's power as to leave it unbalanced. 'Neptune's trident is the sceptre of the world', an 18th Century French poet wrote. 'The empire of the seas', it was said, 'will give a nation mastery of the world.' And when Louisburg fell to English forces, the French ambassador in St Petersburg told the Russians 'The English have so effectively destroyed the balance of power on the seas that there is no further possibility of maintaining a balance of power on the land.'[5]

If strength was sought through mercantilism there was, however, a snag. Mercantilism was a planned development of imperial resources and in such a planned development there had to be a centre which would do the planning. That centre had to be in the most developed part. The interests of the whole were bound to be determined by the centre. And the interests of the whole as seen by the centre would not always be the same as the interests of the whole as seen by the periphery. Expressed in another way, mercantilism was a system primarily in the interests of England. The time was bound to come when the growing strength of the colonies would produce a growing sense of diverging interests, when the interests of England as Englishmen saw them would not always prove compatible with the interests of the colonies as the colonists saw them. That time came in 1775, when our first Empire came to an end. And in its ending a lesson was learned. In that first Empire there had been a sense of imperial propriety, of what was fitting for the whole of which we were the most important part. We had had a tidy and logical plan. The sense of propriety we had shown in the tidy and logical plan of mercantilism. And the lesson taught by defeat and loss was this, that a sense of imperial propriety is a dangerous thing, that a tidy and logical plan is a dangerous thing, that the crystallisation of a particular imperial conception is a dangerous thing. Such a sense of propriety, such a tidy and logical plan, such a crystallisation, ignores reality and therefore ignores life.

Yet lessons can be too well-learned and applied where they are not always suitable. Had the idea of a planned imperial development not been given up, the Dominions with their responsible self-government and the Commonwealth which they constituted could never have emerged, for that implied centralisation while they, as Botha maintained, were fashioned by its opposite, namely devolution. But when Britain acquired its late 19th Century tropical empire, its development, where there was any, was haphazard in the extreme. It ought not to have been beyond our contrivance to make it less so. Yet that colonial empire was as uncoordinated as it was scattered, its most striking feature its complexity, its resources largely ignored. Others benefitted from it as much as we did when development occurred. It was the Japanese, for instance, who began the mining of iron ore in Malaya and the Chinese the mining there of tin. India was an important market for Britain but less important than the Dominions, an important field for British investment but far less important than the USA or South America. A 1918 report had emphasised 'we cannot measure the accession of strength which an industrialised India will bring to the power of the Empire'[6] but unfortunately it was all too easy to measure the very little industrial development which occurred in that country in the years between the two World Wars. What industrialisation there was in Canada qualified but little the statement that Britain was the Empire's sole industrial base. Here again there was failure to develop potential resources. Gladstone was undoubtedly right in saying 'Rely upon it. The strength of Great Britain and Ireland is in the UK.'[7] The Cambridge historian Sir John Seeley was right in saying 'It may be fairly questioned whether the possession of India does or ever can increase our power and our security while there is no doubt it vastly increases our dangers and responsibilities.'[8] The thought must occur to us that France or Germany would not have been as improvident as we had allowed ourselves to become in the matter of developing our imperial power.

It is truly astonishing that a great trading and industrial nation seemed so little concerned to ensure that its Empire added to its industrial and commercial well-being, that our merchants in India were looked down on as not-quite-the-thing. But as Haig wrote to his nephew in 1921, gentlemen were not interested in making money and this was true of our Indian and the Colonial Civil Service in the second half of the 19th Century. Their salaries were not princely, their pensions no more than adequate. They never dreamed of making the fortunes brought home by the Indian nabobs in the late 18th and early 19th Centuries and the Empire they ruled was the most incorruptible that has ever existed. Their reward was honour and honours. The reply given to the eminent businessman visiting one of our African dependencies who asked what attire was suitable for his wife to wear at a reception in Government House – 'We have a very simple rule: Commercial wear short; Government long'[9] – adds to our understanding of our marked failure to develop our Imperial resources.

In fairness to the British it should be added that theirs was an improvidence shared, and greatly added to, by the Dominions. Hughes, Prime Minister of Australia, told the 1921 Imperial Conference 'that the Dominions could not exist if it were not for the British Navy'.[10] Yet Britain could only induce the Dominions to make the slightest of contributions to British naval strength. Malaya paid for a battleship for the Royal Navy, which was more than any Dominion did. Moreover, attempts by Australia and New Zealand to coordinate Imperial defence were always frustrated by Canada and South Africa, so that not only was the armed contribution of the Dominions and of the Empire as a whole to imperial defence as negligible before the event as it was impressive when the fighting began, but it was impossible to work out future strategies as it could never be predicted what assistance could be relied upon. Thus the cost for Great Britain of defending the Empire was greatly in excess of the contribution which it made to that defence.

Moreover, its defence was a strategic nightmare. Since it was geographically so scattered, the concentration of power that affords the best chance of attaining selected objectives became impossible. Power was inevitably dispersed and this added to the difficulties of organisation and greatly lengthened lines of communication, while it lessened the capacity for united and effective action. We were lucky in the First World War in that the threat to the Empire was minimal and we were glad to have the 90,000 Indian troops who served in France. Yet against this figure has to be set the 15,000 British troops who were in India throughout the war. And while a further 51,000 Indian soldiers served in the Middle East then, that area was of primary importance to us because of our interest in India. Even in that war there is something to be said for the view that the Empire distorted our strategic vision while dangerously stretching our power. It is worth recalling, too, that India's contribution to Imperial Defence in 1938 was one division, three out of whose ten battalions were British.[11] And how could it be hoped that the Armed Services would cope if the fears so acutely felt at the end of the 19th Century materialised, if at one and the same time two formidable powers attacked, one at the heart of the Empire and the other at the members? Would it not then become obvious how much more the Empire was relying on our strength than we on its? Such questions were bound to trouble the minds of the High Command but, if so, the mind of Demos did not seem to be so troubled. For him it was axiomatic that we were a great imperial people and if the pomp and pageant of empire, its cloud-capped towers and gorgeous palaces were, in Shakespeare's immortal words, an insubstantial pageant which at the first breath of reality would fade and perhaps leave not a wrack behind, it is also a reminder that, in the years between the wars, it was of Cloud-Cuckoo-Land that the British were truly citizens. Perhaps at no other time in their history did they more convincingly demonstrate the truth of Burke's reflection that the will of the many, and their interests, must very often differ.

After 1918 the British had become well and truly shackled as well as reluctant and improvident imperialists. They had discovered how difficult it is for a people to break away from the chains laid upon them by history. What they had taken they had to hold. How could we say to the Dominions 'if you will not now help us to plan sensibly for your defence you must look after your own if attacked'? How could we blame them for being indifferent to their defence when, facing a far more formidable threat than they did, we continued to neglect our own? How could we build a strategic reserve in India when even conservative Indian politicians let it be known how they would react if we did and when in any event we were so little convinced of its necessity that the Simon Commission repeated the statement made by Lord Derby in 1923 that 'we do not look upon, and never have looked upon, India as being the base of an Expeditionary Force'?[12] We could no more ask 'Is it really in our interests to defend the Empire?' than we could 'Is it really in our interests to defend Great Britain?' They were one and indivisible, and if geography and history cast some doubt upon this proposition, that doubt was brushed aside by the spirit of the people. If that spirit was unfortunately little inclined to heed the advice of the Services, it was adamant that they attend to its command.

After the defence of the home base, it was to the defence of imperial communications and of imperial territory that those Services were committed, and only when these priorities had been attended to was thought given to sharing in the defence of allied territory. After 1918, at any one time roughly half the Army was overseas, there being 106,704 troops at home and 90,634 abroad, the greater part of these being in India. Recollection of the horror of trench warfare confirmed these priorities and never in the between-war years did British grand strategy contemplate such a large-scale continental commitment as that which had perforce been accepted in the First World War. Logically, the signing of the Locarno Treaties would have compelled British strategists to contemplate such a possibility, but they preferred to contemplate the strength of the French Army instead, seeing in it a sufficient reason for not befogging their minds with notions of preparing themselves to discharge a major role in large-scale European war. When in 1936 Germany remilitarised the Rhineland, there was the suggestion that a small expeditionary force be sent to Belgium, to prevent Germany seizing Belgian airfields and being thus in a position from which Britain could be bombed. But the declaration thereafter of Belgian neutrality put paid to that suggestion. Moreover, faith in the Maginot Line reinforced the conviction that if war proved unavoidable a British Expeditionary Force in Europe would not be essential. Even when, having begun to rearm in 1937, Britain got together an Expeditionary Force it was until 1938 destined for Egypt and not France. Had we been better prepared for continental war we would have done better in the fighting in France in the days before Dunkirk than in the event we did. For, as a 16th Century writer expressed it, 'it is an error to think that experimented soldiers are suddenly made like glasses, in blowing them out of an iron instrument'.[13] 'To spend in time convenient is wisdom', Queen Elizabeth I's councillor Lord Burghley said.[14] We paid highly for our folly in neglecting to do so and in not preparing ourselves for the kind of war in which it was so unlikely that we could confine our soldiering to ensuring the security of our Empire. Shackled imperialists, it seems that we could do no other.

Locked into the defence of an Empire inadequately prepared to defend itself, the task of the Army, itself inadequately supported by an improvident people, was greatly complicated by the fact that people had now become reluctant imperialists. We were making it obvious to the Indians that the duration of our stay in India would now be limited. That increased the determination of those who wanted us to leave to bring still further forward the date of our departure. It also stirred up religious ruction since the majority people, the Hindus, naturally looked forward to the sceptre falling into their hands and the minority people, the Muslims, fearing what would befall them, raised the old cry 'Islam in danger' and began to organise to thwart the Hindus. The British now gave free rein to their idealists, to Reading whose strong belief it was that 'justice and sympathy never fail to evoke responsive chords in the hearts of men, of whatever, race, creed or class', to Montague who said 'when we came into India we found that the characteristic of Indian thought was an excessive reverence for authority' and who actually claimed that 'we caused the unrest because we wished to colour Indian ideals with Western aspirations'.[15] He was saying that we do not like excessive reverence for authority, so we will remove that reverence and, *mirabile dictu*, it does not seem to have occurred to him that in so doing we would remove the authority, namely ourselves. We tried power sharing, calling it 'dyarchy', an experiment which did not work then and has never worked since. How could it, when it depended on the good will of those whose reverence for our authority we had deliberately lessened? Events in Eastern Europe since have taught us that if an autocracy can no longer rule by its own force, concessions cannot preserve it. But even then we could hardly have been surprised by the wave of political violence and subversion that confronted us.

And for good measure we made it clear that there were steps we would not take if things went wrong. We cashiered General Dyer who, in the Jallian-wallah Bagh in Amritsar, put down an unlawful assembly with a heavy hand and without observing the principle of minimum force, although in circumstances which made it difficult for him to do so.[16] He pacified the Punjab but official condemnation of his action did not add to the pacification of India. Machiavelli had told us that princes who shrink from resolute action because its cost in human suffering is too great almost invariably find themselves compelled later to inflict still greater woes on their people and the cost of upheaval in India reminds us that so it was there. Before Amritsar the Army felt confident of being supported if it did what it believed had to be done to suppress dissidence. After Amritsar it could no longer be sure of being supported and its task had significantly changed. It was now to contain, not to suppress, upheaval, and that was a much more continuous process and one which made great demands on its time, its training and its discipline. For while the proportion of British to Indian troops in India remained in the years between the two World Wars at about 1:2½, for internal security British troops were used more than Indian, the proportions in this case being 8:7. There was then considerable work for the 60,000 British troops in India at this time, nearly one third of the total strength of the Army.

Nor, despite the hopes of Indian nationalists, did it seem that there could be a quick release for the Army from its formidable task. Idealist Secretaries of State for India and visionary Viceroys might come and go, but none were so idealist as to suggest that India would not for many years to come need the British Army. It was axiomatic that it was essential for Indian defence. And how, the Simon Commission asked, could a British Army be at the disposal of a sovereign Indian Government?[17] Mercenaries had constituted an essential Swiss export in the 15th and 16th Centuries; it was inconceivable that they would become a major British export in the 20th. The

Indian Military Academy at Dehra Dun was the clearest of indications that the British were preparing to leave India, for its job was the training of the officers of what would become an independent Indian Army. But since armies are not created overnight it was also the clearest of indications that the departure would not be immediate.

Extraordinary as was the loyalty of Indian troops to the King-Emperor, the nationalist agitation was bound sooner or later to affect the areas from which India's fighting races came. Indian politicians were excluded from the cantonments in 1922, a measure which showed their interest in them. They could not similarly be excluded from the recruiting fields and, fortunately on very rare occasions, trouble resulted. Thus in the early 1920s disaffection led to the disbanding of the Hyderabadi Lancers. There was also trouble in Peshawar in 1930 when a Garhwali battalion refused duty, the Garhwalis being regarded as being as reliable as Gurkhas and used as frequently as Gurkha and British troops when riots were likely. It was when on riot duty that they gave trouble in 1930. The battalion in question had had a hard day facing the brickbats of the crowd and they had not been allowed to retaliate. On this occasion the three things accepted as being the classical factors causing troop unrest were in evidence. There were ineffective officers: a new Commanding Officer had already earned the nickname 'Perhaps Sahib'. There was general political unease: the United Provinces from which the Garhwalis came was a Congress stronghold. There was a direct military grievance: the subahdar in charge of one of the offending platoons had a grievance and he had engineered the incident as a protest. The refusal of duty was, nevertheless, a very disturbing matter.[18] It is an astonishing British achievement to have kept Hindus, Muslims and Sikhs as loyal comrades-in-arms while in India at large they were readying themselves to cut each other's throats. It is an almost incredible fact that at a time of well-nigh continuous political unrest the number of both British and of Indian troops was reduced and that they were so little in evidence that a German visitor asked where was the military power on which British rule depended. It is a truly magnificent testimony to the Army in India that when it was obvious that self-government was on the way and that Indian troops could not but be affected by the emotions sweeping the country, their loyalty to the King-Emperor was unquestioned when war came. It was a fully stretched Army in an impossible situation that we had in India. That it did so well is not the least of the proofs given throughout its history that it deserved better things at the hands of a rarely sympathetic people.

The AEC in India

As always the AEC was the microcosm reflecting the characteristics of the macrocosm – the Army – of which it was part. With the Army overseas scattered throughout the Empire but mainly in India, it was also fully stretched. Cut down by the Geddes Axe, the AEC numbered no more than 150 in all India. Its highest ranking officer was a Major there at Command. In first class Districts it had Captains, in second class Districts, Brigades and Brigade areas subalterns, while at major British units there were Warrant Officers and Sergeant instructors where needed and when available. It was also in an impossible situation, unable, because not allowed, to give of its best. It also gave proof that it deserved better things at the hands of a rarely sympathetic Army. Abroad, its activity was of the same three-fold kind as at home, although in India one of its functions had a new and most important dimension, namely the teaching of native Indian troops.

Its extra-mural work was always impressive, as was that of its predecessors, the Army Schoolmasters. The leisure which came the way of many soldiers did not come to them. Their job indeed was the job of helping to fill that leisure. They had played a full part in the sporting life of the units to which they were attached, not infrequently captaining their teams. It was altogether fitting and proper that they should do this. Many had joined the Army because they liked its open-air life and the opportunity for sport it provided and there was no more reason why they should be deprived of that opportunity than there was why others of its members should be deprived of it either. Moreover, every teacher knows that if the goodwill of pupils can be won, half the battle is over. The very fact that the successors of the Schoolmasters, the members of the Corps, were often not as *personae gratae* with their units as others might be, made it even more important that nothing should be omitted that might improve their welcome, and identification with the well-being of the unit in matters to which importance was attached was an obvious way of attending to this. Even so, this particular part of the Corps' extra-mural work was not without its attendant danger. When Collison joined his unit in India, his Commanding Officer asked him 'Do you play any games such as soccer, cricket, rugger etc?' On Collison's replying that 'These days I enjoy only an occasional game of tennis', the Commanding Officer pressed him, asking 'Are you sure you don't umpire cricket, referee soccer and so on?' And when Collison answered 'No sir, I don't', the comment of the Commanding Officer was 'Good. Thank God, they've sent me a schoolmaster at last!'[19] There is a lesson there that ought not to be overlooked. The Corps would have been foolish had it not shared the interests of the Army and had it not tried to make itself as useful as possible in promoting them. But it would have been making a heavy rod for its own back had it allowed itself to be content with making itself useful. For its true function was not to make itself useful but to make itself essential, and when effort is limited by the number of those who can make it and by the number of hours in which it can be made, the true ordering of priorities must never be lost sight of.

The Corps conducted its extra-mural work in ways other than on the playing fields, ways that became even more important abroad than at home, where there was far more opportunity for the organised filling of leisure. The response to the AEC lectures in Gibraltar on its history, for instance, left no doubt that they were fulfilling a felt need. Organised trips to the pyramids for families and off-duty soldiers in Egypt, to centres of old buccaneering activity in the West Indies, to still-standing Portuguese emplacements at Malacca, were equally well appreciated. Like all teachers, the Corps members who arranged these visits would be aware of the large areas of legitimate ignorance to which they would have had to confess. But they would also know how to foray effectively in them should occasion so demand. This was welfare work indeed, but who could deny its educational possibilities, could doubt that it might open doors never accessible in classrooms, could be sure that it would not stir into life an interest in things of the mind that would otherwise have remained dormant?

The same would be true of the amateur dramatics often run, and enthusiastically participated in, by the Corps. What finer educational experience could there be than attending a Shakespearean performance in the Curiam, an ancient and open-air Roman theatre overlooking the wine dark Cyprian sea? Gilbert and Sullivan operas, which seem to have had such a wide appeal to widely scattered members of the Corps, could hardly leave as deep an impression as Shakespearean plays, but were they not valiant and successful attempts to refine popular tastes? Addison said that in his *Spectator* essays his great aim was to banish vice and ignorance out of the territories of Great Britain; it seemed to be the aim of later ENSA shows, and perhaps even of the BBC when ENSA departed, to perpetuate it, and one could only be grateful to the AEC for its stand in this matter. Acknowledged or not, and on the whole it was, the Army had cause to be grateful for this extra-mural work of the AEC.

Then there was the very important work of the Corps, its contribution to the schooling of the Army's children. Between the wars there were 190 Army Schools. Sixty were in India, twenty on the Rhine while the Army remained there, four in Gibraltar, eight in Malta, thirteen in Egypt, seven in the West Indies, and nine in China and the Far East. There were sixty-six in the UK, centred on garrison towns such as Aldershot, where there were nineteen. After 1900 there was a tendency to close Army Schools wherever LEAs could look after Army children. But with much of the Army abroad and with the improvement of transport and of living conditions overseas, families moved more frequently than had been the case in the past. Schools had in consequence to be maintained abroad. They were staffed by Army Schoolmistresses, who became the Queen's Army Schoolmistresses when they received their Royal Charter in 1927. In 1938 there were 175 of them serving abroad. There had to be home postings for them too, and in this same year there were 160 of them in home stations, for without these home stations it would not have been possible to maintain an adequate rotation system for the schools overseas, as we have seen.

These schools varied greatly in kind. Most were small with a single schoolmistress looking after half a dozen children. At Quetta there was a big school, attended by over 100 children, and in Cairo there were large schools too. Even in the biggest it was rarely possible to arrange secondary education and the baneful hand of the Treasury made itself felt on what they were able to do. Thus drawing was not included in the syllabus, although this was widely regretted as 'the training for the eye and hand' it provided was valued; the necessary materials, it appeared, were too costly. In many cases the generosity and the ingenuity of local regiments or units made up, as so frequently in the past, for official cheese-paring. The frequent movement of children from school to school obviously suggested that the syllabus to be taught in all Army Schools should be as uniform as possible so that wherever they were the education of the children could continue on the same lines. But the small size of so many of the schools and the consequent intimacy of the atmosphere in them would soon have smoothed down undue rigidity in the system. Moreover, the Home Army children might attend LEA classes in which there was no uniform curriculum, and since children came from and would return to these schools the argument that without Army Schools having a uniform syllabus their education would lack continuity would also be weakened. And when in the 1930s the London County Council seconded women teachers to teach for three years in India, their lack of familiarity with the uniform syllabus would have lessened the insistence on it too. Above all, lack of initiative was never a characteristic of the Queen's Army Schoolmistresses, nor attachment to hide-bound ways.

They might on occasion write as one who found herself in Malta did, 'I cannot help being thrilled at the fact that I can always see lights, houses of a civilised type, shops and even crowds of people – people, too, whom I do not know. That last statement may seem strange, perhaps, but I realise that I have often lived in so small a circle that I knew the names, occupations and characters of every European around me. That is changed.' But as another said 'the *Wanderlust* was in them'. They were of the breed that must go and look beyond the ranges. They thought nothing of travelling alone in the most trying of conditions. They could find beauty even in that most unlovable of animals, the camel: one can sense the contentment of the schoolmistress who wrote 'We were never without the music of camel bells in Multan.' Schools at the back of beyond had their attraction when the smaller children could arrive on the back of elephants. Theirs were not narrow views and the letter of one of their number to their magazine, *The Link*, in July 1932 carries complete conviction. 'I don't contend', she wrote 'that foreign service was solely responsible for broadening my views – the advancing years work their leaven – but I do feel that they contributed much to that end.' Her comment on her pupils, too: 'How often the fine line from Rupert Brooke's *Grantchester* rises to the teacher's lips as she looks at them: Little children, lovelier than a dream', makes one understand how fortunate they were to have her as their teacher.[20]

There were inevitable difficulties and these became obvious when Army Schools had to cope with the annual move from the plains to the Indian hills for six months of the year. As a schoolmistress wrote: 'Owing to the constant moving and subsequent change of teachers, the average child in Northern India is generally backward because teaching is much more trying than in England'.[21] Nevertheless, when it is remembered with what loving care the children were taught one cannot fail to be impressed by the teaching of the Army's children in India and when one takes into account the vivid impression that travel and changing scenes can have on minds opening up, it may perhaps be doubted if Army children were seriously disadvantaged by their many changes of teachers and of schools.

The AEC was concerned to give what help it could to the schools. Older pupils would be taught by AEC Warrant Officers and Sergeant instructors, and AEC Officers would supervise schools and provide such professional support as the circumstances would allow. The schoolmistresses' magazine *The Link* leaves no doubt how much such support was welcomed. It was of importance to the AEC too. For however indifferent a Commanding Officer might be to the education of the troops, and the best of them would never be, he would not be indifferent to that of the children. And to the extent that the Education Officer was welcome in one capacity it became more difficult to harden hearts against him in another. His was an uphill task and he was strengthened in it by his service to the schools.

Whatever the value of these activities, it was on its main work that the Corps would be judged. Abroad its greatest effort was in India where 30% of its members were stationed, these serving the normal five years' tour of duty. Throughout the Empire they were to supervise and assist schools, to be responsible for higher education in them, to run courses at which unit instructors were taught at an elementary level, and wherever possible to run further courses to improve unit instructors. As at home, the role of the officers was supervisory, the teaching being left to the AEC Warrant Officers and Sergeants. This was not to the liking of all AEC officers. One wrote in 1927 'There are quite a number of us who never TEACH and view the prospect of having to do so with some alarm.' The AEC officer in the twenties was forced into this position by the Geddes Axe. The excitement of teaching was denied to those who were not actually in instructional posts.[22] The Warrant Officers and Sergeants were often former Army Schoolmasters, and as Brigadier Wilson acknowledged, 'the Army Schoolmasters were vital to the Corps' success'. Indeed, in the early 1920s 'many units thought so highly of them that they used them as their unit Education Officers'.

The members of the Corps had certain purely military matters to attend to in India, for instance to do one month's attachment to a British Infantry unit (from which war service would excuse them) in their first two years in the country, to do one month's attachment to an Indian Infantry unit, to obtain a Riding Certificate and to attend an Intelligence course. On mobilisation they were at that time ear-marked for intelligence duties. It is, however, to be noticed that there was no pre-ordained role for the attached AEC instructor when a unit was called out in an emergency. It was then for his Commanding Officer to make what use of his services he saw fit to do.[23]

The Corps was most valued in the British Army for what may be called its professional work. It had to deal with the problem of illiteracy. How sizeable that was we can see from the comment of the Director of Staff Duties who said in 1930 that as far as he could see between 7,000 and 8,000 recruits had gained no benefit whatever from going to school. On top of this it had to attend to the education of junior soldiers. In the early 1920s each infantry battalion was allowed sixteen band boys between the ages of 15–18, twelve if the battalion was in India. In the syllabus provided for such units there was a high proportion of general education and it fell to the AEC to attend to this. But above all the concern of the Corps was with the attainment by the troops of their appropriate certificates.

Before 1914 soldiers having the Third Class Certificate received proficiency pay. Thus there was the inducement, which was not without its attractions, that there would be slightly more pay for the slightly more educated. But after 1919 the Treasury would open its heart and its coffers only to those having Second Class Certificates. Since the Third Class Certificate was often referred to as 'licensed illiteracy' perhaps it had a point. There remained, then, inducement to further study. But this encouragement to study was qualified by the admonition that it had to be done in the man's own time. The Warrant Officers and Sergeants of the AEC organised classes for all three certificates. They did all the teaching for the First Class Certificate but not for the Second and Third. The teaching of these was left to the unit NCOs and/or subalterns whom they pushed, prodded and generally persuaded to get on with the job.[24]

There would obviously be local variations, which would sometimes lead to trouble when known but which would continue to work to mutual satisfaction when they were not. Thus when Cameron was in Dublin in the Black and Tan period he agreed with his Commanding Officer that it was impossible to take officers from their military duties to run educational classes for their NCOs and men, even if they knew how to do so. It was agreed that he, together with a Sergeant assistant, would look after the purely certificate side of education. Everything, he says, went swimmingly until the Education Officer from Dublin Castle came along and complained that the scheme was not being carried out as intended. Company officers were to prepare for the Second and Third Class Certificates. 'A good old stand-up squabble, and no holds barred' with the Adjutant in the absence of the Commanding Officer resulted. When the Treaty was signed and the official scheme adopted, Cameron commented wryly 'work was less strenuous for me, but preparation was certainly less satisfactory for the NCOs and Boys'.[25] Macpherson, too, a product of the Shorncliffe Class of '28, as the Americans would say, draws attention to these local arrangements. He writes:

> At times the Unit Education Officer had to be 'carried', usually he was the most junior subaltern and as such had no influence with the Company/Squadron leaders without whose cooperation the Unit Education Scheme would all but founder. The UEO often also had the Messing Officer's job thrust on him and, if they could have got away with it, they would have made him Transport Officer as well. To not one alone of these jobs could he have given his whole-hearted attention, so, as a result, Schoolie often had to cover up for him.[26]

One suspects also, from Wilson's account of his year with the 2nd Gloucesters in a comparatively peaceful part of Southern India, that his interpretation of the scheme was not strictly according to the book. He writes 'The Commanding Officer wanted to get as many men as possible the qualifications needed for Proficiency Pay and to enlarge the field of selection to NCO and WO rank. Over 600 men had 2nds, few 3rds and there were no illiterates. It was a busy year for me.'[27] Since Map Reading was part of the Second Class syllabus and since the AEC was well-known for the excellence of its Map Reading, there can be little doubt that its assistance to the unit instructors in this was as active as the circumstances permitted. Given India's size and the size of the Corps in it, what circumstances permitted was inevitably restricted.

There were those who regretted, as did Wavell, the ubiquity of examinations at this time.[28] And when education in the Army was said, as it sometimes was, to be the finest development to be seen in British adult education, it is worth remembering that there were no examinations in civilian adult education to be prepared for at that time. Those attending civilian adult classes came for the pleasure that attendance gave them, because they enjoyed what they were experiencing now, not because they hoped it would lead to something they would enjoy in the future. But it is difficult to see how examinations could have been avoided and harder still to doubt their worth when we are told by an AEC Sergeant in Bermuda in 1924 that 'we get drafts with less than 54% having 3rd Class Certificates'.[29] NCOs and Warrant Officers were needed and near-illiteracy would not add to their efficiency, and when we read that in the 1930s there was a great increase in those possessing First Class Certificates there can be no doubt that the Corps was making its mark. Even if the Army and Empire syllabus, which was later changed to Imperial History and Imperial Geography, for the Second Class Certificate, covered little more than the most rudimentary forms of Imperial geography and regimental history, it was still a way of building on matters with which the soldier had some familiarity and in which it could be assumed that he would not be entirely without interest. Limited and stultified it may have been, but was it as entirely lacking in imagination as that civilian educational provision, which so completely ignored these things at home?

The philosophy of Utilitarianism as taught by its great exponents, Jeremy Bentham and John Stuart Mill, maintained that an action was good if it increased happiness and bad if it added to pain. So understood, education has always had a strong utilitarian flavour, seeking to add to happiness, however much those exposed to it at such places as Dotheboys Hall may have doubted this. At least its connection with the finding of jobs, the lack of which would not be conducive to pleasure, has been fully understood. The high regard in which education is held by the Chinese is related to the fact that traditionally China was ruled by its scholars, the 'book-perfumed' rulers, the filling of the rice-bowl, to which the Chinese have never been indifferent, being largely determined by performance in the great examinations in which these rulers were selected. In the West, too, however much the universities look upon education as an end in itself, they would not survive if they did not attend to the task of fitting their members for the jobs to which they aspire. The certificate work of the Corps, with its promise of proficiency and higher pay for NCOs and Warrant Officers, was undoubtedly utilitarian. It can occasion no surprise, then, to learn that another kind of education that was always even more markedly utilitarian in its nature was of great interest to the troops. Again and again they have shown a lively interest in that vocational education and training that would increase their prospects of finding a profitable, satisfactory and congenial job on their return to civilian life. This the AEC had long known. To attend to that vocational education it had turned some of its members into technical experts and found that in consequence their technical expertise had become more significant than their Corps membership. When that happened they lost their technical experts to the Ministry of Labour, which became responsible for the former Army Vocational Centres in 1932. How satisfying this vocational work was we can appreciate from the words of the Catterick instructor who wrote in 1924 'It is most encouraging to meet old students now in regular "skilled" employment, who, but for vocational training, would have left the Service with little other hope than casual labour and the dole.' In that same year an officer of the Corps was appointed OC of the Rhine Army Vocational Training Centre. In that year, too, courses were arranged in Gibraltar in carpentry, painting, electric wiring, upholstering, motor mechanics, car driving and smithing. They were much appreciated and many took advantage of them. In Egypt vocational education was carried out by the Royal Army Service Corps and by the Royal Army Ordnance Corps. Men were attached for commercial training to local firms. It was hoped that everyone in possession of a Second Class Certificate would have the opportunity of taking up some form of normal training. Members of the Corps were kept busy attending to the arrangements which all this necessitated.

Vocational education was similarly given high priority in India. So, unfortunately, was the necessity of ensuring that its costs would be minimal. It was emphasised that it must not constitute an additional charge on the Indian or on the Home Government. However, when what ought to be provided is not, those who are convinced that it must be become persistently ingenious in the matter. Years of dedicated neglect had prepared soldiers for self-help at home and abroad. They sought and secured the goodwill of the so-called box-wallahs, the merchants and the industrialists who made it possible for them, if they so wished, to spend their last months in India with a local firm, learning a new trade or refreshing their knowledge of an old one. Nor was such assistance confined to towns. In the wilds of Assam soldiers were included in a party prospecting for oil and they were subsequently offered employment by the Company which had arranged it.[30] Even when it was no longer responsible for vocational education, the AEC inevitably was still called upon to help in its provision, for armies leave it to Trade Unions to work to rule and to measure the help to be given to others solely in terms of what they are paid to do. What the AEC did in this respect was worth doing and if it is to be faulted it is for not making a stronger push to attend to it. The Army, contrary to popular belief, has often been to the fore in matters educational. Perhaps it lost a great opportunity in not pushing itself to the fore in this.

Even before the wielding of the Geddes Axe, generosity had not been the most marked feature of the educational provision intended for the Army in India. Units on draft to India were to take with them one AEC officer and two NCOs. That was half of what units would have at home and a quarter of what would be available on the Rhine. Yet conditions of work there were much easier than they could ever have been thought to be in India and these difficulties would not lessen when that axe had done its work.

There was the enormous difficulty imposed by geography and the attendant isolation which resulted for widely-dispersed members of a very small Corps. The AEC in Egypt was responsible for education in Palestine and in the Sudan as well, and it was a far cry from Sarafand in Palestine to Khartoum in the Sudan. The Education Officer at Calcutta had a bailiwick as large as Europe. When the Duke of Cornwall's Light Infantry was in India in the mid 1930s the Battalion HQ was at Dinapore and Company HQ at Muzafferapore and the Andaman Islands, distant respectively from Dinapore 650 and 600 miles. It was said that their AEC Warrant Officer was their choice for long distance running in the next Army championships. It took more than three days by train to cross Southern Command in India and in the same Brigade area their troops might be separated by 400 miles. They were inevitably more concentrated in the more troubled Northern Command and in the Baluchistan District, but even there distances were far from negligible. In China Command, 1,800 miles separated the Command Education Officer in Hong Kong from his instructors in Tientsin and Peking.[31]

West Indian adult education tutors in the 1960s and 1970s used light aeroplanes to get to their classes. Transport for AEC instructors in the 1920s and 1930s was considerably more lightly-powered and Sergeant instructors cycled along miles of hot and dusty Indian tracks. In England in the 1920s, WEA secretaries cycled through their regions and then and later extra-mural and WEA tutors carried learning from the universities to distant towns and yet more remote villages. In some areas, as in East Anglia, they may well have travelled two or three hundred miles per week. But they did not do so by pushbike under a broiling Indian sun. They were, to misquote Hegel, the owls of Minerva which flew only when the shades of wintry evenings had fallen and if, when coping with ice and snow, they might occasionally have wished for Indian suns, thoughts of much cycling along Indian roads and lanes must soon have reconciled them to their lot. Lack of contact with their fellow tutors during the long winter months when they would be out five nights a week was a constant complaint by those teaching evening classes. It is, however, doubtful if they knew the loneliness of the Sergeant Instructor at Aden who begged his passing colleagues to call to vary the monotony of life there.[32]

The AEC was well used to working in conditions which left something to be desired. Cameron tells us in his *Life of an Army Schoolmaster* 'I was not long at Limerick, but long enough to be stoned regularly every Sunday at the crossroads.'[33] This was not an expression by his pupils of their appreciation of his teaching but a normal hazard of the environment in which he was working, to be philosophically accepted as part and parcel of the job. This was of course Ireland in the troubles and in Limerick, too, where it was legendary that the leading boat in the annual Boat Race was always sunk by the stones dropped by rival supporters as it passed under the final bridge. Conditions in the tropical Empire were usually less exciting but unfortunately more trying than in Ireland. For four months in the year Egyptian heat was such that it was difficult in the extreme to keep the springs of knowledge flowing. In India all out-door training stopped in the hot-weather months from spring to autumn and if during this period education could occasionally be carried on with small groups left on the plains, the combined efforts of many punkah wallahs would hardly have sufficed to solace the unfortunate instructors. When the risk of tropical disease, and perhaps particularly of malaria, is added and the problem presented to families by the early maturing of girls in the Indian sun, it is obvious that the climatic difficulties faced by the AEC overseas are not to be ignored.

The difficulty presented by geography and by climate to the AEC abroad was as nothing compared to that occasioned by the attitude of those they sought to serve. There have been more rewarding pupils than the British. Perhaps the best that could be said of the British soldier in class is that he was as patient under instruction as he was under fire. In each case he put up with it but would have found life pleasanter in its absence. Instructors showed a healthy desire to break away as much as they could from the atmosphere of the classroom and one writer to the *Corps Journal* in September 1925 believed that wonders had been achieved in so doing. 'It is becoming a very rare thing', he wrote, 'now in India to find any hostility to education as carried out on these lines', that is to say in the open, working out problems on the ground, getting away from the classroom, from books, desks and black-boards. Every adult educator knows that the classroom is more suited to the child than to the man and AEC instructors who were successful and ingenious in finding attractive alternative accommodation benefitted thereby. But if classrooms can be dispensed with in the pursuit of education, books cannot, and those who seek to dispense with them will be restricted in their educational achievement. A gentle reminder of the obvious danger of alfresco learning might not, moreover, be amiss. The British soldier has always known how to be absorbed in inattention, an expertise which could easily come to full maturity under the Indian sun.[34]

There is something else, too. As Burke reminded us, those who deal with the affairs of men can never ignore the human nature with which they must work and it is as well to be moderate in our expectations when planning British education. Brigadier Wilson tells us that when he was in India in the years between the wars he 'frequently visited Indian units having educational classes at 9 o'clock at night', an experience that never came his way in the case of British units.[35] At the sight of sepoys spending hours of their leisure squatting about singly or in pairs mastering romanised Urdu and the rules of arithmetic, he asked in 1934 'who has seen the uncertificated British soldier doing likewise'?[36] Here were soldiers applying themselves to education not because authority insisted on them supplying evidence that they had acquired a minimum of it, but because they sought it themselves, seeing in it a passport to better things. In 1989 a comparative survey was made of adult education in South Wales and Durham. The areas compared were the homes of close-knit mining communities, both were under left-wing councils and militancy was highly regarded in each. Both were feeling the pinch of poverty. Yet in South Wales adult education was thriving, while in Durham it limped painfully along. National attitudes can change but the difficulty of changing them ought never to be underestimated.

In an hierarchical society such as the Army the attitude of the leaders must be expected to be of greater significance than that of the led. The Prussian General who said to his men 'The situation demands that you march, my children, and march you shall', expected them to follow him, as of course they did. Inevitably therefore, the attitude of the officers to education was of greater significance to the educator than that of the men. Wavell once said that the officer should be afraid of nothing, not even of a new idea. But British officers were. They were intensely afraid of education. The inter-war Army distrusted serious intellectual effort and considered great interest in books unsound. Brigadier Roe, speaking of his early days in the AEC tells us that he 'found everywhere a very great hostility to the whole question of any Army Education Scheme'. On arriving with his family in India, he found 'in character with the prevailing attitude to education, the Station Staff Officer had made absolutely no arrangements for our accommodation'. On reporting, he was told by the Brigade Major, 'We tried to prevent you being appointed here as we just don't want an

Education Officer on the staff. I'm a Dogra officer and my Dogras have bloody stout hearts and bloody thick heads so just leave it like that.'[37] One is tempted to comment that he possessed the quality of his Dogra soldiers; he nevertheless, with a brevity that was the only commendable feature of the interview, demonstrated to the new arrival the difficult nature of his task. Caution might, however, give charity a hearing. It may only have been prejudice that made the Brigade Major react as he did, but we cannot write off the possibility that it might have been experience. For there are teachers who are so sure that the root of the matter is in them that they feel it their bounden duty to implant it in others too. No one, Fichte said, has rights against reason and if my reasoning is perfect how can I admit that others can legitimately disagree? Must I not rather insist with Comte that 'If we do not allow free thinking in chemistry and biology why should we allow it in morals or politics?' Perhaps that officer had had experience of instructors of the Indian AEC, a Corps which had a span of life which was brevity itself, it having been established in 1922 and disbanded in 1924.

For although the Brigade Major's attitude would not suggest it, interest in education was spreading apace in the Indian Army after 1918. In 1922 an obviously risky, and in the event it seems disastrous, experiment was tried. Perhaps it is no coincidence that it was in Lord Reading's Vice-Royalty that it was begun, his reluctance to acknowledge Indian realities being highly developed. That experiment was the establishment in 1922 of an Indian AEC. It was 300 strong while it lasted, and while allowance must be made for quality as well as quantity, numbers at least suggest that the Indian Army was attaching more importance to education than was the British Army, which was content to have with it in India only half that number of its own AEC. The Indian AEC was drawn not only from educated recruits but from civilian teachers. That was the danger. 1922 was the year in which Indian politicians were excluded from the Army's cantonments and if they were sufficiently interested to go there they would also be sufficiently interested to try to get their supporters into the new Corps. And even if Indian Security Forces could cope with that there was still a problem. For the teachers in particular, and to a large extent the educated recruits as well, must have acquired their learning in the larger towns and cities. Universities, colleges, teachers' training departments were situated there; there there was no tradition of military service; there the outlook was non-military and in so far as it was affected by rising Indian nationalism, as it was bound to some extent to be, anti-military as well. The *Educational Training Indian Army Manual, 1939* stressed the importance of maintaining law and order and emphasised that the soldier should 'understand the benefits which he derives as a citizen of the British Empire and realise that he has a duty to perform in taking part in its defence'. It added 'The History course should stress the need for good government, law and order, as proved by the dissensions and disorders with which the country was affected when stable government did not exist.' It would be reasonable to think that the experience of the 1920s and 30s had focused and clarified Indian Army thinking on these issues; it would be naive to believe that such obvious matters had no place in its thinking in the early 1920s. And we can hardly doubt that those graduating from Indian universities and colleges who joined the Indian AEC would not regard such objectives as their highest priorities. It is at least evident that the Army soon found that the hopes that had been placed in the Indian AEC were ill-founded. It was accordingly disbanded in 1924, its responsibilities taken over, in units, by the personnel of the units, and outside them by seconded Indian officers and NCOs.[38]

Roe leaves us in no doubt how greatly this attitude to education on the part of many officers added to the difficulties of the AEC 'Senior officers', he says, 'came into classes and vetted and made notes of everything that was said.'[39] One of them tells us:

> The newly-come AEC Instructor had to start off by convincing his CO that he wasn't a Red, and that he genuinely wanted to improve the unit's education and asked only to be accepted as one of the family. The Schoolie was up against the prejudice created by the fact that this new element called 'education' had to be squeezed into an already-crowded Unit Training Programme at the expense, the unit felt, of something more important for winning wars. The cynics said that in a future war it would be useless holding aloft your Education Certificates and expecting the enemy to capitulate to a force educationally if not numerically superior to his own.

The attitude of the British officer in the Indian Army to the AEC is strikingly at odds with the importance attached by the Indian Government to military education, for the Indian Government only agreed to the disbanding of the Corps of Army Schoolmasters on condition that each Schoolmaster serving in India should be replaced by an experienced Warrant Officer.[40]

One is again and again struck by the surprise that was expressed when AEC officers were found to be carrying out duties, the discharge of which by other officers would have occasioned no comment, impressed by their ability to do so as they would not have been by competence similarly displayed by officers of other branches. This was not the least of the difficulties faced by the AEC officer in India or elsewhere. He had to be aware of the necessity of continually demonstrating the importance of his specialist knowledge to the Army, as other specialist units had no need to. And he had also continually to be aware, as officers of other departments did not, of the desirability of showing that he had indeed the qualities appropriate to an Army officer. Perhaps few things more clearly reveal that element of artificiality which is inescapable from the Army between the wars than this surprise that was expressed when officers of a small Corps, several of whom had commanded battalions and one a brigade, fourteen of whom had been awarded the DSO, forty-eight the Military Cross and three the Victoria Cross should have been looked at askance as doubtfully possessing officer qualities. Yet there seems to have been genuine astonishment when they demonstrated that they did. The assumption seemed automatic that those who had embraced the profession of arms lost caste when they adopted the scholastic profession too. For the profession of arms, like the profession of diplomacy, was open to the gentlemen of England; others were not. And here perhaps we have the explanation of the eccentric belief that men of these other professions, despite the marriage of younger sons of the gentry with their daughters and with the daughters of commerce, could not be expected to sit with firmness, ease and grace in the saddle. Such a belief was not the least of the difficulties with which the AEC had to cope in the between-war years.

Perhaps this was the nub of it. The AEC was not thought of as 'pukka'. And some of its members, it seemed, reacted stupidly, thereby confirming that prejudice. When Roe reached his unit in India in 1923, he found that his predecessor had been excluded from the officers' mess because he could not afford a dinner jacket. Being interpreted, that means that he considered the purchase of other things more important. And not only are we forced to think that he had got his priorities wrong, but also to suspect that his was the cast of mind that needlessly added to the difficulties of his Corps.

Nor is such a reflection making a mountain out of a molehill. Those who are not esteemed are only too likely to turn in on themselves and, in their turn, think poorly of those whose esteem they lack. Despised by Japanese public opinion in the 1920s, the Imperial Japanese Army reacted *sui generis* and after repeated upheavals and assassinations took over the government in the late 1930s. Affected, as it could not but be, by the wave of anti-militarism sweeping through Britain after 1918, the British Army reacted *sui generis* too. It turned in on itself, back to the comfort of the regiment, and perhaps there has never been a time in its history when its ethos was so different from that of the people it served. That was dangerous both for the Army and the people, not because it raised the spectre of military disobedience to the civil power – that is not the British way nor is it the way of the British Army. It was dangerous because it strengthened the hands of the traditionalists in the Army and in the increasingly menacing inter-war years this was a folly which could not be afforded.[41] Similarly, the slight regard shown by the Army for the AEC cannot but have adversely affected it, lessened its ardour, made it content to continue teaching drearily outworn syllabuses. It is no accident that it was the new entrants into the Corps in the late 1930s who produced their own more relevant syllabuses, greatly to the advantage of the units to which they were attached. It was folly for the British people to treat their Army as they did and as foolish for the Army to treat as it did the AEC.

Moreover, in India the Army was in the most traditionalist part of the Empire and for those who wanted a traditional Army what could be more congenial? This was a society in which card drill was still as important as sword drill was in the old Army, in which the social solecism of turning down the wrong corner of the card could not be survived, in which the officer, but not the box-wallah, was of the Heaven-Born and had the entrée into the club, but not if he was unable to sport black tie and cummerbund. The Public School had from its inception made a great appeal to the Army as the natural growing ground of its officers. Was it not the regiment in miniature? There the boy became the independent man. He left home at an early age and he learned to stand on his own feet. He learned to endure hardship without complaint. He was taught to place a high value on health and on team games. He learned, too, the things that are come by and not taught, the things that are done and not done, the nuances, familiarity with which eases communal living, the ways of protest that are legitimate and those that are not. Forced back on the regiment in an environment which clung to old ways, the Army closed ranks against the new. Absurd as it was, it was not without importance that not all of the officers of the AEC, even those well versed in the ways of black ties, had been to Public Schools.

Cups that are full seem to attract what will leave them running over and there was another reason for the hostility often shown to the AEC. An unfortunate effect of the cutting of the numbers of the Corps was that the ordinary regimental officers and NCOs had to do more in the way of education than could reasonably be expected of them. The trained teachers became so burdened with administration that they had no time to teach. Administrators are not the most popular of beings; the student upheaval of the 1960s was directed against them, not against the teachers. Administrators who are qualified to teach but who do not do so, because their administrative duties leave them no time, must expect to be even more unpopular with those who are not qualified to teach, but have to, and who will readily convince themselves that they would not have to if the administrators would attend to their proper job.

To the resentment of those who were called upon to do what they did not feel up to would also have to be added the displeasure of those who had to suffer the consequences of them not being up to it. Aristotle was right in saying that *hoi polloi* cannot make shoes but that they know when the shoe pinches. The taught know what is indifferent and uninteresting teaching when they have to endure it but they will not look with enthusiasm on what they have to endure and they will never think of it as a means of enriching their lives. As a way of ensuring that education would be well thought of in the Army this way of doing things was not without its peculiarities.[42]

There was yet another and important consequence of this approach to education in the Army. Teachers can never remain separate from their pupils but administrators have no pupils to be separated from. They are remote as teachers can never be. It had been authoritatively determined that the AEC should be fully 'identified with the interests and responsibilities of military life'. It is hard to resist the conclusion, however, that in fact it was not. Given English attitudes that was perhaps inevitable. But what was not inevitable was the great and protracted difficulty of making it so. Had the AEC officer been more of a teacher in the Army he might have been less removed from it and education in it would have been more highly regarded too. There is a revealing comment in Cameron's diary. Gazetted into the AEC in January 1921, he was posted as Officer Instructor to the Royal Barracks in Dublin. The Commandant welcomed him with the words 'As you are an ex-Army School Master, now we'll get something done in the way of education.'[43] There was nothing there of that hostility to education which was later so widely apparent. Clearly the Commandant did not think that the regimental instructor who had been responsible for education before Cameron's arrival had been able to get much done. Equally clearly he paid Cameron the respect of feeling sure that now the job would be properly done. We should remember, too, Brigadier Wilson's comment that the work of the ex-Army Schoolmaster Warrant Officers in the early years of the Corps was 'vital to its success'.

Nor should we forget either two further factors. The first was that to which *The Times* drew attention on 3 February 1938 when it wrote 'It is essential that those who are responsible for the educational training of the soldier shall at least ... carry the same weight, through rank, as the others who are responsible for his teeth, his accounts and his transport animals.' It is odd how this matter of promotion so long bedeviled the Corps. Too great a delay in promoting subalterns added to the difficulty of those who had to overcome unit reluctance to take education seriously before 1939, as too great haste in promoting them increased their difficulty by strengthening the resentment of those with whom they had to deal after 1945. This was a serious difficulty but, even if protracted as it was beyond all reason, one that the years would undoubtedly remove. Doubtless they would the other too, but they would have a greater difficulty since attitudes have a habit of persisting after the circumstances which gave rise to them have changed. Wavell tells us that the headmaster of Winchester wrote to his father regretting Wavell's decision to join the Army class there, saying 'I do not think that you need take this extreme step, since I believe that your son has sufficient brains to make his way in other walks of life.'[44] We can be appalled at the headmaster of Winchester's lack of vision in not appreciating the Army's need of brains nor the great importance of meeting it. But he had seen many of his pupils take commissions and it is clear that their mental abilities had failed to impress him. Some would no doubt have developed as officers the brains they had not chosen to use at school, but many would have remained too limited to understand the importance of further stretching their minds and those of their men. Perhaps, too, the approach of the 'Schoolie' revealed in themselves an inadequacy they would never have felt at the advance of the enemy. When it became apparent that there was no room for the gallant block-head in the officer ranks, and that high intelligence was indispensable, this particular cast of mind, with its mingled disdain for the 'Schoolie' and apprehension lest his presence reveal one's own deficiencies, would at last be a thing of the past.

Unfortunately these were not the only difficulties with which the AEC had to cope. There was one which, as we have seen, played its part in determining the hostility of many officers to education at this time but which was as fundamental as was that hostility. This was the conflict between means and ends which was writ so large over the educational scheme as it developed in the Army after 1918. That end was not the gaining of as many certificates for the other ranks as possible, although that was implied in it. That end was the production of the new type of soldier who would be more suited for modern war than his old-time counterpart. A new type of soldier, it was thought, would be needed: one who, while retaining the old collective virtues, would develop new individual values, who would be able to rely more on his own initiative, to be more aware of his own responsibility, to be more intelligent. It could not be assumed that awareness of this demand would suffice to guarantee the availability of the supply. It could be assumed that there was more likelihood of these qualities being forthcoming if attention was paid to developing them. Since the educated man can be trained more quickly and easily than the uneducated man, it seemed obvious that the educator would have his part to play in developing the qualities now required in the soldier. Yet this, it appeared, was to be the exclusive concern of the regimental officer. This, as we have seen, he greatly resented. He believed that he was not qualified, either by training or by temperament, to carry out the task of a profession he had not chosen to follow. He was told that an officer was an instructor. An instructor was a teacher. Therefore he was a teacher and as a teacher he was told that he could teach whatever he could mug up. This, as *The Times* on 3 February 1938 wrote, was 'unsatisfactory, as they [officers] rarely have the qualifications; and they do not even get the incentive of extra-duty pay such as a physical training instructor receives'. Wavell, with officers in mind, said that there were too many examinations in the Army and that only the crammer benefitted. He believed that Huxley was right in saying of those whose approach to examinations was via the crammer 'They work to pass, not to know; and outraged Science takes its revenge. They pass and they do not know.'[45] There was always the danger that the necessity of ensuring that as many soldiers as possible were in possession of their appropriate certificates would replace the teacher by the crammer. That danger was not avoided and to the extent that it was not, the aim of the educator had not been achieved. How could it be when the instructor was not even a trained teacher and when his performance would clearly be judged by examination results? How could it be when the means were so inappropriate to the end?

Further difficulties experienced by the AEC were as nothing compared with this. Nevertheless, they added to the problems of the Corps. Books were in short supply and available text-books were often so inappropriate that members of the Corps had to write their own, which they did very successfully. In addition, calls upon the Army overseas were insistent and played havoc with educational timetables. During the Spanish Civil War, for instance, troops in Gibraltar had to attend to matters other than educational. There was always the threat of tribal war in India which affected the troops in the Peshawar and Rawalpindi Districts and a Sergeant Instructor speaks of 'the determination necessary to carry on instruction within rifle range of a determined enemy'. That same determination was required too by the teachers who managed to get their required certificates for 150 men of the Royal Welch Fusiliers who spent nearly a year encamped in canvas tents, mud-walled in winter, 6,000 feet up on an exposed and isolated plateau in Waziristan. We read that 'AEC instructors [in Palestine] had not the courage to suggest classes to COs, whose men were lucky if they had two nights in bed in a week'. They added, however, that it still proved possible to hold the First Class Certificate Examination, which was convincing proof that it was believed to be worth acquiring and thus answered a felt need. And we read in the *Journal* of the Corps in April 1939 that 'the civil unrest in Burma since July last has interfered with educational training ... one of the British battalions was called out in aid of the civil power after completing one day's tests in a 2nd Class Examination and did not return for three weeks'. Minor inconveniences inseparable from military life, they nevertheless remind us that the work of the Corps overseas was beset by trials and was not without its hazards.[46]

Perhaps the most important work done by the AEC in India between the wars was with the Indian and not with the British Army. It was seen by some as 'the *raison d'être* of the continued existence of the Corps'. There was special commendation for it in a great state paper. The Simon Report said of it 'The movement for adult education in India – apart from university courses – has with one striking and valuable exception, hardly begun. We refer to the work done by the Army for education in India.' It drew special attention to the fine work done at the Army School of Education in Belgaum, saying 'By this means educational courses are given to the whole personnel of the Indian Army, and many thousands of men return to village life literate and instructed in many matters, from map-reading to the duties of citizenship.'[47] However much we may feel that this does not lack on the side of hyperbole we can still believe that this was a great work done for the peoples of India. If, in the event, the inability of those people to unite prevented it having the beneficial effects that must have been expected from it, like that other great effort in military adult education with which it has much in common, the education of the Austro-Hungarian Army, which also unfortunately failed, it played its part in preserving the unity and the health of an army in an environment in which everything else seemed to be falling into disarray.

The troops of the Indian Army numbered somewhat more than 60,000. That Army had been built up after the Mutiny from areas which had remained loyal. There were many races and religions. They were from the warrior castes which had traditionally kept themselves aloof from politics. They were divided into tribal regiments, themselves sub-divided into companies of separate ethnic units. The troops and the NCOs were entirely Indian, the officers, except occasionally at very junior level, British. Excluding 19,000 Gurkhas, 62% of the whole Indian Army came from the Punjab. Most of the troops came from the villages and were illiterate, as were their NCOs and what junior officers they had. The East India Company had encouraged some higher, and indeed some university education, but it had done little for primary education, particularly in the rural areas. That policy had not greatly changed when Company rule ended. Moreover when education appeared to be the preserve of what the martial races of India contemptuously referred to as 'the fish-eating Babus of Bengal' they were fiercely hostile to it, saying that they would content themselves with the pen of their fathers, namely the sword. From time to time a limited amount had been done by civilians, often clerics, to help soldiers who wished to read and write; there were few, it seemed, who wanted to learn and who were ready to give up their spare time to do so. There was an early attempt, too, to arrange vocational training for the soldier and to help him become literate in his own vernacular. Such effort also had failed.

But times change and as it became borne in on them that education meant jobs, the attitude of the soldiers began to change, too, so that it was not long before the Indian soldier began to look upon education as a privilege to be greatly valued. We have seen how sepoys addressing themselves to it in the 1920s and 30s impressed AEC officers; similarly in February 1940 another was struck by the way 'in which education expands its scope continually'. 'Soldiers on pension', we read 'are keenly anxious that their children should receive the same educational advantages they have obtained in the Army.'[48] Government in the early 1920s felt that the provision of education for the children of the Indian Army was a luxury of which it could afford to deprive itself. But as usual the Army stepped in to do what its lords and masters would not. Many regiments opened schools in which the teaching was done by regimental instructors and by civilian teachers paid from regimental funds. Such Army self-help is sufficiently usual to be hardly worth a comment. What is very striking, however, is this changed view of education in those of whom the commandant of Dehra Dun was reported by *The Times* of 26 October 1922 as saying

> ...the general knowledge of his cadets was very weak, they did not know what countries bordered on India, only one or two knew who Roberts and Kitchener were although they were living in houses in the school which have these illustrious names and this was because the martial races of India are brave and hardy men, accustomed to hardships and life in the open air, who despise cities and the man of the cities and, unfortunately, in the majority of cases, have the greatest contempt for learning.[49]

After 1918 it became obvious that greater attention would have to be paid to the education of the Indian soldier, for there was the need that was felt in the British Army to make the soldier a more highly trained man in peace and a more highly skilled man in war. There were other and special reasons as well. In 1914 there were few Indian officers commanding more than a platoon and after 1918 there were murmurings of discontent in the Indian Army that greater participation in its higher ranks was lacking. It was likely to remain so while excellent, combat-steeled officers had such difficulty in reading and writing. Moreover, Commanding Officers of Indian Regiments have always been interested in the resettlement of their men and as they knew that resettlement prospects were much better for those who spoke English they were the more insistent that the men should have the opportunity of mastering it.

After the disbanding of the Indian AEC in 1924 a later attempt to establish a new kind of Indian AEC was made. It survived longer than its predecessor but it could claim no great distinction. This was the Permanent Indian Service Cadre of the AEC It was formed in 1931 to offset the constant change of personnel brought about by the ending of the normal AEC tour of duty in India. Its members did all their service in India and received Indian Army rates of pay. Few joined it. There were no volunteers to fill its two major appointments. It consisted entirely of Captains and subalterns who had little real authority. Fifteen AEC officers transferred to it and to assist them were twenty Viceroy's-commission officers. Thus the education of the Indian Forces remained the responsibility of the AEC.

That responsibility they discharged very competently. Sound foundations were laid in the establishment of the Indian Army schools for cadets. Apart from Dehra Dun there were King George's Royal Indian Military School, at Jullundar for Punjabi Hindus and Sikhs, at Jhelum for Muslims, at Adjmer for Jats, Rajputs and Mahrattas. They were modelled on the Duke of York's School in England. Their aim was 'to reproduce, as far as is consistent with Indian life and customs, the system of the English public school and, at the same time, to develop the boy's inherited military instincts'. Money for their funding came from the King-Emperor's Patriotic Fund, which was begun in 1918 from the proceeds of the gifts made to King George V from the Indian princes on the occasion of his silver wedding.[50] Originally the schools were commanded by an Indian Army Colonel, below him being an AEC Commandant. Soon, however, AEC Commandants assumed full control of the schools and AEC officers, Warrant Officers and Sergeants were appointed to them. Since many pupils came from villages untouched by modern communications, their task was no light one. Nevertheless the schools became very successful and it is a great tribute to them that they did. They became important sources of recruitment for Kitchener College and for Dehra Dun when the Indian Sandhurst was established there. Many of the senior officers of both the Indian and the Pakistani Armies were from these schools, a factor of considerable importance in speeding the ending of the first war between India and Pakistan.

The schools for the Army itself were as impressive. In 1920 the British Army School of Education in India was set up in Wellington, whence three years later it moved to Belgaum to merge with the Indian Army School of Education which had been opened in 1921. That had been commanded by an Indian Army Major but his Chief Instructor and his three officers were from the Corps. In the combined Belgaum school an AEC officer commanded and he was also responsible for the British wing of the school. Incidentally, the drama figured largely in Belgaum's teaching, an arithmetic lesson became a play showing bargaining in the bazaar and map-reading a team race in simplified orienteering. The theatre, indeed, was a feature of unit education in the Indian Army and we read in the *AEC Quarterly Bulletin* for January 1945 'Great stress is laid on the dramatic method of presentation. This is found to have a natural appeal for Indian troops.'[51] Here again is an illustration of the fertile imagination, the ability to think out new approaches to teaching, that has always been a characteristic of the Corps. Schools in England in the 1970s and 80s were turning to drama in their teaching, years after the AEC had proved its success both at home and elsewhere. Its capacity to teach is only less striking than its willingness to put up with a situation in which its opportunity to do so was so restricted. That capacity was again displayed when in 1922 Kitchener College was founded to give present and prospective Indian officers the opportunity to obtain a wider general education and training than units could provide. The AEC was responsible for education here. In 1932 the Indian Sandhurst was set up at Dehra Dun and as at Sandhurst education figured largely in its syllabus, this being the concern of officers of the AEC.

Languages, understandably, bulked large in the teaching of the Indian troops. There was, in particular, the teaching of romanised Urdu. Urdu had been developed in the Mogul Empire as a means whereby the conquering Muslims could communicate with the conquered Hindus. It was a mixture of Persian and Hindi, the Persian element becoming stronger the nearer one got to the north-west. It was written in either the Persian or the Hindi script. After 1918 it was decided to make Urdu in romanised script the lingua franca of the Indian Army. This had the advantage of being related to all Indian tongues except those of Dravidian origin, this latter disadvantage being minor as few troops were from the Dravidian south. The decision to romanise Urdu script was taken because this was easier to learn than any of the scripts already in use in India. It was the task of the AEC at Belgaum to devise a new romanised Urdu, to draw up syllabuses and to determine the standard for the various Army certificates, examinations for which the Indian troops would be required to sit. Special text-books had to be written. By 1927 this had been done, text-books in geography, history, mathematics, citizenship and map-reading having been produced. Urdu was not a difficult language. It was reckoned that any officer with a reasonable amount of determination should be able to pass the prescribed test in Urdu within twelve months of landing in the country. Regrettably, few AEC instructors knew it. That cannot have facilitated their teaching of English to the troops and it is not something of which they can be proud.

Apart from Urdu, there was the teaching of English. This was the language in which the administration of the Indian Army was conducted. Knowledge of Urdu would suffice only for an elementary level of education and training; above that level English was the language of instruction. It was essential that as many Indian officers and NCOs as possible should be sufficiently fluent in English to administer their own commands, to be potential candidates for the Indian Military Academy and to liaise with British troops. Such was its importance that in Western Command, India, every instructor except one had to teach Indian troops for one hour each day.[52] There were three certificates in English for the Indian soldier. There was the Third Class, which was entirely oral and which required the candidate only to describe what he saw and to ask and answer questions. There was the Second Class, which demanded a knowledge of reading and writing. There was the First Class, the standard of which was good and which was intended for those who would enter for the Indian Army Special Certificate of Education and for those hoping to get into the Indian Military Academy at Dehra Dun.

Apart from studying Urdu and English, Indian troops also studied citizenship, rural reconstruction and general knowledge. It would be naive to imagine that the teaching of citizenship was unconnected with the idea that in this way there could be provided a body of ex-soldiers on whose contentment and loyalty the country could rely. But it was also concerned, as was the syllabus on rural reconstruction, to teach the elementary principles of military hygiene and sanitation and the chief sources of the principal epidemic diseases; the ways in which the health and the sanitation, the social and the economic conditions of the villages could be improved; the village administrative structure; the work of District Soldiers' Boards; the principles on which government is carried out and on which rates and taxes are levied and land revenue collected; and the system of government of a province as laid down in Government of India Act of 1935. General knowledge syllabuses sought to inform the soldier about current affairs.

It is fascinating to find how much appreciated education was in the Indian Army and to acknowledge its impressive achievement. But by the outbreak of the war authority was not satisfied with it and the reason is revealing. The Educational Training Directive Indian Army 1945 said that 'the educational training of recruits in training centres as evidenced by its results is not satisfactory'. It said that 'more intelligent teaching' was needed and closer supervision by AEC officers. 'Getting a student through an examination is less important than developing his intelligence.'[53] Here again more guidance needed to be given to instructors by AEC officers. In other words those who could do the job should give further guidance to those who could not correct their ways. That ways here needed correcting is not in dispute; which ways and whose stood in need of correction is.

Plato, wanting to determine what justice is in the individual, said that he would first define it in the state because it is easier to read things in large letters than in small, and justice in the state is justice in the individual writ large. It is tempting to think that the story of the AEC in India serves the purpose that Plato had in mind in turning to the state. For in India we see writ in larger letters than at home the achievements and the failures, the satisfaction and the frustration, the nature of the task and of its attendant problems, of the AEC in the between-war years.

In these years the Corps did a job the importance of which the Army had to acknowledge and which had to be done. However much we may regret that what was done was not done better, we cannot doubt that without the AEC it would not have been done at all. In those years the Corps did what it could to pay attention to a need still not widely enough recognised in the Army, a need the eventual meeting of which would undoubtedly greatly strengthen it, the need to fashion a modern soldier for modern war. In those years we see the slow strengthening of a Corps, the absence of which would have weakened the Army. We see the reluctant acknowledgement that there was an essential military function for the Corps that only it could discharge. And while we may deplore the reluctance and the slowness alike, what was done was more important than the time which it took to do it or even than the welcome it received. A too thinly stretched and inadequate Army overseas did not disgrace itself, nor did the Corps which was part of it.

Nevertheless what was done fell far short of what had been hoped would be done. If Fisher really believed that Army Education was the greatest military invention since gunpowder we must wonder at his judgement and if he did not, we must wonder still more why he said it. It was no bad thing that the AEC should have left behind it what was referred to as 'that wonderful period of castle-building' of the post-war reconstruction days. But it was highly undesirable for the Army to have lost sight so completely of the need to make the new soldier for the new age, the intelligent, self-confident, self-reliant man whose quick response to new challenges might spell the difference between triumph and tragedy. Perhaps the British Army cannot be faulted for not better preparing itself for large-scale and rapid expansion as it did not envisage a large-scale continental commitment, although no Army has had more occasion than it to realise that there are times when small armies have to become big and that such transformations cannot take place overnight. But what can be done when quick change is necessary by a highly-trained and highly-educated rank and file the Germany Army demonstrated in the early 1930s. And it would have been better for the British Army if it had made as determined an effort to produce the new attitudes in all ranks it said that it was seeking as the German Army had done. When it was said in Parliament in July 1930 that in the Army 'a man can complete his education in a far easier way and with less trouble to himself than if he remained in civil life and went to continuation classes', the assumption was plain to see, namely that he would be under sufficient inducement so to do. The years had shown how ill-founded that assumption was.

What was wrong was not what was taught, it was how it was taught. It was taught in such a way as to leave people unconvinced of the necessity of further teaching.

This was because the teaching was done by those who were not masters of their craft. Those who were did what they could but as they could not do the teaching what they did was not enough to enable the job to be done properly. Therefore it was not done as it ought to have been. There was danger here. A sufficient number of certificates was being acquired and if the Army was satisfied with this why should it wish to change? Would not the regimental officer be tempted to think 'If we have to do this ourselves why should we have to put up with the AEC as well?' Indeed we may think that at this time the AEC worked hard to demonstrate its own dispensability. Of course it failed to do so. What it did was the very opposite; its own indispensability was what was demonstrated. That was an achievement. But it was not one that contained in itself the promise of further advance, of a new and vigorous lease of life. For that an external pressure was required; events were to provide it.

CHAPTER 4

EDUCATION IN THE MILITIA AND IN THE ARMY IN THE PHONEY WAR

War and the mounting loss of the bravest and best, German historians believed, was a principal cause of the downfall of the Roman Empire; it is not difficult to think of it also as one of the great causes of the downfall of the British Empire. For not only did the British lose many of the brightest and best in the Great War, they were exhausted also by that war as by no previous war in which they had engaged. After it their island base was threatened as never before from the air and from the sea, although it was still strong enough to save them in the Second World War. After 1918 they no longer ruled the waves; the 1921 Washington Naval Treaty gave the US naval parity with them, and Japan a comparative status which meant in effect that that country enjoyed naval supremacy in the north-west Pacific. New York now challenged London as the financial centre of the world. The British were more conscious of imperial strains than comforted by dreams of imperial might, more uneasily aware that if the sun never set on their empire it never ceased to reveal their troubles to themselves and all men.

Moreover, despite their victory the war destroyed their old confidence in themselves. This was in fact the direct consequences of the overstrain that war imposed upon them. They became slack as too much stretching slackens a piece of elastic. That loss of confidence was in part the indirect result of the long agony of the trenches, for if that was what conformity to their old ways, the ways of diplomacy, of pursuit of the national interest, of the balance of power, brought them to, then how could it be thought that they would be well-advised to follow them again? Realism appeared to be self-evidently discredited; idealism had long been knocking at the door; the strong idealist element in Gladstonian Liberalism had passed over into Socialism and so dominated the thinking of a new political party, as yet in its early days inevitably inexperienced in the chastening realities of power, as to induce one of its leaders and a future Prime Minister to say 'we have absolutely abandoned any idea of nationalist loyalty'.[1] A greatly extended electorate strengthened this tendency of the people to seek idealistic solutions.[2] It had been said of the British people their strength, politically speaking, lies in their practicality, their acknowledgement that 'circumstances are what render every civil and political scheme beneficial or noxious for mankind'. As Burke said of himself they like to 'heave the lead every inch of the way'. They did not demonstrate this in the inter-war years. If ever there was a people untrue to itself it was the British, torn as they were from their mooring by the storm of protracted war, rendered reluctant by it to exchange the pleasing utopia of dreams for the awareness of increasingly unpleasing reality which wakefulness would have forced upon them, condemned in consequence to be taught only by suffering that 'the worst disorder of the mind is to see things as one would wish them to be rather than as they are'.[3]

As is to be expected of a democracy, the mood of the people determined their choice of leaders. These were no longer the big men, capable no doubt of making big mistakes but also of achieving great things. The people now turned away from the Lloyd Georges, the Churchills, the Curzons; they preferred Baldwin, 'the Methody Machiavelli' who when with the politicians at Westminster was careful to let it be known that he longed only for the management of the pigs at Bewdley but whose inattention to the pigs when at Bewdley left no doubt that it was to the leadership of the politicians at Westminster that he was really aspiring. When bored with Baldwin an uninspiring alternative was found in Ramsay MacDonald whom his irreverent followers referred to as 'the Lossiemouth Loon' and of whom his opponents said that 'he had more than any other man the gift of compressing the largest number of words into the smallest amount of thought'. They had their virtues. Having dawdled his way into industrial trouble Baldwin then handled it admirably; what he referred to as educating the Labour Party was no mean achievement; his coping with the abdication crisis left little to be desired though he might with advantage have faced up to the long-standing problem of the Prince of Wales much earlier than he did. That problem was the Prince's inattention to his duties even more than his attention to other men's wives, and when Baldwin accompanied him on his Canadian visit in the mid-1920s the Prime Minister was already expressing the opinion that the best to be hoped for was that the Prince would break his neck in one of his many tumbles off his horse.[4] MacDonald straightened out British foreign policy for the first time since the war and ushered in the best period of British post-war foreign policy with the exception of Austen Chamberlain's stewardship of the Locarno years.

They were, nevertheless, smaller men than the situation demanded. It could never be said of them what was said of Maurice, Prince of Orange and Count of Nassau 'there was in him such policy that others might never have come upon him with power nor should have gone beyond him with wit'.[5] For them the satisfying of an unsound opinion was a more urgent desirability than its correction. They were not the leaders to change the mood of the people and to conjure up again the pride and the spirit which had made that nation great.

All ages, as Von Ranke reminds us, are equidistant from God; they are equidistant from the Devil too. But if all have their problems some face greater difficulties than others. Those facing the British in the inter-war years, domestic and foreign, would have been sufficient to stretch them fully if even they had not been shaken from their accustomed moorings. They had learned not to push things to extremes, nor to extract the last concession that power could ring from others. Yet after the war they were attracted by the politics of extremism and ideology, although these were known to be incompatible with the preservation of liberty. They were flirting with the notion that nothing should stand between a society and the satisfaction of whatever needs it feels, despite the fact that politics becomes in consequence a process charged with the feeling of the moment and that where wilfulness reigns liberty never can.

They had to digest electoral reform, to educate a new political party in the disturbing realities of power, to resolve a most serious constitutional problem which put at risk the future of a much venerated monarchy. They had to hammer out new relationships with Ireland and India, these difficult as they were to reach, made possible only by the knowledge that the violence which necessitated them would have been as nothing to that which would have resulted had there been failure to find them. They had to do all this while their economy, long past its peak, struggled to cope with increasing poverty and social distress. If in the inter-war years the British people seemed unshakably determined to ignore reality, reality was equally determined to intrude into their world.

Great as were these domestic tribulations, it was their international trials which ought most to have concerned the British people in these hazardous post-war years. All international worlds are dangerous since power unchecked by the rule of law and mitigated only by diplomacy is the greatest reality in them. But some international worlds are more dangerous than others and four factors ensured that that which existed between 1918 and 1939 was particularly so. These were the nature of German power; the nature of the difficulties in the way of establishing a balance of power to restrain the German power; the nature of Japanese power; and the nature of the difficulties in the way conducting a balance of power to restrain that Japanese power.

Europe had often had to corral its own mad dogs, and it maintained its liberties against Charles V, Philip II, Louis XIV and Napoleon. But the power Germany developed in Europe after 1870, though it took some twenty years to do so, was so great as to make it doubtful if Europe alone could tame it. At the cost of great war and gigantic effort Europe, nevertheless, went far to doing so and by 1918 it secured that external help which enabled it to confine German power.

That power, however, though successfully confined, was neither destroyed nor significantly weakened. It therefore followed that after the weakness brought about by war and defeat had passed off, Germany might once again think herself to be, and in certain circumstances might be justified in so believing, in a position once again to flex muscles and threaten neighbours. It ought at least to have been obvious that there was after 1918 a continuing German problem.

This problem might have been solved, at least for the foreseeable future, had German unity been destroyed as it was when the Second World War ended. This problem might have been solved, again at least for the foreseeable future, had the Grand Alliance which pulled Germany down been kept in being. Had the victors wished to make assurance doubly sure they might have done both of these things. As they did neither they made it only too likely that they would have to face that problem again.

It was a tragedy that just when Germany was recovering its strength it should be caught up in the frenzy of Nazism. This was something which deliberately prepared Germany for war and made it impossible to avoid it in 1939. Yet we might have to say that the situation in which Germany found itself, a situation in which it possessed the kind of power that could, it might reasonably think, establish its mastery of Europe, was more dangerous to Europe and to the world than even the evil nature of Nazism. Hitler and Nazism could not wait. They showed their hand repeatedly – in occupying the Rhineland, in seizing Austria and in swallowing Czechoslovakia, and they were not fully prepared even when they invaded Poland in the knowledge that this would almost certainly mean the outbreak of a general war in Europe. They were prepared neither to cross the Channel nor for the battle of the Atlantic. Yet it was this lack of preparation that destroyed Germany. Under another regime Germany might have been more patient and more cautious, might have thereby lulled its opponents and not antagonised them as Hitler did, and when we realise how little even Hitler's actions which antagonised Germany's neighbours sufficiently alarmed and alerted them it is easy to believe that a more patient and subtle Germany might have pulled the wool over the eyes of those neighbours until recovery of sight would have come too late to save them. At all events it would be unwise to believe that Germany under a regime other than that of Hitler but having the kind of power it then possessed would necessarily have been less dangerous.

There can at least be no doubt that a Europe which contained a Germany as powerful as this was a very dangerous place. It was made more dangerous by the impossibility of rebuilding the Grand Alliance which by 1918 had destroyed Germany's first bid for hegemony.

The USA which had joined the alliance in 1917, though not formally as an ally, was determined after 1918 to remain in isolation. It misunderstood the lesson of the First World War. That lesson was that the world was so dangerous that the USA could not safely remain aloof from it. When it seemed that Britain might no longer be powerful enough to maintain the European balance of power and to keep that mastery of the Atlantic which made it impossible for other powers to endanger the USA's position of easy supremacy in the New World, the USA found that this was so little to its liking that it even plunged into war not to maintain British power but to prevent these undesirable consequences of its decline. But the USA forgot this after the war. It convinced itself that it had gone to war not to prevent what it found distasteful and dangerous occurring but to make the world safe for democracy. When the world showed conclusively that it did not want to be made safe for democracy, which to the Americans was tantamount to rebuilding the world in their own image, the USA thought it could safely withdraw from such an ill-conditioned world. Americans are neither foolish nor more indifferent than other peoples to their interests. Had they known that their interests were indeed in Europe they would have looked to them. But Americans had been led to believe that they had not fought because their interests were endangered but out of an excess of altruism, to make the world safer for democracy. They would have been foolish if they had needlessly involved themselves in difficult and dangerous matters because they did not like something which, nevertheless, was not dangerous to themselves. Thinking that Europe did not concern them, as of course it did, naturally they were not going to involve themselves in it. Thus there was no likelihood of the USA taking it upon itself to keep the balance of power in Europe as Britain had so often done: no likelihood, therefore, of the Grand Alliance of 1917 being re-established.

Nor was American isolation the sole reason why it was impossible to recreate that Grand Alliance. Since its revolution in 1917 Russia was no longer available as an ally against Germany. In its new guise as the USSR it was antagonistic to capitalist states, as they were to it. It steadily intrigued against them and they, for the most parts, as steadily sought to isolate it. Far from being available as an ally against Germany, the USSR established close relations with it in the treaty of Rapallo. In view of Hitler's later tirades against Communism it did not seem likely that this accord between Russia and Germany could be re-established in the 1930s. But in 1939 it was and it ought not to be forgotten that the Russo-German Pact of that year which precipitated the Second World War was in the logic of Rapallo. So that the USSR was no more willing to join an anti-German bloc than was America.

Neither was yet another member of the Great War Grand Alliance, Italy. Italy was profoundly dissatisfied with its war gains. Under Mussolini it was determined to expand, a determination which in the Abyssinian crisis of the mid-1930s alienated it from Britain and France, and drove it into the arms of Germany.

For all these reasons, then, it was impossible to recreate the Grand Alliance, an impossibility which greatly increased the dangers brought about by an already too powerful Germany.

The inter-war world was the more dangerous because it contained in the Far East a power as dangerously unbalanced and as dangerously expansionist as was Germany itself. This was Japan. It was not as powerful as Germany, nor indeed as powerful as Britain. It was far less powerful than the USA. But it was far more powerful than its Asian neighbours. It was in the 20th Century and China still in the Middle Ages. It was stronger in the Far East than Britain or the USA, the Washington Naval Agreements having seen to that. It was suffering from dangerous compulsions to conquer raw materials, markets and living-room, compulsions the more driving as they bore on a people more self-centred than most, less inclined than most to consider the interest of others (an inclination not easily to be seen in any of the world's peoples). Japan, moreover, was dangerously susceptible to pressure from its Army and it was always likely to ally with dissatisfied European powers, as indeed it eventually did. It supported Italy and Germany and benefitted from their support even before it allied with them.

Japan's presence was bound to make the world still more menacing. and this the more so as it was impossible to construct a balance of power to restrain it. The USSR was the strongest of Japan's nearer neighbours. But its internal and external situation was such that it was more concerned to get out of Japan's way then to get in it. An unconvincing American effort to draw closer to the USSR and to bluff Japan into fearing that Soviet strength might feature in a power move against it got nowhere and the USSR confined itself to taking those actions, as at Nomonhan and the Hill of Chang-ku-feng, which would suggest to the Japanese that whatever aggressive design they entertained could more profitably be addressed elsewhere than against Soviet territory. However, the fundamental reason for failure to restrain Japan was once again American isolationism. When American pressure induced Britain to give up its alliance with Japan, Britain tried to replace it with an American alliance. But the USA was not interested in making alliances nor in providing the power which would have stopped Japan. American opinion was too pacific and the American Government too unrealistic, with the result, of course, that Japan was not stopped. The menace of Asian war was added to the menace of European war, which is the fourth reason why the international world between 1918 and 1939 was particularly dangerous.

These were not, to use an old phrase, 'trifelous' things and little to be regarded. Yet such was the folly of the western democracies in these years that they were little heeded. Indeed, it was the traditional ways of thought that would have focused attention on them that we looked upon as 'trifelous'. Balance of power was seen as an evil, to be shunned and not sought. It was referred to as having been 'the evil dream of diplomatists since the Renaissance' and that there had been no greater obstacle to 'international thought down to the present day'. It was a 'sovereign specific for precipitating war'. Diplomatists who were traditionally concerned with it partook of its evil too. Delight was taken in thinking of them as 'monocled men who knew nothing and understood nothing and who crystallised in their incoherence, ignorance and incompetence'; the advice was greatly treasured that was given to one of them: 'To be a diplomatist it isn't enough to be stupid. Good manners are necessary as well.' From the idea of balance men turned to that of collective security, which is the opposite of the idea of a balance of power for collective security implies a preponderance of power exercised by a combination of states who are the agents of international society. It is to be doubted if sovereign states can ever be sufficiently unselfish to make a reality of this doctrine of collective security; as the event showed they were not at this time. For the event demonstrated that the dilemma of collective security and of all such suggestions for abolishing international strife from Sully's 'Grand Design' onwards is that if workable they are unnecessary since men will be good enough to do without them and if necessary they are unworkable since men will be bad enough to fall from grace and will not be restricted except by superior force.[6]

This, however, was not understood at this time. Power was ignored as long as it could be and when German misuse of it made that no longer possible German bad behaviour was not attributed to present German vice but to past British immorality. Germany would not be misbehaving if we the British had treated her properly. We went as far as we could to apologise for winning the war. Present woes were always our fault; never that of the Germans. Every now and then we took time off from blaming ourselves in order to abuse the French. We thought it possible that they were worse than we were. We said the Nazis would never have come to power had we not so brutally suppressed the Germans. We said the Germans would get rid of them if we got rid of our animosity to the Germans. We even said the Nazis would turn away from themselves if we did this. So we allowed great increase in German power and subsequently learned the truth of the comment 'He who aims at disarming his enemy by making concessions will never be rich enough to succeed.'[7]

Our attitude to the Japanese was somewhat different, but no less foolish. The excuses we made for the Germans were not to be made for the Japanese. We increasingly annoyed them, as in Manchuria. We increasingly threatened them; during the Manchurian crisis the American Fleet was concentrated in the Pacific. Yet Britain and America were not prepared to make the threats good. They never intended to, thinking talk and expression of disapproval would suffice. There was point to the question which infuriated Stimson when, having proudly asserted that he had assembled the whole of the US Fleet in the Pacific, he was asked if he had assembled the whole of American public option there too, something which all knew he had not.[8] Throughout this period the truly terrifying thing is the neglect by the western democracies of that power without which they could not survive. In the event they almost did not. Woodrow Wilson after 1918 had hoped to make the world safe for democracy.[9] It had been made instead safe for aggression, there being once again demonstrated the truth of Bacon's words 'when a warlike State grows soft and effeminate, they may be sure of a war; for commonly such States are grown rich in the time of their degeneracy, and so the prey inviteth and their decay in valour encourageth war'.

It has, however, been well said that the ebullitions of popular enthusiasm are no safe index to the temper of a people. Thus the distaste of the British for power and their enthusiasm for what seemed to them the costless, or at least cheap, idealism of collective security misled others as to their temper and character. When at last aware of their folly they would fight, as Hitler and Mussolini believed they never would. The British are to be blamed, as Canning condemned those who 'let aggressions ripen into full maturity in order that they may then be mowed down with the scythe of a magnificent war'.[10] Their pride and their spirit, had it been stirred to life in time, might have spared them great tribulation. They could not spare themselves that; they would not spare the war to the outbreak of which their own folly had markedly contributed.

By 1939 their mood was changing. They introduced National Service, a belated and still somewhat half-hearted strengthening of the security measures the Government was now taking. But it was significant that the change of Government mood was itself consequent on the change in the popular mood. Drift had stopped but drive had not yet begun. Backs were straighter and heads were up, but hearts were not yet fiercely resolved. The British people were groping for but had not yet firmly grasped reality; they had not yet sorted themselves out; confusion and not yet concentration characterised their minds.

This was true of British society and Government. It was also true of the British Army. Fortunately for the nation there were maturing in the Army those who would make good its past deficiencies and lead it to victory. They were still, however, making their way and unable as yet to impart to it their ideas, their spirit, their vision. It was unlikely that a long-neglected War Office could at once switch into top-gear activity. Strong, decisive leadership will always have its effect but it cannot dispense with determined and efficient administration, and as it soon became evident that the leadership of the War Office was to be more controversial than inspirational, so it quickly became clear that an urgent desire to waste no more time had not yet seized hold of its administration. Not yet analysing cogently, not yet planning purposefully, not yet rising to new challenges and grasping new opportunities, flustered and somewhat overwhelmed, this is the picture the Army presents in the immediate pre-war days. What else was to be expected of it?

What was true of society, Government and Army was true of the educational stirrings within it. There was little that was planned and purposeful about them either. They too smacked of the haphazard. They were the result of drift rather than design and as National Service seemed to be something that was on top of the War Office, rather than the War Office being on top of it, so these educational stirrings seemed to be little within the control of the AEC, to be no part of its planning, to be occupying little of its attention and less of its thinking. Again one might ask what else was to be expected? These developments had arisen from a situation which the AEC had not anticipated and for which it was as unprepared as was the Army for the position in which it found itself. Habit can take the edge off thought and initiative is rarely speedily shown by the habitually unvalued. The consequences of what we have done have to work themselves out before we can reap all the benefits to be gained from subsequent wiser behaviour. This was true of the Army as a whole, as of the AEC as part of it. With the lapse of time challenges would be welcomed and opportunities eagerly sought by both the Army and the AEC, but for the moment neither were enthusiastically welcomed or indeed clearly seen. For the moment events dominated both Army and AEC; they did not put their stamp on events. Later things would change and the Army and the AEC would reflect the new dynamism that was beginning at last to move Government and nation.

It is in the shadow of these years of confusion and of drift, and perhaps also if it is true to say that coming events cast their shadows before them, in that cast by them too, that we must see the developments that occurred when so very belatedly the nation began to ready itself for the coming storm. In shadow we can glimpse the outlines of things but we cannot see them clearly. To vary the image there is still great confusion and all that occurs partakes of that confusion. We see in the nation and the Government, in the Army and the AEC the beginnings of developments that will assume great importance later. We see them in their first confused beginnings. We are at the opening of a new and most significant phase in the story of the Army's struggle to win recognition from society and of the AEC's struggle to win recognition from the Army, a difficult and protracted phase in which the meeting of new national needs by the Army and of new military needs by the AEC leads to developments as yet undreamed of in the long struggle of both.

In days of old when invasion threatened every man picked up bill and bow. But conscription in time of peace had never been the English way. However, after Munich we knew that if we would not give up what would be shameful to surrender we would have to fight and we were bitterly aware of our lack of preparation to do so. So although it could hardly be said as yet that we were girding up our loins for battle, we brought into being the Militia into which our young men were drafted and it is in that Militia that we can see the stirrings of that great movement of Army Education that was such a striking characteristic of the British Army in the Second World War. It took time for the Militia to be fully incorporated into the Army and time for the educational stirrings in the Militia to become that astonishing surge of education that we can see in the Army in embattled Britain and that still characterised the Army when it ceased to be on the defensive and carried the war to its enemies overseas. In considering what is undoubtedly one of the most extraordinary mass movements of our time, the attempt during the war years to do something that had never before been tried, that is to expose the mass of our people of fighting age to adult education, we shall look in this chapter to its beginnings in the Militia and during the Phoney War. In the following chapters we shall consider its full development in embattled Britain and then its adaptation to meet the needs of the troops fighting overseas.

When in April 1939, 200,000 young men were called up for six months under the Military Training Act to man anti-aircraft defences and to indicate to Germany that there would be an end to British patience, it was from civilians that the first significant move to attend to their education came. Wigg, later a stormy petrel in the AEC but then the District Secretary of the North Staffordshire Workers' Educational Association, believed that an inevitable, and life and death, ideological struggle between democracy and fascism was in the making. He was of the opinion that the Regular Army – in the ranks of which he had himself served – being officered by blimps, would be unable to generate the fighting faith in democracy, in the absence of which fascism would triumph. He was convinced that if Britain were to survive, the Regular Army would have to turn itself into a citizens' army and that only in such an Army was it possible for the indispensable fighting faith in democracy to be developed. In that model of democracy, the USSR, the Red Army had such a fighting faith, whipped up no doubt by its political commissars and, as later events were to show, he was not prepared to let false modesty obscure the fact that he would make an excellent director of them. He persuaded Ernest Green, the WEA's General Secretary, a man who by no means shared all Wigg's naive ideas but who could not cope with his outstanding capacity for intrigue, to set up an Emergency Committee to push this view that a fighting faith must be developed in the Army if conscription were to be introduced.[11] Wigg and Green got together with a group of Labour MPs led by Creech-Jones and Greenwood, preparing in this way to urge upon the Army the need to educate soldiers along these lines.

We have no doubt of the bona fides of Ernest Green and the WEA in this, and the pressures brought on him and it to urge the provision of adult educational facilities in the Army were, on the face of it, respectable enough. For Wigg would have taken care not to put forward extreme views. However anxious he may have been to preach the true faith, he knew that Green was not, nor was he silly enough to reveal that anxiety to those who, as a former soldier, he would be well aware were unlikely to take kindly to it and who were in a position to prevent it. WEA members greatly enjoyed the classes to which they went; otherwise they would not have gone to them, and on bitter winter nights which added to the attractions of the fireside the temptation not to turn out must have been considerable, and yet it was resisted. It is legitimate to believe that they would welcome an opportunity of letting others, who did not know what they were missing, appreciate what they themselves so thoroughly enjoyed. It may, nevertheless, have been true that among those initiating the pressure in North Staffordshire were to be found intentions of not quite so respectable a nature.

North Staffordshire was an area which in the days after 1945 was notorious for the amount of communist influence in its local WEA. That may have been a development to be seen solely in the days after the Second World War, but since the building of influence is apt to take time the chances are that it was not. Nor should we forget that in the mid- and late-1930s there was strong pressure, essentially left wing in character, to spread, through adult education, the view that there must be created 'a new society based on communal rather than individual values'. In modern war, as a Fabian pamphlet put it in 1940, 'the common people must be imbued ... with a belief in their own power to conquer a better future'. It added that Army Education should serve not only 'the military needs of the present Army' but also 'the social needs of the future nation'.[12] Like the notion of 'natural justice', this idea of 'the social needs of the future nation' was capable, it seemed, of almost indefinite extension. These needs would not be attended to, it was said, without the attempt being made to explain to the soldier 'the origin of the incessant strife in which the British Army has been engaged', this being his preparation 'for those inter-capitalist state wars of which the last is the prime example, and of which the next is in solemn preparation'.[13] One may be forgiven for thinking that it was propaganda rather than education that North Staffordshire might have had in mind at this time. It is worth noting that this WEA initiative left the officials at the Board of Education uneasy.[14] They would know, what the Army obviously suspected, that among the civilians, far from such WEA classes being in overwhelming demand, they were for the most part unattended. And since such objectives as those deemed desirable in the Fabian Society pamphlet referred to were unlikely to be accorded high priority by the Army, it is not surprising that the WEA proposals were greeted by it with little enthusiasm.

However, to this pressure from above was added at this time a stirring from below. Once accustomed to their new and unfamiliar life in uniform, some of the Militia began exploring the possibility of finding leisure activities that would occupy spare time when shortage of cash or lack of inclination would reduce the appeal of the NAAFI and the pub. In the short life of the Militia, demand for such activities could only remain spasmodic and occasional, but it was there and not to be ignored. Something else was there and not to be ignored either. Very senior officers were surprised to find how ignorant of current affairs the Militia men were, alarmed that they seemed not to know the reasons for their call-up, anxious that they should be better informed of the nature of their prospective enemy and that they should have a greater awareness of what it was that they would in all probability find themselves fighting for.[15] It is striking that in this immediate pre-war period the shadows cast by coming events are discernible. We see here the individual stirring from the ranks from which the concern develops to do what can be done to satisfy the individual soldier. We see, too, in those in authority the burgeoning desire to improve the citizen, the dawning belief that the fashioning of a better soldier must involve the making of a better citizen. Both of these things are to be seen only in their first and faint beginnings. But unenthusiastic and ambivalent as is the response of the High Command to them, we can nevertheless see in that response an awareness of them too.

The High Command felt called upon at least to take notice of these happenings. The Army Council briefly considered what part, if any, Army Education should have in the training of the Militia. It had no difficulty in concluding that the certificates, the obtaining of which had become the main educational interest of the Regular Army, had no relevance for the Militia. But beyond expressing the hope that the Board of Education, together with university extra-mural departments and other 'responsible bodies', as the phrase went, in Adult Education, included in which was the WEA, would provide evening lectures and classes in the Militia camps, it carried its deliberations no further at this time.[16] It might even have hoped that this would be the end of the matter, but it was unduly optimistic if it did. Since the Army Council seemed devoid of ideas for the promotion of education in the Militia, the WEA felt impelled to come to its assistance. It submitted its own educational scheme, consisting of the provision of lectures and classes in history, economics, economic geography and local government. To arrange, look after and teach these subjects, civilian tutors should be appointed to each Militia camp, after the manner of the WEA tutor organisers later to be found in each WEA District. Regional liaison officers to work with the WEA and the extra-mural departments should be established and there should be a national officer to coordinate all this work and to be responsible to an Advisory Committee of representatives from the various bodies interested in Adult Education and from the Local Education Authorities.

Presented with such a comprehensive scheme the Army must have wondered what would be left in educational matters for it to determine. Nor was it sure that it wanted this to be done. Was there any reason to think that the men would welcome it? They knew that they had to accommodate themselves to military life but why should they have to put up with this as well?[17] The Director of Military Training doubted if they would want it. To make up for the years the locusts had eaten, the men had to be kept hard at it during the day and what interest would they have in attending lectures and classes when the hard day's work was done? Moreover, the Army was clearly unhappy with the leading role which the WEA proposed for itself. If any scheme of Militia education were to be adopted it thought that it should involve the LEAs more and the WEA less. Perhaps it recalled with alarm the attempt of the WEA to insert itself into Army Education in the heady days immediately after the First World War. For indeed it seemed a case of *plus ça change plus c'est la meme chose*, there being little doubt of the place the WEA was seeking to establish for itself in the 'citizens' army' (a phrase already being bandied about and of which a great deal more was to be heard in coming days) if Hitler's continued enormities brought it into being. Military irritation did not, however, remove civilian pressure. The WEA continued to press, much to the annoyance of the Board of Education, whose Chief Inspector deplored the way in which it was trying to force the pace and strongly objected to basing any scheme of education in the Militia largely on it.[18]

Pressures on the Army to be more active in this matter of education mounted from elsewhere too, generated no doubt to some extent by the desire not to leave the running exclusively to the WEA. There was a letter in *The Times* urging the importance of educating the Militia.[19] W.E. Williams, then Secretary of the British Institute for Adult Education, submitted his own scheme for so doing to the Board of Education.[20] MPs who were not associated with the Creech-Jones lobby expressed their interest in it and so did the King.[21] It seemed to be becoming obvious therefore that some scheme of education for the Militia there would have to be. Nevertheless, great difficulties remained to be resolved. If education were to be provided for the Militia, how was it to be paid for? Both the War Office and the Board of Education wanted the other to have the honour of attending to this. Difficulties of this kind might at another time have proved insuperable and it is a testimony to the strength of the gathering civilian impatience at the continuing failure to make provision for the education of the Militia that they were so soon swept aside. By July it was agreed that Board of Education Liaison Officers (Divisional Inspectors) should be appointed to each Command, that some administrative structure would have to be put together so that classes and lectures could be provided, that Regional Committees should be set up on which all adult educational organisations should be represented. It was also agreed that the War Office should foot the bill.

If these developments testify to the remarkable degree of civilian influence in the movement to provide education for the troops so, too, does the absence in the discussions producing them of reference to, of consideration for and of contributions from, the AEC. What was its role at this time? It was continuing its work, at home as abroad, preparing soldiers for their certificates and was becoming increasingly disillusioned with it. That disillusion was increased by the coming of new members into the Corps. There were new men coming into it, fresh from the universities, used to thinking for themselves and not prepared to put their minds into commission with the taking of a commission. In October 1937 six officers joined; never since the foundation of the Corps had so many joined at the same time. Such men had ideas, and able Commanding Officers of regiments to which they were posted encouraged them to produce their own educational schemes. The newcomers were far too few in number but as the fact that they were willing, when given the opportunity by their Commanding Officers, who valued them, to chance their arm in the drawing up of new schemes showed, they were sufficient not only to add to the growing disillusion of the Corps with the old but to bring to it an invigorating readiness to concern itself with the new. They attended, as they always had done, to the map-reading of the troops, those in Catterick using the moors to teach night map-reading. Moreover, at a time when, as in 1938, there was a great shortage of recruits they rendered the Army yeoman service in the training of those who were below the physical and educational standards required for the recruit. There were two units at which such training took place, one near Catterick and one near Canterbury, and when Lieutenant Foxton paid his second visit to them he was greatly impressed by the tremendous change that had taken place in the would-be recruits since his earlier visit.[22]

In addition to these duties the AEC were responsible for the teaching of the Young Soldiers' Battalions that consisted of young men between the ages of 17 and 20. Until they reached the latter age they could not go overseas and this they greatly resented. They were constantly on charges, being high-spirited. They were, as they saw it, subjected to five hours' compulsory education a week and they did not take kindly to it. To overcome their reluctance one AEC officer and four instructors were attached to each of their battalions. They taught Map-Reading, English, Mathematics, Regimental History and the History of the British Army. When, later, ABCA came along they took ABCA sessions too. They encouraged voluntary education and the young soldiers discouraged them by enthusiastically keeping away from it, although even young men are backsliders ever and there was the occasional young soldier who interested himself in handicraft work.

To these their normal duties was added what the AEC could do to satisfy whatever demands of an educational nature the Militia might make. There were requests for classes in musical appreciation and for occasional lectures and, few as they were, members of the Corps did what could be done to meet them. After years in the wilderness the AEC was far from ready as yet to take on a new and demanding role, but it was stirring and could indeed have been made ready had there been sufficient imagination to give it the opportunity to become so.

That hardly seemed likely, however, when on 3 September 1939 war was declared. All arrangements for the introduction of education into the Forces were at once cancelled. It would be silly not to acknowledge how hard-pressed the Army was at that time. The High Command in 1939 faced a far more difficult task than its predecessor in 1914. For then a professional Army had been magnificently prepared for the continental war in which it was to be engaged. It was not big enough for the job that faced it, although when thrown against the flank of the advancing Germans it had so dented that advance as almost certainly to have saved Paris. It had to be greatly expanded as the war continued. But that expansion was based upon a strong foundation that was already there. The morale of the expanding Army was already high and while many newcomers flocking into its ranks had known very little about it before doing so they were not already predisposed to reject its values; the idea that a man owed service to his country had not yet been called in question; the national interest, as elusive a concept as it had always been, was thought to be something that all should forward; patriotism remained a powerful force. Things were very different in 1939. There was no powerful and finely prepared professional Army to be whisked across the Channel then. By a miracle of improvisation ill-prepared and inadequately trained divisions were got over to France. It was expected that there would be time to complete their training there but that expectation itself must have added to the uncertainty of the High Command. For if peace was a condition well known to it and if war was too, war in which there was no fighting was beyond its ken. Training abroad in the face of the enemy, the timing and nature of whose attack could not be foreseen, and training at home under the threat of devastating air attack which must be guarded against, was not the same as training at home in peace, even in the imminence of war.

Moreover, while in the First World War the Army had not felt, and had had no reason to feel, that the civilians joining it rejected its values, it feared, and had reason to fear, that this was the case now. Young people at Oxford had said they they would not fight for King and Country and young people at Cambridge seemed to be more eager to prepare themselves for the class war at home than for the coming struggle in Europe, although none then suspected the extent to which some of them would go in their passionate loyalty to a country other than their own. To many, care for the 'national interest' seemed concerned only for the dividends of the rich, and patriotism not the last refuge of the scoundrel but the first and most obvious ploy in his disreputable bag of tricks. This might have been seen as a passing aberration which would last little longer than faith in the League of Nations. But the Army knew well enough how far it had moved away in the inter-war years from a society which had never appreciated it but whose values it had nevertheless remarkably faithfully reflected, how greatly in those years it had turned in on itself and away from the society whose Army it was.

British society had never sought to understand it but it had had no difficulty in understanding British society. The great role played in both Army and society by the gentlemen of England had ensured that. But the gentlemen of England, while still dictating the mores of the Army, were no longer the prime movers of British society, and the society of which that was true they no longer understood. Thus the Army in 1939 was far more unsure of itself than it had been in 1914 and while this helps to explain its later great concern to educate its soldiers it also helps to explain its priorities when war was declared. Training for it was the most important of all things and to this everything else must be sacrificed. Short-sighted or not, it is very understandable that at this time it should be of the opinion that lectures and classes and all educational activity were a peacetime luxury which must now be dispensed with.

This was a view which civilians, and in particular the WEA, did not share. They believed that the new conscript Army could not safely be left as ignorant as it seemed to be about the issues involved in the war. The WEA, the YMCA and the Universities' Extra-Mural Consultative Committee got together and arranged a conference of all interested in education in the Army at which it was confirmed that the Regional Committees, which it had been agreed before the war began should be set up, should be so constituted and that panels of lecturers should be drawn up. It was also agreed that a Central Advisory Council should be organised and that representatives of the Services be asked to be present as observers at its meetings.[23] This was the time of the 'phoney' war and the Army now faced the problem of keeping men, often in isolated and small anti-aircraft batteries, occupied and interested. So, although no doubt without much enthusiasm, it agreed to cooperate with this civilian initiative.

In fact it soon became evident that the provision of education for the Forces was too big a task for it to be tackled successfully by piece-meal attention of this kind and in consequence, in this first phase of Army Education, the pace of events soon quickened. There was continued civilian pressure against *ad hoc* measures and for the fashioning of an official scheme of Army Education. And this seemed now to be in prospect. Oliver Stanley, who had replaced Hore-Belisha as Secretary of State for War, replying to a question in Parliament, declared that education in the Army was 'of the utmost importance' and that he would do all that he could to ensure that it functioned well.[24] At this time, too, the War Office was considering whether it should find a new role for the AEC.

When war came there was so much to attend to that it is no surprise that the AEC was at once called upon to discharge its wartime role of looking after cipher work. It would not have been easy at that time to have convinced the Army that it should make new arrangements for this. But it is surprising that when strong pressures were developing to provide education for the Militia, when local initiatives to do so, in which the AEC stationed in Britain were heavily involved, were developing, the AEC Directorate in the War Office was not stressing the undesirability if war could not be avoided of its trained educationalists being removed from educational duties. An Army which had shown such little concern for education in the pre-war years could not indeed be expected to become its enthusiastic advocate at once when so many crucially important and long-neglected matters had to be tackled. But to provide education for soldiers was the AEC's job, as it was to think of the best way of providing it. As one of its Captains noted very pertinently at this time 'If lectures on general educational subjects are wanted even in wartime for the troops surely the business should be arranged through the existing AEC organisation. It is the very work in which we have specialised and have long experience.' Its blindness to the opportunities now arising and to the new necessities now presenting themselves may be explained by the long years of neglect; it also increased the possibility that those years might not have come to an end. It had been brought into existence to do the job which now at last seemed waiting to be done, and if it hardly seemed to be aware that that had happened, how could its continued existence be justified?[25]

Yet off to ciphering the AEC went. Thus, of the 70 officers and 280 other ranks of the Corps serving at home, 40 officers and 152 other ranks were at once ordered away for cipher duty and 10 other AEC officers were subsequently given staff appointments. The Army School of Education was closed and educational training for the troops was suspended; only Command Education Officers and those engaged in teaching boys and Army children remained at their pre-war duty. Ciphering was a heavy duty and in addition to it other burdens were laid on AEC shoulders, although few AEC officers could have had such a varied experience as Captain Roe. He was not only in charge of ciphering at Khartoum, but also chief communications officer to the Commander-in-Chief there and general odd job man. The work, he said 'was so heavy that, for a solid year, I was never able to get more than three hours' continuous sleep but became a master of the "cat nap"'. Among multifarious activities which included assuming responsibility for the communications with Wingate's Mission 101, he took the surrender of an Italian officer and his men and commanded a detachment of Madras Sappers and Miners, and a platoon of Indian infantry in clearing a minefield and tank trap; and was responsible for opening the road between Biscia and Agordat.[26] It is pleasant to recall the comment of Major-General Sir Leslie Phillips, Director of Signals: 'My debt of gratitude to you chaps of the AEC is indeed a big one. You have done a magnificent job and I am grateful that you were there when I needed you most.'[27] Yet we can be glad that the High Command was at last beginning to think that the AEC might be of more value in another role.

In confronting the mounting pressures for it to fashion a scheme for education in the Army, the High Command found itself in an unpleasing, and perhaps even threatening, situation. It did not like the WEA and it did not like the pressure for education in the Army that it had generated. It was not as yet convinced that education would be welcomed by the men and had it known that in answer to a questionnaire asking a number of anti-aircraft batteries in the autumn of 1941 to indicate in what subjects the gunners would be interested, 40% wanted no truck with education at all, while what attracted most of the 60% were vocational subjects such as welding and short-hand, it might have concluded that there was, despite the civilian pressure, no great call for it to bestir itself.[28] Yet it did not know that and it had to admit that those might be right who insisted that education would keep isolated anti-aircraft batteries more interested, or at least less bored, than they might otherwise be.

It was useful, but not essential, to have trained teachers doing cipher work. The AEC had not been highly regarded but it was part of the Army and not an outside body which would be difficult to control. Its capacity to bolshevise the Army had been demonstrated over the years to be unimpressive. Would it not be sensible to bring the AEC back into Army education if that would keep the WEA out? The committee which was chaired by Major-General Finch, Director of Recruiting and Organisation, and which submitted its report in early January 1940, considered the possibility of finding a new educational role for the AEC and of expanding its numbers to enable it to discharge it.[29] But if the Corps was expanded additional expense could not be avoided and to that the Treasury strongly objected. That objection was reflected in the rejection of the Stanhope Committee on promotion in the Army of the case of the AEC on the grounds that 'it had been found impossible to effect any marked improvement in the flow of promotion of officers in the AEC without undue expenditure of money'.[30] It was similarly reflected in the insistence of the Brownrigg Committee that the AEC had been excluded from the pre-war amendment of promotion regulations because its officers had security of tenure until sixty whereas in the combatant Corps majors would be compulsorily retired at 47.[31] It was reflected again in the torpedoing by the Treasury of the agreement on the expansion and use of the AEC which was almost reached as a result of the Finch Committee's recommendations. The Treasury withdrew its consent to this on the grounds that other proposals had been put forward and that nothing could be decided until the whole scope of an Army educational scheme had been settled.[32]

It is an indication of how little anything was settled at this time, of how fluid thoughts about Army Education were, that only days after considering expanding the AEC and finding a new role for it, the War Office toyed with the idea of disbanding it.[33] Hore-Belisha gave it a passing thought and the Generals who took such strong exception to many of his thoughts, passing or otherwise, may not have been too disturbed by this one. W.E. Williams, who was in a position to know, seems to have thought that the Corps' disbanding was a possibility, since he refers to a time in 1940 'when the Army might have been willing to leave its education (if any) to be conducted by Regional Committees'.[34] In so saying he is not writing off the possibility that it would have remained on other duties throughout the war. But how likely is it that it would have survived thereafter had this been the case? Need we think, as he seems to have done, that this was a serious possibility?

The might-have-beens of history need not unduly concern us and Cleopatra's nose, be it an inch longer or shorter, can profitably be kept out of our affairs. What is, is what matters and since the AEC was not disbanded the possibility that it might have been is worth only a passing mention. It is of some historic interest as testifying to the lack of universal respect in which the Corps was held at this time. But it would be a mistake to take too seriously the possibility of its disbanding. Interest in the Corps was being expressed in Parliament and it was already clear that, whatever form it would take, education was going to find its place in the wartime Army. Lack of faith in the Corps' capacity to cope with expanding educational needs might lead the War Office to look to others to supervise and satisfy those needs, but if soldiers were silly enough to risk drawing upon themselves avoidable criticism, politicians would have second thoughts and would certainly not be. It seems, therefore, obvious that the continued existence of the Corps would be bound to appear less troublesome than its removal and that its impending demise would remain in the realm of rumour. Only if the War Office had been able to introduce a new and all-embracing scheme that would have satisfied its critics would it have been possible for it to disband the AEC. 'Its disappearance since last September will have been no bad thing if it can be rebuilt upon new and more inspiring lines', the *New Statesman* proclaimed.[35] The proviso is important. If there was nothing on new and inspiring lines to replace the AEC, getting rid of it would have created a major civilian rumpus. Hearing that their demise was in contemplation, officers of the Corps were in touch with their MPs, pointing out that they had by implication been promised that they could serve until they were sixty years old and that this was their compensation for being promoted more slowly than officers of other Corps. Since the War Office had no far-reaching scheme in mind there would undoubtedly have been a spirited defence of the AEC in Parliament and the last thing the War Office and Government could have wanted at that time was to add to their troubles in this way.

The most important thing to notice about this matter, however, is the reaction of the civilian educationalists to the possibility of the disbanding of the Corps. They would have none of it.[36] Aware of the limitations of the Corps, they were not blind to their own. They knew that without those more familiar with Army ways than they were themselves the prospects of developing education in it would be very limited. It would be too much to say that the civilian pressure which brought the Corps into existence assured its continued being, since that, as we have seen, was not seriously in doubt. But it would not be too much to say that here again was demonstrated how mutually beneficial was the close connection between civilian adult educationalists and the AEC. When that connection has been weakest, education in the Army has been least impressive, as it has been most striking when the relationship between them has been closest. Nor is it fanciful to believe that civilian adult education has learned from Army education too, in particular from some of the less formal teaching methods made such good use of by the AEC.

Faced with so many difficulties, the War Office yielded to the attractive alternative of doing nothing and so for the moment nothing was done. This did not please the Central Advisory Council, or its influential Vice-Chairman, Lindsay, the Master of Balliol. The author of a book, *The Essentials of Democracy*, he was familiar with the art of lobbying. He wrote to *The Times* and appealed to Lord Simon, the Chancellor of the Exchequer, and to Lord Halifax, the Foreign Secretary.[37] Another formidable paladin entered the lists too. Lord Gorell castigated the hesitation to do anything about education in the Army. 'No greater blunder', he wrote 'was ever committed by the Government of a democracy; and it must be retrieved without delay if both the Army and the nation are not to reap the bitter consequences.'[38] A flurry of press comment followed his letter to *The Times*. Gorell saw himself as the means of retrieving the situation. 'Unless I throw myself into this again', he confided to his diary, 'it will not be done adequately, and it must be done.' He sought an interview with Oliver Stanley in which he asked to be appointed Director-General, Army Educational Services, with the rank of Major-General. He wanted direct access to the Secretary of State and to the CIGS, and could not be sure of having it if he accepted lesser rank. The scheme he put forward, however, was far too costly, Prime Minister Neville Chamberlain letting it be known that all that could be approved was something on the lines of what had been agreed to for the Militia. Nevertheless some movement now began. In March 1940 the Central Advisory Council received official recognition and a not very generous grant from the War Office. Not until August 1940, however, was there Treasury support for the Council which until then had had to rely on the YMCA and the Pilgrim Trust.[39] In April, too, a committee under Lieutenant-General Sir Robert Haining was set up to prepare an education scheme for the Army, as well as to consider what provision should be made for its entertainment and welfare.

A document published in September 1940 under the heading 'Education in the War Time Army' incorporated its proposals. It acknowledged that Army regimentation could produce 'mental torpor', the attitude of mind of the man who said that what he had liked about the last war was that 'you could cloakroom your brain for the duration'. It believed that to keep morale high and to maximise military efficiency, alert, intelligent minds capable of taking the initiative were required. That being so, it followed that education or 'care for the needs of men's minds contributes quite definitely to military efficiency'. It therefore drew attention to the importance of promoting three types of education in particular. It exhorted Commanding Officers to encourage men to study the humanities, by which was meant the usual civilian adult educational programme of the study of history, geography, economics and international affairs. It hoped that units would remember the importance of education in the utilities, by which was meant training in whatever vocational matters were of especial interest to the troops. It begged them to make provision for education in the arts and crafts, by which was meant the encouragement of hobbies.

It thought highly of the powers of persuasion of Commanding Officers and of the persuadability of the men in whose spare time these three varieties of education were to be pursued. It thought as highly of the ability of the Army, now 'a cross section of the community' containing 'a wide range of knowledge and talent' to contribute to meeting its own educational needs. 'The Army is a community with its own life', it said, 'and should develop its own resources ... in this matter of education the Army may well be expected in considerable measure to live to itself.' But if the Army should continue to live as much as possible 'of its own', the phrase commonly used in late 16th and early 17th Century England to indicate to the Crown the undesirability of persistently seeking to tax, to 'bite in the purse' its faithful Commons, civilian help, where available, should certainly be accepted. Regional Committees, which would have to be suitably supported financially, would be particularly valuable in helping to cope with demand in the humanities and LEAs with that in the utilities. Commanding Officers should designate junior officers to supervise voluntary education in units, it being highly desirable that these should have the support of unit educational committees, which should be run by the men. And to coordinate all this there should be a new War Office directorate.

It is worth noticing that an edition of the *Army Educational Journal*, subsequent to the publication of 'Education in the War-Time Army', emphasised that the new scheme was not only to combat boredom, to stir minds and to give the troops a clear idea of what they were fighting for, it was also to draw attention to 'the essential features of a new and better life' for which the British Empire stood.[40] On the face of it the High Command was sufficiently impressed by the utopian stirrings then making themselves felt in the civilian bodies pressing for education in the Army to genuflect politely before them. It was thought superfluous to spell out in the *Army Educational Journal* what these essential features of a new and better life for which the British Empire stood were, and those who were most determined to secure a new and better life at the ending of the war were most sure that the British Empire could be no part of it. The old lady who in the days of the First World War found 'Mesopotamia' a blessed word would, however, have had no difficulty in entering into the feeling of the *Journal*'s Editor in their appreciation of these noble-sounding words.

The recommendations of the Haining Committee were quickly implemented. The War Office Directorate which it said should be set up to coordinate and supervise the scheme was so established. The Committee wanted it to be headed by an experienced civilian and Bendall was seconded from the Board of Education to control it. Of the three considered for the post he had knowledge of the Army, having commanded a battalion. His new directorate was to work closely with the Welfare Department under Major-General Sir John Brown and both were to form part of a newly-established Directorate of Welfare and Education to be headed by Major-General Willans. Treasury funds were made available for the civilian help sought from the Central Advisory Council and the Regional Committees. Haining had recommended that a War Office branch be set up to arrange correspondence courses in vocational subjects. This was done; arrangements were made with the Institute of Bankers, the main Engineering Institutes, the Chartered Insurance Society and the Law Society to advise on and give their blessing to such courses, and in December 1940 they were begun. By August 1941 chartered surveyors, auctioneers, estate agents and land agents had come into the scheme which was later further extended to the main societies representing accountancy and audit. In later years the range of correspondence courses offered was still more widely extended. A fee of 10 shillings was charged, this to cover the provision of text books and to discourage the taste-and-try-before-you-buy fraternity. As soon as suitable arrangements could be made these courses were available overseas and by the end of the war 222,745 men and women of the Services had registered for them, 117,423 being soldiers. In January 1941 another of Haining's recommendations, *Radio Reconnaissance*, a current affairs programme for the troops, began to be broadcast by the BBC.

The response of the units to the Haining Scheme was, as must always have been expected, very varied. Where Commanding Officers were either so convinced that it was a good thing, or so impressed that the War Office thought it a good thing, that they were determined that their men should have it whether they liked it or not, and arranged in the men's own time the sessions which they had to attend, it is obvious that the men would not share the conviction of the Commanding Officers. Where Commanding Officers gave every support they could, short of ensuring that all their men would volunteer to attend educational sessions, surprising results were often achieved.[41] One unit offered a programme of forty-two talks to be given by those within its own ranks who had volunteered to do so. In many units local talent was similarly found and classes built on it, discussion groups, music circles, dramatic societies and handicraft clubs arranged. Such activity was often most vigorous overseas, as in Gibraltar and Tobruk. Where Commanding Officers were insufficiently impressed by the merits of the scheme they were obviously in a position to ensure that its implementation suffered a little delay.

One of Haining's recommendations was not, however, implemented and this is perhaps to be regretted. He had pointed to the desirability of having enthusiastic supporters of education within the units and had urged that in addition to the appointment of unit education officers there should also be set up unit education committees to be run by the men. The Army would have none of this. Perhaps such committees seemed too much like the cells which had formed in Russian and, later, in German regiments at the end of the First World War. Committees of this kind would not have been without their attendant problems, as later events on the Nile were to show. But, as those events were also to demonstrate, such developments would have been most unlikely to occur in units and since the success of Army Education inevitably depended largely on unit cooperation, unit education committees could have proved very helpful.

There is clearly no possibility of reaching an objective judgement on the success or otherwise of this first phase of Army Education in the war years. Perhaps the nearest we can come to it is to apply to the Haining Scheme the very shrewd comments made much later, and in very different circumstances, by a group of His Majesty's Inspectors. That group, which visited the Mediterranean Area between December 1945 and February 1946, divided the troops into four categories. In the first category they placed 'the top 5% or so' of the Army, in it being the more intelligent and the more academically minded. In the second category were the skilled tradesmen and the men with practical interests and abilities. In the third were the illiterates; the rest were in the fourth category.[42] The HMIs believed that 'the average man is doubtless a misleading fiction' but they sensibly concluded that there were very large numbers of him and his girlfriend about. They thought indeed that 'probably the proportion of such people in the Army is greater than in a normal sample of the population'. So that the fourth category in which the average man was placed was considerably more numerous than the other three. They thought that in matters educational the first three categories were 'well provided for'. However, as concerned the fourth category they found that 'the picture is less cheerful' and in this category, they concluded that the educational scheme 'has been least successful'. This is no matter for surprise, it having also been the experience of the civilian adult educational movements which had sought for so long, and with such limited success, to get into its classes that perpetually elusive body often referred to as the horny-handed sons of toil. Much the same must have been true of this wartime scheme of Army Education. We can at least be sure that it stimulated a great increase in the number of lectures given to the troops. Eight hundred of these were given in September 1940 when the new scheme was announced and 4,800 by January 1941. No doubt where such lectures were compulsory the nostalgia for care-free and lecture-free evenings among many in the fourth category of which the HMIs spoke would have been greatly increased, despite the opportunity for slumbering in collective anonymity which the lectures provided. But who can be certain that interest was aroused in none of them and that none of them profited thereby?

Man's capacity to be dissatisfied is highly developed and the wartime scheme of Army Education came in for much criticism. For some it went much too far, wasting time vitally necessary to complete the training which could alone avoid defeat, if not promoting the indiscipline which would assuredly guarantee it. To others it did not go far enough, failing to address itself to the crucially important task of making soldiers more informed and better citizens, of fashioning the zealous democrat who alone could be expected to stand unbroken in the face of Fascist fanaticism. It was said that it identified education too much with welfare and that by so doing it failed to accord to education the importance it deserved. It was unaware that a great opportunity was presenting itself and being so it was letting it slip unseized away. At home and in peacetime there were many more attractive things to do than attend adult classes. But in war, and in the long periods that seemed likely to elapse between battles, soldiers might not have so many more attractive things to do as to ensure that they would never expose themselves to education. Far more people than had ever heard of civilian adult education might make contact with adult education in one way or another now. And if the Haining Committee was blind to what was possible, it was equally blind to what was not. The stated educational objectives could not be achieved by the means to be employed to secure them. For the Committee seemed to suggest that anyone with the gift of the gab very galloping and with a modicum of knowledge could make a significant contribution to Army Education, whereas what such group leaders might easily do would be to convince soldiers that it would be in their best interests to turn resolutely away from whatever education was offered to them.

Many of these criticisms were to be made of Army Education in its subsequent phases. Those who resented its association with welfare were no doubt placated when, on General Willan's untimely death in an aeroplane crash in 1943, the two were separated, education then becoming the responsibility of the Adjutant-General. It does not follow that their criticism was sound. Education and Welfare have much in common and there is bound to be a grey area between them in which the one merges into the other. And if ever the view had spread among the troops that education was inimical to their welfare, that would have been the end of education in the Army. Throughout the war there were those who thought that Army Education was developing dangerously fast and those who were convinced its pace was hazardously slow. As for the view that the unit officer, untrained in teaching, was not the best of instructors, that was also said throughout the war and its truth remained unquestioned. But there were not enough teachers in the UK to teach all the Army and there could not be education only for that part of the Army which could be taught by what teachers were available. What was true of Army Education in general was true of the wartime scheme of Army Education as well. The alternative was not to do more, it was to do less. The great 19th Century statesman, Lord Salisbury, said there was no error in politics more common than to try to force an issue when that issue was not yet ready to be settled. When the wartime scheme was introduced neither Government nor Army would have accepted more. But time and changing circumstances and the working of the scheme itself induced Government and Army to accept more; time and change alone, in the absence of experience of that scheme, would not have had that effect.

As it was, the essential characteristics of the later, and fully developed, Scheme of Army Education, although not of course all its details, are to be seen in this Haining Scheme. There is here the close collaboration of civilian and soldier which is such a feature of Army Education in the Second World War. Indeed it was the Central Advisory Council that suggested that General Haining chair the committee which would consider education in the Army. When Haldane went to the War Office he was looked upon with considerable suspicion by the High Command who wanted some general idea of the reforms he proposed to submit to Parliament. His reply 'that I was a young and blushing virgin just united to a bronzed warrior and that it was not expected by the public that any result of that union should appear at least until nine months had passed' completely won their hearts.[43] It is, however, an odd fact that the close and harmonious relationship established between civilian and soldier then was followed by the devastating rows between the brass and the frocks which disfigured civil-military relations in the First World War and which were reflected between soldier and civilian in matters educational lower down the scale. It is even odder that the appalling relations which Hore-Belisha, as Secretary of State for War, had with his top military advisers, were followed by the close and harmonious, if not always smooth, relationship that characterised the working together of civilian and soldier from the Prime Minister downwards in the Second World War. For that both soldier and civilian were responsible and we can feel grateful to both in consequence.

Two soldiers, in particular, did much to ensure civil-military collaboration then. There was Major-General Willans who laid down a firm foundation for Army Education and who greatly advanced the task of building an impressive structure upon it. It was while he was Director-General of Welfare and Education that civilian and soldier learned to work so well together. He won the confidence of both. When General Sir Ronald Adam, the other outstanding soldier to whom Army Education owes so much, became Adjutant-General he was capable of ruffling feelings which would have been better left unruffled. General Paget, when commanding the Home Forces, once said that he was undermining the discipline of the Army.[44] That was never said of Willans. His was the way of steady advance, consolidating each step before moving on to the next but always seeing in what had already been achieved the opportunity to achieve more. The history of Army Education registers great lurches, forward and backward, but also steady advance. The steady advance is associated with him and if Army Education would undoubtedly have been less spectacular its achievement might well have been the greater had the lurches been avoided and his the only way to be followed. Those who build up goodwill also accumulate credit which can be drawn upon if occasion demands. Confidence in Willans and readiness to go along with what he had done lessened the reluctance of those who were inclined to be critical of General Sir Ronald Adam when he took further the developments which Willans had begun. It is to be noticed, too, that even in the matter of the introduction of compulsory education in the Army a good deal of the trail-breaking was done by Willans.

But if Adam occasionally aroused opposition which Willans would not have done, he was one of the most powerful supporters of Army Education. As GOC Northern Command he had been eager to provide civilian lectures for his soldiers; he had allowed units under his command to make education part of the official training programme, this being the beginning of the move away from voluntary to compulsory education in the Army; he had worked closely with W.E. Williams when the latter was a War Office liaison officer in Northern Command. Appointed Adjutant-General in June 1941, he was convinced that education was important for the maintenance and improvement of the morale of his troops. The image of the soldier who knew what he was fighting for, and who loved what he knew that Williams could so well evoke, strongly appealed to him. He believed that such a soldier could not be produced if there was no opportunity to fashion him and that he could be if there was. Since the vast majority of those in the Army would not provide that opportunity voluntarily, he had no compunction in making them do so involuntarily. Without him compulsory education might never have been introduced. Without him ABCA might never have been tried. Without him, despite the fact that Sir James Grigg, who was one of the few long-serving top civil servants to leave the ranks of the Permanent Under-Secretaries to become a Minister himself and who succeeded Margesson as Secretary of State for War, was always his own man, it is possible that the influence of Lord Croft when he was Under-Secretary at the War Office, would have turned him against it. Without him the Winter Scheme of 1943 might have been very different. The importance of his support of Army Education is, therefore, unquestioned.

Two civilians also were of outstanding importance in maintaining that collaboration. One was Sir James Grigg. While still Permanent Under-Secretary at the War Office he proved a friend to ABCA. When a group of Conservative MPs alarmed by ABCA approached the Prime Minister, Churchill sought enlightenment from the War Office, this being the first he had heard of it. He did not like what he was then told. He wrote later 'The qualities required for conducting discussions of the nature indicated are not necessarily those which fit for Command in the field. Will not such discussions only provide opportunity for the professional grouser and agitator with a glib tongue? They seem to be in a different category from educative lectures by trained teachers or experts.'[45] He wanted further information and until he got it he asked that action be suspended. The Secretary of State for War replied that he was happy with the scheme, that he would watch its progress carefully and that he did not think it should be killed as he was 'already hearing very good accounts of it'.[46]

Churchill thereupon asked Brendan Bracken, then Minister of Information and a close confidant, for his views. He also shared the Prime Minister's doubts and Churchill wrote to Margesson, the Secretary of State for War, again reiterating his uneasiness. 'Discussions in which no controversy is desired are a farce', he said. 'There cannot be controversy without prejudice to discipline', he wrote, 'The only sound principle is "no politics in Army".' He hoped that ABCA 'would be wound up as soon as possible and the persons concerned in it set to useful work'.[47] Margesson passed the Prime Minister's note to his Permanent Under-Secretary, Grigg, who demonstrated that the resources of the Civil Service are not easily exhausted. Alexander III, one of the strongest of the Tsars, said that, Emperor of all the Russians as he was, some things were beyond his power to do. If his bureaucrats decided that what he wanted should not be done they would prevail. Strong as Churchill was, he did not prevail in this matter either. Grigg ensured that the minute should be lost sight of in the conviction, which proved to be right, that Churchill too would forget it.[48] Later, now himself Secretary of State for War, his influence on Army Education is not to be underestimated. He continued to give it steady support and to resist powerful criticism which, but for him, would almost certainly have prevailed. And he did so even when developments in Army Education at times made him uneasy too.

The other civilian whose contribution to Army Education was of the greatest importance was W.E. Williams. It bears his own inimitable stamp even more markedly than Army Education in the First World War carries that of Lord Gorell. Relentless in pursuit of his objective but never ruthless, he was a man of powerful yet pleasant personality, a very humane and approachable man, widely, typically and affectionately known as 'ABCA Bill', very worthy of the 'K' that eventually came his way. He was a man of great ability, great drive, great determination, great imagination. His was a creative, a probing, an acute and subtle mind. He knew well that circumstances must alter arguments if not cases. He was immensely persuasive and not least remarkable in his capacity to persuade himself. Shrewd and hard-headed, his mind was sufficiently clear, his ideas sufficiently precise, his approach sufficiently down-to-earth for him to get things done. It could not be said of him that he never dented the surface of events.

But there was another side to him. There was in him something of the Celtic visionary and something, too, of the more common conviction that if our hope is sufficiently ardent things are as we want them to be. He would have agreed with O'Shaughnessy that 'each age is an age that is dying, or one that is coming to birth' and his dreams of ABCA are not lacking in the conviction that

> One man with a dream at pleasure,
> Shall go forth and conquer a crown;
> And three with a new song's measure
> Can trample an empire down

Imprecise dreaming wars with precise thinking in him, the dreams of tomorrow colour the reality of today. He can tell us with a sincerity that compels belief that 'the basis of education is the provision of facts'. He can speak of the soldiers' 'determination to get to know the facts' and leave us in no doubt that he was genuinely impressed by that determination. But he nowhere tells us what were the facts that the soldiers were determined to get to know. He is sure that 'some of the best education is that which men acquire without knowing it' and most of us would acknowledge that the theatre, the concert hall, the art gallery have on occasion done more for our education than the classroom. And when he adds that 'education by exposure to knowledge is one of the most fruitful ways of learning' we may think that this is what he has in mind. But in the following sentence he tells us that 'in the Army this process was attained by extensive use of pictorial methods', as demonstrated in Information Rooms.[49] No one will doubt the attraction and the value of such rooms and it is greatly to be regretted that in few public libraries today, or anywhere else outside the Army, are such imaginative and carefully prepared designs to be seen.

But if by 'exposure to knowledge' we mean only being in the most admirable of Information Rooms, we must not only doubt the fullness of the knowledge that will be ours but also the strength of the determination that will thereby be engendered in us to get to know 'the facts'. Napoleon wanted high-flying commanders to expose themselves to the knowledge displayed by the great commanders of the past, as Plutarch believed it would profit men to be exposed to the knowledge embodied in the great men of the classical world. But the exposure they had in mind involved serious study and concentrated application. The facts determined to be got at could only be so in sweat and toil. They were not to be acquired without awareness that they were being acquired, they were not to be plucked from the ambient air in even the finest of Information Rooms. W.E. Williams convinced himself that this was not so, that the citizen could become the good citizen without calling on himself for effort of the kind that would almost certainly prove to be uncongenial.

His was a great achievement during the war, but it was always tinged with illusion. The achievement was the meeting of one of war's urgent needs, the building up and the raising of morale. The illusion was the belief that he had discovered the way in which not only the citizen soldiers during the war but also workers in the factory and in the office in numbers comparable to them when the war was over, could be filled with determination to get at the facts, knowledge of which would transform them as citizens and, by fulfilling them in this way, fashion for us the new utopia. The meeting of the wartime need, and the fog of war alike, had pushed the illusion into the background and minimised its importance. War's ending and with it the ending of the importance attached to the strengthening of morale, together with the blowing away of war's fog by the fresher air of peace, brought the illusion to the fore and maximised its significance, as becomes apparent when the failure of the Bureau of Current Affairs is contrasted with the success of the Army Bureau of Current Affairs which preceded it. Even so we cannot doubt the strength of the impact Williams had on the Army in the years of war. We are told that at the height of the Great Leap Forward in the People's Republic of China a peasant living in a village 'not 100 miles from Peking' had never heard of Chairman Mao. That is so surprising as almost to baffle belief. It would be no less surprising to come across a British Second World War soldier who had not heard of ABCA. That is an indication of the extent of the influence exercised by W. E. Williams on Army Education then.

Others like Moberly, Chairman of the Central Advisory Council and of the University Grants Committee, Yeaxlee, Secretary of the Central Advisory Council who had been closely associated with the magnificent contribution made by the YMCA to education in the Army in the First World War, and Lindsay, Master of Balliol, a man of considerable persuasiveness and great and growing influence, made major contributions to Army Education. They could not remove all friction from civil-military relations in educational matters, for the capacity to see the other man's point of view is not the most highly developed of human attributes. The Army has its own way of doing things, as has civil society, and each at times appears odd and undesirable to the other. And the freedom of expression that might seem damaging to the discipline of the one might appear essential to the well-being of the other. Both judged matters from different standards. That of the Army was the degree to which it would improve morale; that of the civilians the closeness to which it would come to the requirements of liberal adult education and the ends it sought, of which the maintenance of morale had never been one. This meant that the Army would never surrender ultimate control, would insist on the final decision of who was going to talk to it and on what, would reject that 'control from below' which was said to be essential to civilian adult education. This meant that the civilians wanted freedom of choice on the part of the men of the subject in which they were interested – even when it was acknowledged that the Army must insist that some topics, such as its strategy or pacifism, could not be discussed. They found great difficulty in admitting that the final decision about who could lecture to the Forces must rest with them and that the decision might be based on information that could not be divulged.

Moreover, among the civilians was a strong belief that the war must end in a new ordering of things. On what that should be there was no general agreement but there was general agreement that the old order was not good enough. There was little sustained pressure to spell out what the new order should be as everyone knew that would produce disagreement. But there was pressure to convince all that the old order would have to change and that the best way of ensuring that it did was to spell out its manifold faults. That should be part of the task of Army Education. The Army, however, did not believe that, engaged as we were in a life and death struggle, the best way to ensure the future was to denigrate the past.[50] It was for our enemies to make what play they could of our weaknesses and for us to emphasise our strengths and our great traditions, which both resulted from them and had added to them. Such different attitudes were bound to create mutual resentments and suspicions. The written agreement on which the Central Advisory Council insisted, in which the Army guaranteed that 'as in all universities and Adult Education classes, there shall be reasonable freedom of subject and discussion', was a symptom of those resentments, not a cure for them. The Army would not increase its difficulties by making no adjustments to the pressures coming from civilian adult educationalists; still less would it risk weakening itself and undermining its authority by surrendering to them. On the one essential point that, the unquestioned supremacy of the civil power apart, it must retain responsibility for the determination of whatever policies it adopted, it would never yield. So the tension remained and broke surface frequently on complaints made against individual lecturers and even on one occasion in what were referred to as 'first-class rows' between Bendell, Moberly and Yeaxlee, the spokesman of the Central Advisory Council.[51]

Where, however, deeply engrained suspicion easily turns differences into disputes, trust as easily turns disputes which might otherwise fester and become ugly into the differences with which men are content to live amicably together. Army Education could never have developed as it did during the war had that kind of underlying trust not existed. All were pulling primarily against the enemy and not against each other. Men of this stamp were the more important when Civil Servants were put in charge of Army Education, for they could supply what the Civil Servants could not. The making of these responsible for Army Education would ensure that it was well administered; it could not also ensure that it would be outstandingly worth administering. For their experience was not such as to make the imaginative, the innovative and the enterprising responsiveness to the public stirrings, which was forthcoming from the soldiers and the civilians to whom reference has been made, the most prominent of their characteristics.

Besides this close collaboration of soldier and civilian that characterised Army Education throughout the war years, we can notice in the Haining Scheme other things that did too. There was the strengthening emphasis on both individual needs and on collective understanding. Regional Committees were surprised by the extent of the demand for classes in musical appreciation, by the degree of interest expressed in drama and the arts, and not least by the number who were prepared to have a go at painting and drawing. Vocational education was much in demand, although here an important trend soon became apparent. LEAs admitted soldiers without charge to whatever classes in vocational studies they had arranged as part of their own adult educational programmes. The troops, however, much preferred to go to their own centres when vocational opportunities were to be found there, even though such provision would usually be better in LEA classes. These classes were held in schools and freedom from continued attendance at school they apparently regarded as one of the freedoms unaccountably unmentioned in the Atlantic Charter. Study Centres, incidentally, were always popular in the Army. They remind us that welfare and education are as difficult to separate as are the head and tail of a coin. There was little comfort to be found in sitting on one's bed in billet, Nissen hut or tent, less opportunity for concentration and no privacy, whereas some, and at times all, of these benefits, the Centres provided. It was not the least of the services rendered to the Forces by W. E. Williams that he got a grant from the Pilgrim Trust towards furnishing them. The first was opened in York, after which they were soon seen elsewhere and so popular were they that in 1944 there were thirty-five of them in the UK alone, having an average weekly attendance of 1,000 men and women. Where welfare exercised such an attraction, education might make its appeal; at least it had the opportunity to do so and some who came to the Centre for comfort might also find there mental stimulation.[52]

Nor should be forgot the significance of that somewhat coy reference in the *Army Educational Journal*, issued after the publication of 'Education in the War-Time Army' to 'the essential features of a new and better life' for which the British Empire stood. We cannot be blind to the desire expressed by these words to produce a wider collective understanding of them, however inchoate those features were. Increasing interest in the 'citizen army' was being expressed. It was still possible at this time to refer to the Army without mentioning its adjectival nature, as later it was to become very difficult to do. On almost every page of his *History of Army Education*, Williams uses the expression 'citizen army'; his references to the Army unaccompanied by its prefix are rare indeed. Regular soldiers, who would never have looked upon themselves as mercenaries, might have been expected to take unkindly to such usage but they did not. They were not as fascinated by it as they were later to become. But we can already see what a profound effect it was going to exercise on them and to understand that this fascination is the explanation of their interest in making the soldier a better citizen. And if there was at this time the strengthening emphasis on individual needs and on collective understanding, there was also the belief that, as far as it could, and as indeed it would have to when called far away, the Army must be prepared 'to live of its own', a faith which characterises the whole of the later stages of education in the Army during the war.

What part did the AEC play in this first phase of Army Education? The answer to that question is that it was both very little and very important. This was its darkest hour; it was also its darkest hour before the dawn. We have seen that, to misquote Kipling, far-called its members melted away and that the few who were left could do little to cope with the spreading demands already being made. It had become identified with the work that had been its chief concern in the years between the wars. That was second class and it was thought to be too. So poorly was it thought of that Haining, one of the Army's top Generals, who was well-known for his interest in education, thought that it was useless now that a genuinely educational scheme was being fashioned for the Army. 'We have been forced to the conclusion', he said, 'that the Corps cannot reasonably be expected to undertake the effective direction and management of the wider educational services for which provision will have to be made.' Asked to submit a paper on Army Education to the Haining Committee, a paper on which it was obvious that its future might well depend, the Corps replied in a document that reflected finished and finite mediocrity.[53] Nothing about it suggested that careful thought had gone into its composition. It contented itself with imprecision. There were 'approximately' so many of its members at home and 'about' ten had been given staff appointments. It was a dreary compilation of the old inadequacies and its one suggestion was that 'as regards places abroad which are practically under peace conditions, such as India, Burma, Malaya and China ... the normal pre-war system [i.e. the preparation for Army Certificate Examinations] should be introduced', something that it must have known had been rejected by the Army Council as unsuitable for the Militia and something that the Haining Committee at once decided was irrelevant to the Army as it now was. Colonel White, one of the most outstanding and best-loved members of the Corps and author of *The Story of Army Education*

1643–1963, commented on this that none of the fifty officers in Britain who were working with the troops were consulted when this appalling document was being prepared.[54] He added 'It is based on experience of the peace-time scheme, and there is no mention of the current situation, or of publications, handicrafts, music or of any vocational or recreational classes.' The soul of courtesy and charity, he was, nevertheless, impelled to write 'the Corps spent the rest of war in competition with the more imaginative Directors of Welfare and Entertainment'. Only if the purpose of this document had been to convince the Haining Committee of the total unsuitability of the AEC for work with a conscript Army could it have been rationally hoped to be in any way effective.

Fortunately the dawn was at hand. For the War Office was more sensible than the Haining Committee and decided, contrary to the Committee's recommendations, that the AEC should be put in general control of the new scheme. It knew that a uniformed department would be needed to do this and perhaps the thought occurred to it 'better the devil you know than the devil you don't'. Folk memories span the years and perhaps the War Office recollected without pleasure the setting up of a new department, S.D.8, under Lord Gorell as Deputy-Director of Staff Duties (Education). For many thought the odd ideas that the setting up of that department led to unnerving. When Lord Gorell, for instance, said 'there is no reason why the Army should not come to be regarded as the people's university course',[55] Sir George MacDonagh was not alone in calling that 'a fantastic and impractical idea'.[56] Many in the War Office had been shaken by the view that Gorell made no attempt to hide that 'It is possible that in 1930 an army will be synonymous for an educational institution.' They would have been still more shaken had they known that a former member of S.D.8 had written 'It seems to me that before long the Head of S.D.8 will be the most important member of the Army Council, probably absorbing entirely the functions of the Adjutant-General, if not also those of the CIGS.'[57] If new educational departments could turn and swell heads like that there was indeed much to be said for keeping to old ones, undistinguished though they were proving to be.

So that without intending to, the Haining Committee gave a much needed fillip to the AEC, enabling it to get back to its proper work. That return gave it new vitality and new zest, qualities added to by the effect of the new intake into its ranks, for to undertake the supervision now required of it the Corps had to expand. By November 1940 it was twice the size it had been when war broke out. The older members of the Corps had by now lost the crusading spirit of the early 1920s but their experience remained invaluable, and if caution is dispensed with crusaders may be dispensed with too. The new intake were eager crusaders but they had to find their feet and at least to be given the opportunity to learn a little humility, much needed in some cases, in understanding that they had a great deal to learn from the men now in their charge. The old steadied the new and the new invigorated the old; both benefitted thereby. Together they were the channels along which civilian aid to the Forces ran. It was essential that there should be civilians and soldiers whose specific concern it would be to explain each to the other. The secretaries of the Regional Committees and of the Central Advisory Council discharged this difficult function and discharged it very well. Inevitably, however, it was those in uniform who had to pull the labouring oar here, for they knew the Army, its needs, its ways, its quirks, as civilians, however perceptive, could not. They knew what it wanted, what it would insist on having, what it would insist on not having, for they themselves were Army. Important as the civilian contribution was to the maintenance of good relations with the Services and to Army education in general, it was the AEC who were the real engineers responsible for the building of the structure without which Army Education could not have developed as it did. Haining had thought that it could not cope with the educational scheme that would have to be developed; without the AEC no such development could have occurred.

CHAPTER 5

ARMY EDUCATION IN EMBATTLED BRITAIN

We see the ending of this first phase of education in the wartime Army in the devastating defeat of France. The miracle of the Dunkirk beaches, and the momentary uplift produced by it in Britain, could not hide the catastrophic nature of the situation in which we found ourselves, nor the magnitude of the task now facing the nation and the High Command. An ill-prepared Army had been fashioned, based on the assumption that it would primarily, at least for some considerable time, be a defensive continental Army which would be fighting behind prepared positions. That assumption had proved to be unsound when, at French insistence, the British troops had moved into Belgium from their prepared positions, only to find that their flanks were uncovered by the failure of their allies to hold their ground. In consequence a new anti-invasion Army had to be built up and the equipment lost at Dunkirk to be made good.[1]

Moreover, with the downfall of France a new and very great problem began to nag at the minds of our leaders, civil and military alike. French collapse seemed so sudden and French refusal to continue the war from still unconquered French territory so shocking, that much too much was made of the rottenness of French morale as the cause of this catastrophic defeat. The French soldier had fought bravely but this was not sufficiently appreciated nor was the fact that the French Army, clinging to old ways, had been outgeneralled and destroyed by superior strategy and tactics. The morale of the British Army after Dunkirk was also causing concern.[2] On the completion of the successful evacuation, morale, as Eden found when he visited the returned units, was high. Had the anticipated invasion then come we would no doubt have fought ferociously on the beaches and everywhere else. Even then there were grounds for anxiety, there being areas in which morale was less impressive than Eden had found it.[3] Grigg tells us that then 'private property had to be sequestered on the largest scale, and the carelessness and in some cases wantonness with which it was treated was a sure indication how near to breaking point discipline had come'.[4] Sir Ronald Adam recalled how high a rate of desertion there was at this time and how until the summer of 1941 low morale was widespread. Even before Dunkirk the mood of many of the men had left much to be desired. Bishop Hensley Henson noted in his diary in March 1940 'I am distressed to hear from many sides that the prevailing temper of our troops is a half-cynical boredom, as remote as possible from the high crusading fervour which our situation authorises and requires. They are not pacifists or disloyal, but "bored stark". They have neither the enthusiasm of youth nor the deliberate purpose of age, but just acquiesce in an absurd and unwelcome necessity.'[5] Many of the troops were in lonely and scattered anti-aircraft sites, not all of which would be in action, where accommodation was inadequate, pubs distant and beer in any case in short supply; even more of the troops in other Commands were unlikely to see action for perhaps many months to come. That being so, was there not the likelihood that they would become even more bored and blasé and that morale would become even more of a problem? Lord Croft, who had become Under-Secretary of State for War, feared so when he said 'It is vital if the Army is to be kept on its toes there should be no Maginot Complex, no slackening of spirit.'[6]

Two things underlined the urgency of coming to grips with this problem. One was the defeat and humiliation that continued to be our lot after our expulsion from Europe. In North Africa, British Forces were pushed back into Egypt; in the Mediterranean, Greece was abandoned and Crete fell to a numerically inferior air-borne assault; in South-East Asia, a large British force laid down its arms. Inevitably comparisons were made with British troops who had fought to the last shell in the First World War before accepting defeat. What had gone wrong with John Bull? Had we grown too soft to fight?[7] The other was the effect on the Home Front of continued defeat and of the knowledge that, as Harold Nicholson, the diarist and shrewd observer of the political scene, said, 'there is something deeply wrong with the whole morale of the Army'. In the country dissatisfaction, warring with alarm, was growing apace and the agitation that became known as the 'war-to-win-the-war' movement was spreading.

George Orwell was a leading figure in that movement. In his London Letter to the *Parisian Review* of 3 January 1941 and in *The Lion and the Unicorn* of February 1941 he criticised Churchill's leadership and called for radical social and political change, without which, he said, Nazi Germany could not be defeated. Richard Ackland and Tom Wintringham, other leaders of it, calling for an immediate restructuring of society, formed the 1941 Committee and Forward March which later became the Common Wealth Party. Liddell Hart, whose trenchant military writings had never had the influence on the Army for which he had hoped and whose close relations with Hore-Belisha had greatly offended it, was prominent, too, in this 'war-to-win-the-war' movement, proclaiming that Government 'must provide creative ideas from which a positive faith can be generated'. 'To get the best out of men', he said, 'it is not enough to tell them that they must be ready to die in the last ditch. They must be given a new vision of the future and a new hope.' It is an illustration of authority's sensitivity to this kind of thinking that there was consternation in the War Office when it was known that Liddell Hart had been invited to lecture at Coleg Harlech, and that shortly thereafter the Commandant who had invited him was posted and a new Commandant appointed. Tom Wintringham, who had fought in the Spanish Civil War, wrote along similar lines: 'Men must be persuaded, made to understand, given the enthusiasm that will change their discipline from an acceptance of orders to an eager use of all their powers in pursuit of a common aim. They must be made to feel that their own contribution has value – is accepted, that the war is their war.'[8] When we add for good measure that in January 1941 Churchill had his first clash with the *Daily Mirror* (which he later threatened to close down) for undermining public confidence, we can understand how seriously such criticism was taken and how greatly it was feared that it would add to the problem of low morale in the Army. For even though the difficulty of keeping the troops *au fait* with the news was itself a problem, they could not be unaware of the 'war-to-win-the-war' movement and, when available, the *Daily Mirror* was one of their most popular papers.

At least in our large conscript Army this problem of the maintenance of morale was new to us, although since men began to wage war morale has always been known to be of the greatest significance. We had in the First World War taken the soundness of our morale for granted and while from time to time in our long history the morale of our troops must have occasioned concern, that was a matter only for their officers and one, moreover, that had never greatly exercised them. For they knew that leadership, care for their men, even-handed, if severe, discipline and, above all, time, would put things right. They knew that armies cannot be created overnight and that defeat, not victory, is the lot of unprepared armies, a truth clearly stamped on the earlier campaigns fought by the British in their wars. They could say proudly with Napier 'And this is the glory of England; that her soldiers and hers only were capable of overthrowing Napoleon's armies in equal battle',[9] but only when the full price had been paid for the drifting days of peace, when years of endurance had in their turn exacted full payment for coming victory. But in the new situation in which a new kind of Army, a conscript Army, had to be dealt with, could these old means be relied upon to produce, as in the past, the armies that could take the field against their enemies with every hope of success? To take an obvious point: society would not tolerate now the shooting of those who were overcome by fear in the face of the enemy, even though it must have been obvious that knowledge of such a fate might have steadied the nerves of those who might otherwise have given way to momentary panic and that in the absence of that knowledge momentary panic might have more chance of prevailing. In all probability even in its absence, time and discipline, leadership and care, would have had their customary effect, but the High Command was no longer as sure of this as it had always hitherto been.

Hence concern for, and attention to, morale was to characterise it throughout the war. It set up a special Morale Committee; it instructed Commanding Officers to ask their officers to supply information about the morale of their men; it had letters home analysed as they passed through the censor; it used 'spies', such as Lieutenant-Colonel Sparrow who, dressed as a private, travelled on troopships and trains and visited camps.[10] We can get some idea of the importance it attached to morale at this time when we realise that its sensitivity concerning the 'morale returns' that were made to it in the period January to June 1941, returns referred to in War Office discussions, the records of which are available, was such as to lead to their removal from the War Office archives.[11] Concern for morale not only reconciled the Army to having education for its soldiers, it actually made the Army eager for it.

It was to have even more surprising results. The politician might reasonably be expected to be more interested than the soldier in the fashioning of the good citizen but the longer the war lasted the greater grew the interest of the soldier in this and the stronger the conviction of the politician that it was not the proper task of the Army. The politician, less concerned than the soldier with the maintenance of morale, came to the conclusion that the price to be paid for attempting this was too high; the soldier, more concerned with morale than the politician, was sure that it was not, the Army Commanders and the Morale Committee making this very plain, and the view of the soldier prevailed.[12] Or to express the same thing in a slightly different way, education, which initially was reluctantly accepted by the Army under civilian pressure, became of significance to it only when the conviction dawned that education was a means of maintaining morale, and became of major importance to it only when morale appeared to be a major problem and education an essential way of coping with it. Education, in short, would have been greatly curtailed by civilian pressure had the Army not become so convinced that it was an indispensable means of maintaining morale that it resisted the sustained and severe civilian pressure to reduce its scope.

Not that the view that education was unnecessary for the improvement of morale was unrepresented. The appropriately-named Mr Cash of the War Office Directorate of Finances maintained that 'there is no place for organised "Army Education" in wartime in an army composed of all classes from highly educated to illiterate, engaged in fighting or preparing to fight ... what is needed is mainly mental and physical relaxation rather than systematic education'.[13] That view was swept aside when Willans drove home the point that 80% of the soldiers who had so carefully abstained from education were in most cases without 'that most precious heritage the ability to make good use of leisure'.[14] Concern for morale was the mainspring of the astonishing development that took place in Army Education in the war. The new compulsory phase of Army Education that occurred in the months after Dunkirk was a response to the problem of low morale in the Forces and to the broad movement then growing criticizing the present political and military leadership of the country in the war and looking forward to the new Jerusalem at its ending. It is essential to remember this when the difficult attempt is made, as it must be, to draw up the balance sheet and to assess the achievement of wartime military education.

If there were doubts about the efficiency of the old ways of coping with the problem of morale in this new situation, a new way was on offer. This was to create a revolutionary army as France had done when it was invaded by the armies of the *ancien régime*. Those who wanted to do this dispensed with the French Revolutionary threat to throw at invading hordes the head of a king, no doubt finding that both uncivilised and inappropriate, but they would have been happy to hurl at them the head of a Prime Minister. It was the proper task of Army Education, they said, to transform the Army into an Army zealous for democracy, zealous, that is to say, for the kind of democracy they professed, and for no other. A letter written at this time to the *New Statesman* by a WEA tutor involved in Army Education well illustrates their thought:

> It is the function of education to encourage independent thought and this produces discontent, criticism, dissatisfaction and other results which are detested by such traditional organisations as the Army ... Thus genuine Army Education cannot fail to produce anything but serious criticism of the system which men in the army are forced to endure. It would expose the inefficient and incompetent character of those who are in authority. It would lead to a realisation of the ways in which we were led to the abyss through stupidity and ignorance. [15]

The arrogance of this letter ought not to pass unnoticed. We are told the aim of education is to encourage independent thought. We are also told how we can know when it has achieved that aim. It has done so when it has produced discontent with, and criticism of, tradition. It has done so when it has exposed the inefficient and incompetent character of authority, its stupidity and ignorance that has brought us to the verge of the pit. Or, to put it negatively, it has not done so until it has convinced us of these things.

A great political thinker, Burke, had taught us otherwise. Long human experience, which he called 'prescription', was the true criterion of just and unjust action:

> Prescription is the most solid of all titles, not only to property but ... to Government. It is accompanied with another ground of authority in the human mind: presumption. It is a presumption in favour of any settled scheme of government against any untried project, that a nation has long existed and flourished under it. It is a better presumption even of the choice of a nation, far better than any sudden and temporary arrangement by actual election. Because a nation is not an idea only of local extent, and individual, momentary aggregation, but it is an idea of continuity, which extends in time as well as in numbers and in space. And this is a choice not of one day, or one set of people, not a tumultuary and giddy choice; it is a deliberate election of ages and of generations; it is a constitution made by what is ten thousand times better than choice it is made by the peculiar circumstances, occasions, tempers, dispositions, and moral, civil and social habitudes of the people, which disclose themselves only in a long space of time. It is a vestment which accommodates itself to the body. Nor is prescription of government formed upon blind, unmeaning prejudices for man is a most unwise, and a most wise being. The individual is foolish. The multitude, for the moment, are foolish, when they act without deliberation; but the species is wise, and when time is given to it, as a species almost always acts right.[16]

Thus tradition is not an evil to be dispensed with but a good which will greatly strengthen us. It is folly to think that we can safely take the State to bits in order to reassemble it as we think fit.[17] 'An ignorant man', he tells us, 'who is not foolish enough to meddle with his clock, is, however, sufficiently confident to think he can take safely to pieces and put together at his pleasure, a moral machine of another guise, importance and complexity, composed of far other wheels, and springs, and balances and counteracting and cooperating powers.' Men little think how immorally they act in rashly meddling with what they do not understand. We should learn to be 'afraid to put men to live and trade each on his own private stock of reason, because we suspect that this stock in each man is small, and that the individuals would do better to avail themselves of the general bank and capital of nations and of ages'. We should seek to strengthen our individual reason by acknowledging the force of tradition.[18] This, Burke was sure, was the way of political prudence and he would have seen in the cast of mind of the writer above quoted that Jacobinism against which he was making his tremendous stand.

But there were Jacobins in the AEC, too, who, as W. E. Williams expressed it, were 'bellowing for commissars who would enforce in every unit a ruthless analysis of Munich and the rudiments of a political education'.[19] One was Captain George Wigg, who as Secretary of the North Staffs District of the WEA had prodded the WEA into its concern for education in the Militia. Another was Major Gilbert Hall, a stormy petrel whom the Secretary of State for War later described as 'a nasty bit of work who has got to be watched'.[20] ABCA, they said, had shown the need for something more genuinely political in nature. Only if the soldier genuinely believed in 'the faith and practice of democracy' would the war be won and only if men of vision, who were also 'the most ardent disciples' of democracy and who could comprehend the restlessness and subconscious desire at present in the heart of the soldier and mobilise it for a total war effort and for victory, were in charge of Army Education would the soldier develop that genuine belief. They drew up their ideas in a Memorandum which they sent to D.P. Pritt, an Independent MP with well-known communist sympathies, and to Stafford Cripps, the recently-appointed Lord Privy Seal. Aware that they themselves profoundly understood the subconscious desire in the heart of the soldier, and convinced of their ability to enable it to find conscious expression, Hall, in a covering letter to Cripps, felt impelled to add that to head such a scheme men of 'drive, vision, wide-understanding gathered mainly in civilian life, and acute "political sense"' were needed, and they were to be found in Wigg and himself.[21] They both felt that 'we could throw ourselves body and soul into such a job, where we would be doing a vital and most urgent piece of work with profit to the country'. Cripps was unable to forward their cause as he was off to demonstrate to the peoples of India his inability to forward theirs too. But he was able to help them personally by intimating to his colleague at the War Office that he would look with disfavour on the taking of disciplinary action against his correspondent, and prudence, a notable Civil Service characteristic, had not been left behind in that colleague's translation from the Civil Service to the Ministry.

Moreover, the officers in question sought episcopal and press as well as ministerial and parliamentary support. They approached William Temple, then about to be translated to Canterbury. Temple, too, anticipated great things from the release of the as yet fettered spirit of democracy. He had, moreover, divined that 'the AEC's efforts are at present aimless', a revelation which he was kind enough to make known to the Director of Army Education, who was responsible for them.[22] The *Times Educational Supplement* also did what it could to advance the cause, publishing Wigg's letter in which he claimed that Army Education was 'a gigantic fraud', as the civilian bodies engaged in it and the troops who suffered from it well knew, a condition of things for which the dead-wood in the AEC's upper ranks was responsible. Those upper ranks were where they were only 'because the Haining Scheme provided a glorious opportunity to give them promotion they would otherwise never have got'. Hall's effusion to *Reynolds News* remained unpublished but the editor passed it to the War Office.[23] Since it no doubt expressed similar appreciation of AEC senior officers it is unlikely that they looked upon the later promotion to full Colonel of one of these offending officers with unalloyed satisfaction. The services of the other they were no doubt glad to dispense with after the squabbles in Cairo in January 1944 which became known somewhat grandiloquently as the affair of the Cairo Parliament and which will be discussed later. However, supported as they were by politician and blessed by priest, men of this vision, this wide understanding, this acute political sense, this intuitive knowledge of the heart of the soldier, were thus not lost to the AEC, which continued to extract what benefit it could from their further service.

If not satisfied that old ways would suffice to improve morale in new conditions, the High Command was less than impressed with the idea of turning to revolution to ensure victory in a war in which we were already engaged. What, then, was to be done? Nicholson gives us an arresting picture of the doubt and the confusion raised in high circles by the alarmed awareness of this acute problem of morale:

> ...the left-wing people say that you must create a 'revolutionary' army and that our 'class' army can never fight. The right-wing say that we should go back to our old system of regimental discipline. Macmillan says that we have not got the time or scope to create a revolutionary army and that we must go back to discipline. We are between two stools, he says.[24]

Macmillan was wrong. We did not fall between two stools; to use another cliché, we found what would fit the bill. Our old British love of compromise helped us to do so. We looked to leadership, care and discipline and time to work for us, as we had always hitherto done, and to help these things we turned to education, as we have never done before. We sought a way of creating the zeal we wanted without the zealotry we deplored. We did not want an Army of zealots, rightly distrusting them, and therefore we turned away from those who urged it upon us. We did, however, want a zealous Army and therefore we turned to those who said they could get it for us. They were the Cromwellians. We had admitted Cromwell's greatness but our admiration was untinged by affection and his was a name not frequently on our lips. We had grown indifferent to King Charles's head and did not hold it against Cromwell that he had dispensed with it. But we held it greatly against him that he had deprived us of our laws and inflicted military rule upon us. Now, ironical though it was, since the Army had less cause than most of us to think well of him – as he more than any other man, with the governance of England by his Major-Generals, had occasioned English dislike of it – we turned to him as a *deus ex machina*. For he had pointed to us the path of salvation, telling us that what we must seek was the soldier who knew what he was fighting for and who loved what he knew. Now not our loonies, whom very properly we would keep at arm's length, but our middle-of-the-road men in whom we could trust, were telling us that we could have him at a price we could afford. Not by preaching, not by proselytizing, not by propaganda, but by education our dedicated soldier could be produced and that was a price we were prepared to pay.

It was, then, neither in the old nor in the ardently advocated new revolutionary way that the Army sought the answer to its problem of morale, but in this compromise way that took something from both. And if this promised to give the Army what it wanted, it allowed those like W. E. Williams, who were shaping the education from

Places

Tangier 1685 – the first recorded posting of schoolmasters with the Army: Richard Reynolds, MA and Fellow of Sydney Sussex College, Cambridge, and John Eccles, writing master and Gunner

Church parade at the Army School of Education, Bodmin, 1949

The White House Officers' Mess, Wilton Park, Beaconsfield

Accommodation huts at Wilton Park, Beaconsfield, home of the Army School of Education from 1950 – 1995

A general view of the new Army School of Education, Beaconsfield

People

An Inspector of Army Education 1914, one of a series of water colours by Alan M Gladwell

Colonel The Lord Gorell CBE MC, the founder of the Army Educational Corps and architect of the post-World War 1 Army Education System

General Sir Ronald Adam (right), Adjutant General, sponsor of war-time educational schemes, visiting the Army School of Education in Wakefield, 1942

Mr WE Williams, 'ABCA Bill', Director of the Army Bureau of Current Affairs holding a two-weekly production meeting with his staff about the Map Review of the war, October 1942
Photograph courtesy of the Imperial War Museum, London (H25151)

Three holders of the Victoria Cross were amongst the founder members of the AEC in 1920. They are shown here at the Corps' Jubilee Garden Party in 1970. Left to right: Gen Sir Hugh Stockwell, then Colonel Commandant RAEC, Lt Col TE Adlam VC, Col JL Dawson VC, Col ACT White VC MC

Soldiers' Education

Sergeant leading a current affairs discussion in North Italy, World War II
(Photograph courtesy of the Imperial War Museum, London (NA12658)

Warrant Officer instructing a class at 70 AEC, Gillman Barracks, Singapore, 1960s

17th Acting Schoolmasters Class, Aldershot, 1908

Army Travelling Educational Unit, Africa, 1940s

Children's Education

Dr Bell's monitorial system in operation at the Royal Military Asylum, Chelsea, early 1800s

Army Children's School, Eta Jima, Japan – a geography lesson taken by WO2 J Llewellyn RAEC

Regimental School, Poona, 1897, with Army Schoolmasters and Schoolmistresses

Army Schoolmasters with schoolchildren, pre-1914

HRH The Duchess of Gloucester, Colonel-in-Chief RAEC 1977-1992, visiting Alexandra School, Rheindahlen, Germany. The Duchess is now Patron of the RAEC Association

which the Army was hoping so much, to entertain the hope that what they wanted would eventuate too. The genuineness of their conviction that what they were doing would improve morale was unquestioned. But this was not their only goal. They wanted to embark upon the greatest missionary revivalist movement of education in our country's history. Theirs was the hope that the Army would, as it were, break the trail for the nation. Attending to its own needs, it would be focusing the attention of the nation on its too, making it aware of needs of which it had hitherto been unconscious. Army Education would, by making good the failures of the past, be a powerful force in the fashioning of the fine new world of the future.[25]

The report of the Committee set up in February 1942 'to enquire into and report into amenities and welfare conditions in the three Women's Services and to make recommendations' reflects this missionary zeal. It spoke of the generous provision made to meet the educational demands of the men and women of the Services and acknowledged how limited these were, saying 'it would be idle to pretend that the demand is in any respect equal to the possible supply'. 'Many soldiers, like many civilians', it went on, 'have an abysmal ignorance of national and international affairs. If men are apathetic about education, women are more so ... It is a melancholy reflection on the educational failures of the last twenty-five years that many young people refuse to use their minds at all outside working hours, and their only cry is for amusement without any demand made on their initiative, industry or intelligence.' Now an opportunity had presented itself for past failures to be rectified, for young minds hitherto set only on amusement to be induced to appreciate higher things. 'Granted the right approach, appreciation of literature, history, music and art is not beyond the reach of many Service women, and every effort towards this end should be made.'[26] Sometimes difficulties were acknowledged but invariably, it seemed, in the spirit of the exhortation 'let us face the difficulty squarely and turn our backs on it'. 'We take it for granted', an article in *The Highway* on the education of the ATS said, 'that we wish to educate them for a democratic society, but here is the heart of the problem, for can any education for democracy be effective, when in fact for twenty-four hours every day these girls are being taught and conditioned by a (comparatively) benevolent dictatorship?' Conjuring up that particular difficulty was a piece of preposterous nonsense but, great as that difficulty was thought to be, far more important than that was the opportunity now opening up. For the girls, as that *Highway* article went on to say, 'are all under authority, where they can be shaped by their present environment, and encouraged to look forward to and plan their lives and the life of the society after the war'.[27]

The lesson was clear. Even if we had had the right approach before the war, it would not have helped because we could not get at those whom we wished to transform. They were, in T. H. Green's phrase, exercising their right to remain analphabetic. But we have got them now so let us not lose this wonderful opportunity to see what the right approach will do. Granted the right approach, which we will find, great wonders will be done. Those who have thought only of entertainment will see the error of their ways and we will build the New Jerusalem in England's green and pleasant land. This was the hope that swept like a great wave over the country in the war years. It was this, not ABCA which was only a symptom of it, which brought the Labour victory at the end of the war. It was this which was stamped so unmistakably on Army Education during the war.

Common to those whose main concern was with morale and to those others whose interest was also in this great opportunity to develop a mass revivalist movement in adult education, was the conviction that the right of free-born Englishmen and women, or at least of those of them who were in uniform, to remain ignorant could not longer be admitted. The necessity was too pressing, the opportunity too exciting, for such eccentric rights, if rights they were, to prevail. But if they were rights and if they were not to prevail, what was to be made of that? Morale was a military matter and no one doubted that in war some rights had to yield to military necessity. But an educational missionary endeavour was another matter and few would agree that that would justify the overriding of established rights, however eccentric they may be thought to be. Children had no right to remain ignorant but how could 'the free and lawful man' who is the central figure of the Common Law and to whom more than anything or anyone else we owe our liberty, fittingly be compared to a child? Grave constitutional issues might be involved and the Central Advisory Council (with the possible exception of Lindsay, the Master of Balliol, for whom the 17th Century Commonwealth had a great fascination), and the Regional Committees were reluctant revivalists. They were uneasy when education in the Army became compulsory, or, perhaps to speak more truly, when it made the transition from being a supposedly voluntary system, which on the whole it was, to becoming a theoretically compulsory system, which again it was in general, as it did in 1942 for one hour every week. As long as it was justified as being essential for morale, however, they would not withdraw their cooperation.

Athena, we are told, sprang fully-armed from the head of Zeus, but if godhead can produce instant wisdom errant mortals take a little longer to do so. Great issues had to be determined after Dunkirk and even when we had decided to fight on, how best to do so engrossed our attention. We had to feel our way forward and months were to pass before we settled on our compromise way of coping with the problem of morale and of putting it into action. Fortunately, the time we needed to do so was at our disposal. Our success in the Battle of Britain, which demonstrated once again the impregnability of our island base, gave us that and our special relationship with the USA enabled us to make the best use of it. For that relationship depended not on the fact that we and the Americans were both democratic peoples, not on the fact that we had Magna Carta and Shakespeare in common, not on the fact that it could be said, with perhaps a little exercise of charity, that we spoke the same language, but on the fact that we had an identical interest in Europe, in the maintenance of the Balance of Power there, in the prevention of the establishment there of a mistress court, of hegemonic power. It was that identical interest which produced that moment of high drama when, speaking after dinner on the night before his return to the USA, Harry Hopkins, whom Roosevelt had sent to assess our chances of survival before agreeing to let us have the wherewithal to make them good, at last made known how he would report by quoting, somewhat inaccurately, from the Book of Ruth 'Wither thou lodgest we lodge, whither thou goest we go, yea to the very end.'[28] We knew then that we would not be defeated and that we could fashion, if not at our leisure at least at our pleasure, that development of Army Education that would best suit our circumstances. In that development we see the apotheosis of the idea of the 'citizen Army', the Army which, being composed of citizens, could only improve itself, as it must to achieve victory, by makings its soldiers better citizens than they had ever dreamed of being. It was the task of ABCA and *British Way and Purpose* to do that and both would have to be compulsorily attended to enable them to do their job.

ABCA, as it was widely known, was the generally used shorthand to denote the Army Bureau of Current Affairs. It was also intended to convey the meaning ABC of affairs, that basic understanding of the nature of the world in which they were fighting which senior officers were alarmed to find lacking in their men and which was thought to be essential for the maintenance and raising of their morale. It was the brain-child of W. E. Williams. In December 1940 he was appointed to liaise on educational matters between the War Office and the Scottish, Northern, Eastern and Anti-Aircraft Commands. Lieutenant-General Sir Ronald Adam, now Adjutant-General, asked him to report on education within these Commands and to make whatever recommendations seemed good to him. As he was particularly concerned to assess what impact education was having on the troops, it is reasonable to believe that morale was uppermost in his mind and that this was something that he and the Adjutant-General had already been discussing. Williams returned convinced that something new was called for if education was to have a significant impact on the troops.

An obvious explanation of this was the care the troops were taking to give education no opportunity to have an impact on them by keeping away from it. The majority did not go to lectures and discussions and so long as education remained a voluntary activity, Williams was convinced that 'there will never be more than a very limited demand for it'.[29] If education made soldiers better and raised their morale, the majority seemed destined to remain poorer soldiers with poorer morale. If they could not be allowed to remain so, their right to be unexposed to the onslaught of education would have to be overridden. It was thus clear that implicit in the idea of ABCA was the substitution of a compulsory for a voluntary system of education in the Army.

It was Willans who fired the opening salvo in what was clearly a coordinated campaign to get ABCA established. In his report of 4 June 1941, *Education in the Wartime Army*, he made three points. He urged that in the interests of morale, army education should concentrate entirely on Current Affairs. 'It cannot be disputed', he wrote, 'that if we can employ men's minds and stimulate their interests by promoting knowledge, discussion and thought about the affairs of the world in which they live, we go far to maintain their morale and thus to make them better soldiers.' He argued that, so that all troops could be reached, this education must be compulsory and must take place in duty hours. He maintained that in the attempt to economise manpower and draw officers and men together, classes were not to be taken by the AEC but by unit officers. He was strongly opposed by the Secretary of State for War, Captain Margesson, who believed that this would 'lay the door open to political agitation within the Army'.[30] Margesson's alarm was shared by the Army Council, which agreed that 'it would be most undesirable if party politics were allowed to enter into the discussions'.

Willans stoutly defended his ideas. He too was determined, he said, to keep party politics out of the Army but he added that political discussion was already being encouraged by the Haining Scheme. He contended that 'men who wish to discuss politics will discuss them, and it is far better that they should do so openly in the light of facts which have been intelligently and convincingly presented to them, than they should do so in ignorance or behind doors'. He was sure that his scheme would 'militate against political agitation'. 'The agitator', he said, 'invariably thrives where he is dealing with ignorant men or working in secret and fails when brought into open contact with facts and knowledge.' He was doubtless glad to be able to say that political discussions were already being held, that Commanding Officers had become alarmed at them, that a trainee airman at Cranwell had been arrested and jailed for refusing to divulge the names of the others taking part in such group discussion. He would not be forwarding his cause by playing these things down and he must have been aware of the difficulty of persuading people to set alight a back-fire in the absence of a fire. He won his point, although the Army Council remained uneasy. There must, it insisted, be adequate safeguards. ABCA material must be vetted by the Directorate of Intelligence and Commanding Officers must be responsible for ensuring that 'no subjects touching upon party politics be permitted at Unit discussions'.[31]

A number of important consequences followed from this decision to accept compulsory education and ABCA. One was that if the lamb was to be shorn then the wind would have to be suitably tempered to it. Fortunately the very subject in which the military necessity of improving morale made it seem necessary that the soldier be instructed, current affairs, the understanding of which would tell him why he was fighting, what he was fighting against, what he was fighting for, was the very subject which made the greatest appeal to the troops. It 'has been the staple everywhere', Yeaxlee wrote.[32] This was not surprising as men now did not have access to news, papers often not being available in units and BBC broadcasts rarely heard in them. It was the more disappointing, this being so, that the majority still did not feel themselves impelled to attend voluntary current affairs lectures. However it seemed reasonable to think, since most of those participating in voluntary educational activity were interested in current affairs, that there was at least the possibility of interesting the majority of soldiers in it too, if that majority were to be compelled to attend educational sessions.

That would suggest that the task was not hopeless, but if it reduced, it would not eliminate the difficulty of holding the interest and penetrating the understanding of many who would not only be more reluctant, but also less well-informed, less familiar with the things of the mind and in all probability considerably less bright than the minority who voluntarily appeared before current affairs lecturers. If military necessity increased the demand made upon the majority, care must be taken to ensure that it would be the minimum possible demand in the circumstances. The instruction provided, the understanding sought, must be of a very basic nature. It was the ABC of Current Affairs that was to be mastered and it is not wise to introduce to those learning the alphabet the writings of Hegel or Nietzsche.

There was a further important consequence of making ABCA compulsory, a consequence that was itself an equally compelling reason why the instruction to be conveyed in ABCA sessions had to be of a very basic nature. This was that its sessions would have to be conducted by unit officers. It was a civilian who conceived it and the same civilian who headed the department which supervised its working. Most of its pamphlets were written by civilians and it received a good deal of civilian help. This apart, ABCA was exclusively a military affair. There was no alternative to having its sessions arranged and its discussions led by unit officers. Nor was this only because in no other way could it have been part of the Army's life in all the theatres of war in which it was engaged. Even in the Home Commands it would not have been possible for ABCA to be done in any other way, as trained teachers were not to be found in the numbers that would have been needed had they been required to conduct ABCA sessions.

It was tough on the junior officer of the unit to whom this task fell. Lambarde, a 16th Century writer on the governance of England, spoke of 'stacks and stacks of statutes' adding to the labours of the Justice of the Peace.[33] Stacks and stacks of duties were similarly piled on the unfortunate subaltern. Struck by the frequency with which he met the phrase 'It is essential that every officer be able to teach this subject to those under his command' General Paget found that the officer had been expected to cope with 100 different subjects.[34] It was, as he said, 'a load of learning heavy for a subaltern fresh from school'. If, like the Lord High Executioner, the subaltern had many parts to play, it had to be remembered that he was not as yet master of any. It was not an eccentric view that effort in his ABCA role would help him to attain mastery of those that were essential to him. It would have been highly eccentric to have expected him to be well-informed about the topics on which he was to lead discussions, as it would also have been to have expected his men to be knowledgeable about them. It was, therefore, of the very nature of ABCA that its sessions would have to be pitched at a suitably basic level.

There was another consequence of determining that all must participate in ABCA sessions. Hyperbole might suggest, as it did in Lord Eustace Percy's letter to *The Times*, that 'the British Army today is the most intelligent the world has ever seen' and that its leisure would have to be enriched by intellectual interests.[35] It was a large claim which Xenophon's *Ten Thousand* would certainly have wished to contest and it is to be regretted that Lord Eustace neglected to tell us by what standard he was judging. Hyperbole could not alter the fact that before donning uniform the soldier had not felt the need of so enriching his leisure. On the contrary, attention had been drawn to his 'abysmal ignorance'; it had been remarked how 'apathetic about education' he was; it had been stressed how little he sought to use his mind and how he desired to fill his spare time 'only with amusements that made no demands on his initiative, industry of intelligence'.[36] Now that the need, which he himself had not yet felt, to use his mind, was felt for him, a particular problem arose. The teacher of those who came willingly to sit at his feet had their cooperation to build on. But the shining morning face of the schoolboy making his reluctant way to school promised his master an easier task than that of the subaltern confronting the dour expression on the faces of pressed men. If compulsion were to be introduced it would be desirable to introduce brighter and better ways of communicating as well. These brighter and better ways must be as simple as possible and such as could be effectively employed with small groups, for ABCA sessions would be taken by the junior officer with the small group of men for whom he was responsible. The brighter and better ways were to be the ways of discussion. In ABCA sessions the junior officer was to be a chairman, not a lecturer. As chairman there were arts that he must master. He must not allow the group to wander off into irrelevance nor let it be dominated by the talkative and the obsessed. He must encourage contributions from all quarters and see that all important views were considered. He must ensure that all clearly followed the discussion, try to keep it on a logical course and sum up the ground that had been covered and the conclusions, if any, that had been reached. As chairman he would be expected to familiarise himself with the agenda, which would be made available to him in as clear and simple a form as could be contrived. It would be for him also to ensure that propaganda and party politics had no part in the proceedings.

To allay his anxieties every effort would be made to convince him that his was not the most difficult of tasks. He would be inducing others to speak and would not have to prepare monologues. His would not be the sole task of arousing interest, for his men would be speaking and they would be interested in what they and their friends had to say. In this way the mutual agony that might have resulted had he been called upon to lecture would be avoided.

It would be a mortal sin for him to seek to pull the wool over the eyes of his group. But in what was said to reconcile him to his fate the wool was, to some extent, being pulled over his own. For his was not as easy a task as was sometimes suggested. He had to discuss problems and it is the nature of problems to be obstinate, and the greater the problem the more formidable becomes the difficulty of unravelling it. What was required was the ability to define a task, the ability to analyse the problem it set, the ability to assess the priorities in tackling it, the ability to foresee and avoid the pitfalls in the way of its solution, the ability to complete the job. The discussion leader had to be aware of the relevant facts, and these, the ones that are really needed, do not introduce themselves. They are not only passive; like the Scarlet Pimpernel they have the quality of being 'dammed elusive'. We have to go looking for them. The discussion leader had to impose a plan on his material and Montgomery's comments on the General remind us of the difficulty of so doing.[37] 'He must have the ability to simplify a problem, and then to avoid becoming involved in detail ... Of course some details are important; he must be a master of essential detail without loss of vision, and able to express clearly his intentions and plans in simple language which is easy to understand. But that ability to simplify, and to select out of the mass of detail those things, and only those things, which are important, is not always easy. It needs a trained mind.' But if the task of running discussions was trickier than was acknowledged and if brilliance in doing so was rarely to be expected, the willing officer could be shown how to improve, how to strengthen his capacity to analyse, to dissect a problem and to plan a way of tackling it. Moreover, the qualities he would develop if he did so would be of great importance to him in his subsequent military or civilian career. In any case it is hardly to be doubted that discussion was indeed the brightest and best way of handling compulsory ABCA periods, so long, that is, as it was seen as a means to an end and not an end in itself.

When General Willans persuaded the Army Council that a separate small department should be set up in the War Office, under his overall control, to run ABCA he emphasised that it must be under 'an individual of special attainments and great personality, who would supply both inspiration and material'.[38] He believed that a civilian would be more imaginative than a soldier in this job and in August 1941 W. E. Williams was appointed to do it. That appointment ensured that ABCA would be formidably and imaginatively supported. ABCA bulletins, one entitled *Current Affairs*, which concerned itself with the great issues of the day, and the other entitled *War*, which dealt with the fighting fronts, appeared in alternative weeks. The first issues were published in September 1941 and in over four years, between 1941 and 1945, 118 issues appeared. More than 120,000 of each bulletin were printed. There was further help for the discussion leaders. In September 1942 the first ABCA posters were ordered; in November of that year the first copies of the monthly bulletin *Map Review*, a most helpful visual aid, appeared. Both were to supplement the topics discussed in *War* and in *Current Affairs*. Much later, in June 1944, an ABCA Play Unit was set up for the same purpose. Even before that, however, the theatre was called in to help. J. B. Priestley's *Desert Highway* was produced and sent on tour of the units, and this was followed by the staging of plays on other ABCA themes. In the autumn of 1942 an ABCA School was opened in Coleg Harlech where courses were held to train junior officers in running discussions and to win the sympathy of senior officers for ABCA. Some 4,600 officers attended residential courses lasting a week here. ABCA wings were later opened in the Army Schools of Education at Wakefield, Mt Carmel and Perugia. The Central Advisory Council and the Regional Committees helped as well. Fifteen courses, varying in length from two to three days, were held by them before the first ABCA bulletin appeared, seven of these courses being residential. During ABCA's first six months, eighty-three courses and conferences were arranged by them, forty-eight of these being residential. Such courses continued throughout the war. Some Regional Committees set up Current Affairs Enquiry Bureaus to give written replies to queries raised by discussion leaders. Nothing like this assistance had been given to the unfortunate subaltern who, in the years between the wars, had to see to the instruction of men taking the Second and Third Class Certificates; if he was now being asked to tackle a difficult job, he could not complain of being left unaided.

ABCA eschewed party politics and Scarlyn Wilson, who wrote an excellent history of the civilian contribution to Army Education, thought that while lack of knowledge or of experience on the part of the group leader may have allowed some propaganda to creep in, it was 'neither insidious nor deliberate'.[39] Yet it was the introduction of politics into the Army and since many believed with the Prime Minister that the only sound principle was to keep politics out of it, its introduction was bound to be looked at askance. The subaltern disliked it not only because it was another job for him to do but also because it was one that he did not feel up to. The majority of Commanding Officers were dubious about it and even hostile to it. Senior officers were often opposed: Montgomery begrudged the time that might have been devoted to training. Another General is said to have called ABCA 'rank treason'.[40] The AEC was divided about it too. The old hands accepted it as they would have accepted any War Office instruction; many of the new intake shared the doubts of their civilian colleagues about the desirability of allowing amateurs to tackle this job. The Board of Education and the Central Advisory Council and the Regional Committees were also worried by it. Wood, Assistant Secretary of the Board, spoke of the 'suspicion arising, and of the charges being made that the Government is trying to put over some propaganda', and Jack, of the Inspectorate, said that it was 'authoritarian in character'. The Central Advisory Council, which had not been officially consulted about it although Williams had privately spoken to Lindsay, its vice-chairman, was hostile to it, as were the Regional Committees. Like Wood, they thought that the War Office might be attempting to bypass the civilians and to embark upon its own scheme of propaganda. They feared that it might mean a decline in the help required by the Army from them. They doubted if the subalterns could do the job required of them. General Willans had to convene a special meeting of the Central Advisory Council to calm its apprehensions. He succeeded in doing so. But the civilians never liked ABCA and relations between them and the Army became more strained in consequence of its introduction.[41] Sir John Anderson, who held an enquiry into its activities on behalf of the Government, placated his lords and masters, even if he did not entirely remove their fears, by his report in which he said 'The Army Council is to be congratulated in having decided to launch it in spite of the possible dangers; and ... those responsible for this organisation have shown both initiative and restraint.'[42] The Adjutant-General soon assured himself that discipline had not been adversely affected by its introduction, not that he had ever feared that it would be; he was later to say that not one single case of indiscipline arising from ABCA sessions had come his way.[43] Critics like Montgomery withdrew their opposition and he welcomed in North Africa what he had opposed in Britain.[44] Army commanders were vocal on its behalf when its continued existence was in question. They appreciated its effect on the men and they valued its effect on the subaltern; the argument that it was an exercise in the officer's ability to handle his men, calling for judgement, coolness under stress, and the capacity never to lose control, however trying the circumstances, never lost its appeal for them.

'That man thinks much too highly, and therefore he thinks weakly, and delusively, of any contrivance of human wisdom, who believes that it can make any sort of approach to perfection', Burke tells us. No human plans remain unaltered and ABCA was not always carried out according to the book. The Central Advisory Council had feared that with its introduction would come a decline in the help required by the Army from the Regimental Committees. In fact there was a marked increase and an obvious explanation of it was that an appreciable number of Commanding Officers paraded their entire unit for one hour a week to hear civilian lecturers and called this

ABCA, a proceeding which was strictly forbidden by higher authority. In scattered anti-aircraft and searchlight unit officers were not always available to lead discussions and often NCOs were turned to instead. In a number of units, too, ABCA would simply be ignored; in many ATS units, although certainly not in all, this seems to have been the case. Nevertheless there is no doubt that ABCA 'took on'; an Army survey estimated that between 60–80% of units were conducting it with 'reasonable success'. Its budget was expanded and the Army Bureau of Current Affairs continued to expand, as did the Directorate of Army Education. A Basic ABCA was introduced into Young Soldiers' Battalions. It would hardly be too much to say that it became synonymous with Army Education during the Second World War and it is very largely attitudes to the former that determine the very difficult judgements that have to be made about the achievement of the latter.

After nearly a year of ABCA Army Education reached its wartime zenith in the Winter Scheme of 1942–1943 and in the consequent continuation of the *British Way and Purpose* hour in the following months. In April 1942 Brigadier Maude, Inspector of the AEC, outlined an extended Scheme of Education for the Army. ABCA had led the way in showing that education could be accepted as a compulsory part of training. Maude believed that the only way of enabling education to make the contribution it was capable of making to the Army was to make it a compulsory part of that indoor training which in the coming winter would have to replace outdoor exercises. He added that a compulsory educational scheme would be essential during demobilisation and that it would be sensible to make an early start on laying its foundations. He produced a wide-ranging syllabus which included English, history, geography, economics, citizenship, languages, elementary science and handwork. Men would have a choice which would have to be finally determined by the majority expression of local opinion and by instructor availability.

General Willans supported a modified form of this scheme in June, and in September the Army Council agreed that it should operate during the winter months from November 1942 to February 1943. Four hours per week were to be set aside for education in the training programme. One was to be for ABCA and the other three to attend to the needs of man as a soldier, man as a citizen and man as an individual. If these logically-arranged categories seemed designed to give the impression of a thoroughly thought-through Scheme of Education for the Army there was no great harm in that, and if they suggested a balanced and harmonious unity in its application that was not always to be found either, some concessions to spiritual pride are not to be too sharply criticised. It was in any case obvious that the compulsory nature of the Winter Scheme could not be absolute since it had to be conditional on military requirements, Army Commanders thus being free to adopt or put it aside as in their judgement seemed good. Man as soldier, it seemed, needed instruction in map-reading, message-writing, mathematics, mechanics, according to the particular requirements of his unit and the resources at its disposal to satisfy them. Man as a citizen needed to hear about Britain, how it was governed, how it conducted its affairs, its Empire and Commonwealth, its foreign policy. To express his individuality, correspondence courses were at his disposal, hobbies, handwork, lectures, brain-trusts, musical appreciation, private-reading and chess. Meditation with his eyes closed was not specifically mentioned.

It was man as a citizen that was to be the central feature of this new phase of Army Education. ABCA was once described as 'that eccentric theory according to which multiple displays of political ignorance contribute to military cohesion and efficiency'.[45] To some that definition would undoubtedly have borne the sign of the cloven hoof. But the multiple displays of political ignorance to be seen in many ABCA sessions could not be denied, whatever might be thought of their contribution to military cohesion and efficiency. As Bickersteth, who was previously in charge of the education of the Canadian Corps and who, on Bendall's retirement, replaced him as Director of Army Education,[46] noted at this time, 'many of the new intake were completely ignorant of their country's history and institutions'. A course in citizenship was thought to be essential to remedy the deficiencies revealed by ABCA. Stacks and stacks of peripheral duties had been placed upon the subaltern but it was acknowledged that the teaching of this new course would be beyond him. Where available, civilian lecturers could take on this task. However, the new scheme was not to be dependent on them. The Army would have to meet its own requirements and to enable it to do so would look to the AEC and also to whatever suitable talent the unit might find in its own ranks. Detailed briefs were to be prepared for them; these were the monthly pamphlets entitled *British Way and Purpose*, the expression by which the scheme as a whole came to be known.

There were six of these BWP handbooks, each divided into four sections, one covering each week's topic. There were also six method books accompanying them to help the untrained teacher. 1,000 libraries, each containing 400 books, were distributed throughout the Commands for reference purposes. It was a serious and consecutive course in citizenship, concentrating on Britain's political and legal system, its economy, its Empire and Commonwealth, its relations with its allies. It was thus in marked contrast to ABCA, in which there was no relationship between the topics dealt with in current affairs.[47] This Williams admitted, saying that his pamphlets represented 'no more than hedge hopping'. Lord Carrington, who found it a good idea to run discussions with his squadron, was impressed by BWP.[48] He found it less journalistic than ABCA, more informative and better structured, more coherent in its sequence of topics and much better taught.

There was an obvious difficulty attendant on this scheme and it soon made itself evident. A year of ABCA had left no doubt that the concern of the troops was with tomorrow as well as today, a concern which ABCA had done its best to promote. For to the Army Bureau of Current Affairs the war was an attempt not only to ensure that what we had we would hold but also to make what we had more worth having, and ABCA's task was not only to teach the troops what they were fighting for but to make what they were fighting for more worth fighting for. Williams expressed his faith to Lady Cripps:

> The war and the consequent peace are indivisible. We can't afford to wait until Armistice Day before getting down to the puzzles and the headaches of reconstruction.

Even though the plans for rebuilding Britain can't be fully finished in the midst of war, they can and must be sketched in outline. The vital thing is to begin discussing post-war problems now, so that we shall not prove as unprepared for peace as we were for war. There must be no moratorium of social ideas. Some timorous souls too readily seek to 'postpone consideration' of social values and social blue-prints until after the war.[49]

It was inevitable that the BWP pamphlets should reflect that concern with tomorrow, just as ABCA pamphlets did. As Major Marshall, who was closely concerned with them at the War Office at this time said, 'in them we could equip ourselves for the possibility and the desirability of change'.[50] It was equally inevitable that this would occasion dispute between those to whom change was the overriding necessity and who, therefore, wanted as much of it as possible, and those who believed that continuity was the most important element in society and who, therefore, wished to preserve as much of it as they could. Those who want as much change as possible will naturally draw attention to what in the past and the present they believe will most be in need of change. Very conscious of the inadequate lot of those who have not benefitted from the past or who are falling behind in the present, the splendour of tomorrow's dawn will accentuate for them the blackness of tonight. Asking 'for what and for whom has the world's book been gilded when all is for them but the blackness of night', they will inevitably in portraying the past make less of the gilding of the book than of the blackness of the night. Those who want as little change as possible will equally naturally draw attention to what in the past and the present they believe to be most worthy of survival. Very conscious of the great achievement of the ages, they will be less inclined to portray the past so as to compel the asking of the question.

> To be out of the moiling street
> With its welter and its sin!
> Who hath given to me this sweet?
> And given my brother dust to eat?
> And when will his wage come in?

For each his portrayal of the past will be true; to each the other's portrayal of it will be untrue. When change is least in the air this difference in looking at things will matter least; when it is most in the air it will matter most. Change was most in the air at this time and disputes, accordingly, were bound to multiply.

BWP pamphlets met with both left- and right-wing criticism, that of the right being sharper and more persistent. A suggestion that the public schools were socially divisive and that they would in all likelihood be brought into the national system of secondary education after the war brought upon itself, in particular, the adverse comments of Lord Croft.[51] Grigg shared some of Croft's doubts and allowed the BWP scheme to continue only under constant supervision. But continue it did because the Adjutant-General insisted on it doing so. Facing the prospect of a third inactive winter, coupled with the depressing effect of continued defeat in the Western Desert and in the Far East, he feared a lowering of morale in consequence. He hoped the Winter Scheme would 'act as a strong antidote', and thought that this would be especially the case if 'emphasis is laid on what we are fighting for'.[52] The Morale Committee, which the Adjutant-General had set up, came to the conclusion that he was right. Its reports for the months November 1942 to January 1943 stressed that BWP and ABCA had done much to remove ignorance and restore faith in the war effort. One senior commander maintained 'There is no question that the Winter Education Scheme has been a success and has assisted very materially in raising morale and quickening the men's interests and alertness. Even Commanding Officers who at the beginning of the period had grave doubts and little enthusiasm, admit that the results have far exceeded their expectations.' The morale argument prevailed, as it was to do later. Nevertheless, the criticisms were cumulatively important and must have had an effect on significant developments in Army Education that were to occur later in the year. They became of even greater importance when, as in this case, they were the background to a sudden flaring-up of high emotion and to a serious, if to some extent coincident, attack on Army Education.

The sudden flare-up was a consequence of the publication of the Current Affairs ABCA Bulletin No. 33 on the Beveridge Report, a pamphlet written by Beveridge himself. The Report received a great deal of publicity even before its publication; it was given favourable coverage by the Ministry of Information when it was published and it was generally assumed that it was a forecast of future policy. On that assumption it was natural that Williams wanted the troops to hear about it and he asked Beveridge to write a summary of it, which was issued to Home Forces in December 1942. It was seen somewhat cursorily by the Adjutant-General, who was going on leave. He found nothing to object to in it but instructed Williams to show it to the Secretary of State in case there might be political difficulties in publishing it. This Williams did not do and his failure to do so must mean that he is responsible for the subsequent rumpus. Rosebery, when Foreign Secretary, was determined to forward a policy in East Africa to which he knew one or two of his Cabinet colleagues would take exception and therefore, in enclosing in the little red boxes the Foreign Office telegrams and despatches which were circulated to members of the Cabinet he omitted to include the instructions given to his representatives there. The thought must occur that Williams, too, sought to overcome difficulty by giving it no opportunity to arise until the *fait accompli* removed the prospect of it doing so. When Grigg saw the bulletin it was already in the hands of the Home Forces. Williams said of Grigg that he was a man of courage and resolution and he was right. Over Williams's protests he ordered that all copies be withdrawn from circulation. The Beveridge Plan was meeting with heavy weather in Cabinet.

The Labour Ministers approved; the Conservative Ministers, and in particular Kingsley Wood, Chancellor of the Exchequer, doubted if we would be able to afford it. Grigg knew that what Beveridge had written was not yet, and might never become, official policy. It was merely one man's controversial vision of the future, for it was not at that time clear what an important and generally acclaimed reality it would become.

Williams's reaction to the Bulletin's withdrawal smacks of deliberate misunderstanding and dishonesty. He wrote to Beveridge 'I am told that the Bulletin itself is unimpeachable, but that it is not thought desirable to promote formal and organised discussions upon it until Parliament has pronounced! Perhaps they mean "Reichstag" not "Parliament".'[53] This was, to say the least of it, misleading. Beveridge had naturally not drawn attention to the criticism that might be made of his proposals or to the fact that the cost might be such that in the straightened circumstances in which we would inevitably find ourselves after the war we might not be able to afford them. And since the subaltern who had to chair the discussion could only be expected to know about the scheme what he read in the pamphlet there could be no genuine discussion but only general support of it. Abuse was no adequate answer to Viscount Cranborne's question 'If Parliament with all its experience and all its knowledge is not yet in a position to put forward considered views on the subject, how can it be expected that officers and men of the Army who have not the same background ... can as yet take a useful part in a debate on this subject?'[54]

In any case Grigg's point was not that it had not yet been debated in Parliament, but that it was not yet, and might never become, Government policy and that if it did not it would inevitably occasion party political conflict. It is inconceivable that that had not been made plain to Williams. Williams's justification for publishing it was the assumption that it was accepted policy and he must have known this was not and might never be the case.

Cripps, to whom Williams was very close, must also have told him that it would be Labour policy. So Williams must, at the very least, have been prepared to use a compulsory ABCA period to put across what he must have known might well become a party political view and to do so in such a way as to ensure that the opposing point of view could not be heard. Williams contended that the withdrawal of the pamphlet meant that the right of the soldier to take part in free and unfettered discussion was being interfered with. He was wrong. What was challenged was the right to subject him to what might become party political propaganda. When Grigg said 'The factor which principally weighed with me was the absolute necessity of keeping ABCA out of possible political controversy, particularly in view of the fact that attendance at these debates is compulsory' he was so clearly justified that, if he was to make a public reaffirmation of an important principle that had clearly been breached, he had no option but to withdraw Current Affairs Bulletin 33.[55] Williams was grossly unfair to Grigg in mocking a case to which he had no rational answer and his comparison of Grigg's behaviour with that of the Nazis was highly offensive.

But objectionable as this was, it was not so much this as a later, and much more balanced, survey of the Beveridge Plan that appeared in Current Affairs No. 45 in June 1943 that raises doubts about Williams's behaviour at this time. That bulletin was no conservative document and it emphasised that 'whatever the cost the people's health and security should be a first charge on the community'. But it contained not merely a summary of the Beveridge Report but also comments made on it in the parliamentary debates and the text of the Prime Minister's radio address to the nation in which cautionary notes were sounded on the cost of too ambitious social security schemes. Officers, too, were advised to make sure that all understood the cost of great social expectations and to draw attention to all the other needs that would demand satisfaction when the war was over. Current Affairs No. 45 displayed all the balance, all the restraint, all the impartiality so clearly lacking in Current Affairs No. 33.

Aware that he was being watched, Williams was not to be faulted. Unwatched, he was not to be trusted. Was pamphlet 33 a momentary aberration to be attributed to the enthusiasm which at times can unbalance us all? The charitable would say so; the uncharitable might have another explanation. That Williams was willing to try it on is not to be doubted. His words of July 1942 are revealing. The fears aroused when ABCA began, he said, have been allayed and we can, accordingly, move forward.[56] 'Because ABCA has dissolved such nightmares of foreboding it is now in a position to tackle themes which would have been untimely six months ago: Town Planning, the Future of the Land, Public Health.' Such discussions would necessarily involve the politics which the Army Council had decreed must not be introduced. But now, Williams seems to be thinking, we can chance our arm and ignore the Army Council. The Army Council was responsible to the Government and the Government to the people. And the question emerges: to whom was Williams accountable? Ostensibly he was responsible to the Adjutant-General but that responsibility seemed to sit lightly upon him. Yet despite the strengthening of his position after General Willans was killed in February 1943 and despite the continued development of ABCA, his influence was rapidly approaching its meridian.

A number of conclusions from this Beveridge Affair are obvious. The first is that throughout it Grigg's own view of the Beveridge Plan is irrelevant. He was not in favour of it. He wrote to Montgomery 'Unless we make up our minds for a generation of hard-work and self denial (and no Beveridge) we shall be left in the position of the Dutch after Utrecht in 1713, a third-rate nation.'[57] Nevertheless, he made no attempt to stop informal discussion of it in the Army or to forbid the circulation of summaries of it to the AEC, facts which support his contention that it was the official nature of the ABCA discussion which he found unacceptable. A second is that the view expressed by Bickersteth at the time that the withdrawal of Bulletin 33 was 'monstrous', the considered judgement later given by such a sensible and moderate woman as Mary Stocks in her *History of the Workers Educational Association* that it was a 'brainless and wholly pointless action', is patently nonsensical.[58] A third is that Grigg emerges from this episode as far more a man of principle and integrity than his contemporary critics. A fourth is that it was on a principle of fundamental importance that Grigg took his stand and that on that principle he was right to do what he did. The withdrawal of ABCA 33 was not a denial to ABCA of legitimate freedom of discussion, it was a rejection in ABCA of illegitimate advocacy. Those who condemned the withdrawal of the first issue and who were grudging in their acceptance of the second, should have condemned the publication of the first issue and been whole-hearted in their welcome of the second. They had always feared that ABCA would be used to put across a point of view yet they whole-heartedly approved this use of it. It clearly depended on the point of view being advocated. If they approved of it, advocacy was to be approved. If they disapproved of it, advocacy was to be disapproved. It is an old attitude of mind. Orthodoxy, my doxy, is an attractive young lady whom all the right-minded will revere. Heterodoxy, your doxy, is a loathsome hag, to be condemned by all but the ungodly.

A fifth conclusion is that had expediency and not principle dictated his action, Grigg would have adopted another course, that party political interest would have urged another course upon him and that he could have been under no illusion whatever about that when he did what he did. He could have contented himself with taking greater care in the future to ensure that 'the principle of keeping ABCA out of possible political controversy' was not again contravened. In that way he would have pleased those who would have agreed with Sophocles that there are times when justice produces mischief, who believed that it would have been better for this mistake to have been lived with as mistakes so often have to be, than for it to be corrected in this particular way. From the point of view of the interests of the Conservative Party they were undoubtedly right, and the episode played its very minor part in contributing to Conservative defeat at the polls later. But it was not party that dictated Grigg's action. It was principle, and if high-minded action is not always beneficial to interest, it is only the most vital of interests that can be allowed on occasion to tip the balance against principle. The Chinese have a saying 'When a neighbour is in your fruit garden inattention is the truest politeness.' But in matters more important than fruit gardens, inattention is apt not to be the truest wisdom. And those who see value in allowing political discussion in armed forces would be advised to let wisdom and not politeness dictate their behaviour.

One final conclusion is worth emphasising. Grigg must have deeply resented the position in which he had been put and in which he felt compelled to take action that he would know must harm his own party. Williams would find that there was a price to be paid in the future for that resentment.

The Morale Committee had reported in the late summer of 1942 that the troops were very interested in the prospective development of the post-war world. Grigg had not let that alter his decision to recall ABCA Bulletin 33. Indeed, far from believing that there was an argument that withdrawal of ABCA 33 would adversely affect the morale of the troops, he declared in the Commons that he wanted 'to point out the danger of any 'homes for heroes' promises to the Army before we have an authoritative statement on the prospect of being able to carry them out'. He added: 'That, I think, if anything, is calculated to destroy morale and to create difficulty here and hereafter. The making, or anything which looks like the making, of promises on insufficient ground is one of the most fatal things I can imagine.'[59] Grigg was growing sceptical about the argument so often stressed by the Adjutant-General and the Army Commanders that they had cause to be highly sensitive about the morale of the troops. He wrote to his father in April 1942 'I have been going round the troops a lot lately especially those due to go abroad. They are a good lot and their morale is a damned sight better than that of the b.f. journalists who try to frighten us about them.'[60]

Soon after the Beveridge Affair ABCA occasioned further trouble which increased Grigg's irritation with it, which added to his growing doubts about Army Education, and which must have made him still more sceptical of the argument that it was playing a vital role in raising the morale of the troops. As fertile as ever in generating new approaches that would add to ABCA popularity, the Army Bureau of Current Affairs had set up a Poster Department. It produced a poster in April 1943 entitled 'Your Britain. Fight for it Now'. It showed an obviously rickety child playing in a very dark yard. On the crumbling walls of the yard were scrawled the words 'disease' and 'neglect'. A squalid gravestone in a corner of the yard depicted 'death'. The clean lines of a Health Centre representing preventive care were etched across this scene of pre-war squalor and poverty.

That was what we had yesterday; this was what we would have tomorrow. There were those who had always feared that there might be an incompatibility between the two objectives sought by Army Education, the building of morale in the war and of the New Jerusalem after it. Those who were longing for the New Dawn were unlikely to look lovingly on the Old Night. Whether or not they made too much of the lightness of the one they might yield to the temptation of making too much of the darkness of the other. To the extent that they did that would have been an uncovenanted extra for which our enemies would have been duly grateful. But it would not have adversely affected the morale of the nation had the nation been united in its longing for New Dawn and its loathing of Old Night. That, however, was not the case. There were many who disbelieved alike in New Dawns and in the blackness of Old Night and there was the risk of undermining the unity of the nation in stressing these things too much. Extreme, moreover, will always call to extreme. If a *British Way and Purpose* publication on the Empire was heavily criticised by the Left for not spelling out in detail all its imperfections, was it not inevitable that it would be bitterly frowned upon by the Right for being insufficiently lyrical in its praises? And who can believe that morale is thereby improved? When Ernest Bevin, then Minister of Labour, saw that ABCA poster he was sure that the implication that some of the nation's children were like the boy in the picture was far more likely to lower than to raise morale.[61] Was he not right in insisting that it be withdrawn? And was not Grigg also right in thinking that there is much more to be said for the old Greek ideal of the Golden Mean than visionaries are at times prepared to admit?

He was, nevertheless, remarkably tolerant. When the executive Committee of the Army Council accepted General Adam's request that the BWP hour be continued into the spring and summer of 1943, Grigg agreed that it had done much by way of 'fortifying morale', and he supported its continuation. And although he made it clear that the pamphlets must be carefully scrutinised, saying 'We need give no further hostages to fortune' (an indication that he was well aware of having done so in the affair of ABCA 33),[62] he did not object, on the death of Willans in February 1943, to the Directorate of Army Education under Bickersteth and of ABCA under Williams becoming fully independent Directorates responsible to the Adjutant-General, something which increased the stature of both of them. He had been strongly opposed, as Willans had been, and indeed all three Armed Services, to the idea put forward by Cripps in August 1942 that a Super Bureau of Current Affairs be set up 'serving all three Armed Services, and possibly the Civil Defence Services too', but that would have given far greater independence and influence to Williams than the making of

ABCA an independent Directorate under the Adjutant-General could do.[63]

Nor did Grigg prevent an increase in the number of those working in the Army Bureau of Current Affairs, the opening of Coleg Harlech, the introduction of Basic ABCA for the Young Soldiers' Battalions and a very considerable increase in its budget for the year 1943–1944. Nevertheless he still thought that 'citizenship was being overdone' and he shared the Treasury's alarm at the rising cost of Army Education. In August 1943 its representative noted that the Director of Army Education had announced that as two-thirds of his annual budget had been spent in the first four months of the financial year he would be forced to ask for a supplementary grant. This was an Oliver Twist approach to financial management to which keepers of coffers are constitutionally averse. 'This is not', Sir Eric Speed said, 'my idea of financial control.' Supported by General Nye, the Vice-CIGS, the Adjutant-General again prevailed and BWP survived. But it was clear that from now on Grigg was increasingly inclined to listen to his Under-Secretary, Lord Croft.[64]

It was Croft who had appointed Bendall to be Director of Army Education. Williams had been considered for that position and Croft had made it clear that it was not the fact that, unlike Bendall, Williams had not served in the Army that led to his rejection then. Croft wrote later 'With the temptation before me to appoint one who is undoubtedly a very live wire my instinct told me that political trouble was inevitable if he was appointed Director, although he would be good in a subordinate position.'[65] He was to say 'I was frankly alarmed when he was made Director of ABCA.' It was obvious, too, that he distrusted Williams's influence with Adam. He referred to 'the political naivety of generals'[66] and he resented the fact that while he had appointed Bendall he had not been consulted when Bendall retired and when Bickersteth, who succeeded him, was appointed. Croft seems to have had much less confidence in Adam than in Willans, whose comment on the Cripps proposal that a Super Bureau of Current Affairs be established seems to have betrayed some suspicion of Williams. He said that ABCA was 'an immensely valuable but very simple and unofficial affair' and that if it became a 'highly complicated department' it would become 'the centre of political storms'. He added that if taken out of the hands of the War Office, 'the attitude of Commanding Officers who were starting to accept it might change and the resistance to it as something alien to the Army way of life might quickly resurface'. There is no reason why a more highly complicated department should in itself arouse political controversy; there was, however, reason to believe that a more powerful department might encourage its Director to enter upon courses which would promote political controversy and encourage the resurfacing of the initial resistance of Commanding Officers. It seems that Willans was conforming to the old military adage that it is better to base calculations on capacity rather than on intentions and that it is wiser to prevent the concentrations of power arising that might occasion offence than to wait until offence has been manifest and have to meet it then.[67]

Be that as it may, Croft became convinced that both Williams and Bickersteth were dangerous. Bickersteth was 'woolly, verbose ... up in the clouds and useless'. Both were socialists and needed watching. He believed that 'Someone in connection with Army Education is abusing his trust and is in direct contact with extreme left-wing opinion in Fleet Street.' 'The organised campaign in all left-wing newspapers', he said 'indicates concerted action based on information which can only have been supplied by someone in the War Office.'[68] It was Williams whom he suspected. In October 1942 a small War Office committee had been set up under his chairmanship to consider the role of Army Education in the period of demobilisation. He attached great importance to this but strongly urged that someone from outside, 'someone with no political prejudice but with a real knowledge of affairs', should be appointed Director-General of Army Education to keep an eye on both ABCA and the Directorate of Army Education. His recommendation was accepted, it being decided in late 1943 to create a new post in the War Office, that of Director-General of Army Education. The Director of Education for Kent, Philip Morris, was appointed to the post. Morris was a highly respected Director of Education but it was Williams who was identified with the most significant development of Army Education and who had throughout the war been so prominent in it. And whatever the tribute that Morris paid to ABCA and to BWP (in February 1944 he referred to them as being essential to the success of any demobilisation educational scheme) it is inconceivable that Williams was not mortified in being passed over once again. Grigg did not listen to Croft in all things but in this he did. Williams had been too venturesome and his influence was now in decline.[69]

There was, however, only expansion to be seen in Army Education. With the introduction of the compulsory educational scheme there was what had not been expected, an increase in voluntary educational activities in the Army too. Between April and September 1943 45,951 lectures were given and 2,185 courses on current affairs run by civilian lectures. In the peak period, the winter of 1943–1944, more than 110,000 lectures, courses and classes were arranged by the Regional Committees. They planned monthly sessions to help units deal with the monthly BWP booklets; they arranged for Mayors and Corporations to welcome groups studying local government; they even induced the Lord Chancellor and the Speaker to explain the workings of the Houses of Parliament. They had done a great deal but perhaps when Major-General Lloyd, then Director of Army Education, said at the final meeting of the Central Advisory Council that 'had it not been for the far-seeing men and women who had initiated the Central Advisory Council there would be little or no education in the Army today', he was being too generous.

That could equally have been said of the AEC. Without it there would have been little either. Believed, in the war's early days, to have been incapable of supervising the education that would have to be provided for the soldiers, it was now by common consent indispensable: that was the measure of the great improvement that had taken place in its status. Its numbers continued to increase, its strength in 1943 being 1,450 officers and NCOs. A further sixty officers and eighteen NCOs were added in the following year. The HMI's who visited the Mediterranean Area in the months December 1944 to February 1945 were greatly impressed by the activity which characterised its classes; it is that same bursting activity which is such a feature of the whole of its war work. Whether it was in the organising of travelling exhibitions, the arranging of Brains Trusts, the setting up of Information Rooms in camps, the general supervising of the arrangements made by the Regional Committees for the teaching of English to Allied soldiers in the United Kingdom, its work in hospitals (and it is not too much to claim that it was the AEC which first understood and emphasised the importance of therapeutic education there), the somewhat different kind of therapeutic education it provided in military prisons, that same activity was apparent. Its help in attending to the needs of the individual soldier remained crucial. It continued the provision of correspondence courses. It arranged crash courses in the teaching of various crafts for those of its NCOs whose interest was in this. Without its constant care that utterly remarkable interest in music which developed among the troops during the war could never have been so widespread. It must be remembered that such distinguished musicians as Fenby and Rawsthorne came into the Corps at this time. Choirs, glee clubs, madrigal groups, orchestras abounded. There were special music departments set up by ENSA in each Command. There were innumerable gramophone clubs. There were many lectures in music appreciation.

And there was Dobson and Young. They were full-time lecturers on music for the Manchester University Regional Committee. They called their lectures 'Music with a Smile'. They were very amusing and most of their critics conceded that they were a good music-hall turn, although some would have considered this too lavish praise. They held the interest of most who listened to them and most who heard them would not have hesitated to hear them again. But would they have come because they appreciated the slickness of the performance and wanted to enjoy it again, or because they had gained from it a fuller and deeper understanding of music and wanted by building on that understanding to enrich and increase it? No doubt the answer to that question is far from self-evident. One thing, nevertheless, is clear. *The Observer*, which said of them 'no lecturer ever thought more carefully about the nature of his audiences' was abundantly right.[70] It was right, too, in stressing the forethought that had gone into ensuring that the desired contact would be established with those audiences. If what was said was less arresting than the preparation which had gone into making certain that what was said would have the maximum effect, that was no doubt unfortunate. But the lesson was clear and essential all the same. The teacher must give as much thought to his audience and to his approach to it as to his subject. The older members of the AEC had always known that and practised it. Indeed, they had been more aware of it than their civilian colleagues. And if on occasion they praised Dobson and Young too highly, that may have been because this enterprising pair were drawing such remarkable attention to a truth which they themselves had always proclaimed.

And as always the work of the AEC with illiterates was outstanding. This problem of illiteracy was very familiar to members of the pre-war AEC. From 1940 onwards the Corps arranged remedial courses in the various Commands, for this was a continuous problem. The Financial Secretary to the War Office stated in December 1943 'Just under 1% of men enlisted into the Army in the last year and a half were illiterate.' In that year Basic Education Centres for illiterates were set up at which 6,225 men and 75 women had attended courses by May 1945. There is a fitting tribute to the impressive nature of that work in the *Journal* of the Corps for October

1994. 'I was amazed and filled with admiration at what I saw', a specialist visiting one of these centres said. 'Not only has the general public no knowledge of this fine work, but even informed civilian educationalists are quite unaware of the vision, the spirit, and the thoroughness with which it is being carried out by the Army Educational Corps. The results of the six week courses appear almost miraculous.' That visitor noted the difference between the intake – 'slovenly, suspicious, shy, disturbed' – and those completing the course – 'clean, smart, alert soldiers'. 'They were happy, friendly, well-mannered, well-poised and confident', he found. Practically all were able to write home. He drew attention to one of the most pronounced characteristics of Army Education, the imaginative nature of the teaching of the AEC. One of his comments is particularly worthy of attention. He wrote 'The inclusion of handicrafts of various kinds, for example, gives many men who have a deep-seated sense of failure opportunity to achieve immediate success in one direction, and this has an immediate effect on their 'emotional drive' in acquiring reading skills.'[71] Schools now pay more attention to handicrafts than used to be the case and it may be that in consequence those who have left school will think more kindly of it than once they did. At least we are now aware that we benefit ourselves but little in confining ourselves to the recognition of a problem; we need to address ourselves to it as well. Army Education was a striking reminder of that and here again we may think that the AEC was well to the fore in its tackling of the problem of how to overcome the lack of enthusiasm of the English for education.

The Corps played its full part, too, in attending to the needs of the soldier as citizen. Not everyone can run a discussion successfully but Coleg Harlech taught many to do so who would not otherwise have known how to begin and, what is equally important, implanted in young officers who attended its courses the determination at least to have a shot at doing so. The same could be said of other ABCA schools, and of Cuerdon Hall with regard to BWP, and it was the senior members of the Corps whose help to the Director of Army Education made all this possible. Williams was not over-praising them when he wrote:

> Until recently the least-regarded and least-required service in the British Army, its members endured long years of drudgery. These are the officers who now take administrative control of the new scheme and they are proving to be as capable and zealous a crowd as one could hope for. They have not been frustrated by two decades of obscurity: they recognise the difference between Army Schoolmastering of the old style and this vast new network of cultural facilities. Many of them are men of real intellectual quality and they have nothing to learn from their civilian equivalents.[72]

In 1941 the Corps ceased to be purely male, the first Educational Staff Officer being appointed to the ATS. It was an appointment in the War Office and her task was to determine the educational needs of the auxiliaries and how best to meet them. After extensive visiting she concluded that it was essential that the ATS should concentrate on national and international affairs, this in order to raise their morale and to develop in them a sense of responsibility as citizens. It was not obvious why their morale should be low nor, if it was, why it should be thought it would be raised by developing in them a sense of their responsibility as citizens. Their morale would certainly have been adversely affected had the irate ghost of Mrs Pankhurst, roused to wrath at the discovery that 70% of the intake at an ATS Training Depot did not know that women had the vote, stood at the bedside of degenerate femininity banging heads with the statutes giving it to them to remind them of the error of their ways, but presumably this was not expected to occur very widely. And the view that the best way to raise their morale was by pleasing them least was not without its oddity. The Committee, which found that many young people were abysmally ignorant about national and international affairs and were content to remain so, the women even more than the men, had not at this time published its report but it was already apparent that the auxiliaries were far more interested in the problems of individual men and women than in those of states.

The findings of the Staff Officer were what we would have expected the War Office to have expected her to find and when, as soon happened, a number of other women Education Officers were appointed, it was to this task that they primarily addressed themselves. Nor is it surprising that when ABCA came along it was decided that it 'should be invariably applied in the ATS'. Uninterested as the auxiliaries were in current affairs, the numbers of lectures they attended on them given by the Regional Committees increased eightfold between September 1941 and March 1943. But whilst it is not difficult for humanity to reconcile itself to the sufferings of others in a good cause, neither is it beyond its capacity to limit its own, truths illustrated most pleasantly by the ATS Warrant Officer who wrote:

> It was Barrack Night in the Hostel,
> The lecturer's rather a failure,
> Though he's brought a number of lantern slides
> Of business life in Australia.
> The ten back rows are quiet with sleep
> The front rows nod at their knitting.
> Whilst the officer died some months ago
> To judge by the ways she's sitting.

The writer in *The Highway* already quoted believed it eccentric to think that a genuine initiation into democratic life was possible in the Army; these well-written lines leave us in no doubt, that, if this was genuine initiation into democratic life, it would not be endured outside it.

It was always obvious that, given the at times shattering feminine practicality and realism which every married man has if not always appreciated, then at least always acknowledged, a practicality and realism that would certainly not inhibit understanding of national and international affairs if there was also interest in them (and was not Queen Elizabeth I one of our most outstanding statesmen?), a greater realism would soon emerge in ATS education. When in July 1943 ATS Sergeant Instructors were appointed and units more thoroughly canvassed, it was more difficult to ignore what the auxiliaries wanted and to insist on giving them what it was believed they needed. Courses for potential teachers and nurses were arranged; courses in 'minor household repairs' proved very popular; handicrafts were much in demand. Newnham College, Cambridge, put its resources at the disposal of those who wanted to better prepare themselves to teach the academically-inclined, whilst London District in the autumn of 1944 ran well-attended courses in home-making. Two LEA schools with good domestic science facilities and adequate accommodation were given over to those wanting instruction in domestic science and two full-time and two part-time instructors in this subject had their work cut out to cope. Mothercraft and housecraft made much more appeal than ABCA and BWP. When he heard that after sessions of ABCA the auxiliaries had asked for more fact and less discussion, Williams might well have said that this proved his case that ABCA would lead on to the demand that the essential facts be made available, and the auxiliaries might equally well have replied that they found the discussion valueless without the essential facts. All in all, however, the educational scheme for the ATS was a genuine, and on the whole successful, attempt to provide something for everyone who wanted anything; those who wanted nothing would get it when fallen in for compulsory sessions during which they could quietly doze. It no doubt played its part in strengthening the insistence of British women in the post-war years that they had a greater contribution to make to British society, and must be given greater opportunity to make it, than it had ever hitherto been thought possible, or even desirable, for them to do.

'If the world were good for nothing else', Hazlitt tells us, 'it is a fine subject for speculation.' The same might be said of such an immensely variegated mosaic of activity as Army Education in embattled Britain. It was, however, a particular speculation that produced it, the speculation that at a time when the RAF was fully stretched in fighting and winning the Battle of Britain and the Royal Navy the Battle of the Atlantic, and the Army, inactive at home, was training and endlessly training and was suffering from the humiliating and shattering defeats of many of the troops it had sent overseas, extraordinary measures had to be taken to keep it in good heart to go up against an enemy who seemed to be carrying all before him and whose overthrow could only be seen by the eye of faith. Those extraordinary measures appear to have been remarkably well adapted to the situation in which that Army found itself. More must be said about them and not a little against them. But if they were indeed as well adapted to great and greatly pressing needs as seems to have been the case, their importance is unquestioned. They played their part in transforming embattled Britain into Britain victorious.

CHAPTER 6

EDUCATION IN THE ARMIES OVERSEAS IN THE SECOND WORLD WAR

It had always been understood that the Army Education Scheme was not intended for Home Forces only but would apply to troops overseas, at least so far as active service conditions allowed. It was for this reason that it had been insisted so strongly that the Army must 'live of its own', be responsible for its own education, which it could take with it into the war zones, where circumstances permitted. Yet in August 1941, by which time most of the AEC had returned from cipher work to its educational duties, it was a woefully small body of men[1] and only 60 of its officers and 162 of its NCOs were serving abroad, the majority of these being in India. Even when the Corps increased its numbers they were widely scattered and comparatively lonely in consequence. They were to be found in all areas thought at risk. Thus there were small Army stations often in very isolated conditions in the Hebrides, the Orkneys, the Shetlands, the Faroes and Iceland; in even remoter areas such as the Falklands; and in more populous and pleasanter places like the West Indies. There was a larger garrison in Gibraltar, where it was hoped that the effects of the Spanish Civil War and of absolute dependence on sea-borne necessities would keep Spain neutral, but where it was feared that the desire for Gibraltar and Fascist sympathies would push Franco into action.

Where the troops were, they were served by the AEC. Thus in December 1940 a small AEC team was sent to Iceland, where it soon embarked upon what was to be one of the commonest of AEC war-roles, the production of newspapers – in this case the *Midnight Sun* and the *Arctic Times*. Here, in an isolated community which offered little recreation to the troops and where anticipated German attacks did not come, boredom might have been expected to lessen resistance to education. Much substantial educational work was done, the Senior AEC officer said. But, when in later years he recalled his service there, it was not the opportunity Army Education had that impressed him but the failure to make the most of it. 'Broadly speaking', he wrote, 'the Commanding Officers did not value the war-time education schemes.' 'Education was always a side-line, an extra, at best a tedious duty, at worst a confounded nuisance, sullenly performed out of fear of the General's cross-examination', he wrote. 'The belief', he added, 'that education was essential to maintaining the morale of the troops made no appeal.' Though one of them at least could not be thought to be typical of Commanding Officers at this time. There could have been few as indifferent to the morale of their troops as he was. He asked what was the point of educating those who were all going to be killed anyhow?[2]

There was naturally a larger AEC presence in Gibraltar. Here was a small tightly-knit community in a very restricted area, something which provided an excellent opportunity for education. When the war began the AEC stationed there, one officer and seven NCOs, were transferred to cipher work, but they continued to help with the production of *The Rock*, the very popular garrison magazine. They returned to their own work in 1941 with the adoption of the Haining Scheme. Soon 400 officers and men were attending voluntary evening classes. By 1944 there were over 11,000 at such classes. Correspondence courses were much in demand and regular examinations were held for the London University matriculation, the acquisition of which was essential for those who wished to proceed to that University's external degree. Unfortunately, hot heads grew hotter in the Mediterranean sun, as at the other end of the Mediterranean was demonstrated to Goebbel's great delight in the affair of the Cairo Parliament. When Professor Guy Chapman attended the induction course into the Corps at the Army School of Education in Wakefield he found himself in the company of 'a few ardent revolutionaries, young dons eager to air in the ranks the clichés of Left Book Club publications'.[3] Some found their way to Gibraltar where they were said to be 'endeavouring to encourage controversy' by publishing a Forces newspaper which carried a lively political commentary.[4]

At the eastern end of the Mediterranean perhaps nothing more typifies the splendidly solid work done by the AEC than the charmingly named 'Candlelight Cottage' in the Lebanon. This was one of the most outstandingly successful of educational centres. It was on the main shopping street of Tripoli, right on the beaten track. The wife of the local vice-consul started a fund for its furnishing. The Forces themselves decorated it and this they did with a taste not to be seen in the Junior Combination Room of any Oxbridge College. Membership was not free – one shilling a month was charged for what was truly seen as a privilege. Weekly discussion groups met under the title of 'The House of Common Sense': they were reported in the local press, they caused no offence, they were a fine tribute to the AEC instructor who conceived the idea and who was the presiding genius over 'Candlelight Cottage'. No better tribute could be paid to him than that paid by the representatives of the three radically opposed religious bodies, Orthodox, Maronite and Muslim, when they asked that the club be run by the British authorities after the war as a social and educational centre for Tripoli youth.[5]

It was not of course this that caught the eye of Goebbels when he proclaimed that the British Army in the eastern Mediterranean had mutinied. He shared the regard for truth of his lord and master and he was in the business of making mountains out of mole-hills. But the particular mole-hill to which he was referring when he made his claim was not a figment of his imagination. Sir Ronald Adam, the Adjutant-General, said that no threat to discipline had developed as the result of an ABCA discussion.[6] He could not have said that of Army Education as a whole, for in Cairo in January 1944 it produced such a threat. A popular servicemen's club there, attractive because of its musical evenings, set up a discussion group, under the name of 'Thinking Aloud'. The inclusion on its directing committee of Major Gilbert Hall promised that its thinking would be loud enough to be heard. Prompted no doubt by that deep understanding of the heart of the soldier to which he had already drawn attention, Hall seems to have looked upon himself as a modern John Wilkes, gaily challenging authority on behalf of the perpetually oppressed. The executive committee of the discussion group, which contained such stalwart representatives of the committed

Left as Leo Abse, came to the conclusion that the most appropriate place for it to do its thinking aloud would be in its own Parliament. It thought it could find no finer model than the Westminster Parliament and to resemble it as closely as possible it must hold its own general election, as a result of which Government and Opposition would be established. It followed, too, that debate in the Cairo Parliament would be on party political lines. Oddly enough the approval of the area educational authorities was requested and even more oddly, in view of the fact that Gilbert Hall was associated with it, it was forthcoming. An overwhelming Labour Government was returned and presented its programme which was never, however, debated as the Army Commander became alarmed at the attention it was attracting, the Germans saying that the troops on the Nile were mutinying. King's Regulations forbade political activity in the Army and that what was happening was political seemed to admit of no doubt. Accordingly, the Area Commander informed the Parliament that it could no longer call itself such. It would also have to 'spy strangers' and exclude them when civilians were present. No reporting of its proceedings could be allowed; its meetings were to be supervised by the AEC. Those present liked it no more than Queen Elizabeth I's faithful Commons did when she caused the Lord Keeper to inform them,

> For liberty of speech Her Majesty Commandeth me to tell you that to say yea or nay to bills, God forbid that any man should be restrained or afraid to speak according to his best liking, with some short declaration of his reason therein, and therein to have a free voice ... not, as some suppose, to speak there of all causes as him listeth, and to frame a form of religion or a state of government as to their idle brains shall seem meetest. She saith no king fit for his state will suffer such absurdities.[7]

They liked it still less when the GOC British Troops in Egypt imposed further regulations and Hall, speaking on behalf of the executive committee, refused to accept them. This was indeed a *cause celèbre* and Hall tried to make the most of it by rallying support in the Westminster Parliament. He failed, as he was bound to fail when the politics, to the intrusion of which into the Army a blind eye had hitherto been turned, took this blatantly party political form. But it was difficult to deny that when there is genuinely free discussion politics must, sooner or later, become party politics and if this particular manifestation of them in Cairo came to an end, as did Hall's military career, since his resignation was demanded, Parliaments and debates and elections, all necessarily producing division along party lines, cropped up elsewhere in the following months. But when the fighting was over, for the most part the Army tolerated them with what grace it could, sensibly concluding then that the price of doing so would prove less than the cost of suppressing them. But it would be a mistake to believe that those who had looked with disfavour on the introduction of politics into the Army in the first place had not observed what was happening. Perhaps what was most to be regretted about this episode was the necessity of having to end it in this very public way. For the difficulty eventually created could easily be foreseen. It was apparent from the newspapers to which the troops most readily turned as well as from every survey of education in the Army, that change was in the air and that a fairer and finer world was being looked for at the ending of hostilities. That being clear, it was equally evident that what was associated with the status quo of 1939 was unlikely to be hailed, in any mock election, with much favour. The Conservative Party, prominent in the Coalition Government, was so associated and while the Prime Minister had not been, he was associated with the Conservative Party. If mock elections were to be held on a party political basis (and on what other could they be?) few could doubt the outcome. And in the midst of a bitter war in which the Prime Minister was indistinguishable from the British war effort, was it not the most arrant folly to allow a situation to develop in which British soldiers would be expressing what was bound to be interpreted as a vote of no confidence in their war leader? What army in its senses would willingly give such a fillip to its enemies? This Cairo Parliament was important at the time and it is significant for us because it draws our attention to a small but disturbing element that was always present in Army Education during the war.[8]

Insignificant as that element was, even on the Nile, it was completely absent in educational activities further east. Colonel Russell Jones had been in charge of education in the British and Indian Armies in India when war broke out. He became on mobilisation Chief Censor for India and on top of this Director of Army Cinematography. Obviously at this time it was not thought that education would occupy much of his attention. In fact it was soon to do and to necessitate the recall of the AEC to its proper task. Two things made this the case. One was the decision to cut the time devoted to training Indian recruits by half. Unfortunately it was not possible to cut by half the time required to make men literate, and a semi-literate man is not of much greater use to his unit than a wholly illiterate soldier. The second was the great expansion of the Indian Army, nearly two million sepoys now being enrolled. The overriding necessity created by both of these developments was the reduction of illiteracy among the troops so that they could at least communicate with each other in a *lingua franca*, whether it be Roman-script Urdu or English. To enable this to be done the School at Belgaum was enlarged and four regional schools set up. Every graduate teacher who could be spared was attached to the Army, which by 1942 had found 3,000 new instructors and which planned to train a similar number every year. General Tuker underlined the urgency of this problem of illiteracy when he said that some of his Indian battalions were unable to form Intelligence or Signals Sections, or even run an Orderly Room, and he told the AEC sent to help that he depended on them to get his men back into the 8th Army in time for the on-coming battle, something which could not be done until they could communicate with the British battalions on their flanks.[9] The Indian Army certificates were retained as they were of use in selection for promotion and were a significant incentive to the sepoy to apply himself. The Indian Army Special and First Class syllabuses and examinations remained unaltered, as did the examination in the English Language, these being essential for selection to commissioned rank. The syllabuses for the Second and Third Class Indian Army certificates were, however, made less demanding.

Like Tuker, Auchinleck attached the greatest importance to the education of the Indian soldier. He wrote to Wavell 'I think this is of great importance and I hope you will impress it on the Viceroy.'[10] As a result, a Directorate of Welfare and Amenities, a body concerned with both British and Indian troops, was established under the Adjutant-General. In it was an education section, to be known as Welfare Education, the task of which was to explain the issues of the war and to provide information about resettlement plans and about post-war planning in general. It was to produce pamphlets and to introduce group discussion. Only one AEC officer could be spared for this task, all other AEC personnel being engaged in language teaching. He was later joined by other AEC officers from Britain and together they published pamphlets, entitled *Current Affairs* and *Winning the Peace*. The *Map Review*, familiar to the Home Forces, became so popular that it had to be published in Urdu. An *Illustrated Review* was also published in Urdu, Roman Urdu, Hindi, Tamil and Telugu. The sepoy took to discussion at least as well as, and probably better than, the British soldier, for discussion groups were an age-old feature of Indian village life. The citizenship topics introduced on Indian radio by the speaker calling himself Captain T.O. Morrow attracted much interest.[11]

It remained true, however, that language teaching was of most importance to the Indian Army. The Generals wanted it to improve military efficiency and when Auchinleck was GOC-in-C, Middle East, he was anxious that this be continued for his men in Egypt, Syria, the Sudan, Iraq and Persia. Accordingly, an Education Officer was added to the staff of Middle East Command and three educational teams, comprising a British officer, a subadar and four *jemadars* (NCOs) were sent there in June 1942 to act as mobile schools for the training of instructors. The sepoy wanted to improve his job prospects on leaving the Colours. Given this importance attached to it, it is not surprising that in an Indian battalion it was usually the second-in-command who was responsible for educational training, a job in British units normally given to a junior officer.

Auchinleck regarded Roman Urdu as a great achievement. Nevertheless, the Indian Army found it inadequate when the great issue of resettlement had to be tackled. The Indian Army then concluded that it would after all be better to teach the men to read the vernacular scripts. There was no standardised method of teaching these and each unit found its own way of doing so. Things were in consequence somewhat chaotic. Nevertheless it was determined that no-one could attempt advanced academic work until literate in his own vernacular, and as the learning of English, which was greatly prized because of its commercial value, was regarded as advanced academic work, there was a great deal of inducement for the sepoy to master the script of his own particular tongue. It was for the AEC to deal with these problems and it did so as triumphantly as it had coped with similar linguistic differences in South-East Asia in the days of peace. Auchlineck was not exaggerating when he said 'The work of the AEC has borne fruit a hundredfold, and in the armies of India and Pakistan today has made possible standards of efficiency undreamt of in 1914.'

When the war began the certificates, which it had been the main work of the AEC with the British Army in India to help the troops to acquire, were suspended. Then when the Haining scheme was adopted in the Home Forces it was made applicable to British troops in India, Ceylon and Burma. From the units themselves and from the civilian community, panels of lecturers were drawn up. In June 1941 proficiency certificates were introduced to replace the old and now suspended British Army certificates. The new certificates – known as the Third, Second and First Class Proficiency Certificates, India – required proficiency in English, maths and map-reading. ABCA and BWP were introduced for the British troops in India, too, and a Current Affairs School was set up at Ranchi in the foothills of the Himalayas. There was an interesting development in ABCA and BWP sessions for the British troops in South Asia at this time. The pamphlets were briefly, simply and colloquially written and given to the men to read. Platoon commanders were given an *Instructor's Guide*, which suggested the lines on which the discussion might be run. We are told that 'these discussions are in consequence more lively, informed and sustained than their counterparts in British units serving anywhere else'.[12]

In Burma, too, before the Japanese attack, the AEC was trying to carry on its pre-war work, although with the outbreak of war the teaching and examining for the certificates came to an end. As in India, the education of native troops had become very important, although AEC strength in the country was so ludicrously inadequate (in 1939 one officer and two instructors were there) that it could not be properly attended to. When Burma was separated from India in 1937 the native troops there, the Burma Rifles, had no further interest in Urdu. It was not expected that they would be serving side by side with Indian battalions with which they would need to communicate. It was accordingly decided that the training of the Burma Rifles should begin in Burmese and then be continued in English. Just as the AEC had to Romanise Urdu and then write text-books in it, so now they had to produce text-books and new examinations in Burmese. To help them tackle their new work a School of Education was established, all this, however, being ended by the Japanese invasion of 1941.

It was not until January 1944 that the AEC returned to Burma. Here they were responsible, as in other battle areas, for the dissemination of news. How much this was appreciated was made evident during the siege of Imphal when a telegram was received at the HQ of the 14th Army asking for an education officer to be flown in. He published the first daily newssheet in this theatre, the very popular *Manipur Mail*. When the 14th Army began its drive down Burma the first number of the *Jungle Times* was published in the Kabaw Valley and it continued to appear until with the occupation of Rangoon it changed its name and became *The Burma Star*. This continued to appear until it was replaced by the daily newspaper *SEAC* which was published by South-East Asia Command and which was dropped every day throughout the remaining Burma campaign to the troops in the field.[13]

AEC activities in Burma soon diversified as the situation allowed and newspaper publishers became organisers of Brain Trusts, quizzes and classical concerts. As in the Middle East they set up Army Study Centres. And with the happy sense of the appropriate that seems second nature to the British soldier, a highly acclaimed recording of *The Mikado* was played under a brilliant tropical moon amidst the ruins of a monastery destroyed by his troops as their contribution to the occasion. So highly was education valued by the sepoy that there were many times when he insisted on working, and on being examined, for the coveted certificates, despite the often appalling conditions of the campaign. So Viceroy Commissioned Officers would visit the forward units and teach Urdu while the AEC instructor would conduct English classes with the more advanced soldiers, varying this with discussing the news and other topics with neighbouring British units.

From October 1943 there was also an increased AEC establishment in Africa. Here again the AEC was widely scattered and very thin on the ground. Apart from those in Khartoum there was only one AEC officer and one instructor in tropical Africa, these being in Sierra Leone. West Africa contributed two divisions to the 14th Army but the task of preparing the West African Frontier Force for this job was so demanding that there was no time to allot to its educational training. It had been decided in 1940 that English should replace Hausa as the language in which the troops must learn to communicate with each other. As AEC instructors could not be found for this task it was entrusted to civilian African teachers. Unfortunately it proved beyond their capacity and the GOC-in-C called the results truly appalling. This was itself an acid commentary on the totally inadequate numbers of the Corps then available.[14]

But if there was little effective educational training in West Africa, more was done in East Africa. The East Africa Command also sent troops overseas. They also spoke many different languages and dialects. In November 1941 General Sir William Platt, drawing on his experience of the earlier campaigns in Eritrea and Somaliland, produced a compulsory educational scheme. He wanted all the askaris to master Swahili and the British officers and men who were training them to master it too, and to have an inkling also of the background and culture of the askaris. The scheme was to be run by a Directorate of Welfare and Education. In 1943 an East African Education Corps was established to serve both branches of the Directorate. It reached an eventual strength of fifty British officers, and twenty-five British and 800 African instructors. It set up a School of Education, which was also its depot, at Kabete. Here Europeans were taught Swahili and learned something of African ways; Africans were taught Swahili, basic English, map-reading, geography, arithmetic and an elementary course in citizenship known as 'Land and Home Betterment'. *Askari*, a weekly newspaper giving war and general news, was also published by the Corps. The interest of the askari in education was as pronounced as was that of the sepoy and it well justified the greatly increased AEC presence in East Africa.[15]

It was, however, in the active theatres of war that the most impressive work of the AEC overseas was done. In embattled Malta the AEC provided the cipher staff; it maintained a news service for the island and it coped at the same time with a wide-spread demand for voluntary evening classes. Yet for twenty-seven months, from June 1940 to September 1942, Malta was under daily bombardment. Soon a very important new duty was added to its many tasks. In June 1941 conscription was introduced into the island. Since half the population could neither read nor write this meant that a large number of illiterate recruits had to be coped with. It was decided that every soldier must have some English and that a general scholastic background should be provided for the ablest of the recruits who could benefit from it. It was this job to which the AEC now had to address itself and, accustomed to tackling illiteracy, it did so with remarkable success.[16]

It was as active in the Middle East, a most elastic area, it seemed, in the Second World War since it was understood to include places not hitherto thought of as being part of it. It was seen as an extensive area covering Egypt, the Sudan, Palestine, Syria, Iraq, Cyrenaica, Libya and Cyprus. In such a widely scattered area there were in the war's early days only one AEC officer and two instructors to every 10,000 troops. Fortunately the Corps' presence was soon to be strengthened there. In the autumn of 1942 a small AEC team was attached to the 8th Army. Small Education Centres were opened in Tobruk and Benghazi. Not until Tripoli was taken, however, did a full educational scheme develop. Nevertheless, one month before the Battle of Alamein 6,000 soldiers were attending classes. A Middle East School of Education was opened in June 1942, its function being to train Unit Education Officers and newly-transferred members of the Corps. It was not to be compared with the Middle East Army School of Education which was established in June 1944 in Beirut: it was very small, its staff numbering only four. It was peripatetic, moving with the troops and its lecturers serving their needs as opportunity offered. But it was no unworthy predecessor of the later and larger School in Beirut. Early in 1943 an AEC contingent of fifteen officers and forty-three instructors landed at Algiers. They looked after static troops, hospitals and military prisons and two teams, each of four instructors, were constantly on the move not only in the 8th Army but also in the 1st. They brought the news to many who had not heard it since coming to Africa and they were greatly appreciated. As soon as conditions permitted visits were arranged to the ruins of Roman cities, to the markets of Tunis and to the holy places of Kaironan. It was their policy to push forward as far as possible. They had their centres at base and they got together Command, Area, Sub-Area and Centre libraries. But they did not remain at base or on the lines of communication and in consequence they suffered casualties in the battle areas. There is little doubt that the news-hungry men greatly appreciated their efforts.[17]

One of the most arresting things about the activity of the Corps in North Africa is the demonstration it provided that education could be mobile and could keep up with the troops. But this was the result of individual initiative and it was on the Italian Front that there was made the first organised attempt in any theatre of war to carry out 'information work' in forward areas. There, from November 1943, the AEC played a forward role with the troops in action. It gave talks on the military situation based on information supplied by intelligence and these were greatly welcomed. As one AEC officer put it 'We had to learn the art of carrying our education, snail-like, on our backs.' 'The newly-arrived officers from England', he added, 'have been agreeably surprised at the welcome they have received, and it has not taken them long to realise that here, under really active conditions, Education has quite definitely a contribution to make towards the common end.'[18] Education was arranged, too, for the Line of Communications troops. With the capture of Rome in June 1944 the AEC provided guide services and courses in the University of Rome on 'The historical background of Roman civilisation'. These were attended by over 1,000 students. Literary and Debating Societies were organised, as was a Drama Festival. Information rooms were opened, discussion groups set up. There was an educational centre, too, that by the end of hostilities had its own laboratories, technical drawing-office and automobile engineering workshops. Considerable numbers of Italian teachers taught Italian to the troops and lecturers were brought in from the Hebrew University in Jerusalem and the American University in Beirut. Above all there was the great interest the troops displayed in music and the opera. 'The British soldier in Italy', it was said at this time, 'has shown a love – not always informed, but what matters that? – for fine music well-played, which has astonished everyone.' One wonders what Buffcoat, that much-admired Cromwellian soldier who knew what he was fighting for and who loved what he knew, would have made of the opera? Brimstone came readily to his nostrils when he thought of the theatre and he would probably not have been at his most tolerant when contemplating the theatre in Rome. But *autres temps, autres mœurs*, and if his 20th Century counterpart fell beneath his standards in some things, that counterpart knew as well as he did how to make the most of the leisure left him by the enemy and by the Sergeant-Major.

It was on D-Day that the war reached its climax. All the experience culled from all the Fronts had gone into the preparation for and mounting of the invasion of Europe. Here, too, the AEC had its role, which was 'to see that general information circulates at all times'. The main means of information available to the troops was to be the local broadsheet. Every formation, from Sub-Area to Army, was to have its own writing team to produce and distribute these. There were 40 AEC officers and 134 instructors with the initial invading force, the numbers later being increased. Harassed marshals in the sealed invasion areas did not at first know what to do with them but their ability to cope with welfare needs soon altered that. When baths were unavailable they provided them; when baccy was in short supply they found ways of ending the scarcity; with or without the rod of Moses they saw to it that beer continued to flow. Marlborough had never neglected the boots and bellies of his men and it seems to have been something of a surprise when it was found that the AEC was capable of appreciating the importance of these things too. And whatever we think of the admonition that malt does more than Milton can to reconcile God's ways to man, it seems abundantly clear that excellence in the provision of welfare won a respect that nothing else at that time could have done and made it easier for more genuinely educational work to be respected later.[19]

There was a rehearsal of news-sheet production at every large pre-invasion exercise. Unexpected technical hazards were encountered. 'The wireless set or the batteries refused to work. In the summer the duplicating ink ran liquid and in the winter it froze. Paper got damp and would not run through the duplicator. Overwork persuaded the duplicator to abandon its task.' But practice bred the ingenuity to overcome difficulties. As Colonel McGowan said 'We did a job devoid of glamour in vividly exciting circumstances and it was a job of the first importance.'[20]

There were various names given to the news-sheets, *The Triangle*, *The Spearhead*, *The Corps Courier*, *Pegasus Goes To It*, *The News*, *The White Knight*, *The Red Dragon*, *The Tam O'Shanter*, *The Polar Bear*. They all had their own individuality. Those responsible for their production emphasised that it was 'essential that they should not be uniform in type, but that they should suit the needs of the particular formations and should reveal the individualities of the Staff Officers producing them'. It was said that they 'should do much more than give a summary of news from all the theatres of war, together with news from home'. 'There is room for editorials, interpretation of the news, items of local interest and announcements', it was said. 'In addition, material supplied by captured enemy documents has proved to be of great interest to all ranks, as have, too, local items of an historic and geographical nature.'[21]

Here again is to be seen the hard work, the imagination, the elasticity of mind, the individual initiative which was such a marked characteristic of Army Education and of the AEC at this time. Here again is to be seen the keeping up with the troops in the forward areas that had become standard practice. And of course as soon as possible Education Centres were established, as at Antwerp, Lille, Ostend, Ghent, Bruges and Brussels. Arrangements were soon made, too, for local civilians to teach languages and to give lectures. Altogether such manifold activity can leave us in no doubt that by the end of the war the AEC had found for itself a far more important war role than had been planned for it at the beginning.

At the beginning of its life it was decided that the AEC should go where the troops went. It accompanied them on troopships and, willy-nilly, it was with them in POW camps. The troopship might, on the one hand, appear the instructor's dream, some thousands of troops with ample leisure and few competing distractions, ready to respond to any educational activity suggested. On the other hand it might seem an instructor's nightmare for there were no books, no materials and the only accommodation a small patch of uneasily shifting deck. Yet these were the conditions that called forth all those qualities of improvisation on which both the British Army and the AEC rightly prided themselves. Lectures, discussions and quizzes were held during the morning 'stand-to' period, followed by a variety of voluntary activities including a recital of classical gramophone records on one troopship, which proved so popular that scores had to be turned away. A weekly magazine was often produced and essay competitions arranged. There were forty-two entries for one such prize and we are told that 'the standard of essay entries was of an astonishingly high level'.[22]

Nowhere did the British soldier pursue his studies with more zeal than in the POW camps, where the conditions for such study were always difficult and sometimes, it might have been thought, impossible. At first, except possibly in Changi in its very early days, every material thing considered necessary for organised education was lacking in the camps; the scarcity of food tended to reduce mental efficiency, as did the depressing psychological effect of life in a community totally deprived of news and a monotonous routine which seemed likely to continue indefinitely. Yet there were compensating factors. To escape the boredom many prisoners were willing to embark on a course of study and some of the younger ones were keen to use their enforced leisure to improve their qualifications and thus their job prospects when they finally returned home. Most of the camps contained men who were qualified in a wide variety of subjects which they could usefully impart to their colleagues. All that was needed was someone to improvise the material means to at least partially satisfy these demands, to search for potential instructors and generally to organise things. In July 1944 British POWs were held in more than fifty camps in Europe and in Asia, and in many of them the need produced the man; if there was an AEC man in the camp he did the job. One such person was Warrant Officer G. M. Wright, who was awarded the MBE for his work in Stalag 383, a camp of over 5,000 men. There were lawyers, bankers, accountants, farmers, gold miners, lumber-jacks, even safe-crackers and burglars – the services of these latter being it is to be hoped devoted exclusively to teaching the members of the escape club. There were no fewer than 2,500 students and over 130 instructors, a most impressive achievement.[23]

Difficult as conditions were for POWs in European camps, they were infinitely worse for those who fell into Japanese hands, for the Japanese adopted a policy of physical maltreatment of their captives which resulted in what they were seeking, a wholesale mortality among them. For a supposedly civilised and cultured people, the behaviour of the Japanese in war was barbaric in the extreme and whatever the meaning they attached to the conception of *Bushido*, the way or behaviour of the *bushi* or warrior, it soon became apparent that their army was totally lacking in honour in an western sense of the word. After the fall of Singapore some 50,000 British and Australian prisoners were crowded into the British cantonment of Changi, which had been built to house some 8,000 troops. After an initial period of uncertainty and apathy there was set up here what was called Southern Area College. At its peak, it included seven Faculties (Arts, Mathematics, Science, Architecture, Engineering, Law, Theology). 1,500 men sought to enrol but this number could not be coped with and only men under twenty-five who had been attending or who were about to go to University before enlisting were accepted. Another College, the 18th Division College, was set up too, the standard aimed at here being very much lower. Then the Japanese began sending drafts to their notorious working camps and with the decline of the numbers remaining in Changi education declined there too. At the camps for men working on the Burma–Siam Railway education was forbidden. It was, the Japanese knew, a means of maintaining the morale of the prisoners which they were determined to destroy. It went on despite efforts to prevent it and it can be truly said that 'its effect in sustaining morale among the prisoners, especially towards the end, cannot be exaggerated'. It was pointed out with reference to POW camps all over that 'it is interesting to note that some of the men who had no interest in Education were the first to go to pieces when all contact with the outside world was barred'.[24]

There are difficulties, as the British well knew, in the fashioning of large and powerful armies in the shortest possible time. There are easier tasks, as they were also aware, than demobilising them in such a way as to create the minimum of friction and fuss. They had looked to education to help them in the one; they were similarly to turn to it for assistance in the other. As soon as it became obvious to them that the beginning of the end was approaching, they began hammering out what was called the Release Educational Scheme. It was a much more impressive and professional job than the arrangements made during the demobilisation period that followed the First World War and it demonstrates how easy it is to underestimate the administrative ability of the British when they apply themselves to these matters. But before describing it and what became of it, a much more difficult task must be attempted. We have seen how tremendous was the range, how throbbing the vitality, of Army Education during the war. We have seen the careful and imaginative planning that went into it and we have also seen how, like Topsy, it just growed to meet emerging needs. We have underlined the great hopes that it generated and the great claims that were made for it. And difficult as the task is, since the unquantifiable is not to be quantified, an answer must be sought to the questions 'What did it all amount to?' 'How realistic were these hopes, how justified these claims?' It is to these questions that we must now address ourselves, difficult as they are to answer and humbled as we must be by the conviction that fraud lurks in loose generalities.

CHAPTER 7

ARMY EDUCATION IN THE SECOND WORLD WAR: AN ASSESSMENT

By 1945 Army Education was giving rise to increasing uneasiness, but far more impressive than the doubts then expressed was the strength of the confident belief that it had been outstandingly successful. The Secretary of State of War spoke of its 'broad and successful path'. Contributors to a later BBC broadcast on ABCA referred to 'the millions subjected to military education at state expense' and claimed that '60% of units gave it as their impression that it was effective'. An Army survey suggested that the rate of success might be as high as 80%. W. E. Williams was more cautious, saying that Army Education, in his experience, was never more than 50% 'effective'. He added that when it became more ambitious it over-reached itself and became unworkable; when it was most improvised and portable, it came nearer to achieving expectations.[1]

We can agree that what was being attempted during the war in Army Education had never before been tried, the adult education of a great mass of the people. Can we also agree that the success of the attempt was as astonishing as the attempt itself? Did it achieve its objectives? Did it justify the considerable time and effort put into it? Can it still be accounted a success when we consider not just its immediate but its less immediate consequences too?

Some questions are such, Dr Johnson told Boswell, as to make a man want to go out and hang himself. Others, while not having that deplorable effect, must make us wonder whether they can ever be answered. It would certainly tax the wit of any man to provide a definitive answer to the question 'was this great scheme of Army Education successful?' Perhaps the best that can be said of examinations is to apply to them Churchill's famous comment on democracy and call them the worst way of judging things except any we have ever thought of. We accept them as a reasonably but certainly not absolutely verifiable and objective way of assessment, in the knowledge that in their absence we would not even have that. There can be no way of assessing the precise value of any form of education and least of all of those forms of education which do not aim at the passing of a particular examination. The most that can be hoped for is that conclusions come to will carry a little more weight than that reached by the man numbering a cloud of mosquitos who counted until he was tired and then estimated. Nevertheless, whatever judgements are come to must remain in the category of subjective guesstimates and cannot hope to find a place in that of verifiable and objective assessments.

How could it be otherwise given the vast variety of educational activity in the Army, the manifest local differences, the nature of much of the 'evidence' and, not least, the very different standards according to which measurements were made? We must remember that no official returns of ABCA sessions were called for. This was intended to emphasise and to maximise the informality of ABCA discussions, but it would be naive not to acknowledge that it would maximise, too, the temptation of the more heavily burdened, or less conscientious, units to be a little less than punctilious in their ABCA returns. Even when we have no doubt that ABCA discussions were held, how are we to judge of their success? Education, Curtis, the RAF's first educational adviser, emphasised 'endeavours to disabuse minds of the idea that a statement is necessarily true because it appears in print or is repeated sufficiently often. It tries to develop ... a habit of forming an opinion for themselves on the real facts of the case.'[2] Yet we often have to form opinions without knowing all 'the real facts of the case'. States do, too, for despite the existence of diplomatists, journalists and spies they can never know all that other states intend. All that can be hoped for is that sufficient of the real facts of the case can be known to make an opinion worth having. And the great problem that ABCA confronts us with is this: could enough of the real facts of the case be culled from ABCA Bulletins and from the odd facts that might be deeply buried in the sub-consciousness of individual members of the group, and that might be brought to the surface by the subsequent group discussion, to enable a genuinely educated opinion to be generated? This would clearly depend on the nature of the problem being discussed and on the nature of the group discussing it. We know what were the problems that were discussed; some were such as to suggest to us that the answer to our question would be more likely 'no' than 'yes' and others that we would expect to be able to answer 'yes' rather than 'no'. But since the nature of the ABCA group remains an unknown variable, the only safe conclusion we can reach is that it is impossible to reach a conclusion.

There is something else that we cannot know either. Even if we thought that ABCA discussions could not give us enough of the real facts of the case we might still believe that they were valuable because they developed things that were worth developing: leadership, the capacity to plan, the ability to analyse in the discussion leader and, in at least some of his group, increasing stirring of the minds of those attending, the strengthening of their ability to communicate verbally, to present logical arguments and to spot illogicality. How difficult it is to know if this was the case, as the evidence is so contradictory. Thus one full-time lecturer wrote 'An elementary acquaintance with the outlines of the international situation now seems to be possessed by the rank and file in units where a year or so ago one had always to assume a general background of blank ignorance. The questions put at lectures, too, are of a much higher average standard and are in many cases obviously based on intelligent discussions which have been provoked by the material supplied by ABCA.' Another full-time lecturer disagreed. He said 'I can trace no effect of the ABCA talks in improving the level of troops' knowledge. No one in discussion has ever referred to them. Newspapers, the radio and books, in that order, are the sources that men draw on.'[3]

This was what was to have been expected. There were units in which ABCA was well done, units in which it was poorly done and units in which it was not done at all. Where well done it would increase interest in education, where poorly done it would increase determination to have nothing to do with education. One thing it patently failed to do was to increase the wish of the troops to continue with this or any other form of education when, with the coming of peace, there came also the ending of the compulsion so to do. Even so, its failure in new circumstances is not convincing proof of its failure in old. There are too many points of view for an *ex cathedra* generalised statement to be made about them. Many years later some, recalling their experiences, would say of ABCA. 'It didn't really hit us all that strongly. We were more interested in the Naafi. It was all rather boring but we sat it out.' Others would recall, what would be greatly shocking to ABCA enthusiasts, that 'there was invariably a Sergeant or Sergeant-Major to keep his beady eye on you'.[4] There were also those who in later years, recollecting emotion in tranquillity, would remember their visits to isolated anti-aircraft sites in East Anglia, saying 'Our motorbikes danced upon the mud and we used to look more like dirt-track riders than instructors when we arrived.' The men, they said 'used to sit or lie in a compact circle round the stove, trying to keep warm. They were never really rested, clean and comfortable. But the miracle happened. The men not only liked these sessions but demanded more and more. On one occasion there was a discussion until dawn on technical progress and its influence on humanity. We would receive messages that such and such a team wanted a particular theme discussed.'[5] With such varied experience, how can we know what credence to give to Scarlyn Wilson who tells us that 'the innumerable discussions in which to an ever-increasing extent they took part produced in thousands of previously inarticulate men and women a capacity for self-expression and orderly thinking?'[6] How can we be sure that in saying 'increasingly critical judgement is taking the place of prejudice and ill-informed or ignorant dogmatism' among the troops Yeaxlee was right and that a generous enthusiasm was not taking the place of critical judgement in him?[7]

The enormous scale on which things were done, which is such a feature of wartime Army Education, itself defies generalisation. The claim would be accepted that 'never before or elsewhere has anything comparable in quantity or quality been provided in the Army'. The quality again is clearly much more questionable than the quantity. The thousands of lectures given to the troops would not have been, had the troops come to the conclusion that their suffering in consequence was not to be endured. For the spoken word can strike terror even into the stoutest of hearts as soldiers of that much-vaunted New Model Army found when they preferred to face charges for freeing two imprisoned ministers rather than further endure the agony inflicted upon them when the ministers began to carry out their threat to preach themselves to death. Nevertheless, we cannot believe that all of the lectures had educational worth. The stockwhip expert who gave a lecture entitled 'With a stockwhip in Australia', and further talks, with suitably amended titles, on other countries which he claimed to have visited with his whip, and whose lectures consisted in asking a member of his audience to hold at arm's length a newspaper which he would then cut into small pieces with his whip, aroused interest in his skill but added little to knowledge of the countries concerned.

Some of the lectures were frankly fairy-tales. The subject which most interested those attending civilian adult education classes before the war was international affairs and it is not surprising that this proved the greatest attraction to the troops too. They shared the general desire to know more about the USSR when Germany invaded it and those who were willing to speak on it were accordingly in great demand. They were too often the purveyors of ignorant nonsense. They saw with the eye of faith, they spoke with the fervour of the converted, they pictured the walls and turrets of the Kremlin as the seat of a prescient, kindly and indubitably democratic government, shining benignly and resplendently over a happy people and a fortunate land. They kept a sharp eye on the unbelieving too, castigating the malevolent ignorance of a former head of the British military mission in Moscow which had prevented him appreciating the perfection of the USSR, and bringing the heavy guns of the Soviet ambassador, Maisky, to fire against another similarly afflicted with blindness.[8] It was difficult to see in this the 'education in proportion and suitably imparted' which General Sir Archibald Nye believed would make the soldier a clearer thinker.[9] Its connection with education seemed remote, smacking more as it did of Hans Anderson than of Plato and other great educators. He would have been a bold man who had dared to suggest that the Army would benefit by having fairy tales told to its soldiers, but many of them undoubtedly spent some of their time listening to them. One wonders why common sense did not prompt Regional Committees to question whether the starry-eyed for whom the USSR was man's finest, and perhaps his last hope, were necessarily best informed about what went on there and to ask themselves if they would respond to the teacher's call *audire alteram partem*, convinced as they would be that to hear the other side would not be to listen to the voice of God but to expose all to the wiles of the Devil. It is worth noting that where the USSR was concerned balanced discussion did not make a great appeal to the Army Bureau of Current Affairs. ABCA, Williams said, was 'uncompromisingly appreciative of the Soviet Union',[10] another way of saying that it was compromisingly unappreciative of a balanced presentation of the nature and achievements of that country. It is, of course, easier, half a century later, to take a critically balanced view than it was then, when both the USSR and ourselves were up against it.

That common sense did not induce Regional Committees to look closely at some of their lecturers on the USSR helps us to understand the tolerance of the Army – which was remarkable. Dr Osiakovski, a highly untypical Pole who believed that the USSR, and only the USSR, had achieved the virtuous life, was appointed a full-time Central Advisory Council lecturer in January 1940. To enable his audience the better to understand the USSR, he felt it necessary to say that it could want a quick end to the war as it had 'no armament manufacturers to benefit by a long-term policy for the war'. It had no sinister vested interests such as were represented by a former Minister of War and no profiteers, such as the then Minister of Finance who was making enormous profits from the armament companies in which he held controlling shares. There were no pro-Fascists there either, of the kind that had opposed 'the persistent attempts by the USSR to conclude pacts of non-aggression before the war' and that were preventing the immediate opening of the Second Front for which already the USSR was clamouring. Had Britain been serious in its prosecution of the war it would have begun it 'by conscripting the industrialists and their interests'. Refusal, however, to do so was only to be expected in such countries 'of capitalist oppression as Britain and America'.[11] A country fighting for its life might well doubt how much education of this nature, if it could be regarded as education at all, would add to military efficiency and how much it would contribute to the national cohesion in the absence of which military efficiency would be of little use. It might have been expected to ask if it was in our interests to present the USSR as a progressive country from which we had much to learn and which had nothing to learn from us, even to think that such a presentation of the USSR was no educational exercise but only indulgence in propaganda. Yet Osiakovski's nonsense was not ended for a considerable time.

Army tolerance would no doubt have been less had public sense been greater. The Nazi attack on the USSR, however, transformed Soviet vice into Soviet virtue and Russian soldiers, fighting as doggedly in defence of their land as they have always done, into champions of democratic freedom. A fortunate, if obviously transitory, similarity of interests brought about only by the invasion of the USSR by the country with which we ourselves were at war, was hailed as the advent of a new and better world. When after the initial German success the traditional allies of the Russians, space and climate, began to have an effect and Soviet arms to exact a greater toll from the invading forces, when our failures, as at Tobruk and Singapore, seemed to be multiplying, the view that only a 'revolutionary army', which the British was obviously not, could hope to fight successfully, spread. Sometimes, as Sidgwick pointed out, a wave of opinion is so strong that nothing can make headway against it until it has exhausted itself.[12] This was the case with the full tide of pro-Soviet feeling beating on this country at this time. How easily it swept sensible people off their feet we can see from the widespread conviction that the Soviet Union was as democratic a country as our own or the USA. Here is an illustration of that from an excellent little book by two members of the AEC on teaching method, a book containing far better ideas more clearly put forward than anything provided by ABCA. After indicating the differences between British and American democracy the authors went on 'we have to bear in mind that the working out of democratic ideals in countries like China or the USSR may take still more different forms'.[13]

So unchallenged was this kind of collective nonsense that we would have been offended by the suggestion that any of our allies were undemocratic. Everyone knew that Germans, Italians and Japanese were not democratic. They could not be because they were fighting us and we were. From which it followed as the night the day that all people fighting them were democratic and if their practices differed widely from our own that was reasonable as they were different peoples. But it would have been impardonable spiritual pride in us to hint that they were less democratic than we were. A disgruntled subaltern once suggested that some of the Army's educational returns could fittingly find their place in any 'Britain can fake it' exhibition. But the difficulty of determining of how many returns this might be said, pales into insignificance when compared with the enormous problem of assessing how much education in all the absurdities, how much grounding in all the unrealities, how much indulgence in all the illusions, passed under the name of Army Education and how, whatever amount it was, it should be weighed in the scales against the solid, worth-while and indeed splendid work which we must associate with it too.

The difficulty of making a judgement on the wartime Army Education is further increased by the fact that it aimed at two different things. It sought both to improve morale and to start what had hitherto been thought to be impossible, mass adult education. So when success is claimed for Army Education we have to be sure what the success is that is claimed. Is it in the raising of morale or in the promotion of mass adult education? The standards applied to enable us to know if one objective was achieved are not those which will tell us if the other was too. Our victory will convince us that one of our objectives was achieved, for the soundness of the morale of victorious troops is not to be questioned. But here again there is a difficulty. We cannot be sure that the achievement of the one objective that was undoubtedly achieved was achieved because of the development of Army Education and not because of factors that had nothing to do with it. We must be aware, too, that the measuring rod applied by the soldier to judge what was happening to morale is not the same as that used by the civilian to judge the success of adult education. Bendell tells us that the soldier 'tends to measure success by the percentage of men covered by the scheme and to discount the processes by which organised education in a thousand ways meets the uninstructed needs of many individuals'. The civilian, he finds, is more concerned with value than with numbers, more interested in the effect of education on the individual than with the numbers exposed to it.[14] This did not mean that those whose primary interest was in the raising of morale were indifferent to the individual. They were greatly concerned with the morale of the individual fighting man but it was the unit, and not the individual in it, that held their greatest attention, the collective morale of the unit rather than the development of the individual soldier. For those whose primary interest was in the development of mass adult education the unit was of great importance, too, but the greatest significance was the development of the individuals composing it, for it was the individuals, not the units, which would be broken up when peace came, who it was hoped would become the good citizens who would then build better than their fathers had done in 1918. We have to be careful not to imply that if success can be claimed for Army Education in the achieving of one of the two objectives sought, that itself can be taken as proof of success in the pursuit of the other.

We have seen that had it not been for civilian pressure it is unlikely that Army Education would have developed as it did during the Second World War. Even so, we may think it odd that the Army which had never thought highly of education would have turned so readily to it as a means of improving morale. Two or three important matters will help us understand why this was so.

With the shock of British defeat in Norway, the change of Government, the collapse of France and the agony of Dunkirk there was a protracted period in which in the highest circles there was a great deal of alarm and despondency. As late as August 1941 we find Grigg confiding to his father 'The paralysis of action here I find very alarming ... the general tendency of informed opinion is to be very critical and growingly so.'[15] This was perhaps inevitable since in the prevailing blackness vision was necessarily restricted. Government could leave no doubt of its determination to fight on and it made every effort to draw closer to the United States, the better to enable it to do so. But apart from this the utmost it could do was to call upon all for their greatest effort and to raise their morale in the never-to-be-forgotten speeches which the Prime Minister made to the nation.

No government could have been indifferent to the national morale at this time and unfortunately subsequent events were to focus Churchill's attention on the morale of the Army. These events were so devastating that it would hardly be too much to say that they made him lose confidence in its fighting spirit. It has even been claimed that this was why he adopted Bomber Command's strategy of mounting massive raids on Germany and why he was so resolutely opposed to an earlier opening of the Second Front.[16] He had ordered General Percival in Singapore to fight 'to the death'. Britain's 'whole fighting reputation' and 'the honour of the British Empire' were, he said, at stake.[17] Yet the 85,000 strong garrison surrendered in a week. Four months later, in Cyrenaica, 35,000 men surrendered at Tobruk after only twenty-four hours' fighting. He told his doctor 'I cannot get over Singapore.' He said on another occasion 'I am ashamed. I cannot understand why Tobruk gave in. More than 30,000 of our men put up their hands. If they won't fight...'[18] He left that sentence uncompleted but we can have no difficulty in completing it for him and in understanding how great was his concern for the morale of the troops.

The High Command was similarly concerned. Moreover, we have to remember that it was not at this time the impressive collection of soldiers who later came to the top. When Grigg came as Permanent Under-Secretary to the War Office he found that 'Hore-Belisha feels very much like Lloyd George did about the soldiers and the soldiers certainly feel what their predecessors in 1918 did about Lloyd George' and he blamed the soldiers for this as much as he did Hore-Belisha.[19] He was surprised at the length of time they took to sort themselves out. He commented in February 1941 on 'the mulish obstruction and stupidity of most of the soldiers'. Three months later he was still viewing them with great disfavour, seeing them as 'a crowd of snobbish incompetents who at this crisis of our history, almost without exception, are much more concerned with their own personal advancement than with the interests of the nation'.[20] He was appalled at their lack of decisiveness and drive. This was a situation in which, while it was clear that the morale of the troops must be of great concern to them, it was equally clear that they seemed undecided about what should be done to improve it. Grigg could not have written about them as he did had they been giving a firm and decisive lead in this matter. This was a situation in which, not possessing this drive and decisiveness themselves, they were bound to be influenced by those who had both. Generals Adam and Willans had, and both were convinced that education would improve morale, and others, having few ideas of their own, gave them their heads.

Nor is it surprising that after thus capturing the attention of the Army the question of morale continued to occupy it, for it required a long time before the adverse circumstances which pushed this problem to the fore changed for the better. And the readiness, which is no slur on the integrity of the advocates of the remedy adopted, to be persuaded of its success and to be anxious to persuade others of it too, is also very understandable. Is their advocacy as convincing now as it was then? Did education give an essential uplift to morale? We have no means of being sure that it did and certainly no means of knowing that it did not. There are, however, one or two comments that might usefully be made on this matter.

We can be sure that this was not the way in which Buffcoat, if we may use the name which was given to him in the Putney Debates between the Grandees and the representatives of the men, debates recorded by Cromwell's secretary Clarke, became what he was. He, like the 'plain russett-coated captain' of whom Cromwell spoke, was the archetype of that soldier who knew what he was fighting for and who loved what he knew, to whom reference was so frequently made at this time. He was not fashioned by education. He was a soldier of the New Model Army and was a Sectary or, as he came to be known, an Independent. Yet it was not until the close of 1647 that the New Model came to be the great stronghold of Independency, as Parliament was of Presbyterianism. Even after the battle of Naseby in 1645 Richard Baxter found that the Independents in that army were a minority in its ranks. He believed that they would have stayed that way if only more had followed his example in dedicating himself as army chaplain to their defeat. 'I set myself from day-to-day to find out the corruption of the sectaries', he said, 'and to discuss and dispute them out of their errors both religious and political. My life among them was a daily contending with seducers and gently arguing with the more tractable.' He could not get the help he needed. Those who shared his convictions did not, it appears, like the more tractable and they could not stand the seducers. They were a tough lot, these soldiers of Calvinist persuasion. Baxter said of one assistant who was with him for only a short period 'He was a very worthy, humble, laborious man, unwearied in preaching, but uneasy when he had not opportunity to preach.'[21] One wonders how those who heard him felt. But he was not of the calibre to stand up to Dell, Saltmarsh, Sedgwick and perhaps the most famous of them all, Hugh Peters – the men who, as army chaplains, made the New Model the home of Independency.[22] Theirs is an achievement not to be belittled. Neither is it to be thought of as education. It was religious proselytism and it was this, and not education, that produced the soldier who knew what he was fighting for and who loved what he knew.

We can not only be sure that education was not the way in which the soldier who knew what he was fighting for and who loved what he knew was fashioned, we can be very glad that it was not. For the preaching and the proselytising that made him what he was had another effect on him too. It made him a would-be revolutionary and it is no accident that in that New Model bastion of Independency Baxter found those who thought 'God's providence would cast the trust and the kingdom upon them as conquerors'.[23] A minority, they were, nevertheless, ready to look to the sword 'to cast the kingdoms old into another mould', when prodded into doing so by the folly of the Presbyterian Parliament which sought to deprive them both of their pay and of their liberty to worship as seemed good to them. They produced the 'Agitators', the representatives of the cavalry and of the infantry; on Newmarket Heath power was in their hands and not in those of Fairfax, Cromwell and the Grandees, and they came within an ace of launching the country on to new and untried paths. Cromwell's soldiers became even more radical. Their interests clashed with those of the Grandees; the discussions ended and the mutinies and the shootings began. It is, then, obvious from the history of the 17th Century Commonwealth that soldiers who knew what they were fighting for and who loved what they knew could not always be relied upon to fight for what the civil power and their own Generals thought they should. It is equally obvious that the indoctrination and proselytism which alone fashioned them also produced very great problems, greatly increasing the risk that the politics of extremism would prevail.

In the 1940s in Britain that risk was never as great as it had been in 17th Century England. It was possible to believe that Army Education in the 1940s was not impressively educative; it was impossible to portray it as ideological proselytism. We may rightly condemn the Divisional Commander who greeted his newly-arrived Divisional Education Officer with the words 'I don't care what you do to keep the chaps quiet, but don't educate them',[24] and yet believe that those who saw there was a risk attendant on some of what passed for education then were not being blind and blimpish dolts. For there were times when it did not lack the element of ideological proselytism. Consternation at the political ignorance of their men and at their lack of interest in political matters alarmed Commanding Officers and played its part, as we have seen, in the development of Army Education during the war. But not all the men shared these qualities. Many brought with them well-informed and ardently clung-to political views which, since politics meant so much to them, of course they wished to share with their new-found uniformed mates. An ex-Royal Tank Regiment Sergeant draws attention to this very natural activity. 'There were a number of us who were CP members or very close to the CP', he said, 'We got together and decided to initiate some political activity, and started discussion groups in one of the canteens. Here we had discussions and debates on a variety of topics, for example we had one on the Atlantic Charter, one on nationalisation in Britain after the war.' He shows us, too, how difficult, even when the effort was made to find another point of view, it was to do so and how receptive men might have been to any more determined proselytism. He writes:

> We had a captive audience ... As far as the desert was concerned there wasn't anything else to do except have political discussions. There was no alternative. We were stuck out in the desert. You either read a book or you slept or you took part in a discussion. And the fact that there were a lot of politically conscious people made it possible to have these discussions. It was interesting that if we had a political discussion it was very hard to find a Conservative to tackle us. On many occasions we have I know a Labour Councillor who said he was willing to put the case for the Tories in order to make a discussion. He didn't try very hard but at least it made a discussion.[25]

The 'Serving Soldier' who wrote to *The Tribune* on 10 March 1944 was highly critical of Army Education, saying 'All Army Education is based on the notion that the Army is and has to remain a politically neutral body. This so-called political neutrality is the real stumbling-block which makes the development of the Army as a progressive and clear-thinking political force so immensely difficult.'[26] His criticism reminds us of how very far short of ideological proselytism Army Education was. But here was the voice of Buffcoat speaking over the years on behalf of what the Leveller John

Lilburne referred to as 'the honest and gallant blades', the common soldiers of the Commonwealth Army who were seeking 'social justice', who believed that free men ought constantly to assert their authority and who would have their own constitution, 'The Agreement of the people', which, they insisted, must be incapable of being altered by any Parliament and that any attempt to alter it must become an offence punishable by death. And we should remember that, when the Army Command refused to hear Buffcoat's voice, he mutinied. That this was a voice that could stir up trouble became as obvious in the modern Army as it had done in Cromwell's. That trouble broke out in the Middle East, as we have seen, in the Cairo Parliament.

We might be advised, too, to look upon the claims made for the morale-raising effect of Army Education as being lacking in due modesty. They are very sweeping and they are often linked with further claims that make us doubt the soundness of the judgement expressed. Thus Sir Ronald Adam speaks of Army Education as 'a great manifestation of democratic faith which had done much to raise morale and civic consciousness'.[27] As Adjutant-General his claim to know about morale must be respected; his ability to assess the increase in civic consciousness is much more in question. The HMIs, to whom reference has already been made and who were professional judges in these matters, as he was not, were much less aware of such marked increase in civic consciousness. Some of the doubt we feel when we think there is overstatement in the one case begins to gnaw at our minds when we contemplate the other, and we wonder if in the not inconsiderable number of units which had only a fleeting glimpse, if that, of Army Education, morale was manifestly worse than in those which conscientiously applied themselves to it.

We must wonder, also, when sweeping claims are made, if those who make them are paying sufficient attention to other factors that must have played a very important part in the raising of morale. It is worthy of note that neither the Royal Navy nor the Royal Air Force believed they faced such a problem of morale as that which worried the Army. Neither Service was as large as the Army yet both expanded rapidly and those who came into them as conscripts no doubt reflected the same inter-war attitude to the Services as did those enrolling as soldiers. Above all, the circumstances of the Navy and the Air Force were very different from those confronting the Army. The Navy underlined this when it said in January 1940 that 'the Army might have difficulty in keeping its men occupied but it is doubtful if [the Navy] has time to become bored'.[28] The same was true of the RAF. Both toyed with the idea of introducing ABCA discussions. The Royal Navy set up a Naval School for Current Affairs at St Christopher's College, Blackheath, and the RAF opened a School of Discussion in Highgate. But neither attached anything like as much importance to education as the Army did. As for discussions the Navy feared 'the slick, disgruntled mess-deck politician', the development of the 'Political Commissar' attitude, the revival of the lower-deck organisations which had provided a focus for discontent and which, having been held responsible for the Invergordon Mutiny, had been banned thereafter.[29] Its attitude changed somewhat later when there was found to be a disturbing lack of interest among ratings in the war against Japan. 'The average rating in the Navy', it was said, 'is not really very enthusiastic about the war and he would almost certainly react unfavourably to the prospect of continuing the struggle against Japan.'[30] To counteract this it was agreed that lectures and ABCA-style discussions be given by naval officers. It had, however, already become apparent that where there was interest ABCA could add to it; it could not create it where it did not exist. As it did not create interest in the war against Japan it is, therefore, hardly surprising that although many naval officers were trained in the leading of discussions few had the opportunity to put into practice what they had learned.

Clearly it was the very different circumstances in which these two Services found themselves that accounted for the fact that with them the problem of morale never loomed as large as it did for the Army. They were in constant action and while both had their reverses, as any Service must, they had the victories behind them that the Army lacked. And when the same became true of the Army its problem of morale would be solved. Time, leadership and the confidence both brought to the recruit that the new trade of soldiering was being mastered were bound to have their effect and while it is not to be inferred from this that until this occurred education would have no part to play in raising morale, we are entitled to wonder if these things are being given sufficient weight when so much is made of it in raising troop morale. Few would doubt that Montgomery did more than ABCA towards raising the morale of the 8th Army and surely there is great significance in the remark he made to Grigg 'where soldiers win great victories they do not bother over much about the future'.[31] Perhaps we could add that great concern about the future will never have the effect that great victories, and their anticipation, have on the raising of morale.

Top soldiers might stress the importance of making the soldier a more intelligent citizen, as General Adam frequently did. But it is reasonable to think, while the problem of morale is acute, that they were more concerned with making him a better soldier and after extensive enquiries, which must have been made as carefully as possible, they were convinced that education had played an important role in building good morale. Theirs is a view that cannot be ignored. Army Education did not, and could not, produce an Army of zealots; only preaching and propaganda could do that. Nor would an Army of zealots necessarily be well educated; it would only be zealous. Perhaps our safest conclusion is that fortunately our old British love of compromise stood us in good stead here. We educated to the extent that circumstances allowed, perhaps in the process permitting ourselves to think that that extent was greater than it really was and contenting ourselves with what was being achieved. We avoided the preaching and the propaganda as much as we could, perhaps in the process tolerating more of it than we wanted, and contenting ourselves in the knowledge that as we were emphatically not a revolutionary people what was done in the way of ideological proselytism was of such little intrinsic importance that we could afford to turn a blind eye to it. In consequence we produced an Army that was neither very zealous nor well educated. But it was victorious, which was all that the vast majority of us wanted it to be. Perhaps it would have been in any case, even if we had not been so fascinated by that expression 'citizens' army' and even if we had taken our educators with our customary pinch of salt. That we cannot know. But victory was ours and with it the freedom to dream our own dreams and see for ourselves what would come of them.

We have no reason to think that concern for our 'citizens' army' delayed that victory. There seems to have been only one recorded case in which a man was admitted to hospital suffering from discussion.

In the difficult months when our misfortunes, which were far greater than our own folly which had contributed to them, compelled us to stand alone, that concern may have strengthened us. It was a matter of life and death to us then to draw to ourselves all the strength we could. What strength was derived from education in the Army could only have been marginal, but straws can be important as camels well know. We would be wise not to claim too much for Army Education in this matter of raising morale and, at the same time not to look upon it as wasted and unnecessary effort, but as energy and time well spent.

We know, too, that, unusual or not, our way of dealing with the problem of morale had the warmth of British kindliness in it. Towards the end of the war the Russians had to deal with poor morale in their troops. In his *Memories*, Gromyko refers with approval to the 'stern measures employed ... to reinforce discipline among the troops – harsh actions with which Zhukov personally had been associated'.[32] He does not tell us what they were but we cannot mistake the typically Russian note of brutality that he is sounding. Their measures were successful. And so were ours, without the ruthlessness that we can have no doubt characterised Zhukov's measures.

We have seen how for many, even in the early days of the war, entrancing images of the New Jerusalem glimmered on distant horizons. As the war went on those images appeared less distant and assumed sharper outline. Army Education was the road to them and with the passing years increased time was spent on it. At the war's beginning education was compulsory only in Young Soldiers' Battalions. Then in 1941 a compulsory weekly ABCA period was introduced; by 1942 there were four hours of compulsory education in the winter and two in the summer; with the beginning of the Release Scheme in the summer of 1945 six hours a week had to be devoted to education. All-important in the early days of compulsory education in the war-time Army, the morale motive, although always a concern, declines with the passing years. Morale improved and problems successfully tackled make way for those that have yet to be adequately dealt with. The spotlight, moving away from morale, focuses more sharply on New Jerusalem. The introduction of BWP is an indication that priorities are already changing, as it is also a proof that in launching ABCA the morale motive was the strongest in so doing. Then it was said that ABCA could be done in no other way than by the unit officer as there were not enough teachers to do it, and it was good for the unit officer that he should do it. Since the morale of the Army could not, like the curate's egg, be partially good, ABCA had to be done throughout the Army. But now it was said that the unit officer could not be expected to do BWP and that teachers could be found, from civilian sources where they were available and from within the units if they were not, to attend to it. Civilian lecturers could certainly be found for home-based troops if whole units were their audience and not small discussion groups; they were unavailable in sufficient numbers to be sent to these. It could not in any case have been a well-founded assumption that when there were no civilian lecturers and not enough AEC instructors to do the job, adequate BWP speakers would be forthcoming from within units. It must therefore have been anticipated that BWP would be done on a less widespread scale than ABCA. The argument that it would increase the morale of those who did it and that there was no need to worry much about that of those who did not lacks conviction. Morale is surely no longer the driving consideration here. ABCA had revealed such deficiencies as to suggest that uncorrected they would make impossible the building of the New Jerusalem. They must be removed, and if conditions were such that they could not be removed throughout the Army, it was better that they should be removed from that part of it from which this was possible than that no attempts should be made to remove them at all. In this we can see the changing of priorities, the determination to push ahead with mass adult education now taking precedence over the concern to improve morale. In General Paget's Address to an Army Educational Course in Beirut on 19 July 1994 we see the same valuing of education, not because of the effect it will have now but because it alone can 'create that better way of life for which we are now fighting', a 'better way of life [that can be attained] only through good citizenship'. 'In the crucible of war', he said, 'we have a clearer vision of the things that really matter than we have in peace' and in that clearer vision of the things that really matter 'education in the new and great conception of an education designed to make good citizens who will put into life and get out of life its best and fullest value', is seen to have an honoured place.[33]

The Greeks, although they had no compulsory schools, would have raised eyebrows at the suggestion that education designed to make good citizens was a new conception. The city teaches the man, they said, as Homer and the poets, whom Greek boys learned by heart, did too. Arnold also would have queried its newness. The idea, however, that education so understood could become a mass adult movement was certainly new and that was what Army Education was trying to be. For in the words of W. E. Williams 'the ways and means were found and applied to give far more adults a taste of further education than they had ever known in peace-time'.[34]

Moreover, there were developments in civilian adult education at this time that might seem to bear out the hopes that General Paget expressed. There was a positive rash of special classes organised by the WEA for all kinds and conditions of specialist groups. There were discussion groups for Air Raid Wardens, for Casualty First Aid Stations, for Rescue Parties, for the Civil Nursing Reserve. It was claimed that half the Norwich Firemen were taking part in such discussion groups, which sprang up in Durham, Leeds, Hull, Birmingham, the East Midlands, Bristol, Portsmouth, Plymouth and North Wales. Developments in Merseyside were particularly striking: by September 1942 there were eighty-two classes in liberal adult educational subjects and thrity-two of them were in National Fire Stations. In North Staffs similar work with munitions factory workers was begun in January 1942 and we are told that during the next two years 'a very large number of single talks were given, some of which were only of 'propaganda value, but at other times ... work of real educational value' was done. Such was the interest in discussion groups among the London Fire Service and Civil Defence Groups that on 1 January 1944 a Civil Defence Discussion Groups Bureau, much on ABCA lines with 'briefs' and all, was established. To cope with this, too, the WEA set up a special course to train discussion leaders, after the pattern of Coleg Harlech. The City Literary Institute in London came into the picture also and in conjunction with the WEA arranged for talks to be given throughout the country in factory canteens and for construction workers building new airfields, often in the back of beyond. The Women's Land Army and the Women's Timber Corps were not left out – discussion groups were provided for them too. If these new civilian ventures excited the hope that a mass movement of adult education was gathering strength in the country, the old-established adult education movements that kept to the old ways of the extension lecture course and to the tutorial, sessional and terminal class were flourishing as well. Despite the bombing and the blackout, numbers attending University Extra-Mural and WEA classes were increasing also. Marginal as the increase was, it seemed to indicate that there was a stirring in the world of adult education and if even the stick-in-the-mud felt it and reflected it, then how much more would it be galvanised by the new ways associated with ABCA-type discussion?

Whether or not the hopes of those who had, as they rightly claimed, found ways and means of giving more adults than had hitherto known it a taste of further education were sustained by those developments in the civilian world, they were strengthened by the belief in their own success and were certainly very great. 'The lesson which Army Education should bring home to everyone concerned with further education in Great Britain', Williams said, 'is that there is an immense willingness among men and women to make good their educational deficiencies and to explore new worlds of learning.'[35] It took Celtic imagination to see that immense willingness, a quality in which the HMI's were lacking who reported that 'many of the men look upon education at best with philosophic resignation'. How much the immensity of that willingness had escaped them they went on to make clear in saying that there 'were very large numbers who have this in common, that they have no interest in learning as such or in technical avocations and no particular desire for education, as commonly understood'.[36] But for those who were already convinced that the desire for knowledge had been awakened in the troops it was comparatively easy to believe that that desire would enable the dreadful mistakes that had been made after the ending of the First World War to be avoided at the conclusion of the Second. As General Paget said 'We won the last war, but we lost the peace ... we did not recognise our responsibilities as citizens ... Through education such as we have here we shall, I trust, avoid those mistakes after this war.'[37] Williams agreed, although whereas Paget was thinking of avoiding the mistakes Britain had made after 1918 in the international world, it was of Britain's domestic failures then that Williams was thinking.

The thirst for knowledge implanted in the men would not only enable, in effect he meant compel, us to address ourselves in time to the questions that would confront us when the war was over, it would enable us to solve the world's problems, to correct the inadequacies of the past and to ensure that there were none in the future, to usher in the age of plenty and of peace. The task would be hard but the splendid beginning promised a successful conclusion. Could that be doubted now that a great new educational principle had been found to aid us in our task, namely discussion?

How much of this enthusiastic regard for Army Education can we share? It would be unrealistic not to believe that much that was worthwhile was achieved. Undoubtedly one of the great things that Army Education did was to make teachers even more appreciative than they had hitherto been of the importance of liveliness in teaching. Grigg was not unique in his undergraduate experience. He tells us that in the lectures he attended, given by one of the country's greatest mathematicians, there were 'long stretches of profound and disconcerting silence'.[38] He was perhaps fortunate in that he found them disconcerting; there were other undergraduates, and it may be not a few, who found relief in the occasional brilliant flashes of silence that occurred in the lectures they attended.

It was a virtue of Army Education that it realised the limitation of the old English educational ideal that, as Pindar said, 'hath voice for them that understand, but for many an interpreter is needed'. That ideal, which was founded on the old Greek idea of fashioning the cultured man, had never meant much to many who never aspired to be such. Army Education in general, and ABCA in particular, understood this and sought to be that interpreter. The unremitting nature of its imaginative attempts to find ways of popularising education is wholly admirable, however critical one may be of some of its attributes. One cannot praise too highly its ingenuity and fertility of mind. It was constantly searching for new ways of getting across to the troops. Brains Trusts, plays, films, wall newspapers, 'living newspapers' or graphic presentations of the week's news in simplified form, ABCA maps, ABCA song-books, abounded. Perhaps there has never been a more consistent effort on such a large scale to interest every Jack and Jill in the events of the day and to make them aware of the desirability of concerning themselves with the developments of tomorrow. It would be silly to believe that such a sustained effort had not succeeded in stirring minds that would otherwise never have been stirred. It would be idle to deny that lasting impressions may have been made where hitherto finished and finite obtuseness had reigned supreme. It would be churlish to doubt that it led to the development of some who would otherwise have remained among the great unfulfilled. And as development is education, ABCA must be admitted to be an important educational experiment and should not be seen as an unredeemed and unmitigated failure.

It is another virtue of ABCA in particular but of Army Education in general as well that it prompted the asking of all kinds of questions. 'Isn't a question a sort of education?', an ancient Greek once asked. He knew that it was. The unexamined life for the Greeks was not worth living. 'Wanting to know' was their outstanding characteristic. Plato was convinced that the acquisition of knowledge, by which he meant the rational understanding of the causes and consequences of things, was man's duty and delight. Wanting to know came from wonder and wonder generated thought. Or as he expressed it 'It is a happy genealogy which makes Iris the daughter of Thaumas'. Iris was the messenger of the gods, the winged thought that passes between heaven and earth and brings them into communion. Thaumas was the goddess of wonder. Questions may rouse as statements never would and if they do the roused may remain roused and what J. S. Mill called 'the deep slumber of a decided opinion' be decisively ended. Again who can doubt that ABCA was well advised to deal with matters of popular concern, even if we can be critical on occasion of the nature of the topics it selected, of the way in which it dealt with them and of the lack of attempt on its part to establish any connection between them? It is a sound principle of education to proceed from the known to the unknown and this was a great characteristic of all Army Education. Above all one must be impressed by the tremendous energy which is also a marked characteristic of Army Education. No one doubted that the hearts of the teachers were in it. It would seem foolish to deny, too, that Army Education succeeded in awakening an interest in citizenship on the part of some who took part in it. By 1944, we are told, experienced lecturers were saying that men and women in the Services 'had come to regard themselves as participants in, and no longer as mere spectators of, the march of events'. Some went further and saw themselves as determining that march, though whether in all cases this was an unqualified gain may be questioned.[39]

If, however, we believed in fairies at the bottom of the garden, or at least that there were fairies at the end of the rainbow, both Paget and Williams would shatter such illusions. For believing, as they both did, that in education would be found the way of avoiding past errors they both show us, if unintentionally, how limited a part it can play in fashioning the fairer and finer world of tomorrow, which will be transfigured by lack of tension and absence of disagreement. It will be unlikely to produce the Utopia of our dreams for the dream of the one turns out to be the nightmare of the other. For Paget the lesson to be learned was that 'true freedom can be established only through discipline and service', that we can have peace and security only if we are prepared to defend them – even against a former ally should that regrettably prove necessary.[40] For Williams the lesson was that differences between allies must be played down, that we must continue to implant in the British public a sympathetic understanding of the 'Soviet angle', that trust in an understandably edgy ally must at all costs be maintained.[41] But lack of conviction in the arrival of tomorrow's Utopia is not the only thing to suggest to us that it would be even more unrealistic to believe that all that was claimed to have been achieved by Army Education was indeed so, than to be sure that nothing worthwhile was accomplished by it. Its limitations were sufficiently obvious.

If we claim it for a virtue in ABCA that it understood that to convey more widely the old idea of British education a new interpretation was needed, we have to add that the new interpretation it provided did not adequately interpret the meaning of education. Far from stressing the important truth that education is inseparable from effort, it even implied that it was not; it could, Williams suggested, even occur as an unconscious process. So indeed it can and Charles Lamb, speaking of Homer, and his readers, refers to his lessons 'slipping into their minds while they imagined no such thing'. But it is easier to believe that of *The Iliad* and *The Odyssey* than of ABCA pamphlets. General Willans had spotted the danger of allowing people to think that education could be acquired without effort. Handsomely acknowledging the debt Army and nation owed to the AEC, he wrote there was a danger attendant on their success. 'The association of effort, being often less congenial than its absence, with education was minimised at times to the point of suggesting that it was uncalled for in the pursuit of education.' ABCA rightly stressed the importance of asking questions but it did not drive home the fact that it was only the determination to find the answers that made the question important. In much of Army Education the arousing of the determination to find answers to the questions asked was more apparent to those who longed to see it than to normal sight. Army Education was right to insist, as General Willans said, that 'book learning ... is not the sole educational activity', but wrong not to emphasise sufficiently what he also said, namely that it 'is as important as ever'.[42] It is important that we acknowledge the truth of both propositions. We must remember the first and not forget the second. We must induce those to whom book learning comes easily to remember that there are other educational activities, attention to which will aid their own development, and persuade those who turn naturally to those other ways that failure to attend to book learning will limit theirs. We forget at our peril Steele's comment 'Reading's to the mind what exercise is to the body.' That Army Education did not always avoid that peril we can see from an excellent article, 'The AEC and the Second Front', in which the comment occurs, 'handicapped as we all were by a bookish didactic education'.[43] Since this 'bookish didactic education' is said to have been a handicap, 'didactic' cannot be used in one of its senses to mean that which instructs or edifies. It must, therefore, be used in its other sense to mean the giving of unwanted instruction. There is danger here. We may deplore the fact that in our schools insufficient attention has been paid to those who respond best to a non-academic approach. We can think poorly of the headmaster who said that a superb model of an aeroplane which attracted universal approval at a school exhibition had, surprisingly enough, been made by one of his least intelligent pupils. But if we have valued insufficiently the education we will not get from books, we do not help ourselves by deprecating that which we do. We must value music and the arts and crafts more than we have hitherto done; we dare not value books less. And this needs to be said because inevitably in war book learning is at a discount. That did not prevent worthwhile educational activity from taking place during it, but it did mark the limits beyond which that activity could not go.

It must be acknowledged that the Army did not lend itself, correspondence courses apart, to continuous and consecutive study. Its commitments were too heavy, there was always change taking place in its units and in any case few soldiers were attracted to systematic study. Living in conditions which were far more favourable to this, few civilians were either. The tutorial class in which members of the same unchanging group studied a subject for three consecutive years, reading and writing under expert guidance, was the finest development of civilian adult education, but comparatively few attended it before the war; even fewer do today. Nevertheless, smattering does not educate anybody and there was too much of that in Army Education. Technique can catch interest but only substance can instruct.

In true education what we are looking for is the development of the art of analysis, attention to ensuring definition in our use of language, practice in keeping our thinking as clear and as compelling as we are capable of. It could be wished that pursuit of these qualities was more ardent in much of our civilian education today than seems to be the case. Again it is worth reminding ourselves that our inability to get the best does not condemn us to put up with the worst. It does, however, dictate to us a certain modesty in assessing our achievements.

There was, moreover, an obvious danger that Army Education did not always escape. There was always the attendant risk that those who took part in ABCA, or more general educational discussions, might convince themselves that a fleeting, transient, unsystematic and, above all, superficial concern with great and complicated issues was all that was required to master them. Viscount Cranborne in the debate on the withdrawal of the first ABCA pamphlet to deal with the Beveridge Report drew attention to this when he said

> Education in the Army ... is the same as it is elsewhere; it does not consist in encouraging people to reach conclusions on inadequate premises. It must be conducted upon a basis of the fullest information possible ... I would have thought that it would have been quite clear to anybody that to hold a compulsory debate on a subject on which those who have taken part had not had the opportunity to obtain a comprehensive view of the problems that they were discussing would, from an educational point of view, be worse than no debate at all.[44]

So did Ernest Green of the WEA when, addressing those who wanted discussion to be followed by action, he said 'Do you seriously suggest that after one or two informal discussions on any subject of public importance you know enough about it to 'make recommendations' to anyone – least of all the Government?'[45] Some did.

Williams had not succeeded to the extent he thought he had and it would be wrong to number ABCA among the educational wonders of the world. To say as did the editor of *The Observer* that 'though the men and women in the Army who attend the various activities connected with Army Education are rather different from full-time university students, the general principles of adult education inherent in both are very similar'[46] is to say what is obviously and nonsensically untrue. They were not 'rather different', they were totally different. And the 'general principles of adult education inherent in both' were not very similar, they were totally dissimilar. Undergraduates are not pressed men and women, as those attending ABCA and BWP sessions were. Continuity, not discontinuity, is the characteristic of their studies. And their studies are really studies. The heat and the burden of the day is not a meaningless phrase to them. It is in the sweat of their brows that, in the expressive Chinese phrase, they 'enjoy happiness'. They apply themselves to the hard grind of persistent reading and to the harder grind of disciplined and analytical thought. They are under the care of those whose job it is to brace and discipline minds, who do not brush up for the occasion but who are themselves engaged in pushing back the frontiers of knowledge. This is in no sense to denigrate Army Education. It is not to deny that ABCA served a significant purpose. It fitted the occasion and, since that was important, it was too. But what happened to it when the occasion passed is revealing. For if the Army Bureau of Current Affairs was a success, the Bureau of Current Affairs, which succeeded it, was a total failure, as it could not have been had the great claims made for it by those as misinformed as the editor of *The Observer* had any validity. When we look at Army Education we are, then, more likely to see iron pyrites than gold, which is not to be taken as meaning that no gold is to be seen there at all.

Those who are aware of the limitations of Army Education tend to deny its achievements; those who value its achievements tend to ignore its limitations. But what is to be said of its objective as a whole, the objective which became increasingly important as the need to rebuild morale grew less, the making of the men and women of the Services into the better citizens who would transform tomorrow's world? Was it an achievable objective? Was it indeed a legitimate objective in the circumstances in which it was sought? What did it imply, given the way in which it was attempted?

When we seek to know if the hope of Army Education, and of ABCA and BWP in particular, that they would not only make men better soldiers but also better citizens, was achievable we cannot but acknowledge that those exposed to educational sessions so conceived must have become more aware than they had been of the structure of British government, central and local, and of the issues of most immediate concern to the people in general. Such sessions must have dented the ignorance of many of the troops about the nature of British society and about the way the British attend to things. But more than this was aimed at. If it was hoped to provide a knowledge of the things that ought to have been known but that had not been learned at school, it was also intended to ensure that a man would not be what in ancient Greece was called *idiotes*, uninterested in, unconcerned about, politics. The ancient Greeks believed, and men have thought ever since, that this was a function that education could fulfil. That was the conviction of a great Cambridge historian, Sir John Seeley, when he said 'history without politics has no fruit; politics without history has no root'.[47] In emphasising that politics without history has no root he was reminding us that it takes more than a knowledge of the mechanism of government to make the good citizen. It requires, as well as a willingness to attend to our civic duties, the understanding of our society that only a knowledge of our history, of our beliefs, of our ideals, of the literature that reflects them and us, can provide. What has often been referred to as our liberal education has been much maligned, but it was at least the soil in which the seeds of sound citizenship could grow although, as the Cambridge traitors of the mid-1930s remind us, other and more noxious plants could flourish in it as well. Nor need it be believed that only formal liberal education can fashion the good citizen. Good citizenship can be practised at all levels of society, its duties adequately discharged by minds braced by bible-reading, by discussion in chapel, guild, provident club, social club or pub, by mulling over newspapers, radio and television productions, by the interchange of minds that takes place at work. But could it be produced by compulsory attendance at and participation in a smattering of discussions which were lacking in continuity and not all of which would be run in such a way as to arouse interest? Army Education, ABCA and BWP were all determined to prove that it could. Did they succeed in so doing?

If we consider the relationship between ABCA and BWP, the extreme improbability of this particular objective being secured becomes apparent. That relationship was an obvious and sensible one, but not one from which those who believed that together they would produce the better citizens of tomorrow were entitled to derive as much comfort as they contrived to. ABCA revealed deficiencies and

BWP sought to make them good. But the revelation of the deficiencies did not generate the wish in those in whom they were revealed to remove them. Rather they fuelled the determination in those to whom they were also revealed to have them removed. The ignorant soldiers of today did not insist on becoming the informed citizens of tomorrow. Authority that had found the way of revealing their ignorance believed that it must also find the way of removing it. Citizenship, as every ancient Greek knew, was an active, not a passive, affair, a privilege to be carefully prepared for, ardently sought and eagerly seized. The individual wanted it for himself; it was not a case of others wanting it for him. It was his interest to make himself a good citizen. With BWP it was a case of others wanting to make him that. This is not to say that BWP was unappreciated. It was, after all, held in the King's time, and in its absence the King's time would not have become the individual's time, and it would have been surprising had the view not been widespread that it would not be beyond His Majesty's ingenuity to fill it in less congenial ways. It was, however, one thing to think it a good idea to devote an hour of the King's time, which might well have been spent less acceptably, to the acquisition of the knowledge with which good citizens cannot dispense, and quite another to think so highly of that knowledge as to be prepared to give one's own time to mastering it too. The troops were compelled to attend BWP sessions because it was thought to be of the greatest importance that they should learn there what they were taught. They were compelled to attend because it was known that they would not be there to be taught if they were not compelled. Bitter experience seemed to confirm Guy Chapman's view that 'civics' lacks attraction for the adult, that 'the adult rejects effort which will, he thinks, be of no direct practical benefit to him. And unless he has a strong, possibly material interest, he will always shirk the discipline needed to grasp the abstractions of economics and political science.'[48]

One of three conclusions seemed, therefore, inescapable. It might be believed that the soldiers would acquire all that needed to be acquired to become and remain good citizens in the course of the BWP sessions. It could be hoped that, while they would need more than it could reasonably be thought they would get in the course of these sessions to become and remain good citizens, they would, nevertheless, be inspired during them to continue voluntarily as civilians the studies which as soldiers had been forced upon them. Or it could be acknowledged that the soldiers of today would be unlikely to become the good and adequately informed citizens of tomorrow. Many to whom the second eventuality seemed to be as unlikely as the first still, however, refused to admit the probability of the third. Eighteenth Century thinkers believed in a 'hidden hand' that would turn all things to good. Adam Smith wrote 'Every man is by nature first and principally recommended to his own care and therein he is led by an invisible hand to promote an end which was no part of his intention.'[49] Perhaps those who were convinced that the object of the war should not only be the defeat of the enemy of today but the removal also of the inadequacies of yesterday by the development of the better citizen of tomorrow, are rightly to be seen as upholders of this old doctrine of the hidden hand. Many were uncharitable enough to see in them merely the dreamers of the Never Never Land.

There is a further question to be asked. The desire to make men and women better citizens is wholly praiseworthy, but is the wish to do so compulsorily equally so? Is there not something a little bit odd about the view that democratic people should be under compulsion to become better citizens? Most of us believe that there are some things compulsion can never do, even if exercised 'by all the blended powers of earth and heaven'. Rousseau would have it that we can be forced to be free but most of us have been wise enough not to believe him. Grown men and women may legitimately be compelled to refrain from the vice which undermines the rights of others, or perhaps it would be more accurate to say that the attempt to compel them so to refrain may legitimately be made, but not to become virtuous. They may be compelled to become better behaved citizens but not better in the sense that the advocates of compulsion on this occasion had in mind. It could not be said that all that compulsion would do would be to give them the opportunity to become better citizens, for that they already had, and only Hitler could take it away from them. It should be remembered that they were not being demonstrably bad citizens when it was sought to make them good. Many were unlettered citizens in the sense that they were ignorant about the way in which their country was governed. Many had indicated that they saw no reason to change that condition. But their presence in the Army was proof that they were dutiful citizens, discharging their civic duties at great risk to themselves. When the justification for making them better citizens was that this was essential to the process of making them better soldiers, that was another matter – war has its imperious necessities. But this desire was now becoming something in itself, to be sought for its own sake and not for the effect if might have on the raising of morale.

It is to be doubted if this was a legitimate objective for adults who are citizens of a democracy which has not yet determined that free men and women, because they are serving in the Army, do not have the right to be ignorant if they so choose, to be indifferent to citizenship and uninterested in politics. It is particularly to be doubted if this is a legitimate objective when the sovereign people has not yet debated if its life would be improved were all to think politics a worthwhile pursuit; if it has not yet determined that it could contemplate with equanimity the possibly horrendous consequences if many more of us pursued lives of permanent political enthusiasm. In any case is not democracy desirable, not because it maximises wisdom but because it minimises immaturity, because alone of the ways of governing men it tends to secure the indispensable minimum of freedom, rights and dignity for the individual? And is it compatible with that dignity for adults, who are good enough citizens to be prepared to die for their country, to be compelled to subject themselves to the attempt to make them better citizens than they wish to be? The HMIs, whose report on the Mediterranean Area has been referred to, doubted it, thinking that, while it might be allowable for the younger soldiers, older soldiers ought not to be compelled to attend BWP sessions.[50] It would be well if we shared their doubts. A proposal was put to the Executive Committee of the Army Council on 10 September 1943 to the effect that it 'is not a proper charge upon Army Votes to educate the Army beyond the standard requisite for its success as a military machine'. The Army, it urged, should not be concerned 'with the different and wider needs of the post-war period'.[51] That proposal was rejected. But there was more to be said for it than was then admitted. Gibbon, as did Burke, thought that history might be a school of civic prudence. But we must wonder whether there have ever been any teachers in that school, although we can be learners in it, and we can be sure that we will not find them among the writers of ABCA and BWP pamphlets.

We may be the more ready to share these doubts when we realise that what was involved in this attempt to produce the good citizen was the introduction of politics into the Army in a way that had never been intended. For as the months went by it became increasingly obvious that the political education sought could not avoid becoming party political. There was never any doubt that this was true from the first of one of ABCA's Departments, the Play Department, which was to present current affairs in a dramatised form. This unit involved those like Ted Willis and Jack Lindsay who were avowedly committed to left-wing socialist or communist policies. Their plays aimed to stimulate discussion so slanted on social and political issues, as, for instance, their production entitled 'Where do we go from here?' as to promote left-wing thinking. They skilfully interspersed these with plays, for instance on the war against Japan, which would have won the enthusiastic approval of the most right-wing of senior officers. They performed in nissen huts, or barracks or out of doors. They had no stage and they reinforced their message by involving their audience. Their performances were powerful and moving and there was never any doubt about the direction in which they were moving their audience.

The purpose of education is not to shake conviction but emphatically it is not to shape it either. It is to broaden and strengthen minds to the extent that this is possible, to direct them to the stubbornness of essential facts and to leave them to come to whatever conclusions they themselves deem appropriate. It is not the purpose of education to direct minds to a single point of view. Yet there was the increasingly dogmatic assumption to be found in ABCA at this time that post-war problems would have to be handled in a certain way and in no other, and that minds must be so moulded as to ensure that this would be the case. Williams was determined to play an important part in drawing up the plans for rebuilding Britain after the war and in so doing he was proving that he was more interested in politics than in education.

He told Lady Cripps as we have seen 'There must be no moratorium of social ideas.' That was in May 1942, and he would not have said then that there must be no moratorium of political ideas as that would not have sounded respectable at that time and would, as he well knew, not have been acceptable in the Army. But the ideas he had in mind were political, having to do with the way in which society organises its affairs. In the unlikely event of our finding ourselves in unanimous agreement about them they would still be political. In the much more likely event of our not agreeing about them they would be party political. The unit officer who would chair discussions on these topics was no commissar preaching a party line. He had been taught to take the chair and not the floor, and since it can safely be assumed that his own interest in these matters was not overwhelming, it can also reasonably be assumed that he would do his best, and with a fair measure of success, to keep to what he had been taught.

Nevertheless the logical consequence of the position taken up by Williams is that party political matters would be discussed in sessions which the troops were required to attend. When he insisted on war-time discussion of 'social' values and 'social' blue-prints, he could have been under no illusion whatever that these were political issues he wanted to have discussed, and party political issues at that.

Moreover, it is an old truism that appetite grows with eating, and as the Army became more accustomed to ABCA, Williams became the more determined to push these social issues to the fore. When it was generally admitted that the earlier ABCA pamphlets had been free of political bias and that ABCA had a part to play, but only after this had been so admitted, we find Williams writing 'ABCA Bulletins have so far eschewed controversy partly on the ground that none of us knew whether the Army could "take it".' He believed that the Army had demonstrated that it could, and the conclusion he drew from this was that the exclusion of controversy need no longer be given such high priority, when further ABCA topics were determined. 'Themes which would have been untimely six months ago', he said, could now be tackled. 'Timorous persons too readily seek to "postpone consideration" of social values and social blue-prints until after the war', he now maintained. There must be developed in the troops 'a creative determination' to have the social values and the social blue-prints which appealed to them. ABCA would be the means of creating that determination.[52]

'Creative determination', these were fine words and no doubt it was a fine thing too. A soldier who knows what he is fighting for and who loves what he knows, these were also fine words as he also was a fine soldier. But those fine words and the splendid soldier they described had occasioned difficulties, as we have seen. Would not these other fine words and this further excellent thing do likewise? For if ABCA had to develop the determination then it was ABCA's creation. And how could ABCA create the determination of the soldiers to have whatever social values and social blue-prints were deemed worthy of their having without telling them what they were? If it was argued, as it had been by Hall and Wigg, that these values were already bedded deep in the subconscious of the troops and that all that ABCA was doing was to make conscious what was hitherto subconscious, it still followed that without ABCA it would have remained subconscious and so once again we would have to acknowledge that it was ABCA that was creatively determining these things. Williams had criticised those who would enforce 'the rudiments of a political education'. But the way in which society organises its affairs we call politics and what else could we call ABCA's 'creatively determining' what these social values and social blue-prints should be? And if this was politics and if ABCA was compulsory, how did it differ from the enforcement of 'the rudiments of a political education' which he condemned? If the answer to that was that it differed in timing and in degree, its truth would have to be admitted. But would that not be another way of saying that Williams, demonstrating a greater sense than Gilbert Hall and George Wigg had done, of what was timely, was more dangerous than they were? We ought not to forget that very revealing phrase that to discuss these issues six months ago would have been 'untimely'. He would have shown his hand too quickly and would not have got away with it. What could be clearer proof that he knew very well he had something to get away with?

Williams objected to Hall and Wigg because they wanted to go too far and too fast for his liking, but he wanted to go too far and too fast for the liking of those who were not as socialist inclined as he was, and they were bound to oppose him as he had opposed Hall and Wigg. Acknowledging that controversy could no longer be eschewed, he was now ready to accept it. But discussion is one thing and controversy another, and what was to happen to the unfortunate unit officer who had been repeatedly exhorted to take the chair and not the floor? If the pamphlets and topics were now to be such as to invite controversy his job was likely to become not more difficult but impossible. This was a question which does not seem to have concerned Williams and that very fact, together with the further fact that he was ready to accept the consequences of controversy, namely greater opposition, strengthens the feeling that he was increasingly determined, through the ABCA pamphlets, to influence as many as he could to his way of thinking, regardless of what had previously been said. The first Beveridge pamphlet had shown him more interested in advocacy than in discussion. His embracing of controversy does the same, for while discussion can easily proceed without advocacy, it is difficult to see how controversy can. When, no longer running ABCA but the civilian Bureau of Current Affairs, he tells us that in the interests of peace we must see the Russian point of view, he does not mean this at all. He is telling us that we should accept that point of view; advocacy here is very apparent.

This was borne out by the brief history of the Bureau of Current Affairs. Williams had great faith in what ABCA had achieved and as great in what it could achieve. No doubt sustained by the setting up of the civilian discussion groups to which reference has been made, he believed that ABCA would 'take' in civil society, in schools, in factories, in trade unions, as it had 'taken' in the Army. It does not seem unlikely that he hoped in this way to strengthen his political influence too. He obtained a five-year grant from the Carnegie Trust to set up a Bureau of Current Affairs and he was confident that after this pump-priming it would be able to provide for itself. The War Office continued to publish ABCA pamphlets and maps during the early part of 1946, the Directorate of Army Education now assuming responsibility for them. It was, however, announced that when the new Bureau of Current Affairs was ready to publish its bulletins, the War Office would no longer produce its own but would buy the products of the Bureau of Current Affairs.

Morris, who prepared the Army Educational Scheme (Release Period) which was introduced after July 1945, believed that after the war the Army should continue to provide sessions in current affairs. There were important people, like Sir Eric Speed, Principal Under Secretary at the War Office, and Sir Thomas Ridell-Webster, now Quartermaster-General, who were doubtful about this. With the fall of the Coalition Government the country had returned to party politics and they believed that this in itself made it difficult for bias to be avoided in discussions on matters of current political interest and controversy. They thought that the younger conscripts might be easily persuaded, and that instruction in these subjects might become 'scarcely disguised propaganda under official auspices'. General Sir Ronald Adam was worried too. The new Secretary of State, Bellinger, was similarly apprehensive and determined that precautions must be taken against the intrusion of party politics into the Army.[53] Yet at the very time when the Ministry was becoming apprehensive, its control over what was said in the Current Affairs bulletins and in the new Map Review had been removed by the decision to buy from the Bureau of Current Affairs.

Revealingly, in its earlier publications it was as cautious as ABCA's first bulletins had been. But more quickly than had been the case with ABCA the Bureau of Current Affairs soon became less cautious. Williams took pride in the fact that his Bureau was 'entirely independent of Government control and finance'. This meant, he said, that 'it can enjoy a freedom which no Government Department could entrust to the editors and authors of its discussion briefs. While retaining its impartiality it can select themes of interest and controversy without risk of veto.'[54] When controversy is welcomed, impartiality is not the easiest of qualities to maintain, as the BCA publications soon made apparent. It was very stupid of Williams to allow himself to think in this way. If his productions were independent of Government control they were not as independent of Government finance as he claimed. He had forgotten that people will not go on buying what they do not want, and he was to find that when the Army stopped buying his bulletins he quickly ran out of funds and had in consequence to stop producing them. It ought always to have been obvious to him that the veto he said he did not fear constituted the greatest threat to his new venture. His public relations officer warned him that the Government would not continue to accept 'written material which consistently attacks their own policy without putting other views at all adequately', and he sacked her for her pains, thereby demonstrating the old truth that whom the Gods wish to destroy they first make mad.[55]

Pamphlet after pamphlet occasioned controversy and brought people of the stature of Ernest Bevin into the field against Williams. Moreover, Bevin's growing dislike of the USSR and suspicion of its intentions were reflected in increasing hostility to that country in Parliament, in the press and in public opinion generally. Williams was well aware of this but was still determined 'to develop amongst the British public a sympathetic understanding of the "Soviet angle"'.[56] He was convinced that it was the Bureau's duty to stand against transitory public passion and to remain faithful to the great educational task of incalculating in the public responsible, sound and enlightened views, he himself determining what these were. The more the Foreign Office maintained that *Map Review*, in particular, had become no more than a 'coloured supplement to *The Daily Worker*', the more truculent the Bureau became. The War Office was surprisingly patient, despite the Director of Army Education's strengthening belief that 'the War Office is expending large sums of money on an article which falls short of the Army's requirements'. But since the Bureau would not take the many hints that came its way, being still apparently convinced that it must eventually prevail, the end was in sight and it was reached on the 31 December 1949, from which date it was decided to cease buying the Bureau's material. Williams declared that he did not feel 'unduly daunted' by this. He ought to have been since it was the end of his extraordinarily insubstantial vision, which was remarkable for its capacity to convince highly intelligent people that it was ever anything other than a gigantic and costly illusion. That may be too harsh a conclusion for some, but few would dispute the proposition that the BCA was more an essay in politics than in education, and that its history is more in keeping with, than a deviation from, the attitude which Williams had been displaying before leaving the War Office.

If we doubt the legitimacy of the second of the objectives sought by Army Education in the war, if we say that that objective was not in any case attained and that the price to be paid for it would increase and be increasingly unacceptable as time went by, we cannot admit that that education was the great success it was claimed to be. If we judge it from the point of view of the morale motive it was more successful than if considered as a great experiment in mass adult education.[57] That great experiment is, nevertheless, of great importance. For there are well worthwhile lessons to be learned from it.

One very important lesson is that the standard at which we must aim if indeed the cultivated man and the good citizen are to be fashioned cannot be reached by the mass approach that characterised Army Education then. We come to it only by steady persistence. Imaginative initiative alone will not suffice. We need the understanding, in that great phrase, that it is in the completion of the work and not in its beginning that the true glory lies. The voices of the ancient Greeks can help us over the centuries. Plato reminded us that men can come to the doors of the Muses and go empty away, and Hesiod taught us that as concerns vice 'smooth is the way and near at hand its dwelling', but that 'in front of virtue the deathless gods have set sweat; long is the path and steep, aye, rough at the first; but when a man has reached the top, the going is easy'. To some things, it has become clear, there are no short cuts, the developed man and woman and the good citizen being among them. A second lesson is that it is very difficult to persuade people to give education a chance. The gunners in East Anglia were so persuaded; the 'manual workers' whom the HMIs found were 'the only seriously under-represented' section of the Army at the Middle East Army School of Education were not.[58] A third lesson is of the same kind. It is that one must never underestimate the reluctance of the English to expose themselves to education. A comment in *The Times* on 26 March 1990 underlined our regard for education. It ran 'About 50% of teenagers leave school at sixteen and often shun further training – far more than in most other European countries.' In his enthusiastic overestimation of the success of Army Education in the war, Williams must have been attributing to the English the characteristics of the Celts. Army Education was a great experiment to see if mass adult education was possible but not, unfortunately, a proof that it was. It was a demonstration of the strength of the resistance of the English adult to education, not a discovery of ways in which that resistance could be overcome. It was more of an exhortation to the troops to become better citizens than an active encouragement to them to undertake the hard task of enabling themselves to become such. It was the great hope that somehow or other the trick would be done, the hope that if the outsider was backed heavily enough it would contrive to be first past the post.

We can agree with the HMIs, too, when they emphasised that many more of the troops would have welcomed much more in the way of vocational training.[59] The British have been very backward in providing this, and as early as 1920 Lord Burnham, who had been Chairman of the Resettlement Committee under the Ministry of Labour said of it 'In this important matter I am afraid that the state has fallen far short of its duty.' It is to be regretted that the imaginative enterprise which is a feature of much of Army Education is little in evidence here. Guy Chapman had the idea that the evident interest in vocational training might provide a promising approach to the teaching of civics. He thought that the curricula of vocational and technical education should be widened so that the crafts could only be pursued as part of an effort to relate it to society as a whole. He thought that the individual should be taught to approach the state through his craft.[60] It would have been well worthwhile to find out if there was anything in this notion, and in this matter it may be that Army Education missed a trick in making no attempt to see if there was. It had, however, little opportunity to do so. Army Education and trade training were for many years looked upon as entirely distinct processes. Civilian facilities would have had to be used by the Army if it had moved into this field and these were only available in the UK. The 1944 Education Act, too, was most unhelpful here.

There is a fourth important lesson to be learned from Army Education, namely that many more people are capable of reaching the development that could be attained in a good civilian adult education class than had ever in the past found themselves there, if only they could be induced when compulsion was a thing of the past to enrol in one. The AEC instructors who arrived in dirt-track rider condition at those remote East Anglian anti-aircraft sites, who discussed at times abstract topics throughout the night with the men, afford the proof that what is often looked upon as the culture which can make its appeal only to the few may after all mean something to the many. Nor should we forget the appeal of opera in Italy and of music there and everywhere else.

There is enough here to present us with a great challenge, which may not be the least of the achievements of Army Education. Is it only in war, with its squalor, its filth, its danger and its comradeship too that we can find the way to increase the range of adult education? Is it beyond our capacity to do that in peace, and if we refuse to believe that it is, how are we to demonstrate the soundness of our belief? That is the enormous challenge of Army Education to us today. To meet it would no doubt be amongst the greatest of our achievements if, indeed, so much were to be granted us.

When we remember, too, the most important way in which forward units were kept informed by daily newssheets of the progress of the battle, we cannot think only of the shortcomings of Army Education. More impressive in the grey areas bordering on welfare than in matters more strictly educational perhaps it was, as it seems more successful as a means of strengthening morale than as a mass movement in adult education. But just as it seems reasonable to believe that the great effort that went into it was justified from the point of view of its effect on morale, so it would not appear to be stretching charity too far to come to the same conclusion when judging it as a great experiment in mass adult education. It would be an offence against common sense to believe that anything in wartime favoured sustained study, but some few were given a taste for intellectual activity. Their enriched lives might also have enriched others whom they influenced. Indeed, nothing could suggest to us that the world was made poorer by Army Education.

What are we to make of the significance of this great movement for the AEC? Inevitably it benefitted from what continued to be thought well of in Army Education during the war and it suffered from what eventually came to be looked upon with disfavour in it. It was a great fillip for the Corps. The colour, the excitement, the liveliness, the vast activity and variety of war-time education was the greatest of contrasts to the dreary dullness and repetitive sameness of the work of the inter-war years. A Corps which feared that it faced extinction at war's beginning was well aware of its strength and importance at its ending. The excellence of its instruction was widely acknowledged; civilian teachers of distinction noted with appreciation that 'the activity of its classes was the keynote of all the work'. Not least it had demonstrated an important truth that the Army had long refused to admit, and which it would only reluctantly acknowledge in the years ahead, that attention needed to be paid to the education of the officer, that to continue to leave him, as he had been left in the peacetime years, to the mercy of the crammer was unmitigated folly, that the AEC, as Harlech and the other ABCA schools showed, could help him to develop those arts of analysis, of planning, of clear, cogent and concise expression without which he would be unfit for senior command. ABCA's immediate contribution to military morale must no doubt be accounted its finest war-time achievement; its most important ultimate legacy to the Army may well have been this convincing demonstration of its need for the AEC to participate in officer education. General Haining had doubted the Corp's ability to supervise the limited educational provision that he deemed necessary; it had demonstrated its capacity to cope with something that developed into a far vaster movement than he had ever anticipated. And what Wigg contemptuously referred to as 'old guard AEC' continued whenever they could to press for and provide vocational training. It was a measure of his arrogance and his limitation that in his letter to *The Times Educational Supplement* he said that all they were interested in was 'elementary vocational training'.[61] He blamed them for their interest in what the HMIs stressed the men themselves were most interested in.

Yet the Corps paid a great price for its wartime activity. For towards the end of the war it became apparent that a radical mood was gripping the country and that that movement was growing stronger as the war neared its end. As a rule the British have preferred the gradual ascent to the great leap forward. They have sought so to arrange things as to ensure, as Burke said, that 'in what we improve we are never wholly new; in what we retain we are never wholly obsolete'.[62] 'Freedom slowly broadening down from precedent to precedent' has been their ideal. Yet every now and then in their history they have yielded to the sweeping enthusiasm of radical ideas. They had been caught up in such enthusiasm in the great Puritan movement of the 17th Century and the influence of that was never completely lost over the years. In the late 19th Century, we even saw the most unlikely marriage of 17th Century English radicalism with Prussian Hegelianism in the work of the Oxford Idealist political philosopher, T. H. Green. Great and prolonged war seems to stir to life such radical notions, for great suffering, great sacrifice, great effort seem to call imperiously for great reward.

Army Education in general reflected that radical mood. It is to be seen in most

ABCA and BWP publications. Lieutenant-Colonel Sparrow found that most of the AEC officers whom he met in the Middle East were hard working, dedicated men of left-wing views. That was apparent, too, in the issues of the newly-revived Corps *Journal* in 1943. In June of that year articles highly critical of existing educational policies were published and also an extract of a speech given by the President of the USSR to Red Army Commissars. His words, being unmemorable, were soon forgotten; their publication, being memorable, was not.[63] It was always obvious that Army Education in the war could not but have been predominantly left-wing. It is extraordinary what torments liberal adult educationalists inflicted on themselves when contemplating it. They thought to see, or persuaded themselves that they did, as unco' a sight as greeted Tam O'Shanter when uplifted by his Saturday night's potions. But his vision of the warlocks and the witches dancing to auld Nick's piping at Kirk Alloway came to him by courtesy of John Barleycorn; theirs that the soldiers were being 'conditioned into docile totalitarian subjects' was the product only of prejudice and ignorance. One wonders how many soldiers they had ever talked to! A return to a *status quo* which had introduced them to the Sergeant-Major would be lacking in seductive appeal to the troops. Called upon to make a major effort and many sacrifices, it would have been the height of naivety to expect them to content themselves with the knowledge that victory had prevented the world from becoming dreadfully worse. As they saw it the world, and their part of it in particular, must become significantly better. As British society, from which great effort and great sacrifices had also been demanded, was bound to be thinking in similar terms, a tide of opinion was building up against which no amount of unit indoctrination – had such ever been persistently hoped for – could have prevailed. Those who set themselves against that tide would for the foreseeable future be like so many Mrs Partington's trying to push back the inrolling Atlantic. Commanding Officers who saw that tide gathering strength and who were alarmed by it might ensure that the education of which they disapproved would not take place in their units; they could not insist that that which was more to their taste would be provided. We may rightly conclude that the Commanding Officer who told a visiting Education Officer 'I don't want any politics in my unit – the Tory Party has always been good enough for me and it should be for my men' defined politics too narrowly, but we need not also believe that he was able to make use of whatever education his unit was exposed to, to ensure that what he was convinced should be enough for his men, would be.

It is a gross exaggeration to suggest that Army Education created this radical mood. It was a mood generated in civil society and while ABCA, in particular, reflected and perhaps even strengthened a dominant mood, it could not create it. Nevertheless there was a price to be paid for this. It was a high price and the AEC paid it. It learned what guilt by association was. As long as ABCA reflected the mood of the time it, and what was associated with it, was acceptable. But moods change and what was once acceptable no longer is. The change is retrospective, so that what was once seen as reasonable becomes looked on as worthy of blame. Controversial subjects arouse controversy. And since they were to be of a political nature that controversy was bound to be on party political lines. Those who were associated with this scheme, even if theirs was a residual responsibility, would sooner or later be held to account for it.

Perhaps the most flamboyant and outrageous expression of the inevitable back-lash against the AEC was the nonsensical view that the only battle-honour of the AEC was the Labour victory in the 1945 General Election. The facts gainsaid this nonsense but did not prevent continued belief in it. When a special register was drawn up in November 1944 of those of the troops who wished to record their vote 64% expressed the wish to do so. In the event only 37% of these did so, this being a total of 1,701,000. Their vote, which was spread over 640 constituencies, could make little difference to the outcome. It might make a difference in a marginal constituency but not otherwise. Indeed it was always difficult to understand how the view could spread that the Forces' Vote could possibly outweigh the civilian.

Nevertheless it was true that the Forces' Vote was strongly for Labour and that it confirmed, though it did not cause, the swing to Labour in the constituencies. In Reading, where Ian Mikado was a candidate, 90% of the Forces' Vote was for him. Thus Lord Butler could say later 'The Forces' Vote in particular had been virtually won over by the left-wing influence of the Army Bureau of Current Affairs.'[64] This was something the AEC would have to live with in the future when it had occasion to wonder if it was in its best interests that a great political party had been made so suspicious of it. The British Army is not the most revolutionary of institutions and senior officers have rarely been noted for their radical views. And however unjustly, what was held to have been the undue political influence of the AEC was long held against it and long continued to hamper its work.

If wartime Army Education was a great fillip for the AEC and something which exacted a great price from it too, it also marked a great step forward for it. In the history of the Corps a marked rhythm has made itself evident. That history has been characterised both by great rise and fall and by steady advance. Thus much was expected from Army Education in consequence of the great development that occurred in it after the ending of hostilities in 1918; interest in it could hardly have been less by the mid-1920s. Even greater hopes were inspired by it in the Second World War; the reaction was as decisive and as predictable in the mid-1950s as it had been in the mid-1920s. Two world wars proved that moderate expectations are a better foundation on which to build than immoderate hopes. And here a word should be said on behalf of what Wigg called 'the old guard' of the Corps. They were by no means as indifferent as he claimed to opportunities to improve the understanding of the soldiers in civics and in current affairs. But they did not make the mistake of seeing in Army Education a means of transforming society and of effecting great changes in its cultural values. They were more aware than many of the newer members of the Corps of what was and what was not possible in the Army, and the course of education in the post-war Army might well have been smoother had it been more in their hands and less in the hands of the dedicated enthusiasts during the war years. But if the rhythm of Army Education is like the waves of the seas which know striking differences between high and low tide, it also reminds us of the sea on England's east coast which is slowly and steadily advancing over the years. Despite the great rises and falls which have occurred in its history, the AEC has found the way of slowly developing, of continuously building on and going beyond what went before. Its development has rarely been smooth. Perhaps it would be truer to say that it has been growth rather than development. Like Topsy, 'it just growed' and like the growth of that young lady it has not been the result of human planning. It has just happened as the result of adjusting to changing circumstances. And by the ending of the Second World War the AEC had made itself known to society, it had won the respect of the universities and established a close relationship with them as it had never done before, and it had made good its claim to be an essential part of the Army. Its trials were by no means over; its continued existence was no longer in doubt.

CHAPTER 8

THE RELEASE PERIOD SCHEME, 1945–1948

It is to be doubted if the spirit of the troops was markedly uplifted by the notion that they were members of a citizens' army, knowing what it was fighting for and loving what it knew, but there is no doubt at all that their hearts were greatly elated by the imminence of their discharge from it. However, if it takes time, effort and skill to create great and powerful armies, these things are required in their demobilising too. This has not always been realised and occasionally, as in England after the long Revolutionary and Napoleonic Wars, the chaos of peace has been added to the chaos of war.

When it is conscript armies that have to be demobilised there are further pressures to be taken into account and, as we learned in 1918, trouble awaits those who pay insufficient attention to them. Moreover, when Nazi Germany finally accepted defeat we had to relearn the lesson we had mastered in 1815, namely that former allies might become future enemies and that former enemies might have to be seen as future allies, a lesson that reminded us that armed might must not at once be got rid of. In the situation in which the USSR found herself in 1945, devastated by war and aware of the enormous strength of the USA, and of the fact that twice in the 20th Century Germany had been defeated because she had not understood the vital nature of America's interest in Europe and had trampled upon it, the USSR would have been mad to risk war with it by doing likewise. Yet its policy was sufficiently aggressive to suggest that it would. And even if it be said that that was misleading and that its policy, if tactically offensive, was strategically defensive, there could be no certainty of that. Accordingly, international as well as domestic prudence precluded unduly speedy demobilisation. Controlled disarmament, which avoids the complications occasioned by too great haste and is not undermined by the impatience generated by what is thought to be protracted delay, unacceptable unfairness, or even by the leaving of too much time to idle hands, is not the easiest of operations and in that knowledge demobilisation had been carefully and long prepared. It was believed that education would play an essential part in it, keeping the troops fully occupied until such time as they could don their civilian suits and enjoy the happiness they associated with so doing.

Before the end of 1943, though the end of the war was not yet in sight, Sir James Grigg became convinced that the planning for demobilisation should begin. He believed that education must play a big part in preparing the troops for their return to civilian life. The committee which he then set up under the chairmanship of his Under Secretary, Lord Croft, shared the conviction that education would become increasingly important in the period of demobilisation. It recommended that a new post of Director General of Army Education be created, a post to which on 18 December 1943 Philip Morris, one of the country's outstanding Directors of Education, was appointed. He took up office early in 1944. By October he had produced the plan which was then published as *The Army Education Scheme (Release Period)*.[1]

It was a most ambitious scheme and some of the hopes it expressed bore little relation to accumulated experience. It embodied the belief that 'a prodigious demand (for education) will arise from all ranks'. A note of caution was to be heard when an AEC conference to consider the scheme found what it called 'a hint' of this expected demand 'in the Army's call for war news in Europe'. There was greater significance than was realised at the time in the fact that this conference found the hint for which it was looking, not in ABCA or in BWP, but only in something which might turn out to be a specific need expressed at a particular time, a transient need which, however important it was to meet it at that particular time, might well be expected to pass with it. A similar note of realism and caution was sounded when that conference considered what were likely to be the states of mind of the troops when the scheme was being implemented. There would, it was stressed, be anxiety about the family uppermost in the minds of those awaiting demobilisation, anxiety about housing problems, anxiety about resuming old jobs and about embarking upon new ones, about future prospects of employment, about the date of release, about losing touch with home affairs before that happy event. There would be political cynicism in evidence and reaction against military life and routine. These emotions, it was emphasised, 'will be felt against a world background of political uncertainty and turmoil, often in a foreign environment'. One thing above all should not be forgotten: 'There is also the difficulty of general British indifference about education.' But none of these reflections led to any querying of the accepted assumption that 'the demand [for education] will be so great and varied that only the utmost efficiency animated by inspiration will suffice to meet it'.[2] The British indifference to education thus appeared as a blessing in disguise for if, given this, only inspired efficiency could enable the forthcoming educational demands to be met, then what would have happened had the British Tommy been as enthusiastic about education as the Indian sepoy or the African Askari?

The curriculum, it was stressed, 'will be followed by all ranks and will normally, as a minimum, occupy 6–8 hours per week'. The courses it made provision for, the conference was told, 'will normally last for 24 weeks'. It was to be a compulsory scheme and classes were to be held in working hours. And since it was well understood that the desire to get out of uniform as quickly as possible was far stronger and much more widespread than the wish to spend one's remaining time in uniform as profitably as possible, there was to be the guarantee that participation in the scheme would not adversely affect the rate of discharge either of teacher or of taught. The scheme was to prepare the troops for the opportunities that awaited them in civilian life, but it was careful to stress that it could not be a direct preparation for the job market. The Army did not know what that job market would require and if any organisation could pretend to that knowledge it would be the Ministry of Labour, whose functions the Army would not intrude upon. The troops would, however, be given details of what civil trades and professions were available and would be informed of the qualifications required for entering them. A special examination, the Forces Preliminary Examination, would be introduced to enable some of these qualifications to be at least partially acquired. Pre-vocational studies would be provided where possible, it being insisted that there should be no division between these, even when they verged upon the vocational, and general education.

Every effort was to be made to ensure that the individual educational needs of the troops would be provided for and every opportunity given them to enrich their leisure. There was to be Basic Education, General Education, Technical Education and Varied Interest Education, such as social studies. Recreational and cultural activities were to be arranged, choirs, music groups, dramatic societies and sketching clubs. What was on offer was divided into six categories: Technology; General Science; Home, Health and Hobbies; Man and Society; Commerce and the Professions; and Arts and Crafts. In the category 'Technology' would be found courses in engineering, mechanical and electrical, building and so on; in the category 'Home, Health and Hobbies' courses on market gardening, small-holdings and general domestic subjects. 'Man and Society' would cover politics, economics and sociology; 'Commerce and the Professions' would cater for those with business or professional interests; and 'Arts and Crafts' would deal with all the fine arts. Rigidity, it was emphasised, must not be a characteristic of the scheme. The division of subjects into elementary, intermediate and advanced stages, and the arrangement of classes at the level of the unit, the brigade, the local civilian college and the Army Formation College which would be set up, should ensure the maximum flexibility in the working of the scheme. This was essential because many units would continue under operational conditions and because 'the Army not being designed for universal education the Release Scheme of Education will create demands it cannot satisfy'. 'Modification and adaptation will therefore be required', it was said. But there was one thing flexibility must not be, namely, an excuse for failure to implement the scheme. On the contrary 'every possible effort must be made and all ingenuity used' to do so effectively.[3] The conference seems to have held two views, not easily reconcilable, about the problem it was facing. Beginning by declaring that it faced a prodigious educational demand from the ranks which it would have difficulty in satisfying, it ended by saying that the Release Scheme of Education would create demands it could not meet. Neither view was lacking in unreality nor in unbounded optimism.

The Release Scheme was not only to enable the returning troops to make the most of the opportunities awaiting them in civilian life. It was also to prepare them for the responsibilities to which they would be returning. 'The curriculum', it was said, 'must have two elements, the communal and the individual.' ABCA and BWP were to be essential parts of the programme and in addition there were to be 'general lectures all dealing with contemporary events and problems which must affect and interest every man and woman'.[4] The failure to insert the words 'it is hoped' before the word 'interest' was a faithful reflection of the optimism so characteristic of this scheme.

Its impressive and wide-ranging nature is not to be doubted. The fact that under it 2,269,051 books were ordered and 1,697,099 distributed, and this at a time when paper was in short supply, would itself convince us of that. Each unit of 500 or more men and women was to be given a library of 400 books and each Command to have one of 5,000 books.[5] The Release Scheme of Education was on such an enormous scale that there was clearly going to be great difficulty in finding all the teachers who would be required for it. Close collaboration with civilian bodies would continue to be needed. This was regarded as most important and not only as an obvious means of reducing the shortage of teachers, but also as a way of ensuring that the returning soldier would become a better citizen than he had been when joining the Army. The hope was now expressed that the experience of what civilian adult education could provide which would thus be gained in the Release Scheme would attract troops to it on demobilisation. But as there could not be enough civilian teachers to meet all the requirements of the Release Scheme, many uniformed teachers would have to be forthcoming.

They were not, however, to be found in the AEC. The AEC, it was emphasised, could claim 'no proprietary rights' in the scheme; it was, nevertheless, 'a vital element' in it. It would generally supervise the scheme. It would provide expert advice to make possible the effective development of educational facilities in the unit and would, as far as possible, arrange courses in all subjects asked for. It would care for all students for whom no arrangement could be made in the unit, passing unsatisfied demands to the formation immediately above the unit. If courses could be provided more efficiently and economically at Brigade or Sub-District level then this, too, would be done. In general it would keep everything running smoothly and in particular it would take BWP sessions. To enable it to do all this the Corps was to be considerably expanded, the number of its officers serving a Division being increased from one to eight.[6]

Symbolic of that expansion and of the important role of the Corps in implementing the Release System was the announcement at the end of 1944 that Brigadier Cyril Lloyd, Deputy Adjutant-General to 21 Army Group, was being released from that position to become, as Major-General, Director of Army Education, Philip Morris vacating that job to become Vice-Chancellor of Bristol University. The AEC was thus truly coming into its own again. When two not greatly distinguished civilians were put in charge of Army Education that was a reflection of the conviction that the Army's own special department which had been set up to look after this was not up to its job. The third civilian to be so appointed was a much more outstanding educator and it is a very nice judgement that is called for when the decision is taken to depart from a way of doing things that symbolises a relationship with the civilian educational world that is valued and may be thought to be still in need of consolidation. Even so the appointment of an admittedly eminent Director of Education for Kent to supervise Army Education can hardly be looked upon as a vote of confidence in the Army's own educational department. It was, then, very important that when Morris vacated his post the civilian regimen in Army Education came to an end and the Director of Army Education took his proper place in control of the work that was the proper function of his department. The vigour, the confidence, the command of the note now sounded in the Directorate of Army Education contrasts most markedly with the fumbling inadequacy of the reply made to the Army Council and the Haining Committee by those responsible for the AEC at that time.

The main teaching in the unit was to be done by its own officers and other ranks.

Since the Army was now a cross-section of civil society, it was thought to be so rich in varied experience that units could, at least at an elementary level, meet their own needs. 'We shall be working in and for an Army of all the Talents which will be able to produce instructors to meet the formidable other Army of the students of all the Interests'[7] it was claimed. Imaginative administration would bring these two Armies together – if indeed they were other than a figment of the imagination. The key men would be the Unit Education Officers. They were to be appointed in each unit. For a Lieutenant-Colonel's command, the Education Officer was to be chosen from the Majors and Captains. In each unit they were to be supported by one officer and six sergeants who would be full-time instructors. If it was from the privates or corporals that such instructors could best be found, then they were to be made up to sergeants. If still more instructors were needed, part-time instructors could be appointed; as they would not receive pay, in the absence of great enthusiasm on their part they were likely to be absent too. It would be the responsibility of the Unit Education Officer to arrange for the lectures to be given on Current Affairs that were said must affect and interest all citizens. To help Education Officers and their instructors special courses would be provided and there were to be handbooks to cover the six categories under which were listed the courses on offer. These handbooks would supply essential information and they would be accompanied by six additional manuals in which there would be suggestions as to how the various subjects might be taught. Education Officers and their teams would have the additional advantage, too, of hearing experts on the subjects they would be teaching. For in anticipation of the programmes later to be provided for the Open University, or University of the Air as it was often called, the BBC undertook to provide educational talks for the Forces as soon as possible.

At the bottom of the educational pyramid constructed under the Release Scheme was the unit. Above it was the Brigade, Division and Corps, where on the same self-help principle, would be found those capable of teaching the courses and classes it had been thought best to arrange there. And at the top was the Army College, or Formation College as it was called. It was desirable, it was said, that this should be set up within easy reach (approximately ten miles) of a large town containing a University or Technical College. At home Formation Colleges were set up at Newbattle Abbey, Dalkeith, Chiseldon, Luton Hoo and Stockport. Abroad they were to be found at Göttingen, Hanover (later moved to Hohne and then again to Dortmund), Perugia (later moved to Spittal), Mount Carmel in Haifa, Sarafand, Gaza, Victoria College, Alexandria and Mitoqba College, near Cairo. The teachers here, too, were culled from the various regiments and units of the Army. For the organisation and administration of the Formation Colleges the AEC was responsible. One serving officer of the Corps, however, commanded Newbattle Abbey.

This was the scheme of which an advance outline was given in an Army Council Instruction of October 1944. It was made widely known by an ABCA pamphlet published at that time, *Brush up for Civvy Street*. ACIs of February 1945 gave further descriptions of it and emphasised that it would not be implemented until hostilities with Germany were over, except in units specially authorised by the War Office to begin it before then. In May 1945 Gibraltar Command was authorised to implement it and in June it was announced that 1 July 1945 was the date on which it would be generally begun. On that date HM Stationery Office published a pamphlet entitled *The Army Education Scheme – the Plan for the Release Period* so that all could know what was afoot.

Just as Army Education had a dual purpose in the war, so it had a dual purpose in this demobilisation period and the dual purpose was much the same now as it had been then. Morale and New Jerusalem had vied for attention then; they did now too. The primary purpose of the Release Scheme was undoubtedly the maintenance of military morale in the difficult period of demobilisation. It reflected the wartime conviction that education played an important part in the maintenance of morale. Its secondary objective was to inculcate among the troops a taste for education and in this way to make good the deficiencies of pre-war education. In all of this the Release Scheme was an outcrop of the wartime educational scheme. We see this in the way it added to unit education by providing a more advanced education at Brigade and Command, as BWP had in the wartime scheme provided something more advanced than ABCA. We see this in the development of residential Formation Colleges, as residential colleges had been set up during the war in Coleg Harlech and elsewhere. Above all we see this in the great optimism which infused it as it had done the wartime scheme.

The Army Education Scheme (Release Period) would ensure the smooth working of the Demobilisation Plan. The demobilisation troubles of 1919 were not forgotten. On 3 January 1919 10,000 troops had caused trouble at Folkestone; the following day 2,000 were doing likewise at Dover and two days later 8,000 at Brighton, while there were demonstrations also in Whitehall.[8] Now it was believed that a much more carefully prepared demobilisation plan and scheme of education for resettlement than anything that had been available then would sustain the morale of the troops and avoid such unpleasantness.

The Release Scheme would also strengthen the hearts and renew the vision of the faithful. Perhaps the hearts of the hopeful did not beat as high as once they had done, but professional politician, professional soldier and professional educator show us how valiant they still were. For there are fashions in ways of thinking as well as in ways of dress, and the tyranny of time and fashion still decreed that good soldiers should also be good citizens. Thus in his Preface to *The Army Education Scheme – The Plan for the Release Period*, Grigg wrote: 'It has much to offer that is necessary to a good life in an educated community' and he hoped that the returning troops 'will be inspired to make each in his or her unique way, a positive contribution to the future'. The Plan itself contained the words:

> It is a scheme which may have a powerful effect on education generally. The new Education Act has been called a milestone, but there are better metaphors. Soldiers are more likely to respond to the idea that it is a bridgehead, established by planners and specialists – but wholly dependent for its extension and development on the efforts of the common man. It is not too visionary a belief that those thousands of young men and women who participate in the Scheme – as organisers, students or

instructors – will subsequently make their influence felt in securing the full benefits
of educational progress.

General Paget saw in BWP 'a means of developing a sense of citizenship in the Army
which will pay a high dividend after the war'. Major-General Lloyd looked upon
Current Affairs and citizenship as the core of future education in the Army; where
units were unable to implement the full Release Scheme and could only devote three
hours a week to it, one, he insisted, must be spent on citizenship; where it could
manage four hours' education a week two must be given to this. For was not the
Army in this 'embarking on a great experiment in progress'? This same hope that the
Release Scheme could make good the deficiencies of pre-war education shines in the
words W. E. Williams wrote in the *ABCA Handbook* published at this time. 'The
winning of the peace', he said, 'may be a more protracted operation than the winning
of the war', but he was sure that if the soldiers 'leave the Army with a concern for
current affairs, and a minimal knowledge of current affairs, they will become a decisive
influence in winning the real fruits of victory'.[9]

The HMIs who visited Germany in 1946 shared that hope. They were 'in complete
agreement that the provision of education in Citizenship ... is of first-rate importance'.
They said 'Community Education was intended to be at the core of Army Education'
and they left no doubt that in their view it should be. 'What is needed is education in
the enduring problems of modern citizenship', they said. It was 'a large and extremely
important subject' and they wanted it to enjoy 'the full esteem that it demands'. Their
criticism was that the Army was not taking it seriously enough. It was 'too important
to gamble with it' and this, in their view, was what the Army was doing.[10] The needs
of individuals, their preparation for their new occupations, their readjustments to a
new world, were constantly stressed in the Release Scheme. But the needs of the
Army, the maintenance of its morale at a difficult time of running down, the needs of
the community in fashioning in the days of reconstruction a better world in which
returning soldiers would show what better citizens could do, were no less underlined.
Morale and New Jerusalem were still at this time the significant springs of education
in the Army. It was always known that not all units would be able to implement the
Release Scheme since some would have overriding commitments and others would
be too small and isolated to do so. Those not doing so would be expected to continue
with the wartime education scheme, it was somewhat optimistically added. What
was not anticipated, however, was that the implementation of the Release Scheme
would be adversely affected by the increasingly upsetting demonstration of the
unsoundness of the assumptions on which it was based.

The first of those assumptions was that the war against Japan would last at least
a year after Germany's defeat. This, it was thought, would give opportunity for the
Release Scheme to shake down and to be adjusted to actual circumstances so that the
difficulties that would inevitably arise could be removed, or at least greatly lessened,
according to the plans already made and since the call-up would continue while this
was happening, reservists would be coming in and replacing those who were serving.
While this was happening the Release Scheme would gradually become part of Army

life. In fact Japan surrendered only three months after Germany's defeat. This meant that the pace of demobilisation was much quicker than had been expected. This in turn meant that it became impossible to keep classes together for a reasonable period of time or even to be sure that instructors for them would be available. There was thus no time for the gradual absorption of the Release Scheme by the Army. It had to be speedily imposed when everything was thrown out of balance and this frustrated carefully prepared administrative plans, the Scheme in consequence being characterised by rush and not by gradual development.

A second assumption was that the Army would have in its ranks sufficient talent to provide the teachers for the Release Scheme. There was a great deal of talent in the wartime Army, although it was unlikely that when the fighting was over all of it would be available for educational purposes, or if so available would be willing to offer its services. But much of it was in the early release groups. Thus those leaving the Army would be older and more experienced men, while those coming in would be young recruits and it was not reasonable to believe there could be found among the latter the actual or potential instructors that it was not unreasonable to hope to find among the former. Teachers could not be found from elsewhere if the Army could not itself provide them. But how effective could teaching be if adequate teachers were not there to provide it? Too often in the Release Scheme it became obvious they were not. Thus the HMIs in Germany found that many units could not provide their own instructors. They visited 'an infantry battalion of whom less than 2% (including officers) had a secondary education' and 'another in which only eleven (officers and men) had reached school certificate standard'. They spoke to one Commanding Officer who told them 'it was as absurd to expect units to provide their own teachers as to find their own doctors or padres' and who said this ought to have been the job of the AEC. The HMIs added 'We share this conviction about the need for the expansion of the AEC on its teaching side', although they still believed that 'a unit should be definitely expected to make use of whatever talent and ability for educational purposes it can find in its own personnel'.[11] But AEC teaching, too, was not without its problems, as General Lloyd, when drawing attention to the fact that the AEC had to recruit from those coming into the Army to do their National Service, made plain in saying 'The other rank element (the Corps' primary teaching strength) is handicapped by youth, immaturity and inexperience.'[12]

A third assumption on which the Release Scheme was based was that there would be large and reasonably stable field formations with time on their hands. HMIs visiting troops abroad were frequently to meet Commanding Officers whose criticism of the Scheme was that it had been primarily designed for these and that it paid too little attention to the different and more difficult circumstances of their own smaller units.[13] There were large field formations in the demobilisation period, but they were often not stable as they were fast losing experienced officers and NCOs and having to cope with recruits who were frequently poorly educated and very ill-disciplined. Such formations, too, rarely had time on their hands, being committed to many operational and training tasks. It was self-evident that nationalist stirrings in the Middle East and in India would add to the Army's public order duties while even before the end of hostilities Soviet international behaviour began to exercise military minds. The authors of the Release Scheme must have been aware of this; the event suggested that their awareness had not been sufficiently keen.

Duties were too heavy for many units to implement the scheme; the teachers to carry it out were not forthcoming in the numbers required; the suitable accommodation which seems to have been taken for granted did not materialise; and the equipment promised did not either. Thus the HMIs who visited the troops in the Middle East in 1946 found that the claims made for the Scheme did not 'correspond ... with the facts'. 'We cannot expect the Scheme', they wrote 'to be implemented either in its present form or in any other if suitable instructors, accommodation and equipment are not forthcoming.' 'Given these', they added, 'the Scheme is fundamentally sound and finely conceived.' As they made it obvious that in their view those things were not forthcoming this seemed a remarkably round about way of saying that for much of the Army, in their view, the Scheme was fundamentally unsound and poorly conceived. They leave us in little doubt of that when they said that the average Commanding Officer needed to know three things of which he was ignorant, three things without knowledge of which there could be little hope that the Scheme would be successful. He needed to know what is meant by education for his men, how he is to get it laid on and how he is to reconcile its claims with the heavy programme of supply work, repairs or military training which he already has in hand. The thought obviously occurred to them, as it must to us, that an educational scheme which left the average Commanding Officer needing to know such basic things was more lacking in reality than in pretension.[14]

There was yet a fourth assumption made by the authors of the Release Scheme that, as the event also unfortunately proved, was lacking in soundness. This was that the long struggle to convince the Army of the value of education was in fact already decisively won. That was the view reflected by the contributor to the AEC quarterly bulletin for January 1945 who wrote 'as education develops into a normal element in army life'. In view of the impressive development of Army Education in the war that seemed a reasonable assumption. There seems little doubt that Army Commanders accepted it and frowned severely upon those who might still be of the opinion that brawn and backbone were all the soldier required and that brains should not be welcomed in him even as an optional extra. Yet as the HMIs who reported on the Release Scheme in Germany expressed it 'Gods in the shape of General Officers may propose, but it is often the Commanding Officer who disposes.'[15] The HMIs in the Mediterranean at this time noted wryly 'the difficulties of releasing a man for education evaporated when release was required for purposes of competitive sport'. 'Education mindedness', they said 'was at a discount in the Army. Its importance has not been realised.' This, they were charitable and sensible enough to add, was 'a comment on the British character rather than upon the predilections of the Commanding Officers'.[16] These same HMIs reported 'In the Middle East one should be prepared to find not the full War Office Scheme which ... circumstances may well render almost impossible but the best adaptation of it that may be locally possible.'[17] That was almost always the case. The circumstances in which the attempt to implement the Scheme was made were almost infinite in their variety. But varying as they were, they were generally very difficult.

Even at home, where conditions for carrying out the Scheme were much better than elsewhere, geographic conditions were unhelpful. Anti-aircraft units were so widely scattered as to maximise the difficulties which would inevitably present themselves to small units in seeking to adjust to a scheme primarily designed for bigger ones. In Germany these geographic difficulties were still greater as a huge area of territory had to be occupied. Thus 52 Division controlled an area larger than Wales. Units were split up into widely separated Companies or Troops. The 1st Leicesters were stationed in three different towns. Distance was even more of a problem for the Mediterranean and Middle Eastern Forces, whether for those seeking to help widely separated units, to arrange Area and Corps courses or to encourage applications to Formation Colleges. In the Middle East troops were scattered over an area 3,000 miles across. Climatic difficulties in these areas were not to be ignored either. The HMIs in the Mediterranean commented on the lack of heating in, and the bareness of, many of the classrooms they saw. 'The medieval scholar', they said, 'blowing on his fingers and listening enthralled to *Duns Scotus* is an example to be admired rather than followed even in those rare cases where the comparison with the tutor can be admitted.'[18] It gladdens the heart to know that there were apparently some. In the Middle East it was the problem of extreme heat, not of great cold, that concerned the HMIs. Here, they noted, 'summer temperatures of between 110 and 130, or even more, are endured for weeks on end'. They also deplored an absence of hardstandings in classroom tents. 'Where only tented accommodation is available, hardstandings are necessary', they said. 'It is difficult to read, talk, give out books, or take classes, where the floor consists of acrid dust perpetually in motion.'

This was not the only difficulty of which they became aware. They noted that artificial lighting was necessary all the year round in the evenings and they added 'the general level of such lighting is very poor indeed; often one cannot read properly'. Gloom of this kind affected minds, too, and the HMIs added 'the emotional and psychological difficulties engendered in such a climate and in such an environment at the end of a long war are only to be expected; they are far more serious than the physical difficulties of temperature, accommodation, lighting etc'. They spoke of the 'homesick inertia' of the men and said that 'apathy predominates' among them. They found that 'the unconscious influence of those who are tired of everything is one of the chief stumbling blocks in the way of education, welfare and much else'.[19]

Political and military circumstances added to the difficulties of the educators. Those who had been impressed by the famous claim 'Give me a child until he is seven and he will never be altered thereafter' were pleasantly surprised by the absence of attacks on the occupying forces in Germany. There nevertheless had to be constant vigilance. How much that was necessary is shown by the letter Montgomery wrote to Grigg which said 'We have quite recently discovered the first large, widespread, subversive organisation in Germany. This was organised by the General Staff of the Hitler Youth Movement and was financed by Hitler Youth Funds. It was cleverly linked to large commercial firms which were acceptable to our Military Government

Officers. A round-up of leaders is now in progress and the organisation will be crushed.'[20] Apart from the need to guard against such threats, an occupying army has many calls upon it, to say nothing of its normal duties. Guards for POW camps, ammunition dumps and for trains, had to be found. Technical and supply units were as busy as ever they had been, this being particularly true of all units on the lines of communication in the Low Countries. Most units were under strength, with release being speedier than had been anticipated and with only a trickle of reinforcements replacing men who were leaving. Only one or two regular battalions were up to strength. Units, nevertheless, had to carry out all the jobs assigned to them even though they lacked the manpower to enable them to do so. There were few which did not find great difficulty in providing their own instructors and, with leave to be arranged every four and a half months, many found continuity of education almost impossible. Nor should it be forgotten that there was frequent movement as the British Army of the Rhine settled in to its forward positions and that worsening relations with the USSR added to the urgency of training.[21]

Difficult as were the political and military conditions for the forces of occupation, they were much worse in the Middle East and in South and South-East Asia, where nationalist movements had to be contained. Pericles had warned his fellow Athenians that 'to relinquish empire is unsafe' since then 'danger will arise from the animosities incurred in its exercise'.[22] This was the experience of the European imperial peoples and if we are to believe the Americans when they tell us they had not got an empire in the Philippines, at least after the war they encountered the difficulties that would have been met had they had an empire there. The British were luckier than most but British soldiers had occasion to wonder wryly whether the men of the Afrika Korps, had they been on the streets of Cairo and Alexandria, would have been subjected to similar abuse and whether, had this been the case, they would have reacted to such provocation as did British troops.[23] It is a tribute to the British that, speculating on German behaviour in these circumstances, they did not alter their own. There were active service conditions, and casualties, in Palestine, untold bestiality in India and every kind of dacoity, mayhem and murder in Burma. Indeed between 1945 and 1963 not a year passed without British soldiers being in action. In such circumstances the carrying out of any Army Education Scheme could not have priority.

There was yet another problem. The recruits coming in, as the HMIs in the Middle East pointed out, were 'young, unstable and lacking in self-discipline'. Most, they said, had 'finished their schooling in 1939 and have had high wages with little control'. And as they had now to deal with various forms of civil commotion it was essential that they be given as much concentrated training as possible. This had to be done, moreover, as the HMIs said, while 'the most experienced officers, NCOs and men had left, were leaving or were about to leave'. And it was not only the big formations in Egypt and in Palestine which were very hard pressed. 'The average unit', the HMIs found, 'has as much to do as before.' It could hardly be doubted that, given these conditions and the coming into the Army of half-educated and wholly undisciplined youngsters, the high hopes entertained that the Army would pull up the educational standards of the nation were misplaced, since the difficulty of making good existing educational deficiencies was obviously increasing as rapidly as the opportunity of doing so was decreasing.

As ambitious a scheme as the Release Scheme was costly and the Treasury, acutely aware of the horrendous costs of war, was determined that it should not cost more than had been allowed for. Hence when equipment ordered did not arrive in time. local purchase was not permitted. The Army, having liberated much of Europe, proved outstandingly good in liberating much that was in it too. In this it won the unstinted respect of the HMIs, as did the age-old capacity of the Army to help itself. But important as both these kinds of self-help were, they could not suffice. The problem remained. 'Equipment is to be found on paper, to judge by the War Office lists of what may be ordered', the HMIs said, 'But it does not exist in reality ... In respect of both tools, materials and text-books we came across a general sense of fury and frustration.'[24] This was so elsewhere too. 'We suffered badly from the non-arrival of books and equipment', an AEC officer in Germany wrote. 'These did not arrive in sufficient quantity until the run-down of the Army and the release of trained instructors had made the implementation of the Education Scheme almost impossible.'[25]

All of the HMIs who inspected the Release Scheme were warm in their praise of the teaching qualities and of the administrative ability of the AEC. 'The Army owes a great deal to the enterprise of its Education Officers and NCOs', those in Germany said. 'The AEC has kept education going', was the report of the HMIs in the Middle East. 'In the standard of its own best achievement the AEC has set its aim high. The AEC appears to have met the changing needs of the Army during the past year or two with outstanding vigour and resourcefulness, and without losing its sense of purpose and direction in the process'. Nevertheless they revealed that the Release Scheme had been based on yet another fallacious assumption. This was that the AEC would be numerous enough to keep the scheme working properly, to iron out its kinks, correct its deficiencies, give Commanding Officers all the help and advice they needed, encourage the good, support the halting and shame into greater endeavour the bad, if that was possible. In the event, as the HMIs found, they were 'too few in numbers to give the average Commanding Officer the help he needed'. 'There is not nearly enough personnel', they said, 'and during the past few months there has been a constant coming and going of what personnel is available.'[26]

Not all units were 'on the scheme', as the expression went and not all the claims of those which supposedly were, were taken seriously by the HMIs. Those which made every effort to work it had to adjust it to the conditions in which they found themselves, as we have seen. Nevertheless much was done, enough to enable the attempt to be made to distil, as it were, from accumulated experience its failures and its successes and to find what message, if any, it may have for later times.

Let us see what happened to unit education, as this was at the heart of the Release Scheme. 'It was planned', General Lloyd said, 'on the assumption that the Army would provide its own instructors.' The more technical Corps, he said, did and the regiments did not. Yet these, he added, needed the scheme most. They also wanted it least.[27] An AEC officer who was responsible for Army Education Centres in Germany wrote 'In six centres with a majority of infantry students, opinion was against Army

Education. From the six centres with a majority of students of the supporting arms a favourable opinion was received.'[28] 'There were some satisfactory schemes set up, but these', Lloyd said, 'were few and far between.' 'Too much reliance', he found, 'was placed on the Regimental Instructor and the posting of a Regimental Instructor was not under the control of the Education Staff.' These instructors were constantly being released and with them their classes disappeared. There was constant reorganisation of units, amalgamation and disbandment. Such was the difficulty of finding instructors that before the ending of the scheme, a policy change, he admitted, had to be made from providing instructors on a regimental basis to making available what had now become RAEC instructors.[29] Until that happened one Commanding Officer even said 'Unit education generally, unless extremely well run by professional teachers, easily becomes farcical, education in the unit may become just a piece of ABCA – i.e. just a way of spending half-an-hour.'[30] The conviction here that ABCA had little to do with education could hardly have been made more evident.

'Anything like a regular routine', as the HMIs found, 'was well-nigh impossible.' Nevertheless some good work was done in the units, more in the crafts than in the arts. HMIs in the Middle East were happy to acknowledge how much education there owed to the General Officer Commanding-in-Chief, General Paget, and those in Germany gladly paid tribute to the helpfulness of some Commanding Officers. 'There were the few', they said, 'who were genuine enthusiasts and under them education flourished as well as could be expected.'[31] 'Where a unit seemed to us to be good educationally', they added, 'we were often told it also had a good record of military efficiency'. It would be unforgivable, too, not to mention the determination and dedication of some Unit Education Officers. One, writing in March 1946, shows what could be done by a willing Unit Education Officer. He was well aware of the difficulties that faced him. 'I struck an unexpected snag with the word "education"', he says. 'The men, with very few exceptions, shied like frightened horses at the word. If only the Army had invented a new word – something at which it is usually so apt – all would have been well.' He tells us that he was dealing with both old hands and new arrivals. His was an RAOC Holding Company and it seems clear that his old hands had not been among those impressed by wartime Army Education. He adds 'After the students had been along a few times they needed no detailing. On the contrary, the grouse started when they were prevented from coming.' He makes no mention of ABCA and BWP and it is clear that he is not thinking of these but of attention to individual wants. When shortages made it difficult for these to be satisfied he was not blind to the charms of diplomacy, confident that 'a drink in the Mess or some blarney over the phone will often produce the desired results'. This could not always suffice and he was unable to provide a bevy of ATS with dress-making materials or cope with a request to arrange a class in Greek philosophy.[32] In this latter matter, in later years, the RAF successfully demonstrated one-up-manship in keeping an instructor at Cranwell for a year beyond his normal posting to enable a cadet to continue with his classical studies.[33]

The HMIs in the Middle East believed that 'without the high aims of the original Army Education Scheme even the limited achievements we found might not have taken place'. They thought it put pressure on the average unit to allow and encourage voluntary attendance at classes and to meet, wherever this was possible, demands with the appropriate classes. They noticed, furthermore, what seemed to them 'a most important change', namely that classes 'are now generally promoted in working hours'. They thought, nevertheless, that unit education had failed. They reported 'We must, however, ask what real difference the Scheme has made. In the main, education is still voluntary just as before the Scheme was introduced, and over the Middle East as a whole we gain the impression that the number of men enjoying anything like a systematic education is still quite small.' 'Either the Scheme should be modified', they said, 'or education will have to be pressed on very vigorously indeed. Some decision will have to be made about the relation between education and all the other activities that have a claim on working time.' As for the small units, they believed, when things settle down 'we should expect more education and less interruption than at present'.

This same conviction that unit education was the great failure of the Release Scheme was widespread. It was marked even where circumstances seemed most propitious. For some time before the war in Europe ended, Anti-Aircraft Command had not been in action. It was able to make advance preparation for implementing the Release Scheme. It trained nearly 2,000 instructors, benefitting from the many twelve-day courses Regional Committees arranged for it. It held courses to explain the scheme to every officer of field rank in the Command. Group Centres were set up in each of the three Anti-Aircraft Groups to complete the preparation. If elsewhere the Scheme was rushed and thrown off balance by the head-long pace of events, that was less true in Anti-Aircraft than in any other Command. Yet it was obvious that here too unit education was a failure. Colonel Wilson explained why. It was assumed, he said, that 'officers would be instructors in some subjects and students in others. In reality there was always such an obvious shortage of officers that they were able to take only a limited part in unit education in A.A. Command. There were barely enough officers to run the release machinery let alone take part in education classes.'[34] Even the camel can only survive in the desert on its accumulated reserves for a limited period and those of units were disappearing at an alarming speed.

We can learn from our mistakes even more than from our successes, which is no doubt as well since they tend to be more frequent. There is one clear lesson to be learned from the Release Scheme. It is that the unit could not then attend to its own educational needs. It is to be doubted if it ever can unless unit needs become minimal and the unit has its own 'Schoolies' to meet them. 'If a horse is to be compelled to go to the water', the HMIs said, 'the water must be drinkable, abundant and of really good quality. Too many of the compulsory classes that we saw were not suitable and some, it must be plainly stated, were worse than nothing at all. Unit officers should be trained to instruct. Few of them possess this ability in the light of nature. The participation of officers is fundamental to the success of education on a unit basis and they should not be so ill-at-ease and inexperienced in the art of teaching as many of those we saw so obviously were.' The Scheme would have worked in the units only 'had there been a large supply of first-rate instructors capable of improvisation whatever the conditions and of making the right approach to the kind of student with whom they had to deal'. In the absence of such a supply the scheme could not and did not work.[35]

Everything has the virtue that is appropriate to it and it may well be the virtue that is appropriate to Army Education is the course. This was Colonel Wilson's view. 'Anyone who has been closely connected with the Army for any considerable period of time', he said, 'knows that the only way of ensuring continuity of instruction in any subject, no matter what it is by striking men off all other duties for a period of so many working days. To run a course in any subject you like to mention, consisting of one hour a week, for, say twenty-four weeks, will never work in the Army.' 'The great advantage of the short course idea', he emphasised, 'was that one could be almost certain of a 100% attendance.' This, he was sure, 'was the only satisfactory way of pursuing the scheme'.[36] The HMIs in Germany found 'a large number of units favoured block courses of from two to six weeks for men soon to be released who were struck off most, or all, military duties for the purpose'.

The evidence is overwhelming that except in very exceptional circumstances the unit could not provide the teaching to meet its educational requirements and the evidence is equally overwhelming that the educational course could be very helpful. Wherever they came across centralised education HMIs were most impressed by it. They found a great deal of it in Germany and they praised it highly. They met 'quite a number of officers and others who were critical and pessimistic about Army Education'. They thought that they must have 'based their views on the patchy discontinuous nature of the provision known to them in some units' and they added 'a knowledge of what was done in centralised schools might have modified their impressions'. 'Some of the best education work seen in BAOR', they said, 'was at certain of the Forces Study Centres.' They were disappointed that they were not better attended but they were in no doubt of their value. Their strong view was that 'although their voluntary evening activities attract only a small proportion of troops, these few have as great a claim to facilities which enable them to practice their conception of civilian living in a destroyed and foreign land as the many have to lighter forms of enjoyment'. A common remark of those attending centralised schools, they reported, was 'I am getting my mind working again' or 'My skill is coming back.' 'To have made this experience possible for many', they said, 'we regard as a definite and notable achievement of BAOR education.'[37]

The same was true of the Area and Command middle level courses arranged under the Release Scheme. It is easy to agree with Colonel Wilson when he said that these residential courses were 'quite the best feature of the Wartime and the Release Scheme'. Living together in an educational environment, he said, was a new experience for those who left school at fourteen. Even in military premises that experience was an enjoyable one. In a Formation College or better still in a University it was, he was sure, much more so.[38] Morris had spoken of the attraction of 'living and learning in good company'. It was an attraction the unit could not provide; the course could and did.

But for the residential course the ATS would have participated in the Release

Scheme even less than it did. In educational matters men and women in the Forces were in theory treated equally. In practice it was usually more difficult for the ATS to be given time off for education than it was for the men. HMIs visiting the Mediterranean Area found only three instances of time being given to the ATS to attend classes in working hours. It seems, however, that the most ardent of women's lib militants, had there been any about at this time, would not have been able to create great dissatisfaction at this. As an ATS Education Officer wryly noted 'There can be no doubt that the major problem of ATS Education Officers was of overcoming the gloom with which too many auxiliaries remembered their schooldays.'[39]

Visiting HMIs said that of the three main groups of ATS there, 40, 50 and 80% were composed of Palestinians. They noted 'we saw enough to realise the eager, almost avid, desire of Palestinian girls for education. They are keen to take up classes and even agitate for them to be formed; as compared with English girls they seem to find it easier to be released for the classes and courses which they choose.' The HMIs were naive to express surprise at that. If Palestinian girls were not so released there might have been political repercussions which in the case of the English girls Commanding Officers would have no reason to expect; even so the difference in the attitude of the Palestinian and of the English girls to education is sufficiently obvious.

The HMIs added of the English auxiliaries that most expected to get married and that 'what they remember of their schooldays has not suggested that even from the point of view of marriage education may be a help'. But repeated disappointment had not dulled HMI hopes that the Army would be returning to civilian life better citizens than they had got from it. They still thought that the ATS should 'be given some idea of what it means to be a citizen and how they can use their leisure'. They wanted them to be told 'of short courses and LEA provision in existence or planned'; their conviction can hardly have been great that the ATS would make use of their leisure on demobilisation to attend them. The HMIs concluded that 'the general estimate must be that the whole educational scheme for the auxiliaries in the Central Mediterranean Forces has only so far been able to provide something in the nature of a thin top dressing'. They acknowledged that even that could not have been done had it not been easier to secure permission for the auxiliaries to attend full-time courses than to persuade Commanding Officers to release them for odd hours during the working week. They found that 'one out of every seven ATS in the theatre as a whole had attended courses of some kind or other', and this, they said, 'represents something of an achievement in view of the many difficulties'.[40]

Whatever the attraction of the course, however, it could not satisfy those to whom education was a genuinely continuous and progressive process. Thus the Residential course in the Release Scheme was not without its critics then as it has not been without them in later times. For while the educational course might be said to be building education into the pattern of Army life, it was a step away from, not a step towards, the continuity and regularity that had been desired. Courses might be periodic but they were not continuous. They were like inoculations, not necessary, it was hoped, too frequently, conveying immunity whether against ignorance or against that odd preoccupation with it that unaccountably afflicted authority.

That criticism has often had point but it need not always have. Every adult educator knows that if he or she does not express what is wanted in terms of what is attainable nothing worthwhile will be done. And there is no reason why the Army custom of the course should not be so built on as to produce a satisfactory result. The model here might well be Oxbridge. Here undergraduates go to common lectures that can be attended by undergraduates of all colleges. But each college also teaches its own undergraduates, Cambridge in what it calls the supervision and Oxford the tutorial. The purpose of the supervision or the tutorial is not to duplicate the lecture. It is to strengthen, straighten and discipline minds, to develop the arts of analysis and communication and also to ensure that undergraduates are making the effort without which these objectives will not be achieved. There seems to be no good reason why those who have attended courses should, in consequence of that, become immune to further mental effort. Their Commanding Officers could ensure that they were not and a monthly visitation from an RAEC supervisor or tutor could see to the rest. This worked for subalterns in the Junior Officer Education or JOE Scheme and it could be given wider application. If it is thought that the constitution of soldiers is too delicate for them to be exposed to bracing winds so frequently, no doubt the resources of civilisation would not be exhausted, but it should be remembered that nothing is worth having that does not demand effort. In view of the number of language classes which the HMIs in Germany found 'folding up after three weeks when students realised that the study of modern language entailed hard work' this needs saying as it is a truth which soldiers are often tempted to forget. In any case criticisms of the educational course based on its inability to promote long continuity are out of place when applied to the Release Scheme, since however much it sought to develop progressive education in the soldiery, it was totally unable to do so. It soon sought success not in the provision of continuous education, which was early found to be impossible, but in inducing a taste for education in as many as possible of those who might otherwise never have given it a thought since leaving school, if indeed they had done so before then, and in satisfying the comparative few for whom it was a veritable godsend.

The Formation College was described as the apex of the Release Scheme; a description which the HMIs in Germany felt was fully justified. It was the best the Army had to offer and it was very good indeed. The Formation College aimed to admit 1,500 students at a time and they were to attend courses lasting four weeks. Four weeks was a very short period of time, almost certainly too short to have the lasting impression that was hoped for. The principle followed, however, was the old utilitarian principle of the greatest happiness of the greatest number. And in that principle the stress was laid on the greatest number and not on the greatest happiness. It was to the greatest number that authority hoped to give as much happiness as it could. Its concern was not to provide the greatest possible happiness for as many as were capable of appreciating it, even if that number was comparatively small. It calculated that it could at most cater for 10% of the Forces during the demobilisation period and it wanted to spread its net as widely as possible. If courses lasted for two months, only half of those who might otherwise attend them would be able to. It accordingly restricted them to one month and in so doing limited what could be achieved. Unfortunately it did not thereby increase the appeal of the Formation College to the 90% of the Army which, as the HMIs discovered, was unshakable in its determination to stay away. Nevertheless some 200,000 men and women attended Formation Colleges.

But although for too short a time the Formation College encapsulated a spell of college life, its very brevity added to its intensity and gave it an unforgettable sparkle. 'It will be a long time before we forget the keenness and spirit that were apparent', the HMIs said of the Formation College in the Middle East. Wherever it was, the Formation College was more of a University plus than a University minus – for however too brief a time. At certain Oxbridge colleges there are courses lasting a term attended by men and women from the worlds of banking, commerce and the police and those who teach them are always aware of the enormous amount their pupils put into them and of the electrifying effect that has. They are blood brothers and sisters of that great man of whom it was said 'He turned from great affairs of state to Aeschylus and Livy. He threw the Great Seal in the grate and the Privy Seal in the privy.' They have, like him, the ability to turn away from the past and settle with extraordinary concentration on the present, so that all they do stands out with an arresting sharpness. This was true of the Formation College. Perhaps it was the meeting of congenial spirits in a congenial atmosphere, perhaps it was the feeling that this was a wonderful and possibly unique opportunity to do something that had always been at the back of one's mind and that had at last contrived to force its way to the front, perhaps it was the call of the gracious and non-material that had at last made itself heard in an ungracious and most material world, perhaps it was simply the appeal of what was out of the ordinary that was the key to the fascination which the Formation College seems to have aroused in those privileged to attend it. It was an experience not easily forgotten. On occasion the HMIs found the teaching there somewhat unimaginative and they were rude about the vocational courses in the Commercial Wing of the Middle East Formation College at Sarafand, saying that these were so utilitarian in their approach that 'this College scarcely serves an educational purpose in any very wide sense of that term, although it is enormously appreciated by the students'. In general, however, they thought the teaching shared the excellence of the Formation College. The Formation Colleges, they said, were excellently discharging their two main responsibilities, the training of instructors for the Release Scheme and the provision of further education in general and technical studies at a higher level than was possible in lower formations and units.

Apart from its Instructor Wing, each Formation College had Science, Modern Studies, Arts and Crafts, Domestic Science, Commerce and Trades departments. Its courses related to Government training schemes and to professional bodies but did not confer admission rights to either. Education was both general and technical but it avoided narrow specialisation. Current affairs, citizenship and physical training were included in the curriculum. In most cases the requirements of the students were markedly utilitarian. What was looked for was practical experience that would be an asset in applying for entry into a trade or profession, or the knowledge needed for an examination. But while concerned to satisfy these needs as much as possible, the

College aimed to inculcate a concern for the problems of today and tomorrow.[41]

It was a common experience of those who taught centralised courses that 'students were most reluctant to study more than the one subject which they considered might help them in their future occupation'. 'There was', it was found, 'the greatest difficulty in persuading book-keepers that it was worth their while to study economics, or even to convince brick-layers that trade calculations were worth the considerable mental effort which they obviously involved.' Similarly, when Basic Education Centres found it helpful to introduce periods on handicrafts into their programme of remedial education, they met with some hostility. 'What's the use of this?' it was asked. 'I've come to learn to read and write', said one determined to get on with the main task. The HMIs were sure that 'there need be no improper antithesis between vocational training and education'. They insisted 'properly taught in itself and with a background of wider interest, the vocational study can contribute a very great deal to education in the more general sense of the word'. But they had to acknowledge that 'some of the vocational work that we saw, while meeting what was probably the biggest single demand in the Army, was too narrow to be educational in this sense'. They knew how difficult it was to broaden it and they particularly liked the way in which most Formation Colleges insisted on doing so. The HMIs found that the trades students at Mitoqba resented the introduction of theoretical studies in their schemes of work. They wanted to concentrate on the practical handling of the tools of their trade. The plumbers objected to the inclusion of building construction, building science, building drawings and mathematics into their curriculum. The HMIs were greatly impressed and delighted by the Commandant's refusal to modify the course to placate the unhappy plumbers.[42]

The Formation College was not exclusively a development of the Release Period, although the scale on which it operated was. Its predecessors are to be found in places like Coleg Harlech and in the various universities that hosted residential courses for the Regional Committees. It was the culmination of that movement to provide residential adult education, the value of which many University Extra-Mural Boards had found in their Summer Schools but which, apart from these, they had developed little, if at all. It had been left to the Army to realise their full importance. That was one of the great contributions of the Army to adult education.

Yet for all their achievements the Formation College present us with a challenge. The HMIs estimated that from some 90% of the Army no one ever came to them. That 90% stayed away as enthusiastically as the 10% came. The fairness of criticising an institution which specifically and triumphantly sought to satisfy the interest of the interested for failing to attract those who were not must be doubted. Yet if society needs to care for its potential leaders it cannot afford to be indifferent to the development of those whom it does not expect to find among them. In the appalling conditions of the East Anglian anti-aircraft sites where grey matter was successfully stirred and where weighty issues such as the effect of technology on 20th Century living were discussed, it was demonstrated that that 90% was get-at-able. That was not made apparent in the far finer circumstances of the Formation College. That cannot be a criticism of the Formation College but it is a criticism of society generally.

The East Anglian experience presents us with a problem, the solution of which escapes us all but which it is incumbent on all of us to try to find. Meanwhile we can absolve the Formation College for not doing to those whom it could not get what it did so spectacularly for those whom it could.

The HMIs found that the emphasis in all the centralised schools they visited, including the Formation Colleges, was vocational or professional in character. They said that this was also 'mostly true of those schools which offered academic subjects', for their students were preparing for the Forces Preliminary Examination or were interested in the requirements of the professions. The HMIs visiting the Mediterranean Area noted that 'the objective of the courses that we saw was invariably success in an examination'. This was true of the Release Scheme of Education as a whole. Colonel Wilson, in emphasising that interest in it was to a very large extent confined to practical subjects, went so far as to say 'it was occupational and vocational rather than educational'. He added 'Before the ordinary adult with whom we are dealing ("the 90%")' – he meant those who had displayed an apparently finished and finite aversion to education – 'could be interested in the academic side of the scheme he had to be persuaded that it was likely to be of some practical value to him after he left the Service, or else it had to make a direct appeal to his interests.'[43] The unvarying pattern of the Release Scheme was that every trade class was at once over-subscribed. 'What the sóldier usually wanted', the HMIs said after their German tour, 'was something to help him in his civilian career, in his home, or, to a smaller extent, in his leisure activities.'

We can see the same demand for trade training in the very practical help which the Army provided for itself. When the war ended the technical arms began classes to prepare their own people for demobilisation. They also helped neighbouring non-technical units. This was such a real self-help that it led to the recognition of sixteen Pre-Vocational Centres that were attended by no fewer than 2,400 students. Mitoqba College was another illustration of such self help. RAOC and RASC depots had a great deal of equipment that could be used for instruction. They also had skilled instructors, some of whom had taught in technical schools. There were empty hangars at Mitoqba and these were turned into a college which offered courses in building, brick-laying, woodwork, metalwork, fitting, training and machine minding. When the Army turned to self-help in this way it left no doubt as to where its interests lay.

Of all the subjects offered in the Release Scheme 'Man and Society' made the least appeal to the troops. This is a singular comment on that determination which W. E. Williams saw in the troops to familiarise themselves with the essential facts behind the problems of an ever-changing world. Whether they thought that what they already had had was enough to give them the requisite understanding – in which case it was to be doubted how much better citizens the substitution of an unsound judgement for a profound ignorance had made them – or whether they simply concluded that their time could be more pleasurably and profitably spent in other ways, it was obvious that their appetite for such studies had not been sufficiently whetted for them to demand more of the same. A further fact may be of interest too. Colonel White tells us that 'as the older men went, the demand for modern studies grew'.[44] The HMIs commented on the infrequency of ABCA sessions in the Release Period so that it seems that those whose exposure to them had been limited had a greater interest in 'Man and Society' than those who had longer experience of them.

To the Greek of old, life itself was important, but the good life was more important still and the best life was achievable only by the best of citizens. In the average British soldier concern for the good life and the conviction that only the good citizen could achieve it was remarkably little in evidence; much more apparent was his belief that it should concern others no more than it did himself; most unmistakable of all was his interest in preparing himself for a secure and profitable job which would leave him happy in the knowledge that he could then determine for himself without the aid of others the kind of life that would most appeal to him. We ought not, however, to be surprised that what interest the British soldier had in education was of a markedly utilitarian kind. It is an attitude very common in universities. Agreeing with Aristotle that in matters educational curiosity is the beginning of virtue, undergraduates will attend in droves lectures given by visiting celebrities, but they are rarely to be found in lectures given by Faculties other than their own, whatever the cultural interest of these non-utilitarian lectures may be.

The HMIs visiting Germany said that 'Community Education was intended to be at the heart of Army Education'. 'This was not the case', they added. 'In BAOR Community education', they said, 'was neither universally nor regularly done there.' That was true everywhere else too. The HMIs in the Mediterranean found that 'many of the men looked upon education at best with philosophic resignation'. They were doubtless among the 10% of those questioned who said that education gave them an opportunity to relax and get away from military discipline. They were like the corporals, one of whom said 'It's a restive afternoon', and the other 'classes give you a chance to relax a lot and learn a little'. There were more 'who have no interest in learning as such or in technical avocations and no particular desire for education as it is commonly understood'. The RASC driver who said 'once you have been to school no one wants to go again' or the Private, in whose words 'I left school twelve years ago and at the age of twenty-six I have a mind of my own' we can unquestionably hear the voice of what for centuries the English Common Law referred to as the Average Reasonable Man ringing down the ages, are typical of them.[45] There were most of all those who resented being compulsorily got at. The HMIs in the Middle East found that men were saying 'ABCA was an attempt to put over the official version of things' and this was one of the reasons why it was so strongly resented.

The men were right in so feeling, although not in the sense that the Bureau of Current Affairs Bulletins were presenting an official line. Far from this being the case, these Bulletins were infuriating officials and thoroughly annoying General Lloyd and his staff. There was, however, an important sense in which ABCA periods represented 'an official version of things' and one of which the HMIs approved. The official version was that that which would fashion the good citizen must be done. And this seemed so overriding a necessity that the HMIs could even say 'there is not much time to lose'. It is to be regretted that they did not tell us what they had in mind in saying that. But it seems legitimate to infer that they felt 'time's wingèd chariot drawing near', that Armageddon was awaiting the countries whose citizens refused to become good and that the opportunity to compel adult men and women to submit themselves to being done good to in this way was likely to be a passing one. It is not fanciful to say that the British are not to be numbered among the world's most enthusiastic crusaders. If they became convinced, as it appeared they were beginning to be, that they were being forcibly enrolled in a crusade they would soon leave no doubt that they would have to be numbered among the world's most enthusiastic anti-crusaders. Their dislike of official versions, their resentment at being got at, would not disappear and they were beginning to make it evident that the notion of making them better than they wanted to be had better be forgotten as quickly as possible.

The greatest disappointment of the HMIs, they said, was ABCA. 'We expected to find that here, if anywhere', they said, 'we should find interesting and useful work', for ABCA was 'undoubtedly the most publicised part of Army Education'. No one could fault them in saying that, for W. E. Williams was still making great play with that 17th Century Commonwealth soldier who knew what he was fighting for and who loved what he knew. Indeed, his imagination was becoming ever more outrageous as he spoke of 'those squadrons of Cromwell's Ironsides who in their day sat down once or twice a week to debate the issues for which they were in arms'.[46] If this refers to anything at all it would be to the early meetings of those who became known as the 'Agitators' and who were preparing in secret for what happened at the General Assembly of the Army on Newmarket Heath, when those officers whose opposition was known were unhorsed and beaten out of the field in the obviously disapproving presence of the 'grandees', or Generals. The confident submission for the approval of a later set of 'grandees' of this instance of soldiers preparing to mutiny as a worthy example for their own soldiers to follow is not without its piquancy.

Having heard so much of ABCA, HMIs were looking forward to seeing it in operation and they expressed their disappointment forcefully and acidly. They regretted that they saw so little of it. In Germany they noted that 'Regimental Officers were skipping the weekly discussion period', although they seem to have seen more of ABCA than their colleagues did elsewhere. At least they complained less of not seeing it and we cannot assume that they were observing a grateful silence in this matter. They noted with disapproval 'lingering fears' among officers 'that any kind of discussion is subversive of good discipline'. In the Middle East the HMIs spoke of 'the passive opposition of most officers' to ABCA and said that it was 'compulsory only in theory'. They 'formed the impression that in fact there was only a little ABCA going on'. They noted 'a certain disparity between the ABCAs listed as given and those which men say they actually attended'. 'Out of a group of 108 students training to be Unit Instructors', they reported, '80 told us they were not then in units doing any ABCA.' In the Mediterranean Area HMIs 'found it difficult to see much ABCA being done'. Yet they were not unaware that special efforts were made to please them. They came across units which tried to follow biblical precedent, having scoured the hedgerows for those who would take the place of the reluctant wedding guests, 'getting fell in' those who only too visibly would have been greatly relieved had they been 'got fell out'.

Where they saw ABCA being done the HMIs were not above wishing that they had not. 'The majority of ABCA sessions', those in Germany said, 'were poor to bad.' Much more important than that they noted that 'sometimes groups were just intractable'. Dumb insolence has eloquent tongues and even in the Army, where charges were not invariably to be laughed off lightly, insolence was not always dumb. With the bloody-mindedness that they noticed in some groups not even Spenser's 'fair filèd tongue' could always have smoothed the way and not all subalterns spoke with its fluency. 'Even allowing for the effects of visitors walking in, we were struck by the lack of real spontaneity in the discussions that we did see', the HMIs in the Mediterranean Area reported.

For the most part, the HMIs concluded, those who took ABCA sessions were not capable of taking them adequately. 'We are unable to agree that the unit officer is by definition always the most suitable person to conduct an ABCA period', the HMIs in Germany said. 'It depends on him having the relevant knowledge and gifts of leadership. We do not agree that this duty should be laid on him of necessity.' To do this was to gamble with Community Education and too much was at stake for that to be permitted. The HMIs found AEC instructors conducting ABCA sessions and said 'they were often more successful than unit officers'. If officers had to take ABCA 'their training should include, over a long period, instruction in the broad issues of citizenship, as well as in the techniques of guiding discussions'. It was unreasonable to believe that the average regimental officer would necessarily master the art of leading a discussion, the HMIs in the Mediterranean Area believed. Nor would 'more short courses in technique ... supply necessary fundamental knowledge', their colleagues in Germany said. 'This takes long to acquire. Further the art of leading discussions calls not only for the requisite knowledge but also for insight, dexterity, firmness and geniality, if good results are to be obtained. This is not everybody's role.' Their experience greatly concerned the HMIs who were shaken by finding so 'many who disliked ABCA very much indeed'.

They said that it was 'an increasingly distasteful chore' to both officers and men and they added that 'an almost complete absence of enthusiasm for it was most marked'. The abuse piled on it could often be called virulent, the dislike for it something that seemed to verge on hatred. They were appalled to find the community element in the Educational Release Scheme in such poor shape. They attached great importance to education in citizenship, in current affairs, in understanding international reality; they had looked to ABCA to promote interest in these things; they had looked in vain.

They were not sure what it was that occasioned such dislike. 'Was it the study of current affairs, or the use of discussion technique?' they asked. 'Was it the very idea of discussion, or were the discussions not good enough? Was it the element of compulsion, the hour of meeting or simply that a good idea had gone on for too long?' They could not agree about the effect, or the desirability, of compulsion. Some wanted to keep it, others to get rid of it. The majority feeling that was finally found was that while it should be retained for the young conscript it should be abolished in the case of the older soldier. But on one thing they did agree; ABCA had given rise to waffle unstinted, waffle without end. They thought that the method of ABCA had come to predominate over the object of ABCA. 'The idea of discussion', they said, 'has come to matter more than the idea of current affairs.' They thought that 'discussion could not stand the strain of being the principal vehicle of instruction over the years'. The odd thing was that in insisting on discussion when it was not necessary, group leaders turned away from it when it was. The HMIs noted 'In many cases it appeared that the officer in charge of an ABCA period was striving to get discussion going in supposed loyalty to official doctrine; whereas in many BWP periods there was little more than direct instruction without real opportunity given or taken for group discussion.' They said that 'in all periods devoted to Community Education there should be both instruction and discussion, the balance between them being determined by the nature of the topic and the relevant knowledge of the group'. They added 'Occasionally there may be a place for a free-for-all discussion, if the leader is capable of dealing with it; though in general desultory discussion for its own sake is as barren as instruction passively received.' They felt sure that 'the actual presentation of ABCA has aroused distaste and sometimes scorn not always patiently expressed' and they concluded 'In the light of what we saw of the system in operation we are unable to say that these feelings are unjustified.' The troops, they said, 'had had more than enough of ABCA', a point they underlined in the immortal words which would have pride of place in any 'Gems From an HMI's Notebook', the troops 'felt that they had been compulsorily but ignorantly flogging dead red herrings'.

The HMIs drew attention to a significant danger to which the growing dislike of ABCA was giving rise. Current affairs, which they believed to be a subject of intrinsic interest, had become identified with what, they conceded, might at one time have been a lively method of teaching but which had become so formalised as to empty it of content and to deprive it of significance. It was identified with discussion, now the be-all and the end-all of all things. Facts could not be conveyed. They had to be extracted, even if by the crudest dentistry. Any subject to which we were only exposed in the dentist's chair would be unlikely to arouse general enthusiasm and that, the HMIs said, was the explanation of the widespread disenchantment with current affairs they had found in the Army. One thing should be done at once, they suggested. Current affairs sessions must not be called ABCA, that being the kiss of death. They approved of BWP as remedying the deficiencies of ABCA. They wanted to put BWP and ABCA together in a much wider study of current affairs which would include citizenship and which might well be compulsory. And while discussion should be part of all teaching of adults, it should be recognised that on occasion other modes of teaching would be better.

The HMIs touched upon a potentially more deadly danger to which ABCA, it seemed, could lend itself. They did not expand upon it. Perhaps they did not do so in the conviction that as ABCA was increasingly ignored and was clearly on the way out there was no need, as the danger was theoretical only and not real. It was, nevertheless, worth a comment. The troops in the Middle East with whom the Inspectors talked said that discussions did not lead to action. If the HMIs asked the men what action they expected these discussions to lead to, they do not tell us what the reply was; if they did not they missed an opportunity to find out something of importance. For if discussion as such led the men to think that action should follow on whatever conclusions they reached, then it was the greatest danger both to the Army and to civil society, and fully justified those who said that politics ought to have no place in military life. Was it really the dilemma we were facing, that if discussion did not lead to action it would have no appeal to the men and that it would be of the greatest danger to the Army, because it would set men against men and the Army against the state if it did? There was a problem here that ought to have been explored and it must be regretted that the opportunity was not taken to explore it. Clichés are to be avoided because they deaden the truth they seek to convey. But perhaps we should not forget that a little knowledge may be a dangerous thing, however determined we must be never to sing the praises of ignorance.

The HMIs saw the Release Scheme of Education clearly and they saw it whole. Such had been their anticipation of what they were going to see and such their disappointment at what they saw that they could even wonder what difference such an elaborately prepared and costly scheme had made. They could not but be impressed by the marked element of unreality in it and they felt strongly that 'when the flood of release beings to ebb and the Army begins to approach a more ordered mode of life again, the Scheme should be made to correspond more closely with the facts'. Yet they were so well aware of the difficulties that had to be coped with that they could report 'the wonder is not that the Army Educational Scheme had not been more widely and fully implemented but that it had been implemented at all'. That there had been any education at all was an achievement 'and that some very good education has been provided is still more remarkable', they said. They saw much to admire. The libraries, they said, are 'among the best things that Army Education has to offer in the Middle East'. They thought that the Information Rooms there were 'a valuable example of a visual aid in education', although they believed that the judgement of those supplying the pamphlets was sometimes a little eccentric, as when pamphlets on midwifery were sent to the 1st Battalion of the Duke of Wellington's Regiment. They did not share the view of W. E. Williams that exposure to Information Rooms was itself a supremely important education; they found 'tables covered with pamphlets so neat and clean that we doubted if they were looked at'. They were very impressed by 'the remarkable taste for Italian opera that the British soldier has developed' and also 'with the assistance given to him by the Army authorities to indulge it'. And, venturing a judgement beyond their own expertise, they thought that the Educational Release Scheme had achieved its objective at least in this, that it has helped to keep demobilisation smooth and acceptable. Had men been left to await their turn, impatience might have got out of hand. Inaction can breed discontent and the effort put into the Educational Scheme at least conveyed the message that authority cared for the soldier's resettlement.

They were sure that 'the average soldier', like the average civilian, had 'a real interest in education'. Since we must assume that the average soldier belonged to the 90% of the Army which wanted no truck with education, it was obvious that he himself did not know that he had this interest. Indeed he could not know it, because, as the HMIs went on to say, it would 'never awake until awakened'. Things were not even as promising as that suggested since, as the HMIs ruefully admitted, this interest might never be awakened. This was intriguing, if lacking in the clarity that could have been hoped for. As the soldier did not know it we are left to speculate how the HMIs did and to think it a pity that they did not further explore the fascinating implications of the certainty that a mature man's real interests can be better known by someone other than himself.

Two of their conclusions we can find regrettable. The first is that they approved of compulsory education for younger soldiers, not to make them better soldiers but to turn them into better citizens. Perhaps their omission to say at what age the younger soldiers became the older soldiers for whom most of the HMIs thought compulsory education for this purpose undesirable suggests they were not without uneasiness in making their recommendation. Whether that is so or not, we should be. They said if more are taken to water, more will drink. But wanting to raise individual standards and to promote individual development, as we all must, they had forgotten that compulsion can never make men zealous, that it can command outward action but not internal development. They had forgotten how counter-productive compulsory education could be. For if the soldier had to attend compulsory classes essential jobs had to be done, and if they could not be done when he was otherwise compulsorily engaged they would have to be compulsorily done when he was not, in what would have been his own time. One can sympathise with the cook who said 'when a man has been on duty since 0430 hours, it is a big strain for him to finish work at 1400 hours and then attend school for several hours'. Many told an RAEC officer that they were opposed to compulsory education 'as it interfered with the military duties they had to work extra time to get done'.[47] If, as might well be the case, education in the Queen's time spreads in tomorrow's Army there is a problem here which will have to be attended to. The HMIs had forgotten that action will not be successful when it pays inadequate attention to existing conditions and above all when it runs contrary to national sentiments, to the habits, the feelings, the interests, the prejudices which stand rooted in an as yet unchanged national character. There is indeed what T. H. Green called 'the inevitable conflict between the creative will of man and the hidden wisdom of the world which seems to thwart it'.[48] We have to wait until these things change. Our patience will indeed achieve more than our force because in these things our force is incapable of achievement.

The second of their conclusions which must raise our doubts is their view that the unit should still be exhorted to attend to its own educational requirements. It is difficult to deny the truth of those who said that education in the unit could have been provided in no other way since a sufficient number of teachers could not have been brought into it from outside. It is even more difficult to doubt that those who like the HMIs urged that the attempt should still be made to do it in this way had something in common with the 18th Century seller of earthquake pills in Spain – he asked those who asked him what good they would do if they knew anything better to take. However true it was that education in the unit could not have been provided for in any other way than this, it did not follow that it could be done in this. Experience demonstrated the inadequacy both of the earthquake pills and of the view that the unit could attend to its own education.

The faith of the HMIs in the soldier's interest in education, an interest of which he was himself not aware, was indeed in St Paul's words 'the substance of things hoped for, the evidence of things not seen'. We must be grateful to them for refusing to give up the hope that the 90% of the Army, and we may add of civil society too, which looked upon education with great distaste, may at some time or other, in some way or other, be induced to think differently about it. Italian Opera Houses and East Anglian gun sites confirm that hope. Past failure must convince us that future effort to achieve this will be neither easily nor quickly rewarded, but it does not also convince us that it will be vain. Attitudes may take a very long time to change and that time is unlikely to be shorter with the British than with other peoples. But British attitudes have changed and can change again, and the pressures inducing change in our attitude to education seem to be of a constant and compelling kind. As a people it seems obvious that we were not ready for the Educational Release Scheme. Yet we have known many occasions when the time was not ripe for reform but when reform, nevertheless, came in due time. Nothing to be seen in the Educational Release Scheme need deprive us of the hope that the time will come when we will succeed in doing what hitherto has been beyond our best endeavour, namely to create, or, if it is indeed there waiting to be aroused, awaken, in our people an interest in education. We can but agree with the HMIs when they said of the 90% of the Army unattracted by the Scheme 'We have hardly even attempted to teach these people at home, and it is not surprising that there were few units visited which seemed to have found a means of awakening and maintaining the interests of this majority. It remains a challenging field for experiment.'

Caught up as it was in the great activity of the Release Scheme, the AEC had other, and onerous, responsibilities too. There were soon Army schools to be looked after again. In June 1944 Service families began to return to Gibraltar and by early 1946 there was a considerable increase in the number of families overseas. In the Central Mediterranean Area schools were opened in Graz, Naples and Rome by March 1946. In May schools were opened in Tripoli and by October 1946 there were twelve schools fully effective, attended by 500 children. Schools were opened in Cyrenaica and Egypt, in Burma, Singapore, Malaya, Hong Kong and, for a short time for the British Commonwealth Occupation Force in Japan. The great difficulty was to find teachers for these schools, and while the AEC could not be spared to teach in them it had its customary task of keeping an eye on them and of doing everything it could to help them. Immediately after the war in Germany, however, the schools were not the immediate responsibility of the AEC, although it was not long before they once again became so. A civilian organisation, the British Families Education Service, was set up there under the Foreign Office. It maintained a large staff which was responsible for attending to the education of the children of those now engaged in the administration of an occupied land. In July 1946 John Trevelyan, who was Director of Education for Westmorland, was appointed its Director. By December 1948 there were eighty-eight primary schools, two secondary schools and two co-educational secondary boarding schools under his direction. 5,000 children were being taught and 280 British teachers looking after them.

By 1951 the great majority of children were Service children and responsibility for them passed from the Foreign Office to the War Office. In April 1952 the Commander-in-Chief BAOR assumed this responsibility. Support costs were borne by Germany and equipment and staffing were better than elsewhere. In 1955, when Germany joined NATO, the British taxpayer picked up the schoolbill and in 1956 nursery schools were closed in an effort to save his pocket. We have seen what difficulty the teaching of older children occasioned and how the Corps tackled it. In addition, the Institute of Army Education set up an advisory service to help members of all three Services to recruit teachers and to attend to the documentation of the children as they moved around the world as a result of their fathers' postings. Only at home did the AEC lose all responsibility for schools, for at home Army schools were handed over to the Local Education Authorities, the Army retaining control only over two military boarding schools, the Duke of York's Royal Military School at Dover and Queen Victoria School, Dunblane. The hand-over was completed by 1 April 1948. This brought to an end the history of the Queen's Army Schoolmistresses. When the alternation of home and overseas postings was no longer possible recruiting to this body ceased and by 1970 only one Queen's Army Schoolmistress remained in service. That was the end of a long and proud service; with the ending of Empire that ending was also inevitable.

Coping with illiteracy was yet another of the bread and butter jobs of the Corps. It had none of the excitement that attached to the Release Scheme but it was the provision of a service the value of which could not be denied. It remained a matter of great surprise how many illiterates there were, despite the long years of compulsory schooling. By mid-summer 1943 it was estimated that the Army contained 10,000 who could neither read nor write. In June 1946 in one of the smallest of the Home Commands 200 were awaiting places at the Basic Education Centres. In 1946 a battalion commander in BAOR said that 40% of his men needed help when writing home.[49]

The Command Basic Education Centres referred to were five in number. They were later replaced by six Preliminary Education Centres which in 1956 were amalgamated to form a centralised RAEC School of Preliminary Education. This was set up at Everleigh, near Tidworth. It could take 360 pupils at a time and they remained there for twelve weeks. The School of Preliminary Education was called by one who went there 'a dream factory'. The extraordinary hopes expressed at times by some of the RAEC tempt one to think that they were fervent believers in the good fairy's wand, and contemplating the Corps' work with illiterates it is hard to be sure that this useful piece of kit was not available after all. Few things were more civilised, sensible and sympathetic than the approach of the Corps to this problem. Senior Commander Currie's words make that apparent. 'Nor I think were we arrogant enough to believe that to be ill-educated was to be incorrigible', she wrote, 'or that education was a passport to success. We merely held that, in a world of specialisation and competition, literacy was a useful social and commercial accomplishment, and that interests which are capable of development add greatly to the pleasure of life'. 'What is required now is a general education designed to supplement and develop intelligence and to fit it for Service jobs and civilian futures', she added. She quoted Lewis Caroll: '"Curioser and curioser", cried Alice, "Now I'm opening out like the largest telescope that ever was."'[50]

Most teachers have longer to wait before seeing the fruit of their labours, but they have no difficulty in sharing with her and her colleagues satisfaction at a job well done. They will share the pleasure of Colonel Burgess when, stressing the importance of the residential course for those learning to read and write, he said 'The training for leisure proved the wisdom of having residential courses, for many men liked to get on with their work in the evenings. It was an exciting experience to see hardened pub-loafers staying in night after night working on leather purses or patiently enduring the slow polishing involved in perspex work. Provided at first as a refresher, this work had far-reaching effects on the more difficult job of learning to read and write, since it did much to remove the attitude of despair'.[51] When asked why he thought he could do better at the School of Preliminary Education than he had done at school, a soldier replied 'Well, here, the officers care, sir.'[52] Any teacher would be proud to have that said of his or her work. Few things show the strength of the RAEC more than its outstanding tackling of the problem of illiteracy. In this we see the excellence of its teaching, its patient kindliness, its imagination, its persistent ingenuity, its unfailing flexibility, its steady determination. It was careful to arrange classes of low-level equals, it paid special attention to its teaching materials, ensuring their appropriateness to adult soldiers and more often than not having to produce its materials for itself. No instruction was more sympathetic. The job was not entirely without hazard. Teachers were at times assaulted and there was 'a little incident with a knife'. They had to sustain them proof of their success: by the end of the course the great majority of their pupils were writing home.[53] It is pleasant to recall that while so much was being done for the troops there was self-help here as well as on vocational matters as at Mitoqba. There was the Soltau Scheme in Germany. In Thirty Corps districts there were many who were at best barely literate. There were too few, however, in any unit for teaching to be arranged for them there. A Wehrmacht Convalescent Home large enough to feed, teach and sleep 100 men at a time was found at Soltau. Instructors were recruited, an administrative staff found, buildings adapted and units asked to send volunteers. An initial course was planned for six weeks with a further six weeks if the unit could release the man for that time and if this would not delay the man's release. Men came from many arms and services and the Canadian Army also took up vacancies. The results were extraordinary, especially considering that few of the instructors had any teaching experience. Men learned for the first time to read a newspaper and to write a letter home. Soltau was visited and greatly praised by Field-Marshal Montgomery and Lieutenant-General Horrocks.[54]

In areas where the departure of troops was thought to be imminent or where there were few troops, full implementation of the Educational Release Scheme was clearly not to be attempted. Thus there was no Formation College in India, Burma and Ceylon:

300 men a month sailed from South Asia to a Formation College at home. Two residential colleges were, however, opened in India and a residential trade training school was set up as well. This latter school was another excellent example of self-help. It was set up 'by order of the Army Commander' and was not part of the official release scheme. Nor was culture neglected; an excellent orchestra was formed and it toured the units.

There was similar self-help in Burma. The newly-arrived Education Officer found a polytechnic on its last legs there. It had been started by Major Marshall, an engineer officer of great enterprise and energy who arranged courses in brick-building, technical drawing, motor-engineering and other technical subjects. These were much appreciated and well-attended, but they were in imminent danger of ending when Marshall moved on. When Lieutenant-Colonel Mullin arrived he found a lieutenant and a few sergeants coping with the handful of students remaining. Only after eighteen months' continuous effort and repeated failure was Lieutenant-Colonel Mullin able to get it accepted as a proper War Establishment. He came by staff and equipment in ways various and ingenious which might not uncharitably be described as inspired scrounging. 972 British students, 1,419 Indians, eight Burmese, 153 West Africans and 136 of the Indian Women's Auxiliary Corps attended courses at this polytechnic, 'a mite of the pre-release educational schemes of the British and Indian Armies, but all the same a valuable mite'. Apart from this polytechnic, four study centres as well as a school for instructors were opened.[55] In both of these areas, and in Africa too, there was other work for the AEC. Wherever he was the sepoy was always eager for instruction in reading and writing. Many courses were arranged for him, too, in what was called rural reconstruction. There was a scheme to teach the Gurkhas their own lingua franca, Khaskura. There was similar work for the AEC in Africa. A branch of the Army School of Education was established at Gaza to help Africans with agriculture, hygiene and similar matters. In the autumn of 1945 thirteen officers and twenty-one NCOs of the Corps landed at Accra. Twelve Study Centres for British troops preparing for the Forces Preliminary Examination were opened. In February 1946 a West African School of Education was founded at Teshie, near Accra, and in March of that year a West African Army Educational Corps was created. The teaching of English as the lingua franca, if the expression be allowed in this context, went ahead in Sierra Leone. In the summer of 1945 a strong AEC contingent was sent to East Africa too. The contribution of the AEC to the development of countries newly emerging into independence is by no means negligible. It was fully appreciated, as is evidenced by the fact that in July 1947 the Education Officer was asked by Aung San to draw up a plan for the general and technical education of the Burmese Forces.

Never had the AEC been more active and never had its importance been more widely acknowledged than in this Release Period. It was fitting therefore that this should be marked by two major developments. The first was the conferring on the Corps of the title Royal on 28 November 1946, the centenary of the founding of the Corps of Army Schoolmasters. This was followed by His Majesty the King doing it a unique honour. A badge had been designed for it which did not, however, meet with His Majesty's approval. He wanted the Corps to have a badge worthy of it and he suggested what it should be. The College of Heralds objected to the new badge thus proposed, until it was informed who had designed it. It then of course had no doubt that 'His Majesty overrules the College of Heralds'.[56] The RAEC is thus unique in having its badge designed for it by the reigning monarch.

The second event which appropriately marked this great activity of the Corps was its acquisition of Eltham Palace as its HQ Mess. The manor of Eltham is recorded in the Doomsday Book. At the end of the 13th Century it passed into the keeping of Antony Bek, Bishop of Durham. He had the moat dug and laid out the present gardens. At the end of the 15th Century the present bridge leading to the inner court across the moat was built and the Great Hall was finished about the same time. Stephen Courtauld, who took over the estate in 1933, restored the Great Hall and gardens and added the modern dwelling house. R. A. Butler was his guest throughout the war and it was in Eltham that Butler drafted the 1944 Education Act. When Courtauld informed the Crown that he was willing to surrender his lease, Butler expressed the hope that Eltham would be devoted to the cause of Further Education. The Ministry of Works suggested that it might be appropriate for an Army Corps to be housed there and so it came to the AEC. It became the Army School of Education and courses for officers were arranged there during the Release Period. On 1 October 1948 it became the HQ Mess RAEC and the home of a new Institute of Army Education. The Institute, it was said, would be 'an out-station of the War Office, carrying out the detail of executive duties so numerous that they would clog the machinery of the Directorate if they were to be handled within it'. The new Institute housed a Research Wing, a Children's Schools Wing, a Current Affairs and Supplies Wing, an Examinations Wing, an Inspectorate, and eventually an Officers' Education Wing. In 1961 the Institute moved to Court Road, Eltham. In 1982 it was reabsorbed into the Directorate, itself now installed in Court Road. The Corps of Army Schoolmasters would never have dreamed of having such a royal honour conferred upon it or of ever being in possession of such royal quarters.

The activity of the AEC during the war had been far greater than it had ever been imagined it would be. But that activity had owed a great deal to civilians who had inspired much of it and who were in control of it. In the Release Period after Morris's retirement the AEC was its own master and great as was its debt to him, it itself determined how best to interpret the Release Scheme and to ensure the elasticity of approach which was deemed essential to it. The AEC was thus identified more completely and more exclusively with education in the Release Period than it had been with wartime Army Education, and the questions to be asked are what was the significance of this Release Scheme for the Corps? What does it tell us about the Corps' future? In what way does it affect that future?

The Release Scheme of Education, it cannot be doubted, produced a far greater awareness throughout the Army of the existence of the Corps. In reply to a question in the Commons Michael Stewart said that during February 1947 about five-fifths of the Army attended one or more compulsory classes a week.[57] However if many units paid little attention either to the Wartime Scheme of Education to which they were supposed to conform, or to the Release Scheme itself, there can have been few units which were not visited by the AEC in the effort to ensure that they would at least try to do one or the other. However kindly or unkindly Commanding Officers took to instructions from higher authority, they could not have been unaware of them. Since Senior Officers were now known to consider education important it was prudent for officers of less seniority to pay more attention to Staff Officers' Education than had hitherto been thought necessary. If education was now deemed important enough to be made compulsory, even those whose circumstances were such as to free them from compulsion could not but have been keenly aware of the existence of the Corps, the main purpose of which was to look after it.

It is obvious, too, that with the Release Scheme the prestige of the Corps considerably increased. It could not have been only the HMIs who saw and admired the administrative skill of the AEC, its energy and resourcefulness. Its initiative could not have gone unnoticed and when AEC other ranks started the outward-bound courses which later became so popular in the Army, when an experimental farm appeared out of the blue in Palestine, when contrary to all regulations a German POW was seen doing a splendid job as orderly-cum-woodwork instructor in Tripoli, we cannot believe that appreciation was unexpressed or only reluctantly forthcoming. Nor were those who suffered keenly from its absence at all likely to underestimate the teaching skill of the Corps which so impressed the HMIs. Others, too, must have been struck, as were the HMIs, by the sympathetic imagination that infused the AEC's understanding that there is in life a maturity that is unrelated to book-learning, and by the markedly pioneering work of the Corps which was to be seen in its approach not only to illiteracy but to pre-vocational instruction as well. For in insisting that the acquisition of practical skill will always be important but that even more important is the broad and general education without which the mental adaptability indispensable in a world of technological change cannot be mastered, the AEC was indeed engaged in pioneering work of great importance. As we have seen the HMIs were by no means uncritical of the Release Scheme of Education, but theirs was a high appreciation of the work of the AEC and that appreciation must have been made known to the Senior Officers of the Commands visited by them. Certainly no one could have seen in those reports any suggestion that the AEC was not fully capable of doing the work it was undertaking. Nor should we forget the significance of the fact that the Corps was now identified with the resettlement of the soldier. Nothing could have more convinced the soldier that the Corps mattered greatly to him and in the longer term few things could more have convinced the Army of its importance too.

The assumption by the Corps of responsibility for the running of a Resettlement Information and Advisory Service for the Army was one of the more important consequences of the Release Period Education Scheme. For the greatest interest expressed by the troops in the course of that scheme and their most insistent demand had been for vocational training. Authority took the point and, anticipating the ending of conscription, acknowledged for the Regular Army the necessity of providing an organised service offering personal and reliable advice on suitable employment when the troops left the Colours, and of giving this advice well before they did so. A committee met under the chairmanship of Sir Harold Wiles to consider this and its subsequent Report, named after him and accepted by the Government, recognised that the state had a responsibility to resettle the soldier when he returned to civilian life and emphasised that he should have the opportunity throughout his service to prepare for this. To do this he must have the necessary information and there must be the assurance that he understood it. Those whose job it was to explain things should have the task of explaining this too, and so the RAEC took over advising on resettlement from Welfare. How that task was discharged is more appropriately considered when we turn to the Interim Scheme, for that becomes obvious only in the years of that scheme.

Greater awareness of the presence of the Corps and a greater prestige accorded to it can then be seen to be a consequence of the Release Scheme. In so far as this was the case, that scheme must have had a further consequence. It lessened the scepticism with which the Corps had long been regarded. But given the pronounced dislike of ABCA, with which Army Education was so closely associated, that scepticism was by no means ended. Many Commanding Officers doubted, too, if much of the education provided was really of benefit to the Army and it was clear that there would still be an uphill fight to convince them that education was as necessary, and therefore the Corps as important, as their Generals appeared to believe.

We can also, unfortunately, see in the Release Scheme things that should have worried the AEC much more than the continued, if lessening, scepticism with which important elements in the Army continued to regard it. There was the revelation in it of a weakness to which the AEC was prone, had been prone and would continue to be prone. The HMIs stated it with a harshness and a brutality that was unjustified because it was too absolute and all-embracing. They said that the AEC was not using its strength in the most effective way because it misunderstood the true nature of education. The AEC forgot 'that education is not ultimately administered but rather a job done outside in a field where things grow'. Theirs were green fingers that ought to have been out in the soil and the sun and not confined to offices. The HMIs regretted 'the general tendency in the AEC today to think of education as being in the last resort the organising of instruction, not the lively intercourse of mind with mind'. It was 'rare to find the AEC visiting and staying with units as a good inspector would do'. 'The aim of providing really skilled advice to the units', they said, 'should be constantly kept in mind. That advice can only be useful if the givers of it are constantly in the classes and consider that these have first call on their time.' Engaged too heavily in administration, 'too much that was neither constructive nor educational' being required of them, the officers of the Corps were 'too tied to their offices' and 'they were in danger of drowning in a sea of paper'. In consequence of it all they did not do enough teaching and if things were to improve 'more emphasis should be laid on the teaching functions of the AEC', functions they were admirably able to perform but which they seemed determined to deprive themselves of the opportunity of discharging.

It was a hard-hitting criticism and, too sweeping as it was, it could not be said to be undeserved. It was one that could be justly levelled at the officers of the Corps before the war and events were to conspire to ensure that it could be made when the Release Scheme was ended. For the HMIs drew attention, inadvertently it seems, to a great problem faced by the Corps. They gave no hint as to how they thought it might be solved. Indeed, what they said suggested that they did not even see that it was a problem. Speculating on the future of the AEC they said that 'it required an immediate supply of trained teachers having proper status and authority, i.e. rank not inferior to that of doctors and clergymen in the Army'. They wanted arrangements for salary increases, pensions and such to be reasonably interchangeable between Army and Civilian Education. But they also wanted the AEC to retain its NCOs, saying 'There may be circumstances in which the most effective work, in actual teaching as well as in Centres and Libraries, can best be done by NCOs. The NCO has opportunities denied to the commissioned officer of getting to know what the men really think and where the demand for education is so latent this matters greatly.' They did not, however, raise the question what the proper status of the NCO was to be, how arrangements might be made for their salary increments and pensions to be reasonably interchangeable between Army and Civilian Education and how, if such arrangements were not to be made, able teachers could be found to become AEC NCOs. Perhaps the HMIs thought that they were not themselves in the business of squaring circles, perhaps they thought that as the AEC in implementing the Release Scheme of Education had been listening to the whispers of fancy, pursuing the phantoms of hope, there was no reason why they should not continue to do so in facing this particular difficulty too. In the event the RAEC sought to win this tug-of-war by letting go of the rope. The Corps became an all-officer Corps, and while eventually many of its officers found the opportunity to teach, there were so many administrative jobs to attend to that it was still difficult to engage in the teaching that was its strength and that the HMIs wanted to see more of.

Thus if it seemed a reasonable deduction from the period of the Educational Release Scheme that the AEC would have to struggle to fulfil a continuing role in the future, the revelation of AEC weaknesses in that Release Scheme ensured that that would also be a hard struggle. Something else did too, namely the fact that Army Education then, as in the war, was not valued for itself but because it was caught up with pressures that would inevitably be less in the future than they had been in the past. One was the pressure to strengthen morale and the other to build the New Jerusalem. Both had been believed to be of overriding importance and thought to be integrally related. The one could never be lost sight of entirely by the Army, although the importance attached to it could, nevertheless, be expected to decline sharply; the other would soon completely disappear. And with the decline in importance of the one and the disappearance of the other the esteem enjoyed by education because of its close association with both would inevitably markedly decline as well.

Concern with the morale of the troops was entirely understandable in the war and in the demobilisation period. No one could claim that it was unjustified in either. Demobilisation proceeded smoothly but not without occasioning anxiety. In 1945 we are told that an attempt was made to establish a Soviet in an infantry regiment in Egypt. In May 1946 258 men of the 13th Battalion, the Parachute Regiment, mutinied at Muar Camp near Kuala Lumpur. Eight men were as a result imprisoned for five years and 247 for two years. These sentences were later quashed, but Whitehall and

South-East Asian Command were highly alarmed.[58]

But if concern with morale is not surprising, it is astonishing what was done in its name. *Salus populi suprema lex* was the old saw; the morale of the troops was now the supreme law. Even when Prime Minister and Minister of War were agreed in disliking what was done in its name, they had to yield to it. Warwick Charlton, an ex-*Daily Sketch* journalist, edited the first Army newspaper in the Western Desert. He was radicalism personified; as he himself said, he was against everything. The first edition of the *8th Army News* appeared in September 1941. On taking command of the Army in August 1942 Montgomery came to the conclusion that the *8th Army News* had an essential part to play in building the morale of his troops and if thereafter it was an exaggeration to say that Charlton could do no wrong he, nevertheless, contrived to continue to do wrong with impunity, despite Grigg's urging Montgomery to 'curb his exuberance'. Hugh Cudlipp, former editor of the *Sunday Pictorial*, published the *Union Jack* in Algiers. The Prime Minister referred to Cudlipp's 'exceptional malignity' and wrote 'it astonishes me that you cannot find decent men to run these Army newspapers who will present news dispassionately to the fighting lines'. Grigg asked the Commander-in-Chief Central Mediterranean Forces to 'keep your eye on Master Cudlipp', whom he dubbed 'an extreme Leftist'. The Prime Minister returned to the attack, asking 'Is it really a fact that the only journalists who are any good are the malignant scum of the *Daily Mirror*?' He even threatened to bring the matter up in Cabinet. The journalists remained at their posts. When in August 1943 Mountbatten became Supreme Commander in South-East Asia he wanted Frank Owen, the editor of the *Evening Standard*, to edit the paper for the troops there. Once again the Prime Minister and Grigg were unhappy but Mountbatten got his way, helped by Sir Ronald Adam's insistence that this would improve the morale of Mountbatten's command. Sir Ronald, indeed, seems to have been convinced that the more radical the journalist, the better would be his effect on morale. Cudlipp was by no means sure that he wanted such a stormy petrel as William Connor on his staff, but Adam believed that people like Connor would increase the popularity of the paper with the troops and Connor in consequence had to be put up with. Supreme laws are never without their peculiarity. The sins committed in the name of *salus populi* have long been commented on; odd things, too, were done in the cause of morale when that was accepted as imperious necessity.[59]

We had once been well aware of 'the bad use which artful men may make of an irritation of the popular mind'. It was truly astonishing how completely we had ignored this ancient wisdom, but it was always certain that the time would come when we would recall it, beyond doubt that we would begin to question the sense of some of the things that had been done in the belief that they were vital to the strengthening of morale. In the matter of the freedom to be allowed to editors of Army newspapers we see that time coming when, with the removal of the troops from Egypt to the Canal Zone, the AEC was given the task of editing the *Canal Zone News*. The importance attached to the publication of this paper is evidenced by the fact that the Command Education Officer was told that money was no object; the importance of making sure that there would be no opportunity for artful men to make bad use of any irritation of the popular mind on this occasion, however, is demonstrated by the instruction given him that he alone must write the editorial.[60]

Pendulums swing as we see the pendulum swing back here. Education was bound to be affected by that swing. When it was thought that education had a major part to play in satisfying an insistent need, education was believed to be important. When that need appeared less insistent it was only too probable that interest in education would decline, and this was the more likely if it came to be believed, as it did, that the role of education in meeting that need had been greatly exaggerated. The morale of the 90% of the Army that was never attracted to education may have been poorer in the Release Period than that of the 10% that was. But had it been significantly so it is certain that whatever contribution education made to the strengthening of the Army's morale would never have sufficed to prevent tumult in the demobilisation period, and equally certain that many military minds would become convinced of the truth of this. Their regard for education could not but be affected when they did.

The pressure to improve morale was undoubtedly the outstandingly significant pressure with which education was so closely associated both in the war and in the Release Period. But there was another pressure with which it was closely associated then too. This was the pressure to seize the opportunity presented by military discipline to rectify civilian shortcomings, to make better soldiers better citizens, to see in the sword a more effective instrument than the ploughshare in the building of the New Jerusalem. As the pressure to improve morale added to the importance attached to Army Education, so this pressure did too. Its strength baffles comprehension; its long durability would have baffled it still more.

Since the days when ancient Rome settled ex-soldiers on disturbed frontiers it had always been understood that civil society might benefit from military virtues, little as English appreciation of this had ever been. The undesirability of the Army seeking to develop in the soldiery hitherto unregarded military values is not obvious; eyebrows rise, however, when armies seek objectives which can only in the most indirect fashion be looked upon as military. In particular, there are difficulties if armies seek to make of their soldiers better citizens than it is thought necessary to make their civilian counterparts. For a society to seek to improve all its citizens would be no doubt highly desirable. But to select soldiers for this exclusive treatment suggests either that they are in especial need of it or that theirs is indeed a total commitment, not only in the sense that they must be prepared to die in the exercise of their profession, but also in the sense that they have surrendered to the Army the totality of their lives so that they are fit subjects for whatever experimentation their lords and masters think fit.

To suggest that there is a greater need to make soldiers better citizens than there is to make civilians better citizens is to confirm the view that they are indeed poorer citizens than those not in uniform. This is a view already familiar to the English people. It infuses the amazement of their men of letters that soldiers lacked the wit to prefer gaol to the Army as it does the hurt pride of their working classes shamed by those of their family who have gone for a soldier. To confirm it would be to give the stamp of official English approval to the bitter contempt for the soldier expressed in the old Chinese saying 'no good iron would be made into a nail and no good mother's son would become a soldier'. To suggest that the totality of the soldier's life is at the disposal of authority is to see him as a slave and not even the most ardent pacifist could have hit upon a better way of ensuring the disbanding of the Army.

It may indeed be the case that the understanding which would make the soldier a better soldier would also make the citizen a better citizen. This would be true of an understanding of the nature of the international world in which states meet and conduct their business together. The widespread lack of understanding of this by Demos in Great Britain and the USA in the years between the two World Wars almost destroyed him. But continued indifference to it on his part would not make this an illegitimate objective for the Army to have, even though in so far as it was achieved the soldier would be becoming a better citizen than the civilian. For without this understanding the risk would be great that the soldier would be a poorer soldier. That understanding will increase his consciousness of indispensability, his pride in being a soldier. No doubt a nice judgment is called for in distinguishing between instruction in international affairs and in citizenship, and there will be grey areas in which such judgment will have to be exercised. But the principle is clear. What is necessary to improve the soldier cannot be omitted; what can be justified only to improve the citizen cannot be attempted. The surprising thing is not that the Army eventually came to this conclusion, but that it took it so long to do so. But that it would was never to be doubted, nor that when that happened RAEC hopes would become more realistic. Then the Corps would find a more lasting strength because it would become of much more use to the Army. Only when it ceased to pursue ends that were of more significance to civilians than to soldiers would it return to its true function of helping the Army to be better at its job. RAEC hearts had beat highest during the Release Period and the Interim Scheme which followed it. Yet despite appearances this was not the 'full meridian of its glory', which was ahead of it, not behind it.

CHAPTER 9

THE INTERIM SCHEME

It had been hoped that by the time the Educational Release Scheme ended the Army would have found its future form, would have adjusted to its future role and would have fashioned the future educational training appropriate to that form and to that role. But hopes are affected by circumstances and circumstances are always to some extent determined by chance. Planners seek to bind the future and the future has the odd habit of reserving its hardest strokes for those who try to do this. That happened in this case and between the ending of the Educational Release Scheme and the agreeing on the educational provision that would be suitable for the Regular Army of the future, yet another Army Educational Scheme is to be found. This was the Interim Scheme.

It was appropriately named, this post-war period being felicitous at least in the expressions it found for significant developments occurring in it, as witness the description 'Cold War' it gave to the international situation in which it found itself. The words of Tacitus, 'It was rather a cessation of war than a beginning of peace', might seem an appropriate comment on that situation but 'Cold War' is an even better description of it. For not only did we then see the consolidation and the arming to the teeth of the power blocs, acute ideological struggle over Germany, bitter superpower struggle that erupted in repeated and great crises, we also saw how vitally important it is that those who have a sense of power should also have a sense of limit and of law, and what little evidence one of those superpowers gave of having it. Never in Russian history had this sense been highly developed. Stalin quickly make it plain that not closing his grasp on what was in it made little appeal to him. He was also to show that he was not averse to extending it, as his demand for trusteeship in Libya, which Ernest Bevin described as an attempt to come across the throat of the British Empire, makes manifest. There is nothing surprising in this. There are qualities we do not look for, and would not find, in particular peoples – the compulsive desire to be thought well of by other peoples in the Englishman, reticence in the American, moderation in the Slav. Still more important as testifying to the aptness of the description of this international situation as 'Cold War' is the fact that in it the Powers behaved as Powers do when they are not going to draw back from war when all the power realities, which they were careful never to ignore, suggested they would refrain from war, as in the event they did.

The Interim Scheme faithfully reflected the idea of 'interimity', if one may so express it. It is one thing to see clearly after the event that all the power realities suggested that the Cold War would not become hot; it was another to be as sure of this when so much that was threatening was being said and done. We seemed to be in an interim period until war would call again for major effort or peace permit greater relaxation. We had not forgotten the lesson taught us by the inter-war years, that 'early and provident fear is the mother of safety'. So Montgomery concluded that he had been wrong in thinking that we did not need a large army. We did since a substantial part of it must be kept in Europe. But we feared that the USSR might be a greater threat to the Middle East than to Europe, for we thought it possible that what we called 'mutual vulnerability' in the Middle East might precipitate a conflict there that all hoped to avoid. So we had to keep considerable forces overseas. Moreover, we were determined to have in our own hands the new and terrifying military nuclear power which we were already beginning to hope would deter Soviet aggression. All this was very costly and two questions kept forcing themselves into our minds; both strengthened the feeling that it was indeed an interim period in which we were living.

The first was the question 'Could we keep sufficiently large forces to enable us to fulfil all our commitments?' So long as we had conscription the answer would be 'yes'. But could it be maintained? There were strong political arguments against it. We had never before accepted conscription in times of peace. Its absence had been one of the things, so it was believed, which distinguished the British people, who were free, from the Europeans, who everyone knew were not. Political parties began to think there was electoral advantage in promising to rid the British people of this intolerable burden. And although it took a discerning eye to discover that the British people found it intolerable, or indeed ever thought about it at all, once parties saw political gain in its abolition, the difficulty of maintaining it was greatly increased. There were strong economic arguments against it. Factories needed more labour and looked with a jaundiced eye on those whom they thought were wasting their time in the Services. There were strong military arguments against it. The Services believed that conscripts served too short a time to justify the labour and cost of training them. The Services wanted to get on with their own training. But if we abolished conscription could we get sufficient volunteers? Could we afford them if we could get them? We soon had cause to think that the answer to either question would be 'no'.

The second insistent question that kept bothering us was 'If we could not keep large enough forces how could we maintain large commitments?' The answer we eventually gave to that question was simple. It was simply that we could not. We struggled hard not to give that answer. We were becoming convinced that we could not afford both conventional and nuclear strength. We were determined not to give up nuclear power and hoped that it would make up for the lack of conventional strength. Sir Winston Churchill now put forward the view that peace would be the sturdy child of terror. More optimistically, Sir John Slessor looked to nuclear power to serve us in the extra-European as well as in the European world. He thought the dog we kept to take care of the cat would take care of the kittens as well. Sir John was speaking before it had become apparent how remarkably unkittenish the behaviour of kittens was to become, although long before the Vietnam War it was becoming clear that the new generation of weapons would not provide diplomatic leverage in the same direct way that the older weapons had done. We hoped that non-nuclear power, too, would enable us to fulfil our commitments with fewer men and less expense. We contemplated a greater use of Transport Command, hoping to find in increased mobility a way of enabling fewer soldiers to do the work all round the globe of many, a hope which might have had more chance of being fulfilled had we not kept Transport Command so very short of aeroplanes. We carried through a great administrative revolution, the bringing together of the three Service Ministries into a unified Ministry of Defence in the hope of saving every last penny and of making the most of the reduced numbers we were having to make do with. This was praiseworthy ingenuity but it emphasised two things. One was that the realities of power, the 'conjunctures' as the 18th Century called them, were catching up with us and that we would have to conform to them. The other was that in so doing they were heralding the ending of our Interim Defence Policy and with it the winding up of the Interim Scheme of Army Education. Only with its ending could the educational provision for the Army of the future which it had been hoped would follow the Release Educational Scheme be begun.

The Interim Scheme, the broad outlines of which were published in June 1946, when it was said it would begin on 31 December 1948 when the Release Scheme ended, was to be four-fold in nature. It was to consist of Preliminary Education, or education for illiterates or semi-illiterates; of General Education, which would cover education for citizenship, in Current Affairs and in four main subjects, these being English, Mathematics, History together with Geography and Elementary Science, which were said to be 'basic' to a sound modern education; of Individual Education, or education in whatever the individual soldier fancied; and finally of Education for Resettlement. Six hours, in the soldier's working time, were to be devoted to his studies. There could, but it was not insisted that there would, be what were called 'informal tests' in these six subjects that were to be compulsorily studied in working time. If such 'informal tests' were to be held, they were not to be directly linked to pay or promotion although it was hoped they might influence both. This last was a somewhat curious 'looking both ways provision'. The statement that they would not be linked to pay or promotion could only be an inducement not to take the informal tests. The statement that they might influence pay and promotion could only be an inducement to take them. The informality of the tests carried the suggestion that they were somehow lacking in sufficient respectability to become formal and the refusal to link them to pay and promotion also conveyed the impression that they were not quite the thing. The suggestion that they might influence pay and promotion conveyed the impression that they might after all be necessary. The overriding impression left was that this provision could be expected to last only for a brief interim period. It was always likely that the informal tests would become linked to pay and promotion and become formal, or that they would soon be seen to have no relevance for these things and would softly and silently vanish away, the first of these alternatives always being more probable than the second. Whatever the future of the tests, however, it was emphasised that the interrelation between the six compulsory subjects must be made plain, although no attempt was made to inform the possibly unenlightened what this was. It was also stressed that the pace of study was to be unhurried, no doubt by way of ensuring that as the subject matter to be studied was extensive, its study would have to be continued a long time.

This was the scheme, General Lloyd said, which would 'provide the basic requirements of the soldier as a soldier and as a citizen and would also provide the educational requirements of the soldier as an individual'.[1] The General regretted that 'time cannot be spared during the working hours for individual education' but he stressed that 'facilities must be provided for the soldier in his own time'. To make sure that this was done would, he said, be the RAEC's chief problem in the years ahead. It must do all it could to provide such facilities within units. Every unit should have its own library and quiet room. The Corps should realise what a great demand there was among the men for help in elementary calculation, in elementary machine drawing, in certain forms of English, for these things were required before much sought-after Trade and Technical qualifications could be acquired. The Corps must see to it that such help was available. It should not hesitate to make use of civilian teachers and if suitable part-time instructors could be found in near-by technical units there would be money to pay them. But first of all every effort must be made to meet the unit's need from within the unit itself. There would be Army Colleges at home and abroad and Education Centres too, all of which would greatly assist the Corps. BWP pamphlets would help the Corps in promoting the teaching of citizenship. Nor should it forget in this matter of providing individual help for the soldier that there were now 500 different correspondence courses available, going for a song. It must not forget that 'it is laid down that the regimental officer, by which is meant the Sub-Unit Commander, is invariably the Chairman of discussion groups in matters relating to Current Affairs'.[2] Lloyd knew how strongly tempted units would be to leave the whole business of attending to Current Affairs as well as to citizenship to the Corps; since, as he made plain on another occasion, it would not have the time to take this on it must resist the pressures to do so which would undoubtedly be brought to bear on it.

The Army Council Instruction which laid it down that the regimental officer must be the chairman of groups discussing Current Affairs is also a curious document, pointing in two directions. It said of the regimental officer 'The extent to which he will actually guide a particular discussion must depend on his own knowledge and experience and on the nature of the subject. He may make use of anyone who has a particular knowledge of a subject to help him.' It was acknowledgement of the experience that made it abundantly clear that the regimental officer was not necessarily the best man to teach Current Affairs and it hinted broadly that he could not be expected to do this job unless he happened to know something about the topic to be discussed. But it was also clinging to the old ABCA theory that because he would know his own men better than others could, because in running a discussion his own powers of command would be strengthened and because there was to be not lecturing but discussion which he could lead, he was the best man for the job. The ACI sought to reconcile these two contradictory points of view by making the distinction between chairing the discussion period, which the regimental officer was expected to do, and leading the discussion, which it was hoped would be the task of another. But even if it be agreed that there was no difficulty in theory in making this distinction, it must be doubted how helpful in practice it was to make it. For if the junior officer did not know much about the subject under discussion he could only chair the discussion in the sense of ensuring that it remained orderly; there would be no necessity for this if the discussion leader was competent and this would do nothing to ensure the success of the session if the discussion leader was not.[3]

In a much more important sense making this distinction was unhelpful too. In effect the Army Council was now saying that Current Affairs could not be taught if the teacher knew nothing about it and that it could not be taught either if the unit officer was not there to preside. From which it followed that it could only be taught if there was someone qualified to teach it and if the unit officer was present to take the chair. But the Army forgot about the first proviso and insisted only on the second. The ACI in question was permissive and not mandatory. It told the junior officer what he was allowed to do, namely to find help if he could. But if he could not it did not say that the job could not then be done and order him not to attempt it. On the contrary it still expected him to tackle it, despite the fact that it had said that his ability to do so 'must depend on his own knowledge and experience' and that it had already implied that if these were inadequate, so would be his leadership of the discussion.

The Interim Scheme could never be said to be lacking in ambition and it was understood from the beginning that all resources would have to be engaged in it if it was to succeed. Thus civilian assistance continued to be looked upon as essential. There were changes in the administrative structure fashioned to provide this during the war; the closeness of the relationship between civilian and military education was not adversely affected thereby. In 1948 the Central Advisory Council which had served the Army well in the war was replaced by the Army Advisory Board. This had been set up to advise the Secretary of State on educational policy for the Army when Morris retired from his post as Director-General of Army Education and the post itself was abolished. The Army Education Advisory Board was an independent body and on it were represented the universities, the technical colleges, the schools, the LEAs, the Ministry of Education and the Scottish Education Department.

The Director of Army Education and the Director General of Military Training attended its meetings as War Office observers. At the same time the administrative and executive work of the Central Advisory Councils was taken over by a small Central Committee which, like its predecessor, had its own full-time staff. Its function was to coordinate the provision of civilian assistance to the Army and particularly the work of the various university committees which replaced the former Regional Committees. Fifteen Universities agreed that their Extra-Mural Departments would carry on the work previously undertaken by the Regional Committees. Universities and Services alike wished to continue that intimacy which, despite occasional explosions rendered inevitable by different practices and different sensitivities, both had greatly valued. That continued intimacy survives to this day and both the Universities and the Services know that it would be a poor day that saw its ending.[4]

It was obvious that the Universities were best able to provide whatever advanced teaching was required for those National Servicemen whose studies had been interrupted by their call-up and for those Regulars who wished for this. To arrange this and to give whatever further help was needed there were University Tutors at most Army Educational Centres in the UK who were available for interview. In addition Universities continued their well established practice of training RAEC personnel, particularly in Current Affairs, and gave whatever further help they were asked for. With the announcement in 1957 of the intention to abolish National Service and to reduce the size of the Armed Forces it was clear that they would in the future make fewer calls on the Universities than they had hitherto done. The desired continuing intimacy would remain but a good deal of the somewhat heavy top-hamper could be got rid of. It would be enough if there was assured contact between the Universities and the Services whenever it was needed, and it was the work of the Central Committee, whose name was changed to 'The Committee for University Assistance to Adult Education in HM Forces', to provide for this. This change in nomenclature was particularly acceptable to those who believed that the terms 'Army Education' and 'Adult Education in the Army' expressed two entirely different things, that the distinction between them was 'of considerable significance, for these are designations which carry widely different implications concerning the nature of that education'. 'Army Education', it was said, was 'education that is primarily designed to produce the efficiency of the soldier'. 'Adult Education in the Army' was 'education that is primarily designed to educate the man who happens to be a soldier'.[5] The change in the name of the Committee seemed to bear out Lloyd's insistence that, however referred to, education in the Army was 'an integral part of the national system' and to strengthen the care of those who by emphasising that they were participating in Adult Education sought to ensure that it would be liberal, and not in any sense functional or vocational education, they were professing.[6]

There was, as we have seen, an astonishing development of education in the Army during the war and in the following Release Period, but there has been no more extraordinary, indeed one may say fantastic, phase of education therein than that which is known as the Interim Educational Scheme. Its liberal nature was claimed as its great glory. Education of this liberal kind was seen as the antithesis of education that was in any sense functional or vocational. Thus it was said 'the scheme was liberal in its approach and the soldier's efficiency was regarded as only of secondary importance'. To leave us in no doubt that the primary purpose of compelling the soldier to submit himself to education was strictly non-military, we were specifically told that 'the stress was on the soldier as citizen and not on the citizen as soldier'. The aim of the scheme, it was said, was 'to provide a wider usefulness for the citizen who on leaving the Army should be better equipped physically, mentally and spiritually for his work in the community than he was when he entered it'.[7] And we are not listening here to the voice of uninstructed and uninfluential enthusiasm as we appreciate, when we turn again to the Director of Army Education's words to his Conference, that 'Army Education shows to serving men and women how they fit into society as soldiers and citizens and indicates how individual experience and self-expression may best contribute to the common good.' It does not seek to show to serving men and women how citizens may fit into the Army as soldiers, nor how individual experience and self-expression may best contribute to its good. The operative words in what Lloyd says are 'society' and 'the common good'. The scheme is concerned not with the Army as such, but with society and the common good.

If an outstanding characteristic of the Interim Scheme was that it was liberal, at least in this sense of being completely unfunctional, another was that it was consciously modelled, with one striking and strikingly important exception, on that civilian Adult Education of which it claimed to be an integral part. There were no examinations in civilian Adult Education and therefore there must not be in its military version either. To strengthen the case that examinations should have no place in the military counterpart of civilian Adult Education, an extraordinary argument was added and one which made clear how little concerned the Interim Scheme was with purely military matters and indeed how much enthusiasm for the new liberal scheme had undermined any prudent sense of caution in the RAEC. Army examinations, it was said, should have relevance to civilian purposes and have equivalence with civilian examinations. Unfortunately, however, they did not meet this criterion and they should therefore be discontinued. So, for the most part, they were. This was an astonishing achievement, if that is the correct term to use in this context.[8] Because Army examinations had no relevance to civilian purposes they were to be discontinued. Yet if all Army practices which had no relevance to civilian purposes were to be discontinued, what an odd sort of Army the nation would be saddled with. What of the Army would remain if this were to be established as a rule? It is breathtaking to find that the question 'Have Army examinations relevance to Army purposes?' does not seem to have been asked. It is almost beyond understanding that the Army Council did not insist on it being asked and answered before agreeing to the ending of Army examinations. It looks for all the world as if they were so 'groaning under the yoke of this age' as almost to be unable to think for themselves. The attitude of the RAEC also is not easy to understand.[9] When education in the pre-war Army had been solely valued because some exposure to it, however minimal, was essential to other rank promotion, prudence and caution might have suggested to the RAEC that to insist that this was no longer necessary for promotion would be to remove from the soldiery what little attraction education had for it. But in inducing acceptance by the Army of the proposition that education in it must serve a primarily non-military purpose the RAEC was riding high, if not very securely, and prudence and caution are never to be regarded as outstanding characteristics of Crusaders.

That was how the RAEC, or so many of them, saw themselves at this time. Indeed, the single most impressive characteristic of the Interim Scheme was its fervently crusading nature. That scheme was well called 'Interim' in this sense too, that it marked the period, bound in its very nature to be passing, between the last call of the Crusade to be heard in the Army and the Army's return to ordinary life. True to form that great Crusader Sir Ronald Adam appears in his white surcoat with its resplendent red cross. 'There is', he writes, 'immense scope for missionary zeal in spreading the good habit of community discussion, and equal scope for transforming sociable small talk into creative public opinion.'[10] This was belief in the modern version of the philosopher's stone which would turn common metal into gold and it made as much sense as did its medieval counterpart. We can also hear the crusading note in Lloyd's words when contemplating the serious dislocation to civil education caused by the war: 'One of the interesting things to note about the new Scheme is the Army Council's acceptance of the responsibility to overcome the educational difficulties caused by this dislocation'.[11] The authentic voice of the Crusader rings in the Editorial of *Army Education* XXI, No. 2 of June 1947 in which we are told that the Interim Scheme came to the RAEC as 'the fulfilment of many hopes and gave promise of unparalleled opportunity' and in which the Editor received 'with some trepidation news of the curtailment of National Service' as that curtailment 'might adversely affect those hopes and that opportunity'. We can hear it again in the widely held view that 'the Army was the last organised body having a major beneficial influence on the young man still in his formative years' and that 'the opportunity to make good the deficiencies of his background must not be lost'.[12] So strong is this Crusading element in the Interim Scheme that it must be seen as even more important than its liberal nature and than its insistence that it is an integral part of civilian Adult Education. Its preeminence explains yet another and very outstanding characteristic of that scheme and one that can hardly be thought of as liberal, and that is totally alien to civilian Adult Education.

This was its compulsory nature. The compulsion which characterised it sat ill with the liberality in which the scheme took such a pride, with the freedom which it sought so ardently to give to its pupils, always, however, within the context of their remaining pressed men. Thus those attending classes would have freedom from examinations but not from the necessity of attending classes. The framers of the scheme would not have quarrelled with the Oxford Dictionary definition of 'liberal' as that which pertains to a free man, as the arts or sciences that are worthy of a free man. They would have agreed with that dictionary's definition of 'liberal education' as that which is directed to general intellectual culture, not narrowly technical or professional, and they would have agreed too that this type of education is much more appropriate to the free than to the unfree. But they were challenged by questions to which they had no answer. How can liberal education have its longed-for effect when no attention is paid to it? How can the free be liberally educated in their absence? The framers of the Interim Scheme were determined to rectify civilian education and as they had to deal with the products of that inadequate education, who since they were its products would never willingly present themselves to further exposure to education, they felt compelled to use compulsion, for without it they would never have the opportunity of correcting past faults.

The RAEC, we are told, was a somewhat divided body at this time. There were those who never saw themselves as anything but Army officers whose specialist area was education and there were others who saw themselves as education specialists who happened to be in the Army. The first tended to be the conservatives who wanted to build on existing practices and improve them by accepting the necessity of holding examinations, by making the syllabuses for them more imaginative and worthwhile and by compelling students to attend classes for longer periods before being allowed to sit the examinations. The second were the root-and-branch reformers who would be satisfied with nothing less than the abolition of subject syllabuses as well as of examinations. Both had, however, this one thing in common, a strong belief in the necessity of compulsory education. They knew that in its absence their services would be much less in demand. It would be wrong, however, to believe that it was a mercenary self-interest which determined their attitude. They were concerned lest a job they deemed to be of overriding importance could not be done. Conservatives and root-and-branch reformers were at this time great visionaries and they would not contemplate the possibility that the job could not be done. Moreover, they genuinely believed that a salutary compulsion would enable them to do it.[13] For a further characteristic of the Interim Scheme was its marked optimism. It was reluctant to acknowledge difficulties; it is impossible to see in it any reflection of the experience of the Release Scheme of Education. The insistence in the Interim Scheme on the responsibility of the unit for the teaching of Current Affairs is a convincing demonstration that nothing was learned then. It was as unwilling as its predecessor had been to pay attention to the inclinations and the prejudices of the soldiers. It lacked, as the Release Scheme had done, a clear notion of the ways of the common man and a kindly feeling for his limitations. It never acknowledged that if we do not make sufficient allowance for prudence and conformity to circumstances, we have to abide the consequences which are unlikely to be pleasing. It sought unlimited ends with limited means. With teachers as inadequate as they had been shown to be in the Release Period it was, nevertheless, sure that it could do what trained teachers with longer time at their disposal had been unable to achieve. It could be thought that it had one great advantage over those teachers in that it was dealing with mature men. Its task was, nevertheless, immense. Virgil affected to believe that the Roman peasants 'will lay aside their rustic minds, and by continued instruction will quickly follow into whatsoever arts you may invite them'[14] and the Interim Scheme embodied the faith that the same would be true of the soldiers. We are told that education in the armies of Tsar Alexander III had striking success in increasing literacy there; the instruction there would certainly have been continuous, the knout would undoubtedly have figured in that instruction and the desire on the part of the soldiers to become literate would have been unquestioned. But the British Army was no knoutocracy and it had to content itself with the carrot. The days when it knew the lash had long gone by and if it had ever been applied for finished and finite ignorance, British reliance on the Navy would have been absolute and exclusive and the British public would have had no soldiers to deprive them of their liberty as it was so often feared they would. And if the interest of the British soldiers was not aroused and the instruction forced upon them was remarkably uncontinuous, both of which seemed highly probable, then it would soon become apparent that British soldiers, like Rome's peasants, would prove Virgil wrong.

There was a disadvantage, as well as an advantage, in dealing with mature men. Soldiers know better than most men the importance of obedience to command. But their instant acceptance of necessary compulsion makes them resentful of what they believe to be unnecessary compulsion. This is what many at this time never understood. Compulsion might provide classes but it was unlikely to produce more students than would have appeared in its absence. In whatever way, known to the gods but not as yet to men, the great majority of our people can be induced to become better educated, the hope that this can be achieved by compelling mature men and women to attend classes, and thus to become more informed and better citizens, seems to be remarkably without foundation. Yet such was the optimism and the faith in compulsion at this time that it could even be argued that it was the fact that the soldier's Individual Education took place in his own time and that his General Education took place in the King's time that created 'an unnaturally complete divorce between the subjects' covered by the term 'Individual Education' and those that were within the framework of 'General Education', and that it was this divorce which 'goes far to explain why the truly Adult atmosphere created in the former case came to be almost totally absent in the latter – with far reaching consequences'. From this the conclusion, unbelievable though this must appear, could even be drawn that if the soldier could do in the King's time what he wanted to do sufficiently to induce him to do it in his own time, then he would have had the same interest, the same drive, the same enthusiasm (the qualities which created the truly adult atmosphere referred to) when he was compelled to do what he did not want to do in attending classes in which he had no interest, also in the King's time.[15]

There have been non-sequiturs which would demand less ingenuity in the attempt to justify them than that. There was no understanding here that it was the freedom of the soldier to interest himself in Individual Education, or to have nothing whatever to do with it if that is what he preferred, that created the approved-of adult atmosphere and that the only way to ensure that that atmosphere would also characterise General Education was to give the soldiers the same freedom to attend or stay away from the classes devoted to it. If that was done the same adult atmosphere would be found in the classes devoted to General as to Individual Education, always assuming that there would be any classes for it to be evident in. It would, unfortunately, have been safe to bet that there would not have been very many. That is no doubt why those whose faith was in compulsion would never admit reality. It followed that unreality was indeed an outstanding characteristic of the Interim Scheme.

How, one wonders, was a scheme which had these as its outstanding characteristics accepted by the Army? In the nature of the War Office, in the nature of the Army Council, in the nature of the Army and above all in the nature of the pressures on all three at this time we will find the explanation.

If the interests of the Army were not looked after as well as might have been expected when the Interim Scheme was drawn up, then the War Office must accept its share of blame for that. In a letter to Grigg of 14 December 1946 the Permanent Under-Secretary there told him 'the mainspring here ran down the day you left us'. He spoke of his Minister's complete inability to understand or exhibit a point. He thought rather more highly of Lawson's successors, saying 'all three, I think, understand the written and spoken word'.[16] Too much should not be made of such comments. Civil servants feel frustration and like on occasion to let their hair down, as do other people. Moreover if, in the days before civil servants' consciences became so tender as to undermine elementary honesty and self-respect, and before many thought it proper to encourage them to do so by urging that what conscience prompted should be done with impunity, it was always understood that civil servants must be loyal to their Ministers, no one ever maintained that Ministers should always command the private respect of their civil servants.

Since the Civil Service Reforms of 1855 British Government, it has been said, is best described as Parliamentary Bureaucracy. These two elements in our government are organically joined by the Cabinet which has the double function of controlling both Parliament and Bureaucracy, civil servants, however, being the servants not of the Government but of the Crown, which is why, when Governments come and go, they remain. The Parliamentary element in our machinery of government extends from the top to the bottom of its structure, from the House of Commons down to county, district and parish councils. It embodies two great views, the one that the ultimate controlling power over the operations of government is with the whole body of the people and the other that 'talk is an essential element of good government', the subject of the talk being, as J. S. Mill said, 'the great public interests of the country'. The bureaucratic element in our country extends similarly from Whitehall to the city hall, the town hall and the parish hall. It embodies the maxim, to quote Mill again, that 'every branch of public administration is a skilled business'. It was this association of amateur and expert, of parliamentary 'chief' and permanent officials in this combination of Cabinet and Civil Service that Graham Wallace called 'the one great political invention in 19th Century England'.

Not everyone thought so highly of these Civil Service Reforms. Disraeli said that their object 'was to advance the permanent at the expense of the Parliamentary officials' and he added 'Such reform is not our metier, as the Emperor Franz Joseph said to the first French Republicans.' The reformers, he said, 'wanted to turn clerks into Privy Councillors'. Disraeli saw the weakness of Parliamentary Bureaucracy, namely that the balance between the parliamentary and the bureaucratic elements, so essential to its working, is easy to disturb. The external pressures of war and of economic crisis, and the internal pressures of policies of collectivism and of welfare pushed civil servants into increased activity. This and the consequent great growth of bureaucracy that has characterised the 20th Century persuaded MPs that the delicate balance was being upset and brought to the surface the always latent antagonism between them. Each became prone to play up the weaknesses and play down the strengths of the other. The politician became contemptuous of the civil servant's lack of popular appeal and the civil servant of the ignorance of the politician. Each became openly jealous of the other's power, each aghast at the other's pretensions, the civil servant believing that the amateur nature of the politicians and the ignorance of the realities of the world that proceeded from it made statesmen among them rare birds indeed and the politician convinced of the disaster that would result if the never-ending audacity of unelected persons went unchecked.

But if allowance must be made for the occasionally intemperate expression of Civil Service regard for politicians, it seems obvious that War Office direction when the Interim Scheme was decided upon was not at its best and that had it been, that scheme must have been expected to have been somewhat different.

That seems likely to have been the case, too, had the nature of the Army Council at this time been different. Its members were also new and it is tempting to think that they had not as yet found their feet. At least the minutes of their seventy-second meeting held on 31 January 1947 suggest that they were not yet sufficiently determined

to fight for their conviction. That meeting was to discuss the future education of the
Regular Army but it was understood that the Army could only be viewed as a whole
and the discussion concerned Regulars and conscripts. The Council would not give
the Director of Army Education all that he wanted. He wanted one RAEC officer for
every major unit and had to be content with one officer for every three such units. His
more senior officers, who were to supervise this work and to whom he referred as
'travelling headmasters', would have to travel further and more frequently than he
had intended them to. The Army Council could not see their way to recruiting the
5,000 additional RAEC instructors that would have been required had all the teaching
in the Interim Scheme been left to the RAEC. Such a number, the Council made it
plain, could not be afforded and could not be provided. This blunt insistence did not,
however, prevent the Secretary of State for War assuring the House of Commons
some weeks later that 'since the success of this plan depends on the quality of the
instructors ... we have decided that instruction in this compulsory education should
be given by members of the RAEC'. He omitted to add that it had also been decided
that such instruction could not be given exclusively by members of the RAEC but
would be given also by those, the quality of whose teaching was much more in
question.[17]

The Army Council insisted that this would have to be a case of make do and
mend and easily persuaded themselves, although against the evidence at their disposal,
that they had hit upon a workable compromise. They intended that the use of temporary
regimental instructors should be continued, convincing themselves that 'this
compromise solution of an educational staff for ordinary units composed partly of
permanent RAEC instructors and partly of temporary regimental instructors is an
interim solution to the problem'. One would not have expected the politicians to have
read the reports of the HMIs who commented on the Educational Release Scheme,
but one would have expected the soldiers to have some knowledge of them. And in
view of the comments of the HMIs on the capacity of unit instructors it is difficult to
see how the soldiers could believe that a combination of RAEC instructors and unit
instructors could do the job expected of them.

The Army Council had no difficulty in rejecting the title 'universal community
education' which had at first been put forward to describe the compulsory sessions
on citizenship and Current Affairs provided for in the Interim Scheme. That description
was not a happy one. It could be taken to imply that the whole community was
engaged in universal community education and that was manifestly not the case. But
the politician as well as the diplomatist knows the value of the soothing phrase that
does not lend itself to the asking of awkward questions. It is to be noticed that the
soldiers did not seize this opportunity to ask awkward questions themselves and were
glad, as all attending were, to accept the emendation of the Parliamentary Under-
Secretary of State that in future it be referred to as 'General Education'. The soldiers
did not like the compulsory nature of the Interim Scheme. Yet they forbore to ask, as
later they were to, why if young men not in the Army were not subjected to such
compulsion those who were in the Army should be, when no purely military argument
was adduced to justify it. Here it seems we come to the most obvious explanation

why the Interim Scheme was accepted when the soldiers so clearly disliked so much of it. They were overborne by the civilians.

The Secretary of State was not in fact the strongest supporter of such compulsion. He questioned its desirability 'after a soldier has reached the required standard'. He thought it 'wasteful', a word which showed his awareness of the not inconsiderable expense involved, to force the soldier 'to receive instruction which he did not need'. This view, the Minutes record, 'received a great deal of support'. It was, however, strongly opposed by the Parliamentary Under-Secretary of State who 'did not agree that a soldier who had reached the standard of Part I of the Forces Preliminary Examination should be allowed to choose whether he should continue [to attend classes] or not' and who 'believed firmly that general education was good for these young men and that it was the Army's duty to see that they had it'. The Chief of the Imperial General Staff disagreed, saying 'If a soldier had reached a satisfactory standard there could be no sound reason for forcing further study on him; it was a free country and he should decide for himself.' So did the Quartermaster General, who believed that 'the Army should insist only on that standard which it required for its own purposes'. The Deputy Chief of the Imperial General Staff was of this opinion too. He added that 'education was distasteful to many soldiers and the prospect to them of achieving exemption by passing an examination would be a useful incentive to them to reach that standard'. From a somewhat different point of view the Vice Adjutant-General also made known his dislike of what was proposed. He was 'troubled by this rigid right of a soldier in his second eighteen months to take five hours out of his working week for education', since, 'apart from any such urgent call on his services as police duties, there were bound to be specialists and young NCOs whom it would be difficult to spare'. For good measure the Vice Chief of the Imperial General Staff pointed out too that 'working hours at Corps Training Units could not be increased' for 'if more than the two hours a week now provided had to be included men would have to stay longer there', which would have undesirable consequences for their subsequent unit training; alternatively something in the present syllabus would have to go and that also would be most unfortunate.

The civilians were against them, including the Secretary of State himself in one important matter. He 'doubted the propriety of compulsory education for soldiers during the first eighteen months of their service; he was certainly against it during the second eighteen months'. But 'he was in favour of compulsion for all, officers and men, when there were sessions in citizenship and Current Affairs'. For the Finance Member 'the important point seemed to be the provision of full facilities during working hours'. 'If this', he said, 'were genuinely achieved compulsion might be waived after the minimum standard had been reached', it being after all the task of the RAEC to inspire these young Regular soldiers with a desire for further education. But he also 'heartily agreed with the Parliamentary Under Secretary in the value which he put upon general education and with his belief that it was the Council's duty to realise that value; they would thereby create good soldiers and good citizens'. The Permanent Under Secretary seems to have clinched matters. He said that 'rightly or wrongly, public and Parliamentary opinion would force the Service Departments to provide compulsory education for national servicemen and, in his opinion, the Council would do well to accept the situation'. He pointed out too that 'universal compulsion would be simpler to administer', a view which was generally accepted.

Yet the Permanent Under Secretary also discharged the civil servant's job of making sure that the realities of the situation were fully understood. When the Director of Army Education expressed his hopes that 'a central institution of the nature of a polytechnic' should be provided at such places as Aldershot, Salisbury Plain and Catterick, where there were many soldiers and few civilians, that the LEAs should accept these as their responsibility, that there be 'similar provision at least for Middle East Land Forces' to be paid for eventually by the Ministry of Education, which should indeed 'devise [and pay for] some machinery for providing educational facilities for British subjects abroad', the Permanent Under-Secretary uttered the appropriate warnings. 'He thought it would be a long time before the Army colleges and education centres were taken over by the civil authorities.' And he also left the Army Council in no doubt of its extraordinary generosity in devoting a substantial part of its slender resources to what many of them believed to be other people's business. 'He hoped the Council realised how considerable a commitment they were assuming . . . Apart from capital and maintenance expenditure on building, which would be considerable, they were going to spend some £3 million a year and employ some 5,000 men from their slender store on activities, many of which were, in their expressed opinion, the proper duty of the civilian authorities.'[18]

In many ways that must have been an extraordinary meeting of the Army Council. They accepted what they did not want. They did not like the compulsory nature of the Interim Scheme, yet allowed themselves to be overruled by the civilians. They were unhappy at the prospect of military training suffering because more time than they believed could properly be afforded was to be devoted to education, but again they allowed themselves to be overruled. They were told plainly how altruistically they were acting and their reluctance to behave in this way is obvious. But behave in this way they did. It is evident how little they liked the advice of the Permanent Under-Secretary. But they accepted it. They even persisted in the hope that what he told them was misplaced and that the civil authorities would eventually take over from them expenditure on military colleges. Not that their hesitations were unimportant. It was a finely balanced judgment to which they came and if circumstances altered, as they were to, that balance of judgment could be expected to alter too. They would fight back, and fight back successfully, later when they appreciated more fully the absurdity of accepting as their first priority a non-military aim and when they became less impressed by the pressures that would be brought upon them to continue to do so. There is an old Latin tag *errare humanum est, perseverare diabolicum, exire angelicum* – to err is human, to persist in erring is diabolical, to cease erring is angelical. In the implementation of the Interim Scheme the Army showed that there was more in it of the angelical than of the diabolical. But it can hardly be denied that it showed a great deal of human weakness in accepting it in the first place.

The nature of the Army was yet another of the factors determining acceptance by the Army Council of the Interim Scheme. It was no longer an Army which was composed of a cross-section of the nation. It was now made up of two distinct sections. There were the long-term Regulars and the short-term, very young National Servicemen aged 20 or less. By 1951 such had been the decline in the recruiting of Regulars that National Servicemen made up 50% of the Army. A young National Service subaltern in the West Yorks who campaigned in the Malayan jungle during the Emergency had only one regular soldier in his platoon.[19] By that time all battalions had a majority of National Servicemen. This was what made the Army Council so sensitive with regard to their obligations to these young men. The Army Council were acutely aware that the National Service Acts had laid it down that the Services were responsible for the educational welfare of their conscripts. The National Service Act of 1940 had imposed upon the Army authorities the legal obligation to provide instruction in academic and technical subjects for National Servicemen whose pre- or postgraduate studies had been interrupted by their call-up. The National Service Act of 1947, which became operative on 1 January 1949, obliged those authorities to make available to conscripts Further Education similar to that which it was the responsibility of the LEAs to provide under the Butler Act. These were limited obligations but the Army Council was well aware that in the existing climate of opinion they could become less so. The presence of these young conscripts would mean that there would be a greater national interest in education in the Army than would have been the case had it been a purely Regular Army. The experience of the pre-war Militia days proved that. There were those in Parliament who could be relied on to concern themselves with education in the Army. Typical of them was Tom Driberg, who expressed the fervent hope that there would be no 'recession from the new attitude developed during the war ... the attitude that, so far as possible, the soldier should not be cut off from his general civic and political interests and responsibilities'. Driberg was emphatic that the National Serviceman must be seen as what he was, namely 'a citizen in uniform'.[20] So many who were not in the ranks were determined that the citizen should not be less of a citizen because he was in uniform; so many who were in the ranks were determined that they should not be more.

This was a markedly different Army to any hitherto known in Britain. In one sense it was a more stable Army than that which it had replaced, in that it was not subject to the great disturbance occasioned by post-war demobilisation. That increased stability would suggest to the unwary that what had not been possible educationally speaking in the more tumultuous period through which Army Education had passed would have a better chance of being done in the quieter conditions now prevailing. In any case, the very composition of the Army would suggest to its leaders that they would be well advised to see if that was indeed so.

It was above all the external pressures on it that induced the Army Council to accept the Interim Scheme. Those pressures were very formidable. The successful application of great and sustained national effort to the securing of a great objective which it has been very difficult to attain suggests to men that their powers of construction are as extensive, and if they so wish and so organise themselves, can be as successful as their powers of destruction have been shown to be. This chimes well with their natural feeling that great effort should be greatly rewarded and they allow themselves to think that paradise, which hitherto most had not expected to enjoy on this earth, might after all be within their grasp. Society which has shaped them they now begin to think they can themselves shape, removing from it the imperfections of which they are for the moment acutely aware and forgetting, as their hopes beat high, that man's considerable capacity to shape things has always been accompanied by a marked ability to misshape them too, so that the most ardent believers in past golden ages have never been able to furnish us with the records of earthly paradises.

Planning for a better future in the post-war days seemed a natural thing to do. These years have been called 'the golden years' of the social sciences. 'Their high profile', it was said, 'grew after the war.' 'The years of concern with social welfare, coupled with a widespread political move to the left', it was maintained, 'led even sociologists and a new breed of social administrators to a place in the policy sun.'[21] 'It was a seductive time, with a place in the front row of influence' for the social sciences. And no doubt was entertained that they were indeed sciences. It was said that 'what science denotes is the search for truth and a disciplined path towards it not a particular set of methods. And here the social and the natural sciences are alike. There is the same quest for discovery and understanding; the same dependence on empirical data; the same attempts to measure and to intertwine theory and data; to see causal findings; to make predictions.' There was a difficulty here. To those who believed that the Arts were also engaged in a search for truth and were treading a disciplined path towards it, this seemed to be a devaluation of the currency, undervaluing the Arts and conveying the suggestion that the social sciences spoke with a more authoritative voice than experience indicated they were entitled to. But doubts were set aside at this time. For there was now a widespread conviction that humanity itself could be moulded to a tenderer grace, a view shared, as we have seen, even by distinguished members of that profession, the military, which above all others must have been expected to be sceptical of such thinking. The sociologists would shed their light upon us and greatly would we benefit when eventually we understood what they were saying. Typical, too, of these years was the greatly increased influence of the statistical service, dreams seeming less insubstantial if accompanied by an impressive array of figures. In a society so full of high hopes and so fascinated by the prospect of new beginnings, the Army could not afford to be out of step.

Moreover, there was a focusing of these high hopes in a way that seemed of particular significance for it. That was in Butler's Education Act of 1944 and in the White Paper that preceded it. That White Paper emphasised that 'without provision for adult education the national system must be incomplete' and added 'It is thus within the wider sphere of adult education that an ultimate training in democratic citizenship must be sought.' It said that we must have a system of adult education that was worthy of our system of school education. It forbore to add that we already had that and that we were, unfortunately, going to remain contented with it. These high-sounding phrases from the White Paper were, however, weasel words which uttered no lies and spoke no truth. Yet when they were so solemnly uttered how could the Army, or anyone else, know that the appropriate addendum to be immediately affixed was *vox et praeteria nihil*, voice and little else? On the face of it these declarations in Parliament seemed a declaration of intention to develop Adult Education. They were merely a declaration of the conviction that it would be an excellent thing if Adult Education were to develop. The Butler Act declared that LEAs would now have the duty to develop Adult Education but the assistance they were to receive in doing so was restricted. The drive that was hoped for to strengthen Adult Education never came. But the Army could not be sure of that and is hardly to be blamed for mistaking a rhetorical flourish for a substantial advance.[22]

There was a still more particular reason why the Army Council was so acutely conscious of civilian interest in their educational arrangements, very aware that there would be civilian pressure on it if these were thought to be inadequate. They were under pressure from the Minister of War and they had to be the more circumspect as it was not yet sure how much further the considerable changes that had been occurring in the country since the war would go. They knew that the Government was not silly enough to ascribe its victory at the polls to ABCA as some alleged; they knew also that powerful figures in it nevertheless believed that the compulsory sessions on citizenship and Current Affairs had been to its advantage and would insist on their being continued. The Council would know that Shinwell, who as Secretary of State for War had signed the order authorising the Army to take no more of the pamphlets of the Bureau of Current Affairs, had tried to rescind that order when it was represented to him that in signing it he had closed the Army to socialist ideas. It is in character that when he was convinced that the Army's dropping of the Bureau of Current Affairs was in the country's interest he withdrew his opposition to it despite the pressure of some of his party colleagues. Like Bevan he had been a great critic of Government during the war. But unlike Bevan who seemed to welcome disaster, when things looked blackest Shinwell would always rally to his country's cause.[23] Still the Army was cautious and it is interesting that the Minutes of the seventy-second meeting of the Army Council do not record any expression of opposition by the soldiers to the strong insistence of the politicians that compulsory sessions on citizenship and Current Affairs be an essential part of the Interim Educational Scheme.

When we turn from the Interim Scheme to its implementation the first thing we have to note is that it was never properly implemented at all. Almost as soon as the 1948 Handbook devoted to it appeared the six periods of study it envisaged were reduced to three. One of those was to be given to the study of English, another to the study of Mathematics while everything else, Current Affairs, Citizenship, History, Geography and General Science, had to be dealt with in the remaining period. This halving of the time the soldier had initially been intended to spend on education was brought about, ironically, by sustained and successful pressure on the Government by those whose activity in Parliament and Press had originally convinced a reluctant Army Council that they had better accept the Interim Scheme in its entirety. The strong left-wing desire to have National Servicemen educated gave way to the stronger left-wing desire to get them out of the Army. Never liking conscription in time of peace, left-wingers and Liberals together contrived to reduce the period of service from eighteen to twelve months. That was too short a period to enable the Army to profit from conscription, but with such a short time in which to train the conscript the Army now had an unanswerable case that it had little to waste on non-military matters. There had always been those in the Army who doubted whether they could, let alone whether they should, do someone else's job; when it became clear that if the Army persisted in trying to do so it could not do its own their doubts would be greatly strengthened thereby. And when unexpected events on the other side of the world, the Korean War and Britain's participation in it, forced Government to change step and to increase the length of National Service, the Army's case that it dare not devote to purely military training less time than it was doing was not weakened thereby. For if British troops were to be in action all sensible people wanted them to be as fully trained as they could be and the pressures which led to the lengthening of the period of National Service weakened those who had insisted most strongly on the original Interim Scheme, for these were the men of the Left who had already suffered defeat in the lengthening of National Service.

This curtailing of the Interim Scheme was an acknowledgement of evident necessity. Its consequences were unavoidable although, with the wish no doubt to sustain the morale of the RAEC which was so closely identified with, and committed to, the scheme and in the hope of salving something from it, General Lloyd refused to recognise them. He pointed out that the changes thus made inevitable in the scheme were 'as fair as they are unavoidable'. He found the decrease in the number of hours devoted to education 'acceptable'. Feeling perhaps that his case needed strengthening he turned, appropriately, to the Stoics and quoted Seneca to the effect that 'change of mind is not change of will'.[24]

There was comfort from the classics and conformity to command. The reduction of hours was obviously 'acceptable' in the sense that it had to be, and therefore was, accepted. Whether it was also 'acceptable' in the sense that its acceptance left achievable the objective sought in the Interim Scheme is another matter and much more questionable. The Vice Chief of the Imperial General Staff at the seventy-second meeting of the Army Council thought not. He did not think that the Army could afford to give six hours to education. But he said 'to provide less than four hours would be no more than a token implementation of the policy already announced in Parliament' and added 'when considered on educational grounds alone, the inadequacy of less than four hours weekly is obvious'.[25] As for the Seneca adage that 'change of mind is not change of will', General Lloyd was mistaken. This change of mind did imply a change of will. It brought a change of emphasis that was itself a change of will.

We can see that unmistakably in a number of ways. We can see it in the Report of the Army Manpower Committee in 1948. 'We feel bound', that report said, 'to draw attention to the fact that time spent on educating a serving soldier in subjects that do not affect his military efficiency is uneconomical in manpower.' 'Nor', it went on 'do we understand by what right the Army is entitled to submit the soldier to education in such subjects, when the civilian of the same age is not so submitted.' 'We recommend', it concluded, 'that education in the Army should be recast to ensure that every possible facility is given for individual education voluntarily out of working hours, and that compulsory education should be confined to those subjects and standards which are needed by a soldier to fulfil his particular military role.'[26] The phraseology is revealing. Formerly it had been stressed that the soldier should not suffer by being deprived in uniform of the educational opportunities that would have been his had be remained a civilian. Now it was said there was no reason why he should be submitted to something from which he would have been exempt if he had not been a soldier. A right which must not be denied him had become an encumbrance from which he must be freed. He must be able to exercise the right of free-born Englishmen to remain ignorant, a privilege hitherto denied, but now restored to him.

Nor was this a recommendation that remained unattended to. It was one that reflected a developing and fundamental change of purpose. In July 1948 it was emphasised that Army Education, and Current Affairs in particular, had to be made more relevant to military needs, more effective and less controversial. Earlier, in February of that year, HQ BAOR had sent out the directive 'The Army will NOT be used for discussion of Party Politics.' Command Education Officers were told that they must make it plain to all instructors that in whatever classes they took they must be careful to establish a link between 'the subject under discussion ... and military matters of professional interest to the soldier'.[27] In May 1949 compulsion to attend educational classes in working hours was removed and much of the old certificate examination system linked to promotion and to the acquisition of trade qualifications was reintroduced, although the syllabuses for them were revised.

This was particularly significant as an illustration of the fundamental change that had taken place in the Interim Scheme even before any pretence could be made that it had got into top gear. For whereas few academics look upon examinations as anything other than unavoidable nuisances and fewer still believe they are avoidable, this was the conviction of many in the RAEC who were most closely identified with the Interim Scheme. The between-war experience of Army Certificate of Education examinations had been enough to sour any man, folk memories are long and emotion recollected even in tranquillity can be very strong. That may be why in post-war days thoughts of Army Certificate of Education examinations brought to many RAEC nostrils a heady whiff of brimstone. A senior RAEC officer tells us that between the wars the AEC had become little more than an examination machine for arranging, setting and marking tasks. One can well understand him when he adds 'against this background should be measured the grave risk of reintroducing any similar examination system for the post-war period'.[28] The editor of the Corps *Journal* wrote when these examinations were reintroduced 'they had had an electric effect on the troops'. That was not by way of welcoming something that had stirred them out of the apathy habitual to them when education was brought to their attention. It was, on the contrary, by way of deploring the oncoming danger he envisaged, 'the danger of prostituting true educational progress to the frenzied collection of certificates'. The RAEC, he wrote, 'must keep this bogy under control; for to us it means the difference between the joys of skilled craftsmanship and the drab boredom of the conveyor belt'.[29] No one would quarrel with his conclusion that examinations 'must be our servant and not our master'. But not all would think it likely that 'the frenzied collection of certificates' would be a characteristic of Army life or even that the chances of making the Army Certificate of Education examinations respectable education hurdles would be greatly improved if the RAEC in general adopted the attitude to them that stamped this editorial.

But just as recollection of AEC work for pre-war Army Certificate of Education examinations helps us to understand the attitude of this editor, so his attitude explains the at times extraordinary efforts that were made to avoid the necessity of having them. All believed that the intelligence of the soldier had to be developed and that where promotional standards were required they had to be devised, and be seen to be devised, as fairly as possible. But many were sure that the holding of examinations, while providing what would be accepted as a fair way of ensuring that promotional standards had been reached, would also inhibit the development of the soldier's intelligence and destroy his interest. This view prevailed in the Interim Scheme. What was taught was to be valued in itself and not for what it led to. If it was to be tested the product would be valued more than the process and that would be the mark of the cloven hoof. So that the best way of keeping the cloven hoof at bay was not to have tests and indeed to concentrate on what could not be tested. 'The keen specialist', whose specialism could be measured, was thus in the *Handbook of General Education* certified as the villain of the peace. 'The aim of the scheme', it was said, 'is not to cater for examinations, but to help the individual to make his own picture of the world.'[30] Despite the folly and the fallacy inseparable from humankind it is possible to form an impression of how people perform in examinations. But since only God could know how adequate was the picture of the world that each individual had formed for himself no one else, it was hoped, would be sufficiently overweening to make the attempt to examine this; and since it might be prudent to still further discourage the haughty, it was emphasised that the object of it all was not merely to help the individual to make his own picture of the world, but to make him feel at home in the universe as well and who would feel able to ascertain if that aim had been achieved? It is greatly to be regretted that the British soldier was not informed of these objectives as we are deprived of his comments, which would undoubtedly have been pertinent and pithy.

Nor were these objectives the sole line of defence against examinations. As the six titles which were said to be 'associated with General Education – English, Mathematics, History and Geography, Science, Current Affairs, Citizenship' might seem to have a content definite enough to be as objectively assessed as anything in the world of men can be, it was made plain that these indicated 'lines of approach, rather than the final treatment of subjects'. That such subjects can be 'finally treated' would not have been apparent to everyone; that anything in the whole wide world could, with the exercise of a little ingenuity, be represented as being 'lines of approach' to them would, however, have been self-evident to all and the hardiest and brashest of traditionalists would not have thought it possible to attempt to measure them. No one can be surprised if there is a note of testy tiredness in the consequent Army insistence to ensure 'that in future a realistic scheme is in being'.

Indeed, strongly buffeted as it was by post-war winds of change, the Army Council was never completely blown off course by them. At the end of the war there were many Warrant Officers and Sergeants who during it had been given war-substantive rank and who not having the educational qualifications hitherto insisted on for promotion were threatened after the war with demotion. Anxious to retain, or in some cases to regain, their wartime rank they were given an extended period of grace to acquire the educational qualifications they needed so to do. So as early as October 1945 examinations were reintroduced for Regular soldiers in this position and for those, too, who had partially qualified for the pre-war First Class or Special Certificates. The obvious embarrassment of the Army Council in reintroducing these examinations for this limited purpose is itself testimony to the strength of the 'liberal' pressures brought to bear on them. The continued insistence that opportunity be provided for NCOs to acquire the educational qualifications hitherto necessary for promotion was a rejection of the view apparently already accepted that education should have an influence on promotion but that promotion should not be dependent upon it. The further insistence, however, that accompanied the introduction into the examination syllabus of a new paper in English, that there should be no set book on which questions were to be based, was an obvious genuflection before the new gods who had expressed their dislike of all examinations and who were determined to keep them as 'liberal' and as open-ended as possible, if they could not be avoided altogether. One can imagine how unwelcome this proviso would be to the NCOs for whose benefit these great gods had been displeased.[31]

It soon became apparent that there was as great a need in the Interim Army to insist on the attainment of minimal educational standards as ever there had been. For although the standard of the Third Class Certificate which the private soldier before the war had been required to reach was very low, many National Servicemen coming into the Army could not reach it. 1% were totally illiterate, 20–30% were semi-literate and only 10–15% had School Certificate or above. The effects of evacuation, the blitz, the closing of schools, the call-up of teachers, the absence of fathers at the Front proved to be as devastating as they had been expected to be. A survey in 1948 showed that the average fifteen-year old was one and a half years retarded as compared with his 1939 brother. Another made in January 1950 showed that the standard revealed in the worst of sample exercise books taken from local Secondary Schools was much higher than that achievable by many entering upon National Service. It was believed that the below-average boy, educationally speaking, declined between leaving school and embarking upon National Service and since the Army got a major share of such boys, it obviously had a problem.[32]

No one can be surprised that the Army decided that the principle previously announced that promotion should not be conditional on educational achievement was no longer valid, that examinations for its Certificates must be reintroduced and that they must become as functional as military needs dictated. The soldier, it was determined, could not be considered fully trained until he had his Third Class Certificate; without it he would not get his three star rating and the increase in pay that went with it. Without it he could not be promoted to Corporal. The Second Class was necessary for promotion to Sergeant as before and the First Class for promotion to Warrant Officer. The inclusion of English in the First Class and the Special

Certificates was acknowledgement of the fact that the Warrant Officer who lacked the ability to give simple and clear instructions was not to be relied upon. Similarly, when in 1949 Map Reading became a compulsory subject for the Second Class Certificate it was recognition of the fact that maps could remain mysteries to no NCO who was up to his job. The Army Education Manuals of the early 1950s stressed the role of education in improving the soldier's training by making him more alert and self-reliant. And to ensure that it would have the opportunity of doing so, new-fangled theories which frowned upon examinations were put aside.

With the ending of the National Service Army this functional approach to education was to be still further stressed. The General Studies Paper was to be replaced by one entitled 'The Army and the Nation' which made the soldier aware of Britain's international responsibilities and how they affected the Army. This same functional stress is also to be seen in the syllabuses for the Certificates of special-to-arm subjects and in the reiterated comments on the importance of the study of English since 'lucidity in writing and in speech; and quick understanding of what is spoken or written are essential military requirements at all levels'. It would be wrong to think that the wheel had come full circle. The standards which had to be reached before the Certificates were awarded were still distressingly low. Where it had been hoped to promote analytical capacity and to instigate thought, examiners had, for the most part, to be satisfied with narrative and recall. Yet effort was demanded and obtained, and when it is who will dare to say that nothing worthwhile has resulted from it? The syllabuses, even when they seemed to be narrowly 'within the context of the soldier's everyday tasks', were more imaginative than they were before the war. There were interesting optional subjects for candidates to take and they would have been desperately boring to teach only to the desperately bored teacher. The gifted teacher can always find some new approach; when we cannot we would do well to remember the words of Cassius: the fault is not in our stars but in ourselves. And we should remember too, in the knowledge that commercial firms are not the most altruistic or easily deceived institutions, the statement of the Boots Personnel Officer that he looked for leadership qualities in the returning soldier rather than vocational or technical ability and that he valued the Army Certificates of Education where these had been obtained, since their acquisition was proof of persistence and application. In this whole-hearted return to the holding of examinations for the Army Certificates we have convincing proof of how completely the announced aim of the Interim Scheme had changed in its implementation.

Citizenship and Current Affairs were at the heart of the Interim Scheme which embodied the will that the Army should redress the deficiencies of the civilian world. Civilian education had failed to produce the good citizen. Army Education would and with the vision of the New Jerusalem that it had inspired in him the soldier returning from the Colours would fashion it. That, as we have seen, the Army no longer thought of doing. Citizenship and Current Affairs, when the Interim Scheme came to be implemented, shared one hour with Old Uncle Tom Cobleigh and all, while subjects more immediately useful to the soldier such as English, the study of which might help to minimise misunderstanding in communicating, and Mathematics, concentration on which would add to the number of numerate soldiers of whom the Army always stood in need, now took pride of place, being allotted two of the three hours to be given to education. General Lloyd could insist that 'the study of citizenship and Current Affairs will continue throughout the service of every soldier' and derive what comfort he could thereby. But the change that this marked decline in the importance attached to the study of citizenship and of Current Affairs implied was fundamental and he had to acknowledge it as such when he wrote 'In view of the technical needs of the modern Army and because the primary duty of Army Education is to produce an efficient soldier, it became necessary to stress the integration between education and military training.'[33] It had not been believed that the primary duty of Army Education was to produce an efficient soldier and it became necessary to stress the integration between education and military training only when what was accepted as being the primary purpose of Army Education had changed. In the seventy-second Army Council Meeting the argument based solely on educational grounds, in the words of the Vice Chief of the Imperial General Staff, had prevailed. It no longer did. That was not just a change of mind; it was a change of will. It was the end of the Crusade. The Army had at last come to its senses and from now on it would look after its own affairs and leave it to others to get on with theirs.

There seems to have been yet another significant change of will that was a consequence of the reduction in the hours to be set aside for education. The HMIs who reported on the Release Scheme had drawn attention to the way in which Commanding Officers often contrived to ensure that the carrying out of unwelcome instructions suffered a little delay. There must have been many Commanding Officers who, on first hearing how altruistic the Army Council had been in committing them to the Interim Scheme, were of the opinion that if perforce they were to be altruistic they would see to it that altruism adversely affected their interests as little as possible. They knew that leading horses to water is not always the same as inducing them to drink, and experience had taught them that the springs to which the horses were to be led made little appeal to them. Now it was being made clear to them that education would be sacrificed to military training, and not, as they had been led to fear, that military training would be sacrificed to education. Anxious as they were to get on with training, that must have greatly encouraged them. Had they been aware of undiminished enthusiasm for the Interim Scheme and great determination to see it carried out on the part of higher authority, the most recalcitrant of Commanding Officers must, however reluctantly, have made the effort to see that his unit complied with it. But such an early reduction of the time to be devoted to it must, inevitably, have cast doubt upon the will of authority to implement it and have strengthened their own to pay as little attention as possible to it.

We cannot then be surprised that the General Education to which the initiators of the Interim Scheme would undoubtedly have given pride of place fared poorly in its application. Citizenship was soon at a discount. The teachers and the taught vied in disliking it. The wartime BWP pamphlets were still used and there were repeated complaints that these were anachronistic. They had envisaged Brave New Worlds and these seemed much less real than post-war austerity. The Interim Scheme had been conceived in a world of dreams and it was in a world on which reality was impinging that it had to be applied. In such a world the BWP pamphlets were as out of place as they had seemed to be practical primers in that pleasanter world of dreams. Many National Servicemen were firmly of the opinion that had there been Brave New Worlds they would never have been in uniform. If the world persisted in being no better than it had been, why should it be thought that attendance at classes which bored them and which reminded them of a schooling they would rather forget would improve it? As far as they were concerned compulsory education made it worse. If they had to be soldiers they would be soldiers; if they had to fight they would fight with great bravery, as they did in Korea and with even more remarkable adaptability in the jungles of Malaya. But exhortation to know what they were fighting for and to love what they knew they would have regarded as claptrap. England owes much to the great Puritan movement of the 17th Century, but there is a self-righteous note in it which is not in keeping with English kindliness, warmth and humour – Cromwell does not speak with the authentic voice of the British soldier who would be embarrassed if he was thought to be like that Ironside who was said to know what he was fighting for and to love what he knew, if, that is to say, the Tommy did not look upon that idea as plain daft, as he was highly likely to do. He would put up with what could not be avoided, in the classroom as in the field, but he has always found ways of expressing himself and the least sensitive of men would have no difficulty in understanding what he thought of compulsory lessons in civics. And if that was so, who could be surprised if they were not as frequent as those who were sure of their vital importance hoped would be the case?

In the working of the Interim Scheme, Current Affairs fared no better, and almost certainly worse, than citizenship, for that was on the whole better taught, even though many of the RAEC instructors who taught it were poorly qualified to do so. The HMIs reporting on education in the Release Period had emphasised how important it was that the soldier should continue to study Current Affairs and they had expressed the strongest of hopes that this would be done. The Army Council fully acknowledged the importance of such study and did their best to promote it by including a compulsory paper on 'Army and Commonwealth' for the Third and Second Class Certificates and a compulsory paper on 'Current Affairs' for the First Class Certificate. It was not, however, only the ambitious who would receive instruction in Current Affairs. All must do so and the weekly discussions, hitherto known as ABCA, were to continue and be devoted to Current Affairs. They were not to be called ABCA but they were still to be taken by the unit officer. Unfortunately, it could not in this case be said that a rose under any other name would smell as sweet. What had increasingly come to be regarded as unbearably offensive continued to be shunned. The subaltern who suffered from taking the session on Current Affairs, the men who suffered from the subaltern's taking it and the Commanding Officer who suffered from the dissatisfaction which he could sense in his unit and from the continuing necessity of fitting into his programme more than he could reasonably be expected to do, all contrived to ensure that their sufferings were less frequent than the Army Council had intended the Current Affairs sessions to be.

No doubt unintentionally the RAEC made its own contribution to this state of affairs. It deleted the ABCA Staff Officers from its establishment, perhaps prompted to do so by the handing back of Coleg Harlech to its owners. This was a most unwise measure as importance was still attached to the study of Current Affairs. The winding up of the Army Bureau of Current Affairs might have suggested a change in their title and that would probably have benefitted them in view of ABCA's reputation. In any case the function mattered more than the name. Had these ABCA majors, whatever they were called, continued to visit units they might have done something to offset this drift away from the study of Current Affairs. Their removal was an odd way of convincing units that great importance was attached to this study; it was unlikely to induce those who saw the advantage of inattention to repeated injunction to see the error of their ways.

This unit pressure was steadier, more continuous and more successful than pressure on the unit from on high to get on with the job and it was obvious that an increasing number of soldiers were happily uninstructed in Current Affairs. However when the Korean War broke out it was thought to be essential for the soldier to know why he might be called upon to fight on the other side of the world. Appalled by 'lack of knowledge on the part of the average soldier of the facts of the present world situation', the Army Council lent more heavily on units to take up the study of Current Affairs. There was something here of the wartime concern with the morale of the troops. Thus we find Montgomery drawing Grigg's attention to the fact that in the Second World War the percentage of men taken prisoner compared to the wounded and killed was 30%, whereas in the First World War it had only been 6%.[34] It was clearly felt that if discussion of Current Affairs had helped to deal with this problem of morale then it would have a similarly beneficial effect now. 'Psychological warfare', a paper written in 1952 said, 'aims at the destruction of morale by undermining the soldier's faith in the cause for which he fights and in ultimate victory. It has now become a powerful means of attack. The soldier needs to be sufficiently well-informed, through the systematic study of current affairs, to detect the flaws in the enemy's propaganda.' There was now renewed insistence that weekly sessions on Current Affairs be held, courses were to be arranged to prepare unit officers to lead them and briefs, after the old ABCA-style pamphlets, prepared to smooth their way. A series of radio talks was arranged. These were broadcast on the world network of the Forces Broadcasting Service, a practice continued until the ending of the Korean War.[35]

When it was known how United Nations prisoners-of-war had been treated in Korea that, too, gave a fillip to the study of Current Affairs. The 'brain-washing' to which they had been exposed made psychological warfare seem even more important than had been realised and while British prisoners were more resistant to this brain-washing than Americans, the Armed Services were bound to be highly alarmed at what they had learned. A tri-Service panel was set up in 1954 to consider how best to strengthen 'the will to resist' of the troops in battle and after capture, if that should be their lot. As a result in 1957 a new training for 'Combat Survival' was begun, the purpose of which was 'to engender an attitude of mind which will enable a soldier to fight and not be captured, or if he is, to escape and to give him the moral courage and physical courage to resist persuasion and intimidation'. Advances in mass communication, it was pointed out, exposed a country and its armed forces to attack by propaganda and subversion more than it had hitherto been and the best defence against this increased danger was a greater knowledge of the enemy and his unacceptable ways, a greater awareness of one's own practices and of the liberty they provided for and cherished, a more determined study of Current Affairs of which these things would be the fruit.

As a more anxious care for morale had led to ABCA in the Second World War, so this alarm at what seemed to be the onset of a new and deadly menace gave the highest priority to a reinvigorated study of Current Affairs. However, to immunise against Communist propaganda without alienating opinion in a democratic country is no easy task, as the RAEC to whom fell the onerous job of supervising it found. Where troops were stationed in areas subject to heavy doses of Communist propaganda there was the interest to sustain continued attention to that propaganda, its purpose and its sources. Elsewhere it proved impossible to keep that interest alive. It is not, therefore, surprising that, except in the Far East, there was such marked indifference in the Army to 'Combat Survival' that there was general relief when it packed its bags and went quietly away. When it did so this particular pump-priming attempt to stir up the Army into the renewed study of Current Affairs had manifestly failed.

It still, however, remained one of the most important of the tasks of the RAEC to ensure that Current Affairs was taught 'purposefully, systematically and effectively'.[36] Nothing that exhortation could do to bring this about was left undone. Command Education Officers were reminded of the existing policy, namely that all trained soldiers had to attend weekly sessions on Current Affairs lasting one hour in their annual training period or continuously throughout the year. General Officers Commanding-in-Chief were responsible for implementing this policy within Commands. Regimental Officers were to be the teachers of those sessions, it being the responsibility of their Commanding Officers to see that they were prepared to do so. The policy had been enunciated in the *Manual of Army Education*, Part VII, as amended in January 1961 but this, it seems, figured prominently in the category of the great unread. While soldiers had to attend weekly sessions throughout the training period or throughout the year, no one appeared to know anything about it. No orders had been given 'stating the period during which Current Affairs will be taught, the frequency of sessions, those responsible for taking them and those responsible for seeing that they are taken'. There was no direction concerning what was to be studied. Commanding Officers were unpersuaded of the importance and relevance of Current Affairs instruction. Regimental Officers were 'not briefed on current affairs, have received no training in their exposition and lack confidence in their ability to run current affairs periods'.[37] Thus it is clear that the fear of brain-washing, itself transitory, failed to generate a significant and sustained interest in Current Affairs.[38]

The Command Education Officers were to correct this; theirs was the task of putting all to rights. The things they were capable of doing were spelled out for them. They were to see to it that the appropriate orders were published, to ensure that Unit Orders included 'the actual broken down programme of Current Affairs sessions, the topics to be covered, the officers who would deal with them in companies, platoons or their equivalents'. What assistance the RAEC could give must be made known and short courses arranged that would convince Commanding Officers of the importance of instructing their men in Current Affairs.

How they were to deal with other matters for which they were also said to be responsible was not, however, similarly spelled out to the assembled Command Education Officers. They were responsible for seeing that Regimental Officers were briefed on Current Affairs, for ensuring that they received training in the art of exposition, for removing their lack of confidence in their ability to run Current Affairs periods. Command Education Officers would have welcomed hints as to how these things could be done, but these were not forthcoming.

The Director of Army Education then made plain the limited effect of exhortation in dealing with the catastrophic decline of interest in Current Affairs among the troops and the reason for believing that, whatever the pressure from on high, no immediate improvement could rationally be expected. The Regimental Officer must teach Current Affairs. The RAEC Officer could not do this, for if he did he would be in a major unit teaching this subject for thirty periods a week. There were, however, 'two essential conditions' without which there could be no successful teaching of Current Affairs, he said. 'The Regimental Officers must be fully informed on their subject and be able readily and confidently to deal with awkward questions and to teach.' No one could doubt that he was right in emphasising that without these two conditions there could be no successful teaching of Current Affairs by Regimental Officers. And that was the conclusion to which he was pointing when he said 'It is not possible to have a flourishing Current Affairs scheme in the Army unless close attention is paid to Officers' Education.' But he was either not prepared to follow the logic of his own thinking, or other important considerations, such as the subtleties of timing which are so significant and which cannot be known to those who are not feeling the pressures of the day, suggested to him the undesirability of doing so at this particular time. He knew that the close attention to Officers' Education, the importance of which he so wisely emphasised, was not as yet being paid. He, nevertheless, pointed out that Regimental Officers fell into three categories: the Company Commanders who had passed the promotion examination, captains who were studying for it, and subalterns on whose horizons it had not yet dawned. He suggested that units could solve the problems that they had in teaching Current Affairs if the following scheme was adopted: 'All Staff/Promotion candidates should produce a paper on an aspect of Current Affairs within the topics laid down and cover its contents in a lecture/discussion period to the subalterns ... The subalterns in turn would use the material for their own Current Affairs period for their men. Company Commanders and Staff/Promotion candidates should also give direct instruction to the men.' If this scheme was followed, he said, 'there would be no insuperable difficulties over Current Affairs instructions for all men on a weekly or fortnightly programme'.[39]

This was advice of doubtful wisdom. Not all candidates for the Staff/Promotion examinations would reach Staff level. Some who failed to do so would still be of help to the subalterns and perhaps a godsend to the troops. Others, and they might be numerous, would remind us of Hooker's warning 'The pit is ordinarily the end as well of the guided as the guide in blindness.' We must be grateful to the Director of Army Education for seizing upon the connection between Officer Education and successful unit education; however, much more thought was needed to make of this the helpful connection it could undoubtedly be. But there was too much readiness here to think it could be immediately and usefully established. We can hear in the Director of Army Education's words too much of the note sounded by General Duff when he suggested that NCOs retiring from the Army could help to make good the chronic shortage of schoolmasters as 'every junior NCO has to acquire the rudiments of how to teach'.[40] In suggesting that this was all that the schoolmaster requires, in assuming that the capacity to instruct in some subjects was proof of an ability to teach in others, General Duff was greatly undervaluing the teacher's worth, as was the Director of Army Education also. For teaching is an art that, like every art, has its attendant technique and neither are easy to master except by the comparatively few who have what seems to be an inborn capacity in these matters. Neither the art nor the technique are to be acquired in the way suggested by the Director of Army Education.

Interest in Current Affairs could not be whipped up in this way. The ability of inspired teachers to open minds is fully equalled by the capacity of uninspired instructors to close them. And when Commanding Officers saw minds closing and not opening they would be strengthened in their view that irritated and bored men would be less likely to become better citizens than poorer soldiers. A survey taken of Commanding Officers' attitudes made it clear that 'some felt that the instruction provided was generally unpopular, and even the occasion of some resentment among their men'. General Duff was still more critical. 'It is high time', he wrote, 'that somebody said bluntly that education as now practised in the Army is merely a waste of time and money'. He believed that in teaching illiterates and in helping men who wanted to educate themselves the RAEC was doing an important job for the Army. It should confine itself to this. For when recruits had to be trained in eighteen months, something which it had been believed would take three years, the Army must concern itself exclusively with military training, the more so as weapons were now more difficult to master. Yet the attempt was being made 'to use the Army as an agency for raising the general cultural level of the nation by means of instruction given compulsorily to all the rank and file'. This attempt was not succeeding, had not succeeded and could not succeed. 'What else can be expected', he asked, 'when unwilling men are herded into the classroom for an hour a day, an hour reluctantly inserted into a training programme already overloaded; and when continuity is, from the very nature of Army life, almost impossible?'[41] The Command Education Officers in 1956 could burke the truth no longer. They were forced to acknowledge that 'the Current Affairs scheme is rapidly losing ground'. 'Nothing', they said, 'can come of any Current Affairs scheme without the cooperation of Commanders' and they added that 'although the Current Affairs scheme has the full blessing of the Army Council there is no evidence that Commanders really believe in the value of Current Affairs'. 'There is a distrust of Current Affairs by the Army as a whole, dating back to the occasional misuse of ABCA periods during the Release Scheme and a highly misleading version of the unfavourable comments the HMIs visiting Germany and the Middle East made on ABCA at that time.'[42] It might have been thought that it would only have been possible to give a highly misleading version of those comments if it had been said they praised ABCA to the skies. Blaming the past for the difficulties of the present, the Command Education Officers persisted in the belief that these must and could be overcome. They continued to insist that the unit officer must teach Current Affairs and that if he attended a one-day course to consider ways of doing so, that would suffice. This was to deny what they knew the HMIs had said. The Scheme, the Command Education Officers insisted, must be well prepared and they never doubted their ability to make it so. It must, they added, 'appeal to all officers', although they omitted to say how this could be done in the face of the general distaste expressed for it by the unit officers. They acknowledged that if it was not well-prepared and made no such appeal, the 'extinction' of Current Affairs in the Army was 'seemingly inevitable'.[43] As the years went by they continued to acknowledge the difficulties, saying 'too often the teaching of Current Affairs is left to junior officers who cannot have adequate experience' and that the regimental officer's responsibility to teach Current Affairs is one 'which he cannot discharge unless he himself is competent to instruct in this subject'. Yet in 1961 they were still saying of this Scheme 'there is little wrong with this; there is much wrong with its implementation', maintaining that it could be, and was not being, implemented when all the evidence proved that it was not being implemented because it could not be. Such sustained kicking against the pricks, such long belief in the unbelievable, such persistent denial of all experience must make us ask why? The RAEC well knew that it could not itself do the teaching of Current Affairs in the Army. Its teaching strength was not in its officers, of whom there were in any case too few, but in its NCOs, many of whom at this time were not up to the job. The regular NCOs of the Corps with their long experience of teaching would have made a good job of it and would no doubt have gently enjoyed doing so. But only 30% of the RAEC instructors were Regulars and there were other calls on their time. 70% of the instructors were National Servicemen. The great majority of RAEC instructors were too young even to give the impression they would be capable of doing a difficult job. An analysis of instructors in North Midland District in December 1947 showed that 43% of them were below twenty. Their qualifications were not outstanding. 52% possessed School Certificates, 40% Higher School Certificates. Only two had degrees and only one was a trained teacher. The analysis concluded 'they were extremely keen and enthusiastic but the majority lacked the maturity and academic background for such an ambitious scheme of adult education'.[44]

They had but six weeks' basic training at the Army School of Education. For three months thereafter they were on probation as Acting Sergeant Instructors. They were then confirmed as RAEC NCOs. It can hardly be thought they were capable of teaching Current Affairs. How could they convey an understanding when it would have been expecting too much of them to think they themselves understood? Undergraduates in many universities today study International Relations, but the advisability of them doing so is not universally acknowledged. Many remain unconvinced that it is a proper undergraduate study. Minds braced by exposure to old established disciplines seem more immune to the illusions to which contemporary studies so easily lend themselves than do minds not so toughened. An ex-secondary school Corporal pointed the moral and adorned the tail. He told the officer who conducted the inquiry into the RAEC instructors in North Midland district 'most of the teachers don't know what they are talking about and half of them are not as well educated as myself'. Another agreed that 'instructors very often are not competent enough for the job'.[45] *Disce, sed a docis*. Learn but from the learned we are told. Certain truths were belatedly recognised as the Interim Scheme drew to a close. 'The lesson method is certainly simpler than discussion', a paper submitted to the Command Education Conference in July 1959 admitted.[46] But this most basic of all truths, that interest in education will never be aroused until there are teachers who are in love with their subject and learned in it, in love with teaching and masters of their art and greatly concerned about their pupils, was not acknowledged. Why?

Too much depended on the persistence of the belief that perhaps after all these were not truths. The high hopes which had gone into the making of the Interim Scheme had been steadily whittled away. There was little left to the Corps of these hopes other than keeping the Army up to scratch in the teaching of Current Affairs. The Army's commitment to this had been steadily eroded but it had not yet disappeared. It had not done so partly because of its belief that its lords and masters wanted this commitment too. Knowing that in its ranks were fewer Regulars than National Servicemen on whom the eyes of parliamentarians must still be expected to be, the Army doubted if it could afford not to persevere in the teaching of Current Affairs. In any case it thought such teaching would strengthen it; there is no doubting the sincerity of the 1954 ACI which said the purpose of its teaching was 'to enhance the morale of the soldier, strengthening his faith in the ideals for which he may have to fight and inspiring confidence in himself, his leaders and his allies'.[47] Moreover, the teaching of Current Affairs by the unit officer made its appeal to high authority in the Army. The old ABCA notion that it presented a challenge to the young officer which it would do him a world of good to meet, thus strengthening in him the qualities which the Army ardently wished to encourage, never failed to intrigue it. It must, then, have seemed to the RAEC that, tough as it was, this was a fight persistence in which might enable it to win. If officers were too junior to teach Current Affairs, perhaps slightly less junior officers still young enough to benefit from the challenge of having to do so could be made by their Commanding Officers to do it, if sufficiently pressed by their seniors. The Corps said its continued pressure on units to teach Current Affairs was 'probably its most important commitment'.[48] It knew that high authority in the Army would lose much of its interest in Current Affairs, however genuine this was, if it became convinced that the regimental officer was incapable of teaching it. It was most important for the Corps to avoid this. If it did so it would have ensured the recognition by the Regular Army of the importance of education in it. If it failed this would be much more in doubt. However high the price of failure it cannot always be avoided; it was not on this occasion.

In two further significant ways the Interim Scheme must be seen as a failure.

That scheme had hoped to accustom the Army to the practice of continuous and progressive education by insisting that classes must be held regularly in units in working hours. That hope, too, had to be given up. For Army interests having asserted themselves, and having eventually prevailed, against those who sought to make non-military concerns the main aim of Army Education, Army practices similarly began to change, and ultimately to transform, educational arrangements that had been agreed upon when the Interim Scheme was introduced. Only if part of the weekly working time of the unit were to be compulsorily devoted to education would education, it was said, become as much an accepted part of military life as was any military training, or indeed sport. Soon, however, like the time to be spent on citizenship and on Current Affairs, the working hours of study disappeared too. It had always been easier for units to send a small number of men on short concentrated courses of study so that essential examinations could be prepared for than to dovetail educational sessions into weekly training programmes and either work through the unit in this way or be grateful to those to whom such courses had no appeal and to spare them the agony of being further exposed to education.

Now units sought and received what was known as 'authorisation to aggregate periods', an expression which indicated how much close working with the Civil Service had influenced Army writing and which meant permission to send soldiers on courses. In this way Commanding Officers were allowed to abandon the regular weekly provision of education and to send a small number whose promotion would otherwise be retarded on short concentrated courses before taking their examinations. By 1953 the Command Education Officer Northern Command said this was 'the almost universal practice in his command'. Such a typically Army way of doing things could not be expected to remain the exclusive prerogative of particularly favoured, or if one preferred so to regard them, outstandingly difficult, units. It became a general practice which the RAEC might have been advised to accept as the ordinary Army way of doing things and seek to build on and improve. Instead, senior members of the Corps were dismayed. They had, it was said, come to regard 'intensive courses leading to immediate examinations as almost a disease'. One disgruntled senior officer said 'the large scale intrusion of intensive courses with their attendant dangers had convinced many senior RAEC officers that the stars by which they steered were not only remote but receding'.[49]

In yet another way the RAEC had to acknowledge the failure of the Interim Scheme. After the waning of interest in citizenship and in Current Affairs, and after such widespread granting of 'authorisation to aggregate periods' as we have seen taking place it seemed that, apart from Preliminary and Resettlement Education, all that was left of the education envisaged in the Interim Scheme was the support that was still given to the soldier if he chose to devote his own time to his individual studies. This support was indeed generous and not the most severe military critic of Army Education ever begrudged it. Classes and courses were arranged for those who wanted them within units and in the Army Education Centres, of which eighty were set up, often in the charge of an RAEC warden. The teaching for these was done by both civilians and soldiers, as circumstances suggested. The fees for those attending classes in civilian educational institutions were paid. Within units libraries and quiet rooms were provided. Abroad there had to be more reliance on military teachers but there were many areas in which civilian help could be provided. In Greece troops could use the libraries of the British Embassy and British Council; in Eritrea and Tripolitania Italian instructors were employed on the recommendation of the British Military Attaché, and in the Caribbean there were the various extra-mural classes organised by the University College of the West Indies, by St George's College at Kingston in Jamaica and by the Government Training College at Georgetown in British Guiana, which the Forces could attend if they felt so inclined.

Great importance had been attached to Individual Education, it being hoped that the spread of this would create an irresistible pressure on the Army to take all its education more seriously. Its 'truly adult atmosphere' was glowingly referred to and contrasted with the very different, much less splendid and presumably more juvenile, atmosphere to be found in the compulsory classes. But those Commanding Officers who had always maintained that the provision of the most ample supplies of water would not induce all horses to drink had unfortunately no occasion to change their views. In Southern Command, for instance, RAEC officers reported that they had not yet found the secret of attracting the young soldier or young officer to use his spare time to educational advantage. They could at least comfort themselves with the reflection that no one had found the secret of inducing the young civilian to do so either. HMIs had often spoken warmly of the atmosphere in the extra-mural and WEA classes held in the civilian world. But they regretted, as all engaged in that work did too, that there were so few classes for that much-admired atmosphere to develop in. The few who risked exposing themselves to it enjoyed their experience and benefitted from it. That was sufficient justification for the considerable effort that went into providing them. This was true of Individual Education in the Army too. It changed the lives of several, of the Private in Singapore, for instance, who eventually became a doctor, of the girl who left school at the age of fourteen and became a lecturer at London University.[50] We can recall with grateful humility for what small a number the city was saved. To bring contentment and fulfilment to even a small minority is always worthwhile, but it is not to be mistaken for the breakthrough to larger numbers for which so many hoped and which all teachers and democrats must believe to be important.[51] The heading 'Causes of the Comparative Failure of the Individual Education Scheme' in a research paper submitted to the April 1954 Conference of Command Education Officers is the acknowledgement of the failure to achieve that longed-for advance.

That failure is in no way surprising. What is surprising is that anything else should have been expected. For the British Army could not but be a reflection of British society and British society had limited regard for education. In 1988 only 35% of the British age group 16–18 years was in full-time education, this being the lowest percentage of those in a similar age group in any advanced country. This compared with 79% in the USA, 77% in Japan, 76% in Sweden, 66% in France. Of our sixteen-year-olds only half were in full-time education, the lowest proportion in any European Community country, with the exception of Greece. In 1987–1988 45% of our boys and 37% of our girls left school without any O levels, as compared with 10% in France and Germany. A recent survey of seven-year-olds revealed that there had been a 50% rise in the number unable to read properly. One in seven of our youngsters leaves primary school practically illiterate. The salaries we pay our teachers compare poorly with those of non-manual workers in the private sector of the economy. Today they are only 5% above the white-collar average, whereas fifteen years ago they were 37% and at that time their relative decline was already well under way. As a result in 1980 14% of our men graduates and 35% of our women went into teaching, as compared with 34% and 61% in 1960. One in five of our science teachers admit that they lack adequate knowledge to teach their subjects. Less than half those teaching mathematics took this as their main subject when becoming qualified and many did not take it even as a subsidiary subject.[52] Fascinated with Buffcoat, that Cromwellian soldier who knew what he was fighting for and who loved what he knew, we forgot that Mr Atkins had little affinity with him and it was Mr Atkins with whom we were dealing. Kipling spoke for him when he wrote:

> We aren't no thin red 'eroes, and we aren't no blackguards too,
> But single men in barricks most remarkable like you;
> An' if sometimes our conduck isn't all your fancy paints,
> Why, single men in barricks don't grow into plaster saints.

Nor into young men more naturally inclined to study than those not in uniform.

In the Interim Scheme the RAEC wanted to mount a crusade, the Army to get a job done. The RAEC wanted to use the Army to improve the nation, the Army wanted to use the RAEC to improve the Army. And from that Interim Scheme we can see how easy and unwise it is to forget certain basic and essential truths. One is that we cannot afford to forget reality. Horace said of nature *Naturam expelles furca, tamen usque recurret*, if you drive nature out with a pitchfork, she will soon find a way back, and that is as true of reality. Society will be the poorer without its visionaries but it benefits little from the impracticable. There can be no denying how attractive was the conviction that Army Education was an integral part of national education, but here was another case of the cobra lurking under the night-flowering orchid. For it encouraged the thinking that the primary purpose of education in the Army is not a military purpose at all; it is to promote the education of the nation and the educational branch of the Army is more truly to be thought of as a Department of the Ministry of Education than of the Ministry of Defence. Those who advocate such a view are more impressed by the altruism of the Army than by its sense; those who do not believe that altruism is, or ever can be, a marked characteristic of Departments of State must conclude that there can be few more promising ways of suggesting to the Army that its best interests would be served by transferring lock, stock and barrel to the civilian world those of its members who put the interests of that world before its own.

The RAEC was indeed in a difficult position for it was under pressures that were difficult to adjust to, and yet not of such a kind as greatly to discourage impracticable hopes. Thus the Report of the Advisory Committee on Recruiting, the 1958 Grigg Report, which said 'there appears to be some danger that the Services are coming to attach too much weight to educational tests as a qualification for advancement within the ranks – or (perhaps even more dangerous) to make failure to pass them a bar to advancement' and which wanted the tests for advancement to be 'directly related to what is necessary to carry out the duties of the higher position', also stressed that 'Reading maketh a full man' and that 'there should be more such men in the Army'. The Committee could, indeed, see so few of them in the Army that they expressed the hope that 'there is no danger of the Army becoming a cultural desert when National Service disappears', a more polite but no less unmistakable way of saying that they entertained the fear that there was. This, they said, 'would have serious consequences and not only in the context of recruiting'.[53] The Committee wanted education to become more functional. They also wanted it to become more cultural. They were aware that as it became the one the temptation would be great for it to cease to be the other. They believed that the Army was already – before, that is to say, it made its education more functional – yielding to the temptation to be less interested in the cultural development of the troops. They nevertheless urged that education in the Army become more functional. It would have been very understandable had the RAEC allowed their minds to recall those biting lines Siegfried Sassoon wrote of the First World War:

> God heard the embattled nations shout
> Gott strafe England and God Save The King
> God this, God that, and God the other thing,
> 'Good God', said God. 'I've got my work cut out'.

So, too, had the RAEC. But difficult as it was for the RAEC to do all that the Grigg Report wanted, it would see in that Report no reason to give up, but on the contrary further reason to cling to, the continued hope that the way might yet be found of inducing the Army to accept what it had already made it plain it did not want, a much more liberally conceived education than it desired, an education so liberally conceived as in the circumstances to be unfortunately quite unrealistic.

Nothing that had happened during the war or since its ending could justify the assumption the RAEC was making at this time that the great mass of the troops, the 90% whom we dare not think of as ungettable but who had not been got at, could be led in compulsory periods in the Queen's time to 'genuine and enjoyable Adult Education'. Nothing, too, could justify the RAEC if it yielded to the temptation of thinking it had interests distinct from those of the Army. It was always certain that the Army would not long admit this. For the RAEC was part of the Army and the sole justification for promoting the interest of the part was that by so doing the interests of the whole would be advanced. Yet in seeing itself as 'an integral part of national education' it was to this temptation that the RAEC was yielding. In truth Army Education was an integral part of national education only in the sense that it was looked upon by the Army much as the British public looked upon their civilian educational arrangements, with indifference tempered by irritation and not always subdued dislike. The cry of the revolutionary students in Paris at the end of the 1960s *Soyez réaliste; demandez l'impossible* is not, as they learned, a sensible maxim. It is more helpful to take as one's guide the old exhortation 'always seek the best result possible, not the best possible result'. It had been overlooked in the Interim Scheme.

A further basic truth overlooked in the Interim Scheme was that we cannot be effective if we persistently go against the grain of things. It is always more effective to go with the grain than against it and the most successful diplomacy is that which forwards one's interests in such a way as to promote those of others too. Wanting to provide 'a vital service in the recruitment of high quality volunteers' in the Regular Army of the future 'by enabling men to obtain, while serving, qualifications for civilian careers after discharge', the RAEC felt that this could only be done if provision was made for men who wished to do so 'to follow during duty hours a course of self-selected study under qualified instruction'. 'The provision during duty hours', it was said, 'of what is now known as Individual Education will make this type of education fully viable for the first time.'[54] This was said after the number of hours to be devoted to education had already been reduced, 'summarily' as one senior RAEC officer put it, using a pejorative word signifying in this usage unusual behaviour on the part of the High Command, although Army policy has not usually been dependent on the consent of less senior officers.[55] And we must wonder what was the point of continuing to press for more educational hours when high authority had already decreed there would be less.

We see the same insistence on going against the grain of things in some of the experiments in 'liberal' education tried during the Interim Scheme. Typical of them was the so-called 'Colchester Scheme' and it was not lacking in eccentricity. It looked to improve the soldier's 'quality of thought by providing experience in imaginative and conceptual thinking', an objective mercifully not made known to the soldier. It dispensed with a syllabus and with much else that had hitherto been thought valuable in education too, such as continued, coherent and disciplined study. The wind blew where it listeth and discussion should in this be like the wind. Groups would meet once or twice a week for some five months and their instructors would help them to discuss whatever took their fancy. It was said that they would thus have an 'opportunity to discuss subjects of proved interest to them and of a nature that would assist them in coming to terms with their environment'. This would 'put immature and undisciplined minds in contact with one mind more fully developed' so that they 'could experience some of the simpler intellectual pleasures and develop a permanent taste for them'.[56] 'The initiative', it was claimed, 'lay terrifyingly enough with the students' and this 'was the adult approach with a vengeance'.[57] Claimed as a success, it was 'not pursued further'. It was what a senior RAEC officer called 'a revolt against the strait jacket of rigid syllibi and external examinations'. It was also a revolt against common sense and experience which suggested what no educator ever should, that education is possible without effort. Since it minimised the opportunity of those who were to preside over these sessions to prepare them and minimised the opportunity for consecutive, coherent and consistent study while it maximised the tendency to indulge in undisciplined waffle, it was always optimistic to have expected this to be accepted by senior officers as a substitute for more orthodox syllabuses. The spectacle of its authors 'voyaging through strange seas of thought alone' must have increased for those senior officers the desirability of moving in other directions. Only when it, too, took to going with the grain of things would the RAEC occasion no further raising of eyebrows.

Yet a third basic truth lost sight of in the Interim Scheme is that we cannot achieve the ends in the absence of the means. The rapid loss of interest by the Army in Current Affairs is sufficient proof of that. Had the majority of Commanding Officers been convinced that Current Affairs was a worthwhile study it would have survived. As they were not it did not. Yet it is hard to believe that they did not understand that it was important that the soldier should know why his services were required and how it was that the nature of the international world made it unlikely that they would ever not be. The soldier's training ensured that he knew what he was doing; it could only add to his sense of his own importance, and thus to his morale, if he also knew why he was doing it. How could it be assumed that such a staggering glimpse of the obvious would not be vouchsafed to Commanding Officers? Folly is to be found in all professions, not excluding the academic which is usually adjudged to be more learned than the military. But in an Army in which shrinkage was increasing the competition for command, Commanding Officers were unlikely to be foolish and it would be naive of us to find in their inadequacy the obvious explanation of the waning interest of the Army in Current Affairs. The obvious explanation is that their experience had shown them that the study of Current Affairs was not doing what it had been hoped that it would and what, had it been able to do, would have made Commanding Officers as convinced of its value as was the RAEC. It was not making the soldier see why his services were, and would be, required. It was not making him feel the more valued by demonstrating the essential nature of his work which no one else could do. It was, on the contrary, making him feel bored and bloody-minded, and Commanding Officers were to be forgiven for thinking that this was not good for his morale. How could they not conclude that compulsory sessions on Current Affairs were more trouble than they were worth if this was the effect on those who took part in them, teachers and taught alike?

There is something else which the Interim Scheme teaches us, too. It hinted at something which, though rendered of little importance by the conservative nature of the British people and by their strong common sense, is, nevertheless, worth mentioning if only as an indication of how strong the pressures were which were bearing on the Army Council at this time. That something else that we ought not to forget is that dreams if persistently clung to may be tinged with nightmare. We had a hint of that in an article written by Senior Commander James in June 1942. In it she said of her auxiliaries 'We now have for the first time an opportunity to see that some of a large body of women achieve a reasoned and objective view of local and national Government.' She quoted with approval Dr Temple's plea when Archbishop of York that 'education should aim at training men for the social use of liberty'. As her ATS had left school ten years ago she thought that 'to ask them to determine for themselves what they should learn is more than unreasonable'. 'If they have the duty of learning', she said, 'we have the duty of teaching, we have the duty of deciding what they should learn. To throw them wholly on their own resources is not democratic encouragement of freedom of thought, it is an abdication of responsibility towards them. It should not therefore be our policy in the education of the ATS to say "where there is evidence of a genuine demand for a subject we will do all in our power to satisfy it". On the contrary ours should be the much stronger policy of saying "This, this and this are important. How can we stimulate interest in these subjects?"'[58] Senior Commander James is here assuming her auxiliaries have the duty of learning and she has the duty of teaching. Duty is the fulfilment of legal or moral obligation and the decision to impose education as a means of strengthening morale placed a legal obligation on the soldiery to be taught. But here Senior Commander James is concerned not with the maintenance of morale but with making her auxiliaries good citizens. She now has the opportunity of doing so and her duty and that of her auxiliaries derives from that opportunity. The derivation of duty from opportunity is highly questionable and what she says has its dangers for the Army. Such phrases as 'the social use of liberty' may uplift the heart but they do not enlighten the mind. They leave us uncertain what we mean by it and what we have to do to get it. We never agree about these things, and as the Army learned and ABCA and BWP taught, discussion of them, whatever else it achieves, produces division not consensus. If there is danger to the Army in the attitude of mind demonstrated by Senior Commander James, there is even greater danger to democracy, such an attitude being incompatible with it. The 'we know best and should impose on others what we believe to be best for them' cast of mind is not one to be encouraged in a free society which has not yet committed itself to a proposition, the acceptance of which would speedily destroy it.

We can see how nightmarish dreams can become if we remember that such was the importance attached in the post-war years to the education of the young adult that there were those who were willing to toy with the idea of enforcing education on the young civilian adult as well as on his military counterpart. There is a fascinating sentence in the book by Hawkins and Brimble, *Adult Education, The Record of the British Army*. It runs 'It has been suggested ... that, like ABCA in the Army, discussion groups should become a compulsory part of adult education.'[59] That sounds a little better to a free society than the blunter statement that adult education should be made compulsory. But this is what it means, being otherwise either a phrase without meaning or a manifestly absurd proposition. Its only other meaning than that adult education should become compulsory is that all who wanted to attend adult education classes could do so only if, in addition to studying whatever took their fancy, they also attended classes in civics. That would compel those who needed such study least to devote themselves to it most, for as long, that is to say, as there were adult education classes to attend. As a way of promoting adult education this would be highly eccentric, and as a means of advancing the general study of citizenship, totally ineffective.

A further sentence in that book 'Even if one accepts this principle of compulsion – and most people recognise that the nearest we may get to true freedom may always have to be conditioned by some degree of compulsion', suggests that the authors would not have been averse to making adult education compulsory, though they acknowledge the unlikelihood of public opinion agreeing to this. We must be aware how highly dangerous to a free society the view expressed here is. Liberty will be gravely at risk if we do not understand that the relation between it and compulsion is much more subtle than Hawkins and Brimble suggest. For liberty is attained only by the development of the personality of the individual, only by the strengthening and the extending of the individual's rational control over himself or herself. It is the development of these things that enriches the individual and it is the harmonious interaction of developed individuals that enriches society. Hence the ideal society is a whole which lives and flourishes by the harmonious growth of its parts, the growth of these furthering the growth of the whole, and social harmony the consequence of it all. Individuals will not be developed by compulsion. We cannot coerce a man for his own good, not because his good does not concern us but because it cannot be furthered by coercion. It cannot be furthered by coercion because it is not within the capacity of the state to make men act morally. In Hobhouse's words 'To try to form character by coercion is to destroy it in the making.' Thus there is a true sphere of liberty – the moral development of the individual – into which the state cannot intrude without destroying liberty. But liberty is a matter of social interests too. For while the life of society is nothing but the life of individuals as they act upon one another, the life of the individual would be utterly different if he were separated from society. Social liberty must rest on restraint, for a man can be free to direct his own life only in so far as others are prevented from interfering with him. Liberty needs compulsion and it will not be in danger as long as we remember that the relation between them is one of mutual need and that there is no intrinsic and inevitable conflict between them, as there would be if compulsion were allowed to intrude into that sphere, the moral development of the individual, in which the individual must, as of right, reign supreme. It would be so intruding if adult men and women were forced to attend classes arranged for the purpose of making them better citizens. Men are not to be made better by decree; citizens are not to be made better citizens by command.

Exhausted by a great and protracted effort, unbalanced by sweeping change, seeking a respite from reality in dreams and unaware how easily our dreams could turn to nightmare, we were tempted at this time, fortunately not too greatly, to bow the knee to alien gods. And there is a lesson from those days that we would do well not to forget. It is that free men are to be led, not driven. That perhaps is the greatest lesson for us of the Interim Scheme.

CHAPTER 10

THE NON-INTERIM SCHEME
IN THE CONSCRIPT ARMY

Of the many, if one may so call them, bread-and-butter activities of the RAEC, attending to the education of Army children was one of the most fascinating and important of them all. It always produced problems and this was a case, to misquote Shakespeare, of age not withering nor custom staling their infinite variety. It must have been a most odd member of the RAEC who was bored by this particular challenge or blind to the outstanding opportunity presented by the need to teach the Army's children. For most parents are concerned with the schooling of their young and are touched with a due sense of humility, whatever their position, when attending parents' days at school. On such occasions they do indeed come to learn. They want to know what the teachers think and they get to know who the teachers, and those who are in charge of the teachers, are. These in turn get to know the parents and so responsibility for the education of Army children provides opportunity for the RAEC to get to know all ranks and all units.

This problem of Army schools began to concern the Corps even before the end of the war, and as the Interim Scheme replaced the Release Scheme, looking after Army schools made increasing demands upon the Corps. Plans were quickly made to send overseas more Queen's Army Schoolmistresses but for some time a meagre quota of RAEC officers and NCOs, almost invariably having to make do with inadequate supplies of essential equipment, had to set about the task of providing schooling for an increasing number of children. This they had to do while undertaking a whole host of other educational activities, for it was not until 1956 that Staff Officers began to be appointed to Commands for duties solely concerned with children's schools.

Developments in Commands varied significantly, since problems differed greatly. They were often the result of the instability of the countries in which they were located. In some this meant that strict security measures, such as surrounding schools with barbed wire and placing armed guards on school buses, had to be introduced; in other areas it led to families being evacuated and schools closed. There was much troop movement with consequent moving of families in Kenya during the 1952–1957 Mau Mau Revolt and in Malaya during the 1948–1960 Emergency there. Nowhere was the situation less stable than in the Middle East. Deteriorating relations with Egypt, which led to the eventual withdrawal of British troops from the Canal Zone and to the 1956 Suez Crisis, made teaching the children very difficult and the authorities reluctant to invest in new buildings. Yet, while three to five years is a very short time in military planning, it represents a very large proportion of a child's school life. Eventually in 1956 all schools in the Canal Zone were closed, with families moving to Cyprus. This, in its turn, put increased pressure on the schools there and, together with the arrival in Cyprus of the additional forces required to meet the Egyptian challenge to the Canal, occasioned many difficult problems in the provision of adequate accommodation.

Some idea of the extent of the disruption in the region can be seen from the fact that while in March 1955 there were 1,555 children in the Canal Zone and 655 in Cyprus, two years later these numbers had risen to 1,717 in Cyprus and fallen to nought in the Canal Zone. Such an atmosphere of change, instability and unrest was inimical to the best interests of the children and might have been expected to have had an equally adverse effect on the morale of teachers. Yet, almost without exception, they carried on cheerfully and loyally in the face of difficulty, discomfort and danger. Bombs were thrown at their homes by terrorists who murdered the fiancé of one of them. Only one, however, gave up and returned home. They had to cope with the problem of acquiring stores, equipment, books and stationery. All had to be bought at home, and by the time they arrived the demand had usually so increased as to make the supply still inadequate. This problem of inadequate equipment was universal. It was experienced even in Malta, where despite the shortage of classrooms education of the children was outstandingly good. In the provision of school transport, however, inter-Service rivalry reared its head. Naval and Air Force children travelled to school by bus and Army children in three-ton trucks, a discomfort to the children and a danger to life and limb. As soon as the RAEC got a grip on things this particular anomaly was ended.

There were problems which were common to all Commands and which were daunting enough. A major problem, arising from the 1944 Act, was the requirement to provide secondary education for all children up to the age of fifteen, a major difficulty for the schools which before the war had only provided education at elementary level. At home, as we have seen, Army Schools were handed over to the LEAs; this could not be done overseas. Yet how could secondary schools or secondary departments be established where the school population was small, as it often was overseas? They would be economically unsound and educationally unviable. Where there was a large concentration of troops, or where there was a compact area, it would be possible to have day or boarding secondary schools. In some countries, such as Kenya or Jamaica, local civilian schools might be used although there were often problems when they were. Schools in Nairobi, for instance, did not have room to accommodate all Army children under ten years of age and since children could not enter high school before the age of twelve, some had to make do with what could be provided for them, off the cuff as it were, for months at a time. Furthermore, some high schools in Kenya insisted that Army children take the Kenyan Preliminary Examination before they could be admitted, and since the History and Geography syllabuses for this examination had a markedly local flavour Army children could not be expected to do well in them and were often in consequence unable to find high school places. It was very difficult for the Army schools in Gilgil and Nanyuki to prepare candidates for the Kenyan Preliminary Examination without so distorting their curriculum as to adversely affect children who were not hoping to go to the high schools.[1]

We will see how highly the HMIs thought of the teaching the children received in Malta. Secondary education was tri-Service, the Navy as the biggest force running the secondary schools and leaving it to the other Services to see to elementary education. Parents could be very satisfied here. Elsewhere they were not. In the Middle East the lack of secondary education provision led parents in the early 1950s to send their children home; it also encouraged senior NCOs to hesitate to accept re-engagement. In West Africa, the RAEC believed that both from the point of view of health and of education children ought to be left in England. It pointed out the incidental difficulty, namely that 'the apparently uncooperative attitude of most LEAs makes this impossible unless parents are prepared to meet a large part of the fees'.

This difficulty and the link between providing a good secondary education and the Army's recruiting and morale was raised in Parliament, but not before the Services themselves had established an inter-Departmental committee to examine the provision of secondary education by the Services and to suggest ways in which it could be improved. The Committee was fully aware of the problems Service parents faced in educating their children, subject as they were to frequent moves at home and overseas, the limited amount of secondary education available abroad and the cost of boarding school education at home. As a result of its recommendations a scheme of allowances for the Forces was authorised in 1955. Acknowledging both the nomadic nature of Service life and the need for continuity of education, the Treasury agreed to pay up to £75 a year for each child of secondary-school age kept at a boarding school at home, whether or not the parents were overseas.[2] An advice section was established at the Institute of Education to give parents whatever details they required, such as which LEAs and which independent schools offered places to Service children at favourable rates. By 1960 some 5,000 children were boarding. An increasing number of families took advantage of this scheme but the problem of providing secondary schooling for Army children has not been completely resolved, and perhaps it never can be so long as Army families live abroad, for there will always be those who place a high priority on keeping the family together and who are not prepared to face the social and psychological difficulties of separation. However, whether parents determined to keep their children with them or not, all benefitted from the advent of airtrooping. The traditional means of transport for long voyages had been the troopship which meant valuable loss of schooling for many months. Travel was now a matter of days. And for parents who chose to send their children to boarding schools a system of annual free flights for children to visit parents overseas was begun in the late 1950s following the Report of the Grigg Committee in 1958, which looked into the factors that affected the recruiting and the retention of Army personnel.

There was always a further problem that affected Army schools. Frequent changes of school and of teachers created what in the modern idiom was referred to as the problem of turbulence. It was an old problem. As long ago as 1859 Lefroy, the Inspector General of Army Schools, reported that constant movement accounted for the low level of attainment sometimes found there. Almost a century later a review of Army schools in Germany showed that children stayed in one school for just 2.7 terms on average and during this time had to get used to frequent changes of staff. One mother said that her nine-year-old son was attending his twelfth school and that her six-year-old daughter had already had eight teachers. There seems little doubt that such turbulence does adversely affect scholastic performance. But there are compensations, as those who have observed the self-confidence of Army children and their fluency of expression are well aware. Achievement in Army schools was, nevertheless, always incontestable. The HMIs and the RAEC Chief Inspector who visited Malta in 1956 reported not only that all three Services could be satisfied with the schools there, that 'parents could feel confident that their children do not suffer educationally', but also that the work they saw was at least up to the average and that the best was as good as the best they had seen at home. Imtarfa Infants' School they thought the best they had ever seen. Well might the Grigg Report acknowledge the importance of this particular work of the RAEC in meeting the needs of the Army not only by taking such good care of the education of its children, but by thus increasing the attractions of military life also encouraging soldiers to re-enlist and potential recruits to join.[3]

That report drew attention to yet another function of the RAEC which the Army greatly appreciated, its teaching in Boys Units and in Apprentice Schools. Commenting on the Army practice of having Boys Units and Apprentice Schools, the Grigg Report expressed the view that the Regular Army would be able to meet recruiting targets only by attracting young entrants who, when they became of age, would join it. It believed that the Army should aim to get between one third and one half of its recruits in this way. To do that existing schools and training establishments would have to be expanded, but it believed that the cost of doing this would be offset by its beneficial effect on recruiting. It thought, too, that an increased entry of apprentices would be the only way in which the Army could meet the shortage of highly skilled technicians which it feared would inevitably develop in view of its own inability to attract fully trained craftsmen who could earn more money in the civilian world than in the Army.

We have seen that for many years the Army had been enlisting boys. That practice had been given a fresh impetus by the opening of the first Apprentice Tradesmen's School for boys at Chepstow in 1924. It was so successful that a second such school was opened at Arborfield in 1939; the fact that both kept going throughout the war indicated the importance attached to them. A further two schools were opened in 1947, one at Harrogate and the other at Taunton. That at Taunton was short-lived – it closed in 1949 because of lack of recruits. In 1947 these schools were renamed Army Apprentice Colleges. They were commanded by Colonels, usually Guardsmen, and their training Warrant Officers and NCOs were normally Guardsmen too.

There were also Boys' Units which offered specific training for particular Corps and Regiments. In 1926 two Boys' Batteries of the Royal Artillery had been formed to train trumpeters and, although run down on the outbreak of war, they joined to form a new Battery in 1942 and to become one of the first Boys' Regiments, the Boys Regiment RA, after the War.

The job of the RAEC in such units was both important and difficult; as the youngsters were at the Apprentice Colleges for three years much could be done. Its was the teaching role, the task of opening young minds. But it often seemed that the role of those responsible for the military training of the youngsters was to close minds. Life in the units was highly regimented and the atmosphere in them was not such as to produce enquiring and lively minds. Conformity was insisted on and means were found of securing it. For as well as having their Guardsmen NCOs, Boys' Units had Boy NCOs. To the intolerance of youth they too frequently added the arrogance of command. They were much tougher than the Guardsmen NCOs and there was in consequence far too much bullying by them. There was too much forcing boys into becoming men. The RAEC knew what the Guardsmen were reluctant to acknowledge, that maturity is not at the beck and call of impatience. The RAEC knew, too, that once the boys had started to become automatons the teachers had lost them. There was as a result tension between teachers and trainers.

This needed sorting out and tragedy saw to it that it was. In 1954 a youngster belonging to the Boys' Infantry Battalion hanged himself and a committee was set up to look into Boys' Units and make recommendations concerning them. The report of that committee – the Miller Report, named after its military member – suggested that far-reaching changes be made in them and they were. Burke tells us that the deliberations of calamity are rarely wise; this was a case in which they were. The Miller Report expressed the belief that the Boys' Units and the Apprentice Colleges partook too much of the life that was proper to the Army and too little of that which was appropriate to the school. However keen young lads were to become soldiers, they were boys and not soldiers. The Public School had long been thought to be the best source from which the regiment could draw its officers but no one had argued that the best Public School would be that which most closely resembled the regiment. What was needed to improve the existing Boys' Units and Colleges was to make them more like the Public School and less like the regiment. What was needed was the introduction into them of the House system with its stress on competitive sport, its provision of opportunities for hobbies as well as for study, and its closer supervision of individual progress.[4] These recommendations were accepted. To mark the new dispensation a new post of Director of Boys' Training was established and the Boys' Units, which had attracted much more criticism than the Apprentice Colleges, were renamed Junior Leaders' Regiments, a somewhat surprising title in view of the insistence that they must become more like schools than regiments but one which no doubt added to their attraction by emphasising the military connection and the likelihood of those attending them becoming NCOs.

It looked as if the Miller Report might have ended RAEC responsibility for these Junior Leaders' Regiments and Apprentice Colleges. For although it paid tribute to the work done by the RAEC in them it also urged that they should be given greater continuity of staff than could be provided by the Corps with its relatively short length of tours in such units. Indeed, a working party set up by the Directorate of Army Training to look into the Army Apprenticeship Colleges recommended that their RAEC teachers should be replaced by civilian teachers. That this was not done is no doubt a complement to the RAEC; by the mid-1950s there were to be more RAEC than ever in Boys' Units. Its teaching skills were much appreciated and it is as well to remember that it always attached great importance to teaching skills, perhaps more than the civilians attached to them did. Members of the Corps were always great extra-mural entrepreneurs, too, and in this respect as well they did invaluable work in helping to build character and to develop leadership qualities. In the Education Wing in the Harrogate Apprenticeship College, which was headed by an RAEC Lieutenant-Colonel and supported by a further twenty-six members of the Corps, a wide range of activities was organised. As well as providing a great variety of sports, including boxing, canoeing, fencing and sailing, they ran clubs in photography, drama, shooting and mountaineering. The latter was particularly popular, there being opportunity on the moors and great assistance given by the Yorkshire Mountaineering Club. This, however, partook somewhat of sending coals to Newcastle, for such is the enthusiasm of the Corps for life in the hills that one is at times tempted to think that love of mountains is an indispensable qualification for membership of it.

It was a similar picture elsewhere. But as the period of conscription drew to a close and as the RAEC became an all-officer Corps, the RAEC WO and NCO instructor no longer featured in the life of the Boys' Units. To make up for this loss the number of RAEC officers attached to these units was increased. From 1961 civilian teachers were appointed to them. They did not oust the RAEC, there being roughly equal numbers of RAEC and civilians in the Apprenticeship Colleges and twice as many RAEC members as civilians in Junior Leaders' Regiments. We can sympathise with the National Service RAEC sergeant in Germany who wrote 'We only have to teach ridiculously simple stuff – the standard of the highest is about that of a boy of fourteen or fifteen. Not even up to School Certificate standard', even if we think that in his voice there is the ring of inexperience as well as of frustration.[5] Work in the Boy's Units was as exciting as he had found his task to be dull. But both were important and both impressed the Army.

Apart from the work in the Boys' Units the RAEC continued to be responsible for the two military boarding schools at Dover and Dunblane. The excellent work done in them and the importance the Corps attached to it is symbolised by the fact that some of its brightest and best officers served there; among them were those later promoted to high rank; some who were heads of Houses became headmasters on leaving the Army. In addition to these duties the RAEC had many other tasks in the years of the Interim Scheme which had nothing to do with that scheme and which were of greater interest to the Army than it turned out to be.

One of its most important tasks was the teaching of foreign languages. The fluency of peoples in languages other than their own has often impressed the British but rarely to the extent of inducing in them the wish to acquire a similar ability. Since such obstinate insularity seemed hardly to befit an Army which had accepted a great continental commitment, the embarrassment and irritation which such linguistic inadequacy occasioned in the High Command led at times to explosive corrective action. Thus the Commander-in-Chief, BAOR ordered all officers there below the rank of major who were not already proficient in German or not preparing themselves for the Staff/Promotion Examination to undertake the study of German or of French. Some 2,000 officers were involved in this study, the instructors being primarily German. There were the enthusiasts among those 2,000 who were glad to attend more advanced courses run at No 3. Higher Education Centre at Hohne. It is said that most of the others who came reluctantly to school as pressed men would gladly have stayed as volunteers had the press been discontinued. The Royal Navy felt that it could not take the risk in the 18th Century of ending the press and it continued to make use of the press-gang's services; the Commander-in-Chief felt it safer not to rescind his order too. In any case the knowledge of a foreign language to be gained in a single winter may reasonably be expected to be forgotten more quickly and Captains and subalterns were not to be found at every street corner chatting in German to admiring friends and acquaintances.

The Army's concern for the study of modern languages was not confined to such impulsive action as that taken by the Commander-in-Chief in Germany. It had made provision for the advanced study of languages but this was confined to potential interpreters and was the responsibility of the Director of Military Intelligence. There were RAEC officers teaching at the several Joint Service Schools for Linguists where the Slav tongues were being studied, but teaching at them was not a major RAEC commitment. It was clear, however, that the Army was facing a considerable problem. There were fewer officers who were good linguists than there were staff appointments requiring them. In a period of Cold War more Slav and Chinese speakers were needed; the integrated Command Headquarters of a multi-national alliance called for a greater number of officers familiar with European tongues; our East of Suez role, as it was known, a knowledge of Eastern languages; and our Commonwealth connection an ability to get along in those of Africa and other places.

Since each of the Service Directors of Education had greater resources than those at the disposal of the Director of Military Intelligence it was decided in December 1957 that each should become responsible for language teaching in his own particular Service, although the high flyers who aimed to reach Interpreter standard would continue to be looked after by the Director of Military Intelligence. It was no light load that was thus placed on the RAEC. To cope with it Language Schools were opened abroad. There was the Command Arabic Language School established in Aden in 1959. It provided courses in colloquial Arabic for officers and other ranks seconded to the Protectorate Levies, the Trucial Oman Scouts and the Sultan of Muscat's Armed Forces and, as the political situation in Aden worsened, its role expanded to encompass teaching for those involved in Internal Security duties there. At one stage the school was teaching three different dialects – Adenese, Gulf and Muscati. In South-East Asia the Malayan School of Languages ran courses in Malay for British Officers and other ranks. It taught English to students from neighbouring states and during what was called 'Confrontation' former students might have met in battle, although such a meeting, if it occurred, did not have the effect that the meeting in arms of former students in the first Indo-Pakistan War had in shortening the clash of arms.

To enable each of the Services to increase the number of linguists it could teach a new scheme of language training was adopted in July 1960. It aimed to encourage all ranks, and not officers alone as in the past, to learn languages which would be of benefit to the Services by providing a pool of fluent linguists which could be drawn on as required. There was to be a greatly enhanced scale of single payment awards for those who qualified to receive them instead of the previous system under which language pay was only provided when the linguist was in the area in which the language was spoken. Between the two existing linguistic grades, the lower grade of Colloquial speaker and the higher of Interpreter, a medium grade was inserted, that of Linguist. The first examinations for this new grade were held in French, German and Spanish in February 1961 and in September of that year examinations in many other languages, including Chinese and Japanese, were held too.

In 1960 the RAEC assumed a further responsibility. The two Joint Services Schools for Linguists were at Bodmin in Cornwall and at Coulsdon in Surrey. In 1954 Coulsdon was closed and in 1956 the School at Bodmin moved to better accommodation at Crail in Fife. In 1960 it became part of the Army School of Education in Beaconsfield. Here there was further development, 1961 being the first year in which there was a mixed entry of officers and NCOs and in which a member of the Japanese diplomatic service was admitted. In 1964 the Royal Navy began sending its would-be Linguists to Beaconsfield and two years later the Foreign Office sent its entrants there as well. The work done by RAEC officers both in teaching languages and in its accompanying administration both at home and abroad was of exceptional importance and was greatly regarded by the Army. At this time also, Command Education Officers were able to report increased activity in language teaching. There were language classes in Army Education Centres and at local technical colleges. In Eastern District advanced refresher residential courses were held at weekends and in Northern Command there were similar courses, the Universities of Hull and of Durham being to the fore in their provision.

The Corps, too, took great care to keep up with the latest methods of language teaching. It was in close touch with the American Defence Language Institute at Monterey in California, it introduced the American Army Language Aptitude Test, it tried out the Royal Australian Air Force School of Languages Oriental Aptitude Test. It was early in its use of language laboratories, the first being installed at the Royal Military Academy, Sandhurst, and in the Russian Wing at Beaconsfield. These were subsequently installed in all Army language schools and in many Army Education Centres. At the same time the language section of the Institute of Army Education arranged for the revision of the existing colloquial *From Scratch* series and for the writing of new books in that series, in French, German, Italian, Spanish, Russian, Gurkhali, Malay and Swahili. It also produced military vocabularies in Iranian, Mandarin and Cantonese. Altogether this was a most impressive development of language teaching, a fully satisfactory answer to an urgent need, an RAEC service to the Army at which no-one could look askance and which indeed greatly enhanced the reputation of the Corps.[6]

In two further and important matters the Corps continued to attend to its more conventional work, Preliminary and Resettlement Education being also part of the Interim Scheme. Its success in these was impressive. We have already looked at the development of the Preliminary School of Education and have seen how successful it was. In 1962 it moved to Corsham. Here it provided an invaluable service to the individual soldier and the Army for some twenty years, despite an increasing questioning of its necessity. It had been hoped that by the late 1950s the products of the post-war educational development would have replaced those whose poor educational achievement was the result of inadequate pre-war education or wartime educational disruption and that there would therefore be less need for remedial education. It was also felt that in the new Regular Army which would be fashioned to meet the needs of an age of rapidly expanding technology there would be no place for those with educational difficulties. Men persistently entertain the hope experience would deny them; this hope, too, was unfulfilled. Although National Service ended in the early 1960s the Regular Army continued to demand the specialised education which only the SPE could provide.

Not all but the majority of the instructors at Corsham were members of the Corps. Many lacked training in or experience of remedial education. There was a dearth of appropriate books and so the instructors had to compile reading material at the correct age levels based on the Army background and using military vocabulary, as had been done in the inter-war years when the popular *Nobby Clarke* was published. In a typical year about 7,500 men would be graded illiterate or semi-literate. Of these only 2,500 would be deemed likely to benefit from the SPE. Most of the rest went to the Royal Pioneer Corps. Courses at the SPE lasted ten weeks, each intake being of eighteen students. Military training occupied one third of the time there since this was found to be an effective means of restoring the soldier's self-confidence. Student motivation at Corsham was usually very high. The work was far from easy. The final ignominy was often thought being sent there so those joining were often sullen and resentful. Yet of the 992 students attending in its first year 205 were eventually graded tradesmen and sixty-eight became NCOs. It was claimed that remedial education saved the Army each year the equivalent of a brigade by retaining soldiers who would otherwise have been discharged. It is no wonder that the work of the SPE greatly enhanced the status of the Corps. The claim 'the torch of learning of the RAEC is surely never borne so high as at Corsham' was fully justified. And it should be remembered that it was a pioneering venture. As the HMIs said of it 'There is no other school or establishment in the country doing similar work and all inspiration and stimulus have to come within the School itself.'[7]

We have seen that towards the end of the Release Period the Corps was given responsibility for Resettlement in 1948. The hope that men leaving the Colours might find a job with the Royal Corps of Commissioners no longer sufficed. Serious attention to finding them employment must now be given. They must know what prospects there were, what were the difficulties to be encountered and how to benefit from the one and cope with the other. The War Office published its Resettlement Bulletins and there were pamphlets in plenty to be got from the Ministry of Labour and from other Government departments. RAEC NCOs kept unit information rooms stocked with such up-to-date information and in each Command an RAEC Officer was appointed to deal exclusively with resettlement. In active life, however, thoughts of resettlement are unlikely to be in the forefronts of minds. Yet last minute preparations for that leave much to be desired. Accordingly there was to be opportunity for soldiers who had completed three years' service to discuss annually possibly hazy future plans with a resettlement expert. Six months before his final discharge every soldier was to be required to have an interview with a similar expert, or experts, after which arrangements could be made for further instruction or training if that seemed to be indicated. At such interviews the advantage of continued service in the Army was of course discussed. Despite this, however, and despite the fact it had been amply demonstrated that recruitment would suffer if insufficient attention was paid to resettlement, many Commanding Officers were unhappy with the Resettlement scheme, thinking that it turned the soldier's attention away from the Army and towards alternative employment. Their uneasiness led to a modification of the scheme so that resettlement interviews were to take place only eighteen months and then six months before soldiers were discharged.

That still left time for the soldier to prepare for civilian life. He could attend civilian classes held at universities, technical colleges, evening institutes, Army Education Centres or the Higher Education Centres which had been established in 1952. These had grown out of the Formation Colleges of the Release period. Originally intended to provide for a wide range of educational activities at a higher level than could be managed in Army Education Centres, they became primarily concerned with resettlement. They were to be found in Catterick, in Aldershot and in certain overseas Commands. They ran all kinds of vocational courses, the 'Handyman's Course' – or home-owners 'do-it-yourself' course – being particularly popular with officers and senior ranks. Still more popular than those HEC courses were attachments to civilian firms for further training during the last month of a soldier's service. For these held out the prospect of an offer of a job from the firm which provided the training. Thus in Southern Command in 1957–1958 180 other ranks attended courses at HECs and 690 took up vocational training attachments to various firms.

Cash and connection would sort out the Resettlement problems, if any, of most of the pre-war officers whose continued services, through their influential relations and friends, would be of benefit to the regiments they had just left. Their interest in resettlement therefore had been slight. There was, however, a marked stirring of interest in officer Resettlement in 1957. For in that year a considerable reduction in Service strength was announced. In the following five years the Armed Forces were to be reduced from 690,000 to 375,000, a reduction which would involve large-scale redundancies, particularly among officers. To cope with this situation a Resettlement Advisory Board was set up under the chairmanship of Sir Frederick Hooper. It secured Trade Union recognition of more than 100 Army trades as qualifying ex-soldiers for membership of the skilled unions. The Board also established a Regular Forces Resettlement Service. Under it eleven Regional Resettlement Committees were set up, Command Education Officers providing the Service link with the representatives of the industrial and commercial worlds who served on them.

Hitherto there had been no Resettlement service for officers comparable with that already provided for other ranks. Now six Resettlement Interviewing Panels were set up to visit home and overseas Commands to advise officers and Warrant Officers on Resettlement. On each panel was a senior official of the Ministry of Labour and a RAEC Lieutenant-Colonel who was exclusively concerned with Resettlement and who was responsible to a newly-created branch of the Directorate of Army Education, Army Education 5.[8]

A new development in Army Education of great importance for the Army and for the RAEC was the bringing up to the required standard of those regarded as potential officers but as yet falling below it. In 1947 it had been decided that those seeking commissions should be divided into two categories. There were to be those known as 'R' and as 'E' cadets. 'R' cadets were those who had passed the Civil Service Entrance Examination and who, after a short period in the ranks, became officer cadets. 'E' cadets were those Regular or National Service other ranks who, being between eighteen and twenty-one by the time they entered Sandhurst, had been recommended by a War Office Selection Board and had been accepted by the Regular Commissions Board. It soon became clear, however, that those 'E' cadets were much weaker educationally than 'R' cadets. It was questionable how effective as officers 'E' cadets would be until they reached a higher educational standard. Accordingly it was agreed in March 1948 that the Mons Officer Cadet School should be formed and that the RAEC should provide its teachers. The cadets there were to be taught English, History, Geography, Mathematics, General Science and a foreign language which could be French, German or Russian. The School concentrated on awakening the interest of its members and that having been done on creating a will to learn and in this it succeeded admirably. 'Accustomed as most of us were to apathy and sometimes hostility', the then Major Fowler who taught there said – in a phrase which ought to be remembered as faithfully reflecting the difficulties which the RAEC so often encountered and which to an extraordinary degree it ignored and took in its stride – 'we were surprised to find how hard the cadets worked.' The RAEC teachers said 'These cadets were making the Army their career, and we found them humble in the knowledge that they had to be educated to be efficient officers. There was certainly nothing lacking in incentive.'[9]

It is difficult at times not to hear a somewhat cracked note in Army Education as, for instance, when we were told with such strident assurance that to make the soldier a better soldier he would first of all have to be made a better citizen. But there is nothing false about the note that is sounded at Mons. A great effort was being made to make the potential officer a good officer. That effort was a response to a felt need and it was greatly welcomed accordingly. And the response to that need revealed the real strength of the RAEC: imagination, adaptability and teaching skill. It was a most complicated syllabus it had to work out and it did not at first get it right. But it kept at it until it did. It had to improve, as had indeed the Army, and both proved very good at doing so. Both had to try to implement grandiose schemes that may not have been needed and were certainly not wanted, and the record showed that they were not particularly good at so doing. But they were both outstandingly good in coping with the real needs that on a much less elaborate scale were constantly making themselves apparent, as the RAEC teaching at Mons demonstrates so convincingly.

The HMIs who reported on the School of Preliminary Education at Corsham were impressed by the ability of the RAEC to turn its hand to many different tasks. A good example of that is the assumption of responsibility for running the Army News Service. This was transferred from the Army Welfare Services to the RAEC. In 1950 the *British Army News* was sent daily to all units abroad through the Forces Reuter

Service.[10] When this came to an end a daily air-mail news service was begun. Local Army newspapers were dependent on it and so to a large extent were commercial newspapers in Gibraltar, Malta, Singapore and Hong Kong. When economy cuts in 1969 brought BANEWS to an end, there were many protests from those who had hitherto received it. The Army produced many newspapers abroad, these too being run by the RAEC. There were the *Triangle* and the *Quadrant* in BAOR. In Egypt in the early 1950s the Army produced its own paper, which was published three times a week and which ran to forty-four editions. In Aden there was the *Dhow*, in Kenya the *Phoenix*. In Burma there was a paper which included a strip cartoon recording the adventures of the celebrated Jane. There was the *Parbate*, or Hillman, for the Gurkhas when the British Army Gurkha Regiments arrived in Malaya. Its production was indeed a call on the ingenuity and on the hard work of the RAEC. The official Nepalese Government paper, *Gorkha Patra*, was written in too literary a style for the soldiers to be able to appreciate and it was in any case produced in the Nagri script which few soldiers could read. It fell to the RAEC, therefore, to produce a paper in Roman Gurkhali with which semi-literates could cope. Beginning with issuing a double-page cyclostyled news-sheet the RAEC worked up to publishing the *Parbate* every week. This work of the RAEC was greatly appreciated by the Commander-in-Chief, General Sir Neil Ritchie. It would no doubt have been much less welcomed if an unfortunate error in the proofs on one occasion had not been spotted in time. The photograph of General Ritchie on the first page had borne the caption 'an old warship under repair'. But the gods were kind, the error was spotted, the print setter induced to mend his ways and the faces both of the General Officer Commanding and of the Editor duly saved. This was no negligible service that the RAEC was providing in publishing these papers. This practice harked back to something that had been valued in the past and it pointed forward to what must be important in the future. During the war ABCA had spotted the need to keep the soldier informed and it was as well that it had done so. The papers which the Corps published in the battle zones had been greatly valued; to ensure that the soldier knew why he was doing what he was doing would be equally important in the days ahead.[11]

Provision of news for the front-line troops was, after 1945, an established role of the Corps on mobilisation. With the arrival of British troops in Korea when war broke out there, British Forces newspapers appeared and soon enjoyed a high reputation. Within a fortnight of their arrival the RAEC with them was producing a daily paper, the *Korean Base Gazette* and a weekly, the *Round Up*. In 550 days in Korea, the Brigade paper *Circle News* and the *Crown News* which succeeded it as the Divisional paper when the Commonwealth Division was formed, were produced 529 times. Often, we are told, in the early days 'the Brigade newspaper was the only immediate source of news for everybody'. It was said 'there was scarcely a man in the Brigade who did not know that mad sergeant on a motorbike who somehow appeared every morning with the *Circle News*'. In a quickly moving war in which the fog of battle was often particularly dense, this information service of the RAEC was an important contribution to the morale of the troops and was readily recognised as such.[12]

Other tasks carried out by the RAEC which boosted the morale of the troops were more humdrum but not to be ignored. The Corps in these years covered by the Interim Scheme built up an excellent library service. In 1946 the Army Educational Central Book Depot was established and an Army Central Library brought into existence. Command Libraries served as miniature County Library Headquarters. They were of special importance overseas. It was always a problem to find staff for them. But the RAEC did it and 'more than one Corps Officer or Warrant Officer drafted to library work in these years eventually made a civilian career in librarianship'. As the Army became smaller with the ending of conscription the library service improved in quality, range and use.[13] Stocks of books and the rate of their issue rose year by year. 'Reading in the Army', it appeared, was 'far greater in quantity and range than popular stereotypes of the soldier might have led one to suppose.' We would not be well advised on reading that to let joy be unconfined, as the report which told us that also said 'the type of reading is all too frequently inferior or deplorable in quality'.[14] That was regrettable but while those who are content with worthless reading will convince us that we do not have that freedom from trivial foolishness which could be claimed by the men of Athens and of other Greek cities of old, who can say that the habit of reading will not be its own corrective and lead eventually to better things? Soldiers have rarely been what used to be known as bookish. In the pre-war Army, barracks possessed a limited amount of fiction which was issued like blankets under the watchful eye of the Quartermaster. Soldiers could obtain County Library tickets but few took advantage of this. As late as 1972 the BAOR Command Education Officer's driver told him 'libraries are not for such as us'. As a young lieutenant who messed with the 4th Tank Regiment on joining the AEC, that same officer 'never saw an officer take a book or indeed read anything other than a periodical'.[15] It was, therefore, striking that soldiers in the 1950s and 1960s were reading more. We can be grateful to the Treasury for making money available for the provision of recreational reading for the troops, whether or not they had access to public libraries. We can be glad that demand by the soldiers for paperbacks was high. 85,000 went to Korea alone. At the very least it was something the RAEC could be proud of, that there were in Britain in 1958 four Class I, seven Class II and eight Class III Military Libraries. Men will cease to be men before they rid themselves of anomalies and unbroken excellence of leadership is given to no country, to no profession, to no occupation, to no association of humankind. The RAEC has been no exception and one is glad that the fineness of its library service is far more typical of it than that extraordinary question asked of one of his librarians by a Director of Army Education. 'What the hell do you want to give troops books for?'[16] Lest it be thought that folly is to be found only under educational Red Hats it should be remembered that *The Times* of 24 February 1982 reported that a civilian Chief Education Officer said of the University of Oxford 'The place should be destroyed and nothing done to protect it against a deserved fate. I hope no youngsters from my area will go there – that would simply preserve a rotten system by sucking them in.'

A much less interesting but still important job of the RAEC which also contributed to keeping the soldier contented was the running of Correspondence Courses, running in the sense of providing essential information about them, arranging or seeing that they ran smoothly and that costs to the individual soldier were kept very low. This was a continuation into the period of the Interim Scheme of war-time arrangements. Things were named differently, these arrangements now being given the sonorous title 'The Forces Correspondence Courses Scheme'. Nothing of significance was changed and certainly not their popularity. 30,000 of the Services were taking them in 1958. There are those who find difficulty in resisting bargains and these courses were indeed bargains at the price the soldier paid for them. Not all who enrolled would remember that the true glory is not in the beginning of an enterprise but in the ending of the same; were not waysides invented for men and women to fall by? Yet even if the wastage was remarkably high the claim would not be entirely without foundation that in the promotion of large-scale distance learning the RAEC was something of a pioneer. This provision of correspondence courses by the RAEC brought only a little contentment to the troops. Each one of the rods of the Roman lictors was comparatively unimpressive too, but bound together they reflected the formidable strength of Rome. And the many things the RAEC did, and some were not so small, when added together represented significant strength and suggested that the Corps was ceasing to be something that was tolerable because it was useful and was becoming something that was desirable because it was essential.

Another function of the Corps was having this same effect too. This was the running of the Army Education Centre, the popularity of which became evident in the Release period. As an editorial in *Army Education* put it 'Here are books which can be read, comfortable chairs which can be sat on, handicraft benches and tools which can be used.' It was a far cry from the 'wet canteen' of the 19th Century Army. Such Centres retained their popularity in the period covered by the Interim Scheme. The RAEC wardens who looked after them, and their imaginative and enthusiastic approach, prevented Centres becoming purely recreational, and education, particularly of a vocational or handicraft kind, was always to be seen in them. They were primarily concerned with the Individual Education that the Interim Scheme hoped to promote but they also provided General Education for units that were either too small to try to hold classes of their own or unable to supply their own instructors. They were also community centres for Service families, an arrangement which deservedly increased their popularity. They were most important abroad where they were in the grey area into which education and welfare merged and none the worst for that. Good use was made of them in the evenings, for everybody seemed to need further activities to keep boredom at bay and all sorts of subjects might be in demand there, particularly by Service wives. Not that all approved of using Centres to bring units in to get on with their General Education, some believing that it was better to go out than to bring in, for it was only by going out that units would become better known and not all belonging to them would visit the Centres. Such was their popularity that the hope was entertained that this 'will stir up a demand for similar centres in civilian life'. Here again the Corps took the initiative and made a highly worthwhile contribution to civilian adult education. It failed to create an overwhelming demand that similar centres be developed. The creation of overwhelming demands in matters educational is an un-English activity and while there are today admirable civilian counterparts of these Forces Education Centres, they are still far too few. They would be fewer had there not been this Army initiative.

The contraction of Empire was well under way at this time but formally in many cases flags had not yet been lowered. Throughout this period the RAEC was busily occupied overseas. Its task was rarely easy. In Egypt, for example, the rapidly deteriorating political situation led to the withdrawal of Egyptian labour from British military employment, a withdrawal made almost total by the terrorist tactics used against those who would have wished to continue their lucrative employment with the Services. This meant that everyone had to turn a hand to all manner of activity, the RAEC was at everyone's beck and call and far from education having a top priority it could hardly exist at all. Yet when opportunity for diversion was limited and boredom developing, Commanding Officers 'began an increasing demand for a return of educational facilities for their troops'.[17]

With the onset of the Suez Crisis life became very hectic for the RAEC in Malta as well. When the assault Brigade Group arrived in the island in August 1956 the RAEC found itself caught up in a great deal of welfare work. The Rediffusion Broadcasts, which published the news, were suspended then both because of damage done to the Company's installations and because of political difficulties with the Government of Malta. As a result the troops were without up-to-date news of the developing Suez Crisis. The General-Officer-Commanding accordingly asked for the publication of a Daily News Sheet and it was the job of the RAEC to produce it, to write editorial comment and to distribute it. This was the so-called *Radio News*, of which seventy-one issues were published. It had a high reputation for accuracy and honest reporting. It must have been well thought-of as its publication continued long after the restoration of the Rediffusion Broadcasts.

This was only part of the RAEC's task in Malta at this time. There was naturally great interest in the developing crisis and the RAEC put together a course on it for Regimental Officers. A handicraft model-making scheme was introduced at 69 Army Education Centre. A travelling team of instructors was sent to units which wanted instruction for the Army Certificates of Education. Classes were arranged in units and in the Education Centre, and they were well attended. A team visited units to advise on Resettlement and allied problems. Major Hall, as he then was, concluded his report on all this by saying 'Periods of waiting in a high state or preparedness frequently precede operations and produce special difficulties in maintaining morale. The RAEC can readily adapt its resources and utilise them quickly to raise or maintain morale. This should be one of its main roles in active operations or on mobilisation. No one else is better able, or has the resources, to cope with this problem to the extent that the RAEC can in such circumstances.' RAEC activity in Malta during the Suez Crisis seems to have proved his point.[18]

Nowhere overseas was life leisurely and easy for the RAEC. Major Morris in Aden said he often had 'a working day of thirteen hours or more in a climate under which most people have given their all after six hours of work'! We have seen how hazardous and full life was for the RAEC in Burma during the Release Period and this continued to be the case until British troops withdrew. There were 120 members of the Corps in Burma at this time and twelve Education Centres. As we have seen a good deal of educational work was done. There was much activity, too, in the grey area between education and welfare. This was important both for the troops and for the Corps. It added to the interest of both, it brought the Corps increasingly to the fore and in so doing must in some measure have facilitated its more purely educational tasks. Here, too, the work of teaching the Burmese soldier that we saw being done in the Release Period was continued.

In Malaya the RAEC had another difficult job. In November 1947 an agreement was reached by Britain, India and Nepal that of the existing ten Gurkha regiments India should take six and Britain four. These four were transferred to the British Army in Malaya. Many of the soldiers were illiterate and there was the further difficulty that there was no standard speech in Nepal. The Romanised Urdu of the Indian Army would not help the Gurkha because no one would understand it when he was demobilised. So a new Romanised Gurkhali had to be found and the RAEC had to find it. It had to provide a grammar, a pocket dictionary and suitable text-books, all of which it did. It had to do something else too, namely to set up a Gurkha School of Education which would train instructors and which would provide courses in English and in Gurkhali. It is a great tribute to the RAEC that the Major-General Brigade of Gurkhas was able to report to the King of Nepal in 1958 that considerable progress had been made in educating the Gurkha soldier – this despite the difficulties created by the Malayan Emergency.

This work of the RAEC in the last days of Empire in teaching the peoples of former dependencies, teaching that even involved the creation of new means of communication among them, was a most important legacy to the newly-emerging states. This we have seen the RAEC doing in India and in Africa as well. Inculcating a minimum standard of literacy in a regional *lingua franca*, developing general knowledge relating to the soldier's military and domestic environment and seeking to implant in him a sense of civic responsibility as well as improving his prospects when he left the Colours, all this we saw the RAEC doing in the Release Period and it continued to do so while British rule lasted. There was continued development of this work in the days of the Interim Scheme. For now the Army School of Education became increasingly involved in this work. In 1958 long courses in English were arranged there for Gurkhas who were, after receiving initial instruction at the Education Wing of the Gurkha Training Depot, about which more will be said shortly, to join military training courses at Army Training Schools in Britain. Soon after this courses began for African instructors from the West African Forces, Nigeria and Sierra Leone. As a result the School's Overseas English Wing, which evolved from the Gurkha Wing, has included, often at the same time, officers and other ranks from British Guiana, British Honduras, Ceylon, Cyprus, India, Iraq, Israel, Jordan, Kuwait, Malaya, Nepal, Pakistan and the Seychelles. Nigeria and Libya were added later and in 1965 Congolese, Thais and Algerians came. In 1967 the Command Arabic Language School closed in Aden and it became part of the Army School of Education alongside the

Overseas English Wing and the Russian Wing there.

How greatly appreciated this work done by the RAEC was by the newly-independent countries we can see from the fact that, as in Kenya, Uganda and Tanzania, RAEC officers were asked to remain to build on what they had begun in colonial days. It was of national importance in smoothing relations between Britain and her former dependencies. In the case of the Gurkhas this was of immediate benefit to the Army, as they remained its soldiers and the greater their ability to read their own orders and to communicate with their British comrades-in-arms, the more effective soldiers they would be. In the case of the others, when independence eventually came the Army benefitted indirectly in that the good relations thus established with foreign armies increased its influence with them, thus making it easier for mutually beneficial arrangements concerning training to be concluded. And, this being a great service to the Army, in this way too the standing of the Corps in it was enhanced.

Remnants of Empire would linger on and provide tasks for the Corps. But important as these tasks were, they did not point to its future activity. Two further developments, however, did and accordingly are of much greater significance. One was the new thinking that was being directed to Special-to-Arm Education, the new belief that there should be special syllabuses appropriate to each Arm. 'If this were done', it was said, 'both Commanding Officers and soldiers would begin to see there is some purpose in educating their men.'[19] Since this was not as yet done, here was the acknowledgement that the RAEC had not yet succeeded in convincing Commanding Officers and soldiers that there was purpose in Army Education. Its failure was to be regretted but not wondered at, and it is not to be thought especially blameworthy because of it. Its success would have been much more surprising than its failure for was its experience not that of civilian adult education too? Had not those who looked for great expansion in that also looked in vain? But far more important in that comment than the admission of past and present failure was the vision that promised future improvement. While the RAEC bent its endeavours to evoking and satisfying needs of which Commanding Officers and soldiers remained obstinately unaware, however keenly others might have felt them, Commanding Officers and soldiers would continue to doubt that there was purpose in educating the troops. If, however, the RAEC was to address itself to needs of which Commanding Officers and men were very aware, that would be a different matter. The Army existed because of the nature of the civilian world; its job was to cope with the consequences of that nature but not to try to correct it. When the stated aim of Army Education was to make that attempt, that aim would not be achieved. But those who rightly believed that the business of armies was exclusively excellence in the discharge of military function would be irritated and uncooperative. That irritation and that uncooperativeness would be a thing of the past when Army Education was seen to be adding to that excellence, as it would be if special attention was given to the particular needs of each Arm and educational syllabuses devised that would help to meet them. There is a rhythmic movement in driving a car, the foot going down on the accelerator as it comes off the brake. We see that same rhythmic movement in Army Education in the period of the Interim Scheme. As effort is relaxed in the attempt to implement that scheme, which despite what seemed to be its great promise retarded rather than forwarded Army Education, education itself picks up speed, it becomes of a greater significance for the Army and its status is thereby enhanced. This picking up of speed we can see in the thought now being given to working out special educational syllabuses for each Arm.

Above all we can see the picking-up of speed in the development of Officer Education, the second of the important new developments for which the RAEC at this time was responsible. 'Custom is King of all', Pindar said of his world. This was the case in the British Army too. To be educated was a quality not prized in the British officer. Fuller goes so far as to tell us that 'the subaltern was allowed to read Pat Gould and was encouraged to discuss the Pink'un, but if he were caught seriously studying his profession he was for the shore'. 'By the age of twenty-five', he added, 'the brains of the average subaltern had been petrified into Aberdeen granite.'[20] Those more eminent than Fuller, for instance Lord Curzon, shared Fuller's opinion. When Kitchener, Commander-in-Chief India, submitted to Curzon, then Viceroy, a proposal to establish a Staff College in India, Curzon welcomed the idea, characteristically adding that he had yet to find an officer on his personal Staff (and equally characteristically his vanity left him in no doubt that such officers would be 'the pick of the Army') who could converse intelligibly on subjects other than polo and shooting. Warming to his task, Curzon was impelled to point out, with that courtesy he usually displayed to those whom he looked upon as underlings, that the wording of the letter requesting permission to establish a Staff College, was itself proof of its necessity, its illiteracy being the most impressive thing about it.[21] Racked with pain as he so often was, Curzon had a supreme ability to add to his own discomfort. He had no reason to be surprised that Kitchener thought of him very much what he thought of Kitchener.

However in a world which was becoming more dangerous because of the greater concentrations of power in it and because of the impact of technology on weapons, the pressures to change the ways even of the British officer were mounting apace as the 19th Century wore on. Officers seeking promotion had to pass written and practical tests devised to show they were reasonably proficient in the exercise of their craft. After the First World War more, if not as yet much more, was demanded of them. They were required to satisfy examiners that they had, besides adequate skill in the purely military matters in which hitherto they had been exclusively tested, some acquaintance with imperial geography and with military history. At this time, too, a minority of officers were preparing themselves for the entrance examinations to the Staff College at Camberley. In the inter-war period sixty officers joined the two-year course there every year until 1938 when, with the expansion of the Army in view of the threat of German aggression and the need to have more highly trained officers as quickly as possible, the two-year course was reduced to one year and the numbers attending it doubled.

There was no help from the Army for those preparing to take the Staff College entrance or the promotion examinations. They studied in their own time and at their own expense. For the most part they were rarely short of money and they could well afford the fees of the crammer. Whether the Army could equally afford the effect of the crammer on the officer was more questionable, and it was certain that it could not afford to convey the impression, which inevitably it did by doing nothing to help the ambitious officer, that it was indifferent to the development in him of the qualities which the Staff College was seeking to bring out. Fortunately there will always be those who rise above their environment, as Fuller himself and greater soldiers did. We laughed at the cartoons depicting Colonel Blimp and knew nothing of the highly professional younger officers quietly coming to the fore in the British and Indian Armies.

When the Staff College entrance examination was reintroduced in 1947 many, and eventually all, of the subjects required for it were covered by the Correspondence schemes and those preparing for the examination were able to enrol for the courses at a minimal cost to themselves. In 1959 this privilege was extended to candidates for the Promotion examination. The syllabus for the Staff College examination was revised in 1948 when current affairs became a compulsory subject. In 1949 military history did too. When the promotion examination from Captain to Major was introduced in 1950 these subjects were also included in its syllabus. The pass rate was very low in both examinations; this dissatisfied the candidates and their seniors, who did not want too restricted a field from which to select the flyers who would be admitted to Staff College. As a result there was growing pressure for further help for those preparing for this examination.

Given the close involvement of the RAEC in the attempt to develop the study of current affairs in the Army, its briefing of unit officers to help them in the sessions on current affairs they were supposed to take with their men, its harrying of Commanding Officers to commit their subalterns to this work, and its provision of appropriate material for this during the Korean War, it was natural that the Army should turn to the Corps to provide this assistance. This was a new departure for the RAEC for before the war it had very little direct concern with the officer's academic development and advancement. In 1920 members of the Corps had taught at Sandhurst, teaching history, economics, modern languages, science and mechanical engineering there. Also one or two officers of the Corps had taught at Woolwich. When Sandhurst and Woolwich were amalgamated after the Second World War there was the need to employ the civilian academic staff of both institutions. This meant that the RAEC instructors were squeezed out of Sandhurst, although the Corps staffed the Pre-Cadet Wing there that was the forerunner of the Sandhurst Wing that was later established at Beaconsfield. In Scottish Command in the early 1950s RAEC officers taught current affairs and military history to candidates both for the Staff College and for the Promotion Examinations. Elsewhere University lecturers did most of this teaching. By the mid-1950s candidates for both examinations were assigned a visiting tutor to supervise their studies, such usually being full-time tutors employed by the Universities solely for this work. But centralised courses were also organised by the Corps for candidates for these examinations. In Northern Command, for example, a one-week residential course in international affairs and in military history was held annually at Scarborough in conjunction with Hull University, while in Western Command a similar course in current affairs was organised with the assistance of Liverpool University.

Chester was the venue of yet another course for officers from Western Command, and when 85% of Western Command candidates passed the entrance examination for the Staff College no one doubted that the University course could be a much better help to the aspiring candidate than the correspondence course.

For the troops overseas there was a similar pattern of work developing, but the RAEC played a fuller part in it. At No. 3 Higher Education Centre in Germany one-week courses in current affairs were arranged not only to provide students with background information but also to give them the opportunity to write essays and learn something of examination technique. In the more distant and smaller Commands it was rarely possible to make such comprehensive arrangements, but Command Education Officers did everything possible to help the officer to prepare for his examinations. In East Africa Command, for example, officers were able to benefit from the establishment there of a miniature Chatham House, the East African Institute of International Affairs. Once or twice a month officers could attend lectures given by eminent people who passed through Nairobi on their way to or from South Africa. Officers could use the Institute's excellent library too.

Life was simplified for the officers taking the examinations and for the RAEC participating in the teaching for, and in the administration of them, when in 1959 the examinations for the Staff College and for Promotion were combined. The same could not be said of the unfortunate examiners. For in different examinations designed for different purposes the examiners were looking for different qualities, and questions designed to elicit one set of qualities were not best fitted to reveal a different set. Intellectual rigour, communication skills, analytical skills, the ability to handle complex information, to spot the essential detail and ignore the inessential, and above all breadth of view, these were the qualities it was hoped would be revealed in the papers of the potential Staff College man, the qualities which the Staff College could further develop to the advantage of the individual officer and of the Army as a whole. One of the unfortunate examiners was smitten hip and thigh by outraged higher authority which took exception to his view that these were not qualities that could reasonably be expected to be found in the normal run of candidates who were going for promotion only. But in a long experience which brought with it the pleasure of marking scripts on Christmas Day, the errant and unrepentant examiner found these specific qualities only in candidates going for promotion who would indeed, had they so wished, have jumped over this educational hurdle in the path of those seeking entrance to the Staff College.[22]

But interests have often to give way to a greater good and so it was here. When there were two examinations candidates faced great difficulties. The Promotion examination was held in December and the Staff College examination in February. The result of the first would not be known until the second had been sat! Many unfortunate officers had to sit two examinations in a space of two months and very sensibly their feelings were made known. And so in February 1959 the Staff/Promotion Examination, which combined the two, was held for the first time. Perhaps the French comment on the British Commonwealth, *dépourvu de logique mais efficace*, can be applied to this combination of papers looking for different qualities. It lasted for thirty years; it ought to have lasted longer. As examinations go it was very fair and when double-marking became standard practice it was accepted as being so too.

The White Paper of 1957 announced the ending of National Service. Officers of the Regular Army, it was emphasised, must be of high quality and must have some technical and scientific training. This led to the introduction of a military science paper in the Staff College entrance examination. The greater importance now being attached to the education of the officer made it necessary to change the existing position in which no education was provided for him between his leaving Sandhurst and his preparation for the Staff/Promotion examination. This was why much more thought was given to educating the officer; this was why the Junior Officer's Education Scheme was designed. Since this was for the all-Regular Army of the future it will be more appropriately considered when education in that Army is dealt with. The new thinking in Army Education in preparation for its changing role and the fashioning of what it led to were characteristics more of the 1960s than of the 1950s, although, as with Special-to-Arm and Officer Education, forecasts of this can be seen in the earlier decade. That was appropriate to the new Army, the Regular Army of the future. Peacetime conscription, so alien to the British tradition, had ended and with it that great, and greatly eccentric, effort which was also so alien to that tradition, to make use of the British Army to improve the education of the British people. An Army of the kind to which the British people had reluctantly accustomed themselves was returning to win their reluctant respect; an education of a kind which the Army thought might be helpful now had a chance to become more accepted than the education provided for its conscript predecessor.

The nature of that education was indicated by a committee set up in April 1958 to consider the future of the Corps. Army Education, the committee said, 'must give the soldier the kind of education which will help him in his Army career and make him a better soldier'. It must provide vocational training, resettlement advice and further education if required. In making this available the committee said, the Corps should make as much use as possible of civilian resources. The RAEC must attend to the progressive education of the soldier so as to enable him to reach a standard 'whereby he is militarily proficient and qualified to hold higher rank'. It was responsible for the education of the Boys' Units, for the education of Army children overseas, for language training, for the Army News and Library Services and for the teaching of current affairs. The committee added 'It has been agreed that although the educational side of the Royal Military Academy should remain based on a civilian corps of lecturers, there should be openings for an infusion of RAEC officers into the educational staff.'[23]

There is in the committee's report a marked change of attitude to that made evident in the seventy-second meeting of the Army Council in its consideration of the Interim Scheme. At the beginning of that Scheme the then AEC was in the van, showing the LEAs the way. Now there is no longer a question of the Corps leading the field. It has to provide further education on the lines 'of that which, under the 1944 Education Act, LEAs are obliged to provide', but this is only if the soldier wants to devote his spare time to it. The RAEC has, however, another task which civilians would recognise as part of liberal adult education, namely to teach current affairs. The continued insistence that soldiers must be instructed in current affairs is striking. Despite the lack of interest shown in it and the failure to convince commanding officers that it was important to instruct the troops in it and despite the manifest lack of success attendant on the temporary boost to it given by the war in Korea, authority still clung to the conviction that it was important and authority was justified in so doing. That it was appropriate for the Army to be knowledgeable about current affairs was obvious. To understand the nature of the world in which it had its being, to appreciate the changes and chances that decreed its action, to make all know why what at times might seem to be its endless training was necessary, could not but be of the greatest significance to it. And now there was what had hitherto been lacking, the prospect of it being successfully taught.

For the committee envisaged a most significant change in the status of the Corps. It said that the RAEC must become an all-officer Corps of Regular and Short Service officers if it was to do its job properly. The National Union of Teachers, which had become formidably strong, was pressing for this. There was also difficulty in getting well-qualified people to keep up the required number of NCOs, even though fewer would be needed as the Regular Army would be much smaller than the National Service Army it replaced.[24]

Now that the Corps was in a position to attract well-qualified instructors these could reasonably be expected to do the job that unqualified instructors could not. The newcomers were less numerous than could have been wished; were they too few to teach current affairs to the troops? Nor did it seem now beyond the Corps' hopes to enlarge the bridgehead the committee thought would be secured for it in the Royal Military Academy. When 70% of its teaching strength were young conscripts of little training, less knowledge and no experience, the Corps could not have expected the education of officers and teaching at the Staff College to be included among its responsibilities listed by the 1958 committee. With the making of the RAEC into an all-officer Corps hopes could be entertained which could not be before.

There was, then, challenge and opportunity here for the Corps. Since the Army would be smaller it would have to be capable of expansion in an emergency. Hence the insistence that its members must be qualified to hold a higher rank and the view that the soldier's education must be 'progressive'; it was for the RAEC to make a reality of what might easily, if that opportunity was not seized, remain a polite fiction.[25]

There was both challenge and opportunity, too, in the reservations of the Executive Committee of the Army Council, made known to the Command Education Officers' Conference held in 1959 to consider the report of the 1958 committee, about Resettlement being entrusted to the RAEC. The Executive Committee of the Army Council agreed that 'at least for the time being' Resettlement should be so entrusted. It was of the greatest importance that it should remain in RAEC hands; it added to the stature of the Corps and steadily eroded the prejudices with which it had still to contend. It was incumbent upon it to fight off by all means in its power the challenge implicit in the Executive Committee's reservations, to take the opportunity to show how admirable the Corps' handling of Resettlement was and how unnecessary any change would be.

In this there was the certainty that there would be a continuing into the future of the continuous struggle of the past. The RAEC had always fought an uphill battle; it would have to continue to do so. Life would not be easy for it and from time to time threats of its demise might seem to be in the air. In 1959, for instance, there might be the rumour that the question was being seriously considered 'Shall we disband the Argylls and keep the Corps or disband the Corps and keep the Argylls?' The unlikelihood, whether or not the Argylls survived, of the Corps not surviving was always apparent. At this time it seemed to be the case that as the Conservatives were uninterested in education and the Socialists uninterested in the Army, Parliamentary opinion was indifferent about the future of the Corps. Its interest in this was undoubtedly muted. Nevertheless it was always obvious that the disbanding of the Corps would not have gone unnoticed. Universities were too interested for that to happen. But apart from the perhaps exaggerated concern of the Army for its public image, there was an educational job in it that needed doing and that only the RAEC was as yet in a position to do. Everything pointed to the fact that the RAEC would not have an easy ride in the future and nothing to the likelihood of there being no place there for it at all.

In making its recommendations for the future, the 1958 committee took stock of the past. This is an appropriate opportunity to follow its example and see how the Corps stood in the light of its activities in the years of the Interim Scheme.

Perhaps we should start with considering what the Corps had not been able to do and what it would have to find a way of doing before its position in the Army could be said to be consolidated. It had left many in the Army, and indeed perhaps most, unconvinced that education would help a man to be a better soldier. When Napoleon told us that in war intellect reigned supreme it was only the intellect of one man, the Commander-in-Chief, that he was thinking. And when the classical writers spoke of war as being essentially dependent for its outcome on intellect, again it was of the Army Commander they were thinking. They did not expect, and felt that in any case they could dispense with, intellect in the rank and file. However today, while still acknowledging the supreme importance of intellect at the top, we believe that it is of great importance in all ranks. We have no difficulty in convincing ourselves that a man who is alert is potentially a better soldier than one who is not and that a man whose mind has been strengthened and sharpened by education is more likely to be alert than one whose mind has not been so stretched.

Every teacher would like to think that this is a general truth. Nevertheless he will know that it is not a universally accepted truth. His must indeed have been a limited acquaintance who has not met highly educated people who were highly unalert, and highly alert people who were highly uneducated. It is to be hoped that his experience will have been sufficiently limited for him not to have met many highly educated people who were highly unintelligent, but it will have been limited indeed if he has not met any intelligent people who were also very uneducated. And perhaps there is the dawning understanding that we should never underestimate the man whose intelligence expresses itself in the adroit use of his hands any more than we should allow ourselves to believe that 'alert' and 'educated' are synonymous terms.

Perhaps, too, it should be admitted that there was some immodesty, if not arrogance, in the anthems sung in praise of education and its efficacy by the educated. Their faith shone splendidly for all to see. Their missionaries were dedicated and devout. There were few among the RAEC who thought that the best test of the strength of their principles was the demonstration that they were proof even against their practice. But their converts were distressingly few. Vigorous and able as was the presentation of their case the majority remained unconvinced by it. An investigation in one District showed that many of the soldiers there had 'a burning desire to get on'. Among them, it was found, were 'men of skill, brains and ambition'. Two outstanding points emerged from this analysis. The first was the large number who believed that Army Education should 'train people for jobs in civil life'. The second was the very small number who believed that it would help a man to be a better soldier. A questionnaire confirmed that only a handful believed that education would make a man a better soldier.[26]

In one way or other that widespread belief had to be altered before the RAEC could feel that it had securely built itself into the life of the Army. This was the root cause of many of its trials. Ignorance, prejudice and sheer stupidity, qualities of which we all partake to some extent in virtue of our common humanity, added to its woes. RAEC officers were never surprised to be told 'Your Corps put the Labour Government in.' Extreme often calls to extreme and we cannot wonder if at times a silly charge produced a silly reaction. Thus the Commandant at Beaconsfield said to a Sergeant-Instructors' course there that the RAEC did not want 'any dirty pink LSE types', thereby demonstrating the truth of the old adage that a still tongue keepeth a wise head and acknowledging that his experience had left him in no doubt that AEC war-time activities had not been unqualifiedly beneficial to the Corps.[27]

There were, too, the unworthily pretentious who sought by demonstrating their own lack of breeding to keep worthier men in what was arrogantly imagined to be their proper and humbler place. There are misfits in all professions who genuinely believe that it is always the others who are out of step. And they could do considerable damage. Thus in 1956 RAEC officers serving in the Malay Regiment wore the uniform of that regiment, as did officers of the Royal Army Pay Corps also serving with it. A British regimental officer objected to this and as a result they had to give it up. They were not allowed to wear mess kit until later they got their own. The officer whose offended susceptibilities led to all this could hardly have been said to have contributed to military cohesion and efficiency. His action was important not only because of the humiliation which it inflicted on the officers who had to endure such ill-bred malevolence, but because it so clearly revealed the anti-education mentality of many of the regiments. Sometimes it took a peculiar form. When Roy Fairclough was serving in Malaya he passed the practical promotion examination. The training officer of the Cadet Wing of the college at which he was teaching, a Captain in the Middlesex Regiment, failed. At which the Commanding Officer said 'I don't understand the system which allows an RAEC Major to pass while my training officer fails.' Fairclough commented 'The system is at fault not his training officer. And by this curiously inverted logic there is another black mark against the RAEC.'[28] This anti-education mentality in many regiments was not in doubt. Thus a subaltern with the West Yorks tells us how hostile to education that regiment was. Books were bought by the mess to furnish it but were never read. There was a library but it was little used. The odd dictionary or encyclopedia might be referred to in order to settle arguments.[29] Such hostility to education and to the RAEC greatly increased the difficulty of its job. The hostility met from officers and from Sandhurst civilians did not smooth its way there. Nor when the Command Education Officer in Austria visited a Scottish Regiment and was not allowed to visit its Education Centre could that be thought to be merely a personal rebuff.[30] It was a significant professional snub. However much the Corps might add to its own tribulations, as it did by promoting to Captain an eighteen-year-old who was not a graduate, which did its image no good, things would not greatly alter until more were convinced that education would indeed improve the soldier. It was worrying to be made aware how many soldiers did not believe this. Many Commanding Officers were, to say the least, unenthusiastic about education and it could not be assumed that all who were of this opinion had the singular inability to recognise a better soldier when they saw one. Neither that nor the realisation that there were disturbingly few in the ranks who believed that education makes a better soldier will convince those who believe this that they are wrong, but it will convince them that they have failed to persuade many of the correctness of their belief. It will remind them that they have not yet demonstrated its correctness. It would greatly strengthen them if they were able to do this: perhaps in that functional approach to education to which their work in Special-to-Arm education led, and in their work with Officer Education, they were beginning to do so.

The Corps had not yet overcome hostility to it. It had not yet lived down the consequences of having demonstrated its old capacity to seek advance in sudden forward lurches. It had not yet completed the thinking that would open for it new and important avenues of work. It was, however, unquestionably strengthening itself; unappreciated as it might be by much of the Army which judged only by what impinged on individual units, its standing with the Army's higher echelons, few of which were as critical of it as General Duff, was markedly improving; it benefitted from its close relations with the universities which at that time were still basking in the favour of Government and of public opinion. Once again the Corps was showing its old aptitude for slow advance, for putting brick on brick and once again it was finding that this was the best of all ways on which to build itself up. How then are we to assess its standing as the days of National Service drew to an end?

When we try to add up this score there are significant things to be noticed. In this Interim Period in which the Corps had known both failure and success, the failure had been associated with conditions that were ending and that did not seem likely to recur. The success was also to some extent associated with conditions that had come to an end; there would be little call in the future for education solely devoted to the welfare of colonial peoples. But this was only a part, however important, of the RAEC success at this time. For the most part that success was associated with conditions that were likely to persist in the future. Since the unattainable is unattainable, the effort to attain it had not succeeded; there was increasing concentration on the achievable and every likelihood that it would be achieved. The Army was adjusting itself to new circumstances and so was the RAEC. It had learned that eduction, like politics, is the art of the possible; it was now on the true course of making itself as good as possible at that art. Armies would not exist if the world were as our dreams might depict it. The military art requires the insight and the imagination to see what others have not and the intellect to turn to best advantage what insight and imagination have seen. But that art also demands an ever-present and over-riding sense of reality to know what are the limits of the possible. From what is unreal armies will always eventually turn away, as the British Army, and with it the RAEC, turned away from the Interim Scheme.

Too visionary to be greatly esteemed, much too useful to be ignored, this was the position in which the RAEC found itself when the Interim years ended. Yet perhaps we should not forget that we have it on the best of authorities that where there is no vision the people perish. There is a difference between being a citizen and being knowledgeable about citizenship; more people exercise their vote and would refuse to be deprived of it than are prepared to concern themselves with constitutional matters. Not being cordon bleu chefs and unskilled in the making of shoes, they know what is a good meal and where the shoe pinches. Nevertheless, widespread lack of interest in the state and its governance is not the outstanding characteristic of healthy democracies. We may doubt the desirability of compelling mature men and women to sit at the feet of those who profess to teach them citizenship, since the great virtue of democracy is that it treats men as men and not as children, and be advised to remember the old Greek view that teachers teach children and only the poets teach men. We may sympathise with the Army Council when, aware of the importance of ensuring that there should be as much training of the conscripts as was possible in the limited time at its disposal, it concluded that more military aims must have precedence over the attempt to make the soldier a better citizen, particularly as this was a task to which civil society seemed remarkably indifferent. Nevertheless there is something to be said for G. K. Chesterton's view that if we are in the wrong town we may still be in the right place. If citizenship was not to be taught in the way the RAEC sought to teach it, if it was never sensible to look upon this teaching as one of the Army's main aims, the RAEC's calling attention to an important problem was no bad thing. We can be grateful to it for demonstrating how difficult it would be to cope with this problem and how ill-advised we would be to ignore it as completely in the future as we had in the past.

Even in the RAEC's failure here there is much to commend. The Corps drew attention to a problem which others were ignoring at their peril. That problem of educating democratic opinion, if not as old as that rose red city half as old as time, is sufficiently old. 2,500 years ago the Greeks were telling us that all needed education but few wanted it. The Corps failed to find the answer but at least tried to find it and others were not concerning themselves with it. General Lloyd had made two claims for Army Education when he assumed responsibility for it. He said that it was an integral part of the national system of education and that it was the pioneer movement in Adult Education. It had not before he made his claim been the first and it was to be thought as being so only for a short time thereafter. It had always been the second and in tackling this problem when others were not it was confirming that claim. The Corps had not made as much as it might have done of vocational and pre-vocational teaching. But even here it can claim to be a pioneer of that considerable development in practical activities that characterised the further education provided by the LEAs in the 1960s and the following years. The 1944 Butler Act had emphasised the importance of further education after school-leaving age and had laid on universities and LEAs responsibility for developing research into the methods of adult education. The RAEC seems to have taken that responsibility much more seriously than the civilians on whom it was laid. The Corps had nothing to be ashamed of in that.

CHAPTER 11

EDUCATION IN THE NEW REGULAR ARMY

A Chinese gentleman once said to the Australian Foreign Minister, 'If you want to understand the Chinese you must appreciate that there are only two fixed points in the life of a Chinese – birth and death. In between everything is very fluid.' As they tried to fashion the Regular Army of the future the Army Command must have had a strong fellow-feeling for the Chinese. The sun was setting on what coral strands Britain was still responsible for, but there were residual considerations of former Imperial days which must exercise military minds. Thus British Forces had to face down Iraqi ambitions in the Gulf in 1961, put down the Azahari rebellion in Brunei in 1962 and face the further strain imposed on them by the continuing demands of Cyprus and British Guiana. Britain's Commonwealth relations, too, might mean calls on her Armed Forces as Indonesian action against Malaysia involved them in 'Confrontation' in Borneo and as they were asked to suppress the Central African mutinies in 1964. Continental commitment seemed so assured in the foreseeable future that there was a repeated demand, repeatedly ignored, that German should be taught as a compulsory subject in the education of the junior soldiers from whom an all-volunteer Army expected to draw 50% of its annual intake. But Continental commitment apart, the only certainty in the minds of the High Command at this time must have been the certainty of continuing uncertainty.

Everything was in flux. The structure of the Army changed; brigades disappeared and re-emerged; regiments were amalgamated; units were renamed. The Army was at this time groping its way forward, always conscious of having too much to do and too little to do it with, under the constant necessity of cutting down costs and economising in manpower, compelled to be ingenious by the necessity of having to do everything on a shoestring. To find ways of doing this it proliferated committees; committees on every conceivable subject other than the desirability or undesirability of committees, as though domestic pride demanded that it would not only be said of NATO that Soviet armour would never be able to penetrate the thickets they presented. White Papers so filled the air as to ensure that the comparative absence of warplanes in it would be less in evidence. As they were all commonly referred to by their initials the tyranny of initials, beloved of the Services, became ever more monstrous, so that it was almost beyond the power of those who had cracked the Enigma Code to extract meaning from them. Before what conclusions they reached could be adequately considered, further conclusions arrived at by further committees demanded further consideration.

As for Army Education, it necessarily reflected the dominant Army mood. Perhaps not the least of its problems was to know how to prevent itself being swept sinking away in a swirling sea of paper. It seemed, nevertheless, in its continuing addiction to change, determined to show that it too enthusiastically shared the predominant military urge to prove that perpetual motion was no illusion.

But amid all the change certain characteristics of Army Education as it braced itself to meet the needs of the newly-emerging Regular Army remained constant. It was no longer in any doubt that its role was to meet those needs. It had to live with the deficiencies of civilian education and to cope with them to the best of its ability, in so far as Service conditions made that possible and necessary. It had to bring soldiers up to the minimum educational standard deemed essential for military purposes. In so doing it might still be breaking the trail for civilian educators. It might indeed find that it could only fulfil the role for which it existed by continuing its pioneer work, which had always been so outstanding. But its service to the whole community could only be incidental and could not be its primary role, which must be service to the Army of which it was part. It had to make the soldier do what in the view of the Army would make him better able to do what it wanted him to do, and if in the process of doing this it also made him a better citizen that would be something to be devoutly thankful for. All men are entitled to dream and the RAEC is not to be faulted if this was a secondary objective flitting comfortingly through its dreams; it knew now how greatly it would be at fault, and would be held to be at fault, if it allowed this to be a primary aim determining its action.

It was, however, one thing to know that Army Education in the future must be utilitarian; it was another to know how best to make it so. The Army confronted new problems, and while it faced the necessity of speculating about their implications only experience could make fully apparent what they were. For instance, the Army had long made use of junior soldiers and British society had not been adverse to sending them on active service. The Wills Act of 1837 which laid it down that no one under twenty-one could make a will exempted soldiers and sailors from this prohibition. But it had never hitherto thought, as it did now, that about half the total number of its male recruits would come from this source. It had long been known that new and increasingly complicated weapons would affect its training for their use, but it had not hitherto appreciated the difficulty, as it now began to do, of making them 'Jock-proof' when technology was racing ahead, and above all when still greater reliance would have to be placed on emerging technology. The Army could only feel its way in these matters, trusting as it did so that too many shins would not be damaged. The RAEC, whose help would be sought here, would similarly have to feel its way forward. It could only do so and thus prove sufficiently utilitarian if it was also innovative, and this was one of its main characteristics in the early years of the Regular Army.

It had to be imaginative, too, for although in many cases the Army would be well aware of its new needs and would turn to the RAEC for help in meeting them, it could not be assumed that this would always be so. An Army Command which had felt it necessary to urge Army Education to be more realistic might not have considered it sufficiently down-to-earth even to think of it in relation to new and developing problems. Army Education would be advised to think of approaching Army Training, but it might not occur to Army Training to approach Army Education. The professional, too, may be aware of the way in which his expertise may be of benefit to others before those others are fully conscious of newly-pressing needs and the RAEC as a body of professional teachers could simply be aware that it might help others before those others understood this too. However rightly convinced we may be of the great difference between 'education', which seeks the fullest development of the individual and of his intelligence, and 'training', which seeks the mastery by constant practice of specific skills, there is no reason why education, if it is sufficiently imaginative, cannot facilitate the task of training. Imagination was a characteristic of Army Education as it faced its tasks in the new Regular Army, and General Foxton's moving of his HQ to the War Office to be close to the Director of Army Training was symbolic of it.

Difficulty to the idealist is not the steady pressure of reality reminding men of their limitations, but is divine exhortation for them to increase their efforts, the success of which cannot be doubted if they do. To the idealist, what is good for people is so much more important than what they want that what they want cannot stand in the way of what they must be given. Thus when good citizenship as well as victory was to be the Army's gift to the Nation, the soldier's dislike of education was to be regretted; but if it was forced upon him the time would come when he would want what hitherto he had wanted to avoid. Army Education, it was insisted, must always be attentive to consumer needs as the idealist conceived those needs, but while every effort should be made to make it palatable, consumer resistance could not be allowed to prevail, nor should great importance be attached to it. A characteristic of Army Education in the Regular Army, however, was its greater willingness to take account of, and where possible to adjust to, the foibles of the soldiery in thinking poorly of education. Knowing that 'the motivation of junior soldiers to education is not good', it recommended the renaming of Education Wings in Boys' Units as Military Studies Wings 'to blur the connection with school' and to 'emphasise the link with military training'.[1] Its willingness to do so was characteristic of its increased effort, to use computerese, to make education more 'consumer-friendly'. Putting aside the hope of making the soldier feel at one with the Universe, Army Education was now the more determined to make itself at one with the soldier.

In embodying these qualities Army Education was showing itself to be elastic, highly adaptable, very ready to change, on occasion so ready to change as to suggest that the use of a sea-anchor might have been desirable. One thing it was not: it was not in a rut, even if its activities were no longer as highly charged, its drive and its energy no longer what all had acknowledged them to be, as when it was still determined to develop in the soldiery qualities in which they were persistently uninterested. That Army Education now lacked that great drive can be no surprise. For just as it has long been believed that 'the great character and office of governing gives a noble exercise to the reason of the governors which can hardly fail to raise and improve it',[2] so it has long been evident that the pursuit of a great ideal, however unattainable, generates driving energy, as we can see both in Puritan England and in the French Revolution. Yet it would be a mistake to think that Army Education at this time was in any sense lethargic; it could not have had such striking characteristics as we have seen it possessed had it also been that.

Realism, not idealism, now characterised Army Education. That at least was something that was not likely to be quickly changed as it reflected the dominant mood in both Army and Nation. Soon to give up its East of Suez role while retaining its 'fire-brigade' capacity to act overseas, the Army became concentrated at home and in Europe. Its rigid field formations there gave place to more flexible battle groups; its new equipment increased its mobility. As a result its men had to become more versatile, more resourceful, more technically efficient. They had to be quicker in understanding, more adaptable, to possess greater qualities of leadership. Yet it was not easy for the Army to get as many recruits as it needed and very difficult to get men of the right calibre. In 1973 91% of its recruits did not have passes in even a single subject at GCE 'O' level or its CSE equivalent.[3] This obviously increased the need for education to enable each soldier to make the most of himself and to bring up to standard the unfortunately large number who seemed to be below it; in circumstances such as these the Army was convinced that nothing but realism could be afforded. In so thinking it was strengthened by the mood of the Nation. The Nation had seen both the rise and the downfall of the planners. They had captured Labour and the national mood in the immediate post-war years. By the end of the 1940s, the national mood was changing and although the planners remained influential an increasing number of people were turning against them. Swings seem inevitable in these things; people became tired of being planned as the planners did not seem to be producing what had been promised. Men sang the virtues, no longer of planning, but of practicality and pragmatism. Immediately attainable goals became of greater consequence than long-term aims. Army Education could not but reflect this new mood in Army and Nation.

Not that the going was easy for it, however much it wished to do so. Even when it was at its strongest the Army's belief in education was like the faith of the elderly lady who bowed her head in church at the mention of the Devil, saying 'You never can tell and politeness costs nothing'; it was lacking in whole-hearted enthusiasm. What has been called 'the traditional disinclination to assess its [education's] value in contributing to the overall military capability of an army' was still strong. And it is to be remembered that many American regular officers were later to make known their conviction, derived from years of experience in Vietnam, that the purely academic side of their life at West Point added little to their survival and success after leaving it, a view which did not go unnoticed in the British Army.[4] Even so, in the early years of the Regular Army the RAEC found ways of sowing many seeds that would produce a very good harvest. All the impressive developments later to be seen in its work were begun in the mid-1960s. These were years of expansion for the RAEC, the number of its tasks being greatly increased.

It was to educate the soldier that the Corps of Army Schoolmasters came into being; that task continued to concern its successors, the AEC, the RAEC and the ETS. It was always an uphill battle to persuade the soldier to be educated and sometimes, it seems, the struggle was given up, as when it became no longer compulsory for soldiers to acquire the Third Class Certificate, which was abolished. Things changed again and soldiers were to be compulsorily educated until the Second Class Certificate, this compulsion in its turn being eventually dispensed with. The Corps became less interested in soldiers' education when in 1959 it became an all-officer Corps. It was now recruiting highly qualified people and General Foxton did not want to waste them on the grind of preparing the men for the certificates for which the less qualified could teach. In turning to the training organisations he envisaged a new role for his new men. How he thought the less qualified were to be found to do the teaching, what expenses would be incurred in getting them to do the job if found and how they could be met he did not disclose.[5] Not that all agreed with him. Lieutenant Colonel Chris Coplestone, then SO1 Education Colchester, greatly deplored this, believing that the education of the soldier was as important as it had ever been and that whatever the immediate benefit of the Corps' new interest in other matters, this neglect in the long run would cost it dear.[6] Major Bill Lynam, another SO1 Education, similarly deplored this neglect, recalling the constant pressure on the Army of emerging technology and the continued need for more intelligent, alert and adaptable soldiers and fearful of what the ultimate effect on the Army would be if those whose traditional job it was to educate the soldier became convinced it was beneath them.[7] Another dedicated teacher, a former schoolmaster at Eton, Captain Charles James, believed 'The Corps' loyalties were not really to the soldiers but rather to an idealised system of educational administration to which the soldiers were a necessary adjunct',[8] a view echoing what HMIs in the Mediterranean had said at the time of the Release Scheme.

The officerisation of the Corps was the more or less inevitable consequence of the end of National Service, since it was improbable that regular soldiers who were trained teachers or graduates would be willing to serve in sufficient numbers as other ranks and it was also clear that the Corps would lose its credibility unless the majority of its members were qualified; moreover, civilian teachers in service children's schools enjoyed officer status and some of them lived in officers messes. Matters came to a head during the directorship of Major-General Moore-Coulson who obtained agreement to officerisation and wanted an all-regular Corps with a short service fringe. This would have made regular promotion prospects very poor and after much heated discussion he agreed that a proportion of officers could be given Extended Service (ESC) later known as Limited Service Regular Commissions (LSRC) with a promotion ceiling of major. Such officers would, however, be regulars. It was determined that all existing serving NCOs and WOs would be phased out by 1963.

Major-General Tony Trythall, then an SO2 in the War Office, well remembers being given the task of planning the conversion of the Corps within three years from a mixed entity into a body of some 950 officers while at the same time avoiding the disruption of educational provision. It was decided to work inwards from the periphery, the Far East, and this proved successful. The option of allowing some other ranks to serve out their time was not taken, nor was the option of recruiting non-educationally qualified personnel, those with 'O' and 'A' levels only, and allowing them to obtain teaching qualifications during service and subsequently move on to commissioning. Either of these options might have helped, although the second broke the rule of using only graduates or trained teachers. It is certain, however, that the permanent retention of other ranks would not have been an appropriate or successful policy.[9]

However DCI No. 288 emphasised the importance attached to the General Education Scheme for soldiers and the Committee on the Future Structure of the

Army, which examined the long-term commitments of the Corps and which decided that a suitable role for it would be to provide the theoretical background to practical Trade Training, also laid it down that the General Education Scheme for the soldier should be reviewed and that the Corps should be responsible for it. This revised scheme was to begin on 1 April 1971. Its aim was 'to support military training by enabling the soldier to absorb instruction more successfully and to equip him with the wider knowledge of his military calling which he requires in order to assume increased responsibilities'. The 1970s Review of Troops' Education which General Hall undertook resulted from the overstretch and turbulence which was then increasingly plaguing the Army. He realised that a sound defence of Troops' Education based on a systematic and professional poll of opinion, both of Commanding Officers and WOs and NCOs, would stand the Corps and the Army in great stead in the years which lay ahead. He therefore, with the Adjutant-General's support, set up such a review and asked the Chief Inspector to carry it out in the period 1974–1976. The result was a document of general support and warm approval which served as a shield for the RAEC. It is a pity that a similar view of officers' education was not instituted. There can be little doubt that it would have been as warmly approved as was soldiers' education, that the need for it and its importance would have been emphasised, and that such support would have added to the Army's difficulty in substituting for an excellent education scheme the obviously inadequate arrangements which were eventually provided.[10] It could not be doubted that such education was needed. The more educationally qualified to whom Service life appealed tended not to wear khaki. It was said in October 1971 'the overall standard of recruits entering the Army is far below that required for any meaningful civilian qualifications.[11]

The RAEC took up the challenge vigorously and impressively. What was referred to as 'Developmental Education' was far from being only a show. By this was meant the development of standards of literacy, numeracy and self-confidence that would bring the soldier sufficiently close to the standard required for promotion, the model to be followed here being the potential officer's development course. Then there was the idea of the 'marginal man' which had application to all ranks. It provided for the testing of a man at any stage of his career when he was being considered for some rank he was not already holding or for some task he was not already doing. If in this consideration any deficiency was revealed the RAEC would help to remove it. Thus it ran courses for potential helicopter pilots who lacked the knowledge necessary for them to begin ordinary pilot training, for potential artificers and Foremen of Signals, and pre-course training for potential survey technicians. Some 50% of soldiers were tradesmen. Most of their training was done by the particular Arm or Corps in which they served. But some of the more technical trades needed to know more of the mathematics and the physics which were the essential foundations of trade training. This was a need the RAEC met. When, for instance, the Royal Corps of Signals needed refresher courses in these two subjects the RAEC ran them.

In a further development of the courses run for tradesmen, the RAEC branched into Special-to-Arms education. General Foxton admitted that the average soldier did not believe that education could help to fashion a better soldier; he thought Special-to-Arms education might at last so convince him.[12] This was the teaching of those who are to be trained so that they could best profit from their training; it would ensure that it would be completed as quickly as possible and attended to as economically as could be managed. It seems he was right. There was general and great approval of it, expressed by HMIs and by very many Commanding Officers as General Sir Hugh Beach reported, and most important of all by the soldiers themselves.[13] It was most useful and it was complementary to the rest of the Corps' educational work. What was being done needed to be done and it would ensure that the regimental officers would acknowledge that the Corps was an essential part of the Army and not just an appendage to it. It helped to create trust; if that was created a more broadly-based education might follow; without it it never would. Nor should it be forgotten what Colonel Mullin had learned when Headmaster of the Duke of York's School. All but the top stream found no fruit in academic education – but once it was presented as technical education and that this was needed to be backed up by academic knowledge and thought – it all could be accepted.[14] What better way of demonstrating its necessity than that provided by Special-to-Arms education?

Then there was what was called 'orientation' which was carried out by the RAEC and which was much appreciated. This was the briefing on whatever conditions those about to embark on special missions might expect to find. Something else was also important. Discussions on current affairs were no longer regularly held in many units, it being said it was not desirable to make such discussions mandatory because of lack of time and because of what were referred to somewhat coyly as 'different circumstances'. But there was still the need to ensure that men should know about 'current trends and events' which can affect the Army so they can form reasonable opinions on views expressed through the mass media wherever they are serving, and can recognise and counter those reports which could lower morale or alienate loyalty.[15] This was one of the Corps' many jobs. Failing as too often it did to recruit the best, the Army had to make the best of those whom it could recruit. Always conscious of this, these many ways of improving the quality of what was on offer provided by the RAEC were a very ready help and another sure way of winning gratitude to and respect for those who provided it.

Not all parts of this General Education Scheme, however, were equally impressive. Part of it was addressed to ensuring that soldiers of every Arm or Corps would reach the minimum educational standards which each Arm or Corps would, in consultation with a Training Department Adviser or other appropriate RAEC officer, determine were essential to its efficient operation. Even the specific can be specifically ignored; the vague is more frequently than not unattended to; the misty generalisation left undisturbed. The uneasy feeling persists that priorities here were disturbingly reminiscent of those being accepted in the USSR or the People's Republic of China at this time. Policies there were announced which were clearly intended to be in the national interest and then, almost as an afterthought, followed the reminder that these owed their inspiration to Marxist-Leninism or to the great thoughts of Chairman Mao. Realities were recognised and pious platitudes, which cost nothing, were accepted for what they were worth. The education in support of training which it was said would involve a 'greatly increased need for [RAEC] officers able to instruct in technical subjects' who would be frequently called [as consultants] into units for short and specific courses was the important announcement of policy; the bringing up of soldiers to minimum educational standards the pious genuflection.

There was a great deal of talk about general education and general agreement about its desirability. Undoubtedly the RAEC did everything in its power to increase that consensus about its desirability. Again and again it was stressed that 'the Army needed English, not as an academic subject, but for its application to the improvement of communication'. For the Army was now very much concerning itself with the art of communication. The old clichés, the 'fog of war' and the 'din of battle' had at least drawn attention to the difficulty of the Army Commander in seeing all he wants to see and in ensuring that his subordinates hear all that he wants them to hear. The point had been taken that his mind would be the easier if he could be assured that there would be speedy and correct understanding of instructions throughout his Command and that the minds of his subordinates would be the easier if they knew that they would get from him instructions that would be precise and concise. Again and again the RAEC emphasised that communication begins with thinking. Soldiers had to be able to clarify their thinking and to put their thoughts clearly to others. A thought or a fact, it was stressed, which cannot be communicated is valueless. Whatever the instruction that was taking place, it was reiterated that as much time should be spent on correcting what was expressed as on the content of the syllabus itself. Blue pencil was the important thing here. It was vital that opportunity be provided for the setting and marking of written work in quantity as 'improvement in English arises from the study of one's own corrected work'. All this was what the Army wanted to hear. But the doubt persists that much that was said about general education was more the expression of a hope than the expectation of its fulfilment. And some at least will think it a reasonable assumption in a period of turbulence and overstretch that the absence of a specific commitment to undertake it would mean also an absence of sustained educational activity.

A question remains. In the days of Army Certificates soldiers were to be compulsorily educated until they reached the standard of the Second Class Certificate. Now it seemed highly probable that compulsion on the soldier to devote any time at all to education had been dispensed with. If this was so it was either the correction of a long-standing error or the committing of a grave new fault. If reaching the educational standard of a Second Class Certificate was necessary to enable the soldier to carry out his duties adequately then it was not only justified but essential. If it was not, then there was no case for its retention. Young men not in uniform were under no compulsion to reach a higher standard of education than they wanted to, it being apparently accepted that they were fully capable of doing their job without being made to do so. If the same was true of the soldier, the ending of compulsion on him to reach Second Class Certificate level was the rectifying of a culpable error; if it was not, it was making the Army less efficient and a grievous mistake. Which was the right view?

Quite apart from what it did for soldiers' general education the RAEC also contributed to it in other ways. Not the least important of its work was with the Junior

Army. The Junior Army had sustained the manning of a volunteer Army for over thirty years and demographic trends suggested that it would continue to do so. Almost half of the male soldier recruits were enlisted initially into the Junior Army, some 7,500 each year. The majority of these enlisted under the age of seventeen as either Junior Soldiers or Junior Leaders. About 1,500 apprenticeships in over forty recognised trades were offered annually and there were also openings for Junior Bandsmen. After a good deal of sorting out there were in the 1980s three categories of entrants. There were the Apprentices who were being prepared for a technical career in the Army. It was from these that it expected to get the majority of its Warrant Officers and NCOs in the technical and craft trades. They were given a thorough grounding in the basic principles of their trade and also in leadership and sports. They received the military training and the education which would later qualify them for NCO and Warrant rank. All the trades taught qualified for trade union membership. Apprentices could gain credits which would help them acquire the civilian qualifications conferred by the City and Guilds of London Institute or the Business and Technicians Education Council. The course for the Apprentices lasted from eighteen months to two years; they were not charged for it but were themselves paid for attendance. For the most promising of them there was an excellent chance of being selected for a further three years' training which would bring them commissioned rank in one of the technical arms. Then there were the Junior Leaders. They attended a one year's course in military training, leadership, character building and general education either in an Apprentice's College or a Junior Leaders' Regiment. Their course successfully completed conferred on them the Junior Army Education Certificate. Lastly there were the Junior Soldiers who were primarily recruited into specific Infantry regiments. Their six months' training, which included 100 hours of education, brought them the Junior Soldier's Education Certificate.

From time to time there was criticism within the Army of such reliance on the Junior Army. It was generally agreed that the Apprentice Colleges did an excellent job and fully justified themselves. There was, however, often disagreement about the other Junior Entry Units. They gave rise to three criticisms in particular. The very low intellectual level of their intake was frequently commented on; the quantity, it seemed, mattered more than the quality of those admitted. 'When over 40% fail to get an Intermediate Certificate, as was the case in one unit, it must mean that many will never make NCOs and that much work and money is being wasted', it was acidly pointed out. It was thought that if the youngsters in these units took the adult Education for Promotion Certificate 'a pass rate of 10–30% could be expected'. The implications of this were again spelled out: 'The rank of corporal is one which we consider only a very small proportion of ex-junior soldiers are ever likely to attain.' The expense involved in the upkeep of these units was another sore point. 'The Junior is an expensive commodity to train and keep before he becomes militarily useful', critics said. Moreover, the expense increased because of the high rate of wastage; in 1989 it was 26%. Per capita costs for the Apprentice College rivalled those of a good public school.[16] Thirdly, it was often said, these units and their whole approach were far too inflexible. Repeated efforts were made to make sure that this would not be the case, but this charge was still being levelled against them in the late 1980s.

Junior Entry Units were subject to contradictory pressures. It was, as we have seen, difficult to be satisfied with them. And yet it seemed even more difficult to do without them, as in their absence there seemed no way of maintaining recruitment at an adequate level. So that at one time it appeared that their intake would have to be increased and at another reduced. In January 1979 it was agreed that it should be raised to 10,000 in the coming year, to 11,000 in the following year and that it should remain at this constant figure and not be adjusted to meet the vagaries of adult recruiting. In 1982 it was recommended that it be fixed at 7,500.[17]

Given these constant criticisms and the constant necessity of having these units, it was obvious that every effort would have to be made to make the most of those who joined them; their instruction and their education was in consequence of the utmost importance. From the beginning it was difficult to get the balance right between the military training, which as youngsters eager to become soldiers they welcomed, and the education without which their usefulness to the Army would be less than was hoped for, but to which they seemed constitutionally averse. Even after the Miller Report which spoke of 'a cardinal error of approach – treating boy soldiers as soldiers rather than as boys', it was a constant battle to keep the balance between training and education right. By and large in the Apprentice Colleges a satisfactory balance was secured. This was not only because after that report there was a greater appreciation of the role of education and because thereafter less importance was attached to military training. It was also because of the decision to replace the Teeth Arm Commandants at the Colleges with Commandants drawn from the Arm of Service sponsoring the training – thus an officer from REME was appointed at Arborfield and one from the Royal Signals at Harrogate, which covered the Signals trades – and because in consequence the importance of education to bring apprentices up to a good technician-craftsman standard was more fully understood. It was also because of the recruitment into the RAEC of more scientifically and technically trained officers, and the employment in the Apprentice Colleges of more scientifically-qualified civilian lecturers. No doubt also this was not least because of the uncompromising stand taken by the RAEC. In 1970 at Arborfield in the absence of the REME Commandant and his REME Lieutenant Colonel 2i/c, the Administrative Officer, a teeth arm Major, was given command, although the Senior Education Officer was a Lieutenant-Colonel. The Senior Education Officer naturally refused to serve under a Major and he won his case.[18] Much the same happened at Carlisle, with fortunately similar results, although the victory for education won at Arborfield and Carlisle was not always as fruitful in all Apprentice Colleges. There are those who do not see the importance of such struggles for precedence, as there are historians who are outraged at the struggles, often violent and bloody, between 17th Century diplomatists, as for instance between the French and Spanish ambassadors in London and the Hague. Those who underestimate such struggles are much mistaken. The 17th Century struggles were an essential step in the development of the diplomatic art and the fortunately more civilised contentions at Arborfield and Carlisle an essential stage too in the development of education at the Apprentice Colleges. To understand that one has only to contemplate the effect on impressionable youngsters already inclined to attach far greater importance to military training than to education, had the outcome of these particular struggles been different.

There was in fact a question as to whether the RAEC should continue to staff the Boys' Units. The Miller Report had pointed out that 'in one or two units the rate of turnover of staffing, especially in the RAEC, was little short of disastrous'. Civilian teachers would provide greater continuity and the attempt was made to employ more of them. Thus the Director of Army Education's Conference of Command Education Officers was told in 1961 'A start has been made in the employment of civilian teachers in some 50% of the RAEC posts in Army Apprentice Colleges and in other Boys' Units up to 30%.' However the 'slow progress in recruiting civilians for these posts' was noticed. Moreover, the attendant disadvantages of employing civilians in these units soon became apparent. A report of 16 February 1979 pointed out 'Many were too old and most had been at units too long. They were resistant to change, lacking in enthusiasm, unable or unwilling to take a part in outdoor activities as needed.' In such units active and enthusiastic participation in these activities was essential and this was one of the well-known strengths of the RAEC. It was actively concerned with the hobbies and sports which gave some of the young men a chance to escape the roughness of barrack-room life. Under great pressure to reduce its activities because of financial stringency, in 1964 the Corps very wisely refused to drop its commitment to Adventure Training[19] and its concern with this stood it in good stead with the Junior Entry units. So the policy of civilianising the teaching of the Junior Army was reversed and by 1979 an increasing proportion of the RAEC's resources was being devoted to the Junior Army. But the overstretch that was bedeviling so much of the Army was affecting the Corps too. Such were its commitments that it acknowledged 'The policy that a minimum of half the teaching posts [at those units] should be filled by the RAEC was not being achieved.' There was one unit in which all the teachers were civilians.[20]

The education provided in these Junior Entry Units was by no means all that the RAEC wanted it to be. It was often skimped. Education was supposed to occupy 20% of their training programme. Yet despite the review of education in the Junior Army that took place in 1978 and the renewed effort that followed to promote it, it could still be said in 1979 that 'it does not always approach this figure and sometimes falls far short of it'. 'In some units, it was said, 'as little as 12% of the training time was given to education.' A Junior Army Education Certificate scheme was introduced in 1980. This provided a centrally controlled scheme for all the Junior Entry units – except the Apprentices Colleges where the emphasis was on trade-related subjects – but with a built-in flexibility so that the various units could produce unit-designed syllabuses to suit their Special-to-Arm requirements. Each junior had to take eight subject modules (two of which were designed centrally for all units while the remaining six were designed for each unit individually) in order to obtain his certificate. Thereafter, certain juniors who did well in their work for the certificate, and who were recommended by their Commanding Officers, were eligible to sit two subjects of the examination for the Education Promotion Certificate (Military Calculations and the Army in the Contemporary World) before their transfer to adult service. This scheme exemplified the functional concept of education in support of training; the relevance to training requirements and the flexibility of content ensured its adaptability to meet changing training needs; and clearly defined objectives resulted in improved motivation of both students and staff. The teaching, HMIs found, was 'generally satisfactory'. The students, they said, 'invariably worked hard and with determination – even where failure is a likely outcome of their efforts. They are well motivated by frequent testing and they show a determination to avoid the consequences of failure; they are motivated by a desire to avoid letting the squad down and by the intense discipline of Service life.' The HMIs, nevertheless, thought that too much was expected of the young soldiers. They are 'often too tired to learn', they said. They concluded that too much of the curriculum smacked of military instruction rather than genuine education. The HMIs thought this was true even of the Apprentice Colleges and they were critical in all the Junior Entry Units of the overriding influence of the adult Education for Promotion syllabus so early in a soldier's career. They said 'Too much of the work is aimed merely at the retention of facts for examination purposes often at the expense of enjoyment and understanding.' 'Concentration on recruiting junior soldiers to the service', they believed, 'often excludes opportunities to allow the young men to orient themselves for service and to assist them in the process of making radical changes in their way of life.' There were 'few attempts to test the student's ability to understand as well as to memorise'. 'There was insufficient time for general reading, private study and research.' Libraries were little used by the young soldiers – this, said the HMIs 'reflects the very full educational and training programmes of these units'. 'Little opportunity', they said, 'is available for relaxation or for reflection on learning experience.' It is worthy of note that this was the very criticism made of the instruction at the Staff College at Camberley. The education that can come only from quiet reflection has never been sufficiently appreciated in the Army; it has never understood, to use the words of the HMIs, how hard is 'the hard work of reflection'.[21]

Sometimes, however, things may be in some measure excused when they cannot be justified. Steadily and constantly battling, the RAEC had to accept compromise. Is it reasonable to think that things would have been better had civilian teachers entirely replaced them? Is it not highly probable that they would have been a good deal worse if the RAEC had not been prepared to fight for at least the full measure of education that was officially allotted to it? Is it not significant that it so frequently contrived to do more than it was entitled to? It had, for instance, no formal responsibility for teaching map-reading either in the Army proper or in the Junior Army. In fact it taught map-reading in much of the Army. In nine out of the thirteen Junior Entry Units covered by the Report of 16 February 1979 it carried out this teaching too. Despite the obvious need for them in recruiting, the Junior Entry Units might not have survived the criticisms levelled against them and the public alarm occasioned by the suicide of one of their members, alarm which occasioned the Miller Report, had the RAEC not bestirred itself in this matter.[22]

And as the Donaldson Report on Boy Entrants and Young Servicemen made clear in 1970, that would have been a great pity. That report said:

One of the problems which the Services face is to bring out the potential of boys who, for a variety of reasons, have emerged from their school experience much more deficient in the basic skills of reading, writing and arithmetic than their mature ability would warrant. With a renewed sense of purpose, with fresh motivation and with appropriate instructional techniques, the boys who might otherwise be underrated as 'dull' have revealed an unsuspected potential. There is an unacknowledged contribution to an educational problem with which the schools are still wrestling. For their own practical reasons, the Forces are pioneering an important and interesting variant on the theme of Further Education for many young men who need it, if they are to be personally fulfilled and fully productive in the economic sense. The Forces are well equipped to perform this service to the country: they provide for the great majority of the boys in these units a communal life and an environment of challenge stimulus entirely without counterpart in the civilian world.

It is always a difficult question to answer 'For how many can it reasonably be agreed that the city shall be saved?' Yet those words 'without counterpart in the civilian world' are worth pondering on, for the report was right in insisting that those units 'are almost the only residential technical institutions available for successive generations of young people'.[23] The struggle to improve them was a contribution to the Nation as well as to the Army. It was undoubtedly a strain on the Corps' resources but one which equally undoubtedly added to the considerable stock of goodwill which the Corps was accumulating at this time.

Many in the Army had always looked askance at the notion that it was in its interests to educate soldiers. All agreed that finished and finite ignorance in the NCO was unbecoming. It was generally held that to do his job properly he had to demonstrate by examination that he had reached certain educational levels. It was the uniformed educator's job to help him to do this. However unenthusiastic soldiers in general might be about education, those wanting promotion were always grateful for the help they received in their examinations, seeing in this the hidden good at the heart of things that is difficult at times to appreciate. The Committee on the Future Structure of the Army emphasised how essential was Education for Promotion and it followed that to attend to it was one of the RAEC's most important tasks. Its assumption was said to have been 'the turning point in the Corps' role, marking the end of the 'Schoolie' with the old school certificate type of teaching'. It made the Corps 'more vocationally and training relevant'.[24]

The EPC was to ensure that Warrant Officers and NCOs were educationally fitted for their jobs. There were to be two educational qualifications for promotion. There was the Education Promotion Certificate (EPC) without which no one could hold the rank of Sergeant. There was also the Education Promotion Certificate (Advanced) which was required for promotion to Warrant Officer. The subjects in which candidates were to be examined were communication skills (the current military jargon for the use of English), military calculations, military administration and management, and contemporary world affairs. This choice of subjects, it was said, was 'based on the needs of the mature adult with several years' experience in controlling men'. The syllabus was designed 'to test the NCO's ability to meet satisfactorily a specifically military requirement'.

The academic standard of EPC could not be high, though those who taught it – while admitting that that standard was lower than that of the Army Certificates of Education, which it replaced and which had civilian 'O' level equivalents – nevertheless maintained 'in some respects EPC standards were not much below 'O' level and EPC (Advanced) would have merited an 'O' level equivalent'.[25] Such teachers were encouraged by the fact that by 1980 the City and Guilds of London Institutes was acknowledging its respectability.

No one can doubt that many who acquired the EPC certificates put in a great deal of effort in order to do so. One RAEC officer was sure that their acquisition represented 'a real effort by academically ungifted men to achieve a standard some way above what they would have achieved at school'. 'We often found', he wrote, 'that students at Corporal level were unwilling to be "sent to school" again. For them school was a place of failure, often emphasised by the effect of broken families, truancy and the sheer inability to deal with what became insurmountable difficulties, as these boys lost contact with both teachers and subjects. I think that sitting in a desk again was great difficulty for some, especially the tougher, older NCOs of the infantry.' They 'were involved in very hard work, often in their own time'. It is difficult not to feel touched when one reads of the RCT sergeant doing a two-year attachment to the Gordon Highlanders Light Aid Detachment being helped in his studies by his eldest daughter and that 'both were overjoyed at their success'. Candidates were well aware that they had to work and the answer received by a tutor who wished one of his pupils good luck in the examination 'y' know, sir, there's no such thing as good luck – yer makes yer own', indicates that something very valuable had been achieved by insisting that hard work be done even at this low academic level. It would be wrong, too, to underestimate the importance of the gratitude felt by those who passed these tests. 'I thought I'd never pass that education, sir, but I did and I'm real grateful to your lot for that.' The sincerity of that praise speaks for itself and any teacher would have been proud to earn it.[26]

The text-books for the EPC courses were well produced, carefully thought out and written in such a way as to be within the comprehension of the weaker students. 'Brighter NCOs of technical Corps', a tutor said, 'often felt rather insulted [by them], but few went away in my experience maintaining these attitudes after a course.' It was not, however, on the excellence of the text-books but on the skill and the dedication of the teacher that the success of Education for Promotion depended. Of that dedication the appreciation of the work by those engaged in it leaves us in no doubt whatever. There can be few more convincing proofs of that than this comment by one who greatly valued his EPC work: 'There was in the work of teaching NCOs of the less intellectually gifted areas of the Army a real sense that one was teaching very much from the heart to the very men who were at the heart of the system, on whose broad shoulders so much depended.' 'These men', he wrote, 'had often worked their way up literally from nothing – if they wrote in sloping capitals with no tails, because the ruler made it impossible to put them in (although some painstakingly went along afterwards repairing the omissions as the School of Infantry taught them) – they were none-the-less the backbone of the Army and the men on whose loyalty and professional ability the whole system depended.'[27]

The dedicated nature of the teaching is to be seen nowhere more clearly than in Northern Ireland. This stands out from the following account by an EPC tutor there. 'To use the means of transportation we used without carrying a street map, the details of which had to be learned by heart, to carry the minimum of paper which would give away important information if the worst happened, and not only to carry weapons but to ensure that, if ambushed, one could hit back as effectively as possible – all of these skills one had to acquire, often through having to accompany other officers who found themselves in situations that still frighten me today as a result of their anti-military affectations.' 'How I got to one unit', he said, 'is a secret that neither the Commanding Officer of the time nor I dare ever divulge!' Here is an account of a typical day's work. 'One would drive to X, teach there for two hours, see people, correct work and discuss it, then fly to Y, with the suitcase or fishing-bag full of stuff, spend two hours teaching and correcting there and catch the helicopter back to X for a quick lunch with the officers, see the Adjutant or the Second-in-Command about any problems, then drive to Z, teaching another three hours there, then taking a tea-break. The last part of the day could be spent driving a long way to 'D' Company where one dined with the officers at eight, then took two further classes which, with discussions and coaching on the weaker points would go on until 11pm, when the car would be driven out of the gates of the base (with the lights out and the base lights out, then switched on fully to blind any would-be terrorists with ambitions in the shooting line).' EPC tutors had to visit each unit weekly and always on the same day and about the same time, the regularity of the visits greatly increasing the risks. How real they were is illustrated by the fact that on one list of 'Brit' cars discovered was the number and the description of the car of one of the tutors. He was a lucky man. One night he was chased by a big Ford, with four men in it, which had been waiting for him with its lights out. As the tired tutor said he did not wait to see if they were terrorists or merely local drunks, but he was grateful to the Brigade's Light Aid Detachment, the skill of which in keeping his car in top condition deprived him of the opportunity of finding out.[28]

Ingenuity and appreciation were marked characteristics of the EPC tutor's work. Arrangements were such that corrected papers, with advice and reworking instructions, could be in any student's hands within twenty-four hours, and often much less, of receipt of the work. Course materials were photocopied in miniature so that work could be taken in the pocket in the field and done during quiet spells. This had been the practice of the sepoy at home and abroad; no one had thought to see the British soldier doing likewise but this was to be seen on occasion in Northern Ireland. Perhaps we should not be surprised. It was, after all, Ireland that reminded Gladstone that the resources of civilisation are not easily exhausted. In such conditions it is not surprising that mutual respect and sympathy soon developed between teacher and taught there. 'One felt very much drawn to them', a tutor said of his pupils, 'and there was a very real sense of comradeship with them.' 'It was impossible', he wrote, 'not to feel sympathy with those men who had to command and lead their soldiers and study at the same time under very difficult conditions; in the city, "moving target duty" (as the Royal Highland Fusilier CSM put it) was a matter of 100% concentration; for the NCO there was the extra responsibility of leadership and the weight of the responsibility for the lives and actions of his soldiers often in situations where to open fire was almost to guarantee a court appearance as a defendant, whilst to withhold it was to open oneself to a charge of military irresponsibility.' 'Some of our students', he added, 'were murdered before they could take the examinations and others were kept in contact only through the "hospital tutor".'[29]

The tutors were in no doubt, and we should not be either, that EPC was well worthwhile. An EPC pass, modest though its standard was, implied 'the ability to sit and learn over a period in an academic environment and to achieve a satisfactory result'. It increased the value to a prospective civilian employer of those who satisfied the examiners. 'It opened the eyes of many who took it to the possibility of a managerial supervisory course after their time in the Army' and are we not compelled to agree with the sentiment that 'for that alone the EPC was of immense value'? That was of no little importance, but perhaps we should rate another result of EPC even more highly. When we read that 'of the NCOs we educated most learned to treat the idea of education with respect, a considerable advance on their attitudes as school children', that 'many of my students admitted that they now knew something of the value of education, and of those who were married with children a considerable number were determined to see that their children made better use of educational opportunities than they had done themselves', we realise that in this we see the strengthening of the forces that are gradually bringing about the change that is of such importance to our future, the change in our national attitudes to education. But most important of all, since however interested the Army must be in enhancing the job prospects of those leaving the Colours and in ensuring that they are solid citizens, its primary concern must be in improving the quality of its soldiers, EPC tutors were convinced that their work was 'of real value to NCOs in widening their experience, improving their managerial skills and giving them confidence in their own mental abilities'. Tutors were sure that 'success on the educational front gave them a renewed confidence in their own ability to achieve results by a rational and logical approach'. 'After initial failure in the school environment, success was evidence that losing one battle did not mean losing the whole war.' Tutors noticed that 'the feeling of having passed a course in the company of the "brighter" students was an effective morale-booster and gave them added confidence in their work'.

The tutor who wrote this was a fine and greatly experienced teacher. He was a former master at Eton. His dedication is obvious from the fact that in the years 1980–1983 he drove 80,000 miles in Northern Ireland. He was awarded the MBE for his work there. At his investiture he met one of the NCOs he had taught who was there for a Military Medal; he had lost a foot and been shot in the arm but he had also acquired the one subject he needed to complete his EPC. That tutor's colleagues were enthusiastic and dedicated teachers, too. And it is pleasant to record, as they do, what excellent work was done in Northern Ireland by the female officers serving with the RAEC. 'They too', it was gratefully acknowledged, 'shared in the tutorial service in city and country with enthusiasm and high commitment.' They were noted for an ability which was the envy of their male colleagues. 'When things were difficult to get', it was said, 'they could wheedle priceless items out of stony-faced 'quarter-blokes.' 'The letters I received from Commanding Officers', the tutor who was awarded the MBE wrote, 'are a source of never-failing amazement to me.'[30] In this at least his judgement was at fault. Few jobs done by the RAEC could have won from Commanding Officers a greater and more enthusiastic respect than this exceptionally difficult task so well carried out in Northern Ireland. There were those in the Corps in the early 1970s who looked down upon EPC work as merely 'bread and butter' work, to be unfavourably contrasted with other and more glorious Corps activities. They were ill-advised to do so, which is not to say that they were also ill-advised who warned against the danger, as did Lieutenant-Colonel Washtell, that education might come to be seen as a paper qualification, the lack of which is a bar to promotion and not, as it ought to be regarded, as a positive contribution to leadership training.[31]

Circumstances, as Burke reminded us, rule this nether world and so adverse did they become that even this very good system of NCO and WO instruction had to yield to them. Such was the pressure of the clock and the purse on the Army in the 1980s that it concluded that the time and cost of qualifying men and women for promotion would have to be curtailed. The average time spent by the NCOs on courses before getting their certificates was nine to eleven weeks. Commanding Officers urged the RAEC to reduce this; their concern 'over the need to release NCOs for EPC courses at a time when battalions are at full strength and leading a particularly turbulent life' was widespread. The introduction of centralised marking for EPC added to the grievances of the Commanding Officers. Hitherto the RAEC had had centralised marking only for the First Class Army Certificate of Education. Each Command had marked its own papers which meant that results could be produced quickly and NCOs who had not satisfied the examiners could be 'slotted into' the next course while their knowledge was fresh and while the urge to work was still on them. Centralised marking involved official procedures, getting papers there from all over the world, standardising, preparing marking grades and so on. 'It became a way to crack nuts with a gold-plated sledgehammer', as one disgruntled EPC tutor expressed it. The delay meant that failures needed a new course, the full five weeks all over again as sometimes it took as long as eight weeks to get results to units. This procedure was exasperating to Commanding Officers who saw good but slow candidates losing heart and leaving the Army because they could not pass EPC. Aware of the mounting irritation in the Army at the time taken over EPC, the RAEC could with profit to itself have kept to the old flexibility and avoided the new formality, introduced as that doubtless was in the hope of increasing its value in civilian eyes as a professionally conducted examination. There was, however, a reason why EPC candidates were having to retake courses and resit examinations which the RAEC was able to remove. Many had not reached the course standard prescribed when they sat the examinations. The RAEC therefore introduced tests to see whether they were up to the course entry standard and pre-course learning packages for those who were not.

The standard set by EPC could not be very high. Yet it was well worth acquiring. It is a tribute to the teaching skill of RAEC tutors, and this has always been one of their great strengths, that they made of it a genuine educational experience. Perhaps it is not too much to say they made a significant number of soldiers conscious of an educational need of which they had hitherto been unaware. Nor should we forget that even though the Army Certificates of Education were of no high academic standard, they were valued by the manager of Boots who said what importance he attached to their acquisition by men leaving the Colours who applied to him for employment.[32] It is unlikely that he was impressed by their intellectual standard. It is much more probable that he welcomed them as independent confirmations of the qualities he thought much more important than the technical skills to which he paid little attention, as testimony to the character, the determination, the readiness to work hard and to carry through to a successful conclusion an unfamiliar and possibly uncongenial task, for which he was looking. Teachers have sometimes been said to be indifferent to the character of their pupils; in Fagin's Academy or in Dotheboys Hall we would expect them to be; not elsewhere. Education, like the Greek *polis*, aims to fulfil life and if EPC in any way built up the character of those who by sweat and application acquired it, its claim to educational achievement is not lightly to be dismissed.

We have seen what an important expansion in the Corps' work took place when in 1948 Resettlement became one of its commitments. It remained one of its most significant jobs in the Regular Army. The Corps never doubted the truth emphasised in 1948 that 'Resettlement provides the RAEC with a great opportunity of justifying education to the materially-minded'. Nor did it doubt that what it had taken on could 'justly be measured in terms of national dimensions'. For what was involved was the planning and preparing for a second career built into active service life. As an Inter-Departmental Committee said in 1947, to attract Regulars of the right calibre 'potential candidates had to be convinced that they were in no blind-ally occupation but enjoyed prospects beyond their term of service'. Yet it took more than twenty years before this important truth was accepted, it being not only in universities that speedy change is looked upon askance. In those years it was the steady aim of the Corps to drive it home.

It plodded on, providing advice and information on Resettlement, setting up employment-finding agencies, arranging a 'Save-While-You-Serve' Scheme which enabled regular savings to be lodged with Building Societies from which mortgages might be obtained by those leaving the Colours. It encouraged all ranks to prepare early for Resettlement by making use of correspondence courses, evening classes and so on. It expanded the Resettlement Centres at Catterick and Aldershot, running twenty-eight courses at both of them. These were of three kinds. There were General Studies Courses which prepared for the examinations to get into the Civil Service, the Fire Service, the Prison Service and the Police. There were Commercial Courses preparing those wanting to master book-keeping, clerical skills, office organisation and supervision. There were Trades Courses for would-be plumbers, bricklayers and decorators. An additional very popular Course was in household maintenance. In addition to the Lieutenant-Colonels earlier mentioned as chairing the advice panels there were RAEC Majors employed full-time in Resettlement, and instruction in Resettlement duties was part of the normal training of all the RAEC.

It was an uphill battle. The Army was oddly reluctant to acknowledge the reality of the soldier's fear that Army service would not be a sufficient qualification for civilian employment. There is a verse from Juvenal's *Satires* which reads:

> Still we persist; plough the sand, and sow
> Seed after seed, where none can ever grow.

The RAEC must have felt, from time to time, that those lines applied to its efforts to convince senior officers of the great importance of Resettlement work. They were apt to believe that whatever lessened the soldier's apprehensions when contemplating return to civilian life would make him the more eager to do so. Thus they rarely hesitated to say to the RAEC 'your Resettlement service does not help me to retain my soldiers'.[33] Only when Army numbers had to be reduced were Resettlement officers thought to be engaged in virtuous activity; in normal times they were dwellers in the tents of the ungodly. The Army's failure to appreciate that the successfully resettled soldier was its best recruiting officer and that the last significant military experience of a soldier's career was of the arrangements made for his resettlement was remarkable. He tended to remember them. Resettlement involved three activities for the Corps: giving Resettlement advice, arranging Resettlement training; and trying to find jobs for those going out. Of these three only one was labour intensive; the Corps was merely the agent for the other two. The perennial difficulty was getting the man's military experience to count for something in the mind of a prospective employer. This was particularly so when, because of Northern Ireland, the Army was increasingly a closed society and much of its activity somewhat esoteric. In its persistently frustrating fight for Resettlement is to be seen how valuable the Corps can be to the Army, patiently persevering in its pursuit of an objective essential to the good of the whole Army but by no means always accepted as being so by all its parts.

The problem of the illiterate or nearly illiterate soldier had been with the Army for many years. In the days of the Militia and of the conscript Army which followed it the extent of the illiteracy to be coped with shocked the Army. The Home Commands organised an experimental scheme to deal with this problem. In the winter of 1943 and in the following spring five Basic Education Centres running six-week courses for twenty men at a time were set up. After the war these were replaced by six Preliminary Education Centres which ran six courses, each attended by sixty soldiers. There was further rationalisation in 1956 when these were amalgamated to form a centralised School of Preliminary Education, first established at Everleigh near Tidworth and finally at Basil Hill Barracks, Corsham. Courses which had at first lasted twelve weeks were reduced to ten. Soldiers were admitted every fortnight in batches of sixty and up to 360 were admitted at any one time. As the post-National Service Regular Army took shape there were fewer recruits needing the School of Preliminary Education. In 1968 the Army Board agreed to the continuance of the School until March 1973, it taking until then 500 students annually. HMIs reported in

November 1971 on the excellent work it was doing. They strongly urged its continuance and recommended its permanent establishment. In April 1974 the Executive Committee of the Army Board agreed to establish it and ordered all recruits recommended by the Recruit Selection Centres to attend the School of Preliminary Education to be sent there before beginning their regular military training. The School of Preliminary Education was expanded to take 800 recruits each year, a number reduced in 1979 to the 500 pre-expansion level. The School did not have a smooth ride. Many in the Army, including as we have seen a Director of Army Education, thought the Army should not accept illiterate recruits. Many, once recruits came to them at the end of their School course, were reluctant to accept them. They would have liked recruits to have completed their cap-badge indoctrination before being got at by the RAEC. The flow of recruits from the Selection Centres was very unpredictable; when recruiting figures were up the School intake was down and vice versa. In the depression of the late 1970s recruiting difficulties eased and in 1982 the School was closed. During the years 1982–1989 there was no centralised provision of preliminary education in the Army. Sometimes if a knowledgeable RAEC officer was in charge of an Army Education Centre or if a Burnham Lecturer whose concern was illiteracy was available, preliminary education could be provided there. The inability to satisfy needs, however, is not a sovereign specific against their expression and as in the late 1980s the Army again experienced recruiting and retention problems soldiers of poorer quality had to be recruited and the Marilyn Study was set up to see how the problem of recruit shortage could best be tackled. It recommended that a Primary Education Course be put together under the auspices of the Director of Army Recruiting for recruits who failed the Army Entrance Test. They would be given ten weeks of concentrated preliminary education to enable them to pass it. The RAEC provided two instructors. Once again, preliminary instruction proved its worth.

It was to have to do so again when the extent of its recruiting problem shocked the Army into what was hoped would be a temporary re-opening of the School in 1990, this time at Sutton Coldfield. It remains to be seen if the reduction in the size of the Army consequent on the unexpected developments that occurred in the USSR and the Arms Control Agreements which followed will at last relieve the RAEC of this particular task. It is worth noticing that one of its officers who was very familiar with it thought not. He believed that it might not be the case that in a few years the Army could find sufficient recruits from those adequately literate. It seemed to him 'there is a marginal group of up to 10% of youngsters who will continue to be failures in literacy skills in school life'. These could be 'saved from permanent failure by preliminary educational techniques applied in their late adolescence as a result of their being admitted into the new society of the Army – which may still need to accept such recruits.[34] But whether the problem will be removed or not, there can be no doubt that as long as it existed and was tackled so well by the RAEC its expertise was much appreciated by the Army and added to its status in it. It also added to the RAEC's status outside the Army. Its pioneering work had been done long before the civilian Adult Literacy drive began. Open days at Corsham were well attended by representatives of LEAs and voluntary bodies, and became very much a one-day in-service training course for those concerned. The diagnostic techniques, remedial methods and adult material used were much admired.

Gradually throughout the 1960s the RAEC became more and more entrusted with the education of officers, for the greater part of their preparation for the promotion examination which Captains required to reach field rank and for the examination which all seeking to go to the Staff College had to pass. It had been easy to think poorly of the Class III and even of the Class II Certificates of Army Education, although the higher grades might have been beyond the reach of a number of subalterns and some of them might have made heavy weather of the lower grades too. The standard demanded for the education of the officer was another matter. If some 50% of them failed to reach the standard for which they were hoping, it could not be maintained that that standard was not worth reaching. And when aspiring staff candidates welcomed RAEC help it could not be held that that help was not worth having.

When education had seemed to other armies an obvious way of improving them they had turned their attention first to their officers; education in the British Army made its first big impact on the other ranks. There was an odd inversion here when, even more belatedly than in armies, education began to seem desirable for European colonies in Africa. In British colonies, a beginning was made in secondary and higher education in the belief that the elite leaders produced by that education would eventually educate the led, whereas in Belgian colonies a beginning was made with primary education in the conviction that over the years the élite leaders would come up from a broad educational base. Yet the British Army's neglect of the education of its officers had never been absolute and early developments in the 18th and 19th Centuries suggested that it might not have been so marked. An informal elementary school run for officers and other ranks of the Artillery was opened in 1721 and in 1741 a Royal Warrant created an academy at Woolwich to teach cadet officers. In 1764 the Marquis of Granby, Master General of the Ordnance, made of the Woolwich Royal Academy the Royal Military Academy, at which mathematics, classics, French, the art and science of war and fencing were taught. Le Marchant, a Channel Islander of French Huguenot descent, was urging in the closing years of the 18th Century that a school for the education of British officers be set up; joined by General François Jarry, a French émigré general, he set up a Staff Training Establishment at High Wycombe. In 1801 the Government bought an estate to house a Royal Military College which was founded by Royal Warrant in the June of that year. In March of the following year a further Royal Warrant created the Royal Military Cadet College, soon to be called the junior department of the Royal Military College. A Staff Training College for officers in their early twenties, with perhaps two years' regimental service, was also set up; it was not, however, until 1821 that it joined the junior department at Sandhurst, where the Royal Military College had been opened in 1812. It was from this Staff Training College that all but one of Wellington's staff officers in the Peninsula came. It is worth noticing, too, that in 1810 the East India Company, advised by Le Marchant, opened its own officer training establishment at Addiscombe. Officer education was very much in the air at this time and no doubt the continued presence of Napoleon would have ensured its future.

But the sands were running out for him and for officer education too. Years of peace and prosperity were not conducive to military preparedness and Army life as it developed in the 19th and early 20th Century was not conducive to officer education. Few officers would have agreed with Fuller who wrote in 1924 'Whatever confronts us let us criticise it, for criticism is the soul of science, and science is true knowledge. We must learn how to think, not only what to think.'[35] Wavell drew attention to an obvious consequence of the neglect of the education of the officer. 'There is one quality above all which seems to me essential for a good leader', he said, 'the ability to express himself clearly, confidently and concisely in speech and on paper; to have the power to translate his intentions into orders and instructions which are not merely intelligible but unmistakeable, and yet easy enough to waste no time. My experience of getting on for fifty years' service has shown me that it is a rare quality amongst Army officers, to which not nearly enough attention is paid in their education. It is one which can be acquired but seldom is, because it is seldom taught.'[36] That most important lesson had not been learned because there were not many who recognised, as Wavell did, the necessity of teaching it and because in consequence the opportunity of doing so had been denied to those who were able, and would have been delighted, to teach it. The AEC had done so in the 1920s. There were eight instructor officers and a Chief Education Officer teaching at Sandhurst and three teaching at the Royal Military Academy at Woolwich, these, as we have seen, being removed to make way for civilians. The School of Education at Shorncliffe, as we have also seen, ran courses to help the regimental officers who had to teach for the Third Class Army Certificate of Education. The Geddes Axe cut these out, but since it could not cut away the need for them they had to be begun again. The entrance examination for the Staff College was in abeyance during the war. There were no written examinations for officers until 1950 when written and practical examinations for promotion to Captain and Major were reintroduced. There were questions on tactics, administration, military law, military history, current affairs and a special-to-arm paper. In 1952 the examination from Lieutenant to Captain was reintroduced. There were three papers to be taken, one in administration and morale, another in military law and a special-to-arm paper. In 1957 this was changed. The written paper was discontinued and was replaced by a practical test. The first Staff/Promotion examination, as it became known, was held in 1959. The RAEC sought its teaching in the knowledge that they were planning real provision for real need and that in so doing they were rendering a major service to the Army.

The many reviews of, and enquiries into, the Army that occurred in the 1960s and 1970s indicate the great uncertainty that was felt as to how best it should develop in the coming years. Two essential facts were, however, obvious. The first was that in many ways it would be a different Army from its predecessor in the between-war years. The second was that its officers would be very different from those of that Army, in their general background and upbringing, in the attitudes they brought into the Army, and in what would be expected of them when they became fully trained. It had been said of the officer of the old Army that if he only received half a day's pay that was because he gave, and was expected to give, no more than half a day's work.

However adequate or inadequate the remuneration of the new officer, he would no longer be such a gentleman of leisure. No one disagreed with the Howard-English Report of 1966 when it said 'Even today the junior officer often needs to exercise a considerable degree of independent and informed judgement and to possess a high level of technical expertise; while the demands made on his seniors find little parallel in any civil profession.' It followed that the Army would be well advised to attract a reasonable share of intelligent young men to the profession of arms and this it would probably be unable to do if, as the Melville Committee which gave this advice also noted, it did not provide them with adequate opportunities for further education.[37] It followed, too, to quote the Howard-English Report again, that 'to fit officers for so testing a career ... it is as necessary to extend their intellectual abilities as it is to strengthen their moral powers and their capacity for physical endurance'. Which was why in the 1960s and 1970s more thought was devoted than had ever been given to the education of the officer.

Perhaps the outstanding characteristic of that thinking is its volatility. In an astonishingly brief period of time, brief by any standard and extraordinarily so by that of a conservative Army which has often found the slow pace of change congenial to a conservative people undesirably fast, the Army swings from wanting at least as much education as that to be found in other armies to insisting upon considerably less. The most ambitious of all schemes of officer education, that which was prepared in the Howard-English Report of 1966, was accepted by it. That report noted that 'teachers and cadets were virtually unanimous in their opinion that academic activities fail to flourish in a military environment'. It said that what was offered at Sandhurst 'seemed in many ways to be only an extension of school'. 'In general', it said, 'there is no sense that the cadet "changes gear" on leaving school and coming to Sandhurst.' Sandhurst relied too much on the précis and on duplicated notes, a practice which did nothing to encourage original thinking or to develop the power of analysis. Much of its teaching was addressed to 'A' level requirements. The report doubted the necessity of this but said that if it was necessary it would be better to send the cadets to a cramming establishment. It added that if it were really necessary to provide coaching for university entry as Sandhurst did, the crammer again could be employed – a boost to the morale of the crammer by one of our most eminent historians which reflects the value he placed on the degree that might thus be finally achieved, rather than on the services which alone might provide the opportunity of it being awarded.

It was vitally important, the Report declared, that officers 'should receive a course of further education sufficient to stretch their minds fully and give them a thorough grounding in the principles of their profession'. The Services, indeed, could now send a number of their people to universities but they 'should never regard their allocation of university places as an excuse for failing to develop the best facilities for further education themselves that circumstances allow'. Cadets should spend an initial training year, in which some academic work in the form of tutorials should be included, at their Service Colleges. They should then have a period of some two years with the Fleet or with their appropriate units. In this period 'educational activities' should continue. Then there should be an academic year at a Joint Service Royal

Defence College or Academy. This was necessary if able men were to be attracted to the Services and it was essential in order to stretch minds and to develop their critical faculties. This academic year was to be seen 'as part of the initial and probationary period of preparation for the profession of arms'. It was to be understood that 'on his performance during this, no less than in the other phases of his training, the future career of the officer must largely depend'. This year of academic study was to lead eventually to a degree. There was to be an examination at the end of the year which would, when passed, lead to acquisition of the first part of the degree. Part II would be taken after a further two years, which would, when the length of the university year was taken into account, be eighteen months. The authors of the Report believed that at first only 20% of those taking Part I of this degree would be prepared to proceed at once to studying for Part II, but they hoped that those who were unable or unwilling to do so at once would return at a later stage of their careers to complete their degree. Three subjects would constitute the degree course. These would be applied science, weapons and technology; political and strategic studies; and economics and management. There would also be a school of languages where those deemed particularly important, as for instance German, could be studied. It was believed that arrangements could be made with the CNAA for the awarding of a degree. In this way a balance would be maintained between the officers of the various scientific Corps who would get a degree from Shrivenham and the non-scientific officers who would get the degree from the Royal Defence College.

This was to be located at Greenwich. The Directors of Education of all three Services supported this proposal. The Chief of the Defence Staff, Lord Elworthy, did not. He thought the new college would have no more than 300 undergraduates and that this would not be sufficient to make it viable. He believed that the degree to be awarded by it would be valueless in academic eyes but that the existence of the college would prevent officers reading other subjects at other universities and this he would greatly deplore.[38] The Howard-English proposals, however, were supported by Healey, one of the most powerful Secretaries of State for Defence. They got as far as being announced in Parliament. Syllabuses were drawn up for the proposed College and money and manpower ear-marked for it. In fact it proved impossible to provide either. Nor in the event could plans be sufficiently coordinated by the three Services, the RAF being unable to overcome the difficulties raised by what would be the inevitable interruption of its flying training.

This did not put paid to the notion that a way might be found for officers to take an in-service degree. Much of the kind of academic year recommended by the Howard-English Report was introduced at Sandhurst early in 1970. There were to be courses in modern languages, social studies, military technology, mathematics, science and war studies. It was hoped that the Diploma which was to be awarded at the end of the year would be regarded as the first part of an Arts degree. Long, and it seemed encouraging, negotiations with the University of Reading led nowhere and when the Universities of Surrey, Southampton and Nottingham were approached it was with no better result.

Still later, in 1975, another, and this time a royal, attempt was made to push forward the notion of an in-service degree. In July of that year His Royal Highness Prince Philip wondered why there was no military degree, the acquisition of which could be spread perhaps over ten years and completed by the taking of a staff course at Shrivenham. In later elaboration he wrote 'The senior officer is the only "professional" who is unable – let alone required – to take a professional degree course before he is qualified to practise.' The Service officer, the Prince said, should be able to take a degree course that would be as relevant to a professional Service career as the degrees taken by members of other professions were. This, he emphasised, would have two consequences. It would put the non-technical officer on the same level as the parson, the lawyer, the economist among others, each of whom can take a degree appropriate to his chosen profession. This would have an excellent effect on the officer too, enabling him to acquire a solid base in the academic understanding of his profession.[39]

The proposals of the Prince in this matter were no more successful than those put forward in the Howard-English Report. In his reply to the Prince in October 1975 the Adjutant-General, having dutifully said that he was in complete sympathy with what was proposed, went on to explain why he could not be. He had to speak for the needs of the 120,000 and more soldiers who required leadership as well as skills from their officers. The officer was indeed as much a professional as the doctor or the lawyer, but the Adjutant-General doubted if a degree was a suitable recognition of excellence in the profession of arms. The training of a doctor or of a lawyer was more academic and finite and easier to recognise by a degree-earning course than the training needed by a soldier, the skills of most officers being largely concerned with command and leadership which were subjects not suited to academic treatment or classroom examination. The time already devoted to education by the officer was giving rise to the fear that it was curtailing undesirably the regimental life of the young officer. More emphasis on qualification-scoring by young officers could unacceptably reduce the importance of leadership and the need to be close to the private soldier. The need to provide 'family' leadership was the fundamental difference between the profession of arms and the medical and legal professions, which was why he was loath to overemphasise the academic aspects of soldiering at the expense of the practical and personal aspects. The Adjutant-General doubted if such a degree as the Prince wanted would be highly regarded in the academic world and he feared that the introduction of the Army's own non-engineering degree would weaken its case for sending officers to read for normal degrees at universities. The Army would greatly regret an ending of this practice, which he thought would be bad for it, bad for the universities and bad for the country as a whole 'because the Army would be losing one more link with civil life, a link which a professional Army can ill-afford to lose'.[40] Adjutant-Generals came and went; these arguments remained.

A later Chief of the Defence Staff, of all Chiefs of the Defence Staff the warmest supporter of education in the Services, Marshal of the RAF Sir Neil Cameron, was also concerned to find a way if he could to make it possible for officers who so wished to take a degree while serving. He wanted, he said, to take a leaf out of an American book in this. But he was not thinking of officers taking an in-Service degree

Officers' Education

Lt Col Noel Williams lectures officers studying for the Staff/Promotion Examination at 3 Higher Education Centre, Hohne, Germany, 1963

Junior Soldiers' Education

An RAEC Sergeant with Junior Bandsmen of the Parachute Regiment, late 1950s

Preliminary Education

The School of Preliminary Education, Corsham. Shown is the Sandhurst Block which contained the School Headquarters, administration and student accommodation

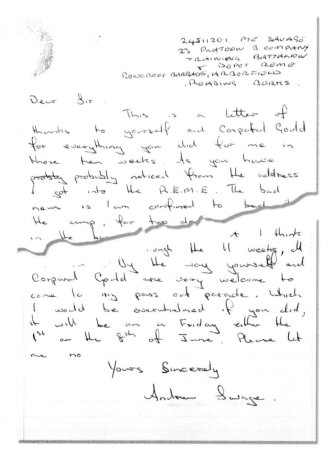

24511201 PTE SAVAGE
23 PLATOON 3 COMPANY
TRAINING BATTALION
& DEPOT REME
ROWCROFT BARRACKS, ARBORFIELD
. READING BERKS .

Dear Sir.

This is a letter of thanks to yourself and Corporal Gould for everything you did for me in those ten weeks. As you have probably noticed from the address I got into the R.E.M.E. The bad news is I am confined to bed in the camp, for two days .... I think .....ough the 11 weeks, All .... By the way yourself and Corporal Gould are very welcome to come to my pass out parade. Which I would be overwhelmed if you did, it will be on a Friday either the 1st or the 8th of June. Please let me no

Yours Sincerely

Andrew Savage.

A 'thank you' letter from a former student of the SPE

Resettlement

Resettlement Centre, Aldershot – Household
Maintenance Course in progress

Army College, Chiseldon – a post-WW2
Resettlement Course in Farmworking

A Final Resettlement Board in the 1950s

A Resettlement Course visit to a Police Training College in the late 1940s

HANC TABELLAM
CORPUS REGALE
EXERCITUS BRITANNICI EDUCATIONI PRAEPOSITUM
IDCIRCO DEDICAVIT
UT UNIVERSITATI GOTTINGENSI
PERENNEM REFERRET GRATIAM
QUOD INTRA ANNOS MCMXLV ET MCMXLIX P. C. N.
TOT MILITES BRITANNICI
COLLEGIO RHENANI EXERCITUS ASCRIPTI
DOCTRINAM CUM LUCE
IN HAC ANTIQUISSIMA STUDIORUM SEDE
HAUSERUNT

The plaque recording the Army College of the Rhine's occupation of Göttingen University, Germany, 1945-49

Troops Information

Commonwealth Division Production Team,
Crown News, South Korea 1950

A selection of news-sheets produced
during various campaigns since 1944

Library Service

34th Division Library, Frevent, February 1916
(Photograph courtesy of the Imperial War Museum, London (WW1 Q8535)

Languages

Lt Col Harry O'Hare (left in beret), the commander of the British contingent of the UN peace-keeping force in Angola, talks to port workers through his interpreter, 2Lt Graham Cable AGC(ETS) (right in beret) at Lobito Port, 1995

Photograph courtesy of Army Public Relations, Plnfo, HQ Land

Maj Alan Cardy interpreting for General Sir Peter de la Billière at the first Gulf War peace talks, March 1991

Some of the Language
Training pamphlets
produced by the Directorat
of Army Education

in a Service institution. He was hoping to make arrangements with universities to enable officers to take degrees on such terms as would be compatible with continued attention to their professional duties, and while he wanted still more the Cambridge M Phil degree in International Relations and War Studies, a one-year postgraduate degree for which officers who had not taken a degree but whose ability as judged by their professional careers indicated they could reach the required standard could be accepted, went some way towards satisfying him.[41] Nor was Prince Philip's proposal fruitless. Cambridge introduced new papers in its Historical Tripos and suitably altered others so that something of what its Chancellor had in mind could be provided. Two Defence Lecturers were appointed and their courses proved to be as attractive to undergraduates as to resident military officers, so that to some extent at least both His Royal Highness and his critics could feel that their views had proved fruitful.

There is a price to be paid for everything and the arguments brought against the Howard-English proposals and those of Prince Philip were weighty. So when these proposals were rejected all did not seem to be lost. There were genuine gains that could still be anticipated. Yet it would be naive to believe that the criticisms to be made of them were not considered by the authors of the proposals against which they were directed. The Prince and Michael Howard and his colleagues had weighed the pros and cons and had concluded that the pros were more weighty than the cons. Perhaps they were right. It could not be said that they were reflecting the old wisdom that a bird in the hand is worth two in the bush, since this particular bird was not yet in the hand. But they were embodying the old utilitarian conviction that the more immediate gain is to be preferred to the more remote. If they had got what they wanted, many more officers would have received much more education than in the event they did. Nothing came of these proposals but what came of their rejection? What followed was not a further development of officer education in other ways as had repeatedly been said would occur. What followed was a continued turning away from the education of the officer. Perhaps His Royal Highness and the others knew that this would happen. As it did it is to be regretted that nothing came of such imaginative and exciting proposals.

Had they been accepted the RAEC would undoubtedly have participated in the teaching involved. For what had been said in the Howard-English Report of Sandhurst teaching could have brought no comfort to the civilians teaching there. Later comments on them would not have added appreciably to their peace of mind. Sir Cyril English took the strongest exception to what they were making of the 'professional studies'. The Sandhurst syllabus, he said, was inappropriate and uncoordinated, and a root-and-branch review was necessary. Civilians, he believed, brought continuity to teaching, not being subject to frequent postings, but they also made it impossible to achieve major change.[42] This latter capability seemed indeed to be a characteristic of civilian teaching at Service Colleges. The Director of Army Training was of the opinion that the RAF had been able to effect radical changes at Cranwell only because the academic staff there were RAF officers.[43] Sandhurst's Academic Council had been firmly of the opinion that the civilians there were pulling up the standard of their RAEC colleagues; it was acidly suggested that they were in fact pulling it down.

The Director of Army Education said that while some civilian instruction there was good the teaching in War Studies was 'dreadful'.[44] The Vice Adjutant-General deplored the fact that graduate cadets at Sandhurst 'found no challenge in the academic standard of either the content or the instruction on "professional studies"'.[45]

Far, however, from restricting the participation of the RAEC in officer education, the failure of the Howard-English and similar schemes greatly increased it. Anticipating the difficulty of attracting a sufficient number of officer cadets, the Army intended to introduce a new short service commission to cope with the shortage. The Director of Army Training hoped that 50% of the officers needed would come from the ranks. They would have to receive further education before they could go to Sandhurst. It was only in 1970 that this was made public, but the RAEC was aware before this that what it had been doing for some of the Mons entry it would have to do for potential officers from the ranks as well. Foreseeing what was coming, the Corps was doing two most important things.

First, it began to prepare itself for its new duties. If it was to widen its responsibilities it would have to ensure that it would be able to do so and also to convince others of this as well. It had to be adequately qualified to do so and it had the foresight to arrange for some of its officers to take second degrees in the subjects they would be teaching. The Corps began to do this even before its role in officer education had been agreed to. The HMIs who had reported on the Educational Release Scheme had urged the Corps to do more teaching. It had been doing a great deal of teaching and it had many other jobs to do as well. Some of the officers of the pre-war Corps had been men of remarkable ease and leisure; there were few of these to be found among their successors. But batteries need recharging, or as Arnold of Rugby put it 'It is ill drinking out of a pond whose stock of water is merely the remains of the long-past rains of the winter and spring.' Those who wished, as he did, to make teaching educative rather than instructive would feel, as he did, 'great need of daily learning'.[46] At the very least the RAEC would greatly benefit, as the universities had long pointed out, if its officers were able to return to them from time to time to refresh themselves there. That had not hitherto proved possible. But for some forty of them it now did. This was the number eventually fully employed in teaching officers.

Secondly, and before any scheme of officer education had been officially agreed upon, the Corps embarked upon its own tentative initiatives in the field of officer education. Southern Command took the lead. Brigadier Frankcom, the Command Education Officer there, established close links initially with the University of Southampton and later with the University of Cambridge. In 1958 in South-Western District university tutors visited units to help Staff/Promotion candidates. This led to the setting up of a pilot scheme to provide education for junior officers. They were to write a series of monthly essays and to attend tutorials. The essays would be corrected and the tutorials taken by the university tutors who were visiting the Staff/Promotion candidates and who would stay on to look after the junior officers. A variation of this pilot scheme was tried out in Aldershot District. This was on a large scale and it involved the use not only of RAEC tutors but also of four full-time lecturers of the Extra-Mural Department of Southampton University and of a panel of part-time specialists. All junior officers in the District were to attend fortnightly discussions lasting 1½ hours. These discussions were to be held in groups of not more than twenty officers. Each group would be the responsibility of a single lecturer who would thus soon get to know the officers, as they would soon get to know him. These discussion periods were to be repeated weekly to ensure the maximum attendance by junior officers. They were to continue throughout the year, with breaks at Christmas, Easter and in August. Throughout Southern Command these ventures aimed to teach junior officers current affairs and military history, and in so doing to practice them in the art of expressing themselves clearly in speech and on paper. In addition to this, potential Staff/Promotion candidates in these groups were to attend short residential courses in current affairs. Candidates for the Staff College attended weekly tutorials in current affairs and military history and they were expected to attend two four-day courses during the year as well. Ambitious as this was, Southern Command hoped to do still more. It contemplated developing more such courses and more courses of a similar nature but at a much more advanced level for Senior Officers. It also had in mind setting up courses to train in map-reading those who would then instruct the junior officer in that subject too.[47]

This was an excellent example of ad hocery and inspired initiative. There was no formal agreement concerning it between the Director of Army Training and the Director of Army Education. But it was so impressive that it was bound to be seen as a precedent, as something that should become formalised and extended to other Commands. Here in embryo was what became known as the Junior Officers' Educational Scheme which would bridge the gap between the leaving of Sandhurst by the officer and the beginning of his preparation for the Staff/Promotion examination.

These seminal developments of the years 1958 and 1959 strongly attracted the attention of Sir Richard Goodbody, the Adjutant-General. In July 1962 he issued an important directive which commented on the inability of junior officers to express themselves clearly in writing and on the generally inadequate standard of education of many officers. He called for something along the lines of the developments that had taken place in Southern Command. This was the official beginning of what became widely referred to as the JOE Scheme. It was not compulsory, at least not until 1974 when, theoretically at least, it became so. But senior officers were urged to give it their full backing and they did so. 'The gratifying thing', it was said, 'is that the response from Commanding Officers is so good.' The holding either of one-day or of residential courses was strongly recommended, as was the maximum use of university tutors to help the RAEC, it being understood that abroad the RAEC would be primarily responsible for JOE teaching. In 1963 the number of full-time university tutors engaged on work for the Services was increased by two and Command Education Officers were given extra funds to find further tutorial assistance, should that be necessary. The Director of Army Training stressed how much he would like to see JOE based on 'a tutor system whereby the student always dealt with the same instructor'. It was the great virtue of JOE that every effort was made to ensure that this should be done. To brace, discipline and fructify minds together over time is the best of all ways of learning; it is the cream of Oxbridge teaching and the tribute paid to JOE in Eastern

District – 'this follows the pattern of most of the best work that has been done for the Services at Cambridge' – typifies what was aimed at, and in great part achieved, by those who taught JOE throughout the Commands. Having one's own tutor was important. The tutor likes to get to know the whimsicalities of his pupil and the pupil the oddities of his tutor, an understanding that, like our tots, takes time to mature. This was understood and appreciated by the officers. The officer who later went on to command the Household Cavalry, and whose irritation at being deprived of his supervisor because his supervisor was required to watchkeep led him to write to the General Officer Commanding complaining of such misemployment, spoke for many who would have hesitated to express themselves so belligerently.

It was noticeable how much like undergraduate teaching JOE teaching turned out to be. It was obviously at a lower level; reading was much less extensive and was less critical; the high-flyers were less in evidence. But the subaltern had a maturity and an experience which bred it which the undergraduate lacked. The subaltern was more sure of himself on his feet than on paper, the undergraduate more at home with paper and less sure of himself on his feet. But for the rest they were remarkably alike. Both shared the misplaced hope that as tutors could not be expected to be familiar with the books they recommended, the eccentricity of the opinions supposedly derived from them would pass unnoticed. They both suffered from the same delusion that excuses which were wearing thin before the Flood would be accepted at face value. There were occasional differences but these were not important. For instance, the auditing of silver seems to have taken up a disproportionate amount of the subaltern's time and colleges had omitted to give undergraduates that particular justification for inadequate preparation of their work. Both subaltern and undergraduate were erroneously convinced that tutorial courtesy would prevent enthusiastic agreement with the time-honoured opening 'I'm afraid this isn't a very good essay'. Both, no doubt to their considerable surprise, were sufficiently susceptible to the sense of shame which prompted them to do what they could to make their subsequent work a little less to be apologised for than their previous efforts. Both, in short, were pupils who needed teaching and who were pleasant and rewarding to teach. In both, too, was the same leaving to the last minute the preparation of their essays in happy oblivion of the fact that as this had been the practice of the tutors themselves in the days of their youth; the signs that this was still being done could not fail to be recognised.

One further point is worth noticing in this developing JOE Scheme. For the most part it was through a study of current affairs that the junior officers were being taught to sort out their ideas, to develop their analytical skills, to express themselves clearly and cogently on paper. The difference between the reception by Commanding Officers of this scheme and of the various schemes so far put forward to teach current affairs is instructive. Then they were unconvinced of the value of such schemes and they disapproved of them. Now they were convinced and they did not. In both cases they saw the effect of the teaching; what they had seen they did not like; what they saw now they did. The difference here was not in the nature of the audience but in the nature of the teaching. There are no absolutes and no certainties in teaching, and a knowledgeable and experienced teacher would never claim to be always a successful one. But to know neither what one is professing nor how to teach it can usually be relied upon to produce boredom and failure. That happened when the teachers were untrained and unlettered in the subject they had to teach; now skilled and well-instructed teachers were available.

Nor was the scientific education of the young officer neglected. In the 1960s a paper on Military Science was included in the examination for the Staff College. It was later withdrawn because it seemed to give an unfair advantage to candidates from the technical Arms and was replaced by the Shrivenham phase of the pre-Camberley staff training.

It was not long before an excellent scheme of officer education began to emerge. It was divided into three parts which corresponded to the three distinct periods of an officer's career. Between the ages of 21–28 when he was mastering the basic skills of his profession his studies would be spread over five months of the year. In these his attention would be directed to current affairs and to military history and, if he felt so inclined, to the acquisition of a language. To help him he would be given an individual tutor, university or RAEC, who would direct his reading and require from him an essay to be gone over at his next tutorial.

Between the ages of 28–31 when he was already a master of his craft and as such pulling his weight in his profession, he would be expected to be turning his mind to higher things. He would, it was hoped, be working at those academic subjects in which he would have to satisfy the examiner before he could go to Staff College. It was also hoped that his preparation to do so would be spread evenly over this whole period, even though human nature and the nature of military life made it unlikely that it would be. Every effort was made to encourage him, in this matter of preparation, to resist the dictates of military life and to withstand the still more imperious dictates of human nature, for as a CAROT paper said, 'tutors are emphatic that the degree of improvement necessary for most candidates to achieve a satisfactory standard can only be achieved by a course of work extending over the major part of a year'.[48] Every encouragement was given to officers to attend residential courses lasting five days and extended throughout the year. International affairs and war studies became, after various changes, the academic subjects in which Staff/Promotion candidates had to satisfy the examiners. Since the qualities sought for in a potential Staff Officer were other than those deemed sufficient to justify promotion, there was an obvious case for having separate examinations for those who would content themselves with the one and for the high-flyers who would only be satisfied with the other. But as we have seen there were good reasons why it did not prevail.

The year's course of study for the aspiring staff officer was carefully prepared and well thought-out. The syllabus was divided into four phases. To deal with each phase five-day residential courses were arranged. They were held in universities and in Army accommodation. The RAEC Officer-Tutors and university lecturers were the instructors on these courses, a feature of which was the inclusion of what Cambridge calls the supervision and Oxford the tutorial. Individual officers brought essays to supervisors who dealt with them as the occasion demanded. This individual supervision was looked upon as perhaps the most important feature of the year's study and it demonstrated the attention that was being paid to directing the officer's mind to analysing problems, to accustoming him to taking things to bits and to putting them together again, to making it second nature for him not to move until he was certain of his objective and certain that his objective was what it ought to be, to compelling him to think for himself, to think clearly and to make his thinking as clear to others as it was to himself. There will always be those who need no instruction in these things, as there will be others who are unable to profit from it. Most of us are in neither category. There were many who needed and who benefitted from the year's prescribed study. It is to be doubted if officers will benefit from its absence.

Each course handled the particular phase of the syllabus with which it was dealing in its own way but it was always understood that Service movement might make it necessary for an officer to take Course A in one university and Courses B, C and D in other universities or Commands and not suffer thereby. He would thus cover the syllabus, he would perforce be made to work over an extended period and since universities are more concerned to induce thought than to impart knowledge, he would be induced to think for himself. An Officer Education Branch (OEB) was established at Eltham Place and its members, accompanied by university lecturers when numbers to be taught warranted it, ran courses at home and overseas. Its tutors were much travelled men. One tutor's itinerary took him in the space of three weeks from the foothills of the Canadian Rockies to the Green Line in Nicosia and thence to Berlin, another from Cyprus to Sharjah and on to Hong Kong.

The University was the ideal setting for the holding of these courses. Its atmosphere encouraged the officer to work as it did not always prompt the undergraduate to do too. Conditions were not always so conducive to application. In the Hong Kong classrooms there was a stark choice: the air-conditioning could be kept on and if it was no one could be heard, or it could be turned off in which case there would be fried officers and boiled officers' tutor for lunch. Nowhere, however, were conditions more trying than in Northern Ireland. Here we are told that 'the well-supported courses upstairs in 32 AEC Lisburn ... seemed filled by very unmilitary hirsute figures who would slink in and then exhausted discreetly fall asleep at the back of the class'. Courses were always held in Lisburn but the resident tutor had to travel throughout the province either by helicopter, by Army transport (the civilianised Army minis) or by private car. One tutor used a bright blue left-hand drive 2CV van carrying a ladder on its roof and emblazoned on its sides 'PQS II Enterprises'.[49] It was remarkable how in successive years such good results were achieved in Northern Ireland. In all of this one thing was very obvious. The old stand-by of the officer in time of trouble, that ingenious gentleman the crammer, was of no use to him now. For the officer was not now required to mug-up a campaign and to memorise the required factors – which is not to be taken as implying that the art and the practice of the military historian is limited to that. The officer was to show that he was capable of thinking for himself; he was required to develop the arts of analysis, to construct and to plan and to write clearly, cogently, concisely and to the point. He was to shun irrelevance and to see in the spot question and the prepared answer the path to perdition. The beneficent rays of the crammer had ceased and he was returned to that outer darkness from which he ought never to have emerged. His place was taken by the teacher whose qualifications were not to be doubted and who was fully committed to the genuine development of his pupils.

To do what the teacher had to do was not the easiest of tasks. He had to induce the officer to see his objective clearly and to make a plan which would enable him to reach it, to sort out the essentials from the mass of available details and not to allow himself to be submerged by the latter. The teacher longed to see at the end of the year a sharp mind dissecting a problem and stating it in terms which made it easy to understand and in language which it was a pleasure to read. Yet every Oxbridge tutor has learned that primeval chaos would be orderly in comparison with some of the undergraduate essays that come his way and officers' essays have not been unknown to be of the same kind. Some officers, too, and not a few, have found great difficulty in resisting the tyranny of the pen which has committed them to many enormities. They tell us that 'our butterfly hopes have no concrete in them'. They say that 'the mess of potage as formulated by the United Nations has given rise to undue hardship and fear'. They inform us that 'prestige the ethos of which is the psychosis of territorial aggrandisement is a highly effective toxin'. After reading that 'the states of the Third World have now been the means where the failure of political diplomacy has broken down the solution of limited war', that 'the action in Hungary and Poland was ideological but not at the involvement of western democracies', that 'the Soviets basically have the problem of the third corner of the three-sided hat', that 'the hubble-bubble of the internal Chinese cauldron has simmered down to its proletarian bottom', a Brigadier marking the papers said that a senior officer must always be among the markers so that he could be aware of what horrendities the younger officer is capable. He was not entirely to blame. One of his recommended books told him 'there is a significant difference between the psychological environment of the decision-maker and his operational environment' and that Governments at times 'suffer from the phenomenon of cognitive dissonance'. The unfortunate officer was meant to understand by this that Governments sometimes misunderstand the situation confronting them and that they sometimes refuse to believe, because they do not like, what they are told. It was a comparatively sensible English book which thus sought to enlighten him. Unfortunately, the syllabus in its early days was too much influenced by the Californian teaching of what came to be known as the Theory of International Relations. A sustained denial that statesmanship was an art, it added incomprehensibility to misunderstanding and called the result a science. There have been more difficult tasks than to persuade officers that the dustbin was the proper receptacle for such learning. They heartily agreed with Carlyle that 'abstract ideas, however they may put on fleshly garments, are a class of character whom we cannot sympathise with or delight in'. Every teacher worth his salt knows he is always taught by the taught and as the months went by the syllabus shook itself free of unnecessary top-hamper and Whitehead's golden rule for teacher and taught, 'seek simplicity and distrust it', began to be fully appreciated. By the time it was decided to move to other and lower things it is not absurd to claim that Staff/Promotion candidates were perhaps to their surprise, genuinely enjoying their year's study. They were unlikely to have done so had they not been convinced that it was also worthwhile.

From the age of thirty-four onwards when the high-flyers were beginning to think of stretching their wings, officers were encouraged to go on courses in world affairs run by the various universities. Norman Gibbs, Chichele Professor of Military History in the University of Oxford, conceived the idea of putting the resources of Oxford and Cambridge together to attract to the joint course they would hold very high-ranking officers. The first course was held in Oxford at the end of a Michaelmas Term; it reassembled in Cambridge at the end of the following Lent Term. This combined course ran for two years. A difference of approach led to Oxford and Cambridge going their separate ways but Professor Gibbs achieved his objective. Courses for senior officers are still run at the older universities, as are various discussion groups for senior officers. Such courses, discussion groups and dining clubs are common in many universities today. The universities and the Services have had their differences but neither are in any doubt about the very considerable mutual gain resulting from the intimacy that now characterises their relations. In these university courses and discussions senior officers tended to concentrate on International Affairs. But the scientific education of those who had every hope of advancement was not neglected, for all officers selected for Staff Training attended the General Staff Science Course at Shrivenham which lasted ten weeks before going on to Camberley.

In a splendid passage in *The Holy Roman Empire* Bryce underlines the significance of the crowning by the Pope of the Emperor Charles the Great on Christmas Day 800. 'The coronation of Charles is not only the central event of the Middle Ages, it is also one of those very few events of which taking them singly, it may be said that if they had not happened, the history of the world would have been different. In one sense indeed it has scarcely a parallel. The assassins of Julius Ceasar thought that they had saved Rome from monarchy, but monarchy became inevitable in the next generation. The conversion of Constantine changed the face of the world, but Christianity was spreading fast, and its ultimate triumph was only a question of time. Had Columbus never spread his sails, the secret of the western sea would yet have been pierced by some later voyager, had Charles V broken his safe-conduct to Luther, the voice silenced at Wittenberg would have been taken up by echoes elsewhere. But if the Roman Empire had not been restored in the West in the person of Charles, it would never have been restored at all, and the endless train of consequences for good and for evil that followed could not have been.'[50] Never since has the idea of the unity of Europe, or Christendom as it was long thought of, disappeared from European thinking. At its lowest level it is to be seen in the great interest which European states have always taken in the doings of their neighbours. If one finds something that will strengthen it, others will not be long in following suit, as we see when War Offices ceased to be and Ministries of Defence took their place. So that when the British Army began to think seriously about the education of its officers it wanted to know how other armies educated theirs.

It looked at the Soviet Army and found that the education of the Soviet officer was 'perhaps the most intensive as well as the most extensive the world has ever seen'. Many officers trained as teenagers in the special or 'Suvorov' military schools. In addition to these there were 140 military colleges in the USSR open by competition to the 16–21 age-groups. Until 1958 these offered a three-year programme of study, later increased to four and five years, at the end of which those successfully completing the course obtained an 'All-Union Diploma', which was the equivalent of a degree. 60% of the curriculum of these schools was devoted to the study of specialised military subjects, tactics and weapons, discipline, army regulations and physical training, 30% to standard academic studies and 10% to political studies.

It was found that there was great competition among Soviet officers for entry to the Staff College. Prospective candidates for it were advised 'to prepare for 2–3,000 hours before the examination'. Assuming that serious preparation would involve an officer devoting three hours per day to study, it would take him two to three years before he felt ready to sit the examination. He would have the opportunity to do this on three occasions. Besides this preparation the officer would also be required to attend classes in political instruction. If admitted to Staff College he would be there for three years if he were on the command course and for five years if he were on the technical course. In each case half the curriculum was devoted to military preparation, the other half to general culture. Attendance at the Voroshilov General Staff Academy was the last step in the officer's education. It was the only Joint Services School in the USSR and it was here that officers were trained for the highest command and staff positions. The course lasted two years and was only open to Staff College graduates. In this academy the continuing academic studies were of PhD standard. Altogether it was an astonishingly long education to which the Soviet officer was exposed, extraordinary even when it is remembered that in the USSR 'the idea of a military career is pursued almost exclusively by the officer corps; that NCOs there are barely more experienced than privates and that, like them, few remain in the army after the obligatory two-year service'.[51]

The British also looked at the education of the American officer and found that the US Army retained all its regular officer candidates at their Academy for four years, after which they received a degree in science and their commissions. It also found that 60% of these regular officers go on to take a Master's degree while serving. It considered the education of the officer in the German Army in which fifteen months' professional training before commissioning was followed by three year's education either for a Science Degree or for a Technical Diploma. A further nine months' specialised training at an officers' school meant that the German officer spent five years in training. There was an annual intake of 400 officers in the German Army and only a small minority of them would take the Technical Diploma and not the degree. Of course it must be remembered that the German Army is a National Service Army and that the young German regular officer is much more likely to be caught up in training National Servicemen than in gaining real regimental duty experience in commanding a platoon in an active unit, as in the British Army. In recent years a simpler and shorter pattern of education for the German officer has emerged. After a year's course in which military training predominates he attends a special Bundeswehr University Course for three years.

The Army of the United Kingdom saw how the French arranged these matters too. The French demanded a very high educational standard on entry for their regular officer candidates (this was the Baccalaureate together with the passing of a competitive examination which was of second year university standard). Successful candidates then passed two years at the St Cyr Academy, at which the course was half educational and half military. No degree was conferred at the end of this course although the level finally reached was probably of degree standard. There was the further opportunity, too, for some 25% of French officers to obtain degrees while serving.[52]

Great peoples borrow but they do not copy. They graft and thus adjust to new conditions. What suited others would not, the British said, suit them. They thought that 'the US Army concept of actively encouraging a second or alternative career qualification is perhaps worthy of study in a forecast era of an increased requirement for career satisfactions'. But though they also agreed that 'the greater the length of time spent on educating a young officer on entry the more satisfying it is in the long run for the officer, and perhaps more economical', they were also sure that 'it is detrimental to the time he is available for desirable regimental duty as a junior officer'. This was the consideration which the British Army was sure must prevail. The ways of others would not suit them and they believed they had found their own way which would.[53] Certainly it seems a reasonable assumption that few officers would have presented themselves at the examination for the British Staff College had they been expected to prepare for it for as long as their Soviet counterparts were advised to prepare for theirs. What was developed in JOE and in the arrangements made to help officers prepare for the Staff/Promotion examination, what was later to be known as the Progressive Qualification Schemes I and II, were designed to meet a felt need. They were an acceptable alternative to what had been prepared in the Howard-English Report. The claim that they had worked well was amply justified. They were very promising indeed.

Above all they taught officers to think. Officers' Tutors were amused at the fact that they were looked at askance for insisting there were no Directing Staff answers to the problems they discussed. As one of them, Major R. Marston, wrote in *Torch* in Summer 1982 PQS II 'is totally different from all other Army courses and examinations ... it is an educational experience whilst most other instruction is "training" ... PQS II is about questions and uncertainties whereas most training deals in answers and the definite'. Those teaching officers were faithful to Lord Acton's dictum on which they had been brought up as undergraduates, that you must make a case for your opponent better than he could make it himself; they made as compelling a case as they could for the view they believed to be wrong and then indicated why they thought it so. Officers had genuine difficulty in understanding that one of the teacher's greatest pleasures comes when his pupil disagrees with his view and produces clear cogent, well thought-out reasons for so doing.

PQS was the high point of the Corps' involvement in officer education. Officer education had originally been provided at Sandhurst and Camberley. After the Second World War Camberley became much less educational in any general liberal sense and Sandhurst, which had been a Sixth Form College which also concerned itself with military training, began to provide an ever shorter, more practical course with little general education as the recruitment of cadets with High School Certificates and 'A' levels, and of graduates, seemed to make this possible. The inability of many junior officers to write English disturbed Commanding Officers and in the mid-1970s the Committee on Army Regular Officers Training (CAROT) was set up. The Director of Army Training and the Director of Army Education wrote the papers for it and produced the excellent Progressive Qualifications Scheme.

Although the recommendations of the Howard English Report were not accepted by the War Office, some of its comments had an inevitable impact on the pattern and practices of officers' education. The Sandhurst academic syllabuses were remodelled and its Military History Department was retitled War Studies. During the inter-war years the academic input by Corps officers at Sandhurst had been considerable, led for much of the time by the distinguished Lieutenant-Colonel A.C.T. White VC. It had ceased during the war and immediate post-war years and resumed in 1949 with the staffing by five Corps officers of Mons and later Anzio Company which had provided a remedial education course for cadets who had not passed the necessary entrance examination. In early 1960 Anzio Company moved to Beaconsfield to become the Sandhurst Wing there. For almost a decade there were no RAEC at all on the academic staff at the RMA. In 1969 two officers returned as lecturers in the War Studies Department where they became particularly involved with the contemporary strategic studies teaching programme. Corps officers were to remain on the academic staff at the Academy in the War or Modern Studies Departments until pressures on the military manpower establishment sadly forced their removal a couple of decades later.

The education of officers in the field commands under the various junior officer and Staff/Promotion schemes which developed in the wake of the Howard-English Report was not the only area of officers' education to which the RAEC was to make a distinctive contribution throughout this period. From 1969 onwards a small team of Corps officers was teaching on the first and some on the second degree courses at the Royal Military College of Science (RMCS) at Shrivenham, where junior officers took science and engineering degrees in preparation for their careers in the technical arms and services. These degrees were awarded initially by London University, later by CNAA and finally, after Government pressure on the Ministry of Defence had resulted in a decision to 'contract out' this educational function, by Cranfield University. Under these changing regimes the Economics, Politics and Social Studies (EP&SS) Branch, which the Corps staffed, had the responsibility of teaching the 'liberal studies' element of the degrees. These courses lasted for two of the three years of the degree course and met the requirement of the Engineering Council for the development of students' written communication skills and the study of the strategic, managerial and economic background to their profession, besides fulfilling the JOE obligation during students' time at Shrivenham. Liberal studies were not a soft option; the courses were all examined and had to be passed. The standards the students attained in them were reflected in the class of their final degrees. In general engineers are not noted for the high quality of their writing skills and the work which the students undertook as part of the liberal studies programme sought to remedy this deficiency.

When the University of Cranfield took over, the Corps' lecturers, who sat on the course and examination boards for the degree courses, formed an important 'organic' element in the monitoring of the contractor's performance in this novel experiment of including a high-level educational process in the Government's policy of hiving off specific functions from its in-house activities and having them delivered by civilian bodies. Freed from the financial and manpower ceilings which had constrained the previous civil service regime, Cranfield was able to expand the range of first and especially second degrees which it offered to its Service clients and to society at large. The College expanded still further when the RAF began sending its in-service engineering degree students to Shrivenham. Soon the EP&SS Group officers were helping to design courses for the School of Defence Management, teaching on new second degree courses as well as continuing their undergraduate work, and educating the light blue and the occasional aberrant dark blue, as well as the traditional khaki. Postings to the staff at Shrivenham were technically subject to vetting by the College's Principal and were very different from mainstream Corps appointments. One ceremonial link with the Corps was retained however: the academic staff processed to the degree ceremonies to the strains of the Corps' quick march *Guadeamus Igitur*, played unusually as a slow march!

Postings to both RMCS and RMAS were a boon for the Corps' officers' education specialists who greatly appreciated the opportunity to deepen their knowledge of their specialist subject, rub shoulders with academics who had the good fortune to teach there permanently and, above all, to assist in the education of a substantial element of the Army's officer corps. They returned to the general work of the Corps enriched by their experience and with a much enlarged acquaintance with the Army's young officers.

One of the most striking of the new developments which became so important for the Corps later began to take shape at this time. It was to become known as Training Support. Training Support is the advice, guidance and assistance given to the Army in its training. Its purpose is to teach the trainers so that they can most profitably conduct the training, to ensure that it is done in the most effective way, completed as quickly as possible, attended to as economically as may be. It embodies the belief that the bark of the NCO is of greater value on the parade ground than in ensuring the mastery of weapons. 'Cleverness' in the 17th Century was a term usually denoting adroitness in the use of one's hands and cleverness in this sense is expected from soldiers. The clumsy soldier would never have been an outstanding archer or a reliable pikeman, and when faults develop in more sophisticated weapons and have to be corrected quickly while battle rages, cleverness with one's hands is indispensable. Practice is inseparable from performance, but the nature of the performance will depend on the nature of the practice and Training Support seeks to produce the best performance by applying the best thought to the discovering of the best practice.[54]

There is an old Yorkshire jingle which runs:

> You live half your life with deception and art
> With art and deception you live t'other part.

It springs to mind when, as frequently happens, we are puzzled by the rapidly changing name of things. We encounter this difficulty when contemplating Training Support. It changes its name with lightning rapidity, the whys and wherefores being more apparent to those who introduce the changes and possibly to the soldiers who benefit from them, than to others less fortunately placed.

In 'Programmed Learning' and in 'Audio-Visual Aids' we heard the first blasts of the trumpet. We were then introduced to 'Educational Technology'. Perhaps it was thought this referred only to the technology that was applied to education and that it was not greatly concerned with instruction; it could hardly have been imagined that education lacked that concern. At all events the term 'Educational Technology' was dropped and replaced by 'Instructional Technology' which had a life span of thirteen years before yielding in its turn to the currently-used expression 'Training Support'. What tomorrow's technology will confront us with we will no doubt learn tomorrow.

However we describe it, it is as well that we should note the universality of Training Support. Armed Services all over believed it to be advantageous to them. We might not think highly of the Joneses and be sure that only the inferior Smiths would feel the need of keeping up with them. But if the Joneses are experiencing a benefit which could be ours and is not we pay them attention. Our interest in training research was quickened by the attention others were paying to it. When NATO allies, to say nothing of the Royal Navy and the Royal Air Force, were developing their training research units it was improbable that the Army would be indifferent to so doing. Except for the RAF's work on simulation, the Army was not, however, behind the other Services in the Training Support field.

Knowledge that others are enjoying something we ourselves have not missed because we have never thought about it might make us aware of a need we had not ourselves felt. This was not the case in the matter of Training Support; we were, on the contrary, becoming painfully alive to its necessity. With the ending of National Service the Army lost a large reservoir of manpower. That was a loss in quality as well as in quantity. At that time, too, new equipment was becoming more complex and more difficult to use. And while this was happening the state felt compelled to curtail its expenditure on the Army. Training had now to be better because those to be trained were less receptive to training than the conscript had shown himself to be, because more was now demanded from the less receptive than had been of their higher-quality predecessors, above all because a way had to be found of reducing the large sums of money already spent on it; the Army's United Kingdom Training Organisation employed, for instance, more than 28,000 soldiers and civilians. In a world in which military technology was racing ahead, in which the soldier had to learn how to handle new, complex and costly equipment, in which the imperative need of economy gave a fresh and clamorous insistence to the arts of costing, of auditing, of management accounting, of ensuring cost effectiveness, everything had to be done to maintain operational efficiency and to prevent the rise in costs which faulty handling of weapons, their poor servicing, inadequate supervision of training in their use, would inevitably entail. It was to Training Support that the Army looked to ensure that its training would be cost effective and that all concerned in it, teacher and taught alike, would be developed to the fullest extent of their potential.

Tackling the most difficult things to begin with is rarely looked upon as the best way of getting into one's stride. To improve training in any branch of the Army is difficult; to improve it in its handling of the newest and most complex weapons is the most difficult of all improvements to bring about; it seemed therefore sensible, as we have seen, to begin by seeking improvement in its trade training. This was the task given to a former REME officer, Brigadier Mellor, in 1963, and he recommended what became known as the Systems Approach to Training. This insisted on as clear a definition as possible of the nature of the problem to be tackled. It emphasised the importance of adopting as open-minded an approach to it as could be done so that all the ways of dealing with it that could be thought of would be considered. Only after this had been done would the best way of solving it have emerged, and when this was embarked upon its effectiveness must be monitored at every opportunity to make assurance doubly sure that the best solution had been found and was being sought in the best way. His report was presented in 1966. It defined the now-famous Mellor 'Loop'; it converted the Army to the Systems Approach to Training; it brought together selection, recruitment, job-design, equipment design, operating procedures and the training required, all integrated for the better achievement of a common aim, the most satisfactory affordable job performance. He recommended that 'the Army should have access to a centre of instruction where the design and management of trade training courses should be taught'.[55]

This was of great interest to the RAEC. In the 1920s the Corps' role in training had been emphasised but it would never have been allowed in its earlier days to be as intimately associated with weapon training of the kind it became so greatly involved in later, and it would have been most odd if it had identified its interests with what was beyond its reach. It seemed to be in its interests rather to make the most than the least of the difference between education and training. It was proud of its title 'Educational Corps' and it was the educational nature of its activities which it stressed. It had always to some extent been involved in vocational education and in the aftermath of the Second World War it became much more so. Some of its members saw in this the signs of things to come. They understood that vocational education would be much more immediately and much more obviously useful to the Army than pure learning or education in the humanities. It seemed sensible to them to minimise the difference between education and training and this they sought to do by connecting them through the common theme of learning, by looking upon education as pure learning and training as applied learning.

The scales were weighted against them for in the days of National Service the Corps had to provide for those engaged in it. It was thought, not necessarily correctly, that public opinion would insist that National Service men and women, wherever stationed, be able to call upon educational facilities which would compare favourably with those available to their civilian opposite numbers. It required all the resources of the Corps to provide for this and to design and teach soldiers' promotion certification courses which would help the later acquisition of the GCE and CSE grades. Fully stretched to do this, the importance of showing how well this work was done continued to make the Corps indifferent to minimising the difference between education and training. The Corps' interest and its thinking in this matter changed with the ending of conscription. This was bound to concentrate the Corps' thinking. Was it entirely unlikely that the Corps would come to an end with the ending of National Service? This seemed the less unlikely as it coincided with Britain's withdrawal from most of its bases overseas; despite the continuing commitment of BAOR more soldiers would now serve at home. Education for them at home might be provided by civilians, by Burnham Lecturers where there were major concentrations of troops, or by local Further Education lecturers specially employed.

The excellent relations the Corps had established with the Universities would have added to the Army's difficulty in closing down the Corps, but public and parliamentary interest in education in the Regular Army was restricted and university support for the RAEC in its struggle to preserve officer education even more so. It was as well for the RAEC to demonstrate to the Army how difficult it would be to do without it. It did this most effectively by moving quickly and decisively into Training Support.

Before the Executive Committee of the Army Council had concluded its consideration of the Mellor Report the RAEC was developing the ideas of self-paced and programmed learning which were current at this time. Too much was claimed for them as when it was asserted that advances were made not through the correction of mistakes but by learning never to make them.[56] Received wisdom had never thought it easy to learn from mistakes, it being part of folk wisdom that while every day teaches that which succeeds it, no day ever learns from that which it follows. But it would not have been thought possible for mankind not to make mistakes. It would have been thought that the teaching that mistakes could be avoided 'must be meant for a new Manufactory of Mankind by God Almighty; for this to be the case there must be a new clay, the old stuff never yet made any such infallible creature'. But if extreme claims are often made for new ideas and practices, they can still be important. Instructional Technology and Programmed Learning had the greatly beneficial effect of making the teacher think about his teaching. No more than anything to do with teaching will it make up for lack of will to improve in the taught. It could aid the understanding of the conscientious student; it could not make the unstudious soldier conscientious. It was an educational fashion, not an educational breakthrough, but in the absence of such fashionable innovations breakthroughs might never come. It was important in itself and even more so because of what it led to, the development of the Corps' new role in Training Support which endeared it to the trainers and greatly raised its standing in the Army.

While the RAEC was interesting itself in programmed learning the Director of Army Training was thinking of it too, hoping it would ease his problems. He had his own team of instructor trainers at the Army School of Infantry at Warminster. They ran courses but they were unimpressively designed and poor in quality; the results obtained there were very disappointing. There are good teachers and bad teachers and many who trained the soldier in the use of his weapons were of the latter variety. They knew little of the art of instruction and many seemed to believe that sound was all that was needed to penetrate the thickest of heads. The RAEC was sure it could make the instructors better and more effective teachers, and in so doing reduce both the time spent on weapon training and its cost; its conviction greatly interested him and eventually it was agreed that the RAEC should take over the Methods of Instruction Centre.[57]

There are few things more highly developed than the capacity of the future to deceive the present: who foretold the collapse of the USSR and the upheaval accompanying it in Eastern Europe? Yet while the future deceives all of the people some of the time it does not deceive all of the people all of the time, as good leadership has shown on many occasions. The most attentive awareness of present development will not always produce this important feel for the future but where present it is a gracious gift of the gods, a great benefit to its possessors and to those they serve. General Foxton, listening to Brigadier Frankcom's views on officer education and to Colonel Hall who was the driving force in these pioneering days in the 1960s of the RAEC's interest in Instructional Technology and Training Support, had it. So, late in 1966, seven RAEC officers were sent to attend a three-month course at Brighton College of Technology on the completion of which six were appointed Educational Methods Advisers to help Arms Directors in their training and one returned as Training Design Officer to the Army School of Education. Of the six sent to aid the various arms one received an MBE for his work in reorganising clerical training in the RAOC. The two specialist wings in the Army School of Education, the Audio-Visual Aids Wing and the Programmed Learning Wing, were now joined by a third, the Army's first Closed Circuit Television Wing. This was the creation of another former Brighton College of Technology student. In recognition of his work he also received an MBE. These specialist wings, together with the transferred Methods of Instruction Centre formed the nucleus of the Army School of Instructional Technology.

In June 1969 the Director of Army Training sent out his letter 'Policy For Instructional Technology In The Army'. The Director of Army Education was made responsible for carrying this out and an MOD Committee on Instructional Technology was set up to coordinate policy and forward its research and development. Training Development Teams were also formed to serve the training groups which required their assistance and RAEC Training Development Advisers to provide them with specialist support were assembled.

The New Army School of Instructional Technology had the task of designing and running a Management Training Course to explain to senior officers the Systems Approach to Training. It also produced 'Yellow Guides' to make known to units the various aspects of the new training which were of special concern to them. It found its home alongside the Army School of Education which, as if to symbolise the new work the RAEC was undertaking, had now ceased its peripatetic existence and moved into its new purpose-built accommodation at Beaconsfield, its buildings spacious, its grounds extensive.[58] In the twilight of Empire spacious new building was invariably a sign of coming departure and so it was to prove here. However, since the new building then came at the end of a role and the new building at Beaconsfield made provision for one which was both continuing and essential for the Army's well-being, it seemed reasonable to pay no attention to old sayings. For not only was the work of all the wings at Beaconsfield of vital importance, one in particular had already proved to be as of great service to the Army in action as the newspapers which the Corps had produced in the Second World War. This was the Television Wing. Again and again the measured, contained yet powerfully appropriate way in which officers, even of no great seniority, conducted themselves when interviewed by television journalists in Northern Ireland soon after incidents of such a nature as to affect the balance of any man, greatly impressed public opinion and further hardened it against the terrorists there. Television which exposes pretence also reveals character and competence, which it did on these occasions. Nor was this the only help given by that Wing to the Army in Ireland. When units are changed incoming units need to familiarise themselves as quickly as they can with the area they have to patrol. And the films held, and made available to units, by the Beaconsfield TV Wing gave them an excellent opportunity of doing so even before they arrived. It was no doubt a compliment which the RAEC could have dispensed with when a bomb was exploded at its Eltham Headquarters in May 1990. Fortunately this recognition of its contribution to the combatting of terrorism killed no-one and did no great damage.[59] The future, unfortunately, was to show yet again its old capacity to bring to naught the dreams of men, to prove the truth of T.H. Green's warning that men's schemes are often frustrated by the hidden wisdom of the world. Its new building at Beaconsfield was also in time to be removed from it.

The RAEC continued to increase its ability to forward Training Support. It sent more of its officers on short courses in Modern Methods of Industrial Training at Brunel University or to a year-long study leading to a degree in Manpower Studies or in Occupational Psychology at Birkbeck College. Such was the relation between Birkbeck and the Corps that in the mid-1970s it had a teaching fellowship there. Sussex, Aston and Bath Universities also held postgraduate courses attended by the RAEC who were going to become Training Development Advisers. They were soon fully employed at the Staff College, the RMCS, the RMAS, the WRAC College, with the major Arms and Services in UKLF, and in BAOR and Cyprus. An RAEC officer was also employed as Training Development Advisor at the Harrogate Army Apprentice College. The continued development of the Corps' activities in Training Support must be left to the next chapter, but the very important theoretical underpinning of Training Support and the Corps' preparation for its later full commitment to it were occurrences of the 1960s which in this as in many other ways can be seen as the seed-bed of so much of its later work.

It was in the late 1950s and 1960s that the Corps, as we have seen, became responsible for the teaching of languages, bringing to the School of Education Arabic Studies from the Middle East and the teaching of Russian from the School in Scotland. The Army had an increasing need of linguists, and since there would be few specialists if specialism was not to be penalised they had to be given the same opportunity as everyone else of gaining the wider experience without which promotion would not come their way. There being thus many calls upon them, nine linguists had to be trained to be sure that every post requiring linguistic expertise would be filled.[60] It is, then, no surprise to find by 1969 some thirty RAEC officers fully employed in teaching foreign languages. Given the importance of BAOR, the teaching of German was bound to appear of great value to the Army and to make it painfully aware how much greater the linguistic ability of allied armies was.

We have seen how repeatedly officers serving in Germany had been exhorted to learn German and how pressure to do so had been put on all those not preparing for the Staff/Promotion Examination. Although German language training had been taking place in Germany since the end of World War Two the first development of a co-ordinated Command scheme took place in the early 1960s when the 'Brewer Scheme' was introduced. This scheme was a major development at that time in language teaching methods and was devised by the late Lieutenant-Colonel G.P.R. Brewer of the Corps in order to provide a system for the mass teaching of German to soldiers. It was based on the use of the tape-recorder and was taught by unit instructors, many of whom had no knowledge of German to start with. They were trained at the Higher Education Centre (Germany) on five-week courses in a near audio-visual method. On their return to their units and equipped with appropriate teaching materials, they then taught groups of soldiers on concentrated two-week courses up to a level where the students were able to communicate with the local population in simple everyday situations both on and off duty. The advantage of the scheme was that it provided a quick, cheap and effective method for mass language training at elementary level and it was employed extensively throughout BAOR.

As language laboratories were introduced into BAOR from 1966 onwards the Brewer Scheme became somewhat dated as it was not suitable for use in them. A new two-week Basic German course was written in 1967 for use in those Army Education Centres which had language laboratories, whilst the Brewer Scheme continued to be used elsewhere in the Command. In 1970 it was decided to produce a new BAOR Basic German Course for use in Army Education Centres, now equipped with language laboratories. This course was taught initially by RAEC officers who had been trained at the Higher Education Centre (Germany) and then later, as the scheme developed, they were joined by local qualified German civilian instructors.

Over the years this scheme expanded and was amended and up-dated, and its importance was stressed in BAOR Command Orders which laid down percentage targets to be achieved by each unit at the different levels of standard. By the early 1980s the Army Education Centres were running short five-day Introductory courses for all ranks and their families who were newly arrived in BAOR and who spoke little or no German, and then the two-week Basic German course for those who had completed the Introductory courses. Certain Army Education Centres also ran Colloquial courses in addition to the Colloquial, Linguist, and Interpreter courses which were run at the Higher Education Centre (Germany). At about this time the Ministry of Defence decreed that senior commanders and staff officers in BAOR were to be qualified at Colloquial level, ideally before taking up their commands/posts. Some of these officers were trained at the Higher Education Centre (Germany) but many of them attended courses at the Defence School of Languages at Beaconsfield. The fact that senior officers attended these courses not only gave them a first-hand acquaintance of the types and levels of courses available, but also gave a marked impetus to the encouragement of the scheme. When the newly-appointed Commander of the 1st (British) Corps attended the Colloquial German course at Beaconsfield this, it was said, concentrated wonderfully the minds of his subordinates.[61]

There was in addition an attempt made by the Corps to persuade those to learn German who were not prepared to make much of an effort to do so. It demonstrated the pioneering spirit it had shown in developing discussion as a suitable means of teaching adults.[62] It was suggested at a cocktail party 'what you want is something like *The Archers* – but with a bit of German in it'. This suggestion was taken up and a programme devised with British Forces Broadcasting Service. A story was made up with fourteen episodes, each lasting for only five minutes. In each the object was to entertain and only incidentally to teach German. The programme limited itself to a few words and phrases which could be easily learned and used without requiring any prior knowledge of the language or its grammar. Episodes involved ordering a beer in a pub, ordering a meal, asking the way, being stopped by a policeman, using the tram. This series ran every day for three weeks. A regular and diligent listener to it would have acquired in this time a vocabulary of about sixty common words and phrases which he could either use or recognise in context.

Emboldened by this, the programme makers tried something else. A newly arrived young broadcaster had ideas about how to present information over the radio to achieve maximum effect. He reckoned that the attention span of the casual radio listener lasted from 45–60 seconds. He believed that the most impact would be achieved by a short, sharp message which lasted just under a minute and which was repeated two or three times a day. He devised a programme 'Say it in German' which took the form of a 'commercial for German', lasting 45 seconds and broadcast three or four times a day. There was to be a different theme each week, 'At the Restaurant', 'Using the Tram', 'In the Department Store', and so on . Each day a maximum of three useful words or phrases relevant to the theme of the week would be featured. These 'slots' would be introduced by an instantly recognisable theme tune. The programme was tried out for five weeks. It attracted immediately favourable comment and it continued to run. A list of the words and phrases it used was printed in the soldiers' newspapers, *Sixth Sense*, *Union Jack* and the *Berlin Bulletin*.[63] It was not a major break-through in language teaching and its lasting effect is to be doubted. It was, however, no more of a gimmick, and possibly less, than the arrangement made by the University of Cambridge to attach a special coach on the Cambridge to London commuter trains in which extra-mural classes were held. That, too, did not last long. Nevertheless these programmes in Germany, and perhaps the Cambridge experiment, were significant attempts to get at the hitherto ungettable; they reflected the dedicated, the imaginative and the pioneering determination which could alone break down the resolve of the 80% of the troops and of the civilian population to shun education as they would the plague, the resolve which no adult educator has as yet been able to remove, and which if not removed must eventually be expected to bring democracy to an unflattering end.

Whatever might be thought of the importance to be attached to the linguistic ability of military attachés (and it was obvious that the senior officer who in this connection expressed his disapproval of what was taught was merely reflecting his dislike of the teacher), the teaching of modern languages by the Corps was highly approved in the Army. There was general agreement with the CAROT Report when it looked to the RAEC to make 'a major effort to meet the training and testing requirements of an increased priority on language teaching', saying this would have to be done 'if the language ability among regular officers is to be ever raised above the abysmal standard at which it has now settled'. The Army was grateful for the ready help given by the Corps to the Special Services in learning whatever languages they might need to know. The outstanding reputation of the Russian Language Wing at Beaconsfield was acknowledged when it was given the task of preparing the Army Central Inspection Team which was to check the disarmament being undertaken in the former USSR. The excellence of the Arabic Wing at Beaconsfield was fully recognised during the Gulf War when American soldiers studied there in preparation for it. The Army could be proud too that its Chinese Language School in Hong Kong had become the premier military Chinese language school in the world. The ending of the Empire had greatly reduced but had not entirely finished the magnificent work done by the Corps in making soldiers of other races literate in their own languages and in teaching them English. That work went on in the teaching of the Gurkha Brigade. It was no easy task and it would hardly be too much to claim that the Corps showed itself possessed of linguistic genius in tackling it. In Malaya, and later in Hong Kong, an effective job was done in teaching Gurkhas who also, as we have seen, became regular attenders at the courses run in the Language Wing at Beaconsfield.[64] In the early 1960s work, in the nature of things temporary, was done by the RAEC with Boys Units of other countries. The Corps trained forty-five boys aged 14½–17½ in the Junior Leaders' Troops of the Royal Malta Artillery. Similar work was done with the Army Boys' Trade School in Singapore which catered for almost 200 boys aged 15–18 years in a three-year course which sought to provide potential tradesmen for technical units of locally-raised British Army units in Malaya. The RAEC also taught 138 enlisted boys in the Junior Leaders' Company of the King's African Rifles. This unit combined the functions of a Pre-OCTU and an Apprentice School as well as those of a Junior Leaders' Unit.[65]

One of the RAEC's most important legacies to the new Commonwealth countries was its work with the Federated Military College in Malaya. Now the Royal Military College, the FMC was founded in Port Dickson, Malaya by Generals Templer and Stockwell in 1952 in order to educate Malay, Chinese, Indian and Eurasian boys up to Cambridge Overseas School Certificate level and then to prepare them for officer training, at first at OCTU or Sandhurst in the UK and later, after 'A' levels were introduced, at the FMC itself. Some boys in later years went on to universities. The FMC was unique among all those colonial institutions and schemes with which the RAEC was associated after the war in that it was designed to produce officers and also leaders in civilian society. It was perhaps analogous to the Indian Military Academy at Dehra Dun where the Corps was represented at Chief Instructor level until 1953. Indeed the FMC eventually came to see itself as a cross between Eton and

Sandhurst, a perhaps somewhat ambitious piece of self perception but a clear indication of how important the college was to the new Malaysia. In its early years the college was staffed by regimental officers, both British and Malay, by seconded Sandhurst lecturers, RAEC officers, Colonial Service Education Officers and a Malay teacher. For some years there were four RAEC officers at any one time and they were extremely influential in the college, carrying out both educational and military duties and carving out for the Corps an important and remembered place in the development of the new country.

With the reduction in the number of British troops in Germany less effort would be expected from the educators and less concern expressed at their failure to induce the uninducible to pick up a smattering of German. However the multinational Allied Command Europe Rapid Reaction Corps led by the British and in which they serve and Common Market developments both compel us to rid ourselves of our old neglect of European languages. There too will always be the more ambitious, the more adventurous and the more far-seeing who will think it advantageous to acquire understanding of extra-European languages. *Options for Change* thus did not give the Army the option for ending, or even of significantly curtailing, language teaching in it. The linguistic tasks of the educator will remain uphill as English reluctance to learn European languages ought never to be underestimated. Coleridge is said to have ended a public lecture by thanking God for having saved him from being able to speak a single sentence in French. If it be God's will that the mastery of European languages should not be sought by the English, in this at least they have always striven to obey Him.[66]

The RAEC had to struggle continually against the Army tendency to take too narrow a view of education; it is a *cri-de-coeur* that was raised at the Command Education Officers' Conference in 1959 'The Army like other strongly individualist organisations, is always in danger of a too narrowly professional attitude towards broad issues including education.'[67] The Army, however, is not to be faulted in its thinking about the Individual Education it provided for the soldier. It was not narrowly professional but it was, on the contrary, as broad as could be desired. It was ready to provide something for everyone. Moreover, it always laid great stress on the soldier's Individual Education as it did again in emphasising how greatly the soldier would benefit if he worked to get suitable resettlement qualifications. The RAEC offered every kind of class and course to units which would accept them. It offered instruction for those preparing for the GCE, for those wanting to enter the Civil Service, the Customs and Excise, Local Government, the Post Office and the Police. It organised classes for the examinations for the Royal Society of Arts and similar bodies, for the theoretical papers set by the City and Guilds Institute and for examinations in foreign languages. It enrolled, at bargain rates, those who wanted to go to civilian educational institutions. It continued to push the Forces' Correspondence Scheme. It worked out a very attractive scheme whereby those aspiring to a university education could be helped to satisfy their ambition. It encouraged soldiers to register for the Open University, the greatest success of contemporary adult education. Its courses were available to Services personnel in home postings on the same basis as their civilian counterparts. Service students, however, were liable to overseas postings, sometimes at short notice, in the middle of a course. The Service Directors of Education therefore approached the Open University to discuss the possibility of continuing their studies overseas. The outcome was a scheme, organized on a tri-Service basis, mirroring UK arrangements. Responsibility for coordination was shared between the Open University, represented by two of its Regional Offices, and the Services, represented in Northern Europe by the Army Educational Services and in Cyprus by the RAF Educational Services. For the Services this entailed designating Education Centres, nominating suitable educational personnel as tutors and arranging summer schools to be conducted by Open University staff from the UK. That the system proved effective was a tribute to all those involved in teaching and administration, but not least to the rapport established at the highest level between OU and the Services. Each side took the trouble to study the other's problems so that demands on both parent systems were reasonable and were met without complaint. Thus the benefit to students was immense, whether pursuing courses as part of their individual development or in preparation for retirement. When moving to or from an overseas posting, they were able to fit into compatible study arrangements without an avoidable loss of momentum in their own studies.[68]

The need for officers with particular academic qualifications to be serving at the Education Centres delineated as meeting places for the Open University and able to act as its tutors was not always easy to satisfy, but the posting authorities generally managed to meet it. The scheme attracted a wide range of Service and MOD civilian students to its courses. There were many officers among them who had entered Sandhurst at the conventional GCE 'A' stage and who now wanted to take their studies further; there were teachers in the Service Children's Schools who wanted to upgrade their teaching qualifications; there were NCOs from all parts of the Army who often built their Open University degrees on relatively modest educational foundations and who frequently gained commissioned rank after taking their degrees; there were Army wives with time on their hands in a foreign land who turned to the Open University for structured and supported study. It is pleasant to record that General Lloyd Howell was awarded an Honorary MA by the Open University for his work in developing the Services' Scheme.

Since at home a great deal of the teaching for soldier's Individual Education was done by the LEAs its provision in the home-based Army did not make great demands on the RAEC. Overseas it was another matter, for here Individual Education took on quite different dimensions and made great calls on the Corps. The Army abroad was to a large extent driven in on itself, and as there had to be plenty of provision for leisure, in Army Education Centres all over the world a great range of day and evening classes was on offer. Centres served as examination centres for many professional examinations as well as for GCE, there being a Special Services scheme arranged with Cambridge University Local Examinations Syndicate for this purpose. Individual Education in a foreign land was more in demand than at home; it made a great contribution to the morale as well as to the self-improvement and to the ultimate resettlement of the soldier. The RAEC provided for the education of the soldier better opportunities than were available to civilians and for the great benefit it brought to the Army and to many of its soldiers and their dependents, soldiers' Individual Education must be counted an outstanding success. If anything was lacking in the matter of the soldier's Individual Education it was neither inducement nor opportunity.

A note of caution is, however, called for. Something was lacking, namely the willingness of far too many soldiers to have anything to do with it. Their unrelenting indifference, though perhaps a stronger word should be used, was as daunting to the adult teacher in uniform as was that of the great majority of civilian adults to the adult teacher out of it.

Yet *Manual* after *Manual of Education*, nevertheless, kept up the pretence that things were other than they were. Again and again the words were printed 'Men who have completed their studies for Army Certificates of Education should be led, as a matter of course, to take up some further educational activity.' Every man speaks two languages, his own and cant, and we can hear it here. This was a well-known waste of paper and it is with a sense of relief that one notes that the ending of the Army Certificates of Education also ended this particular piece of hypocrisy. The uneasy thought occurs to one, however, that the ingenuity of hypocrisy in finding new ways to express itself is never to be underestimated and that it deftly asserted itself in DCI 288 of 1970 when it said the voluntary Individual Education Scheme was being made more effective 'to meet the demand for personal development through culture and education leading to the attainment of skills and qualifications which are of value both in military and in civilian life'. Opportunities abounded for the acquisition of such skills and qualifications as were sought; the excellent abundance was, however, characteristic only of their provision; demand was limited and another word might have appropriately replaced it. Individual Education remained for too many soldiers an area of hopeful provision rather than anticipated use. Had it not been provided, some would have been greatly dissatisfied; as it was some were happy with what was available and more were grateful that what was provided was not forced upon them. The choice was theirs and that was as it should be. Heirs of all the ages in the latest files of time as we believe ourselves to be, we may yet profit from the wisdom of our forebears. Roger Ascham taught us 'No learning ought to be learned with bondage. For bodilie labours wrought by compulsion hurt not the bodie, but any learning learned by compulsion tarieth not long in the mynde. And why? For whatsoever the mynde doth learnt unwillinglie with feare, the same it doth quicklie forget without care.'[69] If the soldier wanted to remain in the Army and if he knew the price he must pay to do so was to apply himself to his books, his choice would be clear. Unwilling to pay the price he could leave the Army; willing to pay it he would no longer be 'learning with bondage'.

The education of the soldier's children remained as it had been for many years, one of the standing preoccupations of the Corps. It was always difficult to attend to. When, for instance, a National Service Battalion of Infantry in Singapore was replaced by the Regular Black Watch the primary school at Changi grew from twenty to 300 overnight, a difficulty which the RAEC took in its stride. Similar problems were to be met elsewhere. With the ending of Britain's East of Suez role 14,000 Army children were brought home by 1972 and the RAEC had to make arrangements for them. It had to attend also to the rise in BAOR of the school population from 13,267 children and 672 teachers in 1956 to 25,679 children and 1,212 teachers in 1969. The Chief Education Officer BAOR reckoned that looking after them took 50% of his time.[70] In 1968 a Youth Service was authorised for BAOR with a civilian Director in charge under the Chief Education Officer, who was thus given all the educational responsibilities of a Local Education Authority for children, youths and adults. On 1 April 1969 came the ending of nearly 300 years of the Army's separate provision of education for its children. On that date the Service Children's Education Authority was set up. It was established in the Directorate of Army Education, which emphasised how little the role of the RAEC in the education of the Army's children had been reduced by this formal change. Control of Service Education overseas hereafter was based on the 'major-user' principle, the Royal Navy being responsible for Service children's education in Malta and Gibraltar, the Army in Western Europe and Hong Kong and the RAF in Cyprus. The three Services in turn appointed a serving education officer to be the head of the Service Children's Education Authority.

The perennial problems of the education of Service children, the problems of turbulence, of schooling frequently interrupted by postings, of the provision of the more advanced types of secondary education, could never be finally solved but only continually addressed. Long and carefully analysed experience reduced these problems as much as could be. There had been long discussions as to whether the problem of the discontinuity of education caused by frequent postings would be better addressed by providing boarding education or by facilitating a smooth transfer from school to school. Both courses had to be followed. The Plowden Report of November 1961 on Service Children put them into the same category as gypsies when discussing the needs of migratory children for boarding education. 6,277 officers' children and 1,225 children of other ranks went to Boarding School. The RAEC played a major part in advising about boarding schools and in facilitating transfer from school to school. Its officers went on short courses to prepare them to do both. It was made clear that they could not provide a professional service but that 'the RAEC officer at unit level must be expected to play his part'. It was very important, it was emphasised, that the RAEC should serve as 'co-opted' members on the boards of LEAs or independent schools and that they should provide 'good offices in bringing parents and Head Masters together'. Its arrangements for the completion and transfer of children's documents when they moved schools were far more comprehensive than anything LEAs gave each other when their children moved. The Corps also developed a GCE examination system uniform throughout Service Schools which ensured that a child moving, for instance from Cyprus to BAOR suffered less syllabus disruption than one moving from Yorkshire to Hampshire. It also negotiated a staffing weighting for Service Schools to take account of their highly mobile populations and did so also with LEAs at home for schools which had a high proportion of Service children, like those on Salisbury Plain where an MOD Terrorist Alert Exercise or the real thing could transform a school's population overnight. No perfect solution to this age-old problem of turbulence presented itself and some of the means adopted led to fresh difficulties, as the making available of Boarding School allowances at home often meant that viable Sixth Forms could not be established abroad. But the determined, the imaginative, the effective contribution of the RAEC to coping with this problem cannot be doubted.

One achievement of the RAEC could not be gainsaid. It had convinced the family soldier of the importance of education for his children. Grateful as he persistently was that he would not have to expose himself further to education, he was determined that his children should have it. The persistent percentage of illiterates which disgraced the national system of education was not a feature of Army schooling, and while this doubtless speaks more for the discipline imposed by the Army than for that exercised by the LEA, it may also be that the family soldier was more convinced than his opposite number in civilian life of the importance of his children's education. In general the soldier had every reason to be satisfied with the education his children received and it is pleasant to record this testimony to the Army Schools overseas from the Annual Conference of the National Association of Head Teachers of 1968: 'It is important that when children come to English schools, for however short a stay, their education should be up to the standards they have been accustomed to overseas.' Few services by the RAEC were more appreciated in the Army than these services to its children.

A development in one of the Army Schools at this time is particularly worthy of mention. It occurred in the Duke of York's Royal Military School when Colonel Mullin commanded it. Before taking up the Headship he visited a number of Secondary Technical and Modern Schools to see how they were implementing the Butler Act. With one exception he found they were following somewhat watered-down Grammar School subjects with the aim of getting GCE passes for their best pupils. Most of the children seemed bored. The exception was Sidcup Secondary Technical School where the Head had abandoned all GCE subjects. He was interesting the children in practical subjects, bricklaying, electrical fitting, carpentry, metalwork, secretarial studies and cookery. There was also basic English and arithmetic. Colonel Mullin found here 'a pleasant hum of fully interested and occupied children'.

Institutions have a duty to teach courses appropriate to the students whom they actually have, rather than to those whom they wish to have. Colonel Mullin knew this and acted accordingly. Installed in the Duke of York's Royal Military School, he found a middle stream and the third stream following inadequately the same subjects as the Grammar 'A' Stream. 'Motivation', he also soon discovered, 'was unfortunately not present.' He was of the opinion that Secondary Education should be extremely practical for 80% of the pupils. Youngsters from the age of fourteen who were in the second Technical stream were of 115–110 IQ on the Moray House tests, that is below Grammar School ability. He designed a practical course for them in woodwork, technical drawing, metalworking and physics. Mathematics and English were compulsory. Pupils took these subjects at 'O' level and could, if they so wished, also take chemistry or French. When they reached the Sixth Form they took 'A' level courses in engineering drawing, physics, pure and applied mathematics. These subjects they studied in school. For one day each week they went to Dover Technical College, where they followed the Ordinary National Certificate curriculum. After the four-year course pupils took three 'A' levels, in physics, engineering drawing and pure and applied mathematics and at the Technical College they took the Ordinary National Certificate examination. Colonel Mullin could only see one set of boys through the four years' examination. All passed the ONC and the engineering drawing 'A' level. Some got 'A' level passes in pure and applied mathematics. A few achieved 'A' level passes in all three subjects. Colonel Mullin directed the Third Stream at the school to the Army Apprentices Entrance examination.

The proof of the pudding is in the eating. At a reunion of Second Stream boys in 1989 one was a prominent manager of an American Company in Geneva, one was head of department of an engineering firm in Reading, one was a self-employed manager-business consultant, one a senior mathematics master at a large comprehensive school. All had enjoyed their schooldays as much as they had obviously benefitted from them. After a lapse of thirty years and more an increasing number of schools were following much the same pattern of education which Colonel Mullin had worked out: here again the RAEC proved to be in the forefront of educational progress.[71] A large percentage of Colonel Mullin's pupils were 'compassionate entry' boys who had been affected by the war years. Only a few of these were academically inclined. By 1967 the entry pattern was different, some two-thirds of new boys having IQs in excess of 115 and only some 12% being 'compassionate entry' to whom precedence was still given. The points system for entry was based on a combination of parent's length of OR service, rank and son's tested abilities. Parents and sons now aspired to Sandhurst and university as opposed to apprentice or craft training. The needs of the less able continued to be catered for by recruiting extra staff and reducing class sizes at the lower end. The school now has a commendable GCE and 'A' level record.[72]

We saw in Chapter 10 how the library services developed when the RAEC became responsible for all General Staff Reference Libraries in 1948. There used to be a Standard Unit Library (a selection of reference texts) in every unit of the Army. The RAEC also used to provide uniformed librarians for the larger libraries, a practice which ended in the late 1950s. In 1970 the Corps reviewed its Library Services, it then being determined that at home existing County Libraries could provide recreational library facilities for soldiers and that the Army need only maintain its own recreational libraries where no suitable library services were available. The RAEC continued to manage the Army (as distinct from the MOD) Library Service based on a large library in each major Command and supporting smaller Army Education Centre libraries. It is a remarkable fact that through all the cuts and reorganisations of the last forty years the Army Library Service in one way or another has continued to function and to provide a service for soldiers, officers, their wives and children, which has been of very great value both to morale and education. The RAEC's maintenance and defence of this service and the loyal contribution of its civilian staff have been outstandingly successful. It was also decided that the Prince Consort Library should become 'a special library' and centre of research. As early as 1857 the Prince Consort had begun a systematic collection of books to set up a military library. Building for this began in 1859 and the library was opened on 5 October 1860. The Prince Consort met all expenses incurred. On his death Queen Victoria ordered that the library continue to be funded by the Privy Purse and the library remained a royal building until she died. King Edward felt that other things had a more pressing call on his purse than the upkeep of the library and the then Adjutant-General persuaded the War Office to make an annual grant for its maintenance. From 1938 until 1948 it was controlled by the Aldershot Garrison; in the latter year all Army Library Services became the responsibility of the RAEC, whence it passed to the ETS Branch of the Adjutant-General's Corps. In the past decade emerging technology has affected the Army Library Service as it has affected all parts of the Army. To meet the increased calls being made on the Prince Consort Library a Military Studies Library Service has been established. The most advanced computers are now in service and computer disc, Diskfax and e-mail make possible the instant transmission of information to any location. 'For an operational deployment', it is claimed, 'the Prince Consort Library will provide an initial batch of raw data on the relevant country or region within one hour and will have a properly formatted and organised background brief compiled within four hours.'[73]

It was said of the Habsburg Empire that had it not existed it would have had to be invented. With so many things done by the Corps which were of such benefit to the Army the same would have had to be said of the RAEC in the professional Army which replaced its National Service predecessor. Moreover, many senior officers would have said this in these years. These were great days for the Corps and they were the days of its mature strength. The Army has often not acknowledged its debt to the RAEC; it was finding it difficult not to now. A further strength at this time was that Army Education still had important outside help, restricted at times as that was. There was not a university in the land with which it had not now established close relations. There were few universities unwilling to consider what help they could give to meet Prince Philip's views on officers' education.

There were many advantages in this close co-operation between the Army and the universities. The courses for senior officers gave them an opportunity to exchange views with distinguished scholars. At a lower level the absence of uniform emphasised the non-military atmosphere of the courses and even Generals whose touring of other units occasionally compelled them when calling to wear uniform apologised for the necessity of so doing. The holding of courses in the universities enabled the Army to do an excellent job of Public Relations and when, for instance, at Madingley Hall in Cambridge, Staff/Promotion courses coincided with courses for the magistracy, the interest taken in and the admiration expressed for the young officers by the magistrates was very striking.

Not least was the effect the running of these courses had on the dons themselves. Accustomed as they were, however little they dared say so, to dealing with those who were wet behind the ears it was bracing for them to meet and discuss with men of a very different experience. When gradually, and with some exceptions such as the long-running relationship with Madingley Hall and with the universities of Birmingham, Wales, Southampton and Leeds, the Army withdrew these courses from universities and held them in its own Education Centres or in hotels in off-peak seasons, a great deal was lost. Non-quantifiable things are not to be quantified, but the young men whom Kipling exhorted Cambridge to look after following the 1918 Armistice – 'Hallowed river, most gracious trees, chapel beyond compare. Here be gentlemen sick of the seas – take them into your care' – gained much from its atmosphere and perhaps the officers in the 1960s and 1970s benefitted from even their brief exposure to university life too. Indeed, the closeness of its relations with the universities was itself one of the reasons why the Army now so valued the Corps.

But no one would pretend that in the great surge of educational activity now occurring in the Army it was any other than the RAEC which pulled the labouring oar. In some things the universities might appropriately feel a sense of shame. They should recall the fully-justified criticism made by Sir Michael Howard of their lack of interest in officer education. 'The largely abortive attempts at reform in officer education over the past ten years', he wrote, 'have not awoken a flicker of civilian interest even in such journals as *The Times Educational Supplement*.'[74] If the Corps was now more generally appreciated throughout the Army than it had hitherto been, it itself, and not the help it got from elsewhere, was responsible for that.

Its high standing at this time was suitably acknowledged. Its new responsibilities increased its numbers and added to the number of its senior posts. In 1959–1960 the heads of its Directorate Branches became full Colonels. Additional Lieutenantt-Colonel's posts were created in Resettlement, in divisions, in BAOR and elsewhere. Three substantive posts for Brigadiers were established; prior to 1965 these had been non-substantive. At this time, too, the Corps was able to take advantage of the rule that a percentage for non-effective strength could be applied to it. This non-effective strength included leave after posting abroad, long courses away from the Corps, necessary intervals between postings. Thus at one stage the Corps list included four Brigadiers, one of whom was employed at E2 (extra-Regimentally) for six months. By the judicious use of this rule it was possible at one time to include in the Corps List some five surplus Lieutenant-Colonels. This was only possible because the Army generally and the powers that were in control, particularly the Military Secretary and the Establishment Committees, held the Corps in such high regard.

That most powerful embodiment of massive English commonsense, Dr Johnson, reminded us that after the sun comes the rain, after the pleasure the pain. These years of the Corps' triumphant expansion were to be followed by marked contraction in some fields, even though this was also accompanied by continued expansion in others. The pressures on the Corps were too strong for it to resist at least for the time being the contraction forced upon it. Yet no Army has a better understanding than the British that withdrawals and lost battles do not necessarily herald final defeat. And a Corps which had achieved so much, displayed such versatility, shown such imaginative ingenuity in meeting important needs and which was strengthening its role in a major and promising new development of the greatest interest to the Army, had no reason, despite difficulties and its disappointments, to belittle the place in the Army it had already won.

CHAPTER 12

EDUCATION IN THE CONTEMPORARY ARMY

The more I turn over in my mind the affairs of modern or of ancient times', Tacitus said, 'the more do I see in all transactions the mockery of human affairs.' There does at times seem to be a perversity in the affairs of man, promising developments being accompanied by forces which restrain and seek to destroy them. Thus throughout the period of its greatest achievement when it was proving itself so useful to the Army, powerful forces were moving against the RAEC. For the days of its most striking success were also the time which saw a great strengthening of its old enemies, the clock and the purse.

The numerous committees investigating this, that or the other aspect of Army life were so many attempts to save money and manpower.[1] The Army had too much to do and too few men and too little money to do it with. It could not reduce its commitments; only the Government could do that and, this it showed no sign of doing. Indeed, later it was to add to them in the Falklands, the Gulf War and Bosnia. Now, with more to do, it had to reduce its expenses. Not wanting to dispense with anything, it had to ask with what it could dispense most and with the least effect on its efficiency. Cuts and clichés abounded; what were described as 'salami' tactics were embarked upon each revolving moon; a Cabinet minister gave us a graphic picture of the Army 'cutting its tail to preserve its teeth'. Want of money, want of men, want of the time that was consequent on both since all had to work longer to do what was essential, affected the whole Army and together with it the RAEC.

'All need education but few desire it', the Greeks said; there had rarely been many in the Army who did. The difficulty of the uniformed educator in persuading the Army to accept him as a member of the family has been writ large over the history of Army Education. Again and again we have seen how strong was the inbuilt prejudice against education in many senior officers. Brigadier Mullin said that in his experience 'Infantry, Engineer, Cavalry officers were anti-education in a not well-defined way. If you got on well with them personally they would be prepared to accept it but often they took dislikes to individuals and this means education lost out. In many senior officers this led to a feeling that education was imposed on them by civilians and politicians. Many said there was little point in providing libraries for the Army. This bias against education revealed itself to me particularly in committees in the MOD. I remember one particularly – investigating in the early 1960s the possibility of setting up a MOD University [Howard-English Report] and it was clear from the beginning that all three Service senior officers were against it.' 'A waste of time and would have an adverse effect on the regimental officer', they said. He also found 'resentment of the policy that the RAEC should assist in training to improve methods of instruction in it [the Army], even to make language training more efficient – the last quality required in a military attaché is the knowledge of the local language'. Experience has taught diplomatists the wisdom of conducting their discussions through interpreters even when familiar with the language of the host country; they have never thought that knowledge of that language was 'the last quality' required. The Brigadier concluded 'All these inbuilt prejudices led to the fact that any Board of Enquiry charged with finding ways to cut expenditure would look at education first. Many (not all) would seize on any stick to beat the RAEC with, to cut the Corps down to size.'[2] Major-General Trythall, too, believed there was some feeling in the Army that the Corps was becoming too powerful an influence in relation to the careers of teeth arms officers and that this played its part in ending the Progressive Qualifications Scheme of Officer Education.[3]

There was the mounting acrimony that was the consequence of past success. A senior RAEC officer who was engaged in many of the battles that took place at this time noted ruefully that 'with a recognition of the new contributions the Corps could make and the influence of officers in key appointments, particularly training, Officers' Education and languages, suspicions grew and we were considered to be becoming too powerful. We were showing our abilities outside the narrow confines of the classroom.' 'The attack on PQS which I had to defend made me conscious that the worry was really the power of the RAEC', he added. A very senior officer went so far as to tell him 'the RAEC must not be allowed to select the future Army Board members'. That the senior RAEC officer to whom this was said interpreted as meaning that 'the regimental system cannot place selected officers in Staff College without being subject to reliance on the RAEC'.[4] It seems indeed to have been a case, in Shakespeare's words, of 'jealousy, the green-eyed monster which doth mock the meat it feeds on'.

The power of jealousy is never to be underestimated. It adds to distrust and generates bitterness. It strengthens other factors which also want what would satisfy it. The often slight regard felt for the Corps was bound to tell against it when the blows began to fall. Nevertheless, jealousy's power is limited and on this occasion too much should not be made of it. The pressure on successive Directors of Army Education which developed in the latter days of the Cold War had less to do with any particular antipathy which may have lurked in the collective breast of the Army Board or elsewhere than with important elements in the ideology of the government of the time. The Conservative Government wished to reduce the power of the State and the number of government servants; it wanted better value for money from the Services (especially more teeth and less tail) and to manage them more effectively. This led to a determination to increase the power of 'the Centre' in MOD as against the separate Royal Navy, Army and Royal Air Force Departments within it. This Centre would coordinate, if not control, what the Single Service Departments could do. Functions which could be rationalised across the board would become tri-Service. Functions which could be carried out by civilians would be handed over to them, 'contractorised' as the ugly phrase went. The Services would be given more freedom to work efficiently but would become more accountable within their defined roles.

In the event what transpired was the adoption of the Government's 'New Management Strategy'. The New Management Strategy sought to identify areas of management to which budgets could be allocated. The aim was to align managerial responsibility with financial accountability and to 'cascade' the budgets down the line of managerial responsibility. Within the system there would be Higher Level Budget holders allocating to and controlling Intermediate Level Budget holders and so on to the point of delivery of the system. As this was discussed and developed, functional Directors argued that the 'cascading' in respect of the functions for which they were responsible should be to and through them so that they could ensure that resources were effectively deployed to carry out agreed policy and could be answerable to Higher Level Budget holders for this being done. In the event the decision come to was to establish and 'cascade' the budgets through the chain of command. Thus the Higher Level Budget Holder in BAOR would be the Commander-in-Chief there and allocations for all services within BAOR would flow through his Higher Level Budget, principally through the chain of command, the divisions and the brigades and garrisons. The Adjutant-General therefore would be a Higher Level Budget holder for only those areas for which he had a direct managerial responsibility.[5] What were called 'Executive Agencies' were also introduced. These became responsible for discrete activities within the Ministry's overall function. They were responsible for the carrying out of the functions they were associated with, the funds for these being directly allocated to them. They did not, however, control policy. The responsibility for this remained a grey area, as it does in civil society – witness the frequent disputes between the former Home Secretary and the Director of the Prisons Agency. SCEA became an Executive Agency as did the Duke of York's School and Queen Victoria's School. They became agencies when the Corps became a Branch. Resettlement, at least as concerns training for it, is to be replaced by a variant of the Agency philosophy, a 'partnership' between the Services and an outside body.[6]

For those whose joy is in complexity, the difficulties it occasions, the unthought of but persistent tensions it creates, what had now to be operated could hardly have been bettered. The problem of Service Children's Schools must have delighted them. HQ SCEA was part of HQ DAEd and was within the Adjutant-General's budgetary area. Service Childrens' Schools (Europe) had its HQ in BAOR and was thus within the BAOR's Commander-in-Chief's budgetary area. Thus one budgetary area was responsible for the policy of Service schools and another for their upkeep, though the adoption of a policy for which the schools could not pay or the imposition on them of financial controls which would not allow them to carry out their policy made little sense. This was a difficulty not beyond the wit of man to solve and those to whom ingenuity is the spice of life tackled it with enthusiasm, finding in the Executive Agency the *deus ex machina*. This did not clear up all complication. As so often happens the solution of one problem creates others, and so it was here. There was left unsettled the question who should be the Agency's sponsor, which in the event proved to be the Adjutant-General. There were other difficulties, too, which had to be lived with and attended to as the years went by. The disputes which have arisen in civilian Agencies in the aforementioned grey area of policy will be certain to occur in the Army's Agencies too. Simpler souls who prefer the paths of simple common sense and who think the more direct ways which do not call for ingenuity are best, deplore the time and energy wasted when they are departed from. Such simpler souls recall that in Marlowe's *Jew of Malta* the cunning Jew weaves traps of such involved subtlety as inevitably to precipitate himself in them; the play should be compulsory reading for all who see virtue in the complex.

It is not then to Shakespeare's green-eyed monster but to Margaret Thatcher's determination to make men and women freer of the state that these developments are due. Heseltine's proposals came in the 1980s, 'contractorisation' followed and the New Management Strategy and the Agencies arrived in the late 1980s and thereafter. Those who are in the profession of education today are under very heavy pressure and have been for years; necessary innovations have prompted the ill-thought out; all called for rigorous discussion and added to the burden of the hard pressed. But it is doubtful if LEAs and headmasters have been subject to the relentless pressures mounting over the years on the uniformed educators. The time they could give to ensuring their services were as good as could be made was infinitesimal compared to that spent in fighting off impractical and damaging attempts to improve them while reducing their cost. They had to fight hard even to keep their services in being at all. Imprecision, ambiguity and contradiction so characterised not a few of the arrangements they had to accept that successive Directors of Army Education who had had the foresight to send many of their officers on post-degree courses must have regretted they did not themselves take postgraduate degrees in double dutch, this it seems being what was most needed at this time.

At the Battle of Maldon the Saxons were defeated by the Danes and Britnoth, the Saxon leader, preparing for the final rally, uttered the immortal words, 'Courage shall grow greater as our strength grows less.' Unlike Britnoth the RAEC leader prevailed. They did not get what they wanted but they wanted what they got. Tough persistence and good diplomacy brought them what had at one time seemed most unlikely, survival in such heart and condition as to give them the hope there would be another day when they would make good their temporary reverse. Army Education owes a great deal to the Directors who fought so valiantly at this time.

Later was to come the first public inkling of pressure for change in the way the Army organised its support services in a parliamentary report which criticised the number of Corps – each with its own administrative structure and regimental organisation. The following debate increased the pressure for change already mounting within MOD and a variety of permutations of amalgamations were advanced, not all of which made sense to the Corps at which they were aimed. Alarmed by the more extreme possibilities being considered, the individual Directors feared not only for the future of their own Corps but for the very survival of the function it provided. Accordingly the Paymaster-in-Chief initiated a series of meetings when it became clear that not only was there pressure for change within the Adjutant-General's area of responsibility but also an imminent possibility of the re-structuring of his area itself.

As time went on yet more extreme ideas for reorganisation were emerging and, fearing that expediency was outrunning sense, the Director of Army Education and the Paymaster-in-Chief proposed that these issues should be addressed in a presentation to the Adjutant-General. The outcome was a session in which it was proposed that if the impetus to change was irresistible it should proceed on the basis of the Adjutant General's Services sharing a common administration structure but with each part retaining its individuality as a specialist service. It was suggested there might be two such groupings – the Medical Services and the remaining Adjutant-General's Services. These suggestions were thrashed out in what must have seemed to the Directors engaged in them such interminable discussions as to make them wonder how to find time to look after their own Departments.

Sandhurst was the first outstanding educational casualty of the new intense attack on the Army's support functions. It fought hard but unsuccessfully against the shortening of its cadet courses. It protested at the way the Army was seeking to cram too much into too short a time when the decision was taken to proceed with the Standard Military Course of twenty-five weeks followed by the Regular Careers Course of twenty-one weeks with only a long weekend between them. The cadets, it said, after the first year's working of that scheme, were not fresh at the beginning of the Regular Careers Course and 'unacceptably stale' at its end. The daily programme was longer than that of any known educational establishment, the period of continuous study being twice the length of the Oxbridge term. There was no time for sport or for cultural activities. It was, they said, an odd comment on the way chosen to achieve the objective sought, which was the creation of an atmosphere of intellectual stimulus and rigorous enquiry.[7]

The Sandhurst Advisory Council took even stronger exception to the recommendations of the CAROT Committee that its academic work be 'stream-lined'. This would, they said, reduce it 'from the perfunctory to something approaching the farcical'. Time was needed for their young men to develop physically, morally and intellectually. The Council agreed that the 'socialisation' of the young officer, 'the inculcation of traditional standards of leadership and man-management', could best take place in the regiment. They appreciated its importance and understood why the Army attached so much weight to it. But it should be clearly distinguished from 'training' and from 'education'. All officers needed all three. Insufficient attention was being paid to education. The CAROT Committee had not distinguished between 'training' and 'education'. It had blurred the distinction by using a phrase which the Council had difficulty in understanding, 'professional academic training'. 'Training' they held to be the development of skills and aptitudes needed for a specific activity or group of activities. 'Education' they judged to be the cultivation of the whole personality and the general development of habits of mind, particularly the ability to see more than one side to a question, to revise and if necessary abandon preconceived opinions, to think fairly, and dispassionately, and to express oneself orally, and in writing, with clarity and logic. The physical and moral development of the young officer could undoubtedly take place in the regiment. 'The development of intellectual maturity', they maintained, 'is a different matter'. That needed 'an environment in which there is time and opportunity for free discussion, for intellectual exploration, for the expression of dissent, at an age when the young men still have relatively open – or at least openable – minds'. The regiment, in their view, could not provide such an environment. It was character-developing but not mind-broadening.

The Council found what CAROT had to say about Progressive Education 'deeply disturbing'. They had been given to understand that the curtailed educational programme at Sandhurst would be 'the foundation for greatly expanded educational activities for junior officers under the RAEC'. Yet CAROT insisted that 'the total amount of time to be devoted to it must not greatly exceed what was already given to it'. There would only be six days' education a year for subalterns for three years and this, the Council said, was derisory. They thought that in the announced objective of the Junior Officers Scheme the confusion between 'training' and 'education' appeared at its worst. That objective was to teach officers to write good English and nothing more. The teaching of English was certainly needed but more was too. They had expected to find some reference to the widening of intellectual horizons, the deepening of understanding and the training of judgement; they had found nothing. The Junior Officers Scheme was too much concerned with 'covering' subjects. It was not attending to the 'awakening of intellectual curiosity' that was 'the only real foundation for any educational programme'.

CAROT said that academic education was no substitute for experience gained in commanding troops. The Council agreed but thought that while for the past hundred years a young officer after joining his regiment could be reasonably sure of seeing action within a few years, that would no longer be true in the future and, unless the commitment in Northern Ireland became permanent, British military activity in the future was likely to resemble that of Continental armies in the past, in that there would be long periods of peacetime soldiering at home in close contact with a civilian population which might not be very sympathetic. The condition which once made it desirable for 'the majority of our officers to go to regimental duty at as early an age as possible' had fundamentally changed; the Council believed that 'the implications of this change for the training and education of the officer had not been taken sufficiently into account'.[8]

General Foxton said when the Army Educational Advisory Board was abolished that he had found it useful as it provided an opportunity for civilian endorsement to be given which might help him to get accepted what might otherwise be rejected.[9] The Sandhurst Academic Advisory Council seems to have been thinking along similar lines, at least to the extent of hoping that the keeping of a civilian eye on the Army's plans for educating its officers might make it more difficult for it to be content with the pretence of doing so. The Council proposed that a new independent academic body be set up as soon as possible to oversee the working of the Junior Officers' Education Scheme and to examine and advise on the whole spectrum of officer education, particularly in its non-technical aspects. They regretted that 'those of us with experience of Sixth Form and tertiary education should find themselves so deeply and unanimously in conflict with the philosophy of education which appears to underlie the recommendations in the CAROT Report'.[10]

It was, as no doubt the Council expected it to be, a last if magnificent flourish of the trumpet. Its notes fell on unreceptive ears; the philosophy with which it was so deeply in conflict prevailed; the new independent academic body which the Council wanted to see set up was never assembled and in July 1975 it was informed that its services would be dispensed with. In its dissolution the Council performed its last service to the Army; the ending of the opportunity to give uncongenial advice ensured that it would no longer have to be listened to.

Ten years after the CAROT Report the ROTE Report reduced still further the academic content of the Standard Military Course at Sandhurst and recommended the abolition of the Regular Careers Course. It proposed a new and much shorter academic 'package' to be tacked on to the professional skills Junior Command and Staff Course; this would have a number of phases. Students must complete four weeks of academic work at Sandhurst, consisting of international affairs, military history and war studies, a three-week military technology course at Shrivenham, and a ten-week course at Warminster. Here they would study elementary staff work, tactics at company level, intelligence and service writing. To round it all off there was to be a correspondence course which Sandhurst tutors would mark. Here again we see the Army's growing disenchantment with education as normally understood and its increasing insistence that everything that passed for it should be 'relevant' to immediate military needs.[11] The same attitude of mind was affecting universities at this time. Their research, they were repeatedly told, must be utilitarian and capable of immediate technological application. In the case of the officers, it was said, education should concentrate on matters affecting BAOR and Internal Security at home or in Northern Ireland. Recent events in Europe and in the Middle East may have convinced the Army that it is not as easy to determine what is relevant as was once thought, although universities have so far failed to persuade Government of this truth. Greater acquaintance with the classics might have made both Government and Army suspicious of the relevance of relevance, more ready to agree with Euripides, who ends one of his great plays with the lines:

> And the end men looked for cometh not
> And a path is there where no man thought
> So hath it fallen here.

It was in any case difficult to reconcile with these developments the hope expressed by CAROT that the junior officer would acquire the habit of learning so that he could the more easily master the hundred and one things he had to know. The RAEC fought hard for its view that 'to halt educational training for two to three years would be detrimental to an officer's academic progress'. It thought it odd 'if he cannot devote a small proportion of his time to the furtherance of the academic part of his training'. It wanted the PQS to be continued, but it was a lost cause for which it was fighting.[12]

As for Sandhurst, despite its spirited defence and the sound points its Advisory Council made and much as its decline might be regretted, it had undoubtedly contributed to its own fate. The criticism made of its courses is hard to refute, its inadequacy being all too patent and the able diplomacy displayed by the RAEC when the blows fell on it too was little in evidence in the Sandhurst authorities. *Do ut des*, give to take, made little appeal to them. They rejected CAROTs recommendation that an RAEC brigadier be appointed there when that indication of willingness to cooperate might have tempered the bitter cold of the winds bearing upon them.

Perhaps the Corps' greatest sacrifice in its new period of storm and stress was its excellent work in officers' education. Important in itself, it was one of the most helpful indications that the Corps might be on the verge of a breakthrough in the job for which it and its predecessors had come into existence, the making of the soldier into a more educated being. If the conviction that the educated soldier was a better soldier was shared by the officers, the RAEC would still have the toughest of jobs in convincing the soldiery of that. But if that conviction was not shared by the officers the RAEC's job would not be tough, it would be impossible. If the officer became convinced of the importance of education for himself he would be more receptive to the view that it would be important for his men too. And if he was grateful to the RAEC for the help it gave him, he would be less likely to begrudge it the opportunity for assisting his soldiers and might even be able and willing to lend a hand in so doing. So that the RAEC's contribution to the education of the officers was not only a present and valuable help to the Army, it was also an exciting promise of a much brighter future both for the Corps and for the Army.

It was this that was now at risk because the great force which had been such a powerful ally in the wartime and post-war days, the force of morale, was now becoming hostile to Army Education. In those days it had been the morale of the troops after Dunkirk, after the defeats overseas which followed and in the long days of waiting and training before action could again be joined that had occasioned the anxiety of the Army authorities. The belief had then been that education would sustain that morale. Now it was the morale of the newly-commissioned officer who the regiment believed found adjustment to it and its ways far harder than did his public school predecessors that was causing alarm and despondency. The conviction was now dawning that education was exacerbating the newly-commissioned officer's difficulty in adjusting to regimental ways and was thus adversely affecting his morale.

This conflict of morale and education was a tragic conflict in the sense that it was a clash not of right and wrong, but of right and right. In the conflict of dark with light choice is easy; when right clashes with right, judgement becomes more difficult. If two desirable things cannot be fully enjoyed at one and the same time it might still be hoped that a balance between the two might be come to; on this occasion such a balance was unfortunately not found. That is greatly to be regretted but it is not to be portrayed as the triumph of darkness over light.

The Army had become much more conscious than it had hitherto been of the desirability of educating its officers. But it had also become more aware of the necessity of exposing its newly-commissioned officers as quickly as possible to the life of the regiment. The regiment had long been the Army's pride and glory. It was peculiar to the British Army. Like Topsy, it had just grown over the years and the British have a great affection for the things that just grow, believing that more than anything else they embody the genius of the race. Great regard for the Army would have been outstandingly un-British; great regard for the regiment by the Army was as outstandingly British. There were few in it who did not acknowledge its virtues, who did not see it as greatly beneficial to, and inseparable from, the Army, essential to its morale and its performance in battle, a supremely effective focusing of loyalties, the envy of other armies. It was a magnificent assertion of the importance of that symbol and ritual which has been well-understood by all healthy societies. It was where each learned to be sure of his fellows as they learned to be sure of him. Homer saw the truth it embodied when he said 'each will fight before his clansman's eyes when clans make up our units in the battle'. Its note is sounded when in the medieval *Romance of Armadis de Gaul*, a knight on learning that the great hero Armadis is his brother exclaims 'now is my life in greater danger for I must be like him'.

It is no surprise that the Army reacted as fiercely to what threatened the regiment as the Psalmist did to those who wanted to 'change their glory into the similitude of an ox that eateth grass'. Wanting to educate its young officers, it wanted still more to have them cocooned in the life of the regiment. If education enhanced the difficulty of doing this it would find a way of convincing itself that it need not. It would not turn its back on education but in the conflict of two rights, in facing the question 'how much of each can we afford to give up, how much of each must we insist on keeping', its answer would be predetermined.

In the old days the great majority of officers had come from public schools and when they joined the regiment they were already familiar with its values and ways, since these were very largely the values and the ways to which they had grown attached in their schools. Now very many of them came from schools of a different kind and the regiment believed, as it had not hitherto done, that it had a difficult job of acclimatising on its hands. It was inconceivable that there should not be a compelling desire in the regiment and in the Army as a whole to enfold in the traditions of the regiment those coming into it who were thought to be inadequately prepared to embrace them. At times this desire led to expressions of doubtful sense, as when it was suggested in the mid-1960s that the new breed of officer would be less well-educated than the old. This seems for a time to have been the view of the Army authorities and if indeed it was it would occasion eyebrows to rise.[13] The high-fliers coming from the public schools would in all probability have been better educated than the majority of officers coming from the state schools but it would have been highly eccentric to believe that the majority of officers coming from the public schools were among the high-fliers. The educational standard of the average pre-war subaltern had often been adversely commented upon and there seems no good reason to think that the average post-war subaltern coming from different schools would necessarily be of still lower educational standard. The Review of Officer Training and Education, the ROTE Report published in 1985, corrected this opinion, acknowledging that officers coming from state schools would be better educated. The view that the new breed of officer would be less well-educated than the old was nevertheless revealing. It showed that what the Army valued most in the schooling its officers had received was the development of leadership, the ability to work in a team, the sporting activities that were thought to be the best way of developing both. It believed with Emerson that it was 'the wise mixture of good drill in Latin grammar with good drill in cricket, boating and wrestling' that was 'of high importance to the matter in hand' and that this mixture was less highly regarded in state schools.[14] Perhaps, too, it was a little afraid of the intellectual ability of the new breed of officer and of his imaginative inquisitiveness that might make him question established practices. There can be no doubt that the Army was convinced that it was facing a real dilemma here. It was from these new, and as it saw them deficient, sources that officers would increasingly have to come. Its very advertising shows us how formidable it believed that dilemma to be.[15] In the early 1980s that advertising emphasised the glamour and excitement of Army life, the travel, the fun, the chances of promotion on merit. The Army would never have welcomed as its officers those to whom the glamour and the excitement of Army life made no appeal, those who were allergic to travel, the sobersides and the lacking in ambition. Nevertheless the Army had traditionally looked for qualities in its officers other than those spelled out in its advertisements; it had sought integrity, loyalty, an understanding of what was done and not done, team spirit and the acceptance of the importance of playing the game, none of these things being highly valued in civilian life in the 1960s and 1970s. This being so, it can be no matter of surprise that the Army would think it desirable to see that these qualities were developed in its newly-commissioned officers and nurtured in that environment which was so congenial to them, namely the regiment.

And when a fundamental change came in Army advertising that, too, convinces us of the sense of urgency it felt in instilling into its officers the traditional regimental values. Officer recruiting advertising in the late 1980s displayed a photograph of the memorial roll call pillar at the Royal Memorial Chapel at Sandhurst. Officers, it was said, should be prepared to follow this example, they must value the precept *dulce et decorum est pro patria mori*. Here was the old appeal to patriotism, to sacrifice, to the traditional military values. The title of the advertisement was 'a tough act to follow'. It is difficult to know if the Army thought that the mid- and later 1980s had brought about such a great change that it could now afford to aver openly that these were the qualities for which it was seeking, or if it had merely become aware that it could hardly continue to stress eagerness to travel as something easily satisfied by Army life. It may be that the Army had simply come to the conclusion that in a period which seemed to abound in City malpractices, to look with contempt upon playing the game, to see as the only acceptable expression of team spirit a willingness on the part of other players to kiss the scorer of goals, to regard loyalty as a meaningless and totally outmoded concept, it had to emphasise that it was looking to its future officers to develop qualities very different from those to be found in civilian life. And we cannot be surprised that it felt it necessary for Sandhurst to run courses which emphasised the importance of integrity and for Commanding Officers to discuss with their officers the overriding importance of it. Here again concern with officer morale is very evident.[16]

There can be no doubt that in exposing its newly-commissioned officers as quickly as possible to regimental ways the Army got what it wanted. There can be no doubt either that what it wanted and what it got was very good. Much was expected of the young officer and much was received from him. Not being allowed to, his standards did not slip. Because the same could not always be said of them, the regard in which the public held great institutions, the Monarchy itself, the Government, Parliament, the Church, the Police and the Judiciary, markedly declined. Because the same could not always be said of them the professions were no longer accorded the respect that was once unquestioningly theirs. The only profession in which standards were as high as they had always been was the profession of arms, an achievement not unnoticed in a country becoming increasingly aware how much had been lost which it still highly valued.

Good shopping, however, demands that attention be paid to prices even when we are highly satisfied with our purchases. And the price paid for great regimental achievement was not negligible.

Knowing that we cannot learn about men from books, the regiment was determined to expose its officers as quickly as possible to that experience from which alone they will learn about men. It is, however, one thing to give priority to experience and another to forget about books. If we thought to learn only from experience our mastery of many essential things would be slowly and painfully acquired. We would not be giving priority to experience if we turned away from other means of learning; we would be giving exclusive attention to it and that we would know to be undesirable.[17] Yet such are the demands in an overstretched Army made upon the officer learning his job in the regiment, learning to know men and how to lead them, that other ways of learning seem so frequently to be put behind him and is it not as likely to be true of him as it was of Mr Podsnap that whatever he put behind him he put out of existence? There is, unfortunately, a difficulty attendant on the practice of clearing the world of its problems by sweeping them behind us. They are sufficiently malevolent to slip in front of us when we least expect them and when, since we have never thought about them, we are unprepared to meet them. We have to rise, or not as the case may be, to unexpected challenges as we cannot prevent them arising. Some problems at least can be anticipated and thought given to enabling us to cope with them, and is it not better that they should be? If the officer aspires to high rank he must, at some stage, make himself familiar with the experiences, the thought, the wisdom which he will get only from the written word. If he has had little opportunity for reading and reflection, reading and reflection will not come easily to him and will have little chance to help him make the best of himself. If no way can be found of ensuring that the young officer growing up with his job in the regiment is benefitting from what is a genuine priority and not suffering from an undesirable exclusivity, he may find that his apprenticeship was not after all as suitable for the complete mastery of his craft as on the face of it it seemed, and the leaders of his craft may have more difficulty than they had expected in finding an adequate number of worthy successors to replace them. Would they not be well-advised to remember the question Frederick the Great asked his generals 'What is the value of experience if you do not reflect on it?' Or to recall Livy's attribution of the successes of one of Rome's greatest generals to 'his perpetual meditation in times of peace as well as war'.

The imperative demands of morale which had once so greatly strengthened Army Education now gravely weakened it. The most promising system of officer education could no longer be afforded. It is a good Stoic principle that men should persuade themselves that what they cannot have they do not need, and this happened when circumstances compelled a cutting-back of education in the Army. The view became widespread that the Army need not concern itself with education to the extent that had been thought necessary recently, the job which it had thought it would itself have to attend to having been adequately tackled by the civilian world before men joined the Colours. This was clearly the case with many of the officers, an increasing number of whom were now graduates. As early as 1958 the steady growth in the number of graduates in the Army was widely predicted; the CAROT Report took it for granted that this growth would continue; years later the ROTE Report was sure that most of the officers in the near future would be graduates. These reports were justified in this belief, although the increase in the number of graduate officers was a slower and more gradual process than had been anticipated; it was not, for instance, until 1984 that the proportion of graduate students at Camberley reached 50%. Whatever the speed of this process, it did not seem manifestly absurd to say that graduates did not need the teaching which it might be maintained was still essential for non-graduates, to exempt them, as they were exempted, from taking part in the Junior Officers' Education Scheme.

What seems obvious is not always the case and the very Army Order which exempted graduates from that scheme leaves us in doubt about the soundness of the judgement which prompted that exclusion. That order, while saying that this is to enable them to catch up their non-graduate colleagues in duties which they were learning while the graduate officer was still at university, also tells us that this is being done 'in order to avoid repetition of intellectual effort'.[18] Too much should not be made of what is perhaps inadequate drafting; the attitude of mind revealed is none-the-less significant. Those who helped officers in the writing of essays never lacked occasion to remind them that repetition was to be avoided. But it had never occurred to them that repetition of intellectual effort was to be deprecated; they had on the contrary sought to promote it.

Universities would not find it easy to answer the charge that they had not had the effect they ought to have had on their graduates if these leave without the desire and determination to continue their education, and not just by growing in the greater school of life. Universities are only too aware how often they fail in this and they could not agree with the view which also became widespread in the Army that graduates would need no inducement to further develop their education. They would be sure that exempting graduate officers from the Junior Officers' Education Scheme was restricting the opportunity for continuing intellectual development of those who might eventually have most to offer the Army. They would strongly agree with the CAROT Report that international affairs and the studies which come under the generic title 'man and society' were professionally relevant to the officer, that graduates in their university studies might not have come into contact with them, that it was essential that all officers practise themselves in the art of clear, concise and cogent writing. Not all graduates had this ability. In the CAROT discussions it was said 'certainly some graduates particularly in the sciences do not show much ability in written expression'. Not all arts graduates did either.

The view was also accepted in the Army that what the officer would lose in the discontinuance of the educational provision hitherto thought necessary for him he would make up for in another way. The 'mind broadening and maturing' of the subaltern would take place 'during a young officer's first tour of regimental duty', CAROT insisted. Years later, the ROTE Report again emphasised that what the subaltern needed he could pick up on the job while attending whatever courses were thought necessary at later stages in his career.

Since men, like foxes, have little difficulty in convincing themselves of the sourness of the grapes they cannot reach, it was soon suggested that this was a much better way than that which it replaced of the officer acquiring the education essential to him. A PQS Review Working Party said in July 1979 that among the officers there was 'a widely held degree of antipathy towards the examination and its purposes'.[19] The careful and thorough scheme of officer education, it now turned out, did not fulfil those exposed to it, rather it frustrated them. And if that was its accomplishment, its ending was timely indeed. That Commanding Officers had never liked it had long been known. They had frequently expressed the wish to lose their officers less frequently on courses and 70% of them, it appeared, had said that preparation for the Staff/Promotion Examination 'placed unacceptable time-demands on units'. But the widely held antipathy now found among the candidates to that examination had not been apparent to many of the Officer Tutors who ran these courses, although they were usually regarded as very well-informed about the opinions and feelings of their pupils. The instructors were of course as anxious that the examination and the preparation for it should continue as the Commanding Officers were not. It is always difficult to know to what extent wishful thinking affects findings, and perhaps our safest conclusion is that however widespread among the officers was the antipathy noted towards the examination and its purposes, it was by no means universal.

The Review of Officer Training and Education effectively ended the education provided by the Progressive Qualification Scheme which was replaced by what was said to be a more 'flexible' two-tier system. The first tier was an examination for promotion only. It consisted of papers in military knowledge, defence and international affairs and war studies. These papers might be taken altogether or singly, and the examination was to be held twice a year. Preparation for it was based primarily on a correspondence course run by civilian lecturers and RAEC tutors at Sandhurst. The second tier was an examination for Staff College so designed as 'to ensure that no detailed factual background for it would be required and that it would not be amenable to any preparatory course so that the fundamental requirements of a good staff officer could be tested', as it was optimistically said.

This was a most important change. There was still to be an examination for candidates for Staff College, its purpose being, as was the purpose of that which it replaced, to see if officers possessed the qualities for which the Staff College was looking, and on which it could build. And since all examinations will be prepared for, this one would be too, despite what was said about it not being amenable to any preparatory course. The wiles of the wily are not easily exhausted. But units would not, or so it was said, suffer from 'preparatory courses' which would occupy the time and attention of their officers. And officers would not benefit from them either. These courses had sought to develop in the officers the qualities for which the Staff College was looking. It cannot be doubted that in many cases they had succeeded in doing so. They had brought over the 500 mark, which aspirants to the Staff College were required to reach, those who but for the help these courses provided would have remained persistently below it. And there is a world of difference between an examination which is merely designed to show if candidates possess certain qualities and one which is part of a process of enabling candidates to develop them. There is little doubt which is the more genuinely educational. Those who taught and who examined PQS II candidates would doubt that if the qualities which were sought in the old examination were genuinely looked for in this new one there would have been as many successful candidates to select from as the old examination produced. They would have felt sure that the Staff College would have had in many cases to do the job that officers' tutors were doing so well, namely to help officers develop them. They would have been wryly amused that the widely-practised eccentricity of officers preparing themselves for the Staff/Promotion examination in leaving their preparation until the last moment, a practice often adversely commented on, seemed to have been paralleled by the equally deplorable eccentricity of the Army authorities in leaving these qualities required by the Staff College to be developed in many of the officers going there only when they got there. They might even have wondered, this task being left so late, if it could adequately be done when they got there. General Learmont, Commandant at Camberley, seems to have doubted it. He said that perhaps his most important task was 'to raise the intellectual level' there and he added, 'cramming and spoon-feeding characterised its proposals'. These were not the ways in which that 'breadth of understanding across a range of disciplines' which the Beach Report stressed was needed if officers 'were to cope with the demands that would be made upon them in senior posts' could be promoted nor in which officers' tutors had tried to prepare their pupils for Camberley. It is easy to understand the dismay of the tutors at the ending of PQS II. As one Naval officer employed with the Army officers tutoring in South West District said, they were 'halcyon days working with a highly professional service in a job which was highly rewarding'.[20]

Many of the officers caught up in the old PQS II preparation for the Staff College examination, we are told, disapproved of it; more seem to have objected to what replaced it. In 1988 the Junior Officers Training and Education Scheme II was introduced. This was to consist of five phases. The first three were residential courses to be held at the RMAS, at the RMCS and at Warminster. The fourth phase was a year-long correspondence course which would consolidate what had been learned in the residential courses. The final phase was a promotion examination in war studies, defence and international affairs. There was also a separate Staff Selection Test for the high-flyers hoping to go to Staff College; the nature of this has already been discussed.

Neither the Beach nor the ROTE Reports sought to justify the ending of PQS II on educational grounds. The case for education admitted of no answer; circumstances were such that it could carry no conviction. These reports were attempts to reduce costs, to save time, to ease the burdens of hard-pressed Commanding Officers. There was to be less time for teaching and fewer teachers. The number of RAEC officers employed in officer education was reduced from thirty-five to eleven. All this was soon strongly criticised. If there had been many before who disliked being taught, it seemed there were more now who objected still more to not being taught. The length of time which elapsed between the holding of the residential courses and the taking of the examination was said to be much too long. The correspondence course and its administration were said to be most inadequate. Such was the unpopularity of this new approach to promotion and the Staff College that the wisdom of ignoring the officer's grievance, and this at a time when so much was expected of him, was not obvious and the Army took steps to end it. The correspondence course was scrapped and replaced by an Interim Scheme called the Directed Reading and Project Scheme. Officers were to write an extended essay during the six months before going on the first of their residential courses. There was also to be a new examination which was to be taken by all officers, whether they were aiming at the Staff College or contenting themselves with promotion. This was the Integrated Promotion and Staff examination. The RAEC tutors still concerned with officer education, renamed Field Tutors, were to hold a one-day course for officers newly embarking on the Directed Reading and Project Scheme; they would teach their pupils how essays should be written.

The making more flexible of PQS affected its first as well as its second stage. The Junior Officers Education and Training Scheme which was now introduced continued to call upon the RAEC, but to a much less extent than had been the case with PQS I. The intellectual development of the young officer again became a Commanding Officer's responsibility and was not mandatory. The commitment of units to it was, as might have been expected, variable. In this respect the Army was back where it had been twenty years before, it thus being evident that as its leading members made their way up in it their encounter, if any, with Army Education had not convinced them of its indispensability. As what succeeded PQS II occasioned dissatisfaction, so too did the replacement for PQS I. The attention paid to the education of the subaltern proved to be inadequate; so too did his education.

Superbly adjusted to the intellectual needs of a small minority, schools in Britain had left a majority uninterested in what had been taught and in matters of numeracy and literacy much less accomplished than could be desired. Many who had attained commissions were of this number, despite the increasing number of officer graduates. Young officers would not have been commissioned had they failed to reach a certain educational standard, but Commanding Officers found some of them less literate than they required them to be. And as the needs of middle-ranking officers forced the Army to make an educational provision which it had thought unnecessary, so now the needs of their seniors brought about a further educational provision which it thought could be dispensed with. So the Junior Officers' Training and Education Scheme began in April 1992. Each young officer had now to undergo, as he or she were only too likely to think of the experience, three years of education in the period between being commissioned and promoted to Captain's rank. In each of these three years there were to be three two-day study periods in which they would study campaigns in North West Europe during the Second World War and also certain current topics to be later determined. We may well believe extremism to be a sin and warm to Bishop Hall when he tells us 'moderation is the silken thread running through the pearl chain of all virtues'. Yet a fleeting regret may still be pardonable that the educational effort demanded of the junior officer by the Junior Officers' Training and Education Scheme was so modest.

There is an even more important reason to wish more attention was paid to the education of officers. Wellington tells us that in India he rose at six and wrote till nine. He does not say that he read, but that he wrote. He insisted that a few written pages of analysis and reflection were more important than a great deal of reading. This was Napoleon's way of study too. High-flyers have no doubt found this for themselves, but the Army might have more flyers to choose from if all officers were pressed more than they are to accustom themselves to writing, reflecting and analysing.

However, if what was demanded of him was less than the subaltern needed it was doubtless more than he desired, and the balance it struck between needs and desires here was itself part of another important balance, that between the imperative needs of acquiring the professional skills which were essential to mastering the military art and the limited time in which they had to be acquired. Without the adjusting of that vital balance the Junior Officers' Training and Education Scheme II would have little hope of success; without it interest might have died which it was of great importance to keep alive, and attitudes which had they hardened would have made difficult later intellectual development might have become engrained. The lesson is striking. The Army, no doubt reluctantly, had concluded that officer education could no longer be afforded; now, no doubt equally reluctantly, it was persuaded that the price for its absence was too high. The significance of that change ought not to be overlooked.

In yet another way the RAEC met the immediate needs of the Army in the field of officers' education. It ran remedial courses at Beaconsfield for officers coming from the ranks. These were not only to bring them up to the required educational standard but also to promote their confidence by showing them how to lead and to practise them in taking discussions. The courses were designed to elicit and strengthen the arts of analysis and of clear and concise writing. The RAEC officers who taught on the courses found them challenging, exciting and stimulating; if this was what the teachers felt about them it is a safe bet that the taught did, too.[21] The Army had every reason to be grateful for this particular essay in officer education, although the RAEC was well aware that since the institutional expression of gratitude is expensive, it is also very rare.

Perhaps it is as well to mention here a further provision for the education of the officer with which the RAEC was not concerned. It was REME's practice to select some thirty WOs every year for Late Entry Commissions. They did not attend the Beaconsfield course, going instead to a short course at the Officers' School to prepare them for their new careers. Such men had qualities of leadership that were not in question and a technical competence which their Corps deemed sufficient to meet the demands which would be made on them in their new role.

The cogency of the reasons for ending PQS cannot be doubted. The Corps' old enemies, the clock and the purse, were now strengthened by the overwhelming financial pressures bearing down heavily on the whole of the Army. The changing nature of the officer corps created new demands, attention to which claimed priority. The increasing number of graduate officers whose degrees were often in disciplines not unrelated to PQS studies led many to suggest their teaching by RAEC officers was no longer necessary. There was also the genuine belief that what would replace PQS, since it was modelled on what satisfied the Civil Service, should be good enough for Army officers. There was in addition a movement directed at the establishment of a Higher Command and Staff Course at Camberley which it was felt could not be set up without releasing the resources used in the PQS. It is also true that the RAEC found it difficult to produce enough tutors of the right intellectual and military calibre to run it.[22] There were other reasons for ending PQS which were less respectable but not less powerful. Some senior officers, particularly fathers of young officers, became upset when their sons failed the examinations. There was also some feeling in the Army that the Corps was becoming too powerful an influence in relation to the careers of teeth arms officers.[23]

But the most important of all the reasons for the ending of PQS was the policy of the government. It was the primary cause of the pressures which bore as heavily on the RAEC and many others in the period before the collapse of the USSR as *Options for Change* did after it. Under previous governments defence and the Services generally had begun suffering what the Chinese described as 'the death of a thousand cuts'. The new Conservative government gave defence a higher profile but brought with it a greater determination to cut costs and a new management policy to enable it to do so which gripped all the Services tighter than before and the non-operational support groups tightest of all. It was this new Conservative drive and determination to cut costs which explains the pressures the Corps suffered in its final phase. Michael Heseltine set out to complete the work of Mountbatten in integrating the Services in MOD and in creating a powerful Centre staffed by a mixture of civil servants and soldiers. He wanted, like a managing director, to know in some detail what was going on and how it was done, and to direct it. He therefore transferred from his previous Ministry the Ministerial Information System. This involved all two-star generals who directed support functions in preparing briefs for discussion with him, this being a good example of the centralising and managerial imperative of the Conservative government. It was these compulsions which account for General Beach's savaging of the RAEC officers' tutors. His Report is one of the most comprehensive reviews of the RAEC ever undertaken and it is made by an officer of considerable intellectual stature. It merits reflection.

The Beach Study was set up in November 1983 to review education in the Army and to define the educational requirements appropriate to career patterns and employments of Army officers and soldiers, both adult and junior. It was established in the context of the LEAN LOOK Studies. which had been carried out in the rest of the Army in 1983 to meet the need to redeploy manpower from the support areas to the teeth arms to cover planned enhancements to the military capabilities of the Army. It was left to the Beach Study to consider to what extent manpower savings could and should be made in the RAEC.

The Beach team consisted of General Sir Hugh Black, Dr M.E. Foss, former Deputy Director of Coventry Polytechnic, and Mr R.A. Wake, former HMI responsible for Secondary Education. It carried out a wide-ranging series of visits, interviews, and discussions with senior officers and other interested parties, and in February 1984 the Commands and Heads of Arms and Services were asked for their comments on the existing system.

The Beach team produced their Report in December 1984. In marked contrast to the Groom Report (April 1983) they found no deep-rooted faults in the system which had evolved for educating soldiers and recommended that the drastic changes outlined by Groom should not be contemplated. The education provided was necessary to the Army, relevant to the soldier's rank and trade, and well constructed and taught. Any serious reduction in the content or time would be to the soldier's disadvantage and to that of the Army as a whole.

The team also visited Junior Entry units when they were undergoing changes of location and reductions in the length of courses imposed by the implementation of the Groom Report. They endorsed the course content and teaching methods in the Apprentice Colleges and commented that the development of the Junior Army Education Certificate in the Junior Leaders units was on the right lines.

On the subject of officers' education the Report was more critical, describing the Progressive Qualification Scheme as 'no longer progressive, leading to no recognised qualification, and can only in a narrow sense be described as a scheme'. Much of the work in the previous syllabus of international affairs and war studies was described as more appropriate to a postgraduate course than to a course for the average Major. It recommended that the first stage (PQS I) should continue in its existing form; that the PQS II examination should become a promotion examination separated from the Staff selection process and consist of four papers (unit administration, morale and man-management; military technology; international relations; campaign studies) and should be taught by a correspondence course system based on RMA Sandhurst. A separate Staff Selection Test on the lines of the Civil Service Selection Board process (i.e. not requiring any detailed factual knowledge or previous preparation or tuition) was proposed. Implementation of the details were left to the Review of Officer Training and Education (ROTE) Study, which was to be carried out in 1985, to follow up the Beach report.

The final proposals put forward by the team recommended no RAEC involvement at all in officers' education but as a result of intervention by the Director of Army Education they were amended at the last moment and it was agreed that eleven Officer Tutors would be retained to provide local tutorial assistance world-wide for the new scheme. (It was a condition of their retention that compensating reductions of another eleven posts from other areas of the Director's responsibilities should be made, which would seem to indicate that manpower savings were the major factor in the Study.)

The ROTE Report recommendations in setting up the Junior Officer Training and Education Scheme (JOTES) Parts 1 and 2 followed broadly the proposals of the Beach Report, although there were some changes in the content and titles of the subjects for JOTES 2. However, within a relatively short time the shortcomings and consequent criticism of the new scheme soon became apparent, particularly in connection with the correspondence course system, and the scheme had to be amended and adapted further.

Overall, the Beach Report could be said to be very supportive of the work of the Corps. With the exception of the recommendations about Officers' Education where there was a reduction of involvement, the other areas of the Corps' responsibilities e.g. Soldiers' Education, Junior Army Education, Training Support, Language Training, Resettlement, Service Children's Schools, in general received a firm endorsement. The continuing need for a uniformed Corps of educators was clearly recognised and the post of Director was acknowledged as a Major-General's appointment. Nevertheless, the Study was set up against the background of manpower savings being required from the support areas of the Army to increase the strengths of the teeth arms. As a result of the Study approximately one hundred posts out of a total of about six hundred were recommended for savings, but this has to be set against the background of similar savings being made in other Corps under Exercise LEAN LOOK.

It seems odd that Beach should acknowledge the importance of education for the Army's middle managers and pass so lightly over the education of those in charge of them. In his tour of units in which he found Commanding Officers most appreciative of soldiers' education he must have gathered what they thought of the literacy of many of their officers. It was later that reports of their examination performance said that much of their writing, despite the fact that 75% of them were now graduates, raised doubts about English being their native language. Highly intelligent as he was it is inconceivable that he was unaware of this. No one could have known more than he the importance of continued education for officers and he leaves it to the ROTE review, the thinking of which he could not have been ignorant of, to suggest what should be done about it. It is difficult to disagree with him when he said PQS II was poorly designed for the average Major. Those who examined for it had said so. They had protested in vain that a single examination for the flyers for Staff College and for those who sought promotion only made little sense. Nor is it difficult to accept his view that the Field Tutors could not do the job. They were too few. They could do their job admirably and help effectively when they could be with the officers, but it was ludicrous to imagine that, hard pressed as they were, they could see officers sufficiently frequently to attend adequately to officer education. Knowing their number would have to be decreased he knew also they could only scratch the surface of things and he did not keep in mind, as the RAEC which fought successfully for the retention of thirteen of them did, the possibility of future expansion. Perhaps he was hoping, as others had often done before him, as we have seen that Wolseley who was also an intellectual did, that with the advance of general education the problem would disappear.

His reasoning, too, is questionable. If PQS II was unsuitable for candidates going only for promotion, why should it be thought unsuitable for Staff seekers? His criticism of the syllabus and the examination for it is based on what it originally was; he cannot have been unaware it was no longer that. His alternative is unconvincing. It may be appropriate for prospective civil servants, although the gobbledegook emanating from them raises doubts about this, and he knew full well that would-be flyers in it face other and more formidable obstacles. He knew what officers thought of the previous correspondence courses designed to help them and could not have been surprised at their speedy demonstration of how they regarded those now proposed. He knew that among those not now being prepared for the Staff College Examination would be a goodly number who without such preparation would never get there, but who would have got there, as the past showed, with it. He is aware of a persistent and most important problem facing the Army and he walks away from it. The report did what it was commissioned to do, it made the savings required. It did so by recommending doing without essential things. The Beeching way also achieved its objective – at a price later judged excessive.

The Conservative government lost no opportunity of saying education was one of its top priorities. It naturally drew no attention to its impact, which was disastrous, on Army Education. The ending of the PQS and the loss of all but a small number of its Officer Tutor posts was a very serious blow for the Corps. The establishment of a unified scheme of education in the Army, covering soldiers, children, cadets and officers had been vetoed by Queen Victoria in 1856. It had taken more than a century to climb back and for the uniformed educator to acquire a role across the whole range of military education. For the Army the reversion to correspondence courses and the severing of the link between progressive military education and entry to Camberley was an even greater blow. As Professor Bond wrote nearly twenty years ago the attempt to devise a satisfactory system of officer education in the British Army has greatly resembled the labours of Sisyphus. It is to be hoped that the new century will at last see the stone reach and stay at the top of the hill.

Hammered by the ending of its fine PQS, the Corps was further weakened by the cutting down of its role in Resettlement, the importance of which was increased by the immediate problem of drastically reducing the numbers of the Army. This would inevitably add to the determination of those who had always resented the RAEC's role in it to redouble their efforts to remove it.[24] Given the fact that the Army Council had before it many supremely important matters demanding as speedy resolution as possible, it could not give sustained and undivided attention to it; it was bound to turn to the time-honoured practice of appointing a committee to consider it and it is an odd committee which does not provide opportunity for the expression of dissatisfaction with existing practices. The RAEC was to learn the truth of Burke's words 'You may depend upon it that when many people have an interest in railing, soon or later, they will bring a considerable degree of unpopularity upon any measure.'[25] The shrinking of the cake sharpens appetite. In his unforgettable portrayal of the evils of war Thucydides reminds us that when shortages oppress knives came out which would not have appeared in the more prosperous times of peace.[26] In dearth Nabab's vineyard which rarely goes uncoveted is bound to seem more attractive. Interests must be expected to be more selfishly and brutally pushed when the consequences of this not being done have become more serious.

While the pressures on it to relinquish Resettlement increased, the RAEC's case for maintaining responsibility for it weakened. This was the consequence of the priorities on which it had itself determined. At this time its first priority was to become an all-officer Corps. It greatly benefitted from this. But there was a price to be paid for it. Sergeants in the Sergeant's Mess would have always had more direct influence than RAEC officers in persuading NCOs and Other Ranks to think about and bestir themselves to prepare for leaving the Army. Had the RAEC Sergeants and Warrant Officers still been there to see to this, the Committee's case for removing it from the Corps would have been weakened.

It is not then surprising that despite the excellence of its Resettlement work, in the 1970s and 1980s the Corps became involved in a bitter and protracted struggle to keep its responsibility for Resettlement. Typical of its determination to spare no effort in helping those nearing the end of their service to prepare for civilian life was its sending of Resettlement Officers to join the British Forces Lebanon in the spring of 1983. Its Resettlement work was imaginative, innovative and persistent. Against formidable opposition it arranged that in the last six months before leaving the Colours the soldier could attend courses lasting six weeks to help him prepare for his new life. It never forgot that it was an intensely personal service it was providing and that it was only through a warm man-to-man relationship that it could be adequately discharged. It had the satisfaction of securing agreement to principles on which a far-reaching Resettlement Plan could be based. Its officers were given further in-service training; they were kept in Resettlement jobs longer than the normal tour of duty time as continuity in Resettlement posts was so desirable. It engaged some of its officers on full-time Resettlement work. It increased the number of Resettlement courses it ran for the soldiers and induced civilian bodies to run such courses, too. In this it worked closely with the Navy and Air Force in the hope of hammering out with them a Tri-Service Resettlement Scheme.

Perhaps the most significant development in the 1970s was its formation of the Army Resettlement Employment Liaison Cell which was set up in the Directorate of Army Education. It built up a database of those seeking employment and of employers who would offer it. It published the Services Resettlement Bulletin Vacancy Supplement which it made available to its sister Services, although the hope of establishing a Tri-Service Resettlement body came to nothing.

The Corps secured agreement to its proposals that the soldier who had no qualifications other than his disciplined service to recommend him to prospective employers should be given additional training, the length of which should depend on the time spent with the Colours, that pre-release training for all should be an entitlement and not a concession, that courses lasting longer than forty-five days should take place after discharge and that adequate allowances be given to those undergoing post-release training. Its satisfaction was but fleeting; its frustration, occasioned by the continued abandonment of agreed principles, lasting. Fine principles, it was evident, buttered no parsnips; these principles, never objected to, were never carried out.

A great cry and little wool, the Devil is said to have exclaimed as he sheared the pigs. The better intentioned might have echoed him when considering the many and varied Resettlement projects put forward. Recommendation followed recommendation. Each was amended, amended again, discussed and fought over; none was ever implemented. A Tri-Service Resettlement Organisation headed by a civilian was set up; it shared the inability of the soldiers to solve resettlement problems. The reduction in the numbers of the Armed Forces envisaged in *Options for Change* concentrated minds. A two-star General responsible for Resettlement was appointed and the Tri-Service Resettlement Organisation was placed under the direction of the MOD Centre.

Resettlement thus passed out of the control of the RAEC's successors. They were still, however, to be concerned with it: 'their role in it', it was said, 'remains unchanged'. It was indeed considerable. The Tri-Service Resettlement Organisation took control of Resettlement training (previously the work of two or three RAEC officers at Eltham arranging courses and looking after two Resettlement Centres) and job finding. The same Corps officers who had carried out this work continued to do so within the Tri-Service Resettlement Organisation alongside their Royal Naval and Royal Air Force colleagues. However, the Director of Army Education remained responsible for giving individual Resettlement Advice, the same thirty of his officers being fully employed on this. The Commandants of the Catterick and Aldershot Resettlement Centres and their deputies remained RAEC officers. They worked not for the Director of Army Education but for the Tri-Services Resettlement Organisation. The Service Directors of Army Education were still concerned with the development of Resettlement policy. The Director of Resettlement is now a Tri-Service appointment. The Director of Education and Training Services (A) is the Army's representative on the Resettlement Policy Committee. It might seem that the Devil's comment on the shearing of the pigs might be applied to these Resettlement changes. Nevertheless the passing of Resettlement to other hands, though relative and mitigated, is a loss to the Army's educators, inevitably reducing their stature.

As the other ways we have considered in which the increased power of the predominantly Civil Service MOD Centre reduced the financial and the executive power of the functional directors in the MOD, these Resettlement developments did too. It has yet to be proved that they were not also a loss to the Army. It was rightly said of those demobilised in the late 1980s who had been helped by the RAEC Resettlement Officers that they returned to civilian life with more generally recognised qualifications than any previous generation.[27] Burke once said that while he could not censure what was done he might be permitted to regret it. This might be an appropriate comment on the taking of full responsibility for Resettlement from the educators.

The Corps made a spirited attempt to retain the ability to do what could be done to enable it to discharge its function. Apart from the various suggestions we have seen put forward to enable it to do so while meeting ministerial requirements, it continued its attention to old needs. It did its best to mitigate the ever-present problem of officer education. It knew its reduced number of Officer Tutors, now called Field Tutors, could not solve that problem. They were far too few to do adequately the job for which they were appointed. Still less could it be done by the handful of Field Tutors *Options for Change* allowed the new Education and Training Services Branch to have. The hard struggle to get them, however, was well worthwhile and its victory of major importance. It drew attention to a problem the Army no doubt hoped that somehow or other the kindly gods would remove but which they had given no sign of doing. The appointment of the Field Tutors was the recognition, strongly endorsed by subsequent findings, that officers still needed further education, graduates though the majority of them now were. It was confirmation of the fact that here there remained a most important job to be done that, requiring a knowledge of regimental ways and an ability to adjust to them which could not be expected from civilians, uniformed educators were best able to do. This was the keeping of the seed-corn which, if there was to be a future harvest, must be preserved. This was the Corps' acid comment on General Beach who had walked away from the problem as it now refused to do.

The RAEC saved much else that was worth saving. It continued to serve as educational advisers on the Regular Commissions Board; as it had done so for nearly fifty years there could be no doubt the Army valued this service. The Corps has been represented at the RCB with one or more officers since 1950; there have also been one or more retired RAEC officers on the staff since 1966. These officers have always had a major influence on the Board, advising on the candidates' intellectual abilities, educational achievements and knowledge of the world. They have also been instrumental in the development of the Board's systems and philosophies. Although the advisers can rarely persuade the Board to pass a candidate it wishes to fail, nor is that their role, they can generally ensure that a candidate with intellectual limitations does not pass, thus saving the Army from many disasters.[28] EPC also remained unchanged and was indeed to receive fresh impetus from future NVQ developments and Language Training continued to expand.

Nor did the pressures now bearing on the Corps prevent the developing of the newer work in which it had been recently engaged. We have seen how in the 1960s and 1970s the Corps laid the foundations for its later contribution to Training Support. In the 1980s we see how impressive this was. The Corps continued to do its homework after sending its officers to take postgraduate degrees in matters connected with instructional technology. Thus one of its postgraduate degreed officers took a shortened version of the course designed for the training of tank crews to enable him to turn his specialist knowledge to that training. One went to the Royal Corps of Transport where he worked in a small team, the Logistics and Development Team, which consisted of two RCT officers, one a Lieutenant-Colonel who headed it, and himself. His job was to assess the effect of existing ways of training on those being trained, to be concerned with the time taken to train them and with the impact of their training on subsequent performance. He had to produce what improvement he could. He had to advise on, and approve, the buying of equipment needed for training purposes. He was a busy man. He produced a report on the Movement Controllers Branch of the RCT, for which he received warm thanks. He contributed to a NATO study of the transportation systems and to a study of close-support staff-car driving in Northern Ireland. He was also a contented man having the knowledge that he was doing an important and warmly-appreciated job. 'The people I work with', he said, 'are a delight; they actually seek me out for my advice, and, what is even more astonishing, they take it without demur!'[29]

The call that is made on services is a fair indication of their value. Calls on the Army School of Instructional Technology, the name it adopted in 1980, were so many and varied that one wonders how it found time for that reflection which its research role necessitated.[30] Fortunately its separate Consultancy Wing was able to relieve it of many jobs. Here is a list of its tasks in the RAEC's last days: to identify requirements for assistance to Intelligence Corps Training Wing; to investigate compact disc technology and assess its potential for use in military training; to identify and recommend methods of training simulator instructors; to write a set of training objectives for the TA Command and Staff Course; to design a training method that maximises the ability of the operator to detect and recognise thermal imagery targets; to investigate the complete artillery ammunition requirements for Regular, TA and training units and to determine how best to meet these needs with the optimum mixture of live firing and simulated training systems; to assess the most effective means of meeting video requirements for training; to advise on computer requirements for Brigade and Battle Group Trainers; to investigate the requirements of all training units for a training management system; to coordinate and monitor the use of computers by the RAEC; to evaluate Smart Ferranti small arms simulators; to train the RAEC in the use of microcomputers and software; to test a distance-learning scheme for the Royal Signals technical training; to advise on the construction of training packages for junior officers and junior NCOs; to advise on the training objectives for All Arms Tactics Courses, for Commanding Officers' Tactics Courses and for Senior Officers' Tactics Course; to advise on technical and training aspects of trainer/simulators; and to advise on the training of Late Entry Officers. The Schools' instructors never suffered from the boredom attendant on frequent repetition; they might have felt a fleeting satisfaction if every now and then the opportunity to experience such boredom had come their way.[31]

Nor was the School left to feed upon itself. It was involved in a great deal of Tri-Service consultation. It worked closely with civilian bodies, the Council for Educational Technology, the Manpower Services Commission, the Business and Technician Education Council, the Association for Educational Training Technology, the Industrial Training Board and a number of others. It acquired an international reputation. It exchanged appointments with the US Army's Training and Doctrine Command and with the Canadian Defence Forces. It sent representatives to international conferences in Europe and in the USA. Such was its determination to keep up-to-date that it sent its people to the only university that as yet gave a degree in Simulation Studies.

Those in the forefront of this new approach to training have not overplayed their hand. They have acknowledged that 'training is one way of helping to achieve satisfactory job performance but it is by no means the only solution'. Their attitude is thus far more realistic than was that of the RAEC officers who made so many extraordinary and exorbitant claims for what they sought to do in, for instance, the Interim Scheme.

They have, nevertheless, succeeded. There has been an improvement in job performance in the Army despite the growing complexity and sophistication of weapon systems and equipment, the increasing competition of civilian life for the kind of recruits it needs, the severe manpower and financial cutbacks in it. It is said there has been substantial saving in money, in the time devoted to training, in the resources it expends in so doing.

Further expansion of this work is hoped for. There is a Persian proverb according to which time is 'the father of miracles, the Prime Minister of all sovereigns with whom they can do everything and without whom they can do nothing'. In great revolutions or when all things seem changing men forget the old truth 'let us change never so often, we cannot change man, our imperfections must still run with us'; experience soon reminds them of it. All things need time to settle down and for some at least of the deficiencies which it reveals to be rectified. Training Support has been pushing at the frontiers of new knowledge and the Education and Training Services Branch of the Adjutant-General's Corps has the job of improving what the years have shown needs improvement in this new work embarked upon by the RAEC in its closing years.

Job analysis, which involves the mastery of what might be unfamiliar details and above all the opportunity to think, is a time-consuming process; inevitably, therefore, since the desire to save time was an important reason for its introduction, there would come the demand that job analysis be itself subject to job analysis in the determination to reduce still further the time to be spent on it. An obvious task facing the new Education and Training Services Branch is, therefore, to seek new techniques in job analysis and its all-important evaluation so that less time need be devoted to it.

Given the general belief that Training Support had proved itself in some areas, the hope was bound to be entertained that it might be equally beneficial in others. Could it be introduced for collective training? Might it not throw new light on an old problem which the rapid advance of technology was making almost unliveable with, the problem of weapon procurement? How far can the increasing use of simulation exercises justifiably reduce the actual use of expensive ammunition and thus also the pressures of Greenpeace and other environmental groups? Can better ways of budgeting which might soften the attitude of Treasury ogres be found? Could the training implications of the introduction of new equipment at the stage at which the equipment was being procured be taken into account? If so it would enable training to be planned as the equipment was being manufactured and ensure that the training costs and manpower implications of the introduction of any new systems could be built into the procurement costs. The RAEC pushed this but met with opposition as purchasing equipment is a competitive process and there is always pressure to hold down full costs until the purchase has been agreed. Queries of this kind constitute a formidable challenge to the new Educational and Training Services Branch. In the growing body of new work bequeathed to it by the RAEC it could find no legacy of leisure.

Nothing in the affairs of men, however, suggests that universal agreement is ever easily reached. It would have been surprising had the achievement claimed for Training Support been uncontested. A paper on it written in 1984 drew attention to the fact that 'many senior officers are unaware of the benefits that Training Support and a Systems Approach to Training can bring to the Training Organisation'. It was said that it had 'alienated a large section of the training community who argued that the Systems Approach to Training was not suited to the achievement of certain learning goals nor to the development of the attitudes which are essential to the successful discharge of military duties'.[32] The utility and the success of a service can, however, as we have seen, be adequately judged by customer demand; that left no doubt how highly valued this RAEC initiative was by most of the Army's leaders. In this the RAEC greatly benefitted by identifying an important market need and satisfying it so well. General Foxton wanted to find a role for the Corps that would be valued, that would continue unchanged if war came and that would ensure that the Corps was seen as an integral part of the Army. Only the future will show if that role has been found in the RAEC's contribution to Training Support, but it cannot be doubted that it has already had a great influence on the Army as it has had on the role of the RAEC in it.

Nor need it be thought that the Corps has been untrue to itself in adopting its new role. Education and training are not synonymous terms as we acknowledge when we speak of 'educational training'; we would look askance at those who spoke of 'educational education'. We know that we must seek clarity in writing, that we must do our best to ensure that it will not be said of us what Horace said of himself, namely that he had laboured to be brief and had succeeded in becoming obscure, that we must strive to follow Quintillian's Golden Rule that 'care should be taken, not that the reader may understand if he will, but that he must understand, whether he will or not'. A sound instinct, however, suggests to us the undesirability of attempting to remove all ambiguity in our use of certain terms. A tolerant vagueness becomes us when we speak of 'nation', of 'nationalism', of 'ideology', since experience convinces us that we cannot find a clear definition of these terms which all would accept. Perhaps we would do well to acknowledge that we should use the word 'education' as we do these words, as something on which we should not seek to impose exact meaning.

It is easy to say that education seeks the fullest development of individual intelligence and training the mastery by constant practice of specific skills; that education involves the development of critical minds and training repeated practice which is not to be questioned but accepted and followed. This is not to be gainsaid, but neither is it to be denied that the practice we associate with training is an essential part of education and that the mental development which we regard as inseparable from education might itself be promoted by that mental disciplining which training provides, while the selection of ways and means, of good ways and means, of the best ways and means, of carrying out training, as of attending to anything else, must always be an intellectual exercise.

It is an old truth that in doing we learn. 'Time shall breed skill and use shall breed perfection', Roger Ascham insisted, and it was of classical education he was speaking.[33] Not everyone who knows the pleasure attendant on the welling up from the subconscious depths of magical lines has a photographic memory; effort, repetition and practice is the negligible price most of us pay for that great joy. All knowledge is of some educational value and so it seems that in matters of education we would do well not to employ the language of millennial expectation. That great educator Gilbert Murray said 'the older I grow I am less sure what education is'.[34] Perhaps it should be added that we should also be less sure what it is not, more ready to admit that there are many kinds of it and all of them important.

There will be those who will believe that the education which enables us to make the most of life is the best kind of education, but there will not be much of a life for us if we cannot make a living and only the foolish will be contemptuous of the kind of education that will help us to do that. Nothing relating to education is unworthy of our attention. The University claims in whatever it teaches to develop thinking and the ability to analyse and synthesise in its students. No one doubts that this is an educational activity and so is that of RAEC in promoting a 'Systems Approach' to training. The University of Cambridge in setting up a new department of management studies is seeking to do much the same for the training of civilian managers. We look to educational training in the civilian world to help us compete more successfully with our industrial and commercial rivals; there is every reason to look to it too to add to our military strength. In pushing educational training it can be said that the RAEC was not just 'practising the manners of the time in order to have favours from it', not that there is anything wrong in so doing, but was meeting a real need and was meeting it effectively. In so doing it was benefitting both itself and the Army and building up a bank of goodwill on which it could draw if occasion so demanded. There is an old saying, 'he that will use all winds must shift his sail'. Perhaps we should add that he who will come safely to port must use all winds. Would uniformed educators have come safely to port if they had not undertaken this new work?

There was besides Training Support a new development which called on the services of the uniformed educator. It was a completely unexpected occurrence which suggested that over the years soldiers' education would be transformed. Hitherto the great determination of the RAEC and its predecessors to provide it had been frustrated by the greater determination of the soldier not to have it. Now something was on offer to which the RAEC had paid only fleeting attention, although it had always proved attractive when, as in the Release Period Formation Colleges, it had done so. What was now available was the result of a change, revolutionary in nature, in the attitude of the English people to education.

The English indifference to education was a centuries' old national disgrace. As early as 1570 in his book *The Schoolmaster* Roger Ascham wrote that the English paid more to the trainers of horses than to the teachers of children, which accounted for the fact that they found more pleasure in their horses than comfort in their children.[35] If a fault is national, a national urge to correct it must be expected to take a little time to develop. Too long-delayed, that national urge was at last beginning to manifest itself in the 1980s and 1990s. This manifestation was not without its oddities. In matters educational the English cannot be expected to be at their best and they can be expected to put their own distinctive stamp on things. Thus it cannot surprise that the English do things that others do not and do not do things that others do. They make universities of their polytechnics and look kindly on their efforts to turn to academic and away from technical education. And this at a time when at last they had begun to understand how important technical and vocational education is to a great industrial nation. Their political parties vie with each other in the production of gimmicks which they hope will receive immediately favourable attention; educational policies which the years will mature are harder to find.

Nevertheless their new interest in education is of profound significance for it is at last developing in them the attitudes to technical and vocational education which so greatly helped to promote the growth of their industrial competitors in the later 19th Century, the Americans and the Germans, and which, clinging to their classical education, they abhorred. Such they thought was the debt of the West to Plato and Aristotle that they deemed no praise too great for them. It did not occur to the English that in some things such reverence might exact too high a price. Isocrates, an Athenian orator and teacher of rhetoric, drew on himself the wrath of Plato and Aristotle. To the Greeks rhetoric was akin to what today might be called communication skills. The Greek philosophers thought of it as vocational, as indeed it was since it enabled its practitioners to make their living as professional pleaders in the law courts. Plato and Aristotle looked on the vocational as not truly education, education as they saw it being concerned with helping men to lead the good life, not the prosperous life. Despite their insistence and that of their great oriental near-contemporary Confucius on the exact definition of things, there is something to be said for the view of that great embodiment of English common-sense, Dr Johnson, that 'sometimes things may be made darker by definition'. The English in following the Greeks and defining education as only that which prepares for the best life were blind to the truth that there can be many different kinds of education, some of which may seek nobler goals than others, none of which will satisfy all, some of which will be congenial to some and anathema to some, and none of which can be neglected. If, however, the English are just beginning to acknowledge that technical and vocational education is as important for them as it has proved to be for their industrial competitors, they are beginning to acknowledge it, as witness the Industrial Training Boards of the 1970s and the Training and Enterprise Councils of the 1980s, and few things today are more important for them than that.

The most striking indication of this welcome if belated recognition is the NVQ scheme put forward by the Government in 1986. It was announced as the passport to a better job and a better Britain. Everyone, it was said, has something to contribute and the qualifications which the scheme would provide would be the recognition that working men and women deserved for the skills displayed in their work, it being thus emphasised that everyone could get them. These qualifications would be worth having since they were based on standards determined by industry and commerce and were specifically designed to meet their requirements. Employers would value them and would welcome applicants who had them. One of the greatest virtues of the scheme was said to be its flexibility. Each qualification was made up of a number of separate units. Each was an indication of what the candidate could do and of the standard to which he could do it. Each unit was thus a mini-qualification, each NVQ covering a particular area of competence. Moreover, these qualifications could be accumulated whenever it suited those who sought them. They were available to all who could achieve the required standard, however long it took them to do it. The scheme recognised five levels of competence. Levels one to four would be completed by 1992. Level five, to be attained thereafter, would be concerned with the qualifications required for professional and higher qualifications; it was assumed to carry 'parity of esteem' with a postgraduate qualification.

Those working for NVQs could get their own National Record of Vocational Achievement. This has four sections. The first is The Personal Record. It confirms what has already been achieved in formal education, in training, in work experience and in leisure time if notable achievement is to be found therein. It includes a personal statement by the holder of his or her interests and activities and strengths. The second part is The Action Plan which records what is immediately aimed at, what it is hoped will be next achieved and the long-term goals that are sought. It indicates what steps will be taken to satisfy these hopes and in what way progress towards them can be assessed. It includes details of on-the-job and off-the-job opportunities. NVQs being made up of units, The Action Plan lists the units still to be achieved for the gaining of the qualification. Should the holder intend to pursue academic qualifications such as GCSE and 'A' levels these will also be included in The Action Plan. The third part of The National Record is The Assessment Record which charts progress made towards reaching the targets indicated in The Action Plan. Over 1.3m people already have this National Record. Among them will be those who find satisfaction and virtue in contemplating clear statements of their hopes and ambitions and who leave it to the high gods to attend to their fulfilment. Most adults, however, expect fairies to remain at the bottom of the garden and it must be the case that a very goodly number are more concerned than they have ever yet been with acquiring qualifications which they can legitimately expect to be of benefit to them. That must be of benefit to the Nation as well.

The seriousness of this attempt to encourage the acquisition of vocational and technical skills is not to be doubted despite the foibles that have accompanied it. The present writer spent many years representing the University of Cambridge on a Local Education Authority without feeling the reverence he ought to have done for the selfless people who devote so much of their time to attending to the affairs of the rest of us. He became acutely aware of the great wish of elected persons to continue to be such. Burke told his Bristol constituents that he was not a weather-vane to twist around to every breath of public opinion and in consequence he forfeited his seat. More successful politicians respect his wisdom and eschew his practice. What appear to be bandwagons, however rickety they may be, seem to have an irresistible attraction for them, as witness the extraordinary appeal of such manifest nonsense as political correctness today.

In his LEA service the present writer saw educational fancies come and go; they had the durability of the wind's soft song. NVQs might be among them but he does not think this is so, for with their arrival there was a difference. An increasing number, which included prominent masters of business and industry who were now taking a much keener interest in educational matters and who were dissatisfied with the educational attainments of those asking them for employment, were determined now, as they had not been before, to find practical ways to improve educational standards and they thought that in the further refining of NVQs they might find what they wanted. They were of the Gradgrind persuasion and it was in a world of facts, not fancies, that they had their being. They were not uncritical of the NVQ scheme but they thought it was meaningful and they wanted to get on with it to see if it was. They were impatient of the long delays which seemed inseparable from its development and their impatience was a new and important factor. Such significant pressure from below in matters educational had rarely hitherto been seen. Direction from above was to say the least unimpressive. The Department of Education and Science seemed ready only to confuse the functions of the accelerator and the brake, applying the first when caution seemed indicated and the second when common-sense suggested increased speed. Even by British standards developments have been slow and there is much to be improved.

There is much the same NVQ Scheme in Europe as there is here but whereas the number of associated qualifications which can be obtained abroad is some 400, with us they run into thousands. In the Malayan Emergency the fortified village was a sturdy defence against communist insurgents; it made a great appeal to the Americans in Vietnam who at once created thousands, which were so inadequately prepared as to be easily overrun. We must trust that we, like the Americans in Vietnam, in introducing a good idea have not overdone it and in doing so have made inadequate preparations to ensure its success. In both France and Germany, too, the prestige of vocational education in recent years has been greatly increased, much more so than has been the case here. In both countries, too, there is an agreed national examination in which what has been achieved can be validated. Not only do we lack that, but our great number of qualifications in so many different subjects makes it hard to see how we can arrange it and even harder to see how in its absence the NVQ scheme can acquire the respectability without which it will not fulfil its purpose. Even so we must not forget the importance of the fact that industry still believes that the NVQ scheme is much more of a policy than a gimmick and that when it shakes down its value will be unquestioned.

The Army, well-aware of the deepening demographic trough of the 1990s and that as a result it would face keener competition in struggling to get the share it needed of the eighteen-year-olds, was at once interested in the NVQ Scheme. It made an even greater effort to draw attention to the educational opportunities awaiting the soldier. The press came to its assistance, *The Observer* saying, with some exaggeration, 'The Army aims to present life as a cross between a traditional apprenticeship and a technical course at the local polytechnic with the bonus of travel and a weekly pay packet.'[36] A new recruitment campaign highlighted the educational and training opportunities provided. Soldiers were promised that their civilian opportunities would be enhanced after three years' service. They were to be given a civilian qualification after studying for level one of the NVQ Scheme. Those showing promise and signing on for longer service would be able to qualify for courses in driving, radio communication and the use and maintenance of mechanical equipment. The slogan 'one career – two qualifications' was made much of. Such was the keenness that the soldier should be induced to participate in the NVQ Scheme that a note for years hushed in Army Education was heard again. The skills to be gained, it was emphasised, did not 'relate to purely fighting skills'. No doubt this was also a reminder that these skills were to be acquired in the soldier's own time. Junior units, presenting their usual crop of problems, needed special treatment; in the Army Apprentice College and the Junior Leader Regiments, the young soldier would be preparing for the gaining of the accumulated credits required for the NVQ in the Queen's time.

It is said that it is better to travel hopefully than to arrive. The truth of that, adult educators in or out of uniform cannot know as they never arrive. They continue to travel hopefully and, such at least is their good fortune, they continue to enjoy the journey. It remains to be seen if the NVQ Scheme will make the uphill task of the uniformed educator more immediately rewarding. The signs are that it will. There had never been much of a problem in relating the work experience and training of soldiers and NCOs in the Specialist Arms and Services to recognised civilian qualifications. This was not true of the soldiers and NCOs of the Infantry, the Armoured Corps and the Artillery, particularly as the Education for Promotion Scheme was now confined to NCOs and directed its subject content and courses more specifically at military requirements. However the development of the NVQ Scheme gave the Army an opportunity to identify in the training and experience of all soldiers the competencies that could be accredited to the appropriate NVQ level. Accordingly the National Council for Vocational Qualifications was asked how the Army could best take advantage of the newly designed qualifications. There were, it was told, two ways open to it – either it could be become an Awarding Body in its own right and, in agreement with the Council, develop and issue its own NVQs, or it could develop the qualifications through an already existing Awarding Body. Given the undoubted advantage of the soldier and NCO obtaining a qualification verified and issued by an external Awarding Body it was agreed with the City and Guilds of London Institute that a pilot scheme for a NVQ at Level 1 should be drawn up. It would be designed as NVQ Public Service; it should be within the reach of the 'trained soldier'. This was approved, the way now being opened for the development of qualifications at higher levels and the widening of the Scheme into other areas.[37]

Apparently arcane military skills could now be evaluated in terms of recognisable civilian competencies and credited under the NVQ system. Its importance for the Army was its potential for Army training and education, for retention of soldiers in the Service and for Resettlement. The NVQ system works on the basis of 'Lead Bodies' which develop and define the qualifications in specific skill areas, and 'Awarding Bodies' which test that individuals have obtained the required skills and merit particular NVQ award. The Army now became a 'Lead Body', DAEd being the appointed 'Lead Director' for the development of the NQV system in it. The 'Awarding Body' was the highly respected City and Guilds of London Institute. In this way the Army had the best of both worlds, itself defining the qualifications needed, the acquisition of which would then be tested by a prestigious civilian authority. The awards are vocational, not academic, though they comprehend a theoretical underpinning of vocational matters. They do not have an academic equivalent but they carry, in the words of the National Council of Vocational Qualifications, 'parity of esteem' with particular levels of academic qualifications. Thus the completion of EFP 1, together with a sergeant's defined military training and experience and some additional work, can qualify him at NVQ Level 3 in Management (parity of esteem with 'A' level) and EFP 2, with similar additions, gains the warrant officer NVQ

Level 4 in Management (parity of esteem with a pass degree). The cost of these qualifications is offset by funding, paid in arrears, from the Further Education Funding Council. The recognition of Army training and experience through the NVQ system is now proceeding through many of the areas of general and technical training under the broad direction of DETS(A).

It is hard to overestimate the great encouragement given to those who have long sought to prod the soldier into greater educational endeavour when this, taken together with his own professional competence and experience, will bring him such attractive civilian qualifications. Well might the last General, Director of Army Education say that the Army will benefit greatly from its early espousal of the NVQ system.[38]

The mental agility which has always characterised the Corps was shown again in its last years. In the early 1980s a Director General of Army Training was appointed to whom the Arms and Services Directors reported, as did the Director of Army Training and the Director of Army Education. Proposals were drawn up to put the Director General of Army Training on the Army Board and for the Director of Army Training and the Director of Army Education to report to him as their Army Board member. This proposal came to nought but the subsequent history of Army Education and the RAEC might have been very different had it been accepted. The Director General of Army Training was also responsible for funding Non-Technical Research as distinct from providing for the great amount expended on technical research. No such funding had ever been allocated previously, despite the importance of the subject. Fortunately a persuasive paper from the Director of Army Education extracted the first £500,000 (reallocated from the underspend on the equipment vote) for this purpose. The Director General of Army Training held wine and sandwich lunches or seminars in his office, these being attended by historians like John Terraine, Correlli Barnett, Brian Bond, John Harding and Shelford Bidwell. Thus a bridge was built between the worlds of military history, war studies and international relations and strategic thought and practice.[39] This initiative by the Director General of Army Training was an important step towards the formation of what later became the Strategic and Combat Studies Institute at Camberley which regularly publishes Occasional Papers on relevant subjects.[40]

The Beach Report recommended the RAEC to make every effort to identify itself with the Army from which it seemed to be becoming more remote. In the 1950s and 1960s many of the RAEC had World War Two experience and sported rows of ribbons; RAEC sergeants lived among their fellows in the Sergeants' Mess and RAEC officers and NCOs were attached to and fully integrated with individual units. By the time of Beach the warriors had all retired, the Corps had become an all-officer Corps and, to become cost-effective, had withdrawn the bulk of its instructors from units to operate as groups in Army Education Centres. All these developments tended to make it seem separate from the Army. For a few years its officers did not even attend Sandhurst. This at least could be corrected. But as it was impossible to reverse the process which had occasioned this feeling of remoteness, the Corps found it easier to express the desire to identify with the Army than to satisfy it. However unexpected events no doubt helped it to do so.

Alice's White Knight was weirdly and wonderfully prepared for every eventuality. His horse wore anklets to guard against the bite of sharks. He had a bee-hive fastened to his saddle so that bees could nest in it and give him honey. He thought it a remote contingency but would have so disliked having mice running over his horse's back that he carried a mouse-trap as well. 'It is as well to be prepared for everything', he said, and never could have been. Typically Britain at this time had to interrupt its preparation for a war it believed it would not have to fight to fight wars for which it was unprepared. These were the wars in the Falklands and in the Gulf. In them the RAEC took up again the role it had assumed in the Second World War and in Korea, and greatly added to it.

The two RAEC officers who sailed with the Task Force to the Falklands took with them two four-tonners laden with material. Among that material, as it turned out, were the only visual aids which could be used for training in the *QE2* and they were in great demand. On the voyage south the officers conducted EPC classes for twenty students, they produced a newssheet ('an extremely popular four page broadsheet'), they organised concerts, they were 'kept very busy until 2130 hours every evening'. So successful were the concerts that when 700 survivors of HMS *Coventry, Ardent* and *Antelope* came on board *QE2* 'the Senior RN officer requested that Willie and I be kept aboard to continue the entertainment service that we had provided on the way down'. So they found themselves back on Ascension Island before setting foot on the Falklands. 'Our role became one of providing for the leisure time of those recovering from their ordeal', they said.

The RAEC officers 'proved without doubt', as one of them said, 'that the Corps had a genuine role to play, prior to and during the post hostilities'. The other underlined the Corps' value in three main areas. The first was 'in entertainment and welfare, where as Army officers conversant with Army practices we were able to respond at short notice, to travel where other civilian specialists could not'. The second was 'in our normal educational work, which remained very important in the pre-hostilities and immediate post-hostilities phases, providing as it did a valuable link to normal conditions and reminding everyone of the military requirement that soldiers be educationally qualified for promotion. At no stage did we have to indulge in "hard selling" in order to drum up customers for our classes.' One is reminded how different it was when audiences had to be found for HMIs visiting ABCA sessions in the Release Period. There could be few clearer indications of what the troops valued and what they did not. The third area of RAEC activity to which Major Coupar drew attention was 'in the information field, through our daily broadsheets and, in our liaison work with the [weekly local newspaper] *Penguin News* reporters, we kept soldiers up-to-date with local and home news which in these circumstances has such an important bearing on morale'. The RAEC officers arranged evening classes. They offered GCE 'O' level history and English, woodwork, military law, conversational french, local wildlife and Scottish country dancing, these classes being open to both soldiers and civilians. 'There was a lot of interest shown by the military', Major Coupar said, 'but not as much as I had hoped from the civilians.' It is not surprising that Major Coupar could say in his report that the Commander Land Forces 'left me in no doubt whatever as to the appreciation of the service which we had provided'.[41]

In the Gulf both elements of the Corps, its generalists and its specialists, were heavily engaged. Twenty-six of its officers were in the Gulf and some forty more at home were involved in non-educational war support roles.

The majority of its officers there were not specialists. They served as HQ watch-keepers, a role which had become theirs on active service. Before the fighting began they acted as education officers to the units assembling in the Gulf and they ran EPC courses. In view of the deployment of British Forces from Germany, HQ BAOR felt it important to keep the families of those sent to the Gulf informed of what their loved ones were doing there. Two RAEC Majors were sent as a Command Information Team. They wrote regular features for *Sixth Sense*, the British Forces newspaper in Germany. They offered a video service to the soldiers who wanted to send to their families videos showing how they were living. The Majors sent back to those about to deploy to the Gulf first-hand experiences of what they should expect. They followed the advancing troops and broadcast to the families in Germany battlefield news. Like all the RAEC they had to turn their hands to anything and they found themselves overseeing the final examination of the eight soldiers taking Open University degrees.

One of the Corps' main jobs in the Gulf was the provision of Forces Information. Lieutenant-Colonel Glyn Jones, who was in charge of this, had to provide a newspaper and radio news and talks. This was the origin of the *Sandy Times* and to produce it was a diplomatic as well as a journalistic task. Nothing could be published in Saudi Arabia without the permission of its Government. It could never permit infidel literature to soil the purity of the Kingdom. Some might have doubted if the *Sandy Times* could properly be called literature but its infidel nature was beyond dispute. This seemed an insuperable difficulty preventing its publication. But when needs must guile can cope. It was agreed that if permission to publish offensive material was not given, if the request for such publication had never been acknowledged, if the Saudi Government remained officially unaware of the publication of what it could never consent to and if when it asked to see copies of what was not published it could be assured that these would be gladly forwarded when permission to publish had been received, all would be well. Thus seventeen issues of the unpublished *Sandy Times* appeared and very popular they proved. The knowledge that the Saudi Secret Service kept an eye on what it could not see removed all fear that what it would strongly object to if it could would never appear. Diplomacy is indeed the most civilised way of conducting the affairs of nations.

The task entrusted to the RAEC to run a radio service was sufficiently daunting as an infrastructure of mains power, leasable landlines, radio masts and broadcasting equipment was not to be found in the Arabian desert. Fortunately Lieutenant-Colonel Jones was able to call on the help of the very well-equipped American Forces Radio and Television Services. Whitehall was unhelpful and it required an appeal from Air Chief Marshal Sir Peter Hine, the Joint Forces Commander, to the Secretary of State for Defence to get the funding for the radio station. With miracles of improvisation the radio service was begun on 17 December 1990. It remained in operation broadcasting to the dwindling British Forces in Saudi Arabia until July 1991. Starting from virtually nothing it provided a full radio service to a very large area with only a staff of five. The American Forces Radio and Television Services had sixty splendidly trained staff, much equipment and five stations. It still had to rely for ten hours of broadcasting per day on pre-recorded material from the USA.

The specialist jobs the RAEC did in the Gulf were very important too; some of them were new. The Corps' linguists came into their own. As soon as it was known that the Iraqi invasion of Kuwait might involve British Forces in action there the Ministry of Defence drew up a list of Arabic-speaking personnel in the Forces. As many had not spoken Arabic for a long time the RAEC arranged refresher courses for them. In October 1990 it sent a number of its Arabic-speakers to be trained as Field Interrogators at the Prisoner Handling and Tactical Questioning Course run by the Joint Services Interrogation Wing at Ashford. Arabic-speaking RAEC officers visited units about to be deployed to the Gulf, explaining conditions there, the character and customs of the Arabs, their culture and the things that would upset them. In the Gulf Arabic specialists served on each of the three Forward Interview Teams assembled there. The interpreting work of the RAEC was greatly valued too. Major Cardy of the RAEC was General de la Billière's interpreter. He and his colleagues also interpreted for the American High Command.

The Arabic speakers of the Corps played an important role in another of the fields in which it was now actively engaged, Psychological Operations. Their work with the Fourth Psychological Operations Group of the US Army was particularly important as that Group was short of Arabic speakers. Psyops, as it was usually known, aimed at weakening the enemy's self-confidence, his trust in his leaders and his will to fight. Now that the mass media could reach whole populations its significance greatly increased. Many armies devoted considerable time and resources to it. So much attention did the Americans now pay to this that they deployed regimental-size Psyops formations in the field, as they did in the Gulf. The Fourth Psyops Group here contained three battalions, two strategic and one tactical. The strategic battalions had the heavy equipment, portable long-range radio transmitters, computer graphics equipment, printing plant capable of turning out 800,000 leaflets a day and even books and an intelligence section to assess the potential audience to be targeted and to determine the best approach to it. The tactical battalion had the light equipment which would enable it to keep up with the advancing troops. RAEC Arabic specialists were prominent in the work of both the US strategic and tactical group. The British 206 Psyops Support Team was particularly active in the production of surrender appeals leaflets. These included 'safe conduct' passes granting deserters safe passage through Allied lines and fair POW treatment. The RAEC Psyops specialists were also engaged in the production of material designed to intimidate, leaflets graphically portraying UN air superiority, leaflets indicating the next bombing targets which were sure to be read and which in view of the overwhelming UN airpower were truthful, thus occasioning alarm and despondency before the actual attacks. There was material undermining faith in Saddam Hussein. There was material to deceive the enemy, to give the impression that the main attack was coming on the coast of Kuwait and not as intended through Southern Iraq. In December 1990 Majors Cardy and Mahon took over the Voice of the Gulf radio station broadcasting daily to Iraqi troops. It is noteworthy that in these broadcasts the Iraqis were never asked to 'surrender' since that word carried implications of cowardice and dereliction of duty that would not appeal to face-conscious Arabs. Members of the Kuwaiti Resistance said later that the Voice of the Gulf was widely listened to by Iraqis and Kuwaitis alike and many Iraqi soldiers gave themselves up in the way it told them to with both hands up, rifle slung over the left shoulder muzzle downwards and safe conducts held in the right hand.

The RAEC in the Gulf attended to one other job of the greatest importance. The Gulf War was the first major conflict in which the Army used computers and information technology in its planning, command and control. The speed of modern operations, the movement of units and their continued supply are such as to tax the best trained and most experienced staff organisation. Computers can greatly ease their load. The RAEC kept itself in the forefront of the movement to introduce into the Army Staff procedures information technology. It was to the fore in the training of soldiers in computer literacy. In the Gulf it supervised the use for the first time in actual operations of information technology. The three services had previously operated their own different information technology systems and in the Gulf it was the RAEC's task to coordinate them and run the coordinated system. This greatly facilitated the movement of men and material from Britain and Germany to the Gulf. General de la Billière stressed 'the most important contribution made by information technology to the British Army's first "high technology" military operation'. He also paid handsome tribute to the work of the RAEC there. He considered 'their contribution to the War to be out of proportion to their relatively junior rank', and said that the role they discharged so ably in the Gulf would be 'of crucial importance in any future campaign'.[42]

Pleasing as this was to the Corps it was accompanied by something that was not. The RAEC who served in the Gulf had occasion to comment frequently on the dislike and mistrust met with there.[43] Their doing of obviously vital military jobs offended. The implication was clear; what right had the Corps to be doing them, how could authority have allowed this to happen? This was not a new experience for the RAEC. It and its predecessors were very familiar with it; it will be odd if it is unknown to its successors.

Sadly, the same mistrust is often met with by teachers in English schools who still do not enjoy the respect accorded to teachers in other lands. Indeed, at a time when much more interest is expressed in education than hitherto it might be paradoxically true that they are less well-thought of than in the past. This must be a temporary phenomenon. Authority cannot continue to think poorly of the teachers without whom educational standards will never improve. And if society wants better education it cannot do so either. In the Gulf the RAEC met with distrust in some units but those higher in command were lavish in their praise of what the RAEC had done. Important as was the distrust expressed at lower levels, it was far less important than the warm praises of the Army's leaders. Which is the more likely, the souring of those leaders by the feelings of some subordinate officers or the changing of their feelings when understanding comes to them, as it must, of the very different views of their chiefs?

There was similar appreciation of the remaining and continuing war role of the RAEC, its part in the war against the terrorists in Northern Ireland. To its normal and hazardous duties there it added its usual, imaginative and exciting extra-mural activities. In 1982–1983 Major Kerslake organised an expedition to the Himalayas for the resident battalion in Ballykelly. It trekked some 180 miles in East Nepal and climbed several peaks between 18,000 and 20,000 feet, this being the first Army expedition on this scale to be organised in Northern Ireland.[44]

To the pre-war AEC such contraction as was to be seen in the work done by its successors in the Corps' closing days would have been undreamed of expansion; that contraction it nevertheless was is not the least tribute to be paid to the post-war RAEC. Few experiences could have been more frustrating than that of the AEC in the years before 1939. Great hope attended the Corps' birth and great disappointment its development in the 1920s and 1930s. Few contrasts could be more striking than that between the Corps in its early days and the closing days of its royal successor. Those closing days were not lacking in disappointment and frustration, nor in developments that are much to be regretted. They nevertheless pulsed with activity, abounded in significant new practices, kept alive the hope that as the Army was winning its fight to persuade the British people that it was no malevolent, outrageously expensive and unnecessary enemy but a great present help and an indispensable future need, so now the Education and Training Services Branch was winning its battle to convince the Army that it was necessary to the Army as the Army was to British society. When we consider the sweeping effect on the Army of *Options for Change*, we cannot exclude the possibility that the RAEC would have had no successors to whom to hand the torch of learning. Asked what he had done in the French Revolution, Sieyes answered that he had survived. In the circumstances he was justified in looking upon that as an achievement; the Education and Training Services Branch of the Adjutant-General's Corps can similarly feel that its very existence is a great achievement of the RAEC. Outstanding services had brought the conviction not always apparent in the Army that its educators, however much weakened as they inevitably were by the demise of the Corps, were still considered indispensable. Acknowledging that the Corps never in its most golden days had 'the strength which in old days moved earth and heaven' might the Corps not be justified in feeling the pride Tennyson ascribes to Ullysses when he writes:

> Though much is taken, much abides; and though
> We are not now the strength which in old days
> Moved earth and heaven; that which we are we are.
> One equal temper of heroic hearts,
> Made weak by time and fate, but strong in will
> To strive, to seek, to find and not to yield?

If there is to be a more hopeful future for Army Education that will not be the least of the achievements of the RAEC.

CHAPTER 13

RETROSPECT AND PROSPECT

With the ending of the Cold War and the collapse of the Soviet Union Britain's expenditure on defence greatly declined. The demand for a peace dividend led to a 24% reduction in the size of the British Army. Dramatic reductions in the fighting units took place. The Royal Armoured Corps lost eight regiments, the Royal Artillery six, the Royal Engineers five and the Royal Signals four; the infantry force was cut from fifty-five to forty battalions. Ten famous cavalry and twelve infantry regiments lost their independent existence in forced amalgamations. Since Britain was determined to retain its capacity for high intensity warfare, it was inevitable that the support services would be squeezed even harder than the teeth arms. Accordingly they were all subjected to swingeing cuts. In addition, in the logistical field, four Corps, three of them Royal, lost their separate identity and formed a new Royal Logistic Corps (RLC). On the personnel side of the Army's organisation six other Corps, four of them with Royal in their titles, lost their sovereignty and formed the Adjutant-General's Corps (AGC). The RAEC was one of these, losing about one third of its strength in redundancies and becoming the Education and Training Services Branch. The change was virtually a seamless one so far as the Corps' educational and training functions were concerned. Indeed, the workload increased as the Branch struggled to cope with the vastly increased Resettlement advice work at the very time when its own manpower was being so drastically reduced. Amidst all this turbulence its Director was also given the invidious responsibility of chairing a committee to suggest improvements to the Resettlement system; though with the proviso that any recommendations it might make were to involve no extra cost! Some of those Corps officers charged with giving resettlement counselling to the many now leaving the Service were themselves on the list of those selected for redundancy, doubly deserving of the gratitude of their clients for so conscientiously bending to their lasts. The demand for Russian language teaching also expanded as arms control and other military exchanges with the Russians grew apace.

The rationale for the formation of the two large support Corps into which so many small and specialist ones had now been moulded was not the same in each case. While both produced savings by the elimination of 'overheads' – headquarters, messes, support services and the like, the RLC brought together cognate functions which could be truly rationalised. In the AGC however, despite great pressure to emphasise their commonality, policemen, lawyers, paymasters and teachers had perforce to continue to operate separately. This only served to emphasise the good sense of the proposal for the 'grouping of AG services' which DAEd and the Paymaster-in-Chief had earlier suggested. The new organisational arrangements involved much turbulence and a great deal of physical change. Eltham was lost as the Corps Headquarters and the splendid Great Hall of King Edward's medieval palace with its exquisite grounds and Stephen Courtauld's unique art deco house alongside no longer provided one of the Army's grandest officers' messes. However, with Worthy Down as their headquarters, the members of the new Branch were now spared the grubby 'slum carriages' of unreliable Network South East, the cramped dormitory arrangements of the Eltham bedrooms and the walk up to the Mess through a not very salubrious part of south-east London where, famously, one Corps senior officer, having recently returned from a tour in riot-torn Northern Ireland was unceremoniously mugged on his way to the Palace. By contrast Worthy Down offered the modern utilitarian offices of a combined Headquarters and Training Centre in the fresh air and greenery of rural Hampshire. The old RAEC was gone but the new Branch stood ready to continue in the educational traditions established by its illustrious predecessor.

It was on 6 April 1992 that the RAEC was disbanded, thus bringing to an end a life-span of seventy-two years. Having, as we have seen, to bear an increased work load the members of the new Education and Training Services Branch of the new Corps continued 'to be a Corps of military educationalists specialising in supporting military training, providing individual educational services and having in addition a range of war roles, some akin to our training roles, some quite different from them; but all providing that reserve of flexible trained manpower which a smaller army will keenly need', as they were told by their Director.[1] This reminder that the specialism of the new Education and Training Services Branch would not be affected by incorporation in the larger unit drew attention to a problem peculiar to itself. This was its work in support of training which had so strikingly developed in the last years of the RAEC; this necessitated its closest relationship with the Director of Army Training. Yet it now belonged to a Corps directly responsible to the Adjutant-General, who was not responsible for training. Now that we all seem to be learning that frontiers are to be more easily crossed than when their function was accepted as being to keep some peoples in and others out, that was no insuperable problem. The Army Board had no difficulty in acknowledging the need of the Education and Training Services Branch to keep close relations with the Director of Training, irrespective of lines demarcating different authority.

It cannot be said that the history of that phase of Army Education which begins with the establishment after the First World War of the now disbanded Corps extends beyond the time whereof the memory of man runneth not to the contrary. Perhaps, however, we may recall the statute of King Henry VIII which laid it down that sixty years outweighed the memory of man and believe that its ending is an appropriate time to draw attention to the achievement of the Corps, to that of its predecessors, the Army Schoolmasters, 'the Corps that never was listed, that carried no colours or crest, but split in a hundred detachments, was breaking the road for the rest', and to what was done before they appeared.

In the history of education in Britain the importance of the educational work done in the Army has never been sufficiently acknowledged. That education made important contributions at all levels of the nation's education, from the teaching of its adults to the teaching of its children; it broke the trail for the nation in its pioneering educational ventures; it played the leading role in rescuing many of the failures who had dropped out of the national education.

In its long-sustained activity Army Education will stand comparison with any of the numerous civilian ventures in Adult Education. Whatever and however important the differences between them, a common, and commonly difficult, task faced civilian and military adult educators. When Lord Brougham in his Inaugural Address to the University of Glasgow on 6 April 1825 defined that task as 'making the highest intellectual cultivation compatible with the daily cares and toils of working men' he was forgetting, as perhaps the occasion justified him in doing, that education has never been unconcerned, to use Aristotle's phrase, with making life possible, however determined it was to prepare its recipients for the good life. It has always known that it must enable rice-bowls to be filled and pockets lined as well as minds to be enriched. The adult educator has, nevertheless, never forgotten that education is the concentrated abridgement of culture and that he must prepare minds as best he can to receive that culture. His failures always have been, and perhaps always will be, more numerous than his successes. It will probably always be true that those who will make the effort to appreciate Brougham's highest 'intellectual cultivation' will remain a minority. But the nation which does nothing to add to the number of those of whom it will not be true is in trouble. And it is difficult to see how anyone, in or out of uniform, could have remained in adult education if experience had not brought with it the conviction that fertile soil can be found even in the most rocky of environments. It was said of the New England colonies of the early 17th Century that the ground was so poor that 'corn had to be shot into it with a musket'. Yet crops were raised there. The adult educator must sometimes feel that his also is the task of shooting corn into the ground with a musket, but his remains the conviction that, like the New England farmer, he will eventually raise something of a crop.

He knows that working men and soldiers have learned to enjoy that 'highest intellectual cultivation' of which Lord Brougham spoke. Here is the testimony of Lord Tweedsmuir: 'I acted as examiner for a prize which was given for essays by working miners in Nottinghamshire. Most of these had been to WEA classes and I can only say that the result filled me with amazement. The essay on Shakespeare, which won the prize, was written by a working miner of twenty-one, and was one of the best pieces of literary criticism I have ever read.'[2] There is the testimony of Newbattle Abbey, and of Ruskin College to which we are told 'young mechanics and miners did not come to acquire an education which is professional and technical but to savour that liberal education which the need to earn a living in their early youth deprived them of'.

We have also the testimony of the anti-aircraft gunners on isolated East Anglian sites who during stand-down hours of the Blitz discussed into the small hours of the morning the future of the race, the evidence of the thousands who listened to music and opera at home and abroad when intervals in the fighting gave them the chance to do so. Commander Currie in her charmingly modest account of her work with the Army's illiterates, in which she expressed the hope that she was opening the door to them through which they would find what gave her such intellectual enjoyment, shares the faith to which Lord Brougham and Lord Tweedsmuir gave expression. She was never alone in so doing. We saw in the Interim Scheme what the Romans referred to as *deliramenta doctrinae*, the wild speculations of learned men. Yet in all its eccentricities, which were no more than the faithful reflection of illusions current at the time, there is one shining light to be seen in it, the dogged determination to introduce the soldier to what Matthew Arnold called 'the high and rare excellence' which has come down to us through the generations. However critical we may be of the ways in which it was thought this could be done, however sure that if it is to be achieved for more than the few approaches more subtle than those then found will have to be tried, we can neither regret nor forget the objective sought. It is the Holy Grail for which all teachers must seek. Time was when civilian adult educators, if they spared a thought for their uniformed colleagues, would have thought themselves a cut above them, although their justification for so doing eludes comprehension. But the many pioneer ventures to the credit of Army Education, its concentration on the most appropriate way of teaching adults, its insistence on careful consideration of audience and method, its use of discussion and of the theatre, its many and varied approaches to the teaching of officers and other ranks, its realisation of the value of residential adult education, its belief in the efficacy of blue pencil in the correction of the writing of soldiers and officers, its provision of Education Centres (and the story of Army Education might be told under the title 'From Wet Canteen to Education Centre'), removed civilian conceit and complacency, and brought the understanding that, different though it was and even though its standard was perforce lower than the highest reached in civilian adult education, the contribution of Army Education to the national effort in adult education was always considerable and was something from which civilian adult education could and did learn.

In one way, the task of the uniformed educator is harder than that of his civilian colleague. The soldier has to educate the young adult who would rarely be found in Extra-Mural or WEA classes and would never be with his age-group peers in colleges and universities. No school-boy with shining morning face or the more appropriate scowls ever went more unwillingly to class than did the young other ranks and the young subalterns to whose unfelt needs the RAEC had to attend.

It is a moot point which produces the better teacher, the voluntary class which wants to learn but will not stay if the teaching is unattractive or the involuntary class which neither wants to learn nor to stay but which must be taught and which will yield to the temptation of being perhaps malevolently inattentive unless the teacher is outstanding. One thing is certain: the indifferent teacher is unlikely to survive either experience.

Civilian adult education, as distinct from the Higher Education to be found in colleges and universities, never concerned itself with the teaching of languages. The literature of Greece and Rome, of the European peoples and even of the Oriental world was another matter, but languages themselves were not attempted. In teaching them Army Education showed itself to be in the top rank of Further Education as well as a significant part of what was usually referred to as Adult Education. Moreover, there was a most important development of Army language teaching which is not greatly in evidence even in the most prestigious of British Centres of learning, the production of new forms of writing better suited to the more backward of isolated peoples than existing scripts may be. The importance not only for the Army but for the nation at large of such developments in South and South-East Asia has already been noted.

Adult Education in Britain has not interested itself in distance learning as has, for instance, Finland. Dr Johnson knew his fellow countrymen when he wrote 'idleness will wait for ever for the moment of illumination' and added 'human nature is such that the drowsiness of hesitation must be wakened into resolve'. In matters educational they require prodding and postal nagging is too impersonal and too easily ignored to partake of that art which is so striking in the hands of the skilled practitioner. So although many soldiers take up correspondence courses they put them down again with almost as great alacrity. Soldiers, nevertheless, are among their steady supporters; they would not have been in the absence of RAEC effort.

Of all the communicating arts that of the TV journalist is perhaps the most immediate in impact, the most assured of its result. For his is the appeal to the emotions, it is for him to touch heart-strings. Our emotions are lively, our sympathies easily aroused, the more so when we are rarely made aware of the cost of indulging them. But the aim of the writer is to promote thinking even more than feeling; it is as Bacon tells us to make us weigh and consider. There will be many who will find it easier to give free rein to emotion than to focus and follow thought, which makes the achievement of the RAEC in providing fine libraries and in encouraging their use the more remarkable. Only 19% of Americans buy a book in a lifetime. Faced with a statistic of that dreadful portent, is it too fanciful to see the spirits of those who fell at Thermoplylae, Salamis, Marathon and Plataea behind the RAEC holding the field against the barbarian onslaught in its great service in supplying books?

However much some may believe that other arts are superior, it would be folly to ignore those of today. We will stand the more steadily if we master them. This, too, the RAEC has done. Its study at Beaconsfield of TV and its impact has been as we have seen of great benefit to the British Forces in Northern Ireland. Not only has it familiarised them with their bailiwick before they enter it, it has also practised officers of all ranks in coping with persistent television journalists there. This has not been a minimal contribution to the long British struggle against the IRA.

This is a long catalogue of RAEC achievements but it has by no means exhausted them. Having shown its concern with culture and the humanities the RAEC has also shown its awareness that these alone will not suffice. It has given a great boost to vocational education. In this it has reflected a swing occurring in society at large, the long-delayed protest against the sacrifice of more than 80% of the community to the academic well-being of the few. It may well be strengthening what it reflects too. Is it not possible that the Army's interest in the National Vocational Qualifications Scheme and its regret at the slowness of its development have done something to sustain interest in it and to speed its further promotion? Indeed it may be that yet another RAEC endeavour, long sustained but eventually unsuccessful, has had a similar effect on civilian education. The Army persisted in its determination to interest soldiers in citizenship and world affairs. The HMIs displayed great interest in these studies and is it not probable that their interest boosted the awareness developing throughout the national education system of the importance of such studies? They have come of age in colleges and schools now.

The unimaginative would do well to select a profession other than teaching. But perhaps the RAEC never showed more imagination than in the handling of a problem with which society which was responsible for it appeared remarkably unconcerned. This is the problem of the numerous illiterates still to be found after a century of compulsory general education. It is a source of never-ending amazement that so many illiterates or near-illiterates still present themselves to recruitment offices. We cannot believe that all illiterates aspire to be soldiers and must wonder how many there are among civilians. It is evident that many of our youngsters have shown far more assiduity in keeping out of the classroom than ever they displayed in it. Illiterates who do aspire to become soldiers cannot be left in their illiteracy and the RAEC's work with them has saved for the Army many serviceable soldiers. In its work with illiterates the RAEC could only go forward by its own inward light. It had to develop its own experience. HMIs waxed lyrical in saying how well the RAEC had done this.

There is an old Sankey and Moody hymn 'Throw out the life-line, someone is drifting away.' The RAEC was very good at throwing out the life-line as HMIs were always pleased to note. They said how greatly they would deplore the closing of all Boys' Units as in their absence there would be a number of youngsters calling in vain for a life-line. This remedial education provided by the RAEC was not the least of its claims on the gratitude of Army and Nation alike.

If the RAEC was skilled in the throwing out of life-lines to the needy at the start of their military service, it found itself similarly employed at the end of the soldier's time with the Colours. It did its best to provide help at every level for those who wanted to prepare themselves for their civilian life, to do what could be done for those who would seek no further qualifications, to help the more ambitious to acquire them, to smooth the path to the university for those who wanted to go there. Its Resettlement work eased a difficult transition for many, undoubtedly did something to improve the Army's public image, to say nothing of the contribution it must have made to recruitment and to the maintenance of high morale in the troops.

The intangible would not be intangible if it could be easily defined, and while the factors which contribute to good morale can readily be enumerated the contribution of a particular Army Service to its maintenance cannot be precisely assessed. We can be sure that the many and varied and much appreciated extra-mural activities of the Corps, ranging from its adventure-training courses at home to its arduous walking in wild country overseas, made an immediate and significant contribution to the soldiers' morale. But what of its steady and persistent bread-and-butter work? The Private in Northern Ireland expressing his gratitude to 'you lot' for the help he received in getting his EPC reminds us how important that work was in the maintenance of sound morale.

The English longbow which at Crécy, Poitiers and Agincourt brought the chivalry of France to the ground continued to affect the tactics followed in the Wars of the Roses. New weapons emerged but not so quickly as to place undue strain on the fighting man. Now military planners who have to cope with emerging technology must often feel inclined to make it their nightly prayer that it will decide that enough is enough and refrain from further emergence. They cannot but feel how much simpler life would be if there were not increasingly expensive weapons for them to acquire and train soldiers in the use of. But difficulties have to be coped with, not wished away, and the new art and science known as Training Support has proved to be a great help in dealing with emerging technology. It was a striking achievement when in addition to all its other activities the RAEC showed itself outstandingly useful in this new art and science, Training Support.

Needs will always call forth attempts to satisfy them as is to be seen in the emergence of what are now accepted as being the war-roles of the RAEC and its successors. They serve at Army, Divisional and Brigade HQ. They have been singled out for commendation of their work here in forwarding the use of computers for military purposes. They act as watch-keepers. They provide all essential news in the battle areas and they keep families at home *au fait* with developments in them. They are responsible for the ready availability of the linguists on whom the Army is dependent in so many different ways and they are prominent in psychological operations. They attend to welfare and provide what education and resettlement advice is called for. When these are compared with the war-role of the Corps at the beginning of the Second World War it becomes evident how restricted and lacking in spontaneity that was. Off the members of the AEC went to cipher duty then. That was important and we have seen how greatly those in charge of ciphering appreciated their help. But it clearly reflected the view that as soldiers must do something in war and that since ciphering must be done the members of the Corps might as well do it. It was not the spontaneous answer to newly felt needs that the presently accepted war-role of the uniformed educator now is, not the acknowledgement that new circumstances will reveal new needs and that a reserve with sufficient imagination and ingenuity to meet them is essential. Necessity has been called wit's whetstone; the AEC responded to it eagerly and imaginatively, and its war-role turned out to be far more important than had ever been contemplated. It was widely believed to have sustained morale in the long period of training after Dunkirk when significant defeats were still being met with abroad; in its preparation and distribution of news-sheets to the front-line troops it performed a service greatly appreciated by them; it did a magnificent job in the maintenance of the morale of British prisoners of war; it helped to relieve the tension and discomfort of troopship travel and in so doing who can assess the significance of its contribution to ensuring that the 'mutiny' on troopship *City of Canterbury* at Durban in January 1942 was a one-off occurrence? When the last Major-General Director of Army Education said that whatever the war-roles of the Education and Training Services Branch might be, they would call upon that 'reserve of trained manpower which a smaller army will keenly need' he was drawing attention to a development which the Army must look upon as among the most imposing of the achievements of its educators.[3]

As most of its work has been with adults it is easy to overlook the important work done by the Corps in the schooling of the young. We have noted the pioneering work done by the Army in the education of its children. It led the way in inducing the state to provide teachers and schools; having been the first to make public funds available for this purpose it was also first in arranging for pensions to be paid for teachers. Typical of its pioneering work was the appointment of Michael Faraday as a master in the Natural Sciences at Woolwich in 1830, this at a time when science education was rare in universities and non-existent in schools. Close attention to Army Schools was always one of the RAEC's greatest concerns. To assess its great value one has only to ask what would have been the effect on the Army if this had not been the case? Would not the Army's morale have been seriously impaired if RAEC excellence in discharge of this function had not been so pronounced?

When one contemplates all the work of the RAEC two questions insistently arise. How could all this have been done if the RAEC had not been there to do it? Would not the Army have been immeasurably the poorer had this not been done? It was far from being an easy task and it was well carried out. We have seen how recruiting posters drew attention to the Sandhurst Role of Honour, saying 'A tough act to follow'. This might be said to the members of the new Education and Training Services Branch as they take over the torch of learning from the RAEC.

We have traced the history of a double struggle which has been taking place over the years, the struggle of the Army to overcome the hostility of the British people and the struggle of the educators to overcome the reluctance of the Army to have anything to do with education. We have seen that that was a struggle in which both the people and the Army showed some of their less endearing qualities.

The British people yielded, as they have not infrequently done, to the temptation to think that if they refused to pay attention to unpleasant realities they would go away. Wanting comfort they forgot lessons which would have denied it to them, forgot that fire neglected is apt to gain in power, forgot that that is a 'just fear which all reasonable men must be possessed with of an ever-growing Power', forgot that it is better not to place too great a trust in the languishing virtue of corrupted mankind, forgot that there are certain periods of time which being once past make all caution ineffectual and all remedies desperate. The Army too showed a similar blindness. The last bastion of the gentlemen of England on whose traditional virtues and values it placed supreme reliance as it had done so often and so successfully in the past, it remained for long remarkably resistant to new ideas and convinced that education could only give it minimal services.

In this protracted and hard-fought double struggle, although for long years there seemed little movement, there was, nevertheless, steady advance. The British people became more reconciled to having an Army and the Army more reconciled to education having a part to play in it. The realities of power, although dangerously slowly in the 1930s, forced the British people to put behind them their old dislike of what Keats called 'the scarlet coats that pester human kind'. That same long-delayed appreciation of reality, which compelled the British people to look differently on their Army, also forced upon the Army a reluctant respect for its educators. We have seen what eventually they were able to do for the Army and the richness of the legacy the RAEC left to its successors.

What stands out both in the history of the British people's attitude to their Army, and of the Army's attitude to education is the ultimate acceptance of reality, however, long-delayed and hard fought against. The story is told of the elder who after heated debates in the presbyteries accepted Church union saying 'I think the scheme of union is impracticable, ill-considered, unjust and absolutely idiotic but there is no doubt it is God's will.' His acceptance of union was not lacking in oddity but no one doubted that the acceptance was more important than the oddity of its expression. He may be said to be typical of the British acceptance of their Army and of the Army's acceptance of its educators. In both the acceptance of inevitability could have been more graciously made apparent, in neither was the lack of grace more significant than the acknowledgement of reality. Most significant was the fact that these changes were not suddenly brought about but were the result of slow growth. For here we see the English at their strongest, acknowledging the truth of Sir Walter Raleigh's words 'The councils to which Time is not called, Time will not ratify.' It is in the slow developments that are ratified by time and not in the great forward lurches which we see occasionally occurring in it that the gathering strength of Army Education is most clearly revealed. A question remains. Is anything to be learned from this unfolding story, of the relationship of its educators to the Army that might suggest anything to us of their likely role in the new Branch in tomorrow's Army?

We cannot know by what door the future will enter, nor calculate its changes and chances. Chance may be what it has been called 'wisdom's creature' but most of us lack the wisdom to tame it. We know it will exercise its usual authority but the way in which it will do so is beyond our ken. Nevertheless there is something to be said for Fielding's view that 'there is another sort of knowledge, beyond the power of learning, to bestow, and this is to be held by conversation'. Talk can trigger thought and even on occasion give us a glimpse of the shadowy outline of coming events. It is in that hope that these concluding comments on the future of education in the Army and of the role of the Education and Training Services Branch are entered upon.

Some of the jobs of the old Corps may not have to be done by the new Branch. It may be, as many will undoubtedly hope, that preliminary or remedial education will no longer be required and that there will be fewer young soldiers' units. Few aware of present educational standards will be readily convinced that the Army has seen the last of remedial education and time will speak authoritatively on the need for young soldiers' units. It would also seem certain that with the reduced size of the Army of the Rhine the schooling of the Army's children will become relatively less significant in the work of the new Branch. The other jobs done by the RAEC will remain to be tackled by their successors; some of its most recently assumed tasks may contract and others expand; it would be to deny its whole history to assume that chores as yet unthought of will not in future come its way.

The days of peace have not been days of quiet and the overstretch and the financial embarrassment which occasioned educational cuts in the last years of the RAEC are still with us and are likely to be so in the immediate future. The British Armed Forces have lived with strategic overstretch for many years; they were almost destroyed by it in the Second World War; no one can have difficulty in understanding the frustration of Admiral of the Fleet Sir Ernle Chatfield when he said at the time of the Abyssinian

Crisis 'The miserable business of collective security has run away with our traditional interests and policies, with the result that we now have to be prepared to fight any nation in the world at any time.' Victory gave the British what they sometimes forget, the greatest of blessings which was the avoidance of defeat. But it did not give their Armed Forces ease from overstretch.

The British ideal was *le practical man* as the French scornfully expressed it, the man who bowed to the here and now and left it to others to acknowledge the lure of the will-o'-the-wisp and no doubt also of things more worth pursuing.[4] Their practicality was at a discount when they persisted in being fascinated by the greatness of their role in the world and in sparing little thought for their capacity to discharge it. Brought by the unkind gods into a war which their fighting chiefs knew could only be won if it was long and the keepers of their coffers only afforded if it was short, they have continued ever since to demand from the Treasury what it could not afford and from their Armed Forces what they could not rationally have been expected to do. How well that was done no doubt convinced them of their wisdom in believing that rationality has a limited part to play in politics. It remained true that they maintained Armed Forces too big for their dilapidated economy to sustain and too small to carry out, without great overstretch and effort, their commitments.

How little that has changed we can see from the exhortation of their Foreign Secretary that they should 'pull more than their weight to make a reality of the new world order'. They cannot make a reality of that since it is only a figment of the imagination, New Presbyter being as the Balkans show Old Priest writ large. If their record is anything to go by they will find great difficulty in not seeking to pull more than their weight. Nor should we forget that public opinion, which is more a matter of the heart than the head, has a new insistency which may pay little regard to what can be afforded and what interests suggest should be done or left undone.

Overstretch and strain must thus be expected to remain a characteristic of the Army at least until such time as sufficiently large numbers of servicemen make known their feelings that enough is enough by leaving it. The old principle that the subaltern should receive half-a-day's pay for half-a-day's work has long given way, and will in all probability continue for some time to do so, to the new that all in the Army should get a day's pay for a day-and-a-half's work. We will eventually realise that as the old principle did not give us the Army that would meet our new needs so the new will not enable us to keep the Army without which the protection of our interests will be impossible. However, while the Army has too many commitments and too little capacity to meet them, the pressures on it will be such as to make it very difficult for the Education and Training Services Branch to be given time to undertake new work. But if we must be aware of pressures on the Army making that difficult we should not be unaware of other pressures on it of a contrary kind which might call insistently for the very expansion, the difficulty of which seems now so evident.

If we allow our hearts to dictate our actions until our heads become too sore to allow that practice to continue, more soldiers might be expected to join up to see the world. Even so it seems likely that the bulk of the Army will be stationed at home. Their regimental life, their messes, their cherished customs which, however weakened, will not be destroyed by the reduction in the number of their bands, will continue to be a hedge between soldiers and society; theirs will remain a total commitment which not even the most dedicated of Japanese firms will ever make of civil occupations. But the mass media have the same regard for hedges that love has for lock-smiths and the direct pressures of contemporary society on its Army are inescapable. What they will be is uncertain; what is certain is that they are bound to be significant and will have to be adjusted to.

There would be no volunteer armies if men and women never felt the appeal of soldiering. A minority no doubt soldier because they can find no other way of making a living, some because they can find, as they think, no easier way of making a living, most because they can find no more congenial way of making a living. The majority join because the Army gives them the satisfaction they feel they will not get in civilian life, the care, or the comradeship, or the pride of belonging, or the sense of worthwhile service, or the opportunity for development, or the open air life, or the adventure; or all of these together. They join because the Army is their preferred way of life. A gentleman has been defined as one who was not solely interested in 'getting on'. With that definition in mind perhaps we can speak of the soldiers as 'nature's gentlemen'. That would have shocked Wellington and it is not normally how we view them. But there would be more sense in so doing than in continuing to refer to them as 'the old and the bold' or 'the brutal and licentious'.

But if it is worth emphasising that the soldiery is less interested in getting on in a material sense than most civilians, it is also worth stressing that all having the interests of the Army at heart should beware of allowing too great a discrepancy in material expectations to develop between society and its Army. Preferences can change and if civilian material prospects become vastly more alluring than those of the soldier, soldiers might be hard to come by. Needing to be superbly fit physically, they retire at a comparatively early age and while few in life's sunny morning spare a thought for its decline more would do so if convinced they had no chance of finding a reasonably paid job on leaving the Army. It is therefore incumbent on it to attend to an insistent need, the need to do all that can be done to strengthen the appeal of soldiering and everything possible to weaken what would undermine it.

This the Army has well understood. Despite its financial embarrassments and their inevitable pressure on the RAEC, its extra-mural ventures, its venture expeditions at home and abroad, have not been curtailed. When many have faced redundancy and when its memory is fresh, care to make the soldier's life as attractive as possible can never be far from the minds of the Army Council. Yet dim as the future must always be, we can already see forces developing, forces still in their early stages which seem unlikely to be halted as the days go by and which as they grow will greatly add to the Army's problem of making and keeping itself attractive if it does not make timely adjustment to them.

One of the strongest pressures now bearing on society and on the Army too is that of the mass media. It has given an immediacy and a power to public opinion which it has never yet had. Its strength has grown over the years and when the New Year 1977 came in it was even claimed that the present wave of alternative music in

Europe symbolising the growing acceptance and advocacy of non-conformity among the young is the result of the widespread influence of the mass media.[5]

Public opinion has always been important. 'Four hostile newspapers', Napoleon said, 'are more to be feared than a thousand bayonets'. It was always impatient, too, for men and women are not the most patient of animals, something which led Hamilton to say he had 'a horror of the momentary action of the public'. But public opinion was always more successful in preventing Government doing what public opinion did not want than in compelling Government to do what public opinion did, which was often no more than a passing, if strongly felt, wish. It has now grown so much more powerful and so much more dangerous that many fear we will soon be suffering the chaotic consequences of government by instant public opinion. The situation which Tennyson feared

> Where blind and naked ignorance
> Delivers brawling judgments, unashamed
> On all things all day long

seems to have been brought about by television. Many who read little see much of that. If we read we may begin to reflect. But if we only see and hear we are much more likely to respond to our emotions since they have been aroused, and not to advance our thinking since that has not been prompted.

The instant transmission of an image not only makes television a most powerful method of communication, but gives it a great influence in moulding public opinion. Brought up in the tradition of investigative journalism, its programme makers are apt to be critical of all authority and to give free rein to their prejudices. They can ensure that their views come with a punch which can be powerfully directed against what the Government believes to be in the best interests of the country, as was seen in Vietnam, the Falklands and the Gulf.[6] They forced President Nixon, elected less than two years earlier by one of the largest majorities ever recorded, out of office, an action unprecedented in American history. In time of war the Head of the BBC would not allow reference to be made to 'our troops' and 'our ships'. 'We are not Britain. We are the BBC', he said. 'We are not in the game of patriotism', his Director of BBC and Current Affairs added. It was even said how better advised we would have been had we been able during the Second World War to listen to Geobbels and Lord Haw-Haw by courtesy of the BBC. That war had been reported 'from a domestic point of view'. In the Falklands War we had at last seen the light as was demonstrated by our 'more two sided presentation of events'.[7] It is worth remembering Admiral Woodward's caustic comment on the BBC at this time: 'I realised that their self-appointed task as "Fearless Searchers After Truth" was, to them, sacrosanct. But their "ratings" that week just may have been paid for with the blood of Captain Hart-Dyke's people'.[8]

We have seen this two-sided presentation of events, on which the BBC prided itself in the Falklands War, in Northern Ireland when the Law Lords upheld the prohibition of the television appearances of hooded terrorists and their supporters.[9]

Television journalists declared that this highlighted 'the unaccountable and unacceptable power wielded by Ministers of the Crown in the British system of government'. It seemed at least evident that they looked on unaccountability as undesirable and it would have been interesting to know how they convinced themselves, insisting as they did on their right to do what seemed good to them and accounting only to their editors who were not themselves accountable to the public, that they were more to be trusted to act responsibly than was a Government which must justify itself in periodic elections.[10]

In this we see an attack not on the Government but on the state, the legal embodiment of the Nation, the possessor of sovereignty, the definer and upholder of all our rights, the focus of our loyalty. It is the organised community and it is the very basis of civilisation since, important as individual effort is, it is only through communal power that great things for the community as a whole can be done. No-one will think that the distinction between the state, which it is our duty as citizens to uphold, and the Government, which it is our right as free men to criticise, can always be made crystal clear, but difficult as that distinction is to make it must, as any healthy state and community will insist, be made in wartime. The reluctance of some of the new breed of journalists to acknowledge this reminds us how formidable is the problem thrust upon us by the recent great increase in the power of the mass media to mould public opinion.[11]

They have brought about what the sociologists call 'the reality of de-authorisation', by which unlovely expression is meant the lessening of respect for and obedience to established authority. As it would be a poor Army which could not command obedience, the Army cannot but be concerned at the prospect of it being undermined. Yet have we not seen television programmes which seem to have that as their objective? When it was said at the 1980 Annual General Meeting of the British Legion 'I have never seen such anti-British and anti-Army propaganda',[12] we might have paid little attention to it in the conviction that hyper-sensitivity is to be expected on such an occasion, had there not been so many programmes of that kind. And we should remember that a British soldier serving in Germany where the mass media was opposed to the Gulf War refused to accompany his unit to the Middle East on the grounds that he was opposed to war against Iraq. We saw demonstrated in the between-war years the truth Juvenal taught when he said of Rome 'now we suffer the ills of lengthy peace, luxury more deadly than arms overwhelms us and makes us pay for our conquest of the world'. We would be ill-advised to be sure we will never see it again. Men and women are as he said, prone to forgive the ravens and blame the doves. We may believe with Shakespeare that 'they that have the power to hurt and will do none ... rightly do inherit heaven's grace' and not look to see many of them in television studios.[13]

Ever conscious of the importance of morale, Montgomery said in his Mansion House Speech of 24 March 1944 'The task of influencing an Army which dwells among an alien population is easy; the thinking and way of life of the people is mainly irrelevant. But an Army which dwells amongst its own folk is a wholly different proposition; it both regards and understands the people amongst whom it dwells, and they pour the ideas and thoughts into the receptive minds of the soldiers all day. Some of these ideas are inimical to battle morale.'[14] He was speaking during a great war and thinking of approaching battle, but his words have meaning for a peacetime Army the bulk of which is stationed at home. They have meaning for the ETS branch too. The searchings of the mass media on matters which bring little credit to the Army must be expected to intensify. It can find no satisfaction in the educational standards of its soldiers. Little public attention is paid to that now. It will be. When it is the Army will be compelled to do more than pay the lip-service to the importance of Army Education with which it contrives to content itself. It will be an offence against common-sense if the long played-down teaching role of the ETS does not in future regain importance.

Yet another of the powerful influences bearing on the Army today is that of technology. The Army has for years been well aware of this. It knew when the National Service Army ended that its rigid field formations would have to give place to more flexible battle groups as new equipment demanded increased mobility. It knew that the troops in consequence must become more versatile, more resourceful, more technically efficient, that they must be quicker in understanding, more adaptable and have greater qualities of leadership. Again and again it has stressed that 'the Army of the future requires a higher calibre man than before', that 'the unemployable civilian is unemployable as a soldier', that 'the soldier of today must undergo longer and more complicated training than before'.[15] As technology developed the Army continued to emphasise how it was 'decreasingly relying on mass and more and more on technology'.[16] It stressed in the words of the Bett Review 'There will be a continuing demand for high calibre personnel able to assimilate information and to establish priorities during the fog of war.'[17] To the effect on it and the challenge to it of technology the Army can be no more indifferent than it can be to that of the media.

No Army can be indifferent to changes in social attitudes and expectations, least of all one which expects its soldiers to be home-based. It has been greatly concerned by the pressures on it of what it has called 'a dramatic shift in attitudes to work'. 'Society', it said, 'has become much more interested in short-term employment and its concomitant higher rewards than in long-term careers.'[18] University Careers Advisory Services have found for some years those seeking their help in finding jobs do not look forward to only a single career; they contemplate changes as they grow older. The Army has always known its soldiers will seek new employment after discharge but it is now more aware than it has ever been that it will not attract as many as it needs and will not long retain those it gets if it cannot make service 'financially worth-while and likely to provide the qualifications necessary for a satisfactory civilian job'. 'Young people', the Bett Review printed out, 'will expect more from their employment: stability, through career development and future employability.'[19] The Army had never been without anxiety lest in an increasingly materialistic and luxury-loving society it might fail to recruit the numbers it must have. The Army could not but be alarmed by these social pressures bearing on it.

One of the strongest forces bearing on the Army seems to be the pressure for educational reform mounting so rapidly today. For the most part we have shown ourselves to be a very patient people with a great capacity for putting up with things, thinking it necessary from time to time to change them but agreeing with Bacon 'it were good that men in their innovations would follow the example of time, which indeed innovateth greatly, but quietly and by degrees scarcely to be perceived'.[20] Now, however, we want amendment without tarrying for any. We are caught up in that great demonstration which we can see throughout East Europe and in the former USSR of the truth Montaigne stressed when he emphasised 'How very incompetently society can go about healing its ills, how impatient it can be of whatever happens to be pressing it at any particular instant, how it can think only of getting rid of this, reckless of the cost.'[21] We are no longer content to live with the consequences of past inadequacy until time and new endeavour have removed them. We look to the stroke of a pen to do this.

Thus we have determined that by the end of the century there will be a 50% increase in the number of our graduates and a 12% increase in the number of our postgraduate students. By then one in three of the 18–21 age group are to be involved in higher education as against the one in five similarly engaged in 1989–1990. To ensure that this will be done we have made all our polytechnics universities, an educational reform the advantages of which no-one else has yet appreciated.

It is to be doubted if our hopes will be fulfilled and if our novel procedures will give us the highly-educated young people we look for by the turn of the century. But since such ways of doing things are not universally approved it is certain that the educational debate vigorously conducted today will no more subside than will the pressure to secure the looked-for reforms. We cannot forget that we have to be as good as the best of our industrial and commercial rivals to compete successfully with them. We cannot be indifferent to the fact that German workers getting apprentice-level certificates in mechanical engineering are five-times more numerous than British workers acquiring similar qualifications; that France and Germany each produce four times as many electricians as Britain does; that 60% of German workers have vocational qualifications which took them two years' teaching to get, that only 37% of them have no qualifications at all. In Britain only 23% have comparable certificates and 69% are entirely lacking in qualifications.[22]

This is what ensures that it cannot be said of the movement for educational reform building up in Britain to-day that it is merely stirring

> ...dust
> Of the windy ways of men.
> That lightly rises up,
> And is lightly laid again.

Unlike youth, it is of the stuff that will endure.

Resident in their own country, soldiers will be more immediately exposed to the currents in it. And if society is now more determined than it was to think education important, if it is associating schools with industry as it has never done before, if it is insisting that more of its young adults should experience higher education and giving them more access to vocational training, if it is providing for those of mature years more opportunity to keep up with the most recent advances in their professions or trades, soldiers will be aware of that. They will know, too, of the benefits such developments bring and will be anxious not to be under a grave disadvantage when leaving the Colours, as they will be if such opportunities have not come their way. If, as is probable, our determination to compete successfully with France and Germany induces us to see that our young in industry and commerce attend day-release classes as their French and German opposite numbers do, will that be something which the Army can look upon as of no interest to it? Not many civilians are willing to attend classes in their own time; not many soldiers will be either. But when others are given during their normal working hours opportunities for advancement which are denied to soldiers in theirs, that will become known and will gradually have its effect and it is to be expected that eventually there will be fewer soldiers to be denied opportunities to.

In yet another way the new attraction education has for the English people must raise a tremor in the Army. It admits the deplorably low educational standard of many of its soldiers. It acknowledges the low educational standard it requires of its recruits and knows too that this cannot be raised since 'any attempt to raise it would have a dramatic effect on the numbers recruited'. It knows how badly its educational requirements compare with those of allied armies, saying 'Our recruits are and will remain of a lower educational standard than that of our NATO allies' and 'Their educational provision makes our level of provision relatively limited.'[23] The Army has avoided the full glare of publicity on this; it has failed to provide the scandals which attract the tabloids and the British public takes little interest in it. But wherever there are matters which seem to reflect little credit on those responsible for them, the investigative journalist can be trusted to make them known with the maximum disregard to the difficulties that have occasioned them and the minimum concern for the national interest in so doing. The Army must be aware that the attention of the ungodly will sooner or later be concentrated on it and that it would be advised to look to its defences against them. If the low standard of our schools focuses the attention of the journalist today, what he will portray as the disgraceful educational attainments of the troops will appeal to him tomorrow as a splendid opportunity to lay bare and to belabour the inadequacies of the top brass. Thus the present national upsurge of interest in education will exercise on the Army as great a pressure as that created by the mass media, technology and the changing social attitudes of the people.

Something else will, too, and that is the nature of the international world in which it is reasonable to think the British Army will be required to operate. That, as we know, will not be a brave new world[24] but it does not seem likely to be as intolerable as old ones have sometimes been. The overwhelming pressure on great states which in Cold War days prevented them fighting still does. The terrible destruction which they know will be the unavoidable price they will pay if they cannot restrain their passions is as likely to keep them at peace now as it did then. That knowledge cannot always make them sensible, but it is likely to keep them sane. Some of the Great Powers are eager that all should honour the rights they cherish, apparently indifferent to the fact that others, to whom they do not appeal and whose different circumstances suggest to them their undesirability, will see in this eagerness only the wish to impose their values on them. This will annoy other Great Powers; it will not make them change their ways. We may deplore what strengthens man's inclination to see the mote in his neighbour's eye and ignore the beam in his own. We should always question, too, the desirability of doing what will arouse the passions of peoples, yet believe that however much they may harden hearts they will not unbalance heads. Great Power war is still remote. Yet our international world has not changed as greatly as is sometimes claimed. In Cold War days Great Power war was unlikely and Small Power war unavoidable. Conditions in the Great Power world made for peace, conditions in the Small Power world for war. The two worlds affected each other but it proved as impossible for the instability of the Small Power world to undermine the stability of the Great Power world as it was for the stability of the Great Power world to bring stability to the Small Power world. We see the same two worlds today and the same relationship between them. The international order which will determine the nature and the activity of the British Army remains one of Great Power peace and Small Power turbulence.

These pressures now bearing on society and the Army have one thing in common. They all stress the increased importance and indeed the overwhelming necessity of paying more attention to Army Education. They have forced from the Army a clearer and stronger acknowledgement of its indispensability than has yet been heard. We see this in an important Army paper which emphasised the importance both of training and of education. 'Training', it said, 'is the provision of skills which are measurable and which can be defined in relation to the objectives. Education is the provision of knowledge and understanding, the development of the mind and the strengthening of its capacity to analyse and look through problems.' 'The distinction between them', it added, 'is in most cases clear but it becomes blurred when training involves personal development. They complement each other with education making training more effective and enhancing the trainee's ability to absorb information.' 'There is', the paper said, 'more need to develop minds than ever before now that quite junior officers have to make more than was the case hitherto important military decisions that may well also have political implications. The Army is now called upon to face many tasks often very difficult to predict. It is decreasingly relying on mass and more and more on technology. Moreover there is developing a significant divergence between the attitudes of society and those on which the Army must insist. Officers at all levels must have the intelligence to do what they are called upon to do and to explain to their soldiers and indeed if necessary to the general public why they are doing it.'[25] This brief and eminently sensible comment on the nature of education and of training and of the relationship between them is important not only because it is marked by a clarity lacking in previous attempts to define 'educational training' but even more because of its insistence on the need for education as well as for training, a need of which the Army has not always appeared conscious.

The Army has paid attention to the threat posed by the media. Defence Council Instruction 288 of 1970 reminded all Commanding Officers of 'The need to ensure that men should know about current trends and events which could affect the Army, so that they can form reasonable opinions on views expressed through the mass media, wherever they are serving, and can recognise and counter these reports which could lower morale or alienate loyalty.'[26]

Thus heeding Montgomery's warning that a home-based soldiery will need defence other than weapons, the Army has also sought to counter the challenge of technology by repeatedly stressing that it has created a demand for the thinking, adaptable, keen-minded and independent soldier called for in situations in which mass has lost much of its military significance. Again and again it has made known its conviction that 'there will be a continuing demand for high calibre personnel able to assimilate information and to establish priorities during the fog of war'. It has said this so frequently that it must now be beginning to listen to what it has said.[27]

Alarmed by the pressures on it arising from changes in social attitudes, the Army has quickly adjusted to them. It has acknowledged, as it has not done before, the driving necessity of ensuring that all soldiers should acquire while they serve the qualifications they will need when they return to civilian life. The new recognition of this urgency is of major importance for hitherto the greatly influential training organisations have seen it as their only role, with which no other considerations must interfere, to train to fight. Nothing they believed must be added to this training requirement. Now the Army knows that it cannot give the trainers their heads, as if they did there might no longer be an Army to train. As the BETT Review emphasised 'Since the Army is bound to face the stiffest competition if it is to attract recruits of the calibre it seeks it must be seen to provide educational opportunities which will help soldiers to gain the qualifications which employers will look for when the soldier leaves the Colours.'[28] 'The education of the young officer must give him the qualifications acceptable in civil society' the Adjutant-General said.[29]

The Army's difficulties in dealing with the trainers have been eased by the development of the NVQ Scheme. This greatly appealed to it. The qualifications which civilian employers will respect can be acquired gradually over the years. Moreover, it has long been apparent that it is in vocational and not academic studies that the soldier can be interested and that it is probably only the minority who cannot be interested in any study at all. This is as true of the great majority of civilians as it is of soldiers and the great change in the attitude of the English people to education in recent years has been the belated recognition of the importance for a great industrial nation of the vocational studies which our competitors have long been promoting.

We have seen how the Army has jumped at the opportunity of making NVQ studies relevant to military training. In its jargon Army courses are 'mapped' into civilian qualifications; a way, that is to say, has been found of meeting the Army's training needs which will also provide for the soldier the qualifications which will satisfy civilian employers. Gone are the years when Commanding Officers, anxious to retain their soldiers and fearing that the better prepared they were for civilian life the sooner they would want to return to it, looked askance at the efforts of Resettlement Officers to persuade soldiers to acquire the qualifications helpful to them in a second career. NCOs were now to keep an eye on soldiers working for NVQs. The NCOs were to be encouraged to train to be accepted as assessors of the standards reached by the soldiers working for NVQs. Being qualified to so act, NCOs would enhance their own market value in civilian life. They had a further inducement to become so qualified in the knowledge that it would cost them the best part of £1,000 to get this qualification in civilian life, but the Army would foot the bill if they got it while serving. NCOs, particularly if they have become certified NVQ assessors, will have much greater effect than Education and Training Services Branch officers in chivvying the slothful and spurring them on to continued effort.[30]

As from 1 April 1990 Level I of the NVQ Scheme has been given to all soldiers holding the Second Class EPC certificate. Foundation Skills in horse care and management, warehousing and wholesaling, light and heavy vehicle mechanics, business administration, light vehicle body repair, catering, security, communication operations, management and training are available to the troops as NVQs. The National Council for qualifications agreed they would be accepted by civilian employers. In addition the Army has encouraged soldiers to work for whatever other qualifications they desire. Under the Individual Refund Scheme soldiers working for approved courses of study can claim up to £140 a year towards the cost of their studies. Roughly 10% of all eligible Army personnel have so claimed.[31]

This is a momentous change in the attitude of the Army authorities to Army Education and it creates a precedent, the significance of which the Army may not yet be aware but which suggests that the uniformed educator may be closer to a long-desired breakthrough than has been thought. Since NVQ studies are now part of training they are done in the Queen's time. The great importance of this is not just that all soldiers are now perforce exposed to education which they can no more escape than they can their drill. It is that soldiers can now legitimately be compelled to submit to one type of education because the trainers have become convinced that without it they might not have an Army to train, and that in consequence it has become very difficult to reject the argument that another type of education, which the Army has no doubt reluctantly been compelled to accept is also vital to it, should take place in the Queen's time too.

Nor has a further change in social attitudes of the greatest importance for the Army been overlooked. The drop in civilian moral and ethical standards in the 1990s created a problem for the Army. Its own standards did not reflect that general decline for it never doubted that if it did not insist on higher moral and ethical standards than those now satisfying civilians it could not do its job. It had to eliminate elements which might adversely affect the morale, cohesion and operational efficiency of units. Yet recruits would bring with them the civilian standards which would no longer suit the Army. Thus as it believed it had to ensure that the officer coming from state schools adjusted to and adopted the ways of the regiment, so now it thought it must see that its soldiers adjusted to and adopted as their own the Army's moral and ethical standards in the absence of which it would be greatly weakened. Its officers, warrant officers and NCOs would have the task of transmitting its values to the recruits, making known the nature of their commitments and why it was essential to the Army's well-being for the highest standards to be maintained. No education mattered more to the Army than that.[32]

We have seen that the Army understood the necessity of educating its soldiers in order to get and retain them. For that and other reasons too it also understood that it must give more attention to the education of its officers. As early as 1993 there was talk again of setting up a Tri-Service University, which senior naval officers took seriously enough to register their alarm, saying it 'would be unable to bring to bear on the maritime domain that sharp focus that Manadon can achieve'. A Tri-Services Command and Staff College was announced as part of the 1994 'Front Line First' reforms. There were difficulties in locating it. The Army Staff College at Camberley and its Naval counterpart at Greenwich were too small to take the required numbers and as listed buildings they could not be altered to provide more accommodation. The accommodation at the Air Force Staff College at Bracknell was shoddy in the extreme. After much wrangling it has now been decided to build a new Tri-Service College in the grounds of the Royal Military College of Science at Shrivenham. There more than 2,000 students, including many from overseas who are always eager to attend such courses, will spend a year of joint training in an impressive environment in which it is hoped they will form lasting friendships which will promote in them the ways of thinking essential to effective Tri-Service operations. Existing Staff Colleges, senior and junior, will eventually be housed in the new Tri-Service College appropriately named Watchfield. Revealingly too, the academic studies in the course are emphasised and it is said that special efforts will be made to increase and have accepted their 'market value' in civilian eyes.[33]

Since Sandhurst, which prepares the junior officer for his first appointment, has little time for his general education that is provided by the first part of the Junior Officers' Training and Educational Scheme before he attains Captain's rank. This Scheme has three parts. There is a period of regimental duty, a practical examination on that and general education, the purpose of which is 'to improve a young officer's ability to write clear and concise English and encourage an awareness of Defence Studies'.[34] It was clearly hoped that Commanding Officers would watch and find means of promoting his education apart from the three two-day courses in three consecutive years. To encourage them and him, the subaltern was given the information and the exhortation to further study he needed in what were referred to as 'stand-alone packages'. Unfortunately it seems they did and complaints about the low standard of the subaltern's education and above all of his writing mounted.[35]

The second part of the Junior Officers Training and Educational Scheme also had limited success. For this a period of regimental duty is required. Officers must attend the Junior Command and Staff Course which lasts ten weeks. They go to a Military Law Course. They spend three weeks of the Junior Command and Staff Course at Shrivenham studying Military Technology and three addressing themselves to Defence Studies at Sandhurst. 'A Directed Reading and Project Scheme prepares them for this course and identifies areas of weakness in written skills', it was said. This Directed Reading and Project Scheme requires officers to study a particular topic and write a 2,500-word mini-thesis on it in the six months prior to attending the residential courses at Shrivenham and Sandhurst. The Education and Training Services Branch Field

Tutors brief officers embarking on the Directed Reading and Project Scheme and give tutorial assistance with the first draft of the mini-thesis. Twice a year they run a revision course for officers, particularly in essay writing.

The greatest success in this Scheme seems to have been in 'identifying areas of weakness in written skills'. The Integrated Promotion and Staff Examination Board reported on the Junior Officers' Training and Education Scheme examination for 1994–1995 'There was ample evidence of poor grammar and spelling. Indeed, some examiners questioned whether English was the mother tongue of some candidates sitting the examination, such was the woeful use of English encountered in a number of scripts.'[36] Some things change slowly over the years. The writer remembers that as Chief Examiner for the Current Affairs paper in the Staff/Promotion examination his Brigadier colleague sent him a script to adjudicate. Its near illiteracy would have created no problem had it not been accompanied by signs of significant thinking and indeed by a touch of originality. Thinking it might have been written by a Gurkha officer for whom he was prepared to bend rules, he asked for further information. It was properly refused and he was told to get on with his job. The candidate's thinking and touch of originality carried the day. Only after he was declared to have passed the examination was the examiner told that English was his native language and that he was a graduate of an English University. Among the examiner's most lively regrets is his failure to sink this candidate without trace. Sandhurst did what it could to correct the officer's deficiency in the writing of English but it had too little time in which to do it. Shocked by this evidence of the great appeal of illiteracy to the officer despite the fact that 75% of them were now graduates, authority declared 'The improvement required cannot be achieved on a "short, sharp shock" basis but must be through a continuing developmental process using relevant subject material.'[37] It is, however, one thing to acknowledge the necessity of a long haul and another to be reconciled to it. Arrangements to deal with this problem suggest that the difference between a 'short, sharp shock' and 'a continuing developmental process' is still as insufficiently understood as it has always hitherto proved to be. The Army Educator has always known that 'continuity is the only lubricant which prevents educational progress from grinding to a halt'.[38] This is a truth which the Army has never accepted. It acknowledges the importance of continuity in training. But not in education which is something it thinks it can get behind it or in front of it as long as it is under its belt. When admitted to be necessary it is thought of as a hurdle to be got over and not as a process to be continued. Perhaps the RAEC made a mistake in speaking of the 'Progressive Qualification Scheme' for officers. For that called attention to what education was but what the Army did not want it to be.

Officer education clearly left much to be desired. In fighting to retain the Progressive Qualification Scheme the Director of Army Education had urged that 'junior officers should not lie fallow for too long'. He had stressed 'the growing need for officers with breadth of mind and knowledge as well as depth of operational skills' and had pleaded that it was vital to retain the Staff/Promotion Examination as an 'intellectual filter' at a time 'when the Officers' Tutors have reported their students as unable to think in conceptual terms and express themselves clearly'. The event had proved him abundantly right.[39]

Senior officers, however, had not been convinced. They had also expressed concern at the attitude to study of the officers involved in PQS. 'The attitude whereby officers expect that facilities for instructing them in their profession should be totally provided is gaining ground', they said, 'but this attitude is the antithesis of many other qualities which are important to the Army. We therefore recommend that wherever and whenever possible an attitude of self-motivation should be developed by young officers and they should be encouraged to realise that they are more likely to advance in their profession in direct proportion to the personal efforts they cultivate.'[40]

This was a dangerous argument. It is one thing to be impressed by the motto of the old Boiler Makers' Union 'God helps those who help themselves' and to be convinced that we will all be the poorer if it is forgotten. It is another to think it desirable to give little or no encouragement to officers to acquire the qualities essential to senior posts in their profession. The senior officers in question could not have been unaware that while their juniors might be self-motivated to prepare themselves for the better discharge of their duties, many in the past had been self-motivated to do nothing of the sort. Times have changed since Fuller said that young officers would be 'for the shore' if they read anything other than the *Pink Un* and Nat Gould's racing novels, and we may think him lacking in the milk of human kindness in speaking of the 'Aberdeen Granite' which he thought to see in the minds of some of his fellow officers. Human nature has not, however, changed and does not find relaxation through unfamiliar intellectual effort after a day's hard work. Tired officers may have less difficulty in resisting the appeal of the *Pink Un* than in finding the works of Nat Gould, but compared with the entertainment they can get by pushing a button the *Pink Un*'s pages might seem a hard academic discipline and Nat Gould one of the minor Edwardian classics.

The high-flyers in any profession will always apply themselves and will make their mark whatever the circumstances. The outstanding have always known that study and learning 'teacheth more in one year than experience in twentie' and that the fees in the school of experience are very high. But there are many perhaps not so outstanding whose talents could be developed to groom them for higher command. Encouraged, they might address themselves to the study and thinking that, unencouraged, might have too little appeal for them. To reach the heights they have to understand before aspiring to them that they will then be directed by their own lights and that unless they know before they get there that 'good principles of learning be the eyes of the minde to look wiselie before a man which way to go right and which not', they will aspire to them in vain.[41]

To instil such 'good principles' had been the object of the Progressive Qualification Scheme and perhaps we can see more clearly now than we could then what a chance the Army was taking in dispensing with it. It is difficult not to agree with the Officer Tutor who said 'We gave our students knowledge and showed them how to use it – to analyse it, interpret the result, and apply what they had learned. How strange and sad that it should now be considered unnecessary'. It is by no means unusual for things to be more valued in their absence than when they were available. That seems to be true of the Army's attitude to officer education today.[42]

What seems likely to be the nature of tomorrow's world and what present developments suggest may be the nature of the Army's commitments in it have also strengthened the Army's interest in education. It has already been engaged and expects to be tomorrow in United Nations multi-national operations. It expects 'to have to deploy at short notice to cope with unexpected emergencies' and believes that 'there will be in consequence a greater demand for mental agility, the capacity to absorb rapidly changing information and on the soldier's ability to make very quick decisions in isolation'. It stresses that 'leaders at all levels will need to understand the tactical and political situation in which they find themselves'. They 'will need an understanding of political, cultural, ethnic and religious differences and a knowledge of foreign languages'.[43] If we persist in efforts to include Eastern Europe in NATO and offer a security pact to the Ukraine, the Army will have to think again and rely more on mass as well as on technology. We must hope that we are not of the Hatter persuasion and will not arouse the jealousy of March Hares. If second thoughts in these matters prevail it seems that, like the pressures from the media, from technology, from the change in social attitudes and the recent upsurge in the country of interest in education, future operations call for education as well as training; they complement each other.

The formidable nature of this cumulative case for Army Education cannot be doubted. Nor can it be doubted that it has still to contend with formidable opposition. How much more concerned prior to 1938 the Camberley Staff College was with instruction rather than with education is apparent when we realise there was very little time there for reading and reflection. The steady growth in the number of graduate officers in the Army was widely predicted as early as 1958. Yet it took thirty years for it to become, as the Beach Report recommended, more genuinely educational to reflect the increased number of officer graduates. However, the prospect of more highly educated officers coming into the Army which took so long to make the Camberley Course more educational took less than ten years to make the Sandhurst Course less so. Here the change was dramatic and not gradual. In this speedy seizing of the opportunity to reduce the time spent on education and in this lengthy and reluctant acknowledgement of the necessity of increasing it, it is difficult not to see a reflection of the attitude of the Army authorities to education.

For as long as they could the trainers stubbornly insisted that 'training must not be distorted to enable civilian qualifications to be gained', as it would be if these qualifications were to be prepared for in the Queen's time. Their influence was such as not only to reconcile the Army to living with contradictions, but to increase them. There is an odd contradiction in the Army Education or Advisory Board's paper already referred to. It repeats what has so often been said that 'the probable nature of future operations will place a greater demand on the mental agility of all soldiers'; having already told us that mental agility can only be expected if intellectual ability is developed by education. To ensure this it reduces the sixteen periods which were devoted to education in the Common Military Syllabus designed for the initial training of the recruits to twelve, this after having admitted their deplorably low educational standards. In this a predominantly English Army fittingly reflects a people who, newly converted to a belief in the desirability of technical education, make its polytechnics universities and smiles on them when they cease to be admirable technical institutions and become inadequate academic establishments. As one of the Government's largest employers the Army makes known its wish to be seen 'Investing in People'. Here again the Army sees clearly and emphasises adequately what is needed; belief in the efficiency of the good fairy's wand still influences its ideas of how to do it. In that it is to be hoped its reflection of its parent society is no longer as faithful.[44]

The same anomaly is to be seen in the education of the NCOs. As the greater complexity of weapons must mean that greater demands will be made on the men who handle them, so it will require more of the NCOs. The Army has long believed a minimum educational standard must be reached before other ranks can become NCOs and NCOs be further promoted. Yet here we have a paradoxical situation; when more is required of them the educational standard they must attain has been lowered and less time is devoted to their teaching. Justification for this has not been sought on the grounds that long experience and further reflection have shown that the former educational standard deemed essential for the various NCO ranks was higher than was necessary and the time taken to reach it needlessly long, for the changes have been recent and no enquiry into these matters has been made. It has not been said that the national system of education has produced soldiers of higher intelligence than their predecessors and that in consequence less topping up will be needed to reach the approved standard, for if this was believed to be true the best proof that it was would have been to maintain the old standards and show that they could be reached with less teaching and less study. This was clearly a case of needs must when the devil drives. An Army with too much to do and too few soldiers to do it had to cut corners.

Yet if corners are cut too finely, trouble may result. A number of Commanding Officers wanted to cut them very finely indeed. Although the EPC courses lasted only five weeks they were wanted to be still shorter. The Commanding Officers who urged this were confusing ends with means and forgetting the purpose of the examination which was not to give to aspiring NCOs the certificates without which they would aspire in vain. Had that been its purpose ingenuity could soon have satisfied the aspiring NCOs and the most impatient of the Commanding Officers. Awards for good conduct are not unknown. EPC's purpose was to ensure that those satisfying the examiners were demonstrating the qualities looked for in the examination, qualities without which candidates could not be expected to do the job required of them.

It was not the certificates that mattered but the effect the preparation for them had on those who acquired them as demonstrated by their acquisition. If that preparation had no effect, the certificates would not be worth acquiring.

We cannot believe that the reaching of certain educational standards by aspiring NCOs would have been insisted on over such an extended period of time if Commanding Officers had not been convinced that this insistence gave them what they wanted, the good NCO. Nor can we believe that Commanding Officers had been deluded in so thinking. If it had been a mistaken view that working for certificates produced better NCOs, that would have become apparent and the Army would have dropped them long ago.

There are dangers in insisting that things be done too quickly. Wishing to improve communications and to build more bridges more quickly to enable this to be done, Mao's China halved the time devoted to the training of the engineers who built them. The bridges fell down, their collapse a testimony to the virtues of patience and the profundity of the thoughts of Chairman Mao. It was odd of him to be surprised when the bridges fell down. Yet even he knew that if he halved the time between the sowing of the seed and the harvesting it would not be worth collecting what came up, and education is more akin to farming than to building bridges. The soil must be prepared to receive the seed and time allowed for it to germinate. Officers anxious to cut down the time spent in preparation for EPC are in the Great Leap Forward business. They would be well advised to look to its consequences in China.

We can hardly fail to be aware of the great oddity here. While the technological developments have made greater demands on the soldier in the handling of his weapons and social and moral developments have weakened the values instilled in him to which he has hitherto looked for support, more alertness is called for in the NCO if Kipling's fine line 'the backbone of the Army is the non-commissioned man' is still to be applied to him. Yet the standard of education he is now expected to reach was lower than it had been and the time devoted to his intellectual development was greatly curtailed. And this was occurring when the pressures on the Army to make itself ever more effective seemed irresistible and when if it was to become so it must ensure the best training of its best NCOs.

However, the Army now maintained that great advances had been made in the education of its NCOs. EPC and the difficulties it created were things of the past. It had been replaced by Education for Promotion which was claimed to be a better way of reflecting 'the progressive nature of the soldiers' training and education'. It provided 'specific training to prepare individuals for a particular appointment or rank'.[45]

It is an old principle of good writing that sound must reflect sense but not that it should be substituted for it. The Army's liking for fine sounding generalities which often do not bear close scrutiny shows it at times yielding to the temptation of thinking it can be. It is comforting to know that EFP is 'in line with the best civilian practices' but it would be more so if we were told what these were and where they are to be found. We need to know this the more as the tests are primarily concerned with the acquisition of military skills which on the face of it must make us wonder what civilian educational practices they can legitimately be compared with. It is good, too, to know they reflect 'the progressive nature of the soldiers' training and education' and it is easy to believe they do indeed reflect the progressive nature of his training. We would be easier in mind if we had been told how they also reflect the progressive nature of his education when the marked distaste for it which he has often shown has hidden even from optimistic eyes its developing progressive nature.

One supreme virtue was claimed for EFP. The reduction of course length led to an annual saving of 24,000 man-training days, a godsend to an increasingly hard-pressed Army. This also must increase our uneasiness. Army statistics do not always convince; the uncharitable would give them an honoured place in the inexact sciences. But they are not to be interpreted as meaning the exact opposite of what they say and it can be safely assumed that those taking the EFP tests spent less time away from their usual unit duties preparing for them than those taking EPC had done. We cannot say that a new educational principle had been discovered here, namely that what adds to its value is the time not spent on it, as it is possible that candidates for the test may in their own time have turned to the RAEC for the additional help it was ready to give them. If EFP lightened any loads, the burden borne by the RAEC was not among them. We must remember the pre-course learning packages for those whom the diagnostic testing, which it undertook, indicated were below the standard for EPC, and it continued to provide help for prospective NCOs studying in their own time. We can, however, say that the arrangements for EFP showed that the less time the Army spent on education the more reconciled it became to it. It must be remembered that not all who had hitherto been able to take EPC and the examinations for the Army Certificates of Education could now do so. Even privates or junior soldiers could take the courses and sit the examinations for them. In view of the vocational principles on which the EFP tests were based, eligibility rules for sitting them were introduced. Only those near in seniority to the ranks for which they were seeking qualification could present themselves for the courses and the examination. The contribution of those now excluded to the impressive number of hours EFP saved the Army is unlikely to have been outstanding, or even to qualify significantly the assertion that in EFP the Army had found a way of spending less of its time on the education of prospective NCOs and WOs.

Attempts to draw a discreet veil over this unpalatable, if unavoidable, truth were unconvincing. The shortage of Army time allotted to EFP was excused on the grounds that as 'the knowledge and skills required were current, the certificates were to be gained by candidates as nearly as possible to the time when they were promoted'.[46] Since they would be promoted only after passing the examination, this was another way of saying they would take it as close as possible to the time their teaching began. This was not what it pretended to be, an argument for curtailing the time between the teaching and the examination, but for shortening the period devoted to the teaching of the required knowledge and skills. The fear that the knowledge and skills taught would change between the beginning of the teaching and the taking of the examination sufficiently to create a problem was convincing only in demonstrating a degree of unease in the propounder of this argument. Is it not significant that when the Army moved away from these 'best practices' it was because an examination thought better of by the civilian world had to be introduced for NCOs and WOs, as it was in April 1994?

Educationally there was more to be said for EPC than for EFP, and the Army can have been in no doubt about that. It knew EPC was well done and worth doing. But like so much else that was valuable in Army Education it had to be dispensed with, the Army being under the pressure which made it impossible to keep it. It came into being when Northern Ireland was pulling additional battalions (up to a third of those available) into the troubled turbulence which was to last more than a decade. This was the context of the subsequent criticisms of EPC. They were born of frustration and necessity. Needs must when the Devil drives and he was driving hard. EFP may indeed have been the best possible practice; it was not best described as the unqualified best practice.

'It's a muddle', Dickens tells us in *Hard Times*. Perhaps that can be said of the present state of Army Education, and yet we can be sure that it will eventually sort itself out. The Army's difficulties in recruiting, its bounty schemes for soldiers who renew their engagement and who bring in other recruits, its very short service commissions which hope to interest young graduates in its ways, will remind us how seriously now it takes the task of improving the attractions of military life. The old enemies of Army Education, the purse and the clock, will strengthen what prejudices there are which impede its progress and will continue for some time the anomalies we have noticed; in the absence of ambiguity the English would not feel at home. Few will think them strong enough to stand indefinitely against the powerful forces still furthering and likely to continue to further education in the Army. Will its Mrs Partingtons prove more successful than she was?

If they do not, what effect will that have on the Education and Training Services Branch of the Adjutant-General's Corps? Should we listen to those, like John Keegan, who say there will be no place for it in tomorrow's Army? He tells us, not entirely correctly, that it came into being because of our imperial role, providing schooling in foreign stations where British teachers were unavailable. Being an all-officer Corps it is disproportionately expensive and scarcely justifiable if most of the Army comes home where educational services can be contracted out. It could therefore be abolished without loss.[47]

This is not a view to be taken lightly when economic pressures on the Army remain as great as they ever were, and when military services, including some hitherto provided by uniformed educators, have already been contracted out. It is most unlikely that a predominantly home-based Army will not continue where possible to ease its burden in this way. If current pressures in society suggest that further developments in Army Education are to be expected, is it possible they will be met not by the Education and Training Branch but by civilians? Universities regretted the ending of the Progressive Qualification Scheme since it curtailed their important contribution to officer education. They would not take amiss appeals to their further help. They would welcome the opportunity to renew their work in officer education if it was thought, as it almost certainly will be, that the help now given by Sandhurst was insufficient. They would not be embarrassed if asked to give more help to the Army in the teaching of languages. The teaching of other ranks might create more difficulty as such is the present furore now occasioned by the standard of our schools that LEAs are unlikely to be able to attend to it. But present difficulties will pass and civilian help could doubtless eventually be provided here. It is, however, entirely improbable that the Army will think it can dispense with the services of the uniformed educator.

It is enough to list the myriad services they perform to be convinced of that. Garrison and unit commanders were unhappy when Army schools became the responsibility of the LEAs, fearing this would result in the loss of the regimental spirit and traditions which always permeated this branch of Army Education. They were reconciled when it was agreed that 'in all cases the local Military Authority will continue to be closely associated with the administration of the schools on local Boards of Management on which RAEC members will also sit'.

The ETS continued to look after Education Centres, the popular cultural focus of the community life of a Garrison and the social activities of its associated units. The Branch continued to look after Garrison libraries and to edit its magazines and newspapers. It staffed, at least for the time being, the five Army Study Centres in Britain, the two in Germany and the single Study Centres in Northern Ireland, Cyprus and Berlin.

It teaches at the Army Apprentice Colleges, where its officers often act also as platoon/troop commanders. It teaches at the Tri-Service Defence School of Languages and at the Salmond House Training Centre in Germany which the Army shares with the RAF. It continues to look after low-level language training, that is to say, up to colloquial level. It also attends to an important pre-operational job: linguistic skills are needed as early as the pre-deployment phase of operations. Others who may have such skills are likely to be fully committed then and they may not have been able to keep their languages up to scratch. So the Branch takes care that 'ETS officers remain both current in language and accessible for deployment'.[48]

The courses studied by EFP candidates are taught by the ETS. Ninety-five of its officers are responsible for the teaching of these courses which are held in Army Education Centres. They are also responsible for what is variously called developmental education or education for commitment. There was indeed a particular advantage of education for commitment and standards being delivered by uniformed education officers, as they have a clear understanding and acceptance of the military culture. Being themselves part of it and skilled instructors into the bargain, the importance of their role can hardly be overestimated in providing an understanding of the high standard demanded by the Army and of the reasons why it is and must be higher than that now contenting civilians.[49] Besides this the Army still persists in seeking to persuade units to teach current affairs; the training, the Branch tells us, is done by unit officers but their material is prepared by ETS Field Tutors who are frequently asked to help in the unit teaching. In addition, Branch Officers take whatever extra-mural classes Army Education Centres overseas or in remote areas are requested to provide. To this must be added the support the ETS gives to the British Forces Youth Service in overseas Garrisons.

It might have been thought that a Branch having only 343 members could not possibly have done more than this but the ETS did. After open competition it was made responsible for office automation training. 'Advice on NVQs', it was said, 'remains an important part of the Individual Education and Training Scheme' for which it was responsible.[50] 'Command Information', the sending of information home for the benefit of families, reinforcement and roulement troops from operational theatres, and Troop Information, the provision in those theatres of non-operational information, were its responsibility. Orientation, or giving the troops the information they need about the areas in which they deploy and the ways of the people living there, is also its responsibility. Army Education Centres have recently produced briefs for Rwanda, Angola, Kuwait, Burundi and Bosnia. An ETS officer serving with the 3(UK) Division Orientation and Briefing Unit, working with a Field Tutor, wrote what was called the *Bosnia Orientation Handbook*. Its success was indicated by the eagerness with which the Americans serving there asked for copies.[51]

The ETS, too, plays a very important role in psychological operations. Psyops, as it is usually referred to, seeks to influence the local populations living in operational areas. It arranges interviews for senior officers on local television and radio and produces newspapers. It sought in Bosnia to secure support for the Dayton Agreement. Psyops is what the Germans did not do in the Ukraine, and what they did there the British soldier could not have done. If, as seems likely, the Army will in future be engaged in humanitarian crisis operations its Psyops specialists will be in great demand. So effective were they in the Gulf that General Jackson 'even referred to Psyops as his main effort'.[52] In the Orbat of 15 Psyops Group there are 118 ETS officers, forty-six of whom are fully trained and a further seventy-two who produce operational support materials. They provide yet another striking illustration of that inbuilt capacity of the Army's educators to turn their hands to the satisfying of significant emerging needs, as did the ETS officer interpreting in Rwanda who found herself acting as midwife.[53]

There remained to the ETS another job to which it attached the greatest importance. This was its work in the Army School of Training Support. At first this had been largely run by postgraduate trained specialist RAEC officers who provided training support to the Army. It was long seen as a jewel in the RAEC crown. It was no longer called that but it was still said to be a 'gem' valued by the Army for its contribution to training. On 3 April 1995, the Adjutant-General opened the new, purpose-built Army School of Training Support at Upavon. In 1996 the training delivery part of ASTS joined thirty other training establishments to form the Army Training & Recruiting Agency (ATRA) under a Major-General at Upavon. The new ASTS with the ATRA was reduced in size to a staff of eighteen, five of whom are civilians and fourteen Army, only four of whom are ETS officers. The former Projects and Training Systems Wing of ASTS (now called Development Projects and Research Group) who continue to provide research and consultancy services,[54] moved under command of Colonel Training Support, an ETS officer reporting to the Director of Individual Training Policy (Army), a part of Headquarters, Adjutant-General. As well as providing training support policy, this post is the professional head of the Training Support function which employs over forty ETS officers amongst the 172 civilian and military working in this area. This makes Training Support the largest specialism within the ETS.

It is a common belief in competitive life that to be away from the centre of activities may be prejudicial to one's career. A senior Cambridge economist wrote to three of his former pupils who were reaching the peaks in British industry and commerce seeking to persuade them and some of their senior colleagues to spend a term in Cambridge which he undertook to ensure they would find profitable. The replies were in essence identical. They all acknowledged the importance of having such a sabbatical term; two thought it essential for men in their position; all regretted their inability to get away when important decisions had to be taken. Their former supervisor commented dryly that they were reluctant to leave when in their absence decisions might be taken more profitable to those present than to absentees.

Army officers and industrialists are in this respect brothers under the skin. They do not like to be long away from the main life of their unit in which they find fulfilment. They do not want to be away for a long time as specialists must expect to be. Away from its main life they are stepping off the normal road to promotion; doing so, the thought will be in their minds that out of sight might be out of mind, that they will be ill-advised to be away when colleagues who are present might be considered for a promotion that would pass the absent by. They distrust the specialist appointment. To go on Training Support would be considered by many as a backward step in their career. The members of the ETS Branch do not think in this way. They belong to a Branch of generalists which highly respects its specialists. Its Training Development Advisers still serve on every Training Development Team and the Branch believes its role in training will remain one of its most important tasks. There are many graduates serving in the Army who have also gained wide experience in training and would be more than capable of completing the postgraduate degree required for a TDA appointment. What they do not have, however, is the lifelong experience of how people learn and of teaching and training in many different parts of the Army. This is the added dimension that makes the ETS officer so successful as a Training Development Adviser.

Even when civilians can do the jobs now done by the ETS Branch, the uniformed educator has advantages over them. Colleges such as Farnham Castle provide the information industrialists going abroad need about conditions in the countries to which they are going. Lessons, however, are not always learned and the teachers of the institutions specialising in preparing those who are to work overseas are not present when their pupils find themselves in the countries they have been studying, and their expertise cannot be called on in the unanticipated situations which always arise. The ETS are present and can thus make orienteering more helpful than such institutions can.[55] It is because things always turn up and not only abroad that the Army has always insisted, and the uniformed educator always understood, that Army Education must be 'dynamic and flexible'.[56] Thus the Army educator has always had to cope with a problem in his teaching which his civilian colleague rarely knows and with which it would not be easy for him to cope. Pupils are often not available when from his point of view they should be; their frequent movement and unexpected calls upon them necessitated the uniformed educator being more adaptable and a more skilled administrator than that colleague to cope with the upsets and absences to which he has to accustom himself. Those who think that when the bulk of the Army is at home there is no further need for Army educators overlook this inevitable situation.

The ETS has another important advantage over civilians, too. It is much cheaper. The overheads of colleges such as Farnham Castle are not minimal nor are their charges. The Army cannot look to them for the bargains it gets from the ETS. Two for the price of one has always had its appeal and the ETS gives more than this. Few supermarkets can compete with what it offers. Three or four or more for the price of one is its standard rate and bonuses on top of this are not unknown. Now that the Army has begun to interest itself in the financial details which hitherto it left to the Treasury, the buying more dearly of a less satisfactory product is unlikely to appeal irresistibly to it.

It made that clear when it accepted the findings of a study made of the possible privatising of the Army School of Training Support which was opposed to it, saying that the School 'provides a considerable wealth of expertise dedicated to the Army's interest at little cost' and that 'experience has shown when employing civilian agencies a high degree of detailed specification, direction and close monitoring is necessary if the outcome of any study is to be relevant to the terms of reference'. It made this manifest too when it agreed with a 'Market Testing Scoping Study' into 'the Army Education Function'. This concluded 'The Army Education function contributes to the efficiency or well-being of the Army and should continue. Its overall functions should not be considered for strategic contractorisation.' Unwelcome to the ETS as a striking reminder of its immensely difficult task in persuading officers to write English, this must, nevertheless, have greatly raised its spirits. As must the Army's second thoughts in the matter of ending ETS support of Part I of the Junior Officers Education and Training Scheme. When it was found that the civilian help which would have been necessary to replace that of the ETS could not be afforded, that the correspondence courses which could easily have been provided could not on past experience have been expected to be adequate, and that it would not be desirable to leave this to Commanding Officers, not all of whom would have the ability or the capacity to provide it, it was decided to continue ETS support of JOTES I.[57]

We are no longer a great imperial people and our relative strength has grown less, although we should remember that Britain always added more strength to the Empire than it gave to Britain. We should also say that we need to become leaner and fitter and to make the most of ourselves. We have to get the best out of our institutions and to make the Army even more professionally expert than it is now widely acknowledged to be. We would be well-advised also to be more determined than we have hitherto been to do what the German Army did so successfully when in the days of defeat following the Great War its size was internationally restricted and it followed what the British Army said perhaps with its tongue somewhat in its cheek 'has long been an accepted principle in the British Army that every member of it shall be capable, in war, of assuming the responsibilities of at least one rank higher than he holds in peace, and that higher rank must be matched by a corresponding increase in educational attainments'. From their earliest days those who specialised in teaching soldiers have served it well. If any lesson is to be learned from their history it is this – they will continue to do so. It would be foolish to believe that the ending of a phase in their story is the ending of their history. Cicero said he did not know how soothsayers could refrain from bursting out laughing when they met in the streets of Rome. Conjecture, which must always raise doubts may surmise, but only tomorrow can show what will be the tasks which will face the Army educator then. The years and the realities have brought to both the Army and its educators what they sought, the abandoning of old animosities, the ending of the long nurtured and deeply cherished suspicion of the Army by the British people and of the dislike of its educators by the Army. To the predecessors of the ETS in the RAEC and the AEC it must often have seemed that the tired waves were vainly breaking, and for years the Corps of Schoolmasters must have felt that there was here no painful inch to gain. But if, as seems likely, we can now believe that 'far back through creeks and inlets making comes silent flooding in the main', we can drink a toast to the Corps of Schoolmasters which began the long fight. *Gaudeamus igitur*. What they began has endured. A 16th Century diplomatist who had the unenviable task of portraying to his sovereign what manner of woman was the prospective royal bride, reported 'what is wanted, she has it'. This could truly be said of them and their successors. That those successors will be present to tackle whatever tasks the never ending flight of future days may bring does not admit of doubt.

BIBLIOGRAPHY

Archives
Royal Army Educational Corps Archives

Churchill College Archives:
    The Croft Papers
    The Grigg Papers

War Office Publications
    Current Affairs (Army Bureau of Current Affairs, 1941–1945)
    War (Army Bureau of Current Affairs, 1941–1945)
    Map Review (Army Bureau of Current Affairs, 1941–1945)
    The British Way and Purpose: Consolidated Edition of British Way and Purpose Booklets 1–18 (Directorate of Army Education)

Reports of Conferences and Discussions
'Arms and the Man', course for senior officers at Nottingham University, 16–19 January 1950

'Education and the Armed Forces', report of a seminar held at the Royal United Services Institute for Defence Studies, 15 November 1972

Theses
Jones, D.R., 'The Reverend G.R. Gleig and Early Victorian Education', MA thesis, University of Bristol, 1983

Mackenzie, S.P., 'Politics and Morale', D. Phil. thesis, Oxford University, 1988

Smith, E.A., 'The Royal Commission into Military Education, 1868–70, with Special Reference to the Education of the Non-Commissioned Officer and Soldier', MA dissertation, University of London, King's College, 1985

Secondary Sources
Books
Barnett, C., *The Collapse of British Power,* London, 1972
Barnett, C., *Britain and Her Army,* London, 1974
Bart, Sir G.D. (ed), *The Panmure Papers,* 2 Vols, London, 1908
Bartley, G.F., *The Schools For the People,* London, 1871
Bond, B., *British Military Policy Between the Two World Wars,* Oxford, 1980
Borden-Turner, Colonel D. (Lord Gorell), *Education and the Army. An Essay in Reconstruction,* Oxford, 1921

Brett, Maurice V., *Journals and Letters of Reginald Viscount Esher,* London, 1931

Brougham, Henry Parker, Lord, *Works of Henry Lord Brougham,* 11 Vols, Edinburgh, 1883

Bruce, H.J., *Silken Dalliance,* London, 1946

Bryce, Viscount James, *The Holy Roman Empire,* London, 1928

Butler, R.A.B., *The Art of the Possible,* London, 1971

Calder, Angus, *The People's War. Britain 1939–45,* London, 1969

Callwell, Major-General Sir C.C., *Field-Marshal Sir Henry Wilson, His Life and Diaries,* London, 1927

Chapman, Guy, *A Passionate Prodigality, Fragments of Autobiography,* London, 1965

Chapman, Guy, *A Kind of Survival,* London, 1975

Churchill, W.S., *The World Crisis: The Aftermath,* London, 1929

Churchill, W.S., *The Second World War,* 6 Vols, London, 1948–54

Clive, L., *The People's Army,* London, 1938

Colville, John, *The Fringes of Power. Downing Street Diaries,* London, 1987

Cockerill, A.W., *Sons of the Brave. The Story of Boy Soldiers,* London, 1984

Cowles, Virginia, *Looking for Trouble,* London, 1941

Crick, Bernard, *George Orwell. A Life,* London, 1980

Croft, Henry Page, Lord, *My Life of Strife,* London, 1945

Curtis, S.J., *A History of Education in Britain,* London, 1957

Dilks, D. (ed), *The Diaries of Sir Alexander Cadogan, 1938–1945,* London, 1971

Dunlop, K., *The Development of the British Army, 1899–1914,* London, 1938

Eden, Anthony, Earl of Avon, *The Eden Memoirs. The Reckoning,* London, 1965

Fieldhouse, M. (ed), *The Political Education of the Servants of the State,* Manchester, 1988

Ford, Boris, *The Bureau of Current Affairs,* London, 1951

Firth, Charles Harding, *Cromwell's Army,* London, 1902

Fortescue, J.W., *A History of the British Army,* 13 Vols, London, 1899–1930

Fox, K.O., *Making Life Possible. A Study of Military Aid to the Civil Power in Regency England,* privately published, 1982

Froude, J.A., *Liberty and Property,* London, 1889

Fuller, J.F.C., *Memoirs of an Unconventional Soldier,* London, 1936

Gibbs, Philip, *The Pageant of the Years,* London, 1946

Gilbert, Martin, *Winston S. Churchill,* London, 1975

Gilbert, M., *Churchill: A Life,* London, 1991

Girouard, M., *The Return to Camelot. Chivalry and the English Gentleman,* New Haven, 1981

Gleig, G.R., *The Life of Arthur, Duke of Wellington,* London, 1864

Godwin-Austen, A.R., *The Staff and the Staff College,* London, 1927

Gorell, Colonel, Ronald Barnes, Lord, *One Man – Many Parts,* London, 1926 *[see below]*

Gorell, Colonel, Ronald Barnes, Lord, *Education and the Army: an Essay in Reconstruction,* Oxford, 1921 *[see entry for Borden-Turner]*

Gordon, H., *The War Office,* London, 1935

Grigg, P.J., *Prejudice and Judgement,* London, 1948

Hackett, General Sir John Winthrop, *The Profession of Arms,* London, 1963

Haldane, Richard Burton, *Sir Richard Burton Haldane. An Autobiography,* London, 1931

Harrington, W. and Young, P., *The 1945 Revolution,* London, 1978

Harris-Jenkins, G., *The Army in Victorian Society,* London, 1977

Hart-Davies, Duff, (ed), *Letters and Journals of Sir Alan Lascelles from 1920 to 1936,* London, 1989

Hawkins, Major T.H. and Brimble, L.J.T., *Adult Education. The Record of the British Army,* London, 1947

Henson, H.H., *Retrospect of an Unimportant Life,* London, 1950

Johnson, B.S., (ed), *All Bull. The National Service Man,* London, 1973

Kelly, T., *A History of Adult Education in Great Britain,* Liverpool, 1962

Laffin, J., *The Story of the English Soldier,* London, 1966

Langer, W.S., *The Diplomacy of Imperialism,* New York and London, 1935

Lefroy, General Sir J.T. (ed. Lady Lefroy), *The Autobiography of General Sir John Henry Lefroy,* London, 1895

Liddell Hart, Basil Henry, *Memoirs,* 2 Vols, London, 1965

Lloyd, Major-General C., *British Services Education,* London, 1950

Luvaas, Jay, *The Education of an Army. British Military Thought 1815–1940,* Chicago, 1964

Maclaren-Ross, J., *Memoirs of the Forties,* London, 1965

Macleod, R. and Kelly, D. (eds), *The Ironside Diaries,* London, 1962

Mansbridge, Albert, *The Trodden Road. Experience, Inspiration and Belief,* London, 1940

Mansergh, N., *The Commonwealth and the Nations,* Oxford, 1948

Mather, T.C., *Public Order in the Age of the Chartists,* Manchester, 1959

Minney, R.J. (ed), *The Private Papers of Hore-Belisha,* London, 1960

Morgan, Sir Frederick Edgworth, *Peace and War. A Soldier's Life,* London, 1961

Nicholson, Harold, *Diaries and Letters, 1939–1945,* London, 1967

Orwell, S. and Angus, J., *The Collected Essays, Journalism and Letters of George Orwell,* London, 1968

Pease, T.C., *The Leveller Movement,* London, 1996

Preston, Adrian, *In Relief of Gordon,* London, 1967

Prothero, G.W., *Select Statutes and other Constitutional Documents of the Reigns of Elizabeth and James I,* Oxford, 1913

Reese, P., *Our Sergeant,* London, 1986

Reese, P., *Homecoming Heroes,* London, 1992

Robertson, Field-Marshal Sir William, *From Private to Field-Marshal,* London, 1921

Rothstein, A., *The Soldiers' Strikes of 1919,* London, 1980

Royle, T., *The Best Years of their Lives. The National Service Experience, 1945–63,* London, 1986

St John Williams, N.T., *Tommy Atkins' Children. The Story of the Education of the Army's Children, 1675–1940,* London, 1971

Scott, Drusilla, *A.D. Lindsay. A Biography,* Oxford, 1971

Shinwell, Emmanuel, *Lead with the Left. My First Ninety-Six Years,* London, 1981

Shelley, A.R., *The Victorian Army at Home,* London, 1977

Slim, Field-Marshal Viscount, *Defeat Into Victory,* London, 1972

Smyth, J., *Sandhurst. The History of the Royal Military Academy, Woolwich, The Royal Military College, Sandhurst and the Royal Military Academy, Sandhurst, 1741–1961,* London, 1966

Spies, E.M., *The Army and Society,* New York, 1980

Stocks, Mary, *The Workers' Educational Association. The First Fifty Years,* London, 1953

Strachan, H., *Wellington's Legacy. The Reform of the British Army, 1830–54,* Manchester, 1984

Tropp, A., *The School Teachers,* London, 1957

Turner, E.S., *Gallant Gentlemen. A Portrait of the British Officer 1600–1956,* London, 1956

Watson, Sir C.M., *History of the Corps of Royal Engineers,* Chatham, 1915

Wardle, D., *English Popular Education, 1780–1970,* London, 1970

Wavell, Field Marshal Sir Archibald, *Soldiers and Soldiering,* London, 1953

White, Colonel A.C.T., *The Story of Army Education,* London, 1963

Wigg, George, Lord, *George Wigg,* London, 1972

Wilson, Field-Marshal Lord, *Eight Years Overseas, 1939–1947,* London, 1959

Wilson, N. Scarlyn, *Education in the Forces, 1939–1945. The Civilian Contribution,* London, 1948

Wintringham, T., *New Ways of War,* London, 1950

Wolseley, Field-Marshal Lord, *The Story of a Soldier's Life,* London, 1903

Wolseley, Field-Marshal and Lady, *The Letters of Lord and Lady Wolseley, 1870–1901,* London, 1922

Wyndham, H., *The Queen's Service,* London, 1899

Articles

Adam, General Sir Ronald, 'The Sequel to A.B.C.A.,', *Journal of Education,* 78, No.919, February 1946

Adam, General Sir Ronald, 'Education in the Army. Needs of the Future', *The Times Educational Supplement,* 6 December 1941

Adam, General Sir Ronald, 'Adult Education in the Forces', *Adult Education* XVIII, 1945

Amisson, Capt. D.P., 'G5 in Central Bosnia', *Torch* 4/1, 14, Summer 1995

Anglim, S.J., 'The Royal Army Educational corps in the Gulf Conflict of 1990–91'. Produced by the Directorate of Education and Training Services

Aris, R., 'Problems of Army Education', *Contemporary Review* CIXVI

A Serving Soldier, 'The Inarticulate Revolution', *Tribune,* 10 March 1944

Bartlett, O., 'Soldiers and Politicians', *Spectator,* 19 January 1945

Bates, Captain Louise, 'The E.T.S. in Ruwanda', *Torch* 4/1, Summer 1995

Bendall, F.W.D., 'Education in the Army – Purpose and Plan of the Work', *The Times Education Supplement,* 1 November 1941

Bickersteth, J.B., 'Soldiers and Citizens', *Public Opinion Quarterly* VIII, 1944

Bishop, Lieutenant-Colonel J.S., 'Education in the 8th Army', *Journal of the Army Educational Corps* XIX, No.2, October 1944

Bonney, Warrant Officer II, 'Books for All. The Army Educational Corps' Network of Libraries in the Middle East', *Journal of the Army Educational Corps* XIX, No.3, May 1945

Bowyer-Boyer, Major F.A., 'Some early educational influences in the British Army' *Journal of the Society for Army, Historical Research,* 33, 1955

Brock, Dryden, 'Where are we going', *The Highway* XXXI, 1938

Bruce, Maurice, 'Army Education', The Spectator, 1 November 1946

Burgess, Colonel J.T., 'Ten Thousand Tragedies', *The Army Quarterly* IV, July 1944

Burslam, Captain G.C., 'A Day in the Life of a U.E.O.', *Army Education* XX, No.1, March 1946

Cable, Lieutenant Graham, 'Minerva Turns Sky Blue – E.T.S. Go Live in Angola', *Torch* 4/2, Winter 1995

Cabley, Major P.R., 'Officer Training in the Soviet Ground Forces', *The Army Quarterly and Defence Journal* 115, No. 4, October 1985

Cannon, Lieutenant-Colonel P.S., 'Education in Chains', *Journal of the Army Educational Corps* XX, No.4, December 1946; Vol XXI, No.1, March 1947; Vol XXI, No.2, June 1947

Chapman, Guy, 'A Note on Morale', *Adult Education* XIV, 1942

Chapman, H., 'And then there was one', *Army Education* XX14, No.3, September 1950

Congreve, G.T., 'Education in the Armed Forces', *The Citizen* X, 1940

Coville, Colonel K.N., 'Prospects and Experiments: Recreational Handicrafts', *Journal of the Army Educational Corps* XVII, No.3, March 1942

Deakin, S., 'The British Army and Society in the 1980s', *British Army Review* 91, April 1989

Dobrée, Major Bonamy, 'A.B.C.A. gets going', *The Spectator* January 1942

Duncan, J., 'Basic Education', *Journal of the Army Educational Corps* XIX, No.2, October 1944

Editorial, 'Teething Troubles of the Army Educational Corps', *Torch,* 1924

Fairclough, Colonel T.R., 'Resettlement', *Torch,* Summer 1992

Fowler, Colonel A.L., 'The Army School of Education', *Torch,* Jubilee Edition 1920–1970

Fowler, Major A.L., 'Mons Company, R.M.A. Sandhurst', *Journal of the Army Educational Corps* XXIII, No.4, December 1949

Fuller, J.F.C., 'Mind – the Man', *Journal of the Army Educational Corps* No.1, 1924

Gadd, Major-General A.L., 'Remembrances of Things Past', *Torch,* Winter 1978

Gleig, G.R., 'National Education', *Edinburgh Review* XCV, No.194, 1952

Gloden, Gill, Douglas and Dallas, 'Mutiny at Etaples Base in 1917', *Past and Present* 69, 1975

Gorell, Lord, 'Back to War', *The Quarterly Review* 555, 1943

Gould, Lieutenant-Colonel E.A., 'Following the Drum', *Journal of the Royal Army Educational Corps* XXIV, No.1, March 1950

Gould, Lieutenant-Colonel E.A., 'Education in a British Unit', *Journal of the Army Educational Corps* Vol XIX, No.3, May 1945

Graubert, S.R., 'Military Demobilisation in Britain following the First World War', *Journal of Modern History* 19, 1947

Grimsey, Major G.E., 'Looking Back on Korea', *Army Education* XXVI, No.2, September 1952

Gunner, Colonel G.E., 'The Formation College on the Rhine', *Journal of the Army Educational Corps* XV, March 1946

Hall, Rear Admiral, 'Educational Work in the Navy', *Army Education* XVII, 1942

Hawkins, Major W.C., 'Cipher Duties, 1939–1941', *Torch,* Jubilee Edition 1920–1970

Highway, The, 'The A.T.S. Girl and Her Future as a Citizen', *The Highway* XXXV, 1943

Howard, Michael, 'Army Education', *The Times Literary Supplement,* 30 May 1975

Hudson, Lieutenant-Colonel E.V.H., 'The East African Educational Corps', *Army Education* XXV No.2, June 1951

Hunter, Captain H.L., 'The Work of the A.E.C. in Hospitals', *Journal of the Army Educational Corps* XVII, No.2, December 1941

James, Senior Commander C.W., 'Education in the A.T.S.', *Journal of the Army Educational Corps* XVII, No.4, June 1942

James, L., 'Education and the Army', *The Highway* 34, 1942

Jay, Captain K.F., 'Education Under Fire', *Journal of the Army Educational Corps* Vol XX, No.3, September 1946

Leese, Major J., 'The A.E.C. and the Second Front', *Journal of the Army Educational Corps* XXX, No.22, October 1944

Lindsay, A.D., 'Education in the Army – Interest and Incentive', *The Times Educational Supplement* 29 November 1941

Lloyd, Major-General C., 'The Beliefs Behind the Interim Scheme', *Army Education,* December 1949

Luckhart, Major H.W., 'Army Courses in Rome', *Journal of the Army Educational Corps* X, No.4, December 1946

Macfarlane, Brigadier J.M., 'Language Training', *Torch,* Summer 1992

McGowan, Colonel L., 'News-Sheets in the Field', *Torch,* Jubilee Edition 1920–1970

MacGregor, Warrant Officer II J.H., 'Candlelight Cottage', *Journal of the Army Educational Corps* XIX, No.4, December 1945

MacKenzie, S.P., 'Vox Populi in the British Army: Newspapers in the Second World War', *Journal of Contemporary History* 24, 1989

McNeill, Colonel D.M., 'Formation Colleges', *Torch,* Jubilee Edition 1920–1970

Mansbridge, A., 'Army Education', *Journal of the Army Educational Corps* XXVII, No.4, June 1942

Marshall H., 'The Soltau Scheme. Work in N.W. Europe 1944–46', *Torch,* Winter 1978

Marston, Major R., 'Ongoing Meaningless Situation', *Torch* 16, No.1, Summer 1982

Maude, Brigadier C.J., 'Compulsory or voluntary Education?', *Army Education* XVII, 1941

Montgomery, Field-Marshal Bernard, 'Military Leadership', lecture given at the University of St Andrews, 15 November 1945

Moss, Major B.V., 'Vee Haff Vays', *Torch* 14, No.2, Winter 1988

Mountain, Warrant Officer II J., 'With the A.E.C. in Burma', *Army Education* XIX, 1945

Mullin, Lieutenant-Colonel W.S., 'The "Poly" in Burma', *Journal of the Army Educational Corps* XXI, No.3, September 1947

Pafford, Major G.H., 'Books on Army Education 1944–5', *Aslib,* 1946

Page, Air Commodore H.M., 'War-Time Education in the Royal Air Force', *Army Education* XVII, 1944

Raybould, S.G., 'The Commanding Officer and Army Education', *The Highway* XXXV, 1942

Reeves, Brigadier B., 'The Junior Army', *Torch,* Summer 1992

Roe, Brigadier F.P., 'Thirty Five Years in the Corps', *Torch* II, No.2, 1977

Roe, Brigadier F.P., 'War Again' *Torch* 12, No.2, Winter 1978

Royal United Services Institute, Open Forum on 'Officer's Education – the Users' Views', 6 October 1978

Sergeant-Instructor, A.E.C., 'Education in a Detention Barracks', *Journal of the Army Educational Corps* XIX, No.1, June 1944

Stockbridge, Lieutenant-Colonel W.S., 'The Army Library Service', *Torch,* Jubilee Edition 1920-1970

Suckling, B., 'Experiments in Teaching Illiterates', *Journal of the Army Educational Corps* XVIII No.1, September 1942

Summerfield, Penelope, 'Education and Politics in the British Armed Forces in the Second World War', *International Review of Social History* XXVI, 1981

Thompson, E., 'The Army Discussion Group', *Army Education* XVII, 1941

The Times Educational Supplement, 7 March 1942, 'A Staff Officer on the State of Army Education: an Appraisement and Some Criticism'

The Times Educational Supplement, 24 October 1942, 'Education in the A.T.S.: Impressions and Some Queries'

The Times Educational Supplement, 15 January 1944, 'Army Education Overseas. Developments in the Middle-East – a Correspondent'

The Times, 22 September 1942, 'ABCA and its Work – a Correspondent'

Trease, Warrant Officer II R.G., 'Army Education Afloat', *Journal of the Army Educational Corps* XIX, No.41, December 1945

Turner, Lieutenant-Colonel P.J., 'A Review of the Recent Activities of the R.A.E.C. with the British Troops in Egypt', *Journal of the Army Educational Corps* XXVI, No.2, September 1952

White, A.C.T., 'Educational Training', *Journal of the Army Educational Corps* XVII, No.4, June 1942

White, A.C.T., 'The Men were surprisingly well-informed', *Journal of the Army Educational Corps,* II, 1925

White, A.C.T., 'Education in the Army: Points within the Unit', *The Times Educational Supplement,* 2 November 1941

Willans, Major-General Sir Harry, 'The Progress of Army Education', *Journal of the Army Educational Corps* XVII, No.4, June 1942

Williams, W.E., 'Projects and Experiments: Army Study Centres', *Journal of the Army Educational Corps* XVII, No.1, September 1941

Williams, W.E., 'Projects and Experiments – ABCA', *Journal of the Army Educational Corps* XVII, No.2, December 1941

Wilson, Colonel A., 'Some Thoughts on the A.E.C. (Release Scheme)', *Journal of the Army Educational Corps* XX, No.4, December 1946

Wilson, Brigadier C.A., 'The Education of the Soldier. 1920–1939', *Torch,* Jubilee Edition 1920-1970

Wilson, Lieutenant E.G., 'Education in a Young Soldier's Battalion', *Journal of the Army Educational Corps* XVII, No.3, March 1941

Wilson, Major E.F., 'News-Sheets in the Field', *Journal of the Army Educational Corps* XIX, No.2, October 1944

Yeaxlee, Basil, 'Adult Education in H.M. Forces: the Central Advisory Council and the Regional Committees', *Adult Education* XIII, 1941

Yeaxlee, Basil, 'The Civilian Contribution to Adult Education in the Armed Forces', *Army Education* XVII, 1942

NOTES

Chapter 1 – The Origins of Army Education

1   Prothero, G.W., *Select Statutes and other Constitutional Documents of Elizabeth and James I*, 4th Edition, p.175 (Oxford, 1973).

2   Barnett, C. W., *Britain and Her Army 1509–1970. A Military, Political and Social History*, p.35 (London, 1970). 'The trained bands were hardly called out once in five years for exercise; few men knew how even to load the muskets and the majority were afraid to fire a shot.' Fortescue, Sir J., *History of the Army*, Vol.I, p.194 (London, 1899).

3   Barnett, op. cit., p.35.

4   Barnett, op. cit., p.47. Only the Muster-Master in each county was a paid Crown Officer. His duty was to check that the numbers said to be enrolled were indeed so, 'a duty', Fortescue tells us, 'which was often most dishonestly performed.' Fortescue, *The British Army 1783–1802. Four Lectures Delivered at the Staff College and Cavalry Schools*, p.2 (London, 1905).

5   ibid. Until reorganised in 1757 it was a thoroughly inefficient force: Wellington relied on it for the defence of the country *faute de mieux*. 'I should infinitely prefer and should have more confidence in an Army of regular troops', he wrote, but he knew he could never get them. Howard, M., *Studies in War and Peace*, p.63 (London, 1970).

6   Firth, C.H. (ed), *The Clark Papers. Selected from the Papers of Williams Clark, Secretary to the Army, 1647–1649 and to General Monck and the Commanders of the Army in Ireland, 1651–1660* IV, p.62 (London, 1901). This referred to 'the part of the Army that hath broken uppe the Parliament, by which means all the whole people of England are likely to loose their liberties.' Or as Swift expressed it in *A Letter to the Whole People of Ireland*, 'Eleven Men well armed will certainly subdue one single Man in his Shirt.'

7   *The Federalist*, p.264 (London, 1911). 'In framing a government which is to be administered by men over men, the great difficulty lies in this: you must first enable the government to control the governed; and in the next place oblige it to control itself.' This was essential because 'there is a degree of depravity in mankind which requires a certain degree of circumspection and distrust.'

8   Fortescue, op. cit., p.11. 'Though barracks were early introduced into Ireland, the British politician saw, or affected to see, in these the riveting of chains for the British nation. The particular fear might vary. Some saw in the proposal to build barracks an excuse for enlarging the Army. Watson, Sir C.M., *History of the Corps of Royal Engineers*, p.133 (Chatham, 1915). The Chinese who thought of the soldier as poorly as did the English agreed with Lao-tse who said 'where armies are quartered, briars and thorns grow.' The appropriate English version of that would be 'where briars and thorns grow, armies are quartered.' When built they were so spartan that it cost considerably more to keep criminals in

prison than soldiers in barracks. Bond, B. 'The Late Victorian Army', *History Today* XI, No.9, pp.616–24 (September 1961).

9   Fortescue, op. cit., Vol.XI, p.47. For the popular suspicion of the officer clubs *see* Howard, M., *Studies in War and Peace*, p.59 (London, 1970) and Fortescue, op. cit., p.9. 'The institution of half-pay ... formed a reserve for the filling up of vacant commissions in the next war.'

10   Smith, E.A., 'The Royal Commission Into Military Education, 1868–70. With Special Reference to the Education of the Non-Commissioned Officer and Soldier', p.20. Dissertation submitted in partial fulfilment of the requirement for the degree of Master of Arts, in the Faculty of Education, University of London, 1985. For the view that 'to be gone for a soldier was a crushing disgrace', *see* Wavell, Field Marshal, *Soldiers and Soldiering*, p.125 (London, 1953).

11   Howard, op. cit., p.52.

12   Barnett, op. cit., p.237. Fortescue, op. cit., pp.53–4. Of the 1784 Flanders Campaign Fortescue writes 'Some of the Commanding Officers were worthless, drunken blackguards, who never dreamed of marching with their men.' It was of them, he added, that 'the Hanoverian General Walmoden wrote to Dundas the most terrible words ever written of a British force: "Your army is destroyed; that is to say the men are. The officers and their baggage are safe."' It must be remembered that although in the early modern period standing armies were developing and great soldiers emerging to make them more formidable and to show how effectively they could be used, soldiering could still be remarkably slap-dash and amateur. When Charles I invaded Scotland in 1638 only 200 of his 5,000 men could fire a musket. That was typical of military training at the time, even though the incompetence of all but one of the Stuart kings was highly developed. We must be aware, too, that a misleading impression can be gained by the absence of Colonels from their regiments or by their age and condition. 'Before the middle of the 18th Century Colonels had become rather figure-heads than actual commanders of regiments. They pocketed the emoluments and occasionally interfered with the management, but they left the actual work to Lieutenant Colonels.' Fortescue, op. cit., p.10. It seems that Americans as well as the British are attached to old ways. When contributions to party funds indicate the desirability of appointing ambassador the possibly better-heeled than qualified donor, the State Department ensures that there will be a Minister under him of sufficient ability to carry His Excellency. The modern American practice seems to provide a better insurance than did the old English way.

13   Turner, E.S., *Gallant Gentlemen: A Portrait of the British Officer 1600–1956*, p.236 (London, 1956).

14   Ridley, J., *Lord Palmerston*, pp.442–3 (London, 1970).

15   Spiers, E.M., *The Army and Society*, pp.13–14 (New York, 1982).

16   Wavell, op. cit., p.125.

17   Fortescue, op. cit., Vol.II, p.44.

18   Johnson, F.A., *Defence by Committee* (London, 1960). For his view that the War Office was 'a citadel of mismanagement, inefficiency and administrative

chaos', *see* p.14. For the Secretary at War, *see* Fortescue, op. cit, Vol.IV part 2, pp.871–2. For the Horse Guards and the Queen against the Secretary of State *see* Gordon, H., *The War Office*, pp.54–5 (London, 1935) and White, A.C.T., *The Story of Army Education*, p.36 (London, 1963).

19 Fortescue, op. cit., p.24. The Bow Street Runners did their best but as Fortescue observes 'It was impossible even to put down a powerful gang of poachers without the help of the Army.'

20 *The New Cambridge Modern History* (Cambridge, 1957). *The Old Régime 1713– 63* VIII, p.181.

21 Carlyle, T., *The Letters and Speeches of Oliver Cromwell* III, pp.64-5.

22 Jones, Revd D.R., 'The Rev. G.R. Gleig and Early Victorian Army Education'. A thesis submitted in the Faculty of Arts of the Queen's University of Belfast for the degree of Master of Arts, July 1983. 'I could seldom prevail on even the uneducated to enlist when they were sober-living and industrially inclined', wrote Recruiting Sergeant Robert Macdonald, 'It was only in the haunts of dissipation or inebriation and among the very lowest dregs of society, that I met with anything like success.' Recruiting, Gleig said, 'begins in falsehood, continues in intemperance and ends in remorse', p.59.

23 Pease, T.C., *The Leveller Movement*, p.174 (London, 1996).

24 Simes, T., *The Regulator: or Instructions to Form the Officer and Complete Soldier upon Fixed Principles*, pp.15–18 (London, 1780). Colonel White in the *RAEC Gazette* Jubilee Year Edition, November 1970, Vol.2 reminds us of this same age-old need for the educated soldier. He quotes from Vegetius's *De Re Militare* which was written about AD400: 'As there are several educated men in the legions recruit trainers should note those able to write, to calculate and to keep books. The legion has its daily rosters, its parades and its pay sheets to attend to and such men can be used for this.'

25 Sheridan, R., *Complete Plays*, pp.99–108 (London, 1954); Williams, N. St J, *Tommy Atkins Children. The Story of the Education of the Army's Children 1875–1970* (London 1971). Only a literate NCO could prevent his men 'being fleeced at every turn', pp.3–4.

26 For Sir John Moore's System of Training see Cope, W., *History of the Rifle Brigade* (London, 1924). 'Had he lived he might have done for the Army what Elizabeth Fry did for the prison system and Jeremy Bentham and his disciples for the law.' Howard, op. cit., pp.56–7.

27 Lefroy, J.H. 'Report on the Regimental and Garrison Schools of the Army and on Military Libraries and Recreation Rooms', pp.29-30 (1859).

28 Smith, op. cit., p.43. *Parliamentary Debates*, House of Lords, 3rd Series, Vol. 207, col.1813, 17 July 1871. 'Modern warfare was no longer force opposed to force – in the Army, as elsewhere, it was intellect opposed to intellect and it was necessary to have officers with better professional attainments of a far higher standard.' (Lord Truro). This was an argument which became stronger as the years went by.

29 Williams, op. cit., p.21. It was said to be 'pregnant with mischief'. It would

'enable people to read seditious pamphlets and vicious publications against Christianity'. *The Parliamentary Debates from the year 1803 to the Present Time*, p.798 (London 1812).

30   Third Report from the select committee on the education of the lower orders. House of Commons 1818 (426) IV, p.56. Brougham's widely reported Inaugural Address to the University of Glasgow on 6 April 1820 was a fine profession of his faith. 'The highest intellectual cultivation is perfectly compatible with the daily cares and toils of working men', he said. Of significance for the future of Army Education, however, was the lack of support for his bill, which he had to withdraw, to make education available to more than the one fourteenth or one fifteenth of the population to whom he said it was already available.

31   Sergeant William Lawrence, who wrote an account of his service in the Peninsula, tells us that he only once attended a service by a chaplain but that was very brief as the chaplain lost his nerve and 'jumped up with his traps and made a bolt.' In 1811 Wellington had only one chaplain in the Army. Methodist prayer meetings were common and he was alarmed at 'the zeal and enthusiasm growing around him which he wanted to moderate'. 17th Century zealotry had brought Lilburne and the Levellers startling success in the General Assembly of the Army on Newmarket Heath; Wellington's alarm at the spreading of early 19th Century zealotry in the Army was not perhaps baseless. Jones, op. cit., pp.8–10. White, *The Story of Army Education*, p.23 (London, 1963).

32   It was an age which would never have coined the saying 'when drink is in wit is out'. It was not unusual for the Prime Minister, the Younger Pitt, and his friend the Secretary of State at War to come drunk to the House of Commons. They were never censured for so doing by the Opposition which was itself so drunk as to have regarded sobriety with considerable surprise and indignation. Lord Brougham as Lord Chancellor was more than once too drunk to rise unaided from the Woolsack. As usual the Army reflected society. There was a famous occasion when every man of the Light Division was more or less drunk, including the GOC who was so drunk that he insisted on taking the division on a night march. This was not a normal practice and 'there were regiments in which drunkenness was considered disgraceful in an officer; and that feeling was gaining rather than losing ground'. Sir John Moore spent years in purging his regiment of hard-drinking officers, thinking it wrong to trust them with the lives of soldiers. Fortescue, op. cit., pp.35–6. *The Sanitary Commission Report of 1858.* Smith, op. cit., p.24.

33   Opposition in Parliament to the frequent and brutal flogging of soldiers was growing and Government appointed a Commission on Military Punishment which recommended the establishment of libraries. These and reading rooms were provided in 1838. Five years earlier the East India Company had set up libraries for its troops in India's seven principal stations; British and Indian Army establishments were separate at this time. White., A.C.T. in *Journal of the Army Education Corps*, June 1931. Hansard Parliamentary Debates, Supply, The Army Estimates, Vol.46. col.1126, 22 March 1839. For the introduction of

games *see* Strachan, *Wellington's Legacy. The Reform of the British Army 1830–54*, p.85 (Manchester 1984).

34   White, op. cit., p.19.

35   Second Report of the Royal Commission on Military Education, 1870. Minutes of Evidence. Colonel Eltrington was CO of the 4th Battalion of the Rifle Brigade at Aldershot. Sir John Moore would not have thought highly of him.

36   White, A.C.F., 'A Note on the History of Army Education', *Journal of the Army Educational Corps* XVII, No.4, June 1942.

37   Farwell, Byron, *For Queen and Country. A Social History of the Victorian and Edwardian Army*, p.141 (London, 1981).

38   White, *The Story of Army Education* op. cit., p.34; for Gleig's view *see* Jones, A.C.J., 'My Predecessor in Office: the Reverend Prebendary George Robert Gleig, M.B.' *The Royal Army Chaplain's Department Journal* IV, No.22, July 1931.

39   White, op. cit., p.265. 'Although a man of great experience the Duke was not a man of wide views. He said 'the right time for any change is when you can't help it.' He was said to be a man to whom a new idea was perdition.' Gordon, op. cit.

40   Shelley, A.R., *The Victorian Army at Home*, p.92 (London, 1977).

41   Wolseley believed that 'the more highly a man is educated the better soldier he is.' Report of the Committee on Army Schools and Schoolmasters 1887, *Minutes of Evidence*, p.75. He was also a realist and it is worth recalling what he said of an officer he knew well who could not pass the examination to go to the Staff College. 'I often think when men talk of military examinations and the Staff College that the only one of my four ADCs who could not pass a scientific examination as a Staff Officer is worth the other three put together.' This is something to be remembered with befitting humility in the belief that as the lawyers say exceptional cases make bad law, in the knowledge that Wolseley strongly supported the Staff College. *The Letters of Lord and Lady Wolseley 1870–1901*, p.123 (London, 1922). For his view that 'with an Army of short service men we have to use short training time to maximum advantage', *see* Report of the Committee on Army Schools and Schoolmasters 1887, *Minutes of Evidence*, pp.75–6. A comment by Major Addison bears reflection too. He said that education would no doubt make an excellent Staff Officer 'but for one quality, in which he may after all be wanting, and which education can scarcely convey – common sense.' Jones, op. cit., p.145. In the early 18th Century Steele draws our attention to that companionship of the ranks which has persisted over the centuries. Comparing them with their officers he writes 'they have the same taste of being acceptable to their friends and go through the difficulties of that profession by the same irresistible charm of fellowship and the communication of joys and sorrows which quickens the relish of pleasure and abates the anguish of pain.' Steele, L.E., *Essays of Richard Steele*, p.256 (London, 1937). That companionship helps our understanding of Wolseley's priorities.

42   Hawkins, T.H. and Brimble, *Adult Education. The Record of the British Army*,

p.34 (London, 1947).

43   Kipling, R., 'Drums of the Fore and Aft', *Wee Willie Winkie Stories*.

44   Wolseley, Field Marshal Lord, *The Story of a Soldier's Life* Vol.II, p.252 (Westminster, 1903).

45   Rhodes James, R., (ed.), *Winston S. Churchill. His Complete Speeches, 1897–1963* Vol.II, p.214 (New York,1974).

46   Williams, op. cit., p.9.

47   Hawkins and Brimble, op. cit., p.16.

48   ibid., p.17.

49   White, op. cit., p.17.

50   Hawkins and Brimble, op. cit., p.21.

51   White, op. cit., p.27.

52   Shelley, op. cit., p.104.

53   *Journal of the Army Educational Corps*, June 1931, commenting on an article in *The Quarterly Review* 1845.

54   Smith, op. cit., p.52.

55   White, op. cit., p.21.

56   The first library was opened in Gibraltar in 1793, every officer contributing a day's pay to it. By 1800 the Rifle Corps set up a library for a course of lectures then given. In 1813 the Royal Engineers founded their Corps Library at Chatham to keep its members professionally up to date. Its success encouraged engineer units at home and abroad to do likewise. In 1820 the Chaplain's Branch issued a pack of twenty-eight books to all Corps orderly rooms. In 1825 the Regimental Surgeons of the 80th Regiment of Foot set up the first general library for the NCOs and men of the battalion. The Royal Commission on Military Punishments which met in 1838 suggested that libraries and reading rooms would improve morale and it was decided to install them in every major garrison. By 1844 there were thirty-eight libraries at home and forty abroad. All soldiers could use them on payment of one penny a month. They were well-stocked. Thirty-eight papers and periodicals were provided at the Gunner's library in Woolwich in 1860. Clearly a good standard of literacy was expected from the Gunners. Books were thus obviously becoming part of Army life. In 1857 Prince Albert began the systematic purchase of books, this being the beginning of the Prince Consort's Library, the jewel in the crown of the Army's library services. Swift., L., 'The Library Service', *Torch*, Summer 1992.

57   When Mr Leggat, the Chaplain at Portsmouth suggested in 1824 that a library be formed there the Duke of York thought it most imprudent; libraries he thought unnecessary and objectionable. White. 'A Note on The History of Army Education, in Army Education XVII, No.4, 4 June 1942, p.134. *See also* Hawkins and Brimble, op. cit., pp.12–13.

58   Jones, D.R., op. cit., p.81; Jones, A.C.J., 'My Predecessor in Office: The Reverend Prebendary George Robert Gleig, MA', *The Royal Army Chaplain's Department Journal* IV, No.32, July 1931.

59   Jones, D.R., op. cit., p.50.

60   White, op. cit., Appendix A.

61   ibid.

62   ibid., p.38.

63   An act of George III abolished the sale of offices in departments of state but
     gave to the Crown the discretion of retaining this practice in the Army. Gladstone
     was determined that 'the nation must buy back its Army from its own officers';
     see Morley, J., *The Life of William Ewart Gladstone*, p.361 (London. 1911).
     This could have been done by having Parliament vote the money to compensate
     officers who had bought their commissions. If this had been done the Crown
     could have been persuaded to forego its discretion to retain the buying of office
     in the Army. Gladstone preferred to abolish purchase by Act of Parliament. He
     failed to do so as the House of Lords would not pass his bill. Determined to get
     his way he turned to the Royal Prerogative, making use of the Royal Warrant to
     end purchase and justifying Disraeli's criticism 'No Minister acts in a wise
     manner who finding himself baffled in passing a measure ... comes forward and
     tells the House that he will defy the opinion of Parliament and appeals to the
     Crown to assist him in the difficulties which he himself has created.'
     Moneypenny, W.P. and Buckle, G.E.R., *The Life of Benjamin Disraeli, Earl of
     Beaconsfield*, p.481 (London, 1929). For the bitterness of the debates *see
     Parliamentary Debates*, House of Lords, 3rd Series, 14 July 1871, Vol.27,
     col.1799.

64   Turner, op. cit., p.236.

65   Jones, D.R., op. cit., pp.173–4. While Britain spent about £1,300 annually on
     the education of officers, Prussia spent £26,000, France £48,000 and Austria at
     least £127,000. On Staff Officer education in 1856 France spent £5,814, Prussia
     £3,230, Austria £4,300 and Britain nothing at all. Report of the 1856 Panmure
     Committee, quoted in Bond. B., *The Victorian Army and the Staff College, 1854–
     1914*, p.65. (London, 1972).

66   4th Report of the Director General of Military Education, 1889, p.14–15.

67   Shelley, op. cit., p.91.

68   ibid., p.86.

69   Hawkins and Brimble, op. cit., pp.21ff.

70   White, op. cit., p.33.

71   Hawkins and Brimble, op. cit., p.28.

72   ibid., pp.23–4.

73   Shelley, op. cit., p.119.

74   Leaver, W.R., *Reminiscences of Schoolmaster W.R. Leaver*, RAEC Archives.

75   Hawkins and Brimble, op. cit., p.25.

76   White, op. cit., p.41. Wolseley's words strongly suggest that he was hoping not
     only to dispense with Army Schoolmasters but to forget about Army Education
     as well.

77   Smith, A.E., op. cit., p.74.

78   White, op. cit., p.61.

79   Shelley, op. cit., pp.99ff.

80   White, op. cit., p.44. There were warnings in the 19th Century that we neglected technical education at our peril. In 1852 Lyon Playfair published a lecture 'Industrial Construction on the Continent.' It was a forceful reminder of the competition we were facing and an exhortation, which we ignored, to follow continental example. In 1879 the City and Guilds of the London Institute was set up, but its institution did not sufficiently encourage us to turn to vocational training. Thirty years later the Samuelson Commission was again reminding us of the importance of vocational education. 'An extended and systematic education,' it emphasised, 'is a necessary preliminary to the fullest development of industry.' We were reluctant to listen. While Dickens in his early years hoped much from industry, in his later works he turned against industrial and commercial ways. In *Domby and Son* (1846–8) he wrote 'The earth was made for Domby and Son to trade in, and the sun and the moon were made to give them light. Rivers and seas were formed to float their ships; rainbows gave them promise of fair weather; winds blew for or against their enterprises; stars and planets circled in their orbits to preserve immaculate a system of which they were the centre.' Hardy despised Carthage as a trading nation and feared England was going the same way. And when the University of Cambridge began, belatedly, to establish connections with industry one of its most prestigious professors, Sir Ernest Barker, deplored this, fearing that 'the University would degenerate into the provider of recruits even for the world of business.' Wiener, M.J., *English Culture and the decline of the Industrial Spirit, 1850–1980* (Cambridge, 1981).

81   For poor attendance at schools abroad *see* Smith, A.E., op. cit., p.66. The legal difficulty which had long bedevilled compulsory education was now removed, no doubt not to the satisfaction of all. The Law Lords, concurring that compulsory education was essential in a modern army, gave it as their opinion that it was illegal. They suggested that the Articles of War be amended to make it an offence for a soldier to absent himself from school if ordered to attend. In 1859 the Articles of War were so amended.

82   ibid.

83   Report of the Harris Committee, *Minutes of Evidence*, p.43.

84   Leaver, op. cit.

85   Smith, A.E., op. cit., p.81.

86   White, op. cit., Appendix A.

87   Cameron, R.J., *Life of an Army Schoolmaster as seen through my Experiences 1889–1920*, RAEC Archives.

88   Ruthven, W.J., *Memoirs of an Army Schoolmaster, 1890–1920*, RAEC Archives.

89   Meckiff and Meckiff, *Memoirs of Army Schoolmasters Meckiff and Son, 1880–1933*, RAEC Archives.

90   Smith, op. cit., p.87.

91   ibid., p.88.

92   ibid.; Trapp, A., *The School Teachers*, pp.35–6 (London, 1957).

93   Smith, op. cit., p.89.

94   White, op. cit.
95   Smith, op. cit., p.87. Well might Schoolmaster Kemshead speak of 'the impassable barrier to commissioned rank'.
96   White, op. cit.
97   Smith, op. cit., p.85.
98   Tropp, op. cit., quoting a letter to the Papers for the Schoolmaster. 'His social position is much below that belonging to other professions whose equal he is in intellectual and literary attainments; whilst he is prevented by the very attainments from cordially sympathising with his equals in social position.'
99   White, op. cit.
100 Collison, A.L., *Extracts from the Memoirs of an Army Schoolmaster, 1904–1927*, RAEC Archives.
101 Leaver, op. cit.
102 ibid.
103 ibid., 'There was little room for individuality or self-culture', he added. The Schoolmaster poet James Thompson described his work as 'pumping muddy information into unretentative schools'. 'The Ex-Army Schoolmaster's Association', in *RAEC Gazette* 3, No.5, Dec. 1973.
104 White, op. cit., p.43.
105 Leaver, op. cit.
106 ibid.
107 Jones, D.R., op. cit., p.175.
108 Howard, op. cit., pp.54–5.
109 Jones, D.R., op. cit., p.20.
110 ibid., p.37.
111 *The Times*, 30 December 1854.
112 Jones, D.R., op. cit., p.173.
113 ibid., pp.138ff, 180.
114 Spiers, op. cit., p.151. 'A quick eye, personal courage and the qualities of an English Gentleman had been all sufficient.'
115 *Parliamentary Debates*, House of Lords, 3rd Series, Vol. 27, col.1799ff, 14 July 1871.
116 Second Report of the Royal Commission on Military Education 1870, p.IX. 'Keenness is out of fashion – it is not correct form.'
117 Bond, B., *The Staff College*, p.56.
118 ibid., p.205. Some thought it made a difference, saying 'It was where you went to learn how to combine arrogance with ignorance.'
119 Spiers, op. cit., pp.209–10. In the 1880s the Staff College had only thirty-two officers a year, which was insufficient to fill vacant places.
120 Farwell, B., *For Queen and Country. A Social History of the Victorian and Edwardian Army*, pp.141–149 (London, 1981).
121 Farwell, B., *The Great Boer War*, p.87 (London, 1977).
122 The great difficulty in changing this was that gentlemen were expected to serve the state 'because they had the qualifications in an unspecialised age to do so'.

Spiers, op. cit., p.1. In an increasingly specialised age this was no longer true. Officers did not find it easy to adjust to the times. There was little change in the social composition of the officer class in the 19th Century which, as with purchase which gave the officer no inducement to change his ways, added to his difficulty in doing so. The dictates of the time were, nevertheless, imperious as Cardwell insisted. 'We live in times when heroism will not do – when natural ability will not do – when all the virtues which adorn the British officer will not do, if not coupled with the most careful professional training and the most unremitting attention to his duties.' *Parliamentary Debates*, 3rd Series, House of Commons, Vol.206, col.292ff, 11 May 1871. Thirty years later Viscount Esher had still to make the same point. Our best officers understood this and would compare with the best in any profession. He doubted if the average British officer of high rank and middle life would. 'In the possession of qualities other than those which relate to the intellect the great majority are truly outstanding. In intellectual qualities the average officer is unimpressive.' Esher, Viscount, *Today and Tomorrow and Other Essays*, p.47ff (London, 1910).

123   Lloyd, E.M., *A Review of the History of Infantry*, pp.118, 124, 145 (London, 1908).

124   Bruce, R.J., *Silken Dalliance*, p.101 (London, 1946).

Chapter 2 – The First World War and Education at Home, 1920–1939

1   Report on the Army Scheme of the Ministry of Reconstruction Adult Education Committee, 1919.

2   Gorell, Lord, *Education and the Army: an Essay in Reconstruction*, pp.8–9 (Oxford, 1921). It was said, as it frequently had been and was to be again, that the needs of training left no time for education.

3   ibid., p.14.

4   ibid., p.5.

5   *Journal of the Army Educational Corps* IV, No.4, March 1927.

6   White, A.C.T., *The Story of Army Education. 1643-1963*, p.53 (London, 1963).

7   Gorell, op. cit., p.19; Borden-Turner, D., 'Education in the Army', *Army Quarterly* 1, 1920.

8   White, op. cit., p.47.

9   ibid.

10   Gibbs, P., *Realities of War*, pp.436–8 (London, 1920).

11   Bonham-Carter papers, quoted in MacKenzie, S.P., 'Politics and Morale: Current Affairs and Citizenship in the British Armed Forces, 1919–1949', p.11. D. Phil. Thesis, University of Oxford, 1988.

12   Gloden, G., 'Douglas and Dallas'; 'Mutiny at Etaples Base in 1917', *Past and Present* 69, 1975. Men wearing arm-bands with the letters 'SWC' (Soldiers and Workers Councils) on them, imprisoned the officers and informed them they would be shot. The mutiny was quelled and the ring-leaders shot.

13   White, op. cit., p.53.

14   ibid., p.51.

15   Gorell, Lord, *Education in the Army: an Essay in Reconstruction*.

16   Fisher, H.A.L., 'Report on the Army Scheme'. He also called it 'the greatest invention since gunpowder'. Gorell, op. cit., pp.175–6.

17   Gorell, op. cit., p.34. An infantry captain, he was awarded the Military Cross after the battle of the Somme. After recovering from his wounds he was appointed a Staff Major. On becoming a Deputy Director of Staff Duties (Education) and head of SD8, he was promoted to Staff Colonel. It was by an unfortunate oversight which he greatly regretted he was not invited to the garden party at Eltham Palace held to mark its becoming the HQ of the RAEC.

18   ibid., pp.34–7.

19   Gorell, Lord, *One Man, Many Parts*, p.210 (London, 1956).

20   ibid., pp.209–10; Gorell, *Education and the Army*, op. cit., pp.261–3. He was accused of bolshevising the Army and General Childs, Director of Personnel Services, said that he had turned an Army which before the war had been 'well-disciplined and ignorant' into one which was now 'educated and ill-disciplined'.

21   Gorell, op. cit., p.219; Borden-Turner, op. cit., p.138ff.

22   Told to the author in Malaya by the Commanding Officer in question.

23   Gorell, op. cit., pp.209–210.

24   Army Order, 24 September 1918, RAEC Archives; White, op. cit., p.50.

25   Fisher, op. cit.

26   Army Order VII dated 13 May 1919, RAEC Archives.

27   MacKenzie, op. cit., p.15.

28   White, op. cit., p.54.

29   Mansbridge, 'Address of 7 May 1919'. It was, he said, 'a movement which is destined to have a profound effect upon the life of the whole nation'. For Fisher *see* Gorell, op. cit., p.269. For Robertson *see* Mackenzie, op. cit., p.34. Robertson believed that education 'was the most useful kind of propaganda and very helpful from a discipline point of view'.

30   Froude, J.A., *Liberty and Prosperity* (London, 1889).

31   Paul, H., *Letters of Lord Acton to Mary Gladstone*, p.76.

32   *Parliamentary Debates*, 5th Series, XCVII, col.810, 10 August 1917.

33   Gorell, op. cit., p.11.

34   Graubert, S.R., 'Military Demobilisation in Great Britain following the First World War', *Journal of Modern History*, 19, 1947. Borden-Turner wrote: 'The people are in a mood when they are ready to receive instructions from incompetent and ill-informed teachers, from social and political propagandists of every kind and description. The provision of sound teaching in the Army upon citizenship in all its aspects should result in the accession to the community of numbers of men not only disciplined in body and mind but intelligently informed of their duties, rights and responsibilities as citizens. This cannot fail to have a profound influence on future developments in social and industrial politics.' Borden-Turner, 'Education and the Army', *Army Quarterly* Vol.1. 1920.

This was the note sounded more loudly in the Second World War than in 1919, as then those who feared that education would undermine morale could not prevail against the confident conviction that it would, on the contrary, greatly strengthen it. Churchill reminds us how real was the fear then of social disruption; to him it appeared that 'everywhere subversive elements were active'. Churchill, W.S., *The World Crisis. The Aftermath*, p.60 (London, 1929).

35   Morgan, Sir Frederick, *Peace and War: A Soldier's Life*, p.126 (London, 1961). For regiments requiring private means, ibid., p.125.

36   Army Order 3, 9 December 1918.

37   Gorell, op. cit., p.51. The CIGS, Sir Henry Wilson, initially no supporter of this great development of Army Education, changed his tune and called it, 'probably the biggest step the Army has ever taken'. White, op. cit., p.56.

38   Gorell, *Diary*, 1919, p.35.

39   MacKenzie, op. cit., p.44.

40   3 August 1919.

41   Army Order 231, 15 June 1920, RAEC Archives.

42   Liddell Hart, B.H., *Memoirs* I, p.50.

43   Collison, A.L., *Memoirs of an Army Schoolmaster, 1904–27*, RAEC Archives.

44   Army Order 231, 15 June 1920, RAEC Archives.

45   Gorell, op. cit., p.37.

46   The 1920 *Manual* defined education as 'the systematic endeavour of intelligent people to help others to make the best of themselves'. The persistence of the belief that such systematic endeavour would characterise the Army is striking. It is to be seen again in the *Manual of Educational Training* issued in September 1923, which emphasised that the aim of military training was the production of 'a highly efficient Army composed of individuals who are good and capable citizens'. It was 'within the power of the army to develop the mind of the recruit on such lines as to give him a wide outlook and the power to improve' and this would 'react profoundly on the national life'.

47   *The Times*, 3 February 1928.

48   'Teething Troubles of the Army Educational Corps', *Torch*, 1924.

49   'The Final Report of the Committee of the Ministry Reconstruction Adult Education Committee 1919'.

50   Dilks, D. (ed.), *The Diaries of Sir Alexander Cadogan 1938–1945*, p.50 (London,1971).

51   Preston, A., *In Relief of Gordon. Lord Wolseley's Campaign Journal of the Khartoum Relief Expedition 1884–1885* (London, 1967). Wolseley yearned for the day 'when the license of democracy and socialism will be conquered by the sword and succeeded by cruel military despotism. Then it will be that the man of talk will give way to the man of action and the Gladstones, Harcourts, Morleys and all that most contemptible of God's creatures will black the boots of some successful cavalry colonel. A new Cromwell will clear the country of these frothing talkers and the soldiers will rule. Would that my lot could have been cast in such an era.' He wanted to see Gladstone and Harcourt lynched and torn

limb from limb. Tar and feathering would suffice for Northcoate.

52 MacCleod, R. and Kelly, D. (eds.), *The Ironside Diaries*, p.366.

53 Calwell, C.C., *Field Marshal Sir Henry Wilson. His Life and Diaries*, p.238 (London, 1927). For civil/military relations see *also Blake*, R., *Life and Times of Andrew Bonar-Law, 1858–1922*, pp.187, 193 (London, 1955). Cooper, D., *Haig*, Vol i., p.131 (London, 1935). Magnus-Allcroft, Sir P., *Kitchener: Portrait of an Imperialist*, p.279 (London, 1958).

54 Pease, *The Leveller Movement*, p.174 (London, 1996).

55 Gorell, *One Man, Many Parts*, op. cit., p.210.

56 *Manual of Educational Training* Part I, 'General Principles'. 'The officer', it declared, 'cannot excel unless he cultivates his power of instruction.'

57 Borden-Turner, op. cit., p.138.

58 Collison, op. cit.

59 'Educational Training in the Regular Army. PROWO 32/5436'. Copy in RAEC archives. Gorell, *Diary*, 1919, p.64. 'It is possible that in 1930 an army will be synonymous for an educational institution', he wrote.

60 White, A.C.T., 'Educational Training' in *Journal of the AEC* VII, No.4. June 1942. For his view that 'it was probably meant to be a tactful means of acquiring training hours for the education of young soldiers' and that 'supposed to represent the fusion of two ideals, it really carried an inherent disunity, for the results produced by training represent to a large extent the will of the trainer, whilst, as the manual pointed out, a prerequisite of any form of education is the provision of freedom and choice', *see also* White, *The Story of Army Education*, op. cit., pp.69–70.

61 ibid., p.74.

62 ibid., p.73.

63 Hawkins and Bramble, op. cit., p.82.

64 Cameron, R.J., op. cit.

65 Sherry, Brigadier T.C., 'Service Children's Schools', *Torch*, Summer 1992.

66 'The Report of the Committee on the Education of the Army's Children', The Onslow Committee.

67 'The Report of the Consultation Committee of the Board of Education on the Education of the Adolescent, 1926' (The Hadow Report).

68 White, op. cit., p.78. How well justified and deserved was the Corps' reputation for teaching is fully borne out by an article, 'Army Education and the Dalton Plan', *Journal of the AEC* I, No.3, July 1924. 'No individual', it said, 'can be fully developed by another person. The learner must be induced to cooperate with the instructor. The responsibility for finding things out for himself must, as far as possible, be thrown on the learner and the task must be made sufficiently attractive to arouse his interest.' That comment encapsulates the essence of teaching.

69 Gorell, op. cit., p.11; White, op. cit., pp.78–80; *The Times*, 3 February 1938.

70 Hawkins, Major W.C., 'Cipher Duties, 1939–1941', *Torch*, Jubilee edition. While it was only in 1931 that the AEC was given this responsibility, the cipher work

in India during the Great War was entrusted to some thirty Army Schoolmasters. The cipher section in Mesopotamia was largely staffed by them. One of them, Jack Charmian, together with the cipher books, was among the last to evacuate Kut and when General Dunsterville entered Hamadan a Schoolmaster, Bill Waterson, was with him. Collison, op. cit.

71   'The AEC in Thrace', letter to the Editor of the Corps *Journal* 1922. Quoted in *Torch* Commemoration edition, Summer 1992.

Chapter 3 – The AEC Overseas in the Interwar Years, 1920–1939

1   Langer, *The Diplomacy of Imperialism 1890–1902*, p.78 (New York and London).

2   ibid., p.85.

3   ibid., pp.83–4.

4   Gooch and Temperley, British Documents London, 1926, Vol.XI, pp.228–9.

5   Windelband, W., *Die Auswärtige Politik der Groszenmächte in der Neuzeit 1494–1919*, p.194 (Vienna, 1941); Postlethwaite, *Britain's Commercial Interest Explained*, p.16 (London, 1956); *Mémoires pour servir à l'Histoire de Notre Temps per L'Observateur Hollandais*, p.VIII (Frankfurt, 1757); Pownall, T., *Mémoire adressé aux Souverains de l'Europe*, pp.5–6 (London, 1781); Barner, N., *A Discourse of Trade*, p.14 (London, 1690); Butler, R., *Choiseul. Father and Son. 1719–1754*, p.750 (Oxford, 1980).

6   Barnett, op. cit., p.78.

7   Mansergh, N., *The Commonwealth Experience*, p.126 (London, 1969). For once Disraeli agreed with him. Monypenny and Buckle, *The Life of Benjamin Disraeli. Earl of Beaconsfield*, Vol.II, p.1476.

8   Barnett, op. cit., p.134.

9   Gerouard, M., *The Return to Camelot: Chivalry and the English Gentleman*, p.227 (New Haven, 1981).

10   Yet at that Conference, Hughes was well aware that British naval power would not have sufficed to deal with both Germany and Japan together. Barnett, op. cit., pp.81 and 252.

11   ibid., p.165.

12   ibid., p.134.

13   Hale, J.R., *War and Society in Renaissance Europe*, p.68 (London, 1985).

14   ibid., p.70.

15   Barnett, op. cit., pp.151–3.

16   ibid., p.152.

17   ibid., p.163.

18   Omissi, D., *The Sepoy and the Raj. The Indian Army 1860–1940. Studies in Military and Strategic History*, p.139 (London, 1994); Mason, P., *A Matter of Honour: an account of the Indian Army, its officers and men*, p.452 (London, 1974).

19   Callinson, op. cit.

20   *The Link*, July 1939; July 1931; July 1932; Leaver, op. cit.

21   *The Army Schoolmistress*, July 1925; *Parliamentary Debates*, 5th series, Vol.197, col.227.

22   Fowler, Colonel A.L., in *Torch*, Jubilee Edition 1920–1970.

23   Macpherson, W., *Good-Bye to Quetta*, RAEC Archives.

24   The main educational programme for soldiers was provided at regimental depots during basic training. They had five hours of education each week for four months. They then sat for the Third Class Certificate of Education, being examined in reading, writing, arithmetic and regimental history. White, op. cit., p.71.

25   Cameron, S.J., *Life of an Army Schoolmaster as seen through my experiences 1889–1920*, RAEC Archives.

26   Macpherson, op. cit.

27   Wilson, Brigadier C.A., 'The Education of the Soldier', 1928, *Torch*, Jubilee Edition.

28   Wavell, Field Marshal Lord, 'Minerva's Owl', pp.8, 9. He said that when he became General 'I did my best to have written examinations abolished or at least reduced.' He said of the AEC 'the examination complex cramped its style'.

29   Cameron, op. cit.

30   JAEC Vol.I, No.1, January 1924; JAEC Vol.I, No.2, April 1924.

31   Leaver, op. cit.

32   Quarrell, W.O. C.J., JAEC Vol XII, No.3, July 1935.

33   Cameron, op. cit.

34   If classrooms can be dispensed with in the pursuit of education, books cannot. The professor in charge of the class of creative writing in the Faculty of English at Harvard University bemoaned the fact that his students were not of this opinion. Soldiers in India who did not share it either were restricted in their educational achievement as those unlettered members of the class of creative writing in Harvard University will be too.

35   Wilson, Brigadier, 'The Education of the Soldier 1920–1939', *Torch*, Jubilee Edition.

36   JAEC Vol XII, No.1., January 1934.

37   Roe, Brigadier, 'Thirty five years in the Corps', *Torch* II, No.2, 1977. It was not only in India that he encountered this hostility. He writes of his experience as Lieutenant Colonel in AA Command 'The Corps and its work were beset by the most bitter and sustained hostility.' Lest it be thought that Brigadier Roe was unduly sensitive the writer may be forgiven for recording that Bill Lynam recollected that on going as Education Officer to a Division he was told 'You are an Army nuisance and we don't need you.' When for good measure we remember there were periodic calls in Parliament for the abolition of the Corps in the inter-war years (*Parliamentary Debates*, 5th Series, Vol.182 col.228, Vol.225 col.220), we cannot be surprised that there were those in it who gave up the struggle, content to enjoy what privileges and life-style they could and to find satisfaction, if they thought of so doing, outside the hours they were officially required to put

in. The Corps' Journal reflects its morale. In its first number it published a tremendous onslaught against the unthinking senior officer by Fuller – 'Mind – the Man'. It attracted the unfavourable attention of Lord Caven, the CIGS, whose ire together with the repeated blows coming the Corps' way, turned the Journal into a dull catalogue of special events, its most interesting pages being of extensive travels, the difficulties of teaching in adverse conditions, the upheavals occasioned by the annual movement of families in India to the relative cool of the hills. The wonder is not that the morale of the Corps suffered but that the Corps continued, as in adverse circumstances the Corps of Army Schoolmasters had done, to do the jobs it was allowed to do as well as they could be done and to make the most of the few opportunities that came its way. 'In a small command, like Malaya, very little happens that is of interest to those in other commands. We just get on with our jobs' one of its members wrote. That comment reminds us that there was sufficient conscientiousness and dedicated toughness to bring it through its despondent years. JAEC I, No.2, April 1934.

38   White, op. cit., p.67; *The Times*, 11 August 1922.
39   Roe, Brigadier, op. cit.
40   White, op. cit., p.64.
41   We laugh today at Lord Cardigan refusing to allow some of his horse-lines to be moved to dry ground from a muddy patch where horses stood knee-deep in mire because that would spoil the symmetry of the lines. We should not forget that other times have other ways and we should expect future generations to be more aware than we are that we also live in glass houses. But we can still acknowledge how long it takes for attitudes to change and remember the difficulties occasioned by the building of an airfield at Gibraltar between the wars. The need was seen by all to be vital yet when it came to the point objection was raised in the highest quarter because the plan put forward, to which there was no alternative, was to involve the demolition of a newly built cookhouse in the neighbouring Infantry Barracks. Morgan, op. cit., p.124. Tradition is a source of strength but it is a weakness when traditionalists are too strong.
42   The Corps was well aware of the inadequacy of the teaching the Units could provide. It did what it could to help. As we have seen it ran courses for Unit instructors at Shorncliffe and it did so abroad. It ran annual six-week courses in Egypt and in India for them. Such courses would undoubtedly benefit the instructors but they did not remove the widespread conviction that it would have been much better if those whose ability to teach the teachers was not in question but whose capacity to teach them sufficiently in six weeks was, had done the job for which they themselves were so well qualified instead of expecting the unqualified to do it. Given their many commitments and their fewness in number this was not possible. But this teaching of the teachers did not enamour the taught nor add to the prestige of the Corps. 'The AEC in Egypt and the Mediterranean', *Army Education Journal*, 4 December 1926.
43   Cameron, op. cit.
44   Wavell, 'Minerva's Owl', op. cit., p.3.

45   ibid.
46   For these hazards of teaching overseas see JAEC X, No.4, October 1933 and
      JAEC XVI, No.2, April 1939.
47   Hawkins and Bramble, op. cit., pp.85–6.
48   JAEC XI, No.2, April 1934.
49   Lunt, Brigadier W., Letters, RAEC Archives.
50   JAEC X, No.4, October 1933.
51   The *AEC Quarterly Bulletin*, January 1945.
52   JAEC XII, No.3, July 1935.
53   *Educational Training Directive*, Indian Army.

Chapter 4 – Education in the Militia and in the Army in the Phoney War

1   Harris, K., *Atlee*, p.116 (London, 1982). It was his theme at this time that Labour
     supported internationalism and not nationalism. We paid no attention then to
     what the Federalist called 'the natural and tried course of human affairs'. We
     ignored its warning that 'to mould our political systems upon speculations of
     lasting tranquillity is to calculate on the weaker springs of the human character'.
     What it called 'the necessity of proper exertions' was a truth beyond most of us
     then. Hamilton, A., Jay, J., and Madison, J., *The Federalist*, pp.160, 161, 123
     (New York, 1911).
2   Burke, E., *World's Classic Edition of Burke's Collected Works IV*, pp.312–3
     (London, 1906); Figgis, J.N. and Lawrence, R.V., *Historical Essays and Studies
     of Lord Acton*, p.130 (London, 1907).
3   Bassuet, J.B. and Bouillon, A., *L'Esprit de Bassuet: Chain des Pensées Tirées
     de Ses Meilleurs Ouvrages* Paris. MID CO LXXI.
4   Hart-Davis, Duff, *Letters and Journals of Sir Alan Lazcelles from 1920 to 1936*
     Vol.II, p.50 (London, 1989).
5   Hill, D.J., *A History of Diplomacy in the International Development of Europe*
     Vol.II, p.596 (London, 1906).
6   For 'the old and false idea of the Balance of Power' see Campbell, E.H.T,
     Christianity and International Morality, p.63 (Cambridge, 1921); for the Italian
     Prime Minister's view of diplomatists as ignorant monocled men see *Commission
     d'Enquete parlementaire sur les énvénements survenus en Frame de 1933 a
     1945. Rapport de M. Charles Serre*, p.86 (Paris 1951); for a similar view
     expressed in the House of Commons in March 1918 see Craig, G.A., 'The
     Professional Diplomat and his problems, 1919–1939', *World Politics IV*, January
     1952, p.147; for the Spanish ambassador at Tokyo's advice to the young British
     attaché there that the diplomatists needed to be stupid as well as courteous see
     Bruce, op. cit., p.94; for the Balance of Power see Bacon, Francis, *Essayes*,
     p.58 (Dent, 1906) – 'First for their neighbours; there can no general rule be
     given (occasions are so variable), save one, which ever holdeth; which is that
     princes do keep due sentinel that none of their neighbours do overgrow so (by

increase of territory, by embracing of trade, by approaches or the like) as they become more able to annoy them than they were'; for the idea of Collective Security and its weaknesses, see Hinsley, F.H., *The Pursuit of Peace Through Power* (Cambridge, 1965); Barnes, H.H., *Perpetual War for Perpetual Peace* (Princeton, 1953); Brugière, P.F., *La Securité collective 1919–1945* (Paris, 1946).

7   Crick, B. (ed.), *Machiavelli. The Discourses*, p.313 (London, 1970). He added 'If you yield to a threat, you do so in order to avoid war, and more often than not, you do not avoid war. For those before whom you have thus openly demeaned yourself by yielding, will not stop there, but will seem to extort further concessions and the less they esteem you the more incensed will they become against you'; in January, 1907, Sir Eyre Crowe had given us this very warning against Germany. 'For there is one road', he said, 'which if past experience is any guide to the future, will most certainly not lead to any permanent improvement of relations with any power, least of all Germany, and which must therefore be abandoned; that is the road paved with graceful British concessions – concessions ... not set off by equivalent counter-services' – quoted in Diplomacy in Fetters, *Sir Victor Wellesley*, p.10 (London, undated).

8   Bassett, R., *Democracy and Foreign Policy: A Case History. The Sino-Japanese Dispute, 1931–33*, p.249 (London, 1952). This was what was criticised at the time as his 'policy of bluff' for his faith, from which he never departed, was solely in the force of public opinion of which he said 'Never before has international opinion been so organised and mobilised'. See also pp.145–6.

9   Bacon, op. cit. p.172.

10   Temperley, H., *The Foreign Policy of Learning, 1822–1827*, p.81 (London, 1925).

11   Wigg, G., *George Wigg*, p.90 (London, 1972).

12   Stevens, T., 'Army Education', *Fabian Research Series*, No.53, (London, 1940).

13   Clive, L., *The People's Army*, pp.210–11 (London, 1938).

14   Mackenzie, S.P., *Politics and Military Morale; Current Affairs and Citizenship Education in the British Army 1914–1950*, p.62 (Oxford, 1991).

15   White, op. cit., p.96, citing General Sir Ronald Adam's letter. 'Like other Army Commanders, I was horrified at the utter lack of knowledge of the average man as to the war, what we were fighting for, and what we were fighting against.'

16   Mackenzie, op. cit., pp.61–2.

17   ibid., p.62.

18   ibid., p.63.

19   *The Times*, 11 May 1939.

20   Mackenzie, op. cit., p.63.

21   ibid., p.67. His Majesty made it known that he desired that men should go back to civilian life after their term in the Militia with wider ideas about citizenship.

22   Communicated by Major-General Foxton.

23   Mackenzie, op. cit., p.65.

24   *Parliamentary Debates*, 5th Series, Vol.156, cols.31–2.

25   Letter from Captain Carris-Wilson, 20 February 1940, RAEC Archives.

26   Roe, Brigadier T.P., *Torch* 12, No.2, Winter 1978.

27 Hawkins, Major W.C., 'Cipher Duties, 1939–1941' in *Torch*, Jubilee Edition.

28 Scarlyn Wilson, N., *Education in the Forces 1939–1946: the Civilian Contribution*, (London, 1948).

29 Report of the Committee chaired by Major-General L.K.H. Finch, Director of Recruiting and Organisation on 'The War Time Role of the Army Educational Corps'. Paper for consideration by War Committee, 5 January 1940, RAEC Archives.

30 The Stanhope Committee on promotion in the Army, ibid.

31 The Brownrigg Committee, 'The Interim Report of the Committee on the Organisation of the Army Educational Corps, 1938', ibid.

32 Mackenzie, op. cit., p.67.

33 Gorell, *One Man, Many Parts*, op. cit., pp.341–2.

34 Williams, p.194. Creech-Jones raised in Parliament the question of the Corps' demise and was assured that it had not been abandoned. Mackenzie, op. cit., pp.66–7.

35 17 February 1940.

36 Scarlyn Wilson, op. cit., The officers of the CAC were asked if the AEC should be disbanded and education in the Army handed over to civilians as to a great extent Haig had done in France in 1916. The CAC was sure that education could never become part and parcel of the Army without a strong AEC. Asked if they would prefer a military or civilian Director of Army Education with whom to work, they said that everything depended on the individual chosen. They added that whoever this was he should have a deputy who should be military if the Director was civilian and vice versa. The CAC suggested that General Haining head the committee which would consider education in the Army.

37 *The Times*, 9 February, 1940; Wigg, G., op. cit., pp.94–5, 97.

38 Letter to *The Times*, 26 January 1940.

39 Report of the Committee on Educational, Welfare and Recruiting Needs of the Army (The Haining Report), May 1940, RAEC Archives.

40 ACJ 1415/1940, ibid.

41 White, op. cit., p.92; 'Education and the Army: Possibilities within the Unit', *Times Educational Supplement*, 22 November 1941; a staff officer, 'The State of Army Education: an Appraisement and Some Criticism', *Times Educational Supplement*, 7 March 1942.

42 HMI's Report on Army Education. Middle East Command. 9/11/1945-15/2/1946. RAEC Archives.

43 Maurice, General Sir Frederick, *The Life of Viscount Haldane of Cloan, Vol.1*, p.169 (London, 1937).

44 Letter to Grigg. Grigg Papers 9/7, 13, 29 October 1942, Churchill College Archives.

45 Churchill, Sir W.S., *The Second World War: The Grand Alliance III*, Appendix G (London, 1950).

46 Mackenzie, op. cit., p.100.

47 ibid., p.101, note 48.

48   Grigg, op. cit., p.351.
49   Williams, op. cit., p.134.
50   Mackenzie, op. cit., p.80.
51   ibid., p.81. The CAC at this time was under heavy pressure from WEA Tutors and even from a highly-respected Professor of Adult Education. With a lamentable lack of what the French call *le tact des choses possible*, Professor Raybould maintained that education in the Army would be possible only if control of it could be taken away from Commanding Officers and entrusted to those experienced in adult education. See *The Highway* XXXV, November 1942. A memorandum for lecturers and tutors to the Army asked them to be careful to avoid anything which 'might be regarded as defeatist'; this a number of them looked on as an undesirable infringement of tutorial liberty. See James, L., 'Education and the Army', *The Highway* XXXIV, October 1942. The Aberystwyth and Hull Regional Committees demanded that 'the principle of academic freedom should be affirmed and no longer trammelled by considerations of expediency and security'. 'Where are we going', another *Highway* article asked and left no doubt that in the writer's view we were in Army Education on the slippery slope to that totalitarian state against which we were in arms.
52   White, pp.106-7; 'The Study Centre or Forces Education Centre as a pioneer initiative', editorial, *Army Education*, March 1946. 'Here are books which can be read, comfortable chairs which can be sat on, pictures which can be looked at, handicraft benches and tools which can be used. The Army has shown what can be done and hopes this will stir up a demand for similar centres in civilian life'. Here again the Army took the initiative and made a highly worthwhile contribution to civilian adult education. It failed to create an overwhelming demand and while there are today admirable civilian counter-parts of these Forces Education Centres they are still far too few. They would be fewer had there not been this Army initiative.
53   The Haining Report, op. cit.
54   Brigadier Maude, having been Inspector of the AEC, had become its 'Controller', 'A change', White tells us, 'intended to emphasise his executive functions'. White, op. cit., p.111.
55   Paper by Gorell, 'Educational Training in the Regular Army', W.G.32/5463, RAEC Archives.
56   Mackenzie, op. cit., p.49.
57   Mackenzie, op. cit., p.49

Chapter 5 – Army Education in Embattled Britain

1   Grigg, op. cit., p.337.
2   Eden, A., *The Eden Memoirs. The Reckoning*, p.113 (London, 1965); Cowles, V., *Looking For Trouble*, pp.412, 416 (London, 1941).

3   Grigg, op. cit., p.339.

4   ibid., p.355; Nicolson, H., *Diaries 1939–1945* (London, 1967); Chapman, Guy,
     'A Note on Morale', *Adult Education* XIV, 1942; Summerfield, P., 'Education
     and Politics in the British Armed Forces in the Second World War', *International
     Review of Social History* XXVI, 1981, p.138.

5   Henson, H., *Retrospect of an Unimportant Life*, p.85 (London, 1950).

6   Croft Papers 2/6, 'The Army 1940. Mental and Recreational Stimulant', 12
     August 1940, Churchill College Archives.

7   Nicholson, op. cit., p.211.

8   Summerfield, op. cit., p.139; Crick, B., *George Orwell*, p.271 (London, 1977).
     Wintringham, T., *New Ways of War*, p.50 (London, 1950).

9   Napier, Major-General Sir W., *The History of the War in the Peninsula and in
     the South of France 1807 to 1814*, p.194 (London, 1890). Napier added
     'Napoleon thus made his troops not invincible, indeed nature had put a bar to
     that in the character of the British soldiers.'

10   Mackenzie, op. cit., p.89.

11   Summerfield, op. cit., p.140.

12   ibid., pp.140–1; Adam, General R.F. 'Adult Education in the Forces', *Adult
     Education* VII, 1945; Gilbert, M., *Churchill: A Life* (London, 1991) cites Wavell's
     comment to Churchill 'Neither British, Australians or Indians have shown any
     real toughness of mind and body' on the surrender of Singapore.

13   Spead, Sir E., PUS Finance, quoted in Mackenzie, op. cit., pp.155–7; for the
     view of Cash, T.C., of the Directorate of Finance see Summerfield, op. cit.,
     p.135; for the view that it was a fallacy that morale would be improved by the
     Winter Scheme see Mackenzie, op. cit., pp.160–1; for the view that the morale
     of the troops was higher than many thought see Grigg's letter to his father, 26
     April 1942 in Grigg Papers, PJGG 9/6 11, Churchill College Archives.

14   Summerfield, op. cit., p.138.

15   James, L., letter to *New Statesman*, 21 June 1941; 'Education and the Army',
     Highway 34, 1942, p.62.

16   Speech on Reform of Representation, House of Commons, June 1784.
     'Imperceptible habits and old custom, the great supporter of all the governments
     in the world', he said.

17   Appeal from the New Whigs to the Old, 1791, Works IV, the Nimmo edition of
     1899.

18   Reflections on the French Revolution and Other Essays, *Everyman*, 1955 p.84.
     Disraeli agreed. 'The traditions of a nation are part of its existence', he said.
     Moneypenny and Buckle, op. cit., p.605.

19   Williams, W.E., 'Education in the Army', *Political Quarterly* 259.

20   Mackenzie, op. cit., p.139.

21   ibid., pp.134–5.

22   ibid., p.138.

23   ibid., p.136.

24   Nicolson, op. cit., pp.211.

25 Summerfield, op. cit., pp.134–5.

26 Hawkins and Brimble, op. cit., pp.145–7.

27 ibid., pp. 147–8; 'The A.T.S. Girl and Her Future as a Citizen', *Highway* XXXV, 1943; Senior Commander C.M. James. 'Education in the A.T.S', JAEC XVII No.4., June 1942.

28 'Now that I am here and on my feet, I might say in the language of the old book to which my grandmother from Auchterarder, and no doubt your grandmother too, Mr Chairman, paid so much attention that (and here Hopkins paused and looked straight down the table at Churchill) wheresoever thou goest we go, and where thou lodgest we lodge, they people shall be our people, thy God, our God, even unto the end.' Churchill was in tears. Johnson, The Rt. Hon. T., *Memories*, p.146, (London, 1952).

29 Mackenzie, op. cit., p.113; Maude, Brigadier C.G., 'Compulsory or Voluntary Education', JAEC XVII, No.1, September 1941; Williams regretted how 'tardily conceded' this principle of compulsion was. He said education 'remained until very near the end low on the list of occupational priorities in the Army'. Williams, op. cit., pp.1–2.

30 For the plan put forward and vigorously defended by General Willans and Margesson's opposition to it see Sommerfield, op. cit., pp.140–1.

31 ibid., p.142.

32 Yeaxlee, B. 'Adult Education in H.M. Forces: the Central Advisory Council and Regional Committees', *Adult Education* XIII, 1941; *The Times Educational Supplement* 1 November 1941.

33 Tanner, J.R., *Tudor Constitutional Documents 1445–1603*, p.457 (Cambridge, 1940).

34 White, op. cit., p.98; Macpherson, W., 'Goodbye to Quetta', RAEC Archives.

35 Quoted in Hawkins and Brimble, op. cit., p.113.

36 Committee on Women's Services, op. cit.

37 Lecture on Military Leadership, University of St Andrews, 15 November 1945.

38 Mackenzie, op. cit., p.117.

39 Scarlyn Wilson, op. cit., p.52.

40 Harrington, W. and Young, P., *The 1945 Revolution*, p.111 (London, 1978).

41 Scarlyn Wilson, op. cit., p.47.

42 Mackenzie, op. cit., pp. 188–9.

43 White, op. cit., p.103; Summerfield, op. cit.

44 Mackenzie, op. cit., p.122. He wanted to save time for training by making ABCA part of the Chaplain's hour.

45 Communicated by an officer of the Household Division.

46 Mackenzie, op. cit., p.159.

47 Williams, W.E., 'Projects and Experiments ABCA', JAEC XVII, No.2, December 1941.

48 Carrington, Lord, *Reflections on Things Past. The Memoirs of Lord Carrington*, p.478 (London, 1988).

49 Mackenzie, op. cit., p.178. Williams was, however, still cautious. 'I have been

in hot water', he said, 'for crying up Russia so much', for over a year ABCA pamphlets kept off Russia.

50   ibid., p.163.

51   Croft Papers 2/6, 'ABCA and Political Reactions', Churchill College Archives. 'If every officer is teaching his men on these lines week after week what, we may well ask, are we going to see when the Army through its official machinery has built up a divine discontent which no power on earth can appease?'

52   For the A-G's fear that the prospect of a third inactive winter coupled with the depressing effect of defeats in the Far East and in the Western Desert would bring about a lowering of morale and efficiency and his hopes that the Winter Scheme would 'act as a strong antidote', see Mackenzie, op. cit., p.161. For the views of the Morale Committee and of senior officers, see ibid., p.167.

53   ibid., p.180.

54   *Parliamentary Debates*, House of Lords, 5th Series, Vol.125, cols.99ff, January 1943.

55   *Parliamentary Debates*, House of Commons, 5th Series, Vol.386, cols.851–853, January 1943.

56   Mackenzie, op. cit., p.144.

57   Letter to Montgomery, 25 July 1944, Grigg Papers PJGG 9/6, Churchill College Archives. Grigg wrote to his father on 30 July 1944 'We are going to have a baddish time when the war is over. Both the Russians and the Yanks are jealous of us and will try to reduce us to a third rate power .... it does mean that all these promises of a good time to be had by all won't materialise, that the people who believed them will be pretty sore for a bit'; ibid.; see also Barnett, C.W., *The Lost Victory. British Dreams and British Realities, 1945–1950*, pp.395–7, (London, 1995).

58   Stocks, M., *The Workers' Educational Association. The First Fifty Years*, p.127 (London, 1953).

59   *Parliamentary Debates*, House of Commons, Vol.386, cols.851–853, January 1943.

60   Grigg Papers, PJGG 9/6, Churchill College Archives.

61   Churchill, W.S., *The Second World War IV. The Hinge of Fate*, p.847 (London, 1951). Bevin wrote to the PM who expressed his feelings strongly.

62   Summerfield, op. cit., p.149.

63   Mackenzie, op. cit., p.145. It is interesting that it was Cripps, a committed socialist, who urged this and that it was Grigg, a Conservative Secretary of State, who thought Churchill dangerously indifferent to the undermining of conservative ideas that was going on, who opposed it.

64   ibid., pp.222–4. A proposal was put to the Executive Committee of the Army Council on 10 September 1943 to spend no more on efforts to make soldiers better citizens. It was not a proper charge upon Army votes to educate the Army beyond the standard requisite for its success as a military machine. The Army, it was urged, should not be concerned 'with the different and wider needs of the post-war periods'. Summerfield, op. cit., p.149. That proposal was rejected.

But there was more to be said for it than was then admitted.

65   Croft, op. cit.

66   Mackenzie, op. cit., p.228.

67   ibid., p.146.

68   Croft Papers, 2/6 'Welfare and Education ABCA', V/15/2, Churchill Archives.

69   Mackenzie op. cit., p.241. In the 'ABCA Handbook' Williams wrote 'Victory in war, real victory, is in a sense a delayed action affair. It reveals itself, not merely in the defeat of an enemy, but in the positive achievements of peace'. This is the acknowledgement that ABCA was to have not merely a political aim but a party political aim as well. No one could have been so naive as to think there would be general agreement on what constituted 'the positive achievements of peace'. The only general agreement to be expected was that so vague a phrase needed defining if it was to have any meaning at all and that agreement on its meaning could never be unanimous.

70   Williams, op. cit., p.105; Hawkins and Brimble, op. cit., pp.198–203.

71   Hawkins and Brimble, op. cit., pp.225, 232; White. op. cit., p.74. 'Between 1926 and 1938', he tells us, 'the number of illiterates and near illiterates among recruits was never less than a quarter.' 'In 1943 some 10,000 men', Wavell tells us, 'were practically illiterate'. He writes 'illiteracy tended to distinguish the individual from his fellows who could not but be aware of it. That distinction was not good for his morale nor was his inability to write home'. 'Minerva's Owl'. Speaking of his first course for illiterates Colonel Burgess has this to say of their morale: 'They were the sorriest crowd I ever saw, the flotsam and jetsam of life's backwaters, their eyes dull, their faces strained and cheerless, their clothing and in not a few cases their bodies too dirty.' 'Ten Thousand Tragedies', op. cit.

72   Williams, *The New Statesman*, 1 March, 1941.

Chapter 6 – Education in the Armies Overseas in the Second World War

1   White, op. cit., p.90. There were only 113 officers and 238 instructors in the Corps at the beginning of the war.

2   Gould, Lieutenant Colonel E.C., JRAEC XXIV, No.1, March 1950.

3   Chapman, G, *A Kind of Survivor*, p.156 (London).

4   White, op. cit., pp.135–6.

5   MacGregor, WO J.H., 'Candlelight Cottage', JAEC XIX, No.4, December 1945. Among its many activities was the holding of a French tea once a week, when a dozen soldiers would meet a dozen local ladies for tea and conduct the entire proceedings in French. There were fines for lapses into other languages. So successful were these that an English tea had to be given for the local ladies who wanted to brush up their English.

6   White, op. cit., p.103.

7   Tanner, op. cit. p.553.

8   Mackenzie, op. cit., pp.165–70.
9   White, op. cit., p.147.
10   ibid., p.151.
11   ibid., p.149. 'Captain T.O. Morrow' was Major A. Myers.
12   ibid., p.149.
13   Mountain, WO J., 'With the AEC in Burma', JAEC XIX, No.4, December 1945;
       White, op. cit., p.152.
14   White, op. cit., p.153.
15   ibid., p.154.
16   ibid., pp.136–7.
17   Bishop, Lieutenant Colonel J.S., 'Education in the 8th Army'. JAEC XIX No.2.
       October 1944; Diary of Curtis, W.O., 'The AEC at the Front', RAEC Archives.
18   ibid.
19   Leese, Major J., 'The AEC and the Second Front', JAEC XIX, No.2, 1944; Jay,
       Captain J.F., Army Education XX, 1946.
20   McGowan, Colonel L., Torch Jubilee Edition.
21   Wilson, Major, E.J., 'News Sheets in the Field', JAEC XIX, No.2, October
       1944.
22   Trease, WOII R.G., 'Army Education Afloat', JAEC XIX, No.41, December
       1945; Broad, Captain A.H.R., 'Education on a Troopship. The University of
       F.18', RAEC Archives.
23   Cannon, Lieutenant Colonel P.S., 'Education in Chains', JAEC XX, No.4,
       December 1946; Vol.XXI. No.1, March 1947; Vol.XXI, No.2. June 1947.
24   ibid.

Chapter 7 – Army Education in the Second World War: an Assessment

1   Parliamentary Debates, 5th Series, Vol.143, col.1945; Williams, op. cit., p.28;
       an unofficial assessment of the number of units doing ABCA placed it as low as
       10%; see Craig, J.A., 'Politics on Parade. Army Education and the 1945 General
       Election', History, April 1996, p.224.
2   Mackenzie, op. cit., p.288.
3   Scarlyn Wilson, op. cit., pp.54-5; Williams claimed that 'even when clumsily
       conducted it could often reveal its value as a means of making men think and
       express themselves'. Williams, op. cit., p.50.
4   BBC discussion on Army Education, 1996.
5   Jay, Captain K.T., 'Education Under Fire', JAEC XX, No.3, Sept 1946. When
       V-bomb attack shifted to East Anglia, battery officers no longer welcomed AEC
       sergeant-instructors who nevertheless continued to visit during stand-down hours.
       One wrote 'men who had never heard Delius or Beethoven would listen patiently
       and attentively – and like it'. That instructor writes 'After VE Day I was stopped
       by a gunner who said that he still remembered our talks.'
6   Scarlyn Wilson, op. cit., p.28.

7   Mackenzie, op. cit., p.336.

8   ibid., p.198. He complained of the 'misinformation and slander' contained in lectures given by Rosita Forbes: she was forbidden to lecture to the troops. Others were cautioned against indulging in anti-Soviet propaganda. The Government was anxious to strengthen relations with the USSR and wished not to offend its susceptibilities. The Ministry of Information published a special manual which gave journalists 'arguments to counter the ideological fear of bolshevism'. This was too much for Orwell who gave up his BBC commentaries on the war to write *Animal Farm*, his biting satire on Soviet life. He thought Stalin's dictatorship 'a more hopeful phenomenon than Nazi Germany' but continued to denounce Soviet oppression. Avery, R.. *Why the Allies Won the War*, p.287 (London, 1995). Churchill at this time had no wish to strengthen Cripps whose conduct as British ambassador in Moscow had greatly displeased him and whose growing influence might have been dangerously increased had it been suspected that the Government was encouraging anti-Soviet attitudes in the Forces.

9   Mackenzie, op. cit., p.225.

10   ibid., p.170.

11   ibid., 190ff.

12   Sidgwick, H., *The Development of European Policy*, p.375 (London, 1903). He maintained that democratic majorities could be as tyrannical as any despot.

13   Phillips, Major J.A.R. and Curtis, Captain S.J., *Teaching Method*, (Glasgow, Leeds, Belfast, Undated).

14   Hawkins and Brimble, op. cit., p.112.

15   Letter to his father, 15 August 1941. He added 'I have never known the governing clique to be so devoid of capacity and morals.' Grigg Papers 9/6 11, Churchill College Archives.

16   Churchill cursed 'this bloody Second Front' and Sir Alan Brooke, CIGS, said *Overlord* was not 'the pivot of our whole strategy'. However the Americans at Teheran without prior discussion with the British told Stalin about *Overlord*, which greatly pleased him. Overy comments '*Overlord* was approved not on its strategic merits alone, but also to seal the alliance'. Overy, op. cit., pp.142 and 144.

17   Moran, Lord, *Winston Churchill: the Struggle for Survival, 1940–1965*, p.27 (London, 1966). Wavell had reported on the Singapore Garrison on 11 February 1942 'Morale of troops is not good and none is as high as I would like to see'. Moran comments on Churchill as the news of the surrender was received 'There is never any danger of his folding up in dirty weather. At this game there is no one of his weight. He has made use of the crisis as an argument for postponing the Second Front'. ibid pp.36–7.

18   ibid., p.27.

19   Letter to his father, 25 May 1939, Grigg, op. cit.

20   Letter to his father, 23 February 1941, ibid.

21   Baxter, M. (ed. Sylvester, M.), *Reliquine Baxteriance 1696*, pp.41, 50–1, 53.

22   Aylmer, G.E., *Rebellion or Revolution*, pp.127, 179 (Oxford, 1986): see reference to 'the volatile (in all likelihood manic depressive) Hugh Peters'.

23   Baxter, op. cit., He said the sectaries were 'not one to twenty throughout the Army'.

24   Communicated by Brigadier Mullin.

25   Summerfield, P., 'Education and Politics in the British Armed Forces in the Second World War', *International Review of Social History* XXXI, 1981.

26   Mackenzie, op. cit., p.231.

27   ibid., p.178.

28   ibid p.320.

29   ibid p.326.

30   ibid p.324.

31   Letter from Montgomery to Grigg, 15 September 1944, Grigg Papers 9/8, Churchill College Archives.

32   Gromyko, A.A. (trans. Shukman, H.), *Memories*, (London, 1989). On the Eastern Front the Germans shot the equivalent of a whole division for indiscipline, defeatism or dereliction of duty. In addition 42,000 were imprisoned for similar offences. Figures for the British Forces numbered only forty deaths. Overy, op. cit., p.22.

33   Letter from General Paget to Grigg, 19 July 1946, including copy of address to Army Educational Course, Beirut, 11 July 1946, Grigg Papers 9/7, Churchill College Archives.

34   Williams, op. cit., p.195.

35   ibid.

36   HMI's Report on Army Education, Middle East Command, 9.11.1945 – 15.2.1946, RAEC Archives.

37   Grigg Papers, op. cit., 19 July 1946.

38   Grigg, *Prejudice and Judgement*, op. cit., p.29.

39   Scarlyn Wilson, op. cit., p.37.

40   Grigg Papers, op. cit., 19 July 1946.

41   Mackenzie, op. cit., p.205.

42   Willans, Major-General H., 'The Progress of Army Education', JAEC XVII, No.4, June 1942.

43   Leese, Major J., 'The AEC and the Second Front', JAEC XIV, No.2, October 1944.

44   *Parliamentary Debates*, House of Lords, 5th Series, Vol.125, cols.699–705.

45   Mackenzie, op. cit., p.306.

46   *The Observer*, 8 October 1944.

47   Seeley, Sir J., *Introduction to Political Science*, p.4 (London, 1911).

48   Chapman, Guy, *A Kind of Survivor*, pp.46, 203 (London, 1975); Coville, Colonel K.R., 'Projects and Experiments: Recreation Handicraft', JAEC XVII, No.3, March 1942.

49   Smith, A. *The Wealth of Nations*, pp.148, 154, 232 (Cambridge, 1955).

50   HMI's Report on Middle East Command, op. cit.

51   Mackenzie, op. cit., p.157.

52   ibid., p.115.

53   ibid.; for Speed and Riddell-Webster see p.253; for Adam and Bellinger see pp.254, 260.

54   Williams, 'Civilian ABCA', *Army Education* XXI, March 1947.

55   Mackenzie, op. cit., p.262.

56   ibid., p.262.

57   Williams, *History*, op. cit., p.192; Scarlyn Wilson, op. cit., p.43 where he tells us that upwards of 120,000 copies of each ABCA bulletin were printed. *The Economist* of 18 December 1943 sounds, however, a warning note. It writes 'the temptation to see army education through somewhat romantic glasses is too seldom resisted. The picture of a great civilian Army pulsing with interest and information on world affairs and civic problems is almost certainly a well-meaning myth. The mass of soldiers, like the mass of citizens, is mostly unmoved and unaffected by matters outside daily work'.

58   HMI's Report on Middle East Command, op. cit.

59   ibid.

60   Chapman, op. cit., p.203.

61   *The Times Educational Supplement*, 17 October 1946.

62   Burke, E., 'Reflections on the Revolution in France', *Everyman*, No.460. Dent, 1955. p.32.

63   President Kalinin, 'Problems of Army Technique', JAEC, June 1943.

64   Butler, Lord R.A.B., *The Art of the Possible*, p.49

Chapter 8 – The Release Period Scheme, 1945–1948

1   *The Army Education Scheme (Release Period)*, W.O. Pamphlet, October 1944. Forward by General Adam.

2   Course for AEC personnel to prepare them for taking part in the Release Scheme, 1944, RAEC Archives.

3   ibid.

4   ibid.

5   Pafford, Major J.H.P., 'Books and Army Education', *Aslib*, 1946. A new W.O. Department was established, run by two officers, one sergeant-instructor and three clerks. It sent out nearly 2,600,000 books; see also Bonney, WOII A.E., 'Books for all. The Army Education Corps' Network of Libraries in the Middle East', JAEC XIX, No.3, May 1945.

6   Course for AEC personnel, op. cit.; Wilson, Colonel C.A., 'Some Thoughts on the Army Education Scheme (Release Period)', JAEC XX, No.4, December 1946.

7   Lloyd, Major-General C., in *The AEC Quarterly Bulletin*, January 1945.

8   Graubert, op. cit.; Rothstein, A., *The Soldiers' Strikes of 1919* (London, 1980).

9   Letter from General Paget to Grigg, 19 July 1940 including his address to Army

Education Course, Beirut, 11 July 1944. Grigg Papers, PJGG 9/7, Churchill College Archives; Summerfield, P., 'Education and Politics in the British Armed Forces in the Second World War', *International Review of Social History* XXVI, 1981; Course for AEC personnel, op. cit.; *The AEC Quarterly Bulletin*, January 1945; Williams, op. cit.; ABCA Handbook; *The Army Education Scheme (Release Period)*, Preface by the Secretary of State for War.

10   Report by HMIs 1946, RAEC Archives.

11   ibid.

12   Letter to Adjutant-General, December 1947, RAEC Archives.

13   Report by HMIs, op. cit.

14   ibid.

15   ibid.

16   Report on Army Education. Middle East Command 9/11/1945 – 15/2/1946, RAEC Archives.

17   ibid.

18   ibid.

19   ibid.

20   Letter from Montgomery, Grigg Papers PJGG 9/6, op. cit.

21   On 3 April 1946 Montgomery wrote to Grigg 'We do not want, nor are we likely to be given, a large Army', see ibid. Nevertheless the Soviet threat to Europe was taken seriously in 1945. However, this threat was thought to be less immediate than the threat in the Middle East. It was believed that deterrence would keep Europe at peace; it was feared that 'mutual vulnerability' might precipitate conflict in the Middle East. cf Paper Summarising Minutes of Chiefs of Staff Committee Meetings, CAB 79 and CAP 80, 1945, RAEC Archives.

22   Crawley, Richard, *The Peloponnesian War Thucydides*. Temple Classes Vol.1., p.139 (Dent, 1903).

23   Macpherson, Major W., 'Awaiting Posting', Memoire in RAEC Archives.

24   Report of HMIs, op. cit.

25   Marshall, Lieutenant Colonel W.P., 'Army Education Work in N.W. Europe, 1944–46', *Torch*, Winter 1978.

26   Report of HMIs in BAOR. They spoke of 'the patchy, discontinuous nature of the provision in some units'.

27   Address by Major-General C. Lloyd, 'Educational Training. Release Period/ Post War', March 1948. RAEC Archives.

28   Baxter, Lieutenant Colonel C.B., 'The Report of a Survey carried out in the North Midland District. December 1947–January 1948', RAEC Archives.

29   Lloyd, Major-General C., 'Consolidated Report on Army Education. October– December 1946', RAEC Archives.

30   Report of HMIs, op. cit.

31   ibid.

32   Burslem, Capt. G.C., 'A Day in the Life of a UEO', *Army Education* XX, No.1, March 1946.

33   'Education and the Armed Forces', Report of a Seminar held at the Royal United

Services Institute for Defence Studies, Wednesday 15 November 1972.

34   Wilson, op. cit.

35   Report of HMIs, op. cit.

36   Wilson, op. cit.

37   Report of HMIs, op. cit.

38   Wilson, op. cit., In this article he quotes the remark made by Sir Philip Morris.

39   Mackenzie, op. cit., p.340; see also 'Education in the ATS', *The Times Educational Supplement*, 24 October, 1942; White, op. cit., pp.119–123.

40   Report of HMIs, op. cit.

41   McNeill, Colonel D.H., 'Formation Colleges', *Torch*, Jubilee Edition 1920–1970. The Formation Colleges at Goettingen and Perugia were located in the universities there. The Corps expressed its thanks by presenting a marble plaque which was placed in the auditorium of the universities recalling that it was here *quod tot milites Britannie doctrinam cum luce in sede hauserunt*; see also Gunner, Colonel G.E., 'The Formation College of the Rhine Army', JAEC XX, 1 March 1946.

42   Report of HMIs, op.cit; Luckhurst, Major K.W. 'Educational Courses in Rome', JAEC, XX, No.4, December 1946. The DAE had emphasised that 'there must be no division between vocational and general education' and the Corps had always recognised that the aim of all its teaching was to give width of view and depth of insight, to develop the ability to analyse, to strengthen the critical faculty and accustom pupils to the weighing of evidence. In matters vocational it had to find a balance between the academic and the practical, between what will help us to live and what is essential if we are to live well, between general culture and vocational training. The Corps was well aware that for all vocational work there is essential supporting academic knowledge, a 'know-why' behind the 'know-how'. It was an important truth on which the Corps was insisting, namely that in a world of rapid technological change, mastery of a single technique will not suffice. It may add to difficulty, some men resist changes that will make old and once lucrative skills no longer useful. What is needed is the adaptable mind which is much more likely to come from understanding the theoretical knowledge that led to the acquisition of the practical skill than from the practical skill itself. The practical skill will always be important but even more important is the broad and general education without which the mental adaptability indispensable in a world of change cannot be acquired. Universities which teach the science not the practice of law, the science not the practice of engineering, the science not the practice of medicine, are not unaware of undergraduate pressure to get on with more vocational matters. Such pressure on the Corps is greater, as is the honour of resisting it. Course for AEC personnel, op. cit.; White, op. cit., p.168.

43   Wilson, op. cit.

44   White, op. cit., p.178.

45   Baxter, Lieutenant Colonel C.B., 'The Report of a Survey carried out in the North Midland District, December 1947–January 1948', RAEC Archives.

46   Williams, ABCA Handbook.

47   Baxter, op. cit.

48   Green, T.H., *The Principles of Political Obligation*, p.167; for his view that 'there is an agency which is not ours' see ibid.; and for his view that 'men's actions may be overruled for good' see ibid., p.134.

49   White, op. cit., p.181.

50   Suckling, B., 'Experiments in Teaching Illiterates', JAEC XVIII, No.1. September 1942.

51   Burgess, Colonel J.T., 'Ten Thousand Tragedies', *Army Quarterly* IV, April–July 1947.

52   ibid.

53   Suckling, op. cit.; Duncan, J., 'Basic Education in the Army', JAEC XIX, No.2, October 1944; White, op. cit., pp.112–115, 181–183.

54   Marshall, H.P., 'AEC Work in North West Europe. 1944–46', *Torch*, Winter 1978.

55   Mullin, Lieutenant Colonel W.S., 'The "Poly" in Burma', JAEC XXI, No.3, September 1947.

56   Mullin, Brigadier W.S., '"Royal" on RAEC', *Torch.*, Spring 1987.

57   *Parliamentary Debates*, 5th Series, Vol.434, col.1526, February 1947.

58   Royle, T., *The Best Years of their Lives; the National Service Experience, 1945–63*, p.21 (London, 1986).

59   Mackenzie, S.P., 'Vox Populi. British Army Newspapers in the Second World War', *Journal of Contemporary History*.

60   Roe, Brigadier F.P., 'Full Circle', *Torch*, Summer 1979

Chapter 9 – The Interim Scheme

1   *Handbook of General Education* 1948; Lloyd, Major-General C., 'The ideas behind the Interim Scheme', *Army Education*, December 1949.

2   Minutes of a Conference of Command Education Officers, 18–19 January 1946, WO 165/85, Part IV, RAEC Archives.

3   White, op. cit., pp.188–9.

4   McKenzie, op. cit., pp.239, 271ff. The change from the Central Advisory Council to the Central Committee and the ending of the Regional Committees occurred with a good deal of avoidable friction and unnecessary heat. Common sense and common interest prevailed and an acceptable relation between the Universities and the Services was again established.

5   Salisbury, Col., Head of Research Branch, RAEC Archives, Undated but after 'second half of 1957' to which it refers.

6   Lloyd, Minutes of a Conference of Command Education Officers, op. cit.

7   Bond, Col. J.J., 'The General Education Scheme, 1945–1970', RAEC Archives; Lloyd, 'The ideas behind the Interim Scheme', op. cit.

8   The Army Education Advisory Board's Views on Examinations, October 1946,

RAEC Archives.

9   The Army Council at this time obviously agreed with Swift who said 'What a Weakness and Presumption it is to reason against the general Humour and Disposition of the World.' Swift, J. (ed. Eddy, W.A.), *Satires and Personal Writings of Jonathan Swift* (London, 1932).

10   Adam, General Sir Ronald, 'The Sequel to ABCA', *Journal of Education* 78, No.919, February 1946.

11   Minutes of a Conference of Command Education Officers, March 1948, RAEC Archives.

12   'Arms and the Man', Course for Senior Officers, Nottingham University, 16–19 January 1950. Lloyd.

13   Lloyd, Minutes of a Conference of Command Education Officers, March 1948, RAEC Archives. This difference was important as the idealists who were very influential at this time did not always have their way. Notes not lacking in realism were to be heard at this time. A paper in the RAEC Archives (R.R. 210 (7) 1952) emphasised that 'the Army is one vast school of instructors, these being its officers, warrant officers and NCOs who would need a sound educational foundation to enable them to do their job which has become more important in view of the complicated nature of modern weapons and of the need to fortify against psychological warfare'. Here was the true note of the Army Education which could not have grated on the ears even of its bitterest critic. This all had to do with meeting legitimate military needs. It almost seemed that Cromwell was safely back in the 17th Century, no doubt happy to think that his mutinous soldiers would no longer be held up as a model for other armies to follow.

14   Virgil, *Georgics* 2, p.51.

15   Salisbury, 'The Historical Significance and Value of the Colchester Scheme', RAEC Archives.

16   Letter to Grigg by PUS MOD, The Grigg Papers, PJGG 12/1, 14 December 1946, Churchill College Archives.

17   *Parliamentary Debates*, House of Commons, 5th Series, Vol.409, col.410, 13 March 1947.

18   Extract from the Seventy-Second Meeting of the Army Council, 31 January 1947, AC/M (47) 2, 4 February 1947. For the idea of an Army Polytechnic see ibid., Memo by Adjutant General, Appendix B.

19   Communicated by Lieutenant-Colonel Peter Reese, the subaltern in question.

20   *Parliamentary Debates*, House of Commons, 5th Series, Vol.409, col.1307, 13 March 1947.

21   Moser, Sir Alan, 'The Need for an Informed Society', August 1990, p.1.

22   White Paper submitted to House of Commons, 1943. For the Army's awareness of its legal obligation under the National Service Act 1940 see paper, General Aims of Army Education, Research Records, 210 (7) 1952.

23   McKenzie, op. cit., pp.267–270. It was Lloyd who insisted that BCA pamphlets no longer be bought by the Army. His colleagues at the Admiralty and Air Ministry, while equally discontented with the pamphlets, were hesitant because

of the political objections all foresaw. Lloyd's view was accepted and the letter he drafted for the Minister was signed. When under pressure from his party colleagues Shinwell ordered the Adjutant-General to continue buying the BCA Bulletins. The Adjutant-General said that as he could find no reason for doing so the Minister would have to supply it himself. Shinwell let the matter rest. The Adjutant-General's reply was of course drawn up by his expert advisers in the DAE. Communicated by Brigadier Mullin.

24 Lloyd, *Army Education* XXI, No.2, June 1947.

25 Extract from the Seventy-Second Meeting of the Army Council, op. cit.

26 The Report of the Army Manpower Committee, 1948, RAEC Archives.

27 McKenzie, op. cit., p.263.

28 Payne, Col. T.W., 'The Soldiers' Education Scheme', RAEC Archives.

29 Editorial, JRAEC XXIII, No.4, December 1949. Two years earlier another editor had written of the Interim Scheme that it came to the RAEC 'as the fulfilment of many hopes and gave promise of unparalleled opportunity'. He said that he had 'read with some trepidation' the curtailment of national service since it might adversely affect those hopes and that opportunity', *Army Education* XXI, No.2, June 1947.

30 *The Handbook*, op. cit., p.29.

31 ACI 1247, 31 October 1945.

32 'Arms and the Man' course, op. cit.

33 Lloyd, Liaison Letters 1948–56 in AEI/BM/63, 30 November 1948, Modification to the Army Education Scheme (Interim Period) 5 May 1949, RAEC Archives; Lloyd, *Army Education* XXIII, No.4, December 1949. In 1946 the purpose of Army Education was said to be 'the production of the well-informed soldier-citizen'. WO32/12007, *The Future of Army Education*, 13 May 1946, RAEC Archives. In 1949 the teaching of citizenship was absorbed into the General Education syllabus which aimed to provide 'the greatest possible practical connection with soldiering'. Lloyd, *Army Education*, op. cit. By 1952 the aim of Army Education had become 'increasing the soldier's understanding of his task as a soldier, strengthening his faith in the ideals for which he may have to fight, reinforcing his pride in his Regiment and in his country and her achievements and inspiring confidence in himself, his weapons, his leaders and his allies to obtain victory in the event of war'. *The General Aim of Army Education*, 1952, Appendix G 1,16, RAEC Archives. The *Manual of Education* 1954 states the aim of general education as being 'to develop the soldier's mental alertness, intellectual capacity and initiative to heighten his response to training and to help him cope effectively with the military situation in which he finds himself'. The dreamers still dreamed but the cold winds were blowing strongly. In Korea and the Malayan jungles dreamers did not thrive.

34 Letter to Grigg, 3 April 1946, 11/1, Churchill College Archives.

35 White, op. cit., p.189; McKenzie, op. cit., p.278. The pamphlets bore 'no trace' of the Brave New World philosophy which had underlain so much of the material produced by ABCA. They focused exclusively on the NATO alliance and why

we were fighting in Korea.

36   Quoted in 'The Consolidated Quarterly Report on Army Education. January to March 1947', RAEC Archives.

37   ibid.

38   ibid.

39   ibid.

40   Duff, Major-General, 'The Shortage of Recruits', *The Army Quarterly* LVIII, No.2, April 1949.

41   ibid.

42   'Proposed Scheme for Current Affairs in the Army'. Undated but probably part of agenda for Conference of Command Education Officers, 1956, RAEC Archives.

43   Conference of Command Education Officers, 1956, RAEC Archives.

44   Baxter, Lieutenant-Colonel C.B., 'Attitudes Towards Army Education. The Report of a Survey carried on in the North Midland District. December 1947– January 1948'; Letter from Lloyd to Adjutant-General, December 1947, RAEC Archives.

45   ibid.

46   Conference of Command Education Officers. July 1959, RAEC Archives.

47   'The General Aim of Army Education', 1952' op. cit.

48   1961 Paper for DAE's Conference of Command Education Officers BR4/1961 (AEI), RAEC Archives.

49   Salusbury, 'The Historical Significance of the Colchester Experiment'.

50   Communicated by Brigadier Mullin.

51   Research Branch, 'Matters in hand along with Certain Recommendations Concerning the Future of the Corps Paper to CEOs Conference 1954', 8 April 1954, RAEC Archives.

52   Moser, op. cit., pp.31–2.

53   CEO (p.7) 1959, Conference of Command Education Officers 1959, RAEC Archives.

54   Salusbury, op. cit.

55   ibid. In the early 1960s a comprehensive scheme of education which began with the needs of the recruit up to what was required for promotion to Warrant Officer was hammered out. An effort was made to provide for the needs for the different Corps and Arms and to allow for a degree of local assessment in determining fitness for promotion. It was too ambitious and complicated and it made too great a demand on the soldier's time. Yet it is another indication of the more realistic note to be heard occasionally at this time.

56   Salusbury, op. cit.

57   Bond, Colonel R.J., 'The General Education Scheme 1945–1970', RAEC Archives.

58   James, Senior Commander C.M., 'Education and the ATS', JAEC XVII, No.4, June 1942. 'The great inlet by which a colour for oppression has entered into the world is by one man's pretending to determine concerning the happiness of

another.' Acton, Lord, *Lectures on the French Revolution*, p.30 (London, 1925).

59   Hawkins and Brimble, op. cit., p.383

Chapter 10 – The Non-Interim Scheme Activities of the RAEC in the Conscript Army

1   White, op. cit., p.217. Where there were no Army secondary schools but there were local secondary schools, as in Nairobi, Cairo, Hong Kong, Jamaica and Paris, fees for attendance at these were refunded.

2   ibid., p.218.

3   ibid., p.214. Williams, *Tommy Atkins' Children*, op. cit., p.155 shows how helpful and hardworking the RAEC and the Queen's Army Schoolmistresses were at this time. Schools were established in Japan for British, Australian, New Zealand and American children. Only one sixth of the pupils at these schools were British; over half the teachers were Queen's Army Schoolmistresses and RAEC sergeants.

4   White. op. cit., p.193.

5   Royle, op. cit., p.61.

6   Gadd, Major-General A.L., 'Remembrances of Things Past', *Torch*, Winter 1948; Macfarlane, Brigadier J.M., 'Language Training', *Torch*, Summer 1992; Moss, Major B.V., 'Vee Haff Vays', *Torch*, Winter 1980. The RAEC pioneered a revolutionary breakthrough in the traditional forms of language study. It was found that the traditional language teaching did not meet the immediate need. It was necessary to develop intensive courses based on what were called 'language laboratories'. Electrical connections were so developed in these that all attending the laboratories could work as a class or, by the turn of a switch, teacher and pupils could speak privately. The University Grants Committee commented on this development 'the Universities and the country as a whole have reason to be grateful for the uncovenanted benefits of this service training'. White, op. cit., pp.237–8.

7   White, p.183; HMI Reports on Corsham. While acknowledging the excellence of the work done at Corsham Major-General Foxton nevertheless felt too much time was being wasted on it. 'I can see many other opportunities for useful work which my chaps could do were they not ham-strung by the present out-dated system', he said. If the Army had to accept illiterates or near-illiterates, remedial education, he thought, should take place during basic training and no soldier should go on to full training until he had reached the required educational standard. Interview with Major General Foxton.

8   Major-General Gadd was the initiator of officer resettlement. He had a questionnaire sent to officers who had retired in the last three years; 90% said they would have liked advice. Communicated by Brigadier Fowler.

9   Fowler, Major A.L., 'Mons Company, R.M.A. Sandhurst', JRAEC XXIII, No. 4, December 1949; Fowler, Colonel A.L., 'The Army School of Education', *Torch*, Jubilee Edition 1920–1970.

10   White, op. cit., p.190.

11   ibid., pp.190–91; ibid., p.195 for Major Meerendonk and 'the Hillman'.

12   ibid., p.192; Grimsey, Major G.E., 'Looking Back on Korea', *Army Education* XXVI, No.2, September 1952.

13   Stockbridge, Lieutenant-Colonel W.S., 'The Army Library Service' in *Torch*, Jubilee Edition 1920–1970. The Prince Consort Library remained in royal possession until Queen Victoria's death. It was taken over by the War Office then. It became the responsibility of the RAEC in July 1952 and remains in their custody today.

14   'Reading in the Army. A Report on a Survey of the Reading Habits and Interests of Men and Women in the Army Conducted in 1954', RAEC Archives. To the question 'Do you generally have to be forced into reading by bad weather, illness, travel or 'waiting?', 59% of the men and 12% of the women answered 'Yes'.

15   Communicated by Brigadier Mullin.

16   Communicated by Major W. Lynam.

17   Turner, Lieutenant-Colonel P.J., 'The RAEC in Egypt', *Army Education* XXVI, No. 2, September 1952.

18   Command Report Malta, 5617, RAEC Archives.

19   Interview with Major-General Foxton.

20   Fuller, JAEC I, No. 1, January 1924.

21   Wavell, Field-Marshal Lord, 'Minerva's Owl', op. cit.

22   The author is the unrepentant examiner referred to.

23   DAE's Conference of Command Education Officers 1959. The Charter of the RAEC CEO Cp.11 1959, RAEC Archives.

24   ibid.

25   Index No. RR 210 (7) 1952, RAEC Archives. 'It has long been an accepted principle in the British Army that every member of it shall be capable, in war, of assuming the responsibility of at least one rank higher than he holds in peace and that higher rank must be matched by a corresponding increase in educational attainments'. The British Army was content to call this an 'accepted principle'; the German Army did better – it acted upon it.

26   Baxter, op. cit., Baxter added something that ought not to be forgotten. He found many opposed to the Interim Scheme because it interfered with their military duties and therefore they would have to work extra time to get these done. A cook told him 'when a man has been on duty since 0430 hours it is a big strain for him to finish work at 1400 hours, and then attend school for another 2½ hours'.

27   Royle, op. cit., p.62.

28   Communicated by Colonel Roy Fairclough.

29   Communicated by Lieutenant-Colonel Peter Reese, the then subaltern referred to.

30   Communicated by Brigadier Lawrence Fowler.

Chapter 11 – Education in the New Regular Army

1   'Report on the Education of the Young Soldiers', 16 February 1979, RAEC
     Archives.
2   Halifax, Marquis of (ed. J.P. Kenyon), 'The Anatomy of an Equivalence',
     Halifax's Collected Works, p.143 (London, 1969).
3   A/43/ED/5130. (D.A.Ed.), 14 October 1974, RAEC Archives.
4   Simpson. K., 'The Art of War', RAEC Archives.
5   Communicated by Major-General Foxton.
6   Communicated by Lieutenant-Colonel C. Coplestone.
7   Communicated by Major W. Lynam.
8   Communicated by Captain C. James.
9   Communicated by Major-General Trythall.
10   'The Executive Committee of the Army Council', discussed in DAE's
     Conference of Command Education Officers 1959; The Charter of the RAEC,
     RAEC Archives.
11   'The Army's Future Requirements', paper by the Adjutant-General; ibid.
12   Communicated by Major-General Foxton.
13   DAE's Conference for Command Education Officers 1959, RAEC Archives.
     Payne, Colonel T.W., 'The Soldiers' Education Scheme', *Torch* Commemorative
     Edition, Summer 1992.
14   Communicated by Brigadier Mullin.
15   Minutes of the DAE's Annual Conference of Command Education Officers
     1979, RAEC Archives, CAP 1970 p.198.
16   In the Miller Report on Boys' Units training, it was said, 'too much emphasis
     was placed on quantity rather than quality'; see also Wood, Major, 'The Future
     of the Junior Army', *British Army Review* No. 91, 1989; Bowyer, Major, 'The
     Young Soldier', *Torch* Jubilee Edition, 1920–1970.
17   The Donaldson Report on Boy Entrants, RAEC Archives; Bramley, Major W.,
     'Survey of Educational Provision in Junior Entry Units: Report of Working
     Group B', 14 February 1979; Bowyer, op cit.
18   Communicated by Colonel Fairclough.
19   Communicated by Brigadier Mullin.
20   Minutes of DAE's Annual Conference of Command Education Officers, 1979,
     RAEC Archives.
21   HMI's Report on Junior Army Education in the 1980s, RAEC Archives.
22   The Committee on the Integration of Technical and General Education in
     Apprentice Schools which was set up in January 1958 recommended that
     Apprentices should follow four courses of study, ONC, GCE, City and Guilds
     and the Army Certificate of Education Senior Test, this being equivalent to, and
     giving exemption from, the Army Certificate of Education First Class. The
     Command Education Officers Conference of 1959 was told 'this recommendation
     was being implemented'. See HMI's Report on Junior Education in the 1980s,
     RAEC Archives.

23   The Donaldson Report on Boy Entrants, op. cit.; Bramley, op. cit.

24   Communicated by Colonel Fairclough. He was sure that stubborn attachment
      to old ways and old values which left no opportunity for new endeavour would
      not have been acceptable to the Army. He stressed that the functional approach
      to education was still an approach to education and that the academic approach
      to education was not leading there since few soldiers were attracted by it and
      most were careful to keep away from it., 'We were not blind to the consequences',
      he said, 'and knew our educational influence on the individual soldier would be
      lessened. We inevitably began to edge our academic inclinations aside' he added.
      'We never doubted the value of the Army Certificates of Education or EPC but
      knew that increasingly the rest of the Army did question their value and the
      time and manpower spent on them. We were at that time led to believe that the
      schools gave pupils all they needed for certain levels of employment in the
      Forces and it was convenient for some to argue that the RAEC was no longer
      required.' He knew how this changing role could not but affect the Corps. 'Our
      changing role', he said, 'and these new tasks we developed changed our
      uniqueness as teachers and educationalists and this is a pity. I always saw myself
      as a military educationalist and my strength as a Staff Officer Education in
      Arborfield lay in the identification of education weaknesses which when
      corrected led to a technical development of the apprentice which would not
      have been possible without us being present'. 'There was, and indeed still is',
      he added, 'a danger in our more functional orientations.'

25   Communicated by Captain James.

26   ibid.

27   ibid.

28   ibid.

29   ibid.

30   ibid.

31   Minutes of the DAE's Annual Conference of Command Education Officers
      held at the Army School of Education, 1–5 July 1963, RAEC Archives.
      Lieutenant-Colonel Washtell said 'We had to remember that in wartime most
      Warrant Officers would be promoted to commissioned rank. The ability to think
      quickly is essential to good leadership.'

32   Bramley, op. cit.

33   Communicated by Colonel Fairclough.

34   Bramley, op. cit.

35   Fuller, J.C., *Journal of Army Education*, No. 1, January 1924.

36   Wavell, op. cit.

37   The Howard-English Report, RAEC Archives.

38   Papers concerning Howard-English Report in RAEC. Archives.

39   ibid.

40   ibid.

41   Communicated by Chief of the Defence Staff, Marshal of the Royal Air Force
      Sir Neil Cameron.

42   'The Regular Commissions Course; its length and Contents and its Relation to the Junior Officers' Education Scheme', CAROT 2471, undated, RAEC Archives.

43   ibid.

44   ibid.

45   ibid.

46   McCrum, M., *Thomas Arnold – Headmaster, A Reassessment*, p.57 (Oxford).

47   Brigadier Frankcom was Command Education Officer, Southern Command from 1958 to 1960. He was in Aldershot when the Aldershot Scheme which was subsequently extended throughout Southern Command was begun. During this time many Staff/Promotion courses were run at Oxford too.

48   The aim was 'to provide a continuous and progressive course of education from Commissioning through to the Staff/Promotion Examination. 'This was sought by improving the standard of written English among Junior Officers ... and teaching them to marshal facts, to reason logically and to express concise and coherent conclusions.' HQ Southern Command paper dated 18 September 1968, RAEC Archives. In the following discussion the DAE said the Regular Commissions Course was intended to be the foundation course in a system of military education extending from the RMAS to the Staff/Promotion examination but that at present its relationship to the Junior Officers Education Scheme was nebulous. It was most important, he stressed, it should be so related.

49   Communicated by Captain James.

50   Bryce, Viscount J.R., *The Holy Roman Empire*, p.509 (London, 1928).

51   Cabley, Major, 'Officer Training in the ARA and Soviet Ground Forces' in the *Army Quarterly and Defence Journal* 115, No.4, October 1985.

52   'Officer Training in Foreign Armies', CAROT/G/73A/ 3 September 1973, RAEC Archives.

53   ibid.

54   Atkins, Lieutenant-Colonel B.M., 'The Army School of Training Support: past, present and future', *Torch*, Summer 1996; 'Review of the Training Support Functions within the Army', RAEC Archives; AGA Vol. 1, Chapter 17, Training Support 109, March 1994, RAEC Archives; 'The Systems Approach to Training in the Army', RAEC Archives; Mackay, Colonel A.E. and Flower-Smith, Major M.A., 'Instructional Technology and Training Support', *Torch*, Commemorative Edition, Summer 1992.

55   Mackay and Flower-Smith, op. cit.

56   Minutes of the DAE's Annual Conference of Command Education Officers held at the Army School of Education 1–5 July 1963. 'In such a method of teaching', it was said, 'machines were more effective than teachers.'

57   Mackay and Flower-Smith. op cit.

58   ibid.

59   'The IRA Bomb at Eltham', 14 May 1990, in *Torch*, Summer 1990.

60   Communicated by Major-General Foxton.

61   Macfarlane, op cit.

62 Moss, Major B.W., op. cit.

63 ibid.

64 Aston, Major P.G., 'Education in the Brigade of Gurkhas. 1957–1973', paper in
    RAEC Archives. Recruits to the Brigade of Gurkhas came from two Recruiting
    Centres in Nepal, Paklikawa in the West and Dharan in the East. Few were
    literate in Nepali and none could speak English. Classes were conducted in
    Roman Gurkhali, the then *lingua franca* of the Brigade. The RAEC had done
    the pioneering work in developing Roman Gurkhali before it became an all-
    officer Corps. There were five Recruit Training Companies in the Depot and in
    each was an RAEC Sergeant or Staff Sergeant and five or six Gurkha Education
    Instructors. There was one RAEC Warrant Officer and a Gurkha Staff Sergeant
    in the Depot Administrative Company. On joining their battalions soldiers would
    continue working through the Education syllabus and it was not uncommon for
    soldiers on operations to continue working for their certificates while waiting
    in ambush positions., 'All the Gurkha instructors were incredibly keen', an
    RAEC officer said. 'In the evenings when I walked round the lines I would find
    them in tented classrooms repeating the day's work by the light of hurricane
    lamps. It was I believe the only unit in the British Army where Unit Orders
    forbade recruits to get up until a certain hour. The Commandant was disturbed
    by the instructors' habit of rousing recruits at some unearthly hour to put in
    extra training before the first official parade'. This work with Gurkhas was
    considered of the highest importance as they formed a highly important part of
    the Army. It was not the only RAEC work with non-UK troops which brought
    it kudos. Since 1950 students from seventy-seven countries have participated in
    the various courses on offer at Beaconsfield. Between 1989 and 1999 200 Turkish
    officers will have attended six-months courses at the Defence School of
    Languages. There was something else too of great value to Army and nation
    alike. The Corps left behind it in the developing countries a general educational
    scheme to ensure that a basic standard of literacy and of general knowledge
    could be developed there. It established a Corps of educational instructors which
    would eventually take over the bulk of this work including the teaching of English
    on a large scale. In the 1960s RAEC officers transferred or were seconded to
    the armies of Tanzania, Kenya and Uganda. Their pupils played a considerable
    role in the development of their countries. The overseas graduates of Oxbridge
    have not always been cherished in their memory, as witness Bose, the leader of
    the Indian Nationalists who joined the invading Japanese armies. The RAEC,
    too, does not look with great pride on its pupils Idi Amin and Colonel Gadaffi.
    Murray, Lieutenant-Colonel P.S., 'The Corps and Non-UK Troops', *Torch*,
    Commemorative Edition, Summer 1992.

65 DAE's Conference of Command Education Officers, 1961, op. cit.

66 The Collected Works of Ralph Waldo Emerson. Vol V. p. 82. op. cit.

67 DAE's Conference of Command Education Officers. 1961. op. cit.

68 Communicated by Major-General Howell.

69 Wright, W.A. (ed.), *English Works of Roger Ascham*, p.198 (Cambridge, 1970).

70   Communicated by Brigadier Mullin.
71   ibid.
72   Communicated by Major-General Howell.
73   Swift, L., 'The Library Service', *Torch* Commemorative Edition, Summer 1992.
74   Howard, M., 'Army Education', *The Times Literary Supplement*, 30 May 1975

Chapter 12 – Education in the Contemporary Army

1   Communicated by Major-General Foxton.
2   Communicated by Brigadier Mullin.
3   Communicated by Major-General Trythall.
4   Communicated by Colonel Fairclough.
5   Communicated by Major-General J. S. Lee.
6   Communicated by Major-General C. A. Kinvig.
7   The Tillard Committee which reported in autumn 1971 recommended that all
      officer candidates, whether for short-term or regular commissions, should do
      six months' military training at Sandhurst after which they would be
      commissioned. Those seeking regular commissions would return for a further
      six months' Regular Commissions Course of which between thirteen and eighteen
      weeks would be devoted to 'military-related academic studies'. The Sandhurst
      Academic Council was outraged at this, calling it the end of Sandhurst as an
      important educational institution. The Academic Council was even more outraged
      when only two years after the introduction of the Regular Commission Course
      in March 1973 which laid it down that 186 periods be devoted to War Studies
      and a further 102 to International Affairs, it was decided in March 1975 that
      these would both have to be covered in 175 periods. The bitterness occasioned
      by the imposition on Sandhurst of a much tighter and fuller programme which
      left no times for sports and relaxation is easily understandable. 'Comments of
      the Sandhurst Academic Advisory Council on the CAROT proposals. Paper
      submitted 1974', RAEC Archives. The Sandhurst Advisory Council was made
      up of dons and headmasters from a variety of Universities and Schools. The
      Director of Army Education was not a member of it.
8   ibid.
9   Communicated by Major-General Foxton.
10   Paper submitted by Sandhurst Academic Council, 1974, op. cit.
11   PQS Review Working Party Final Report, D/AET/12/19/1/AT4, July 1979,
      RAEC Archives.
12   The Review of Officer Training and Education (ROTE) Report.
13   Communicated by Major-General Foxton. He thought this was their belief. If it
      was it, was not shared by the ROTE committee which was concluded in 1985
      and chaired by Major-General Rougier of 'Sandhurst Today'. 'The ROTE Report:
      A Synopsis', RAEC Archives.
14   Wilson, D.E. (ed.), *The Collected Works of Ralph Waldo Emerson* V, English

Traits, p.110.

15   Deakin, S., 'The British Army and Society in the 1980s', *British Army Review* 91, April 1989.

16   ibid.

17   Ascham, R., *English Works*, op. cit., 'Learning teacheth more in one yeare than experience in twentie, and learning teacheth safelie, when experience maketh more miserable than wise. He hasardeth more that wacseth wise by experience. An unhappie Master he is that is made cunning by manie shipwreckes. A miserable merchant that is neither richer or wiser but after some banknoutes. It is costlie wisdom that is bought by experience.'; *The Scholemaster* p.196.

18   PQS Working Party Report, op. cit.

19   ibid.

20   Communicated by the tutor in question, one of the writer's pupils in the Fitzwilliam courses for PQS tutors.

21   Fowler, Major L., 'A new development in Army Education: the Mons Company', JAEC XXIII, No.4, December 1949.

22   Communicated by Major-General Kinvig.

23   Communicated by Major-General Trythall.

24   Communicated by Major-General Ryan.

25   Burke, E., Speech in House of Commons, 11 February 1780.

26   Thucydides (trans. R. Crawley), *Peloppenesian War*, p.224, The Temple Classics, (London, 1903). 'In peace and prosperity states and individuals have better sentiments because they do not find themselves suddenly confronted with imperious necessities; but war takes away the easy supply of daily wants, and so proves a rough master that brings most men's characters to a level with their fortunes.'

27   Reese, Lieutenant-Colonel P., *Home Coming Heroes: An Account of the Reassimilation of British Military Personnel into Civilian Life*, p.10 (London, 1992).

28   Communicated by Major-General Trythall.

29   Communicated by Major K. O. Fox, the officer in question.

30   Atkins, Lieutenant-Colonel B.M., 'The Army School of Training Support: past, present and future', *Torch*, Summer 1996; 'Review of the Training Support Function within the Army', RAEC Archives; AGAI Vol 1, Chapter 17, Training Support 109, March 1994, RAEC Archives; 'The Systems Approach to Training in the Army' op. cit.; Mackay and Flower-Smith, op. cit.

31   'Review of the Training Support Function within the Army', op. cit.

32   'Training Support: the 1984 View. Training Organisation', RAEC Archives.

33   Ascham, op. cit., p.199.

34   Murray, G., 'Religio Grammatici: the religion of a man of letters', in *Essays and Addresses*, p.11 (London, 1922). 'On these matters', he said, 'I cannot argue but only feel.'

35   Ascham, op. cit., p.196.

36   *The Observer*, 7 November 1992.

37   Communicated by Major-General Lee.
38   Communicated by Major-General Kinvig.
39   Communicated by Major-General Trythall.
40   Communicated by Major-General Kinvig.
41   Pilley, Major D.V., 'Operation Corporate. To the South Atlantic with the Task
     Force (April–September 1982)', RAEC Archives; Coupar, Major M.A., 'To the
     South Atlantic with the RAEC April–September 1982', RAEC Archives.
42   Macfarlane, Colonel J.M., 'A Letter to the Editor', in *Torch*, Winter 1991; Robins,
     Captain S., 'Letters from the Front'; Barnes, Major A.D. and Bristow, Major
     C.D., 'The Second Eighty Days of Operation Granby'; Mahoney, Captain M.W.
     'Operation Granby'; Nichols, Major D.J.G., 'OP. Granby's German Dimension';
     Williams, Captain P., 'O.P. Haven – The Gulf Sequal; Holley, Lieutenant W.,
     'An Innocent in Iraq', *Torch*, Winter 1994.
43   Anglim, S.J., *The Royal Army Educational Corps in the Gulf Conflict of 1990–
     91*, Directorate of Educational and Training Services (Army), RAEC Archives.
44   Kerslake, Major, 'The RAEC in Northern Ireland, 1982–83', *Torch*, Summer
     1983, vol.1, no.1.

Chapter 13 – Retrospect and Prospect

1   Kinvig, Major-General, letter of 18 December 1990 to RAEC Members.
2   Tweedsmuir, Lord, *Canadian Occasions*, p.112 (London, 1940).
3   Kinvig, op. cit.
4   Disraeli shared the scorn of the French, 'A practical man', he wrote, 'is a man
    who practices the blunders of his predecessors.' Moneypenny, W.T. and Buckle,
    G.L., *Life of Disraeli; First Earl of Beaconsfield*, p.675 (London, 1929).
5   *The Times*, 1 January 1977.
6   In Vietnam such was the American insistence on freedom of information and
    such the American capacity to take things to extremes that the media there
    became 'a highly credible, never-tiring political opposition, a maverick third
    party which never need face the sobering experience of governing'. Hallin,
    D.C., *The Uncensured War: the Media and Vietnam*, p.42 (New York, 1986).
    The American military defeated the North Vietnamese forces in the Tet offensive
    while building up the South Vietnamese Army. But the American media, and in
    particular television, turned against the war. The effect on the morale of American
    troops was shattering. GIs printed on their battle-dresses and painted on their
    helmets initials expressing their hatred of and their contempt for their own Army,
    conveying in the language of the gutter the sentiments appropriate to it and its
    accompanying practice 'fragging', or the shooting in the back of officers and
    NCOs. Hasek, J., 'Military Isolation and the Media: the Vietnam Case', *The
    Army Quarterly*, October 1985. For the Falklands see Woodward, Admiral J.,
    One Hundred Days, pp.109–113, 276ff, 324 (London, 1992); Hooper, op. cit.,
    pp.155–160. For the Gulf War see notes to Chapter 12. For the view of American

journalists that in war 'that their main task was to seek out and report' the horrors which are being committed in our name, 'to find the bit of right on the other side' and for their view that 'British journalists have not been sufficiently critical of British troops' see *The Sunday Telegraph*, 3 February 1991.

7   Cockerell, M., *Live from No.10*, p.269ff (London, 1980); Barnett, S. and Curry, A., *The Battle for the BBC*, p.160ff (London, 1994); Franklin, R., *Recharging Politics: Political Communications in Britain's Media Democracy*, p.130ff (London, 1994); Harrie, C. and Clarke, S., *Fuzzy Noosters*, p.11 (London, 1994); Annan, 'Broadcasting and Politics' in *Journal of Communication* 28, No.3, 1978.

8   Woodward, op. cit., p.299. The BBC published the failure of bombs dropped on HM Ships to explode. Two days later those dropped on HMS *Coventry* sank her. Many will wonder, as he did, if the Argentinians would have known of this fault in their bombs and have corrected it but for the BBC revealing it. He reminds us that 'Argentinian generals and admirals admitted after the war that they had gained ninety per cent of all their intelligence from the British press', see ibid., p.112. He had wanted to keep the joining up of the Battle Group and the Amphibians Group secret until after the landing but this was announced by the BBC. 'Not for the first time', he wrote in exasperation, 'they have blown our cover.' The BBC announced that the attack on Goose Green in which Colonel Jones was killed was imminent and Woodward comments 'there are still some who believe that the BBC was responsible for the Argentinian 'ambush' in which Colonel Jones and many others died. 'The Commanding Officer of 2 Para wanted to sue the BBC for manslaughter', see ibid., p.239. A still photograph of a Rapier anti-aircraft missile which was better than anything that could have been obtained by Argentinian low-level photo reconnaissance was available for Argentinian study by courtesy of the British press, as was an interview with a Harrier pilot who had just flown a combat mission and who discussed the best tactics to employ against Argentinian fighter aeroplanes. The clash between the interests of the media and the Armed Services here is obvious. War Correspondents have never been beloved of the Armed Services, as witness Russell in the Crimean War. For War Correspondents wish to reveal what Commanders want to conceal. Sometime, as was the case with Russell, that is to the advantage of the Services. Woodward did not find it so in the Falklands. He said of the journalists there 'they were outsiders looking on; we were insiders watching out. We just operated on completely different mind nets', see ibid., p.112. He added what could never have been said of Russell: 'Theirs was a mixture of "It doesn't matter much who wins or loses as long as we report it fairly and as in our judgment we see it".' Alistair Burnet thought it was 'natural that there should be conflict between the Armed Services and journalism', see Hooper, op. cit., p.211. It is in the interests of both to make it as little as possible; it is in the interests of neither to deny its existence. Technology has now made that conflict absolute in major war. Journalists now have the facility to transmit pictures from the battlefield, thus bypassing editorial processes and making military censorship impossible. Could any Commander allow revelation of what

might ensure his defeat to the enemy?

9   *R. v. the Secretary of State for the Home Department, Briand and Others*, 7
      February 1991, The Law Reports 191, House of Lords Committee of the Privy
      Council and Peerage Cases 1, London.

10   Believing that the Falklands War did not endanger the security of the country,
      that many were opposed to it, that as the Labour Party was in disarray and that
      as its leaders supported the Government those opposed to the war would go
      unrepresented if the BBC did not represent them, it took on itself the task of so
      doing. How it knew this duty was imposed on it and that the Labour Party was
      so demoralised by electoral defeat that in supporting the Government it could
      now be deemed so incapable of discharging its opposition responsibilities as to
      justify a body which did not share its accountability to the people usurping its
      role, were questions it forbore to say.

11   Lord Annan had pointed out in the 1977 Committee he chaired on broadcasting
      that while journalists owe no duty to the elected government they owe the same
      loyalty to the state, particularly in time of war, that all citizens do. In his 1982
      Report to the House of Commons on the BBC, he made plain his view that in
      the Falklands War it had not acknowledged this truth. Whereupon Ludovic
      Kennedy accused him of being 'prejudiced and biased .... hysterical, intemperate
      and obsessional'. Annan's view that the BBC had been blind to the truth that
      statements which 'discredited not merely the politician but the whole concept
      of government, without which a society cannot exist, destroyed public confidence
      in the nation in a peculiarly poisonous way' echoed Chief Justice Camden's
      findings in a famous case, *Entick v Carrington*, in 1765 which is generally
      regarded as one of the great bulwarks of the liberties of England. 'All civilised
      governments', he said, 'have punished calumny with severity, and with reason.
      For these compositions debauch the manners of the people. They enervate the
      authority of government. They provoke and excite the passions of the people
      against their rulers and the rulers often times against their people. Liberty became
      in consequence in the utmost danger because tyranny, bad as it is, is better than
      anarchy and the worst of governments is more tolerable than no government at
      all.' Grant Robertson, Sir C., *Select Statutes, Cases and Documents to illustrate
      English Constitutional History, 1660–1892*, p.472 (London, 1943); The Annan
      Reports of 1977 and 1982; Barnett and Curry, op. cit.

12   Reese, Lieutenant-Colonel P., *Home Coming Heroes*, pp.240–1 (London, 1992).

13   What can harm can also benefit. The mass media, while occasioning problems
      for the Armed Services, also provides them great opportunities. 'The Army
      itself', *The Economist* wrote, 'accepts that television is the best recruiting officer'.
      Important documentaries, *Sailor*, filmed on board HMS *Ark Royal* which was
      an outstanding success, *Warship*, *The New Officers*, a Panorama Special shown
      on 15 September 1975, *Spearhead*, viewed by 10 million people, and *Fighter
      Pilot* brought the Armed Services great and favourable publicity. These
      documentaries would not have been possible without the full cooperation of the
      Forces, which did not shrink from a 'warts and all' presentation of their lifestyles.

That cooperation did not lack imagination and it is interesting that it was the Army, calling on its experience in Ulster, which took the lead in establishing Unit Press officers and in designing a training course which they had to attend. Hooper, op. cit., p.194.

14   Speech at the Mansion House, 24 March 1944.

15   Conference of Command Education Officers, 1959, RAEC Archives.

16   'The Army's Future Requirement for Developmental Education and Options for Delivery. A Note by the Secretary', ECAB/P/1 (95) 22, dated 6 September 1995, RAEC Archives.

17   Independent Review of the Armed Forces Manpower, Career and Remuneration Structures (The Bett Report).

18   Annex A to ECAB/P/1/(95) 22, op. cit.

19   Bett Report, op. cit.

20   Bacon, Sir F., Lord Verulam, *The Essays of Francis Bacon, Lord Verulam*, p.74 (London, 1907).

21   *The Complete Works of Montaigne* (translated by Donald M. Frame), p.731 (Lexington).

22   Moser, op. cit., pp.31–2.

23   'The Army's Future Requirement. A Paper by the AG', op. cit. One hundred and fifty years ago we were admitting our inferiority to continental armies in educational matters and we still are. If soldiers are unable or unwilling to reach the educational standard deemed desirable they could, if recruiting were satisfactory, be discharged. But such is the shortage of recruits that since October 1995 soldiers in the Infantry, the Armoured Corps and the Artillery have been paid bonuses for serving for a further two years and for bringing in recruits. It being essential to make the best of what is available, greater effort is now made to raise the recruit's educational standard in his initial period of training; see note 41, Chapter 11.

24   Confucius tells us the price we must pay if we want this. His ideal state was 'the State of Great Similarity'. In it 'a public and common spirit ruled all under the sky'. If this was not achieved men would find themselves living in 'the State of Small Tranquillity', this being made tolerable only by observance of the rules of propriety, by which men must be guided back to 'the State of Great Similarity'. Before that state can be reached a proper government is necessary based on the 'Five Social Relationships with their moral responsibilities, the relationship between ruler and subject, father and son, elder and younger brother, husband and wife, friend and friend'. Only when these are what they should be can we hope to enter 'the State of Great Similarity'. We may express the price to be paid for such a transition somewhat differently today; in essence it remains the same.

25   'The Army's Future Requirements. A Paper by the AG', op. cit.

26   So the great concern with morale which so furthered Army Education in the Second World War and in the immediate post-war years, and then, in the closing 1970s and 1980s when time spent on it was deemed to be at the expense of the

regiment, weakened it, now once again came to its assistance.

27   'The Army's Future Requirements. A Paper by the A-G', op. cit.

28   The Bett Review, op. cit.

29   'The Army's Future Requirements. A Paper by the A-G', op. cit.

30   ibid., Appendix D.

31   ibid.

32   'The Army's Future Requirements Paper by the Secretary, ECAB', op. cit., A letter to *The Times* 2 April 1997 asserted that the culture of the Forces must be changed to bring it in line with the culture of the rest of society. If this were done both Education for Commitment and the high reputation of the Army would soon be heard of no more.

33   *The Daily Telegraph*, 5 February 1997.

34   'The Army's Future Requirements', op. cit., Appendix 1 to Annex B.

35   PQS Review Working Party Final Report, D/DAT/12/19/1/AT, 4 July 1979.

36   ibid., 'The ability to write simple, clear and concise English was lacking in graduates too', the Report said. It was this inability of science graduates that was first noticed but this report found arts graduates were often no better. It would be interesting to know whether in the last two centuries the Army has more frequently insisted on the need for a more educated soldier to cope with advancing technology or on the necessity of improving the officer's capacity to write straightforward and intelligible English. Fortescue wrote at the beginning of the 20th Century 'Although I have encountered cases of officers, even of high rank whose letters showed symptoms of illiteracy, I should say that the officer of a century ago wrote better and corrector English than the officer of the present.' He might have found difficulty in finding an historical comparison with officer literacy today. The persistence of the problem, the persistence of the acknowledgement of it, the persistence of the belief that continued exhortation and minimal provision of help will solve it are striking. In the 19th Century Sir De Lacy Evans said that £46,000 was spent on the education of other ranks and their children and £1,300 on the education of officers; see James, op. cit., p.175. Lord Abinger bemoaned the fact that Parliament 'would not vote a sufficient sum of money to enable the officer to carry out his professional studies'. He said that when his Guards Battalion got a class together of those who wanted to learn practical engineering and asked the War Office to find a teacher all the War Office could do after much delay was to recommend a sergeant in a Volunteer Corps and to refuse to defray the cost of the necessary material; see *Parliamentary Debates*, The House of Lords, Vol.207, col.1798, 17 July 1871. And so it continues. It is a safe bet that future examiners will still feel impelled to make caustic comments on the literacy of many officers.

37   PQS Review Working Party Final Report, op. cit.

38   Reeves, Brigadier B., 'The Junior Army', *Torch*, Summer 1992.

39   Command Education Officers Conference 1959, RAEC Archives.

40   PQS Review Working Party's Final Report, op. cit.

41   Ascham, op. cit.; Bacon, 'Advancement of Learning', *Everyman* 719, p.56

(Dent,1958). 'The unlearned man knows not what it is to descend into himself or to call himself to account'.

42   Communicated by Major K.O. Fox.

43   'The Army's Future Requirements', op. cit.

44   ibid., Annex A.

45   ibid., Appendix 1 to Annex C.

46   ibid.

47   *The Daily Telegraph*, 6 February 1990.

48   'The Army's Future Requirements', op.cit, Annex F.

49   ibid.

50   ibid.

51   *Torch* 1/1 14, Summer 1995; *Torch* 5/16 16, Summer 1996.

52   ibid.

53   Bates, Captain L., 'Have Languages, Will Travel', *Torch* 4/1, Summer 1995.

54   'The Army's Future Requirements', op. cit., Annex F; Mackay and Flower-Smith op. cit.

55   Cable, Lieutenant, G., 'Minerva Turns Sky Blue. ETS Go Live in Angola', *Torch* 4/2, Winter 1995. The Angolan Government was greatly impressed by the ETS briefing of soldiers. It was pleased that so much was being done to familiarise them with Angolan ways. This was a small matter but host governments at times give a luke-warm welcome to the providers of the UN assistance for which they have asked and the good impression made by the British soldiers helped the UN in the discharge of its mission.

56   'The Army's Future Requirements', op. cit., The Report by HM Inspectors on the Army School of Preliminary Education, Corsham, 17–21 October 1966 said of the RAEC 'its adaptability in the use of manpower and facilities has been developed to a high degree'.

57   'The Army's Future Requirements', op. cit.

INDEX